13

A History of the United States

PRIMARY SOURCES

Our Land, Our Time

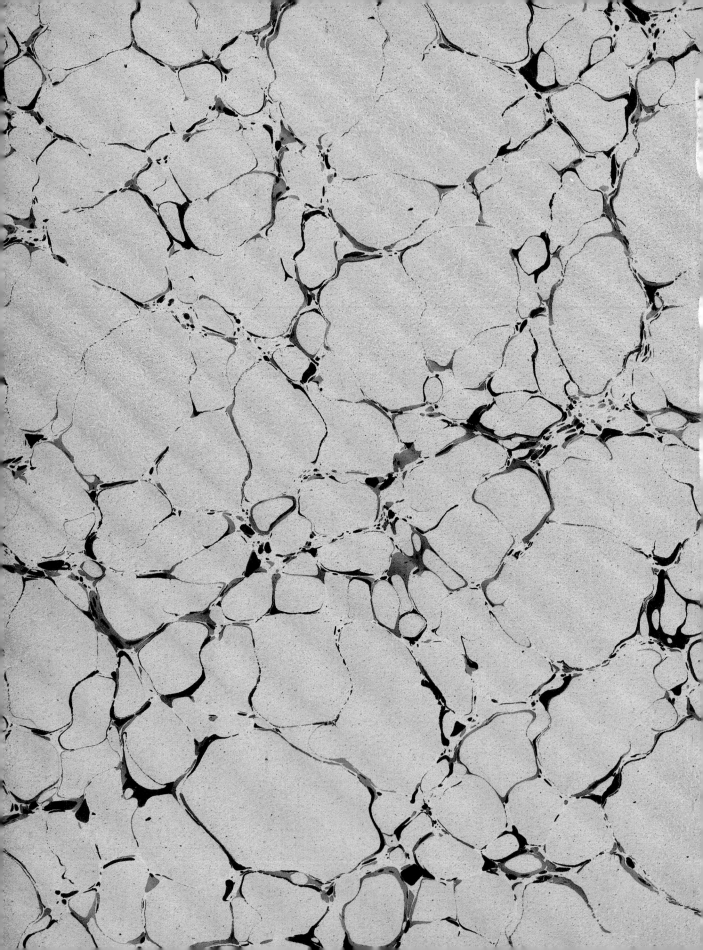

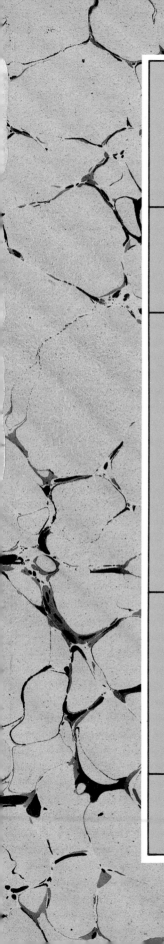

A History of the United States

PRIMARY SOURCES

Our Land, Our Time

Joseph R. Conlin

CORONADO PUBLISHERS

San Diego   Chicago   Orlando   Dallas

Joseph R. Conlin is Professor of History at the California State University in Chico, California.

REVIEWERS

The publisher wishes to thank the following reviewers of *A History of the United States: Our Land, Our Time* for their comments. They provided specific comments on the content, organization, and difficulty level of the material. Their assistance has been invaluable in creating a textbook that will be usable for the teacher and profitable for the students.

Henry Billings
Social Studies Educator
Hamilton-Wenham Regional High School
South Hamilton, Massachusetts

Gerald Jackson
Social Studies Educator
Caney High School
Caney, Oklahoma

Leone Little
Director of the Social Studies Department
Thomas Carr Howe High School
Indianapolis, Indiana

Suzanne McDaniels
Social Studies Consultant
Spartanburg County School District No. 7
Spartanburg, South Carolina

Clifford O'Harrow
Social Studies Department Coordinator
Sandy Union High School
Sandy, Oregon

John Porterfield
Secondary Curriculum Coordinator
and General Supervisor
Lewis County Schools
Weston, West Virginia

Margaret Ward
Social Studies Curriculum Program Supervisor
Polk County Schools
Bartow, Florida

Karen Wiggins
Consultant for Social Studies and Foreign Languages
Richardson Independent School District
Richardson, Texas

James Wilson
U.S. History and Government Educator
Bonita Vista High School
Chula Vista, California

Acknowledgments for material quoted from other sources will be found on page 411 which is an extension of this page.

A *History of the United States: Our Land, Our Time—Primary Sources* is organized to make your study of American history more valuable. Following a helpful **Table of Contents,** you will find a 32-page **Prologue** titled *A Brief History of the United States.* This prologue provides a sweeping overview of America's history. A running-frieze illustrates this prologue and serves to introduce some of the people who played parts—large or small—in the pageant of American history.

The 10 units and 34 chapters that make up this book of primary source readings correspond to the units and chapters found in *A History of the United States: Our Land, Our Time.* If, when studying the basic textbook, you turn to the corresponding unit of this book of readings, you will find a selection of written documents and special visual resource features that will further explain and illustrate the events of the time. The reading selections will help to point out the complexity of the issues facing Americans throughout our history and the diversity of opinion and political approach that have been a part of our democratic society.

Each unit has features that offer interesting sidelights to the period you are studying. *Written* primary-source materials from the period covered in each chapter of the unit include personal letters, diary and journal entries, speeches, and other documents. Among these written primary sources is one Key Document titled **Unlocking History.** In addition to the Key Document itself, there is a Commentary explaining the significance of this document.

Other *nonwritten* sources are titled **Artifact as Document, Picture as Document,** and **One Point of View.** The first two features show that nonwritten materials from a particular period can be just as valuable as primary sources of historical information as written documents. One Point of View highlights paintings, photographs, and other illustrations done by individuals who lived during certain periods and recorded insights into their times as they saw them.

The paintings, artifacts, and photographs in this book document the people, places, and events discussed in the text and add visual information about American history. The captions next to the pictures identify them and bring together information in the text or add relevant, new information.

Each written and nonwritten source document is followed by a grey-screened box of **Critical Thinking** questions. The questions are designed to provoke individual analysis of the particular written or nonwritten "reading" they follow.

Following Chapter 34, you will find a copy of **The Declaration of Independence** and an in-depth section covering the **Constitution of the United States.** A convenient **Index** completes the book.

UNIT 1

A BRIEF HISTORY OF THE UNITED STATES xviii–31

READINGS 32

Chapter 1 • 25,000 BC–1754 AD 33

1. Prince Henry the Navigator Encourages Exploration 33
2. Christopher Columbus Discovers a "New World" 36
3. Hernando Cortez Describes the Gold Gifts from Montezuma 37
4. Montezuma's Followers Lament the Conquistadors' Greed 39

Chapter 2 • 1525–1625 42

1. Bartolome De Las Casas Condemns the Spaniards' Treatment of Indians 42
2. Robert Coopy Pledges Himself to a Contract of Indenture 43
3. The *Mayflower* Passengers Pledge Themselves to a Compact of Government 44
4. Edward Winslow Describes the Pilgrims' First Thanksgiving Celebration 44

Chapter 3 • 1625–1732 48

1. Thomas Dudley's Unexaggerated Account of Life in the Massachusetts Bay Colony in 1631 48
2. An Exaggerated Account of Life in the Colony of Baltimore in 1633 49
3. Roger Williams Writes about the Civil Affairs of Providence 50
4. The Toleration Act of 1649 Provides for Religious Freedom in Maryland 51
5. William Penn Frames a Government for Pennsylvania 52

Chapter 4 • 1650–1754 56

1. Jacques Marquette and Louis Joliet Explore the Mississippi River 56
2. William Fitzhugh Describes a Colonial Plantation 60
3. Thomas Danforth Writes to Increase Mather about Governor Andros 60
4. Peter Kalm Observes England's American Colonies 62

UNIT 2

READINGS   66

Chapter 5 • 1754–1774   67

1. Lieutenant Governor Robert Dinwiddie Protests French Occupation in the Ohio River Valley   67
2. Christopher Gist Accompanies Major George Washington to the Ohio River Valley   67
3. American Colonists Assert Their Rights and Air Their Grievances   68
4. Ephraim Bowen Recounts the Burning of the *Gaspee*   70
5. A Popular Song of the American Revolution   71

Chapter 6 • 1775–1783   74

1. An American Woman Writes of Her Active Support of the Revolution   74
2. Ann Hulton Gives an Eyewitness Account of the Battle of Bunker Hill   75
3. John Dickinson's Plea for Conciliation   80
4. The Declaration of Independence Is Celebrated   80
5. One Patriot's Attack on the Tories   81
6. Elias Boudinot Tells the Tale of Benedict Arnold's Treachery   82

Chapter 7 • 1783–1789   85

1. Alexander Hamilton Criticizes the *Articles of Confederation*   85
2. The Confederation Congress Seeks Additional Powers   86
3. Benjamin Franklin Urges Passage of a New Federal Constitution   87
4. Patrick Henry Speaks Out about the Proposed Constitution   89
5. Edmund Pendleton Speaks Out about the Proposed Constitution   90
6. Patrick Henry Speaks of the Necessity of *A Bill of Rights*   91

Chapter 8 • 1789–1801   94

1. Colonel John May Celebrates Independence Day, 1788   94
2. George Washington Arrives in New York City To Be Inaugurated   94
3. Thomas Jefferson Appraises the Character of George Washington   96
4. A Broadside from the Presidential Election of 1796   100
5. Federalists Succeed in Passing Four *Alien and Sedition Acts*   100
6. State Legislatures Respond to the Alien and Sedition Acts   102
7. Abigail Adams Reflects Upon Her Experiences as the First, First Lady to Live in the White House   104
8. Manasseh Cutler Informs His Daughter about His Life as a Congressman in the New Capital   105

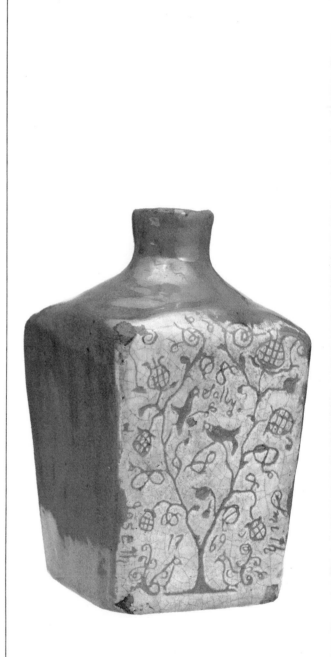

UNIT 3

READINGS	**106**
Chapter 9 • 1801–1824	**107**
1. President Thomas Jefferson Expresses Concern about France's Control of Louisiana	107
2. Napoleon Considers Selling Louisiana to the United States	108
3. The Senate Debates the Purchase of Louisiana from France	109
4. Explorer William Clark Describes the Events of November 7, 1805	111
5. Tecumseh Speaks Eloquently against the Sale of Indian Lands	112
Chapter 10 • 1800–1825	**116**
1. The Rules and Regulations of New England Mills	116
2. Eli Whitney Invents the Cotton Gin	117
3. Elijah Iles Recalls His Move to Illinois in 1821	118
4. John Fitch Describes a Demonstration of His Steamboat	119
5. Robert Fulton Describes His First Successful Steamboat Voyage from New York to Albany	120
6. Thomas Woodcock's Account of a Trip through the Erie Canal	121
7. Charles Fenno Hoffman Describes Travel on Henry Clay's National Road	124
Chapter 11 • 1824–1844	**125**
1. Presidential Candidate Andrew Jackson Is Accused of Serious Crimes	125
2. President Andrew Jackson's Inaugural Celebration Gets Out of Hand	126
3. Senator Daniel Webster Responds to President Jackson's Veto of the Bank Bill	132
4. A Baptist Missionary Tells of the "Trail Of Tears"	133
Chapter 12 • 1815–1850	**135**
1. Transcendentalist Amy Reed Writes of Her Experiences at Brook Farm	135
2. Philosopher Henry David Thoreau Addresses the Question of Civil Disobedience	136
3. Dorothea Dix Pleads the Plight of the Mentally Ill	138
4. Abraham Lincoln Expresses His Opinion about the "Know-Nothings"	140
5. Sarah Grimke Suggests Reasons for the Situation Women Found Themselves in, in the 1800s	140

UNIT 4

READINGS   144

Chapter 13 • 1820–1860   145

1. Former Slave Solomon Northup Tells His Story   145
2. Josiah Henson Recalls the Day His Family Was Sold   147
3. Underground Railroadman William Still Remembers the Courage of Harriet Tubman   149

Chapter 14 • 1835–1860   154

1. Sam Houston Speaks Out in Support of Texas Joining the Union   154
2. John O'Sullivan Proclaims America's "Manifest Destiny"   155
3. Runaway Slave Anthony Burns Is Arrested in Boston   156
4. English Traveler Thomas H. Gladstone Witnesses the Sack of Lawrence, Kansas   158
5. A Popular Song Celebrates John Brown's Raid on Harper's Ferry   162
6. Abraham Lincoln Speaks about the Incident at Harper's Ferry   162

Chapter 15 • 1861–1865   164

1. Southerner Mary Boykin Chesnut Describes the Attack on Fort Sumter   164
2. President Abraham Lincoln Offers Emancipation Amendments to the Constitution   168
3. Citing the *Emancipation Proclamation,* a Slave Serving in the Confederate Army Frees Himself   169
4. "Johnny Reb" Encounters "Billy Yank"   170
5. General Ulysses S. Grant Recounts the Surrender of the Army of Northern Virginia at Appomattox Courthouse   172

Chapter 16 • 1865–1877   174

1. Northern Newspaper Correspondent Sidney Andrews Dispatches Reports from Postwar South Carolina   174
2. President Andrew Johnson Extends Amnesty to Most Southerners   175
3. William H. Crook's Eyewitness Account of the Senate's Impeachment Proceedings against President Andrew Johnson   177
4. *Ku Klux Klan* Member Robert Hayes Mitchell Is Tried on a Charge of Murder   178

UNIT 5

READINGS   **182**

Chapter 17 • 1865–1900   **183**

1. Railway Worker Alexander Toponce Remembers the Day the Transcontinental Railroad Was Finished   183
2. Simon Sterne Criticizes the Railroads   183
3. Journalist Henry D. Lloyd Warns Against an "Age of Combination"   184
4. John D. Rockefeller Defends His Business Practices   185
5. Russell Herman Conwell's Speech Captures the Spirit of His Age   186

Chapter 18 • 1868–1896   **192**

1. Sociologist William Graham Sumner Describes the Health of American Politics in 1876   192
2. President Rutherford B. Hayes Favors Civil Service Reform   192
3. Robert Ingersoll Waves a "Bloody Shirt"   193
4. Editor Richard Watson Gilder Defines a New Type of Patriotism   196

Chapter 19 • 1865–1900   **197**

1. American Capitalist Andrew Carnegie Recalls Receiving the First Dividend Check   197
2. Italian Dramatist Giuseppe Giacosa Offers His Assessment of American Slaughterhouses   198
3. Joseph Kirkland Tells of Working Conditions in Manufacturing "Sweatshops"   199
4. The *Knights of Labor* Lists Its Aims   200
5. Immigrant Mary Antin Arrives in America—"The Promised Land"   206
6. President Grover Cleveland Vetoes a Bill Proposing Literacy Tests for Immigrants   207
7. Suffragist Susan B. Anthony and Senator Joseph Brown Take Sides on a Woman Suffrage Amendment   209

UNIT 6

READINGS   214

Chapter 20 • 1865–1900   215

1. Ogalala Sioux Chief Standing Bear Analyzes the Indian Way of Life   215
2. Sioux Chief Red Cloud Speaks Sadly about Old Wrongs   216
3. Cowhand James H. Cook Reminisces about the Adventures of a "Long Drive"   217
4. Cattleman John Clay Recalls the End of the Open Range   219
5. Mark Twain Spins a Yarn about Tarantulas in Carson City   220
6. Artemus Ward Pens a Dubious Account of the Silver-Mining Towns of Nevada   224
7. A Colorful Memoir of Life in Virginia City, Nevada, in Its Heyday   226

Chapter 21 • 1873–1896   227

1. Writer Hamlin Garland Fictionalizes the Midwestern Farmer   227
2. The Populist Party Drafts a Controversial Platform in 1892   228
3. President Grover Cleveland Upholds the Dignity of Labor   229

Chapter 22 • 1896–1903   232

1. Admiral Alfred T. Mahan Analyzes the Influence of Sea Power on International Politics   232
2. President William McKinley Decides to Annex the Phillippines   232
3. Indiana Senator Albert J. Beveridge Envisions the "March of America's Flag"   233
4. Missouri Senator Carl Schurz Questions American Military Expansion   234
5. Hawaii's Queen Liliuokalani Calls on Americans to Not Annex Hawaii   235
6. William Randolph Hearst—Young, Brash, and Ambitious—Seeks His Own Newspaper   237
7. William Dean Howells Visits a Spanish Prisoner-of-War Camp in New Hampshire   238
8. Frederic Haskin Proudly Recounts the Cutting of the Panama Canal   242

UNIT 7

READINGS   246

Chapter 23 • 1890–1910   247

  1. French Newspaper Correspondent Charles
    Bourget Reports His Observations of an
    American College Football Game in the
    Autumn of 1894   247
  2. A Glimpse of the Rich at Play, in Saratoga   248
  3. Muckraker Lincoln Steffens Questions the
    Practice of Running the Government Like a
    Business   249
  4. Wisconsin Governor Robert La Follette
    Argues in Favor of Primary Elections   250
  5. Frederic Howe Shows Democracy Works in
    Wisconsin   251
  6. Muckraker Upton Sinclair's *The Jungle*
    Exposes the Meat-Packing Industry   253

Chapter 24 • 1901–1916   258

  1. Progressive Writer Amos Pinchot Relates a
    Personal Story about the Famous "TR" Style   258
  2. President Theodore Roosevelt Names the
    Virtues Needed by a Practical Politician   259
  3. American Conservationist Gifford Pinchot
    Puts Forth Three Principles of Conservation   262
  4. President Theodore Roosevelt Speaks on
    the Relationship between Big Business
    and Government   263
  5. Presidential Candidate Theodore Roosevelt
    Campaigns for the "Square Deal"   264
  6. President William Howard Taft Sends a
    Message to Congress Concerning Seal
    Hunting   265
  7. Presidential Candidate Woodrow Wilson
    Sees America Changing   267

Chapter 25 • 1914–1920   268

  1. Nebraska Senator George Norris Opposes
    United States Involvement in World War I   268
  2. Former President Theodore Roosevelt
    Writes a Letter about the War in Europe   269
  3. An American Soldier in France Writes
    Home from "The Front"   272
  4. American Ambulance Driver Guy Emerson
    Bowerman, Jr. Records His Experiences in
    the Final Days of World War I   272
  5. Massachusetts Senator Henry Cabot Lodge
    Demands Harsh Peace Terms   274
  6. Suffragist Carrie Chapman Catt Tells Why
    the League of Women Voters Was Formed   274

UNIT 8

READINGS   278

Chapter 26 • 1920–1929   279

1. German Tourist Count Felix Von Luckner Observes the Effects of Prohibition   279
2. Historian Frederick Lewis Allen Reports How the Younger Generation Ran Wild   282
3. Langston Hughes Remembers Harlem in the Twenties   284
4. Mordecai Johnson Speaks Out on the Testing of Black Faith   285
5. Massachusetts Senator David I. Walsh Opposes the New Immigration Quotas of 1924   287
6. Sociologists Robert and Helen Lynd Study "Middletown"   288

Chapter 27 • 1923–1929   290

1. Edward Earle Purinton Offers a Tribute to the Business Game   290
2. Wisconsin Senator and 1924 Progressive Party Presidential Candidate Robert La Follette Speaks Out against Monopolistic Power   290
3. President Calvin Coolidge Vetoes a Reform Bill   291
4. President Calvin Coolidge Defends American Intervention in Nicaragua   294

Chapter 28 • 1929–1937   295

1. Iowa Lawyer Remley Glass Relects on the Hardships Facing Farmers in the Corn Belt during the Great Depression   295
2. Writer James Agee Brings to Life the Plight of the Sharecropper   296
3. President Herbert Hoover Rejects Major Governmental Controls of the Economic System as a Cure for the Great Depression   298
4. Presidential Advisor Raymond Moley Reminisces on the "First Hundred Days" of FDR's Administration   304
5. *New Deal* Programs Are Created to Help the Transient Unemployed   304
6. New York Governor Alfred E. Smith Talks Plainly about His Catholicism   305
7. A Miner's Son Talks about Growing Up in the Hard Times of the Great Depression   306

UNIT 9

READINGS	**310**
Chapter 29 • 1930–1945	**311**

1. President Franklin Delano Roosevelt
   Addresses Congress on the Problems of
   American Neutrality — 311
2. President Franklin Roosevelt Calls
   December 7, 1941, a Date of Infamy — 312
3. President Franklin Roosevelt Broadcasts a
   Fireside Chat about War — 313
4. American Novelist John Steinbeck Reports
   on the Job of a War-Correspondent — 316
5. War-Correspondent Ernie Pyle Sends Home
   a Report on the Bravery and Spirit of
   American Soldiers — 317
6. Defense Worker Rachel Wray Reminisces
   about Her Wartime Experiences as a Riveter — 318
7. Margaret Takahashi Describes the
   Internment of Japanese-Americans after the
   Japanese Attack at Pearl Harbor — 319
8. President Harry S. Truman Reveals the
   Dropping of an Atomic Bomb on
   Hiroshima — 324
9. A Description of the City of Hiroshima
   after the Dropping of a Single Atomic
   Bomb — 328
10. Writer Dwight MacDonald Presents a
    Pacifist's View of the A-Bomb — 328

Chapter 30 • 1945–1952 — **330**

1. The *Truman Doctrine* Is Established to Halt
   the Spread of Communism — 330
2. Secretary of State George Marshall Devises a
   Plan to Rebuild Europe — 331
3. President Harry Truman Speaks Plainly
   about Civil Rights — 332
4. Victor Navasky Tallies Up the Costs of
   "McCarthyism" — 333

Chapter 31 • 1952–1960 — **336**

1. The Supreme Court's Decision of *Brown* v.
   Board of Education of Topeka Begins the
   Process of School Desegregation — 336
2. Rosa Parks Refuses to Give Up Her "Seat on
   the Bus" — 337
3. President Dwight Eisenhower Writes about
   the Sputnik Satellite — 338

UNIT 10

READINGS   342

Chapter 32 • 1960–1968   343

1. Massachusetts Senator John F. Kennedy Calls on Americans to be New Pioneers on the "New Frontier"   343
2. Poet Robert Frost Recites at President John F. Kennedy's Inauguration   344
3. President Lyndon B. Johnson Offers Americans His Vision of a "Great Society"   344
4. Stokely Carmichael and Charles Hamilton Discuss "Black Power"   348
5. Arkansas Senator J. William Fulbright Opposes American Military Involvement in the Vietnam War   349
6. President Lyndon Johnson Reaffirms His Administration's Foreign Policy Goals   350
7. Essayist Dave Dellinger Visits North Vietnam   350

Chapter 33 • 1968–1976   354

1. The American Space Program Proves Successful   354
2. Secretary of State Henry Kissinger Explains the Meaning of *Detente*   355
3. President Richard Nixon Establishes Diplomatic and Economic Relations with the People's Republic of China   356
4. Political Writer Elizabeth Drew Recounts the Vote to Impeach President Richard Nixon   357
5. Writer Seymour Hersh Dissects the Henry Kissinger-Richard Nixon Team   358
6. Betty Friedan Looks at "The Feminine Mystique"   362

Chapter 34 • 1976–Present   363

1. First Lady Rosalynn Carter Recalls President Carter's Energy Program   363
2. Presidential Adviser Hamilton Jordan Recalls the Morning He Learned American Diplomats Were Being Held Hostage in Iran   364
3. President Ronald Reagan Delivers His First Inaugural Address   365
4. Writer Ellen Goodman Contemplates the Drafting of Women   365
5. And May the Best Woman Win!   367
6. The 1984 Summer Olympics—On Your Mark, Get Set, Go!   368
7. The Robots Are Coming! The Robots Are Coming!   369

Declaration of Independence   372

Constitution of The United States of America   374

Index   404

UNLOCKING HISTORY / KEY DOCUMENT

The Adventures of Marco Polo	34
Thomas Paine Pushes for Common Sense and Independence	76
President Andrew Jackson Champions Opportunity for Individuals and Argues for a Strong National Government	128
William Lloyd Garrison Attacks Slavery through *The Liberator*	152
Jacob Riis Tells Americans about Their Slums	202
William Jennings Bryan Exhorts the Democratic Party Not to "Crucify Mankind Upon a Cross of Gold"	240
President Woodrow Wilson Proposes a Fourteen Point Peace Plan	276
President Franklin D. Roosevelt and the Great Depression	300
President Harry Truman Faces the Awesome Decision of Whether or Not to Drop the Atomic Bomb	322
Reverend Martin Luther King Jr.'s Dream for America	346

ONE POINT OF VIEW

John White	46
John Singleton Copley	58
Amos Doolittle	78
Gilbert Stuart	92
Paul Petrovich Svinin	114
John James Audubon	142
William S. Mount	150
George Catlin	160
Thomas Eakins	190
Thomas Nast	194
Jacob Riis	204
Frederic Remington	244
Charles Dana Gibson	256
Georgia O'Keeffe	292
Margaret Bourke-White	302
Bill Mauldin	326
Norman Rockwell	334
George Segal	370

PICTURE AS DOCUMENT

POLITICAL CARTOONS—The Quarrel with
Great Britain   72
IRON: The History of an American Industry,
1800-1825   122
THE RIGHT TO VOTE—The Spread of
Democracy in America   130
CIVIL WAR PHOTOGRAPHERS—The New
Documentors   166
WASHINGTON, D.C.—Home of the Nation's
Government   180
THE PHILADELPHIA CENTENNIAL—America
Demonstrates Its New Industrial Power   188
ELLIS ISLAND—Gateway to America   212
CUSTER'S LAST STAND—A Romantic Subject for
Illustration   222
PIONEER HOUSING—American Ingenuity Turns
Logs, Sod, and Adobe into Homes   230
THE TWENTIES—Taking Time for Fun and Games   280
FSA PHOTOGRAPHERS—Recorders of the New
Deal Programs   308
LIFE MAGAZINE GOES TO WAR—A
Photographic Record   320
FREEDOM RIDES—The Quest for Racial
Integration and Equality   340
AMERICAN SPACE PROGRAM—A Success Story   352
AMERICA'S BICENTENNIAL—1776–1976   360

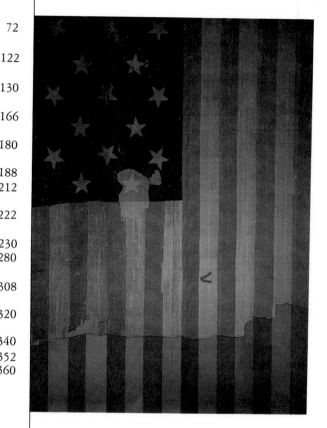

ARTIFACT AS DOCUMENT

AZTEC ARTIFACTS—A Legacy of Craftsmanship   40
PURITAN GRAVESTONES—The Puritan's
Graveyard Documents   54
COLONIAL CRAFTS—Objects of Daily Life   64
GEORGE WASHINGTON—Tributes to the First
President   98
"TR" MEMORABILIA—A Popular President Is
Remembered   260
WORLD WAR I POSTERS—Building Public
Support   270

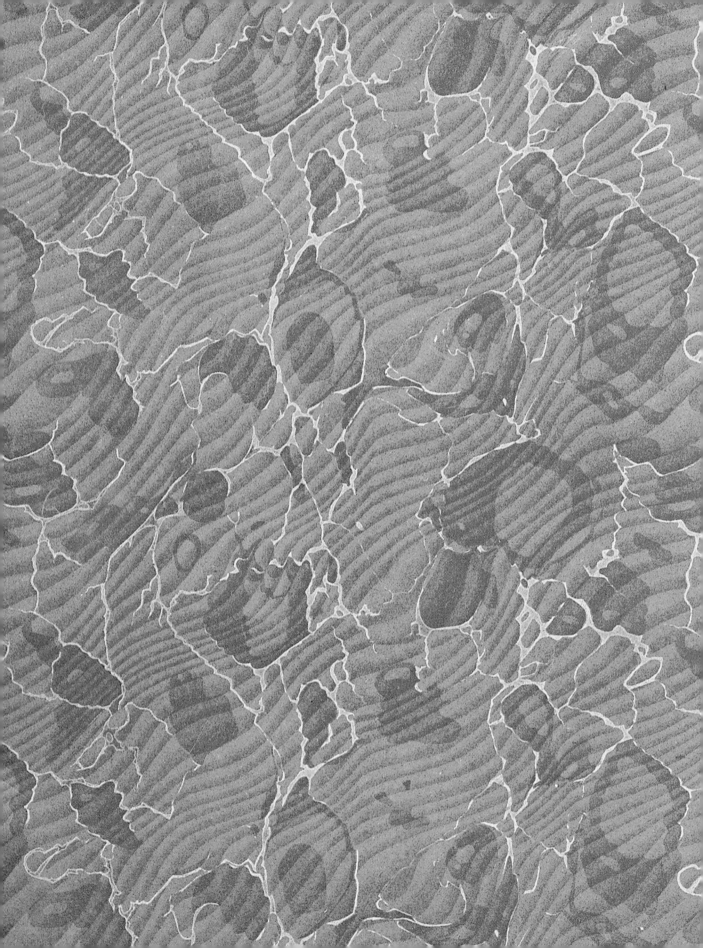

A BRIEF HISTORY OF THE UNITED STATES

25,000 BC–Present

1. ONE LAND, MANY PEOPLES

The first Americans were Asians. More than 25,000 years ago, small bands of primitive hunters crossed a land bridge that then connected Alaska with Russian Siberia. Over the centuries, warmer temperatures drew their descendants to the south where they spread out over the two huge American continents. Melting polar ice raised the waters of the Pacific Ocean and the land bridge was submerged.

So much room was there in the Americas, and so many different kinds of land—forests, mountains, plains, prairies, deserts, and in Central and South America tropical jungles—that the first Americans developed an amazing variety of languages, economies, and cultures. Not until the year 1492 A.D. would they come into contact with a new group of immigrants, this time from Europe. Not until the 1500s would the newcomers be so numerous that they began to conquer the Americas from the people they called Indians.

How the First Americans Lived. In what is now Mexico, and in Peru and Equador in South America, the Indians developed very advanced cultures. The Incas of Peru and Equador built stone roads and ruled an empire that stretched for thousands of miles. The Aztecs of Mexico created

MAYAN RULER
Pre-Columbian times

MARCO POLO
Adventurer and chronicler

1

a huge city, Tenochtitlan, where Mexico City is today, and ruled the most heavily populated part of the Americas.

Comparatively fewer people lived north of the Aztecs in what is now the United States and Canada. When Europeans first arrived at the end of the 1400s, the total population of North America, above Mexico, was no more than one or two million people. (More than 235 million people live in the United States today, more than 25 million in Canada.) Because they were so few, the Native Americans lived in small groups called tribes and developed different ways of life.

In the Southwest, Pueblo Indians lived in villages made of adobe brick perched high on cliffs for easy defense against enemies. They were very skillful farmers. They had to be in order to coax corn and beans out of their harsh desert homeland. In California, on the other hand, nature was kind. The large number of small California tribes lived largely by gathering or hunting their food.

In the Pacific Northwest, including British Columbia, lived the tribes that created the famous totem poles so fascinating today. They too had an abundant life with a good diet based on salmon. They traded actively with the Indians of the mountains to the east such as the Nez Perce.

On the great plains and prairies that reach up and down the center of North America, the native Americans lived by hunting the bison, the American buffalo. Not only did the huge beasts supply food, their hides were used for shelter (teepees) and clothing, their bone for tools and weapons. Not until after the arrival of Europeans, however, did the plains Indians reach their highest development. They captured and tamed horses that had escaped from the Europeans and were soon among the most skillful riders in the world.

In the eastern third of the present-day United States, vast forests sheltered game animals and many kinds of plant food which, along with fish and shellfish gathered in coastal waters, supported the Eastern Woodlands Indians. Almost all of these peoples spoke Iroquois, Algonkian, or Muskohegan language but, except for the Iroquois tribes, which were allies, they were often at war with one another. The Eastern Woodlands Indians farmed corn, beans, squash, and tobacco in clearings in the forest. But they depended on hunting and gathering for much of their food.

An Age of Discovery in the Old World. During the 15th century (the 1400s), the Portugese, who lived in the far west of Europe, began to explore the coast of the huge continent of Africa. While they were interested in trading with West Africans (and making slaves of some of them), the chief object of their long voyages was

PRINCE HENRY THE NAVIGATOR
Sponsors voyages and founds a school of navigation

CHRISTOPHER COLUMBUS
Discovers America, October 12, 1492

to find a new route to *the Indies*, as Europeans then called Asia.

Europeans valued the products of the Indies: fine tapestries, silk and cotton cloth, and most of all spices—cinnamon and nutmeg and allspice and black peppercorns—which brought new pleasure to eating. These goods were imported into Europe by Italian merchants after a long caravan trip across the Asian continent. Because the Italians made so much profit from this trade, they prevented their customers from sailing to the eastern end of the Mediterranean Sea and buying Asian goods for themselves.

This is why the Portugese attempted to bypass the Italians by looking for a route to Asia around the unknown tip of Africa. They wanted Asian goods cheaper so that they could replace the Italians as suppliers to all Europe. In 1487, a ship's captain named Bartholomew Dias reached the southern tip of Africa. After that date, the Portugese lost all interest in getting to Asia by sailing westward across the Atlantic, as an Italian sailor living in Portugal, Christopher Columbus, had advised them to do.

Columbus Discovers America and Cortez Discovers Its Riches.
Leaving Portugal, Columbus went to Spain where he convinced Queen Isabella to raise the money to finance a voyage of exploration. On October 12, 1492, he reached an island he believed was on the outskirts of the Indies. For this reason, he named the people he met there Indians.

Columbus, though, had not reached Asia. Columbus had discovered a *New World*, as Europeans would soon call it. And at first, the new land disappointed the Spanish soldiers called *conquistadores*, or conquerors, who flocked there. Not only were there no valuable Asians goods, all of the Indians seemed to be poor and weak. Infected with Old World diseases for the first time, and treated brutally by the rough Spaniards, the Native Americans died off in horrible numbers.

Then, in 1519, one of the most rugged of the *conquistadores*, Hernando Cortez, gave Spain good reason to be thankful for its New World colonies. Although it took him several years, Cortez and his soldiers conquered one of the world's greatest and richest empires, the realm of the Aztecs in Mexico. Ships laden with gold and silver sailed back to Spain every year, especially after another *conquistador*, Francisco Pizarro, conquered the equally rich empire of the Incas.

The Hispanic Empire.
Except for Brazil, which was controlled by the Portugese, Spain ruled all of South America, Central America, and most of the islands of the West Indies for 300

WALTER RALEIGH/
VIRGINIA DARE WITH
MOTHER
Virginia Dare is first English child born in America

JOHN SMITH/
POCHAHONTAS
Help settlers of early Jamestown

years. As far north as St. Augustine, Florida; Santa Fe, New Mexico; and Sonoma, California, Spanish soldiers and friars (Roman Catholic priests and brothers) brought the New World under the Spanish flag.

The Spanish introduced the tragedy of slavery to America. They captured black people in Africa and brought them to the New World to do their heavy labor. But the Spanish also created a glorious civilization that is today the heritage of all Hispanic Americans (*Hispania* is Latin for Spain) from Argentina and Chile to Mexico and Puerto Rico. They built magnificent cathedrals, founded universities, encouraged poets and artists to practice their skills. The friars and monks of the Catholic Church fought against the harshness of the great landowners toward the Indians and blacks and were often successful in protecting them.

The wealth of the Hispanic Empire aroused the envy of other nations of western Europe. Beginning in 1607, England, France, Holland, and Sweden also carved out colonies in the New World, north of the powerful Spanish. In 1607, English settlers founded a colony in Virginia. In 1608, Frenchman Samuel de Champlain founded Quebec. In 1626, the Dutch West India Company founded New Netherland. And in 1638, Swede Peter Minuit founded New Sweden.

2. ENGLAND'S COLONIES BECOME AN AMERICAN NATION

The first permanent English settlement in America was Jamestown, Virginia, established in 1607. The next year, Jacques Cartier founded the first French colony at Quebec in what is now Canada. During the years that followed, the Dutch and the Swedish settled little communities on the Hudson and Delaware Rivers. The Dutch took over the tiny Swedish colony and England conquered the Dutch town of New Amsterdam, renaming it New York. By the end of the 1600s, only France and England held real claims to North America north of Hispanic Mexico, New Mexico, Texas, and Florida. The French controlled the middle of the continent down the Mississippi River and the English pushed slowly westward from the Atlantic shore.

England's Southern Colonies. In the first two English colonies in the south, Virginia and Maryland, the raising of tobacco created a prosperous and sometimes elegant society. Many Europeans had the tobacco habit. Consequently, when John Rolfe, the husband of the Indian princess Pocohantas, developed a way to prepare the native plant into a product that pleased smokers, the people who owned land around the Ches-

*MILES STANDISH/
WILLIAM BRADFORD
Pilgrims land at Plymouth,
Massachusetts, November, 1620*

apeake Bay found it possible to create a comfortable life where at first they had struggled to survive.

By about 1660, Virginians and Marylanders borrowed the institution of slavery from the Spanish. Slave laborers captured in West Africa were cheaper than free workers hired in Europe, and the tragic institution of slavery became a part of southern life. When North Carolina was founded, also as a tobacco colony, and South Carolina as a place where rice and *indigo* were grown (indigo is a plant used to make blue dye for cloth), the wealthy planters there also legalized slavery. Georgia, the last of the southern colonies, was founded in 1732, in part, to provide a new life for the poorest English people. Slavery was forbidden there. However, once Georgia developed a plantation economy, slavery became a way of life there, too.

New England. Some people who lived in New England—the colonies of Massachusetts, New Hampshire, Rhode Island, and Connecticut—owned slaves too. But using slave labor was never important in the northern colonies because there were no large plantations there. A short growing season and poor soil meant that most farms were small, worked largely by family members. Fishing, whaling, and trading overseas were much more important than farming in the New England economy.

The first New England settlement was Plymouth. It was started in 1620 by *Pilgrims* or Separatists, members of a religion that was persecuted in old England. Massachusetts Bay, begun at Boston in 1630, was also begun for religious reasons. The Puritans who founded it wanted to create a community that was run according to God's law, as they believed God's law to be. Rhode Island, Connecticut, and Rhode Island were founded by people who disagreed with the Puritan religion and were persecuted by the leaders of Massachusetts.

The Prosperous Middle Colonies. The Middle Colonies of New York, New Jersey, Pennsylvania, and Delaware were in many ways the most fortunate of all the English settlements. Their moderate climate and rich soil enabled settlers to create farms that produced far more grain and livestock than the people of those colonies needed for themselves. However, because foodstuffs were the chief products, rather than tobacco, rice or other plantation crops, the middle colonies were a country of family farms instead of large plantations worked by slaves.

New York was originally Dutch. In 1664, however, an English fleet seized the colony from

ANNE HUTCHINSON
Banished from Massachusetts, Hutchinson starts a settlement in Rhode Island, 1638

PETER STUYVESANT
Loses Dutch colony of New Netherlands to the English, 1664

5

Holland without firing a shot. For a year, in 1673 and 1674, the Dutch ruled "New Netherlands" once again. But by that time the colony was more English than not, and England easily won it back.

Pennsylvania was founded in 1681 as a haven for Quakers, members of a religion called the Society of Friends. William Penn, a wealthy English landowner who had become a Quaker, persuaded King Charles II to repay a debt he owed Penn in the form of American land. The Quakers opposed persecuting anyone for religious beliefs. People of all faiths flocked to Philadelphia and spread out over the rolling countryside to the west and north.

New Jersey was also populated heavily with Quakers. As for Delaware, it was actually a part of Pennsylvania. Not until shortly before the American Revolution did Delaware become a truly independent colony.

Growth and Prosperity.

So rich were American resources that the thirteen colonies were able to grow large and prosperous during the 1700s. English North America was a place where, through hard work, ordinary people (except for the oppressed slaves) could hope to prosper as a merchant, an artisan making goods needed by others, or as a planter. By the 1750s, a million and a half people lived in England's American colo-nies. The population of the "Mother Country" was about 6 million at that time, just four times larger than the colonies.

Some observers realized that the colonies would, in time, be larger than the Mother Country. They suggested that when that day came, Americans would demand to be free of English control, or at least to be put in charge of their own government under the English Crown. However, there was no sign that many Americans felt that way during the 1750s, when Great Britain went to war against France. Most colonials thought of themselves as loyal subjects of the Crown. They depended on England's army and navy for defense against the nearby French.

The Long Contest Between England and France.

Canada had grown too, although the French colonies in America had expanded over huge tracts of territory rather than growing much in population. Farming was not extremely important to the French in Quebec and Louisiana (then the whole Mississippi Valley). Instead, the French used their friendly relations with the Indians to trap, hunt, and trade for deerhides and the furs of beaver and other native animals. Skins and furs brought good prices in Europe.

Between 1688 and the 1750s, the French and British fought several wars for supremacy in Eu-

WILLIAM PENN
Founds Quaker colony of Pennsylvania, 1681

ROBERT LA SALLE
Explores the Mississippi River to its mouth, 1682

rope and in North America. At first, the American part of the war was important to neither nation. By 1754, however, it was clear that war would go on indefinitely there unless one side could win a decisive victory.

The British won that victory. Instead of fighting skirmishes in the forests and picking away at the outposts of French Canada at the mouth of the St. Lawrence River, English General James Wolfe daringly struck at the heart of the French colony, the fortress city of Quebec. He captured it and, at the Treaty of Paris in 1763, France turned over Canada to Great Britain and Louisiana to Spain. Britain—and the thirteen colonies—were supreme in the eastern part of North America.

A Quarrel Becomes a Revolution.

The *French and Indian War*, as it was called, nearly bankrupted the British government. Because the Americans had gained the most from the victory—security from French attack—King George III's ministers believed that the Americans should help pay off the large debt. When they tried to tax the colonies, however, Americans responded with riot and economic boycott.

No doubt, many Americans simply did not want to pay any taxes, no matter how much they owed to the Mother Country. However, there was also a principle at stake. It was a traditional right of British subjects that they could be taxed only by an assembly that represented them, made up in part of elected representatives. In Britain, Parliament, and not the king, had the right of taxation. However, Americans elected no representatives to Parliament. They said that only their own thirteen elected assemblies had the right to tax them.

Although the British Parliament backed down after colonial protests against the Stamp tax of 1765 and the Townshend taxes of 1767, Parliament refused to give up its claim that it held the power to tax the Americans. In the early 1770s, however, neither Parliament nor American protesters forced the issue. Even when, in the *Boston Massacre* of 1770, British soldiers opened fire on a crowd of Bostonians that had backed them to a wall, killing five, the large majority of Americans thought that the mob, rather than the British soldiers, were responsible. The colonials seemed to be more deeply devoted to the British empire than ever.

British Blunders Lead to Rebellion.

In 1773, Parliament passed a law giving the Great East India Tea Company a monopoly on all tea, a favorite drink, that was sold in the thirteen colonies. It was not a tax law. In some places, tea actually dropped in price as a result of the act. But

JAMES OGLETHORPE/
MARY MUSGROVE
Founds the colony of Georgia,
1733

BENJAMIN FRANKLIN
American printer, statesman,
and inventor (1706-1790)

Americans who were opposed to British rule, organized in secret clubs known as the *Sons of Liberty*, were angered by the idea of Parliament telling them where they had to buy their teas. In Boston, in December 1773, Sons of Liberty dressed as Indians and led by Samuel Adams and John Hancock, boarded the tea ships and threw their cargo into the harbor.

Parliament did not find the *Boston Tea Party* amusing. A series of extremely harsh laws aimed at punishing Boston and the colony of Massachusetts, which many Parliamentary leaders thought was the most troublesome colony, resulted in an angry reaction throughout the thirteen colonies. The *Intolerable Acts*, as Americans called them, led to the first united action in the history of the colonies, the *First Continental Congress* of 1774.

Meeting in Philadelphia, this assembly (and the Second Continental Congress of 1775) tried to compromise with Great Britain so as to end the crisis peacefully. But George III and his chief adviser, Lord North, were determined to establish their authority over the Americans once and for all. They rejected every proposal to restore peace, from both the colonies and Parliament.

With tempers strained, the inevitable occurred in April 1775. British troops, marching from Boston in an attempt to arrest protest leaders Samuel Adams and John Hancock, opened fire on armed farmers at Lexington, Massachusetts, and fought a pitched battle with American militia called *Minutemen* at Concord. When the smoke cleared, Boston was surrounded by thousands of anti-British American soldiers.

Independence Declared. For more than a year, the Second Continental Congress continued to search for a way to stay within the British empire. However, there was no ignoring the armed conflict in Massachusetts. Congress also sent George Washington, of Virginia, to Boston in order to take command of the American forces in the name of *all* the colonies.

As for King George III, instead of recognizing that he was not dealing with just a few radical protesters, he refused to give an inch and, slowly, Americans began to think of independence. When a radical English immigrant named Thomas Paine published a blistering attack on all kings at the beginning of 1776, his readers nodded their approval. In June, Congress resolved to fight for independence. The great statement of the human right to liberty, to which Abraham Lincoln would refer at Gettysburg, the *Declaration of Independence*, was adopted by Congress.

Independence Won. Defeating the professional British army took six years. The American

PAUL REVERE
Rouses American Minutemen, April 19, 1775

GEORGE WASHINGTON
Leads Continental Army to victory, 1775-1781

troops, called *Continentals*, were rarely a match for the redcoats on the battlefield. However, George Washington proved to be a pillar of strength. He refused to give up despite repeated defeats in the field and poor support from quarrelsome Continental Congress. In the early fall of 1781, with the invaluable assistance of a French navy, Washington forced the surrender of a large British army at Yorktown, Virginia.

The British still held Philadelphia and New York. But the Crown had had enough fighting. England agreed to the independence of the United States of America in the *Treaty of Paris* of 1783.

Experimenting with Government. For the first few years of independence, Americans were governed by a basic law known as the *Articles of Confederation*. In effect, the thirteen states were independent nations. For Congress, the chief governing authority, to accomplish anything important, such as a tax law, it was necessary to win the approval of all thirteen states.

There was almost always one state which refused its consent, and the Articles of Confederation government was plagued by financial difficulties. Moreover, the nations of Europe did not respect the independent confederation. They claimed that it was too difficult to deal with thirteen separate governments.

Leaders who wanted a strong and single *national* government, like George Washington and James Madison of Virginia, and Alexander Hamilton of New York, called a meeting in Philadelphia in 1787. Although its announced purpose was to improve the Articles of Confederation, this Constitutional Convention actually wrote an all new frame of government. This new document was the *Constitution*, under which we are governed to this day. The Constitution has at times been changed ("amended"), of course. The *Founding Fathers*, as the men who wrote the Constitution are called, were shrewd enough to know that changing times would require changes in the work they did. In 1789, when the Constitution went into effect, they were happy enough to have a strong central government that could rule the sprawling republic efficiently. Some of those Americans who worried that the Constitutional government was too strong, were won over when all agreed to a *Bill of Rights*, ten amendments to the Constitution which guarantee basic freedoms to individual citizens.

3. THE AMERICAN REPUBLIC

The Consitution created a *republic*, a form of government in which laws are made not by kings and queens but by elected representatives and

THOMAS JEFFERSON
Becomes first Secretary of State,
1789

WILLIAM CLARK
SACAJAWEA/MERIWETHER
LEWIS
Explore the new Louisiana
Territory, 1804

those they appoint to office. But it did not create a democracy, a form of government in which all citizens participate in electing their leaders. Only in time would all adult Americans win this right.

The Constitution also created a *federal* form of government. That is, power was divided between all the states on the one hand, and the central "federal" government on the other. Although the Founding Fathers gave considerably more power to their federal government than had been the case under the Articles of Confederation, it remained a matter of dispute just where the line between the two was drawn. Not until the Civil War was over, was it resolved that the federal government was supreme.

The Federalist Era.
The first two presidents, George Washington and John Adams, were *Federalists*. Their political party believed that the federal government should be strong, that an educated and usually wealthy elite should govern the country, and that the United States should establish a strong economic and financial system that favored trade and industry over agriculture.

Alexander Hamilton, who was Secretary of the Treasury during Washington's first term, designed many of the policies of the early Republic. He established the financial credit of the government by taking over all of the Confederation and the state governments' debts and arranging to repay them. He also set up the Bank of the United States, which would make it easier for business people from all parts of the United States to do business by controlling the national currency.

The Jeffersonians.
Washington's Secretary of State, Thomas Jefferson, opposed most of Hamilton's policies, particularly Hamilton's belief that trade and industry were more important to national prosperity than agriculture. When war broke out in Europe between France and England, Jefferson and his supporters also tended to favor France while Hamilton was pro-English.

Jefferson resigned from the government and, in 1796, he ran for president against Federalist John Adams. Adams won, but a peculiar provision in the Constitution—later changed—put Jefferson in the vice presidency. During the four years of Adams' presidency (1797-1801), the disagreements between the Federalists and the Jeffersonian Republicans deepened.

Because most Americans were farmers, a majority of citizens had a natural reason to favor Jefferson. President Adams, however, became even less popular when congress passed and he signed a series of *Alien and Sedition Acts* that seemed designed to defeat Jefferson by reducing the civil liberties of people who favored him.

STEPHEN AUSTIN
Settles with 300 American families in Texas, 1821

DAVY CROCKETT
Fights and dies defending the Alamo, March 6, 1836

The Nation Expands.

Elected president in 1800, Thomas Jefferson's major contribution was the purchase of the *Louisiana Territory* from France. This was not just the present state of Louisiana, but the center third of the United States, from the Mississippi River to the Rocky Mountains. In making this tremendous real estate bargain—it cost only $15 million—Jefferson put the world on notice that his country was an expansive nation. A rapidly growing population needed room and Americans were ever moving westward in search of land.

Jefferson and his hand-picked successor, James Madison, were less successful in their attempts to keep the United States out of the series of wars that engulfed Europe in the early 19th century. Americans were involved, despite their resistance, because of the importance of worldwide trade to the New England states. Both French and British warships seized American merchant vessels that were trading with their enemy. However, British affronts were more insulting to the United States because of the practice of *impressment:* crew members of American ships were often forced into service on British warships. Relations between the former Mother Country and colonies were also tense because many Americans, particularly westerners, wanted to capture Canada and expand the nation to the north.

An Unhappy War and an Upsurge of Democracy.

The *War of 1812* between the United States and Britain was not a happy one for either side. American naval captains won some exciting one-on-one battles and the British invaded and burned Washington D.C., almost capturing President Madison. But the war solved nothing, not even when a general from Tennessee, Andrew Jackson, won America's sole great land victory, the battle of New Orleans, after a treaty had been already signed in Europe.

Many New Englanders hated the War of 1812 because it severely damaged their overseas trade. Before bad feelings turned too sour, however, the war was concluded and the United States entered an "era of good feelings" such as had not been known before, and would not be known for two generations. The president lucky enough to oversee this calm period was James Monroe, the fourth Virginian to hold that post.

Monroe's successor, John Quincy Adams, the son of the second president, was not so lucky. In 1824, he actually won fewer votes than his chief opponent, Andrew Jackson. But becuase neither candidate had a majority in the electoral college, the decision was left to the House of Representatives, which chose Adams. Jackson's supporters cried "Corruption!" and vowed to put their man in the White House in 1828.

SAM HOUSTON
Defeats Santa Anna, April 21, 1836

PRESIDENT JOHN TYLER
Supports the annexation of the Lone Star Republic, 1844

They were aided by a great upsurge in Democratic feeling. Responding to popular demand, state after state dropped rules that required people to own property in order to vote. The Age of Jackson was also the *Age of the Common Man* for Jackson insisted that every free white male should have the opportunity to elect his government and to participate in it.

Jacksonian Democracy did mean democracy only for free white males. Few people believed that women should be able to vote and Indians and blacks were largely viewed as despised minorities. Jackson's supporters, democratic among themselves, believed in pushing the Indians off their ancestral lands and keeping blacks in slavery. After Jackson was elected president in 1828, only the opposition Whig party, led by men such as Henry Clay and Daniel Webster, spoke out in favor of justice for the Indians. Many northern Whigs, furthermore, were increasingly convinced by abolitionists that slavery should be abolished as a crime against decency and the promise in the Declaration of Independence of equality for all. Few American men of any political persuasion believed that women should have equal rights. Nevertheless, in the great social tumult of the era, a small group of women and men met in *Seneca Falls*, New York in 1848 to proclaim a Declaration of Independence for women.

The Slavery Issue.

The greatest reform movement of the era was the anti-slavery movement. Abolitionists were a tiny minority. Although no northern state allowed slavery, not all whites were concerned that southerners continued to own human property. However, a growing number of northerners demanded that the western lands be reserved for free farmers. They wanted slavery kept out of the federal territories.

Until 1848, the issue of slavery in the territories seemed to be settled for all time. Under the terms of a compromise in Congress in 1820, a line had been drawn through the Louisiana Purchase at the latitude line of 36 degrees, 30 minutes. Slavery was forbidden north of this line.

Then, in 1845, American annexation of the independent Republic of Texas led to war with Mexico, from which the Texans had rebelled in 1835. After a string of military victories, the United States added the old Spanish lands between the Rocky Mountains and the Pacific Ocean to the Union. The United States truly stretched "from sea to shining sea." Suddenly, the question of slavery in the territories took on new urgency. Would the "peculiar institution," as southerners called slavery, be allowed in these new lands? Most southern political leaders were determined that it would. In the North and West, popular opinion was increasingly anti-slavery.

HENRY DAVID THOREAU
MARGARET FULLER
RALPH WALDO EMERSON
American Transcendentalist writers

North versus South.

There was no time to settle the disagreement coolly. In 1848, gold was discovered in the new acquisition of California and in 1849, tens of thousands of Americans rushed to the slopes of the Sierra Nevada Mountains. In 1850, California applied for admission to the Union as a free state, that is, a state in which slavery was forbidden.

Pro-slavery southern senators and congressmen vowed to resist. California was widely viewed as the most desirable part of the land taken from Mexico and many southerners lived there. If California became a free state, it was very likely that no new slave states would ever develop in the territories. Angry southern leaders like John C. Calhoun of South Carolina threatened that their states would secede from the Union if their interests were ignored.

The California issue was eventually compromised, but only at the cost of angering many northerners who opposed slavery. Under the terms of the *Compromise of 1850*, the question of whether slavery would be allowed in New Mexico Territory (which included present-day Arizona) was left open and Congress enacted a strong *Fugitive Slave Law* which enabled law enforcement officials to seize slaves who had run away from their southern masters and successfully escaped to a free state or territory.

The Republican Party Forms.

After the Compromise of 1850, tempers cooled until, in 1854, Senator Stephen A. Douglas of Illinois introduced a bill that provided for the organization of the Kansas and Nebraska Territories on old Louisiana Purchase lands. The *Kansas-Nebraska Act* provided that the people who would actually settle the two territories would vote for themselves as to whether or not they would allow slavery.

Douglas was not pro-slavery. His chief purpose in pushing this law through Congress was to make it possible for a transcontinental railroad, which nearly everyone agreed was necessary, to connect with Chicago, in his home state. Previous to the Kansas-Nebraska Act, such a route was impossible because the federal government did not have territorial officials in Kansas and Nebraska.

A miniature civil war between pro- and anti-slavery settlers in Kansas aroused anger back in Washington. However, the most important result of the Kansas-Nebraska Act was the formation of a new political party, the Republicans, whose guiding principle was: no slavery in any of the territories whatsoever.

Although the Republicans did not advocate abolishing slavery in the southern states, most abolitionists joined the party because of its anti-slavery leanings. This led southern Democratic

FREDERICK DOUGLASS
Writes and lectures in support of the abolition of slavery

HARRIET BEECHER STOWE
Writes Uncle Tom's Cabin, *1852*

party leaders to state flatly that if the Republicans came to power, they would have no choice but to take their states out of the Union. They could not remain under a government which threatened their basic social institution—slavery.

Lincoln and War. In November 1860, Republican candidate Abraham Lincoln was elected president. The party had selected him because he was a moderate. Unlike some Republican leaders such as William H. Seward and Salmon B. Chase, Lincoln emphasized the fact that he did not think the government should attack slavery where it already existed.

This did not satisfy the southern extremists called "fire-eaters." By March 1861, when Lincoln was inaugurated, seven states of the lower South seceded from the Union. Lincoln hoped to keep the other eight states, where slavery was legal, within the Union. If he could do so, the new Confederate States of America would almost certainly fail, and the seven rebellious states would have to return to Washington.

However, Lincoln insisted on exercising his presidential power in one of the few places in the deep South where it still existed—Fort Sumter, in the harbor of Charleston, South Carolina. When Fort Sumter needed supplies, he informed the governor of South Carolina (Lincoln refused to recognize the president of the Confederacy, Jefferson Davis) that he was sending only food and medicine to the fort—and no arms. Nevertheless, Confederate guns opened fire on Fort Sumter and the long Civil War was underway.

Americans Fight Americans. The Confederates regarded themselves as the true heirs of Thomas Jefferson and the American Revolution. As far as they were concerned, they were fighting for their independence against "foreign" rulers, just as the thirteen colonies had fought against Great Britain. Southern leaders also believed that they were defending the Constitution, which allowed slavery and implied clearly that slavery was a state institution in which the federal government had no right to interfere.

On the other hand, Abraham Lincoln and the supporters of the Union, including many leaders of the loyal slave states of Delaware, Maryland, Kentucky, Missouri, and West Virginia (which "seceded" from Virginia), insisted that the Constitutional Union and Liberty were one and inseparable. Only when all the states were united could the principles on which America was built be defended.

To this belief, Abolitionists added that the Declaration of Independence held that "all men are created equal." In fighting to bring an end to

ULYSSES S. GRANT
Commands the Union forces

ROBERT E. LEE
Commands the confederate forces

slavery, they believed that they were the true heirs of the American Revolution.

Confederate Hopes Soar.

For two years, the Confederates won most of the victories. With superior commanders like Robert E. Lee and Thomas "Stonewall" Jackson, southern armies in the East defeated advancing Union armies that outnumbered them, over and over again. Only when Lee went on the offensive himself in September 1862, was his army defeated. The battle of Antietam was important to President Lincoln because the rare Union victory enabled him to take the first important steps against slavery. He issued the *Emancipation Proclamation*, which declared that all slaves held in rebel territory as of January 1, 1863, were thereby freed. This presidential order turned the North's Civil War into a war "to make men free" as well as a war to save the Union.

In the West, the war went somewhat better for the Union. By the spring of 1863, Union armies and navies had captured the entire Mississippi River except for a short stretch dominated by the city of Vicksburg, Mississippi. If Vicksburg (and Port Charles, Louisiana) could be captured, the Confederacy would be sliced into two and the southern economy badly crippled.

General Ulysses S. Grant surrounded Vicksburg and sat down to starve the city out. The people of Vicksburg held out heroically. Eventually they ate virtually every animal in the town in the hopes that Lee or another Confederate general from the East would speed west to save them.

Instead, Lee, tried to lift the siege of Vicksburg by invading Pennsylvania. He hoped that his threat would force Lincoln to call troops from Vicksburg in order to defend the North. Instead, Lee was defeated at Gettysburg on July 3, 1863 by troops already in the East. On the next day, July 4, Vicksburg surrendered to Grant. It was the turning point of the war.

Grant's War of Attrition.

Lincoln made the Union hero of Vicksburg, Ulysses S. Grant, commander of all Union forces. Unlike his predecessors, Grant had an overall plan to win the war. While his most trusted aide, William T. Sherman, continued to fight in the West, before advancing across Georgia, Grant would grind away at Lee's courageous army.

The population of the Union states was more than twice that of the South. In addition, by 1863, freed slaves rushed to join the Union army by the tens of thousands. While Grant's forces continued to grow, Lee's shrunk with every casualty.

Lee was so skillful a commander that he delayed final defeat throughout 1864, the year Grant and Lincoln expected to finish the war. By April

PRESIDENT ABRAHAM
LINCOLN
*Preserves the Union,
1861-1865*

LOUISA MAY ALCOTT
*Publishes popular fiction during
Reconstruction*

1865, however, to fight further was suicide. Many of Lee's troops did not even have shoes to wear and food was in critically short supply. On April 9, 1865, at Appomattox Courthouse, Virginia, Lee surrendered. During the next several weeks, the other Confederate armies in Texas and elsewhere also laid down their arms.

But there was one more casualty to be counted. On April 14, 1865, accompanied by his wife, Abraham Lincoln attended a play at Ford's Theater in Washington. Into his private box slipped an actor who was a zealous pro-Confederate, John Wilkes Booth. Booth shot Lincoln in the head at point-blank range and the president died a few hours later.

"Sic semper tyrannis!" Booth had shouted as he escaped, "Thus always to tyrants!" In fact, he had killed a president who hoped to restore the Union by treating the rebel South with generosity. At his second inaugural just a few months after his Gettysburg Address, Lincoln had said, "With malice toward none; with charity for all; with firmness in the right, as God gives us to see the right, let us strive on to finish the work we are in; to bind up the nation's wounds; to care for him who shall have borne the battle, and for his widow, and his orphan—to do all which may achieve and cherish a just, and a lasting peace, among ourselves, and with all nations."

4. THE TRANSFORMATION OF AMERICA

Putting the Civil War behind them, Americans started an era that would see a basically agrarian, or farming, society become a modern industrial nation. The United States again achieved a stable political environment. As a result, both foreign and domestic *capital*, or money, became available for investment. Having vast stretches of usable land, large pools of *labor*, and seemingly unlimited natural resources, the United States found itself to be the right country, at the right place, at the right time.

The period between 1865 and 1900 was an era of rapid growth and rushing progress: the population of the United States more than doubled; the number of states increased from 36 to 45; and annual production of goods increased six-fold.

Between the day General Lee and General Grant met quietly at Appomattox and the noisy celebrations of New Year's Day 1900, the United States became the wealthiest and most powerful country in the world.

Railroads Crisscross the Nation. By 1865, the United States was already the world's leading

SOJOURNER TRUTH
Abolitionist and Feminist

DRED SCOTT
Slave who sued for his freedom

railroad country and long-distance construction had only begun. The Union Pacific-Central Pacific system, the first railroad to cross a continent, was built by mostly immigrant European and Chinese laborers. The first *transcontinental railroad* was completed at Promontory Point, near Ogden, Utah, on May 10, 1869.

Before 1900, five railroads tied the Pacific Coast to the population centers of the South and Northeast. Thanks in large part to the generosity of the federal government, which granted 131 million acres (53 million hectares) to railroad companies as both an incentive and as a way of financing construction, the length of American railroads increased from 35,000 miles in 1865 to 259,000 in 1900!

The Railroads, the Buffalo, and Indian Culture.
While the new rail-transportation network made the creation of a truly national economy possible, it also destroyed the culture of the last truly independent Indian tribes, the Plains Indians. The Sioux nations, the Crow, Cheyenne, Commanche, Arapahoe, Nez Perce, and Blackfoot tribes depended for their survival on the gigantic herds of bison—perhaps 15 million of them in 1860—which roamed the unbroken grasslands of the Great Plains. From the buffalo, the Indians got their food, clothing, shelter, tools, and weapons.

The great beasts had played a major part in their religion, too.

The railroads led to the near extinction of the bison. At first, to feed the gangs of workers building the Union Pacific and Northern Pacific, then to provide buffalo hides for the eastern and European markets, and finally simply to get rid of herds so that trains could run smoothly across the Plains, hunters like the famous Buffalo Bill Cody systematically destroyed the herds.

Without the bison, the Plains Indians were doomed. They fought valiant battles against units of the American army such as the Seventh Cavalry and the *Buffalo Soldiers,* black troops who were stationed in the West. But by 1880, almost all of the Plains people had been moved to reservations and encouraged to become farmers.

Agriculture's Extraordinary Growth.
The railroads, "two streaks of rust and a right of way," reached into the most isolated corners of the United States, ready and willing to haul farm produce to the cities. This opportunity sent farmers from the old states and people from abroad flocking to the great West. Between 1870 and 1900, they cultivated more new farmland than all American farmers had tamed during the preceding 263 years!

American farmers produced so much more

STEPHEN DOUGLAS/ABRAHAM LINCOLN
Lincoln-Douglas campaign debates

JEFFERSON DAVIS
President of the Confederate States of America

than the people of the cities could consume that the prices they received for their crops steadily declined. In 1896, an American farm family had to produce twice as much as they had in 1870, in order to maintain the same standard of living.

The result of this profit squeeze was a "farmer's revolt" during the 1890s. There were no outright battles but the anger of farmers was real and deep. They believed they had been betrayed by bankers, railroaders, and food processors ("middle-men"), who reaped the benefits of their toil while they, the farmers, were impoverished.

An Industrial Giant.
Another reason for the farmer's discontent was their feeling that they were no longer so important to the nation as they had been. In fact, agriculture did become less important because of the more rapid growth of industry in the final part of the 19th century. While land under cultivation doubled between 1865 and 1900, the value of manufactured goods increased more than six times.

Many companies involved in mass production sought to create a working monopoly of their business—that is, they wanted to control the entire business like John D. Rockefeller controlled oil refining. Fearing such concentrations of economic power, numerous Americans called on the government to regulate the *trusts,* as huge compa-

nies were known. Congress responded by creating the Interstate Commerce Commission in 1887 (to regulate railroads) and by passing the Sherman Antitrust Act in 1890 (to regulate monopoly in manufacturing). But because the laws were vague or poorly enforced, "Big Business" contined to be a dominant force in the United States at the end of the century.

Labor Tries to Organize.
The Knights of Labor, founded in 1869, signed up workers in secret, because many employers fired anyone who joined a union. The Knights believed that some-day the capitalist system—wherein property is owned by private investors—would have to be replaced by a society in which all citizens owned the factories in common and decided democratically on how to use them. While the leaders of the Knights of Labor believed firmly in working toward this goal through peaceful means, and even opposed strikes against employers, the Knights enjoyed their greatest success as a result of a series of sometimes violent strikes.

The American Federation of Labor, which took the place of the Knights as the nation's leading labor organization, was more conservative. Founded in 1881, A.F. of L. leaders like Samuel Gompers accepted capitalism as the best economic system possible. The A.F. of L.'s goals, Gompers

FORT SUMTER
*Civil War begins,
April 12, 1861*

PRESIDENT LINCOLN'S
FUNERAL TRAIN
Assassinated April 14, 1865

said, were to get *more* for its members within the system: better pay, shorter hours at work, better conditions of labor at the workplace. Only skilled workers were welcome in the A.F. of L. Not until after the turn of the century would unskilled workers have success in forming effective labor unions.

The "New Immigration." Labor unions had their greatest strength among native-born workers rather than with immigrants from abroad. In fact, because immigrants were generally willing to work for lower wages than native-born Americans, many unions opposed allowing more newcomers into the United States. In California, workingmen were staunch opponents of the Chinese immigrants who had begun to come to America during the Gold Rush of 1849 and continued arriving to take jobs constructing the railroads.

In 1882, Congress passed a law excluding most future Chinese immigration. But Congress did not restrict the flow of immigrants from Europe.

The New Immigrants came from southern and central Europe and the Near East. The fabulous growth of the economy meant that new labor was much in demand. Beginning about 1880, the *New Immigration* reached its peak in the early years of the 20th century, when more than a million Europeans entered the United States each year.

5. AN AGE OF EXPANSION, AN AGE OF REFORM

In the presidential election of 1896, the Republican party candidate, William McKinley, soundly trounced the hero of the angry western and southern farmers, Democratic and Populist party candidate, William Jennings Bryan. McKinley hoped to have a peaceful administration, to calm down the tempers that made the election campaign so furious., McKinley was not to get his wish for peace. Within two years, the President was pressured into supporting a war against Spain.

America Reaches Out. In 1892, wealthy Americans living in the kingdom of Hawaii had seized control of the islands and tried to join them to the United States. However, an investigation by President Grover Cleveland in 1893 revealed that most Hawaiians wanted to remain independent. Cleveland was an anti-imperialist. He was opposed to annexing a country against its people's wishes.

By 1898, however, the spirit of expansionism had grown in Washington. Cuba, one of the last Spanish colonies, was involved in a rebellion against Spain. Many Americans were sympathetic with the rebels. When an American battleship, the *Maine,* was destroyed by an explosion in Havana's

MOUNTAIN MEN
Early explorers of the West

HOMESTEADERS
Pioneer farmers

harbor, newspaper publishers, seemingly eager for war, convinced many Americans that Spain was responsible for the disaster.

Spain was no match for the energetic and powerful United States. Within a few months, Cuba was independent and the United States took control of the Spanish colonies of Puerto Rico and the Philippines. In the excitement, Hawaii became an American colony too.

Under President Theodore Roosevelt, who succeeded McKinley in 1901, the United States built and controlled the Panama Canal between the Atlantic and Pacific oceans. This vital waterway allowed the growing American navy to move easily from one part of the world to another.

Roosevelt practiced *gunboat diplomacy* in Central America. In order to prevent European nations from interfering in Central American and Caribbean affairs, he sent the United States marines into any country that became so unstable that European nations were tempted to move in. These policies kept European empires out of the western hemisphere, the goal of the Monroe Doctrine. But they also made many Central Americans bitterly resentful of "Yankee" interference.

The Progressive Era.

One reason some Americans felt justified in interfering in the affairs of other countries was their belief that American political institutions were superior to those of other nations. This self-confidence became all the keener in the early years of the 20th century because a great reform movement was underway. The *progressives,* as the reformers called themselves, cleaned out corruption in city governments; made state governments more democratic by introducing secret ballots in elections and allowing voters to remove officials from power before their terms were expired; and used the powers of the federal government to regulate big business.

President Theodore Roosevelt became known as the "trust-buster" because he used the courts to break up monopolies in several industries. He was just as popular for fighting big business at home as he was well-liked for using his "big stick" in keeping the nations of the Caribbean and Central America in line.

The Triumph of Progressivism.

Roosevelt retired in 1908 and was succeeded in the White House by William Howard Taft, a man of strongly conservative tendencies. Within a year, leading progressives in Congress like Robert M. "Fighting Bob" LaFollette were attacking Taft for opposing democratic reforms in Congress and reversing Theodore Roosevelt's campaign to conserve forest and mineral resources in the western states.

FOURTEENTH AMENDMENT PASSED, 1861
Black male citizens gain the right to vote

TRANSCONTINENTAL RAILROAD
Completed May 10, 1869

When the Republicans nominated Taft, Roosevelt ran for president as the candidate of the new Progressive party. It was called the *Bull Moose party* when Teddy told reporters that his health was excellent: he felt as "fit as a bull moose."

The split in the Republican party allowed the Democratic nominee, Woodrow Wilson, to win the presidency. Wilson too was a progressive, although, at first, he favored breaking up big companies rather than regulating their activities. Under Wilson, progressivism flourished. Not only did political and economic reforms continue, moral and social reform won widespread support. In 1913, the states ratified constitutional amendments allowing a *progressive income tax* and the election of senators by *popular ballot* rather than in the state legislatures. *Prohibition,* the movement to outlaw the manufacture and sale of intoxicating liquors (aimed at improving the morals of the nation), steadily won new support. Much more important was the *woman suffrage movement.* By 1916, when Wilson ran for re-election, most women sensed that their half-century fight to win the vote was near to success.

America Goes to War. By 1916, Woodrow Wilson's main concern was his struggle to keep the United States out of the World War that had broken out in Europe two years earlier. Steadily during those years, American opinion had shifted from a near unanimous desire not to get involved to an increasing determination that Germany, seen as an anti-democratic nation, be prevented from defeating democratic Great Britain and France.

American anger towards Germany also increased as a result of a new German weapon, the submarine. In order to defeat Great Britain, Germany's leaders concluded it would be necessary to starve the island nation's citizens. This meant torpedoing merchant vessels trading with Britain, even though that meant sinking ships of neutral nations like the United States.

Until early 1917, Wilson worked to come to an agreement with Germany. But by February 1917, the Germans had decided to take a calculated risk. Although they knew that *unrestricted submarine warfare* would bring the United States into the war, the German General Staff believed that Great Britain could be defeated before the Americans could take effective action. In April 1917, President Wilson asked Congress for a Declaration of War and, over some opposition, he got it.

The Sour Taste of War. Germany lost its gamble. After a few worrisome months when submarines devastated British shipping, the American and British navies took control of the North Atlantic. Ships carrying food, medicine,

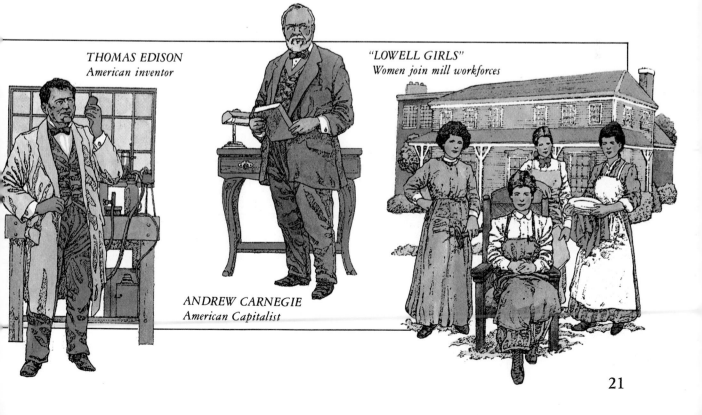

THOMAS EDISON
American inventor

ANDREW CARNEGIE
American Capitalist

"LOWELL GIRLS"
Women join mill workforces

war materiel, and American troops—called "doughboys"—streamed across the ocean. While American soldiers played an important part in the final year of battle, it was American industrial might that tipped the scales in favor of the allies.

With the people of Italy, France, and Britain deeply grateful for American help, Woodrow Wilson believed he could use the influence of the United States to establish a peace that was fair, instead of, as was traditional, punishing to the loser. Wilson wanted to create a Europe in which each nationality had its own country. He listed the terms of a fair and lasting peace in a document called the *Fourteen Points*.

Most important to Wilson was Point Fourteen. In order to resolve future disputes between nations without resorting to war, Wilson proposed the formation of the *League of Nations,* a kind of congress of all countries which would find peaceful solutions to international disputes.

The League was all-important to Wilson. To win approval of it by European leaders, he dropped his insistence that Germany not be punished by forcing the Germans to make large reparations payments to the victors. At home, Wilson refused to compromise with critics, who said that as the Covenant (or agreement) of the League was written, it seemed to deny the United States freedom of action in international affairs.

If he had agreed to the ratification of the Treaty of Versailles and the League Covenant with certain "reservations," Wilson could have won its approval. But the President was exhausted and ailing as a result of his trying schedule. He fell victim to a serious stroke while campaigning for the League in Pueblo, Colorado, and he refused to compromise. The United States never did join the League of Nations and, in 1920, tired of wartime idealism, the American people elected an easy-going senator, Warren G. Harding, as their president.

6. THE GREAT DEPRESSION, THE NEW DEAL, AND WORLD WAR II

Warren G. Harding presided over a sadly corrupt administration for little more than two years. When he died in 1923, he was succeeded by Calvin Coolidge, a shrewd politician who believed that the less a president did and said, the better off the country was.

Like many Americans during the "Roaring Twenties," Calvin Coolidge believed in business and businesspeople. Under "Silent Cal," as President Coolidge came to be known, the economy appeared to boom. Except for farmers, miners, blacks, and other disadvantaged groups, the entire

BOOKER T. WASHINGTON
Founds Tuskeegee Institute, 1881

ARRIVAL OF IMMIGRANTS
America as a land of opportunity

22

American people seemed to be prospering.

But there were serious weaknesses in the economy. In October 1929, just seven months after Coolidge had turned the presidency over to Herbert Clark Hoover, a panic on the New York Stock Exchange led to the worst economic depression in the history of the United States.

The New Deal. Just as they had admired big business during the prosperous 1920s, Americans blamed big business and the Republican party for the depression that followed. The Democratic party became the nation's majority party. Franklin Delano Roosevelt, a cousin of former-president Teddy Roosevelt, was easily elected president in 1932 and quickly set about a sweeping program of reform known as the *New Deal.*

In order to help people laid low by the depression, the New Deal created agencies to put people to work. There was an "alphabet soup" of temporary relief agencies such as the CCC (the Civilian Conservation Corps), a military-type body that put young men to work in the national forests and parks building trails, windbreaks, and recreational facilities. The PWA (Public Works Administration) hired unemployed workers to build roads, post offices, and other projects for which the federal government was responsible. The WPA (Works Progress Administration) did similar things but also hired unemployed workers, actors, and artists to do guidebooks to each of the states, bring theater to isolated parts of the country, and beautify federal buildings.

These agencies were intended to be temporary. But their success in relieving poverty helped create one guiding principle of contemporary liberalism, that curing economic and social problems is the responsibility of the federal government.

Longer lasting New Deal reforms included *Social Security,* retirement pensions for the elderly established in 1935; the steeply graduated income tax which made the rich pay a higher percentage of their income in taxes than the poor; and close regulation of finance and business by a number of alphabet agencies.

The Rise of Totalitarianism. But the New Deal did not conquer the Depression. Prosperity returned only when war in Europe and Asia brought increased orders for American manufactured goods and preparation by the federal government for the possibility that the United States would be dragged into a world war.

In Europe, Italy and Germany had fallen under the control of brutal right-wing governments: the *fascists* under Benito Mussolini in Italy, the *Nazis* behind Adolf Hitler in Germany. In Japan, aggressive army officers who wanted the military to be

JANE ADDAMS
*Founds Hull House
settlement, 1889*

THEODORE ROOSEVELT
San Juan Hill, 1898

supreme in their country, launched attacks on China designed to turn that huge but weak and divided country into a Japanese colony.

Because the United States was determined to keep China open to the trade of all nations, relations with Japan declined steadily throughout the 1930s. President Roosevelt stayed wide of the European troubles, however, because of the strength of isolationists—Americans who regarded World War I as a mistake not to be repeated—in both Congress and the country at large.

World War II in Europe.

The debate between the isolationists and those Americans who wanted to intervene in a war came to an end on December 7, 1941. On that day, Japanese planes based on aircraft carriers launched a devastating attack on the American Pacific Fleet in Pearl Harbor, Hawaii. Outrage against the Japanese was so great that every member of the Senate and House of Representatives but one, voted to declare war on Japan and Germany.

American strategy was to defeat Germany first. Japan was the weaker enemy. However, if the German Nazis had too much time to entrench themselves in Europe, there was a serious question as to whether or not they could ever be completely defeated.

During 1942 and 1943, the United States flooded the Soviet Union with materiel with which to fight Germany. While the Russians bore most of the burden of combating the efficient Germany army, the Americans and British first tried to invade Hitler's "Fortress Europe" through Italy. While most Italians favored the allies, that nation's mountains proved too effective as defenses. The Germans were able to hold the line.

Then, on June 6, 1944, came the greatest amphibious attack of all times, the D-Day beach-landings of 176,000 mostly American and British troops in Normandy, France. Supervised by General Dwight D. Eisenhower, more than 4,000 ships, 600 warships, and 11,000 planes were involved in the massive attack. It took a year for this army to join the Soviet forces driving from the east and successfully defeat the German forces, bringing Germany's surrender.

The War in the Pacific.

Because most American power was concentrated in Europe, the war against Japan actually took longer. The tide was turned against Japan by the middle of 1942 when, at the Battle of Midway Island—named because it is in the middle of the Pacific Ocean—the American fleet inflicted serious losses on the Japanese Navy. Japan was not wealthy in resources. When an aircraft carrier was lost to the Japanese navy, it could not be replaced. In contrast, America was so

WRIGHT BROTHERS
Wilbur and Orville fly
the first airplane, 1903

AMERICAN SOLDIERS
America enters World War I, 1917

wealthy and efficient, that shipyards and aircraft factories turned vessels and planes out faster than the Japanese could destroy them.

Slowly, and at the cost of high casualties in each battle, the American Navy under Admiral Chester Nimitz closed in on Japan through the Central Pacific. At the same time, U.S. Marines under General Douglas MacArthur "island-hopped" through New Guinea and the Philippines towards Japan. Once within the range of aircraft, the Americans steadily bombed Japan, hoping to break the people's morale.

But the lesson of bombing civilian targets in World War II and since has been that it does not destroy morale. Rather, people become all the more determined to fight the enemy. By August 1945, American commanders estimated that American troops would suffer a million casualties if they attempted to invade Japan. One alternative, a negotiated peace short of surrender, was unacceptable. American public opinion demanded the complete defeat of Japan.

The other alternative was to use the atomic bomb that had been developed secretly in the United States. No one was sure that the nuclear device dropped on Hiroshima, Japan, on August 6, 1945 would actually work. If it did not, then the United States would have to invade Japan for there was only one other atomic bomb then in existence. But the bomb did work, and, because Japan did not surrender immediately, the second bomb was dropped on Nagasaki several days later. World War II was over. The Nuclear Age had begun.

7. AMERICA BECOMES A SUPERPOWER

The postwar years saw the United States grow to become a "Superpower" among nations. Americans prospered as never before during the late 1940s and early 1950s. Industries producing *consumer goods,* from new homes and cars to completely new commodities like home television sets, more than took up the slack created in factories that had produced goods for the war effort. The unemployment rate took a number of dips and climbs but never did it approach the disheartening levels of the 1930s.

The president during most of the 1950s was the hero of the war against Germany, Dwight D. Eisenhower. "Ike," as Eisenhower came to be known, was widely perceived as a man who knew how to lead. Conservatives in his Republican party urged him to do away with the New Deal reforms that gave the federal government responsibility for many social welfare programs. Eisenhower

NINETEENTH AMENDMENT PASSED, 1920
American women gain the right to vote

GEORGE GERSHWIN
American composer for the "Jazz Age"

agreed not to expand them, but at the same time he faced up to the fact that in the modern world, government could no longer function as it had in the 19th century.

Cold War Abroad. In foreign affairs, Eisenhower was a voice of moderation. He had to be, for practically as soon as World War II was over, relations between the Soviet Union and the United States went sour. Whereas the United States wanted freely-elected democratic governments established in the nations of Eastern Europe, the Soviet Union was determined that the countries of the Balkans—Hungary, Czechoslovakia, Poland, and East Germany—be friendly to them. Twice in the 20th century Russia had been invaded and devastated by a powerful Germany. The Soviet dictator, Josef Stalin, and his successors, intended that it never happen again.

By 1947, in the words of British leader Winston Churchill, an *iron curtain* descended across Europe between democratic west and Soviet-dominated east. When the Soviets perfected their own nuclear weapon in 1949, the world was faced with the possibility that a third world war would mean the end of civilization. President Eisenhower refused to go along with the reckless threats against the Soviet Union by his secretary of state, John Foster Dulles. Eisenhower believed that it would be better to have a "Cold War," a war of chilling words, than the last war.

The Korean Conflict. Eisenhower and President Harry S. Truman before him, practiced the foreign policy of *containment.* By 1949, both men believed that Soviet influence must be contained where it already existed, in eastern Europe and in the People's Republic of China. In Europe, Containment was highly successful. In the Marshall Plan and Truman Doctrine, the United States pumped millions of dollars into the western European economy and those nations remained allies.

In Asia, however, Containment policy led to an undeclared but bloody war. In 1949, troops from Communist North Korea invaded the Republic of Korea, an American ally, in the south. President Truman immediately sent troops there under the flag of the United Nations, which had been founded in 1945. When these troops approached Korea's border with Communist China, China entered the war with hundreds of thousands of "volunteers." For three years, the Korean Conflict was deadlocked. Neither side was able to score a decisive victory. But neither were the Chinese or Americans able to come up with a compromise for ending the bloodshed. It was Eisenhower's promise to find a compromise that helped him win the presidential election in 1952.

CHARLES LINDBERGH
*Flies the first nonstop solo
trans-Atlantic flight, May 1927*

A Spirit of Restlessness. President Eisenhower managed to avoid all-out war in crises over Berlin in Germany and over the Suez Canal in the Near East. He also agreed to exchange goodwill visits with Premier Nikita Khruschev of the Soviet Union. When Khruschev visited the United States in 1959, he won the approval of many Americans during his good-natured tour of the country.

But before Eisenhower could visit the Soviet Union, an American U-2, a spy plane, was shot down while flying over Soviet territory and the pilot captured alive. Tired of Democratic party criticisms that he let his advisers make foreign policy, Eisenhower accepted full responsibility for the U-2 flight and Khruschev cancelled his invitation to the President to come to Russia.

By 1960, there was a spirit of restlessness loose in the United States that found the elderly and easy-going Eisenhower to be more a symbol of the past than an inspiration for the future. In 1960, a young and energetic senator from Massachusetts, John Fitzgerald Kennedy, exploited this restlessness by narrowly winning the Democratic nomination for the presidency and the election.

The Civil Rights Movement. John F. Kennedy presented Congress with a reform program he called the *New Frontier.* It was an expansion of the New Deal approach to government, providing for such things as government-funded medical care for the elderly and programs for winning friends abroad, such as the Peace Corps. Kennedy also responded to the increasing demands of black Americans that they be granted equality by sponsoring a Civil Rights Act in Congress.

The *Civil Rights Movement* had its beginning under Eisenhower in 1954 and 1955. In 1954, the Supreme Court reversed its approval of racial segregation in *Plessy v. Ferguson* and ruled that separate segregated schools were unequal by definition. The Court ordered southern school districts to desegregate "with all deliberate speed." In 1955, blacks seized the leadership of the movement for equality for themselves. Led by a young Baptist minister, Martin Luther King, Jr., blacks living in Montgomery, Alabama, boycotted the city's bus system because city law required black people to sit in the rear of buses.

King's doctrine of non-violent civil disobedience, violating unjust laws but peacefully submitting to arrest, aroused the enthusiam of black and white people throughout both North and South.

A Decade of Turmoil. President Kennedy never saw the triumph of the Civil Rights movement. In November 1963 he was touring Dallas, Texas when an assassin, Lee Harvey Oswald, shot and killed him. Just two days later, Oswald himself

FRANKLIN DELANO ROOSEVELT
Delivers a radio broadcast about
Pearl Harbor, December 1941

AMERICAN WORKINGWOMEN
Women replace the male
factory-workers-turned-soldiers

was murdered in the basement of the Dallas Police Department building. The American people were stunned. For years, authors and politicians suggested that Oswald had not acted alone but had been part of a conspiracy. Some suggested that Fidel Castro's Cuba, a nation Kennedy had helped invade unsuccessfully in 1961, was responsible. Others believed the conspirators were right-wing extremists who believed that Kennedy and all liberals were tools of the Communists.

Suspicions and impatience with government were typical of the 1960s. On the right was the John Birch Society, people who believed that the United States should be consecrated to a holy war against Communism. In 1964, this group supported Arizona senator Barry Goldwater's campaign for the presidency against Kennedy's successor, Lyndon B. Johnson of Texas. Goldwater was badly beaten, in large part because the American people feared that he would be reckless with America's nuclear arsenal.

At the other end of the spectrum were young black militants who had become impatient with the non-violent approach to equality of the Civil Rights Movement. The advocates of *Black Power* said that blacks should withdraw from political association with whites and work to win power for themselves. Black Power rhetoric was often violent and the movement never won any substantial gains. Young white militants, chased out of the Civil Rights Movement, came to concentrate their political energies on a long, drawn-out war that had broken out in Vietnam.

The Great Society and the Vietnam War.

Lyndon Johnson of Texas succeeded in carrying out his *Great Society* reform program in the wake of President Kennedy's assassination. The Great Society guaranteed black voting rights, launched a "War Against Poverty" in city slums, established Medicare for elderly citizens, and generally expanded social services throughout the country. Johnson would no doubt be remembered as one of the greatest reformer presidents because of his success in getting his programs enacted, if he had not become mired in an unwinnable war.

Although President Johnson implied in his re-election campaign of 1964 that he would not expand the American presence in Vietnam, by 1969 he had "escalated" the war until there were more than half a million young Americans fighting South Vietnamese guerrillas and regular troops from North Vietnam in the southern half of that troubled country. The United States was also bombing Communist North Vietnam with more munitions than had been dropped during the whole of World War II.

As the war dragged on, more and more Ameri-

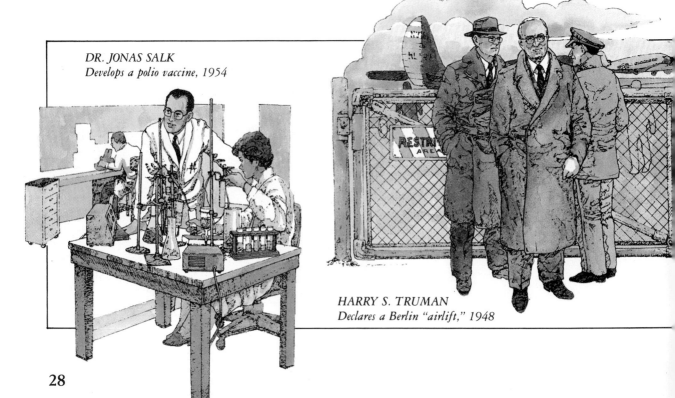

DR. JONAS SALK
Develops a polio vaccine, 1954

HARRY S. TRUMAN
Declares a Berlin "airlift," 1948

cans came to question the soundness of the United States' involvement in Vietnam.

The Nixon Presidency.

Confusion over the proper role for the United States in Southeast Asia, and distress about the increasing inflation that Johnson's costly social programs caused, led to the narrow victory in the presidential election of 1968 of Richard M. Nixon. In fact, Nixon did not end the war in Vietnam for four more years, and actually expanded it into neighboring Cambodia and Laos, resulting in the loss of friendly governments in those nations.

On the foreign front, however, Nixon earned himself an honored place in American diplomatic history by ending the quarter-century old refusal of the United States to recognize the government of Communist China. His active Secretary of State, Henry M. Kissinger, convinced the old Cold Warrior that China feared Russian power as much as the United States did. By establishing friendly relations with Peking, the capital of China, the United States could help prevent the possibility of a third world war.

After visiting China, Nixon and Kissinger also pursued a policy of *Detente* with the Soviet Union.

Watergate.

If Nixon helped the United States regain the initiative in relations with the other great powers of the world, he undercut confidence in the integrity of the United States government at home. Suspicion of political enemies led him, in the presidential election of 1972, to approve, at least after the fact, the actions of his aides in burglarizing and wiretapping the national headquarters of the opposition Democratic party in Washington's *Watergate* apartment and office complex.

After easily winning re-election by a landslide, Nixon step-by-step trapped himself in lies that were proved to be such by tape recordings he himself had made. In October 1973, Vice President Spiro Agnew was forced to resign over charges that he had taken bribes as governor of Maryland. In August 1974, ailing with phlebitis, a disease that nearly killed him, Nixon too had to resign in order to avoid almost sure impeachment and removal from office. He was succeeded by the vice president he had appointed to replace Agnew, Gerald R. Ford of Michigan.

Ford was welcomed by many American people as a simple, honest man. However, he damaged his reputation by extending a complete presidential pardon to President Nixon. Many critics regarded the pardon as part of a deal, although Ford insisted the pardon was necessary so that the American people could put the agony of Watergate behind them once and for all. To many

UNITED NATIONS HEADQUARTERS
The Secretariat building completed, 1952

REV. MARTIN LUTHER KING, JR.
*Leader of the non-violent civil-rights movement
and winner of the 1964 Nobel Peace Prize*

Americans, the political lesson of Watergate was that in a democracy, no one is above the law; even the president is to be held accountable.

Jimmy Carter Becomes President.

By November 1976, the luster had worn off Henry Kissinger's foreign policy. Right wing extremists regarded recognition of Communist China and detente with the Soviet Union as encouraging those powers to stir up discontent in the undeveloped Third World. Many liberals were aghast that Kissinger supported brutal right-wing movements such as that led by the army officers who overthrew the democratically-elected government of Chile and murdered its leader, Salvador Allende.

Even more important, the Watergate affair had caused many concerned citizens to question the integrity of their government at home. Two political outsiders, men who had never been involved in the federal government, rose to the fore in both the Republican and Democratic parties.

In the Republican party, ex-movie star and governor of California, Ronald Reagan, spoke for the far right in calling for a tough foreign policy and a cutback in social programs at home. He mounted a substantial challenge for the Republican presidential nomination but incumbent President Gerald Ford held it off and represented the Republican party in November, 1976.

Jimmy Carter, the moderate and amiable governor of Georgia, was practically unknown nationally when the long season of caucuses and primaries that made presidential nominations began. A few early victories, however, rolled into a bandwagon that gave him the nomination. Carter insisted he would bring refreshing new policies to Washington and won a narrow victory in November.

The Carter Presidency.

As president, Jimmy Carter's personal decency and call for the respect of human rights throughout the world won approval almost everywhere. He sponsored a major breakthrough in the hope for peace in the Middle East by pressuring Egypt and Israel into a treaty of accord. And as president, Carter also furthered the hopes of disarmament by pursuing SALT, the Strategic Arms Limitation Talks, with the Soviet Union.

But Carter was plagued by a runaway inflation he could do nothing to halt. Indeed, the economy was faced with an unprecedented woe, *stagflation,* in which prices continued to rise while the economy stagnated. The greatest disaster to befall him, however, was the fall of America's longtime ally, the Shah of Iran, and the seizure of 53 American hostages by the fanatical right-wing government that succeeded the Shah, followers of the Ayatollah Ruhollah Khomeini.

RICHARD M. NIXON
Offers friendship between America and
the Peoples Republic of China

ASTRONAUTS ARMSTRONG AND ALDRIN
America puts the first men on the moon, July 1969

30

The Conservative Surge.

American support for Carter's attempts to rescue the hostages helped him beat off an attempt by Senator Edward M. Kennedy to win the Democratic presidential nomination in 1980. But in the fall election, he was buried by the landslide victory of Republican candidate Ronald Reagan, who shed his image as a rightwing extremist during the campaign by presenting the public with moderate rhetoric.

But Reagan had no intention of leaving the reforms of the preceding half-century untouched. He introduced budgets that slashed federal expenditures on domestic programs and increased defense spending. Although he had campaigned on a promise to balance the budget and reduce the national debt, Reagan actually pushed federal indebtedness to heights never previously known—over one trillion dollars. However, because the economy did improve dramatically in 1983, Reagan's popularity remained high.

The Election of 1984.

Despite the efforts of the Democratic party, President Reagan and Vice President George Bush easily won re-election. Reagan won 525 electoral votes, while Walter Mondale won only 13. Ten of Mondale's electoral votes came from his home-state of Minnesota, with the remaining three votes coming from the District of Columbia. In a landslide victory, President Reagan carried the remaining 49 states, winning 59 percent of the popular vote. Whether because of the improving economy or the renewed spirit of confidence and patriotism that characterized the American mood in 1984, the "great communicator," as Ronald Reagan was called, had a second term in which to carry out his policies.

Toward the Year 2000.

The United States faces the final years of the 20th century with both challenges and opportunities. Uppermost is the hope, voiced by all sides, that the arms race with the Soviet Union can be halted and then scaled down. Without an end to the construction of more weapons capable of destroying the earth, there can be no security, nor can there be the economic development necessary to improve life for Americans or the citizens of the undeveloped nations.

In foreign relations, the question arises, how is the United States to react to turmoil in the Third World? What kinds of governments should Americans support? What kinds should be opposed?

The issue of equal rights remains a pressing concern for every group of Americans. And issues of access and opportunity for all remain to be addressed.

In these areas, it is the historian's task to show what went before. In a representative democracy, it is the citizens' task to determine the future.

One Land, Many People

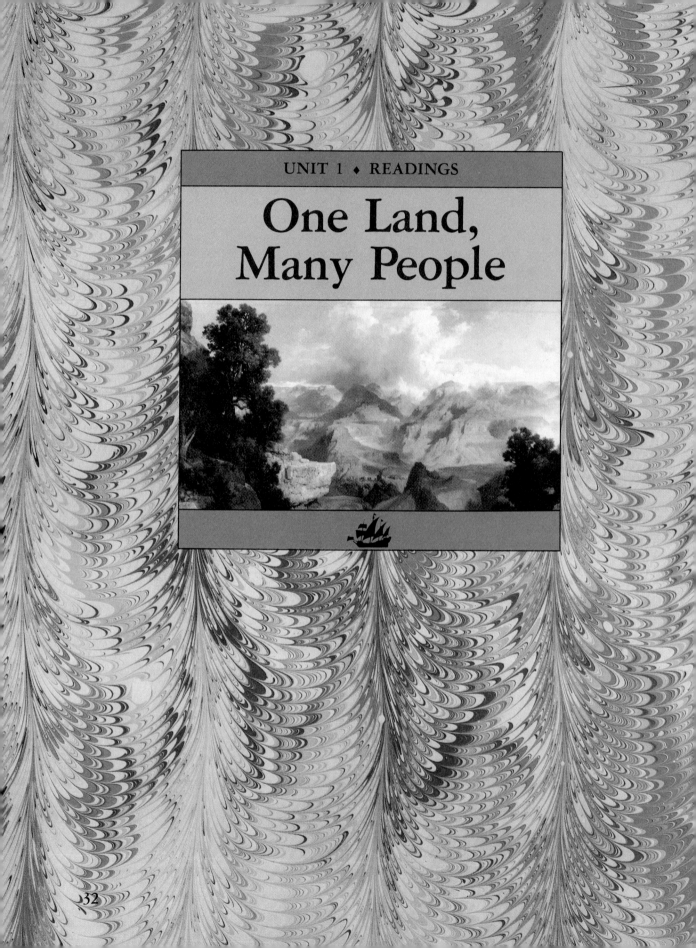

A MEETING OF TWO WORLDS

25,000 BC–1754 AD

1. PRINCE HENRY THE NAVIGATOR ENCOURAGES EXPLORATION

Prince Henry the Navigator of Portugal encouraged explorations of foreign lands and was responsible for improvements in ship-building and navigational instruments. His accomplishments were set down in writing by Gomes Eannes de Azurara, who lived during Henry's time. The following selection describes Henry's motives for exploration.

The praises which I tell you of our noble Prince Henry were not invented by my own wit, but are the living voices of his virtues and his great merits, which would be of great profit to every one of you, if you could keep them whole and sound in your thought, not desiring that I had related them more briefly, since it would be difficult to find anyone like him among the men of our time.

The noble spirit of this Prince was ever urging him both to begin and to carry out very great deeds. For which reason he always kept ships well armed against the Moors, both for war, and because he had also a wish to know the land that lay beyond the isles of Canary and that Cape called Bojador [NW Africa], for up to his time, neither by writings, nor by the memory of man, was known with any certainty the nature of the land beyond the Cape. Some said indeed that Saint Brandan had passed that way; and there was another tale of two galleys rounding the Cape, which never returned. But this doth not appear at all likely to be true. It seemed to him that if he or some other lord did not endeavor to gain that knowledge, no mariners or merchants would ever dare to attempt it (for it is clear that none of them ever trouble themselves to sail to a place where there is not a sure and certain hope of profit) and seeing also that no other prince took any pains in

this matter, he sent out his own ships against those parts, to have manifest certainty of them all. And this was the first reason of his action.

The second reason was that if there chanced to be in those lands some population of Christians, or some havens, into which it would be possible to sail without peril, many kinds of merchandise might be brought to this realm, which would find a ready market because no other people of these parts traded with them; and also the products of this realm might be taken there, which traffic would bring great profit to our countrymen.

The third reason was that, as it was said that the power of the Moors in that land of Africa was very much greater than was commonly supposed, and that there were no Christians among them; and because every wise man is obliged by natural prudence to wish for a knowledge of the power of his enemy; therefore Prince Henry exerted himself to discover how far the power of those infidels [non-Christians] extended.

The fourth reason was because during the one and thirty years that he had warred against the Moors, he had never found a Christian king who would aid him in the said war. Therefore he sought to know if there were in those parts any Christian princes, in whom the charity and the love of Christ was so ingrained that they would aid him against those enemies of the faith.

The fifth reason was his great desire to make increase in the faith of our Lord Jesus Christ and to bring to him all the souls that should be saved.

Selection adapted from Gomes Eannes de Azurara, *The Chronicle of the Discovery and Conquest of Guinea*, Vol. 1, translated by Charles R. Beazley and Edgar Prestage. Originally published by the Hakluyt Society, London, copyright © 1896; reprinted by Burt Franklin, New York.

CRITICAL THINKING

1. Why did Prince Henry think it was important to know "the power of his enemy"?
2. Without his encouragement of foreign exploration, what did Prince Henry predict would happen?
3. Why was it to Prince Henry's advantage to be the first prince to send his ships to foreign lands?

The Adventures of Marco Polo

Marco Polo was not the first European to make the long dangerous trip to Cathay, as China was then known, nor even the first to write about it. A hundred years before him, between 1160 and 1173, a Spanish Rabbi named Benjamin of Tudela traveled to the borderlands of China. Between 1245 and 1255, two Roman Catholic priests, John of Plano Carpini and William of Rubruck, visited the capital of the Mongols who had conquered China and most of Siberia and Central Asia.

But those men merely visited the Mongol empire and returned home. Their written accounts, which existed in only a few copies, were known to only a handful of people. Marco Polo actually lived in East Asia for fifteen years, working as a high official of Kublai Khan, the greatest emperor in the world. Polo's *Book of Various Experiences,* about what he saw in China, Burma, and Indo-China, was an instant "best seller." The printing press had not yet been invented. But Polo's writings were copied by hand, and copied again and again. They were carried carefully to the farthest corners of Europe where kings, queens, priests, and merchants read and reread them. (Or, because only a few people could then read, they had the *Book of Various Experiences* read to them.)

Because of this book, Marco Polo played a part in the history of America, even though he lived and died two hundred years before the voyage of Columbus. For it was he, perhaps more than any other single person, who set into motion the desire of Europeans to learn about the world beyond the boundaries of Europe. It was the combination of curiosity and the desire to trade for the exotic goods of East Asia, which Polo described, that led to the Age of Exploration.

Marco Polo was born, about 1254, into a wealthy Venetian family. He was perhaps twelve when his father, Nicolo, and uncle, Maffeo, returned to Venice in 1266, after a long absence. The Polos were merchants. It was natural that they began to think about how they might use their friendship with the Mongols to establish regular trade with China. In 1271, after long preparation, Nicolo and Maffeo left Venice. Seventeen year old Marco went with them.

Marco Polo remained in the Chinese capital, present-day Peking, for fifteen years. The emperor was impressed by young Marco, and made him a kind of diplomat. Marco visited far-off possessions of the Khan, carrying instructions and returning with reports. Thus he became, probably the most widely-traveled human being of his times.

In 1295, Marco Polo returned to Venice to find that his country was at war with its chief competitor in trade, the city-state of Genoa. Marco was captured and spent two years as a prisoner-of-war. It was while he was in prison that he wrote his book about what he had seen in Asia.

Not everything in this document should be accepted as pure fact. Marco Polo surely exaggerated many of his tales of the splendid wealth of Kublai Khan's empire, and he told of what he had heard as well as of what he had seen for himself.

But that is not as important as the fact that for two centuries the *Book of Various Experiences* fascinated Europeans and aroused their interest in the lands of the East and the spices, fine silk cloth, tapestries, carpets, and magnificent porcelain that could be found there. Just as important, were Marco Polo's descriptions of the coasts of China. Could there be any doubt that the waters that washed the coasts of Europe were the same waters that crashed against Chinese beaches? The question was: which was the best way to go to reach those shores? Christopher Columbus's answer was to sail west. Such a course, however, resulted not in reaching the land of Marco Polo—Asia—but, rather, in the discovery of the New World of the Americas.

UNLOCKING HISTORY
KEY DOCUMENT

*I*t is the custom in making presents to the grand khan, for those who have it in their power, to furnish nine times nine of the article of which the present consists. Thus, for instance, if a province sends a present of horses, there are nine times nine, or eighty-one head in the drove; so also of gold, or of cloth, nine times nine pieces. By such means his majesty receives at this festival no fewer than a hundred thousand horses. On this day it is that all his elephants, amounting to five thousand, are exhibited in procession, covered with housings of cloth, fancifully and richly worked with gold and silk, in figures of birds and beasts. Each of these supports upon its shoulders, two coffers filled with apparatus for the use of the court. Then follows a train of camels, in like manner laden with various necessary articles of furniture. When the whole are properly arranged, they pass in review before his majesty, and form a pleasing procession.

In Zipangu [Japan], they have gold in the greatest abundance, its sources being inexhaustible. But as the king does not allow of its being exported, few merchants visit the country, nor is it frequented by much shipping from other parts. To this circumstance we are to attribute the extraordinary richness of the sovereign's palace, according to what we are told by those who have access to the place. The entire roof is covered with a plating of gold, in the same manner as we cover houses, or more properly churches, with lead. The ceilings of the halls are of the same precious metal; many of the apartments have small tables of pure gold, of considerable thickness; and the windows also have golden ornaments. So vast, indeed, are the riches of the palace, that it is impossible to convey an idea of them. In this island there are pearls also, in large quantities, of a pink color, round in shape, and of great size, equal in value to, or even exceeding that of the white pearls. It is customary with one part of the inhabitants to bury their dead, and with

another part to burn them. The former have a practice of putting one of these pearls into the mouth of the corpse. There are also found there a number of precious stones.

Java abounds with rich commodities. Pepper, nutmegs spikenard, galengal [ginger], cubebs [peppercorns], cloves, and all the other valuable spices and drugs, are the produce of the island; which occasion it to be visited by many ships laden with merchandise, that yields to the owners considerable profit. The quantity of gold collected there exceeds all calculation and belief. From thence it is that the merchants of Zai-tun and of Manji in general have imported, and to this day import, that metal to a great amount, and from thence also is obtained the greatest part of the spices that are distributed throughout the world.

On one island I visited, sappan, or brezil wood, is produced in large quantities. Gold is abundant to a degree scarcely credible; elephants are found there; and the objects of the chase, either with dogs or birds, are in plenty. From hence are exported all those porcelain shells, which, being carried to other countries, are there circulated for money.

Selection adapted from *The Travels of Marco Polo, the Venetian*. Edited by Thomas Wright. Published by Henry G. Bohn, London, 1854. Facsimile Reprint published by AMS Press, Inc., New York.

CRITICAL THINKING

1. Summarize, in one sentence, what Marco Polo was trying to convey to Europeans in the passage you just read.
2. How might Marco Polo's words have influenced the early voyages of discovery and, consequently, the exploration of the New World?

2. CHRISTOPHER COLUMBUS DISCOVERS A "NEW WORLD"

The journal that Columbus kept during his voyage in 1492 was lost, but parts of it were copied before it disappeared. This explains why much of the selection that follows is written in the third person.

Thursday, 11th of October.

The course was west-southwest, and there was rougher sea than there had been during the whole of the voyage. The crew saw sandpipers, and a green reed near the ship. Those of the caravel *Pinta* saw a cane and a pole, and a land plant, and a small board. The crew of the caravel *Niña* also saw signs of land, and a small branch covered with berries. Everyone breathed afresh and rejoiced at these signs.

After sunset the Admiral [Christopher Columbus] returned to his original west course, and they went along at the rate of 12 miles an hour. Up to two hours after midnight they had gone 90 miles. As the caravel *Pinta* was faster, and went ahead of the Admiral, she found the land, and made the signals ordered by the Admiral. The land was first seen by a sailor named Rodrigo de Triana. But the Admiral, at ten o'clock, saw a light, though it was so uncertain that he could not affirm it was land. He called Pero Gutierrez and said that there seemed to be a light, and that he should look at it. He did so, and saw it. The Admiral said the same to Rodrigo Sanchez of Segovia, whom the King and Queen had sent with the fleet as inspector, but he could see nothing, because he was not in a place whence anything could be seen. After the Admiral had spoken he saw the light once or twice, and it was like a wax candle rising and falling. It seemed to be an indication of land; but the Admiral [wanted to make] certain that land was close. The Admiral asked and admonished the men to keep a good lookout on the forecastle, and to watch well for land; and to him who should first cry out that he saw land, he would give a silk jacket, besides the other rewards promised by the Sovereigns. At two hours after midnight the land was sighted at a distance of two leagues. The vessels waited for daylight; and on Friday they arrived at a small island called, in the language of the Indians, *Guanahani* [San Salvador]. Presently they saw naked people. The Admiral went on shore in the armed boat with Martin Alonso Pinzon, and Vicente Yañez, his brother, who was captain of the *Niña*. Having landed, they saw trees very green, and much water, and fruits of diverse kinds. The Admiral called to the two captains, and to the others who leaped on shore and said that they should bear faithful testimony that he, in presence of all, now took possession of the said island for the King and for the Queen, his Lords.

Presently many inhabitants of the island assembled. What follows is in the actual words of the Admiral. "I," he says, "that we might form great friendship, for I knew that they were a people who could be more easily freed and converted to our holy faith by love than by force, gave to some of them red caps, and glass beads to put round their necks, and many other things of little value, which gave them great pleasure, and made them so much our friends that it was a marvel to see. They afterward came to the ship's boats where we were, swimming and bringing us parrots, cotton threads in skeins, darts, and many other things; and we exchanged them for other things that we gave them, such as glass beads and small bells. Finally, they took all, and gave what they had with good will. It appeared to me to be a race of people very poor in everything. They go as naked as when their mothers bore them. All I saw were youths, none more than thirty years of age. Some paint themselves white, others red, and others of what color they find. Some paint their faces, others the whole body, some only round the eyes, others only on the nose. They neither carry nor know anything of arms, for I showed them swords, and they took them by the blade and cut themselves through ignorance. They have no iron, their darts being wands without iron, some of them having a fish's tooth at the end, and others being pointed in various ways. They are all of fair stature and size, with good faces, and well made. I saw some with marks of wounds on their bodies, and I made signs to ask what it was, and they gave me to understand that people from other adjacent lands came with the intention of seizing them, and that they defended themselves. I believed, and still believe, that the other people come here from the mainland to take them prisoners. They should be good servants and intelligent, for I observed that they quickly took in what was said to them, and I believe that they would easily be made Christians, as it appeared to me that they had no religion."

Saturday, 13th of October.

"As soon as dawn broke many of these people came to the beach, all youths, as I have said. They came to the ship in small canoes, made out of the trunk of a tree like a long boat, and all of one piece, and wonderfully worked, considering the country. If the canoe capsizes they all promptly begin to swim, and to bale it out with gourds that they take with them. . . . I was attentive, and took trouble to ascertain if there was gold. I saw that some of them had a small piece of gold fastened in a hole they have in the nose, and by signs I was able to make out that to the south there was a king who had great cups full, and who possessed a great quantity. I tried to get them to go there, but afterward I saw that they had no inclination. I resolved to wait until tomorrow in the afternoon and then to depart, shaping a course to the southwest, for, according to what many of them told me, there was land to the south, to the southwest, and northwest, and that the natives from the northwest often came to attack them, and went on to the southwest in search of gold and precious stones.

"This island is rather large and very flat, with bright green trees, much water, and a very large lake in the center, without any mountain, and the whole land so green that it is a pleasure to look on it. Here is found the gold they wear fastened in their noses. But, in order not to lose time, I intend to go and see if I can find the island of Cipango [Japan]."

Selection adapted from *The Journal of Christopher Columbus (During His First Voyage, 1492–93)*, translated by Clements R. Markham. Originally published by the Hakluyt Society, London, copyright © 1893. Reprinted by Burt Franklin, New York.

CRITICAL THINKING

1. Describe the attitude of the Indians toward Christopher Columbus and his men.
2. What evidence did Columbus offer as proof of the Indians' intelligence?
3. How does the statement " . . . I intend to go and see if I can find the island of Cipango [Japan]" relate to Columbus's belief that he had reached Asia?

3. HERNANDO CORTEZ DESCRIBES THE GOLD GIFTS FROM MONTEZUMA

After swearing their allegiance to the Spanish king, Montezuma and other Aztec chiefs turned over much of their treasure to Hernando Cortez. In the following excerpt from a letter to Charles V, Cortez describes that treasure; one-fifth of it which was to go to the king, one-fifth to Cortez, and the rest to be divided among the members of the expedition.

I spoke to Montezuma one day, and told him that Your Highness was in need of gold, . . . and I besought him to send some of his people, and I would also send some Spaniards, to the provinces and houses of those lords who had there submitted themselves to your Highness to pray them to assist Your Majesty with some part of what they had. Besides Your Highness's need, this would testify that they began to render service, and Your Highness would the more esteem their good will; and I told Montezuma that he also should give me from his treasures, as I wished to send them to Your Majesty. He asked me afterwards to choose the Spaniards whom I wished to send, and two by two, and five by five, he distributed them through many provinces and cities. He sent some of his people with them, ordering them to go to the lords of those provinces and cities and tell them that I had commanded each one of them to contribute a certain measure of gold. Thus it was done, and all those lords to whom he sent gave very compliantly, as had been asked, not only in valuables, but also in bars and sheets of gold, besides all the jewels of gold, and silver, and the feather work, and the stones, and the many other things of value from which I assigned and allotted to Your Sacred Majesty your share, amounting to the sum of one hundred thousand *ducats* [gold coins] and more. These, besides their value, are so marvelous that, because of their novelty and strangeness, they have no price, nor is it probable that all the princes ever heard of in the world possess such treasures. Let not what I say appear exaggerated to Your Majesty, because in truth, all the things created on land, as well as in the sea, of which Montezuma had ever heard, were imitated in gold, as well as in silver, and in precious stones, and feather work, with such perfection that they

Montezuma (left) was emperor of Mexico when the Spanish arrived. Never imagining that Hernando Cortez (right) meant to conquer the Aztecs, Montezuma welcomed him with gifts of gold.

seemed almost real. He gave me a large number of these for your Highness, besides others, he ordered to be made in gold, for which I furnished him the designs, such as statues, crucifixes, medals, jewelry of small value, and many other of our things which I made them copy. In the same manner, Your Highness obtained, as the one-fifth of the silver which was received, one hundred and odd *marks* [more than 800 ounces], which I made the natives mold in large and small plates, bowls, cups, and spoons, which they executed as perfectly as we could make them comprehend.

Besides these, Montezuma gave me a large quantity of stuffs, which considering it was cotton, and not silk, was such that there could not be woven anything similar in the whole world, for texture, colors, and handiwork. Amongst these were many marvelous dresses for men and women, bed clothing, with which that made of silk could not be compared, and other stuffs such as tapestry suitable for drawing-rooms and churches. There were also blankets and rugs for beds, both of feather work and of cotton in various colors, also very marvelous, and many other things so curious and numerous I do not know how to describe them to Your Majesty. He also gave me a dozen *cerbatanas* [blow guns] with which he shoots, and of their perfection I likewise know not

what to say to Your Highness; for they were decorated with very excellent paintings of perfect colors, in which there were figures of many different kinds of birds, animals, flowers, and various other objects, and the mouthpieces and extremities were bordered with gold. He gave me a pouch of gold net for the pellets, which he told me he would give me also of gold. He gave me also some turquoises and many other things, whose number is almost infinite.

Selection adapted from *Fernando Cortes, his five letters of Relation to the Emperor Charles V*, Vol. I, translated and edited by Francis Augustus MacNutt. First published in 1908. Reprinted by the Rio Grande Press, Inc., Glorieta, New Mexico, 1977.

CRITICAL THINKING

1. How did Hernando Cortez persuade Montezuma to help him gather Aztec treasures?
2. Why did Cortez think it necessary to write that his description of the treasures was not an exaggeration?
3. Why did Cortez write that the Aztec treasures were priceless, aside from their value in gold and silver? What was so unusual about them?

4. MONTEZUMA'S FOLLOWERS LAMENT THE CONQUISTADORS' GREED

The following passages are taken from written Aztec accounts of the conquest of Mexico. Notice that in the first passage the Europeans are referred to as "gods." This is because the Mexicans believed them to be descendants of the Aztec god, Quetzalcoatl. The second narrative refers to events that took place after Montezuma was imprisoned by the Spaniards. Following these passages is a poem that describes the once great Aztec empire after its conquest.

Then Montezuma dispatched various chiefs to meet the Spaniards. They gave the "gods" emblems of gold and feathers, and golden necklaces. And when they were given these presents, the Spaniards burst into smiles; their eyes shone with pleasure; they were delighted by them. They picked up the gold and fingered it like monkeys; they seemed to be transported by joy, as if their hearts were illumined and made new.

The truth is that they longed and lusted for gold. Their bodies swelled with greed, and their hunger was ravenous; they hungered like pigs for that gold. They snatched at the golden emblems, waved them from side to side and examined every inch of them.

They went to Montezuma's storehouse, where his personal treasures were kept. The Spaniards grinned like little beasts and patted each other with delight.

When they entered the hall of treasures, it was as if they had arrived in Paradise. They searched everywhere and covered everything; they were slaves to their own greed. All of Montezuma's possessions were brought out: fine bracelets, necklaces with large stones, ankle rings with little gold bells, the royal crowns and all the royal finery—everything that belonged to the king and was reserved to him only. They seized these treasures as if they were their own, as if this plunder were merely a stroke of good luck. And when they had taken all the gold, they heaped up everything else in the middle of the patio. . . .

The Mexicans were too frightened to approach. They were crushed by terror and would not risk coming forward. They shied away as if the Span-iards were wild beasts, as if the hour were midnight on the blackest night of the year. Yet they did not abandon the Spaniards to hunger and thirst. They brought them whatever they needed, but shook with fear as they did so. They delivered the supplies to the Spaniards with trembling hands, then turned and hurried away.

Flowers and Songs of Sorrow

Nothing but flowers and songs of sorrow
are left in Mexico . . . ,
where once we saw warriors and wise men.

We know it is true
that we must perish,
for we are mortal men.
You, the Giver of Life,
you have ordained it.

We wander here and there
in our desolate poverty.
We are mortal men.
We have seen bloodshed and pain
where once we saw beauty and valor.

We are crushed to the ground;
we lie in ruins.
There is nothing but grief and suffering
in Mexico . . . ,
where once we saw beauty and valor.

Have you grown weary of your servants?
Are you angry with your servants,
O Giver of Life?

CRITICAL THINKING

1. Why does it seem as if the Spaniards "had arrived in Paradise" when they entered Montezuma's hall of treasures?
2. Explain why the Spaniards are called "slaves to their own greed."
3. Why did the poet think the Aztec Empire had fallen?

AZTEC ARTIFACTS
A Legacy Of Craftsmanship

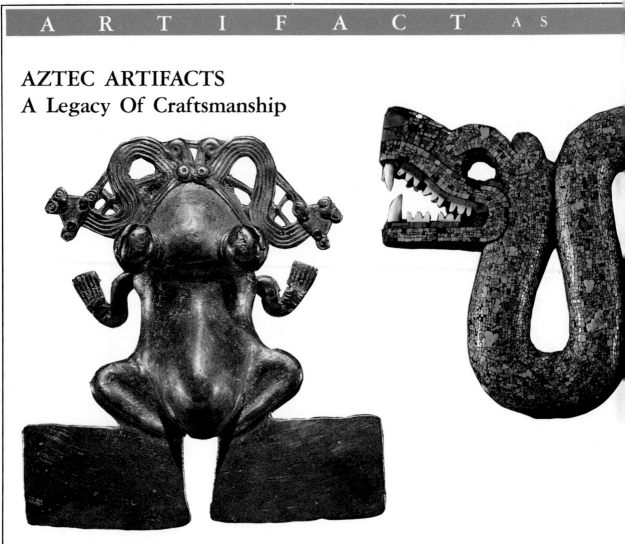

Note the exaggerated and highly stylized design. The artist gave the frog an elaborately forked tongue that curls mystically from the frog's mouth.

Small animal sculptures were made by the Aztecs who ruled in what is now Mexico when the Europeans discovered the New World. The small gold, ceramic, and stone animals provide several clues about the Aztecs. Such mastery of craft and variety of subject is likely to be the product of a developed culture. Since these figures existed in fairly large quantities, it is apparent that gold was plentiful.

Historians have concluded that many of these animals were parts of jewelry worn by Aztec priests, rulers, and some warrior heros. Pendants were attached to necklaces or other body ornaments. Aztec sculpture and painting show that people of high rank wore adornments in their ears, noses, lips, and on head dresses and body garments as well as around their arms and legs.

The sculptures depict animals that played an important role in Aztec religion. Gods were often shown as animals, such as the feathered snake named Quetzalcoatl. Rattlesnakes were honored because they were believed to have links to the world of the spirits. The Aztecs saw themselves as part of nature and felt that they shared the world with the animals.

D O C U M E N T

Another example of jewelry was a gold lip plug made in the shape of an eagle. An Aztec nobleman wore this ornament through a hole in his lower lip.

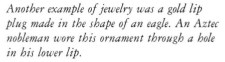

A turquoise-encrusted pendant represents Tlalhoc, the two-headed serpent god whom the Aztecs believed to be the source of rain and abundant crops.

CRITICAL THINKING

1. Summarize the manner in which these three artifacts and others like them tell about Aztec culture.
2. Archeologists may not know as much about the lives of the poor in an Aztec community as they do about the lives of the rich and powerful. From your reading, can you suggest some reasons for this?
3. Why might the artist have made the back feet of the golden frog so plain?

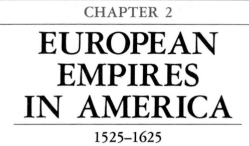

CHAPTER 2

EUROPEAN EMPIRES IN AMERICA

1525–1625

1. BARTOLOMÉ DE LAS CASAS CONDEMNS THE SPANIARDS' TREATMENT OF INDIANS

Bartolomé de las Casas was a Christian friar who witnessed the degrading working conditions under which some Indians in the New World were forced to work by the Spanish. In the following account, he describes the plight of the Indians and condemns their persecutors.

At first, the Indians were forced to stay six months away from home at work. Later, the time was extended to eight months and this was called a shift, at the end of which they brought all the gold for minting [making into coins]. During the minting period, the Indians were allowed to go home, a few days' journey on foot. One can imagine their state when they arrived after eight months, and those who found their wives there must have cried, lamenting their condition together. Of those who had worked in the mines, a bare 10 percent survived to start the journey home. Many Spaniards had no scruples about making them work on Sundays and holidays, if not in the mines, then on minor tasks such as building and repairing houses, carrying firewood, etc. They fed them cassava bread, which is adequate nutrition only when supplemented with meat, fish, or other more substantial food. The minero [Spaniard in charge of the mines] killed a pig once a week, but he kept more than half for himself and had the leftover cooked daily for thirty or forty Indians, which came to a bite of meat the size of a walnut, per individual. While the minero was eating, the Indians were under the table, just like dogs and cats, ready to snatch a bone. This ration applied only to mine workers; others never tasted meat in their lives and sustained themselves exclusively on cassava and other roots.

In exchange for his life of services, an Indian received 225 *maravedís*, paid them once a year as pin money or *cacona*, as Indians call it, which means bonus or reward. This sum bought a comb, a small mirror, and a string of green or blue glass beads.

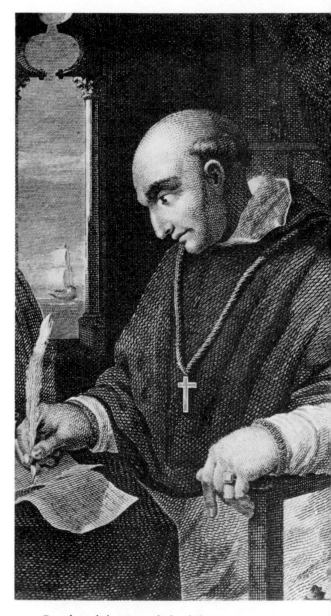

Bartolomé de las Casas deplored the Europeans' inhumane treatment of the native peoples they found living in the newly discovered lands.

I believe the above clearly demonstrates that the Indians were totally deprived of their freedom and were put in the harshest, fiercest, most horrible servitude and captivity which no one who has not seen it can understand. Even beasts enjoy more freedom when they are allowed to graze in the fields. When the Indians were allowed to go home, they often found it deserted and had no other recourse than to go out into the woods to find food and to die. When they fell ill, which was very frequently because they are a delicate people unaccustomed to such work, the Spaniards did not believe them and pitilessly called them lazy dogs, and kicked and beat them; and when illness was apparent they sent them home as useless. I sometimes came upon dead bodies on my way, and upon others who were gasping and moaning in their death agony, repeating "Hungry, hungry." And this was the freedom, the good treatment, and the Christianity that Indians received.

Is there a single nation which would not think that the world is full of just such evildoers as the Spaniards if their first experience with that outside world was with a people who entered territories by force, killed the people, and deprived them of their rights? Just because the Spaniards told them to obey the King of Castile [Spain], supposing they understood, what obligation did they have to obey since they already had their own kings? Or rather, if they had consented, would they not be judged as ridiculously stupid for doing so? Was trying to defend oneself from Spanish cruelties such a crime? Even beasts are allowed the right of self-defense.

Selection adapted from Bartolomé de las Casas, *History of the Indies*, translated and edited by Andrée Collard. Published by Harper & Row, Publishers, New York, 1971. Copyright © 1971 by Andrée M. Collard. All rights reserved.

CRITICAL THINKING

1. Using Bartolomé de las Casas' account, summarize what daily life was like for the Indians who worked for the Spanish.
2. Why might de las Casas have felt moved to write his account of the conditions he witnessed?

2. ROBERT COOPY PLEDGES HIMSELF TO A CONTRACT OF INDENTURE

In return for their passage to the colonies, indentured servants agreed to serve a master for a specific period of time—usually between four and seven years. The following document is one of the earliest contracts of indenture, dated September 7, 1619. In this agreement, signed in England, Robert Coopy hired himself out to four men who owned a plantation in Virginia.

That the said Robert does hereby covenant [pledge] faithfully to serve the said Sir William, Richard, George, and John for three years from the day of his landing in the land of Virginia, there to be employed in the lawful and reasonable works and labors of them and to be obedient to such governors as they shall from time to time appoint and set over him. In consideration whereof, the said Sir William, Richard, George, and John do covenant with the said Robert to transport him (with God's assistance) with all convenient speed into the said land of Virginia at their expense, and there to maintain him with convenient diet and apparel suitable for such a servant; and in the end of the said term to make him a free man of the said country, thereby to enjoy all the liberties, freedoms, and privileges of a freeman there; and to grant to the said Robert thirty acres of land within their territory.

Selection adapted from Abbot Emerson Smith, *Colonists in Bondage: White Servitude and Convict Labor in America, 1607–1776*. Published by The University of North Carolina Press, copyright © 1947. Reprinted by Peter Smith, Gloucester, Massachusetts, 1965.

CRITICAL THINKING

1. What benefits does this contract guarantee Robert Coopy?
2. What will Sir William, Richard, George, and John gain by bringing Robert Coopy to Virginia?

3. THE *MAYFLOWER* PASSENGERS PLEDGE THEMSELVES TO A COMPACT OF GOVERNMENT

The Mayflower Compact *was drawn up by William Bradford while the Plymouth settlers were still aboard the* Mayflower. *Its purpose was to legally bind the group together so that once ashore, the colony could run smoothly.*

In the name of God, Amen. We, whose names are underwritten, the loyal subjects of our dread Sovereign Lord King James, . . . having undertaken for the glory of God, and advancement of the Christian faith, and the honor of our King and country, a voyage to plant the first colony in the northern parts of Virginia, do . . . solemnly and mutually, in the presence of God and one another, covenant [pledge] and combine ourselves together into a civil body politic, for our better ordering and preservation and furtherance of the ends aforesaid; and by virtue hereof do enact, constitute, and frame such just and equal laws, ordinances, acts, constitutions, and offices, from time to time, as shall be thought most meet [fitting] and convenient for the general good of the colony; unto which we promise all due submission and obedience. In witness whereof we have hereunto subscribed our names at Cape Cod the eleventh of November, in the reign of our Sovereign Lord King James of England, France, and Ireland, . . . and of Scotland. . . . Anno Domini, 1620.

Selection from *Documents of American History*, edited by Henry Steele Commager. Published by Appleton-Century Crofts, Division of Meredith Publishing Company, New York, copyright © 1963. All rights reserved.

CRITICAL THINKING

1. Summarize what the passengers aboard the *Mayflower* pledged to do once they were ashore?
2. What reason might William Bradford have had to draw up a compact before everyone got off the *Mayflower?*

4. EDWARD WINSLOW DESCRIBES THE PILGRIMS' FIRST THANKSGIVING CELEBRATION

Writing in 1681, Edward Winslow describes the Pilgrims' first settlement, and includes an account of their first Thanksgiving. Since he is writing this letter to a friend in England who is planning to come to Plymouth, Winslow ends with some helpful advice.

In this little time that a few of us have been here, we have built seven dwelling-houses and four buildings for the use of the colony, and have made preparation for various others. Last spring we planted some twenty acres of Indian corn, and sowed some six acres of barley and peas. According to the example of the Indians, we fertilized our ground with herrings, which we have in great abundance. God be praised, our corn did well, and our barley did fairly well, but our peas were not worth gathering. We feared they were planted too late, for they came up very well, and blossomed, but the sun dried out the blossoms.

After our harvest was gathered, our governor sent four men out to hunt wild birds so that we might have a special celebration after we had reaped the rewards of all our hard labor. During this time, many of the Indians came amongst us, including Massosoit, their greatest king, with ninety of his men. For three days we entertained and feasted them; and they went out and killed five deer, which they bestowed on our governor. Although food is not always as plentiful as it was at this time, by the goodness of God we are so far from want, that we often wish you could partake of our plenty.

We have found the Indians very faithful in their pact of peace with us, very loving, and ready to please us. We often go to them, and they come to us. We walk as peaceably and safely in the woods as in the highways in England. We entertain the Indians in our homes, and they, in turn, give us their deer meat. They are a people without any religion or knowledge of God, yet they are very trustworthy, quick to understand, intelligent, and just.

The climate here is similar to England's. If there is any difference at all, it is somewhat hotter here in summer. Some people think it is colder in winter, but I cannot say so from my own experi-

Pilgrim Edward Winslow, a founder of Plymouth Colony, came to America aboard the Mayflower.

plums of three sorts—white, black, and red; and an abundance of roses—white, red, and pink. The country needs industrious men to employ. It would grieve your hearts if you had seen as I have, so much land, near good rivers, uninhabited; while those parts of the world in which you live are so overcrowded with people.

Now, because I expect your arrival among us, I thought it would be good to advise you of a few necessary things. Do not rely too much on us for corn at this time, for we shall have little enough till harvest. Build your cabins as open as you can, and bring a good supply of clothes and bedding with you. Bring a musket or hunting gun for every man. If you bring anything for comfort in this country, butter or salad oil, or both, is very good. Do not bother to bring rice, unless you plan to use it during the voyage, since our Indian corn is just as good. Bring paper and linseed oil for your windows, with cotton yarn for the wicks of your lamps.

I will write no further for the present, since I hope to see you when the next ship arrives. So I take my leave, commending you to the Lord for a safe journey unto us.

> Your loving friend,
> E.W.

Plymouth, in New England, this 11th of December, 1621.

CRITICAL THINKING

1. How does Winslow's account compare with popular ideas about the first Thanksgiving?
2. What contrast does Winslow draw between Plymouth and England?
3. Who seems to gain most from the relationship between the Indians and the Pilgrims? Explain.

ence. The air is very clear and not foggy, as has been reported. I cannot remember a more seasonable year than the one we have enjoyed here. Once we have cattle, horses, and sheep, I do not doubt that men might live as contented here as in any part of the world. For fish and fowl, we have a great abundance. Fresh cod in the summer is commonplace. Our bay is full of lobsters and a variety of other fish, all summer long. We have no oysters nearby, but we can have them brought by the Indians when we want. During the spring, the earth produces wild salad herbs. There are grapes, both white and red, and very sweet and strong; strawberries, gooseberries, raspberries, etc.;

JOHN WHITE

As modern newspapers send photographers to document newsworthy events, the English sent artist, John White, to observe the New World in the late sixteenth century. Probably accompanying explorer Martin Frobisher, White went to the Baffin Islands, off the coast of Greenland, in 1577. While he was there, White painted watercolors of Eskimos he found living there.

In 1585, he landed with the first Englishmen on Roanoke Island, off North Carolina. His task was to paint the people, the flowers, and wildlife of this uncharted world. In this way, he hoped to supply information for the English and perhaps encourage prospective settlers.

Between 1585 and 1597, John White was governor of the Roanoke Colony. He produced simple and direct watercolors showing aspects of the native people and their surroundings. He depicted no warlike or aggressive behavior but rather chose to show the people as farmers and fishermen.

After White returned to England, his drawings were copied and became popular advertisements for the new land across the Atlantic. When he returned to Roanoke in 1591, he found that the colonists had mysteriously disappeared. The only record of Roanoke Colony is the art that John White left behind.

An Eskimo who lived on Baffin Island is shown wearing a warm parka and heavy boots. The style and material of his hardy outdoor apparel caught John White's eye, because such clothing had never been seen in England.

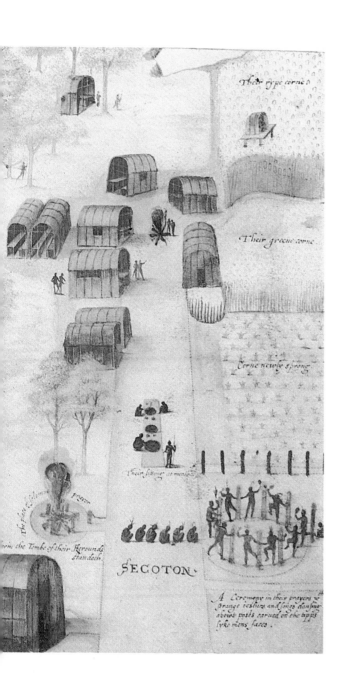

Secotan was a farming community. In this drawing White documents the different stages of growing corn, the Indians planting corn, cooking and eating meals, and celebrating the harvest in a vigorous dance.

John White's drawings, like the one reproduced above, provide a unique record of the native American people's appearance and style of dress in the sixteenth century.

CRITICAL THINKING

1. Cite ways in which John White's drawings might be compared to postcards of our time.
2. From these three drawings, what might late sixteenth century Europeans notice that would encourage them to consider making a visit to the New World? What might frighten them?

CHAPTER 3
THE THIRTEEN COLONIES
1625–1732

1. THOMAS DUDLEY'S UNEXAGGERATED ACCOUNT OF LIFE IN THE MASSACHUSSETTS BAY COLONY IN 1631

Thomas Dudley was a leader of the Massachusetts Bay Colony. His letter to Bridget, Countess of Lincoln (the wife of his former employer), is one of the earliest accounts of life in New England. The following excerpt illustrates Dudley's reason for coming to America—the search for religious freedom that led many other Puritans to join him.

Thomas Dudley, a stern Puritan, arrived in America in 1630 and served four times as governor of the Massachusetts Bay Colony.

12th of March, 1631

If any come hither to America, to plant for worldly ends, that can live well at home, he commits an error of which he will soon repent. But if he comes for spiritual reasons, he may find here what may well content him: materials to build, fuel to burn, ground to plant, seas and rivers to fish in, a pure air to breathe in, good water to drink till wine or beer can be made, which together with the cows, hogs, and goats brought hither already may suffice for food, for as for fowl and venison they are enjoyed here as well as in England. For clothes and bedding they must bring them with them till time and industry produce them here. In a word, we have little to be envied, but endure much to be pitied in the sickness and mortality of our people. And I do the more willingly make this open and plain, lest other men should be disappointed when they come hither, as we were because of letters sent to us from America to England, wherein honest men, out of a desire to draw over others to them, wrote somewhat exaggerated accounts of many things here. If any godly men, out of religious ends, will come over to help us in the good work we are about, I think they cannot dispose of themselves nor of their estates more to God's glory and the furtherance of their own reckoning.

Regarding the discouragement which the sickness and mortality among us may give to such who have cast any thoughts this way, the natural causes seem to be in the lack of warm lodging and good diet to which Englishmen are accustomed at home; and in the sudden increase of heat which they endure that are landed here in summer. Other causes God may have, which I forbear to mention, leaving this matter to the further dispute of physicians and divines.

CRITICAL THINKING

1. According to Thomas Dudley, why would a settler who desired only worldly gains be committing an error by coming to New England?
2. Why might Dudley want to be truthful about the hardships that were a part of life in New England?

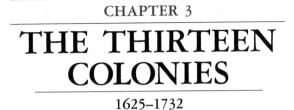

2. AN EXAGGERATED ACCOUNT OF LIFE IN THE COLONY OF BALTIMORE IN 1633

In 1633, an account of the colony of Baltimore was published to encourage settlers to emigrate to Maryland. The following selection describes the origins and advantages of the colony.

This province is near the English colony in Virginia. The Most Serene King of England, Charles I, desired that it should be called the land of Maria or Maryland, in honor of Maria, his wife. The same Most Serene King, out of his own noble disposition, recently, in the month of June 1632, gave this province to the Lord Baron of Baltimore and his heirs forever; and this gift he has confirmed and ratified by the public seal of his whole kingdom. Therefore, the Most Illustrious Baron has already determined to lead a colony into those parts, first and especially, in order that he may carry both here and to the neighboring places, the light of the Gospel and the truth; then, also with this intent, that all the associates of his travels and toils may be invited to a share in the gain and honor, and the empire of the King be more widely extended.

For this purpose he is seeking, with all speed and diligence, for men to accompany him on this voyage, both such as intend to try their fortunes with him, and others also. Indeed, after attentively considering the whole matter, and taking the advice of men, distinguished for their experience and wisdom, he has now weighed with great care all the advantages as well as disadvantages which have hitherto advanced or hindered other colonies; and found nothing which does not tend strongly to confirm him in his design, and promise him the most prosperous success.

The first and most important design of the Most Illustrious Baron, which also ought to be the aim of the rest who go in the same ship, is not to think so much of planting fruits and trees in a land so fruitful, as of sowing the seeds of religion and piety. Surely a design worthy of Christians, worthy of angels, worthy of Englishmen.

It is acknowledged that the situation of the country is excellent and very advantageous. The climate is serene and mild, not oppressively hot like that of Florida and old Virginia, nor bitterly cold like that of New England; but a middle temperature between the two, and enjoys the advantages, and escapes the evils, of each. It has two very large arms of the sea, both of them bays abounding in fish. One of these, named the Chesapeake, is twelve miles wide, and spread out between two districts, runs from south to north 160 miles. It is navigable for large ships, and is interspersed with various large islands suitable for grazing; and at these islands can be caught, in the greatest abundance, the fish called *shad*.

The other bay they call the Delaware, in which codfish are caught all the year round; but the most convenient time to catch them is in the colder months, for the warm weather interferes with salting them.

There are various notable rivers. The chief of these they call the Attawomech [Potomac], a navigable river running eastward 140 miles, where there is such a lucrative trade with the Indians, that a certain merchant in the last year exported beaver skins to the value of 40,000 gold crowns, and the profit of the traffic is estimated at thirty fold.

On the plains and in the open fields there is a great abundance of grass; but the country is, for the most part, thickly wooded. There are a great many hickory trees, and oaks so straight and tall that beams, sixty feet long and two and a half feet wide, can be made of them. The cypress trees also grow to a height of eighty feet, before they have any branches, and three men with arms extended can barely reach round their trunks. There are plenty of mulberry trees to feed silkworms.

The woods, moreover, are passable, not filled with thorns or undergrowth, but arranged by nature for pasture for animals, and for affording pleasure to men. There are fruitful vines, from which wines can be made, and a grape as large as cherries, the juice of which is thick and oily. There are three kinds of plums. Mulberries, chestnuts, and walnuts are so plentiful that they are used in various ways for food. Strawberries and raspberries are also to be found there.

Of the fishes the following kinds are already known: sturgeons, shrimps, skates, trouts, white salmon, mussels, periwinkles, and numberless others of that sort, the names and species of which are unknown.

For the rest, there are such numbers of hogs and deer that they are rather an annoyance than an advantage. There are also vast herds of cows and wild oxen, fit for beasts of burden and good to eat, besides five other kinds of large animals unknown to us, which the neighboring people use for food.

There are also great quantities of wild turkeys, which are twice as large as our tame and domestic ones. There are blackbirds, too, and thrushes, and many and various kinds of small birds, some red, some blue, etc., etc. In the winter, there are plenty of swans, geese, cranes, herons, ducks, parrots, and a great many others, unknown in our country. Peaches also are so abundant that an honorable and reliable man positively declared that he gave a hundred bushels to his pigs last year. Even the peas in those parts grow ten inches long in ten days. It is such a good grain country, that, in the worst years, the seed yields two hundred fold, while the soil is so rich as to provide three harvests a year.

It is probable that the soil will prove to be adapted to all the fruits of Italy, figs, pomegranates, oranges, olives, etc;—to pass over the rest briefly. There is also hope of finding gold, for the neighboring people wear bracelets of gold and long strings of pearls. It is also to be expected that the provident industry and long experience of men will discover many other advantages and sources of wealth.

Selection adapted from *Narratives of Early Maryland, 1633–1684*, edited by Clayton Colman Hall. Published by Charles Scribner's Sons, New York, copyright © 1910. All rights assigned to Barnes & Noble, 1946.

CRITICAL THINKING

1. In order of importance, state Lord Baltimore's reasons for establishing a colony in Maryland.
2. Why would it be important to a potential settler to know that the colony is near two large bays?
3. What expectation is raised by the statement that "the provident industry and long experience of men will discover many other advantages and sources of wealth?"

3. ROGER WILLIAMS WRITES ABOUT THE CIVIL AFFAIRS OF PROVIDENCE

Roger Williams wrote the following letter to Governor Winthrop of Massachusetts shortly after establishing the settlement of Providence. The exact date of the letter is unknown; it was probably written in 1636 or 1637. It is particularly interesting because it provides the earliest account of the civil affairs of Providence, Rhode Island.

Much Honored Sir,

The frequent experience of your loving ear, ready and open toward me, (in what your conscience has permitted), emboldens me to request a word of private advice with the soonest convenience.

The condition of myself and those few families here planting with me, you know full well: we have no Patent [Charter], nor does government by civil authorities suit with our present condition. Hitherto, the masters of families have ordinarily met once a fortnight and consulted about our common peace, watch [guard duty], and planting; and mutual consent has finished all matters with speed and peace.

Now of late some young men, single persons (of whom we had much need) being admitted to

In Rhode Island, in the 1630s, clergyman Roger Williams established a democratic government based on religious and political freedom.

freedom of inhabitation, and promising to be subject to the orders made by the consent of the householders, are discontented with their condition, and seek the freedom of vote also, and equality, etc.

I have, therefore, had thoughts of proposing to my neighbors a double subscription, concerning which I shall humbly crave your help.

The first concerning ourselves, the masters of families, thus:

We whose names are hereunder written, former inhabitants of the Massachusetts (upon occasion of some difference of conscience), being permitted to depart from the limits of that Patent, came over into these parts, and being cast by the Providence of the God of Heaven, remote from others of our countrymen amongst the barbarians in this town of New Providence, do with free and joint consent promise each unto other, that for our common peace and welfare (until we hear further of the King's royal pleasure concerning ourselves) we will from time to time subject ourselves to such orders and agreements as shall be made by the greater number of the present householders. In witness whereof we hereunto subscribe, etc.

Concerning those few young men, and any who shall hereafter desire to plant with us, this:

We whose names are hereunder written, being desirous to inhabit in this Town of New Providence, do promise to subject ourselves to such orders and agreements as shall be made from time to time, by the greater number of the present householders of this Town. In witness whereof, etc.

Hitherto we chose one officer to call the meeting at the appointed time; now it is desired by some of us that the householders perform that work and also gather votes and see the watch go on, etc.

I have not yet mentioned these things to my neighbors, but shall, once I receive your loving counsel.

Also, since this land I have purchased at my own charge, my question is this:

Whether I may not lawfully desire this of my neighbors, that as I freely subject myself to common consent, and shall not bring in any person into the town without their consent, so also that against my consent no person be violently brought in and received.

I desire not to sleep in security nor dream of a nest which no hand can reach. I cannot but expect changes, including the change of the last enemy—death—yet dare I not despise a liberty, which the Lord seems to offer me, if for my own or others' peace; and, therefore, have I been thus bold to present my thoughts unto you.

R. Williams.

Selection adapted from *Old South Leaflets*, Vol. III. Published by Directors of the Old South Work, Old South Meeting House. Boston.

CRITICAL THINKING

1. Although Roger Williams was forced to leave Massachusetts, he remained on friendly terms with Governor Winthrop. How does this letter demonstrate that fact?
2. What motivated Roger Williams to propose two "subscriptions" to his neighbors?
3. Why does Williams feel it is his responsibility to do what he thinks is best for the colony?

4. THE TOLERATION ACT OF 1649 PROVIDES FOR RELIGIOUS FREEDOM IN MARYLAND

The Maryland Toleration Act, passed in 1649, was designed to prevent the Catholics in Maryland from being persecuted. This document achieved lasting importance as a model for the legal concept of religious freedom.

Forasmuch as in a well governed and Christian Commonwealth, matters concerning religion and the honor of God ought in the first place to be taken into serious consideration and endeavored to be settled, be it therefore ordered and enacted by the Right Honorable Cecilius Lord Baron of Baltimore that whatsoever person or persons within this Province shall from henceforth blaspheme God, that is, curse him, or deny our Saviour Jesus Christ to be the son of God, or shall deny the holy Trinity, the father, son, and Holy

Ghost, shall be punished with death and confiscation or forfeiture of all his or her lands and goods.

And be it also further enacted that whatsoever person or persons shall from henceforth in a reproachful manner or way declare, call, or denominate any person or persons any name or term in a reproachful manner relating to matter of religion shall for every such offence forfeit and lose the sum of 10 shillings sterling.

And whereas the enforcing of the conscience in matters of religion has frequently resulted in dangerous consequences in those commonwealths where it has been practiced, and for the more quiet and peaceable government of this Province, and the better to preserve mutual love and amity amongst the inhabitants thereof, be it therefore enacted that no person or persons whatsoever within this Province, professing to believe in Jesus Christ, shall from henceforth be any way troubled, molested, or disapproved of because of his or her religion nor in the free exercise thereof, nor any way compelled to the belief or exercise of any other religion against his or her consent, so long as they be not unfaithful to the Lord Proprietary, or molest or conspire against the civil government. And that all and every person and persons that shall wrong, disturb, trouble, or molest any person whatsoever within this Province professing to believe in Jesus Christ for or in respect of his or her religion, or the free exercise thereof, shall be compelled to pay triple damages to the party so wronged.

Selection adapted from *Great Issues in American History, From Settlement to Revolution, 1584–1776*, edited by Clarence L. Ver Steeg and Richard Hofstadter. Published by Vintage Books, a division of Random House, Inc., New York, copyright © 1969 by Random House, Inc. Copyright © 1958 by Richard Hofstadter.

CRITICAL THINKING

1. According to this Act, what matter is considered to be of greatest importance in a well governed and Christian commonwealth?
2. Explain why the Maryland Toleration Act refers to religious problems in other commonwealths.

5. WILLIAM PENN FRAMES A GOVERNMENT FOR PENNSYLVANIA

William Penn wrote the following "Frame of Government" for Pennsylvania in 1682. While the document itself remains important, its Preface has become an enduring tribute to the potential for justice and mercy in government.

Government seems to me a part of religion itself, a thing sacred in its institution and end. For, if it does not directly remove the cause, it crushes the effects of evil, and is as such an emanation of the same Divine Power that is both author and object of pure religion; the difference being that the one is more free and mental, the other more corporal and compulsive in its operations. But that is only to evildoers; government itself being otherwise as capable of kindness, goodness, and charity as a more private society.

They weakly err that think there is no other use of government than correction, which is the coarsest part of it. Daily experience tells us that the care and regulation of many other affairs, more soft and daily necessary, make up much of the greatest part of government.

For particular frames and models of government, it will become me to say little. My reasons are:

First, there is nothing the intelligence of men is more busy and divided upon. It is true, they seem to agree to the aim of happiness; but in the means, they differ, and the cause is not always lack of light and knowledge, but lack of using them rightly. Men side with their passions against their reason, and their sinister interests have so strong a bias upon their minds that they lean to them against the good of the things they know.

Second, I do not find a model in the world that time, place, and some special emergencies have not necessarily altered, nor is it easy to frame a civil government that shall serve all places alike.

Third, I know what is said by the several admirers of monarchy, aristocracy, and democracy, which are the rule of one, a few, and many, and are the three common ideas of government. But I choose to solve the controversy with this small distinction, and it applies to all three: Any government is free to the people under it (whatever be

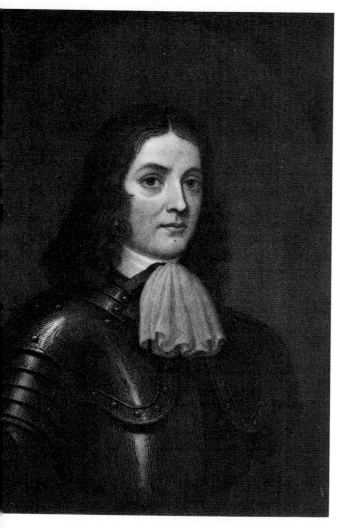

William Penn founded the colony of Pennsylvania in 1681 as a refuge for English Quakers.

the frame) where the laws rule, and the people participate in making those laws, and more than this is tyranny, oligarchy, or confusion.

But lastly, when all is said, there is hardly one frame of government in the world so ill designed by its first founder that in good hands would not do well enough. Governments, like clocks, go from the motion men give them; and as governments are made and moved by men, so by them they are ruined, too. Wherefore, governments rather depend upon men than men upon governments.

I know some say let us have good laws, and no matter for the men that execute them; but let them consider that though good laws do well,

good men do better; for good men will never lack good laws, nor submit to ill ones. That, therefore, which makes a good constitution must keep it, namely: men of wisdom and virtue, qualities that —because they descend not with worldly inheritances—must be carefully propagated by a virtuous education of youth.

These considerations of the weight of government, and the various opinions about it, made me uneasy about publishing the ensuing frame and conditional laws, foreseeing both the censures they will meet with, from men of differing temperaments and interests, and the occasion they may give of discourse beyond my design.

But the power of necessity induced me to a compliance that we have (with reverence to God, and good conscience to men) to the best of our skill, contrived and composed the frame and laws of this government, to the great end of all government, namely: to support power in reverence with the people, and to secure the people from the abuse of power; that they may be free by their just obedience, and the magistrates honorable, for their just administration; for liberty without obedience is confusion, and obedience without liberty is slavery. To carry this balance is partly owing to the constitution, and partly to the magistracy. Where either of these fail, government will be subject to convulsions; but where both are lacking, it must be totally subverted; then where both meet, the government is likely to endure. Which I humbly pray and hope God will please to make the destiny of Pennsylvania. Amen.

Selection adapted from *The Annals of America*, Vol. I. William Benton, Publisher. Published by Encyclopaedia Britannica, Inc., Chicago, copyright © 1968. All rights reserved.

CRITICAL THINKING

1. Why does William Penn feel that government is "a part of religion itself"?
2. Although people may agree on the goals of government, what prevents them from carrying out their aims?
3. Explain why Penn believes that governments depend upon men rather than men upon governments.

ARTIFACT AS

PURITAN GRAVESTONES
The Puritans' Graveyard Documents

The Latin inscription cautions the living to "remember death." Another popular motto was "time is passing."

Two messengers of death poke arrows into a winged skull on the stone marking the grave of Elias Row, who died in 1686.

The early settlers often visited cemeteries. Many people could not read, but the images on the gravestones could be understood by everyone. The graveyard became a place for quiet reflection on the hardships that were part of their daily lives.

The earliest Puritan gravestones were wooden markers inscribed with the name of the deceased, his or her age, and year of death. Eventually the markers were made of more durable sandstone, granite, and slate, probably furnished by masons and bricklayers. In the late seventeenth century, stone carvers began to specialize in the gravestone as an art form, and some even signed their work.

On these stones are pictured images of death such as skulls; skeletons and crossbones; the gravedigger's pickaxe and shovel; and candles with snuffers. Some carvings symbolized the passage of time with the hourglass and Father Time with his reaper's scythe.

Other less grim images included faces with wings, and swords or coats of arms indicating the deceased's profession or family status.

CRITICAL THINKING

1. What did some Puritan gravestone cutters do when they made a mistake or ran out of room? What spelling errors can you see?
2. Compare similarities of the art style shown on the tombstones here and the style used in the Aztec artifacts shown on pages 40 and 41.

D O C U M E N T

On Richard Kettell's (1680) gravestone, the carver conveys the fleetingness of life by using a death's-head, pickaxes, coffin, and hour-glass. This stone is an example of simple Puritan style.

On this red sandstone marker for Elisha Stanley (1786, East Hartford, Connecticut), the carver departed from traditional symbols and instead attempted a portrait of the deceased.

The stone of Captain John Fowle (1711), with its coat of arms in the center panel, is found in the Phipps Street Burial Ground, Charlestown, Massachusetts.

CHAPTER 4

COLONIAL AMERICANS

1650–1754

1. JACQUES MARQUETTE AND LOUIS JOLIET EXPLORE THE MISSISSIPPI RIVER

The St. Lawrence River was the principal trade route from Quebec, the first permanent French settlement in North America. But because the river was frozen for half the year, trade was difficult. Consequently, New France's priests and traders were encouraged to search for new waterways. In 1673, Jacques Marquette, a French priest, and Louis Joliet, a fur trader, set out to explore the Mississippi River. In the following passage, Marquette relates the first part of their expedition.

Here then we are on this renowned river, of which I have endeavored to remark attentively all the peculiarities. The Mississippi River has its source in several lakes in the country of the Indian nations to the north. Its current, which runs south, is slow and gentle; on the right is a considerable chain of very high mountains, and on the left fine lands; it is in many places studded with islands. We gently follow its course, which bears south and southeast till the forty-second degree. Here we perceive that the whole face is changed; there is now almost no wood or mountain, the islands are more beautiful and covered with finer trees. From time to time we meet monstrous fish, one of which struck so violently against our canoe, that I took it for a large tree about to knock us to pieces.

We advanced constantly, but as we did not know where we were going, we kept well on our guard. Accordingly, we made only a little fire on the shore at night to prepare our meal, and after supper kept as far off from it as possible, passing the night in our canoes, which we anchored in the river pretty far from the bank. Even this did not prevent one of us acting always as a sentry for fear of a surprise attack.

At last, on the 25th of June, we perceived footprints of men and a beaten path entering a beautiful prairie. We stopped to examine it, and concluding that it was a path leading to some Indian village, we resolved to go and explore. We, accordingly, left our two canoes in charge of our people, cautioning them strictly to beware of a surprise; then M. Joliet and I undertook this rather hazardous discovery for two single men, who thus put themselves at the discretion of an unknown and barbarous people. We followed the little path in silence, and discovered a village on the banks of the river, and two others on a hill. Then, indeed, we recommended ourselves to God, with our all hearts; and having implored his help, we passed on undiscovered, and came so near that we even heard the Indians talking. We then deemed it time to announce ourselves, as we did by a cry, which we raised with all our strength, and then halted without advancing any further. At this cry, the Indians rushed out of their cabins, and having probably recognized us as French, especially seeing a black gown [priest's robe], or at least having no reason to distrust us, seeing we were but two, and had made known our coming, they delegated four old men to come and speak with us. Two carried tobacco pipes, well-adorned, and trimmed with many kinds of feathers. They marched slowly, lifting their pipes toward the sun, but yet without uttering a single word. They were a long time coming the little way from the village to us. Having reached us at last, they stopped to consider us attentively. I now took courage, seeing these ceremonies, which are used by them only with friends, and still more on seeing them covered with stuffs, which made me judge them to be allies. I, therefore, spoke to them first, and asked them who they were. They answered that they were Illinois and, in token of peace, they presented their pipes to smoke. They then invited us to their village where all the tribe awaited us with impatience. These pipes for smoking are called in the country *calumets*.

At the door of the cabin in which we were to be received, was an old man awaiting us. When we came near him, he paid us this compliment: "How beautiful is the sun, O Frenchman, when thou comest to visit us! All our town awaits thee, and thou shalt enter all our cabins in peace." He then took us into his cabin, where there was a crowd of

French missionary Jacques Marquette made a daring expedition on the Mississippi River in the company of Louis Joliet, a fur trader.

people who devoured us with their eyes, but kept a profound silence. We heard, however, these words occasionally addressed to us: "Well done, brothers, to visit us!"

As soon as we had taken our places, they showed us the usual civility of the country, which is to present the *calumet*. You must not refuse it, unless you would pass for an enemy, or at least for being impolite. It is, however, enough to pretend to smoke. While all the old men smoked after us to honor us, some came to invite us on behalf of the great sachem [chief] of all the Illinois to proceed to his town, where he wished to hold a council with us.

Having arrived at the great sachem's town, we saw him at his cabin door. He presented us his *calumet* and made us smoke; at the same time we entered his cabin, where we received all their usual greetings. Seeing all assembled and in silence, I spoke to them. First, I said that we

marched in peace to visit the nations on the river to the sea. Second, I declared to them that God their Creator had pity on them, since, after their having been so long ignorant of Him, He wished to become known to all nations; that I was sent on His behalf with this design; that it was for them to acknowledge and obey Him. Third, that the great chief of the French informed them that he spread peace everywhere, and had overcome the Iroquois. Lastly, we begged them to give us all the information they had of the sea, and of the nations through which we should have to pass to reach it.

When I had finished my speech, the sachem rose and spoke thus: "I thank thee, Blackgown, and thee, Frenchman," addressing M. Joliet, "for taking so much pains to come and visit us; never has the earth been so beautiful, nor the sun so bright, as today. I pray thee to take pity on me and all my nation. Thou knowest the Great Spirit who has made us all; thou speakest to him and hearest his word: Ask him to give me life and health, and come and dwell with us, that we may know him." He begged us, on behalf of his whole nation, not to proceed further, on account of the great dangers [Spanish settlers, the enemies of the French] to which we exposed ourselves.

We slept in the sachem's cabin, and the next day took leave of him. He escorted us to our canoes with nearly six hundred persons, who saw us embark, showing, in every possible way, the pleasure our visit had given them.

Selection adapted from *The American Reader* by Paul Angle. Published by Rand McNally & Company, New York, copyright © 1958. All rights reserved.

CRITICAL THINKING

1. What evidence in the selection shows that Jacques Marquette was familiar with Indian customs?
2. From what information can you conclude that the Illinois and Iroquois Indians were enemies?
3. Marquette referred to the Indians as "barbarous people" before he met them. Why might he feel this description was no longer true after spending time with the Indians?

ONE POINT OF VIEW

JOHN SINGLETON COPLEY

John Singleton Copley [1738–1815] is remembered as the master painter of the Colonial period. A Bostonian, Copley had a difficult childhood. His father disappeared at the time of his birth. Later his mother married Peter Pelham, a successful engraver who began to teach art to Copley.

Colonial artists typically received their art training as sign painters and house decorators. Young Copley was fortunate to have the instruction of his stepfather, as well as of John Smibert, an English portrait painter living in Boston. Copley was 13 when his stepfather died and he suddenly found himself the head of his family. He began to draw portraits for money—first crayon sketches, then watercolor miniatures, and finally oil paintings.

Copley tried to show people honestly. He had a special talent for depicting both his subjects' expressions and forms. When he drew figures, he was aware of light and shadow, and his brushwork was smooth and finished.

Copley painted numerous children and adults, ordinary people as well as the famous. He left a true picture of his generation, as he saw it.

This painting, titled "Governor and Mrs. Thomas Mifflin," shows the governor of Pennsylvania and his wife at home. The clothing and furnishings detailed by Copley reveal the couple's wealth.

CRITICAL THINKING

1. Portraits of this time often picture people with treasured objects or implements of their trade. What might you assume about the people in these paintings?
2. Although these portraits were beautifully done, they also are very honest. Look at the faces, and point out examples of realistic treatment.

Copley painted his half-brother, Peter Pelham, with a pet squirrel. This work is an example of his love of detail—the chain, the animal's fur, the shiny fabric. "Boy with a Squirrel" (1765) may have been the first American painting exhibited in Europe.

During the Revolution, Copley, a Tory, took his family to England. In the portrait below (1776-1777), Copley can be seen smiling over the head of his father-in-law. Copley's wife and children are dressed in the striking clothing he liked to paint.

2. WILLIAM FITZHUGH DESCRIBES A COLONIAL PLANTATION

William Fitzhugh was the owner of a prosperous plantation in the Chesapeake Bay region. The following letter written to a friend in England provides a vivid description of a colonial plantation. Because he was homesick for England, and thinking of returning, Fitzhugh wrote this letter hoping to attract a buyer for his estate.

April 22nd. 1686

Doctor Ralph Smith,

The plantation where I now live contains a thousand acres, at least 700 acres of it being rich thicket [shrubbery], the remainder good, hearty, plantable land, without any waste either by marshes or great swamps. The spaciousness, convenience, and pleasantness you well know. Upon it there are three Quarters, well furnished, with all necessary houses, ground, and fencing, together with a choice crew of Negroes at each plantation. Upon the same land is my own dwelling house, furnished with all accomodations for a comfortable and refined living, with thirteen rooms in it, nine of them plentifully furnished with all things necessary and convenient. Utility houses include a dairy, stable, barn, henhouse, kitchen, and all other conveniences, and all fairly new. There is a large orchard of about 2,500 apple trees, well fenced. There is a garden a hundred foot square, a courtyard wherein is most of the foresaid necessary houses, together with a good stock of cattle, hogs, horses, mares, sheep, etc., and necessary servants for the supply and support thereof. About a mile and a half distant, a good grain mill provides my own family with wheat and Indian corn for our needs. Up the river in this country there are three tracts of land more. One of them contains 21,996 acres; another, 500 acres, and one other 1,000 acres, all good, convenient, and spacious, and which, in a few years will yield a considerable annual income. The yearly crops of corn and tobacco, together with the surplus of meat, more than will serve the family's use and will amount annually to 300 lbs. per year. The orchard in a very few years will yield at least 15,000 lbs. tobacco annual income. What I have not particularly mentioned, your own knowledge in my affairs is able to supply.

Sir Your W. ff.

Selection adapted from *William Fitzhugh and His Chesapeake World, 1676–1701*, edited by Richard Beale Davis. Published for the Virginia Historical Society by the University of North Carolina Press, Chapel Hill, North Carolina, copyright © 1963.

CRITICAL THINKING

1. Does Fitzhugh succeed in painting a picture of a pleasant way of life? What persuasive words does he use?
2. Based on the information in this letter, what were money crops for the Chesapeake Bay area?

3. THOMAS DANFORTH WRITES TO INCREASE MATHER ABOUT GOVERNOR ANDROS

When William of Orange, a Dutch Protestant replaced James II as king of England, New Englanders rebelled against Governor Andros, an unpopular magistrate appointed by James II. Thomas Danforth describes that rebellion and the imprisonment of Governor Andros in a letter to The Rev. Increase Mather, dated July 30, 1689.

It's now fourteen weeks since the revolution of the government here. Future consequences we are ignorant of, yet we know that, at present, we are eased of those great oppressions that we groaned under, by the exercise of an arbitrary and illegal commission.

The business was acted by the soldiers that came armed into Boston from all parts, being greatly animated by the Prince's declarations, which about that time came into the country, and heightened by the oppressions of the governor, judges, and the most wicked extortion of their debauched officers. The ancient magistrates and elders, although they had strenuously advised to further waiting for orders from England, were compelled to assist with their presence and counsels for the prevention of bloodshed, which had most certainly been the result if prudent counsel

CHAPTER 4

Colonists disliked Sir Edmund Andros (left), the governor of New York colony. The Rev. Increase Mather (right) was a Boston churchman who later became president of Harvard College.

had not been given to both parties. A copy of that paper sent Sir Edmund Andros I have herewith sent you, upon which he forthwith came and surrendered himself.

The same day, about thirty more of the principal persons of that group were secured, whereof some were quickly released, and some yet remain under restraint.

I am deeply sensible that we have a wolf by the ears. I do therefore earnestly entreat of you to procure the best advice you can in this matter that, if possible, the good intents of the people and their loyalty to the Crown of England may not turn to their prejudice. The example of England, the declarations put forth by the Prince of Orange, now our King, the alteration of the government in England making the arbitrary commission of Sir Edmund null and void in the law; these considerations, in conjunction with the great oppressions the people lay under, were so far prevalent in the minds of all, that although some could not advise to the enterprise, yet are hopeful that we shall not be greatly blamed, but shall have a pardon granted for any error the law will charge us with in this matter.

We do crave that the circumstances of our case and condition in all respects may be considered. Nature has taught us self-preservation. God commands it as being the rule of charity toward our neighbor. Our great remoteness from England denies us the opportunity of direction for the regulation of ourselves in all emergencies, nor have we means to know the laws and customs of our nation. These things are our great disadvantage. We have always endeavored to prove ourselves loyal to the Crown of England. And we have also labored to attend the directions of our charter, under which were laid by our fathers the foundation of this His Majesty's colony; and we are not without hopes but that we shall receive from Their Royal Majesties the confirmation of our charter, with such addition of privileges as may advance the revenue of the Crown, and be an encouragement to Their Majesties' subjects here.

Selection adapted from *Readings in American History*, edited by Oscar Handlin. Copyright © 1957 by Oscar Handlin. All rights reserved. Published by Alfred A. Knopf, Inc., 1966.

CRITICAL THINKING

1. What justification does Thomas Danforth give for the rebellion of Governor Andros?
2. What problems does Danforth fear may result from the rebellion?
3. What does the statement "Nature has taught us self-preservation" have to do with the case Danforth is making?

61

4. PETER KALM OBSERVES ENGLAND'S AMERICAN COLONIES

Peter Kalm was a Swedish scientist who came to America in 1748 and stayed until 1751. He kept a diary during his travels throughout the colonies. In the following excerpts, he discusses his visit to New York City—and makes a startling prophecy about the American Revolution.

November 2d

New York, the capital of a province of the same name, is extremely advantageous for trade, for the town stands upon a point which is formed by two bays; into one of which the river Hudson discharges itself not far from the town. New York is therefore on three sides surrounded with water. The ground it is built on is level in some parts, and hilly in others. The place is generally reckoned very wholesome.

Toward the sea is a pretty good fortress, called Fort George, which entirely commands the port, and can defend the town, at least from a sudden attack on the sea side. Besides that, the city is likewise secured on the north, or toward the shore, by a palisade [fence], which, however, (as for a considerable time the people have had nothing to fear from an enemy) is in many places in a very bad state of defence.

The port is a good one. Ships can lie in it, quite close up to the bridge, but its water is very salt, as the sea continually comes in upon it; and therefore is never frozen, except in extraordinary cold weather. This is of great advantage to the city and its commerce; for many ships either come in or go out of the port at any time of the year. The entrance, however, has its faults; one of them is that no men of war [warships] can pass through it, for though the water is pretty deep, yet it is not sufficiently so for great ships. Sometimes even merchant ships of a large size have slightly touched the bottom, though without any bad consequences.

New York probably carries on a more extensive commerce than any town in the English North American provinces. The trade of New York extends to many places; and it is said they send more ships from thence to London, than they do from Philadelphia. They export to that capital all the various sorts of skins which they buy of the Indians, sugar, rum, mahogany, and many other goods which are the produce of the West Indies. In return for these, they import from London stuffs, and every other article of English growth or manufacture, together with all sorts of foreign goods. England, and especially London, profits immensely by its trade with the American colonies; for not only New York, but likewise all the other English towns on the continent, import many articles from England. From hence it appears how much a well-regulated colony contributes to the increase and welfare of its mother country.

By 1750, New York already had become a flourishing city. This view of Manhattan island from the Brooklyn shore shows the ferry landing at the extreme right and New Jersey in the distance.

The governor of the province of New York resides in this city and has a palace in the fort. Among those who have been entrusted with this post, William Burnet deserves to be had in perpetual memory. His great diligence in promoting the welfare of this province is what makes the principal merit of his character. The people of New York therefore still reckon him the best governor they ever had, and think that they cannot praise his services too much.

An assembly of deputies, from all the particular districts of the province of New York, is held at New York once or twice every year. It may be looked upon as a parliament in miniature. Everything relating to the good of the province is here debated. The governor calls the assembly and dissolves it at his pleasure.

The king appoints the governor according to his royal pleasure; but the inhabitants of the province make up the governor's salary. Therefore, a man entrusted with this job has greater or lesser income, according as he knows how to gain the confidence of the inhabitants. There are examples of governors, in this and other provinces of North America, who, by their disagreements with the inhabitants of their respective governments, have lost their whole salary, his Majesty having no power to make them pay it.

At the assembly, the old laws are reviewed and amended, and new ones were made, and the regulation and circulation of currency, together with all other affairs of that kind, are determined. For each English colony in North America is independent of the other, and has its proper laws and currency, and may be looked upon in several lights as a state by itself. Consequently, in time of war, things go on very slowly and irregularly here; for not only the sense of one province is sometimes directly opposite to that of another; but frequently the views of the governor, and those of the assembly of the same province are quite different. So that it is easy to see, that while the people are quarrelling about the best and cheapest manner of carrying on the war, an enemy has it in his power to take one place after another.

It is of great advantage to the crown of England that the North American colonies are near a country under the government of the French, like Canada. For the English colonies in this part of the world have increased so much in their number of inhabitants, and in their riches, that they almost compete with Old England. Now in order to keep up the authority and trade of their mother country, and to answer several other purposes, they are forbidden to establish new manufactures, which would turn to the disadvantage of the British commerce. They are not allowed to dig for gold or silver, unless they send them to England immediately; they have not the liberty of trading to any parts that do not belong to the British dominions. These and some other restrictions cause the inhabitants of the English colonies to grow less tender for their mother country. This coldness is kept up by the many foreigners, such as Germans, Dutch, and French, settled here, and living among the English, who commonly have no particular attachment to Old England.

I have been told by Englishmen, and not only by such as were born in America, but even by such as came from Europe, that the English colonies in North America, in the space of thirty or fifty years, would be able to form a state by themselves, entirely independent of Old England. But as the whole country which lies along the seashore is unguarded, and on the land side is harassed by the French in times of war, these dangerous neighbors are sufficient to prevent the connection of the colonies with their mother country from being quite broken off. The English government has therefore sufficient reason to consider the French in North America as the best means of keeping the colonies in their due submission.

CRITICAL THINKING

1. According to Peter Kalm, what accounts for the fact that New York engaged in more commerce than any town in the English North American provinces?
2. Summarize Kalm's theory regarding England's desire to keep the French in North America.
3. Which statement of Kalm's could be considered a prediction of the Revolutionary War?

COLONIAL CRAFTS
Objects Of Daily Life

Pelegrine White, born aboard the Mayflower *and the first baby born in the New World, used this hooded wicker cradle.*

The candlesticks above were produced by Caspar Wistar's glass factory before the Revolution.

At the time of the first settlements, living conditions were primitive as the colonists struggled to grow food and keep alive. Basic utensils, such as cups and shovels, were imported from Europe. As the Colonies prospered, people demanded better things and began to import more goods from England. This suited the English who passed laws restricting what could be manufactured in the Colonies.

Few craft products made before 1650 have survived. After that date the manufacture of simple wares began. Coins were melted down and made into silverware. Many wealthy colonists felt this was a safe substitute for money. If the uniquely crafted and engraved silver were stolen, it could be identified. By the early 1700s, many colonial silversmiths were making beautiful and elegant wares.

Glass and ceramic manufacture developed more slowly. In 1739, a German immigrant living in New Jersey, Caspar Wistar, was the first settler to manufacture glass in the colonies. He produced simple glassware for those who could not afford the more expensive imports. Twenty years later, other German settlers established more elaborate factories and produced more refined glass.

Most ceramic ware was imported from Europe. However, simple pottery was made in Jamestown as early as 1650. Everyday objects such as crocks, mugs, pitchers, and jugs were common. Since these objects were valued only for their usefulness, few have been preserved.

Textile manufacture was a very active home industry in the colonies as early as the 1640s, when both the Massachusetts and Connecticut colonies required that all families grow flax, the plant from which linen was made. Cloth was often dyed or embroidered. Women did most of the textile work.

D O C U M E N T

Embroidery was the most common decoration in Colonial homes. The ornamental wall hanging of a woman in a pastoral setting was made in New England in the 1750s.

A quart tankard, made by William Bradford Jr. in New York City, is a rare example of pre-revolutionary pewterware.

A red earthenware tea cannister was made in Pennsylvania in 1769. Simply crafted from the abundant native clay, it is one of the earliest examples of decorated American pottery.

CRITICAL THINKING

1. These objects are elegant but very simple in their design. Suggest reasons why the pre-revolutionary artisans did not produce more ornate or complex products.
2. Archeologists use many clues to date artifacts style or what the object was made of to help them place the artifact in time. Why is one of these artifacts easy to date?

The Making of a Nation

CHAPTER 5

THE QUARREL WITH GREAT BRITAIN

1754–1774

1. LIEUTENANT GOVERNOR ROBERT DINWIDDIE PROTESTS FRENCH OCCUPATION IN THE OHIO RIVER VALLEY

Acting under orders from Great Britain, Lieutenant Governor Robert Dinwiddie of Virginia wrote the following letter to Monsieur de St. Pierre, a French military leader in the Ohio River Valley. In the letter, Dinwiddie protests the French occupation and fortification of the area. Dinwiddie also introduces the bearer of the letter, George Washington.

SIR,

The lands upon the river Ohio, in the western parts of the Colony of Virginia, are so notoriously known to be the property of the Crown of Great Britain that it is a matter of equal concern and surprise to me, to hear that a body of French forces are erecting fortresses and making settlements upon that river, within his Majesty's dominions. The many and repeated complaints I have received of these acts of hostility lay me under the necessity of sending, in the name of the King, my master, the bearer hereof, George Washington, Esq., one of the Adjutant-Generals of the forces of this dominion, to complain to you of the encroachments thus made, and of the injuries done to the subjects of Great Britain, in violation of the law of nations, and the treaties now subsisting between the two Crowns. If these facts be true, and you think fit to justify your proceedings, I must desire you to acquaint me by whose authority and instructions you have lately marched from Canada with an armed force, and invaded the King of Great Britain's territories, in the manner complained of; that according to the purport and resolution of your answer, I may act agreeably to the commission I am honored with from the King,

my master. However, sir, in obedience to my instructions, it becomes my duty to require your peacable departure.

ROBERT DINWIDDIE

October 31, 1753

Selection from "Governor Dinwiddie to Monsieur de St. Pierre" in *Readings in American History*, edited by James Alton James. Published by Charles Scribner's Sons, New York, copyright © 1914.

CRITICAL THINKING

1. What was Robert Dinwiddie's main objective in writing the letter and sending George Washington to de St. Pierre?
2. In the British view, what made the lands in the Ohio River Valley "the property of the Crown of Great Britain"?

---

2. CHRISTOPHER GIST ACCOMPANIES MAJOR GEORGE WASHINGTON TO THE OHIO RIVER VALLEY

Christopher Gist accompanied George Washington to deliver Lieutenant Governor Robert Dinwiddie's letter to the French military leader in the Ohio River Valley. The entries are from Gist's journal. The second entry describes an incident on the return trip.

Wednesday 14 November, 1753.—Then Major George Washington came to my house at Will's Creek, and delivered me a letter from the council in Virginia, requesting me to attend him up to the commandant of the French fort on the Ohio River.

Thursday 27.—We rose early in the morning, and set out about two o'clock. Got to the Murthering town, on the southeast fork of Beaver Creek. Here we met with an Indian, whom I thought I had seen when on our journey up to the French fort. This fellow called me by my Indian name, and pretended to be glad to see me. He asked us several questions, as how we came to travel on foot, when we left Venango, where we parted with our horses, and when they would be there, etc. Major Washington insisted on travelling on the nearest way to forks of [the] Alleghany. We asked the Indian if he could go with us, and show us the nearest way. The Indian seemed very glad and ready to go with us. Upon which we set out, and the Indian took the Major's pack. We travelled very brisk for eight or ten miles, when the Major's feet grew very sore, and he very weary, and the Indian steered too much northeastwardly. The Major desired to encamp, to which the Indian asked to carry his gun. But he refused that, and then the Indian grew churlish, and pressed us to keep on, telling us that there were Ottawa Indians in these woods, and they would scalp us if we [stopped]; but to go to his cabin, and we should be safe. I thought very ill of the fellow, but did not care to let the Major know I mistrusted him. But he soon mistrusted him as much as I. He said he could hear a gun [from the direction of] his cabin, and steered us more northwardly. We grew uneasy, and then he said two whoops might be heard [from the direction of] his cabin. We went two miles further; then the Major said he would stay at the next water, and we desired the Indian to stop at the next water. But before we came to water, we came to a clear meadow; it was very light, and snow on the ground. The Indian made a stop, turned about; the Major saw him point his gun toward us and fire. Said the Major, "Are you shot?" "No," said I. Upon which the Indian ran forward to a big standing white oak, and to loading his gun; but we were soon with him. I would have killed him, but the Major would not permit me to kill him. We let him charge his gun; we found he put in a ball; then we took care of him. The Major or I always stood by the guns; we made him make a fire for us by a little run, as if we intended to sleep there. I said to the Major, "As you will not have him killed, we must get him away, and then we must travel all night." Upon which I said to the Indian, "I suppose you were lost, and fired your gun." He said, he knew the way to his cabin, and 'twas but a little way. "Well," said I, "do you go home; and as we are much tired, we will follow your track in the morning; and here is a cake of bread for you, and you must give us meat in the morning." He was glad to get away. I followed him, and listened until he was fairly out of the way, and then we set out about half a mile, when we made a fire, set our compass, and fixed our course, and travelled all night.

Selection adapted from "George Washington and the French Posts on the Ohio, 1753" in *Readings in American History*, edited by James Alton James. Published by Charles Scribner's Sons, New York, copyright © 1914.

CRITICAL THINKING

1. Why might George Washington not have wanted to kill the Indian?
2. In what year did Washington and Gist bring Dinwiddie's letter to the French military leader? How do you know their mission was unsuccessful?

3. AMERICAN COLONISTS ASSERT THEIR RIGHTS AND AIR THEIR GRIEVANCES

The Stamp Act was the British Parliament's first attempt to tax American colonists directly. Some colonists responded with violence. Others—the delegates to the Stamp Act Congress—responded by addressing to King George III the following list of rights and grievances of the colonists in America. The proceedings of the delegates to the congress were recorded in an official journal from which the following was taken.

Saturday, Oct. 19th, 1765, A.M.—Then congress met and upon mature deliberation, agreed to the following declarations of the rights and grievances of the colonists in America, which were ordered to be inserted.

The members of this congress, sincerely devoted, with the warmest sentiments of affection and duty to his majesty's person and government; inviolably attached to the present happy establishment of the protestant succession, and with minds deeply impressed by a sense of the present and impending misfortunes of the British colonies on this continent; having considered as maturely as time would permit, the circumstances of the said colonies, esteem it our indispensable duty to make the following declarations, of our humble opinion, respecting the most essential rights and liberties of the colonists, and of the grievances under which they labor, by reason of several late acts of parliament.

1st. That his majesty's subjects in these colonies, owe the same allegiance to the crown of Great Britain, that is owing from his subjects born within the realm, and all due subordination to that august body, the parliament of Great Britain.

2d. That his majesty's liege subjects in these colonies are entitled to all the inherent rights and privileges of his natural born subjects within the kingdom of Great Britain.

3d. That it is inseparably essential to the freedom of a people, and the undoubted rights of Englishmen, that no taxes should be imposed on them, but with their consent, given personally, or by their representatives.

4th. That the people of these colonies are not, and from their local circumstances, cannot be represented in the house of commons in Great Britain.

5th. That the only representatives of the people of these colonies, are persons chosen therein, by themselves; and that no taxes ever have been, or can be constitutionally imposed on them, but by their respective legislatures.

6th. That all supplies to the crown, being free gifts of the people, it is unreasonable and inconsistent with the principles and spirit of the British constitution, for the people of Great Britain to grant to his majesty the property of the colonists.

7th. That trial by jury is the inherent and invaluable right of every British subject in these colonies.

8th. That the late act of parliament, entitled, an act for granting and applying certain stamp duties, and other duties in the British colonies and plantations in America, etc., by imposing taxes on the inhabitants of these colonies, and the said act, and several other acts, by extending the jurisdiction of the courts of admiralty beyond its ancient limits, have a manifest tendency to subvert the rights and liberties of the colonists.

9th. That the duties imposed by several late acts of parliament, from [the] peculiar circumstances of these colonies, will be extremely burthensome and grievous, and from the scarcity of specie, the payment of them absolutely impracticable.

10th. That as the profits of the trade of these colonies ultimately centre in Great Britain, to pay for the manufactures which they are obliged to

King George III's inability to handle the grievances of the colonists led to Great Britain's loss of its American colonies.

take from thence, they eventually contribute very largely to all supplies granted there to the crown.

11th. That the restrictions imposed by several late acts of parliament, on the trade of these colonies, will render them unable to purchase the manufactures of Great Britain.

12th. That the increase, prosperity and happiness of these colonies, depend on the full and free enjoyment of their rights and liberties, and an intercourse, with Great Britain, mutually affectionate and advantageous.

13th. That it is the right of the British subjects in these colonies, to petition the king or either house of parliament.

Lastly, that it is the indispensable duty of these colonies to the best of sovereigns, to the mother country, and to themselves, to endeavor by a loyal and dutiful address to his majesty, and humble application to both houses of parliament, to procure the repeal of the act for granting and applying certain stamp duties, of all clauses of any other acts of parliament, whereby the jurisdiction of the admiralty is extended as aforesaid, and of the other late acts for the restriction of the American commerce.

Selection adapted from *Chronicles of the American Revolution* (originally compiled by Hezekiah Niles as "Principles and Acts of the Revolution in America"), edited by Alden T. Vaughn. Published by Grosset and Dunlap, New York, copyright © 1965.

CRITICAL THINKING

1. Give some examples of language used by the delegates to assure King George that they did not intend treason or revolution.
2. In the Declaratory Act, passed after repeal of the Stamp Act, Parliament asserted the principle that it had the right to tax and make law for Americans. Which items in the list above oppose this principle?

4. EPHRAIM BOWEN RECOUNTS THE BURNING OF THE *GASPEE*

Although the delegates to the Stamp Act Congress expressed their opposition to Great Britain in a moderate way, other Americans turned to violence. The burning of the Gaspee *is one example of such violence. The* Gaspee *was a British revenue vessel patrolling in an effort to prevent smuggling. Ephraim Bowen, a Rhode Islander who took part in the incident, when the* Gaspee *ran aground in Narragansett Bay, gave the following account.*

In the year 1772, the British government had stationed at Newport, Rhode Island, the schooner [ship] called the *Gaspee*, of eight guns, commanded by Wm. Duddingston, a Lieutenant in the British Navy, for the purpose of preventing the clandestine landing of articles, subject to the payment of duty [an import tax]. The Captain of this schooner made it his practice to stop and

board all vessels entering or leaving the ports of Rhode Island, or leaving Newport for Providence.

On the 10th day of June, 1772, Capt. Thomas Lindsey left Newport in his packet [boat] for Providence, about noon, with the wind at North; and soon after the *Gaspee* was under sail, in pursuit of Lindsey, and continued the chase as far as Namquit Point. Lindsey was standing easterly, with the tide on ebb about two hours, when he hove about, at the end of Namquit Point, and stood to the westward, and Duddingston in close chase, changed his course and ran on the Point, near its end, and grounded. Lindsey continued on his course up the river, and arrived at Providence about sunset, when he immediately informed Mr. John Brown, one of our first and most respectable merchants, of the situation of the *Gaspee*. He immediately concluded that she would remain immovable until after midnight, and that now an opportunity offered of putting an end to the trouble and vexation she daily caused. Mr. Brown immediately resolved on her destruction, and he forthwith directed one of his trusty shipmasters to collect eight of the largest long-boats in the harbor, with five oars to each, to have the oars and row-locks well muffled, to prevent noise, and to place them at Fenner's wharf.

About the time of the shutting up of the shops soon after sunset, a man passed along the Main street beating a drum and informing the inhabitants of the fact, that the *Gaspee* was aground on Namquit Point, and would not float off until 3 o'clock the next morning, and inviting those persons who felt a disposition to go and destroy that troublesome vessel, to repair in the evening to Mr. James Sabin's house. About 9 o'clock, I took my father's gun and my powder horn and bullets and went to Mr. Sabin's, and found the southeast room full of people, where I loaded my gun, and all remained there till about 10 o'clock, when orders were given to cross the street to Fenner's wharf and embark; which soon took place, and a sea captain acted as steersman of each boat, of whom I recollect Capt. Abraham Whipple, Capt. John B. Hopkins, (with whom I embarked,) and Capt. Benjamin Dunn.

The party proceeded till within about sixty yards of the *Gaspee*, when a sentinel hailed, "Who comes there?" No answer. He hailed again and no answer. In about a minute Duddingston mounted the starboard gunwale in his shirt and hailed, "Who comes there?" No answer. He hailed again, when Capt. Whipple answered as follows—"I am the sheriff of the county of Kent. I have got a warrant to apprehend you, so surrender." I took my seat with my gun by my side, facing forwards. As soon as Duddingston began to hail, Joseph Bucklin, who was standing by my right side, said to me, "Ephe, reach me your gun and I can kill that fellow." I reached it to him accordingly, when, during Capt. Whipple's replying, Bucklin fired and Duddingston fell, and Bucklin exclaimed, "I have killed the rascal." In less than a minute after Capt. Whipple's answer, the boats were alongside of the *Gaspee*, and boarded without opposition. The men on deck retreated below as Duddingston entered the cabin.

As it was discovered that he was wounded, John Mawney, who had for two or three years been studying physic and surgery, was ordered to go into the cabin and dress Duddingston's wound, and directed to assist him. When finished, orders were given to the schooner's company to collect their clothing and everything belonging to them and put them into their boats, as all of them were to be sent on shore. All were soon collected and put on board of the boats. Soon after, all the party were ordered to depart, leaving one boat for the leaders of the expedition, who soon set the vessel on fire, which consumed her to the waters' edge.

Selection adapted from "1772—Rhode Islanders Burn the Gaspée in *The American Reader: From Columbus to Today,* edited by Paul M. Angle. Published by Rand McNally & Company, Chicago, copyright © 1958.

CRITICAL THINKING

1. Are the attitudes of the Americans involved in the burning of the *Gaspee* similar to or different from the attitudes of the delegates to the Stamp Act Congress as described in the previous selection? Explain what you mean.
2. In your opinion, were the motives of the Americans who burned the *Gaspee* primarily patriotic? Give reasons for your opinion.

5. A POPULAR SONG OF THE AMERICAN REVOLUTION

"Yankee Doodle" was a patriotic song of the American Revolution. The words of another such song are given below. Even though Parliament had repealed most of the taxes on imported goods, the hated tax on tea remained. (Bohea is the name of a China black tea. The "Green Dragon," a Boston tavern, was a meeting place for Boston radicals such as Sam Adams. "North-Enders" were residents of a section of Boston.)

1773

Rally, Mohawks! bring out your axes,
And tell King George we'll pay no taxes
    On his foreign tea;
His threats are vain, and vain to think
To force our girls and wives to drink
    His vile Bohea!
Then rally, boys, and hasten on
To meet our chiefs at the Green Dragon.
Our Warren's there and bold Revere,
With hands to do, and words to cheer,
    For liberty and laws;
Our country's "braves" and firm defenders
Shall ne'er be left by true North-Enders
    Fighting Freedom's cause!
Then rally, boys, and hasten on
To meet our chiefs at the Green Dragon.

Selection from *The Spirit of 'Seventy-Six: The Story of the American Revolution as Told by Participants,* edited by Henry Steele Commager and Richard B. Morris. Published by Harper & Row, New York, copyright © 1958.

CRITICAL THINKING

1. Explain the references to "Mohawks" and "axes" in the first line.
2. Which do you think had a greater influence on the thinking of ordinary Americans: a song like this or a document like the list of rights and grievances found in Selection 3, above? Why?

POLITICAL CARTOONS
The Quarrel With Great Britain

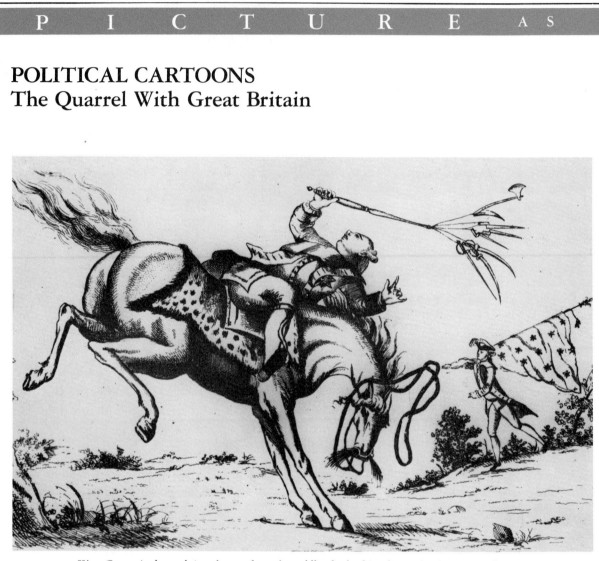

King George is shown being thrown from the saddle of a bucking horse. An American colonist is approaching, carrying a battle flag.

During the eighteenth century, graphics that satirized political figures or events were known as caricatures or engravings. Unlike present-day political cartoons, they almost never appeared in newspapers, but were sold in print shops throughout Europe and the United States.

Most of the caricatures depicting the American Revolution were produced in England—and nearly all were favorable to the American cause. Much of the British public strongly disapproved of its government's policy towards the American colonies, and expressed its sentiments by frequenting London's 140 print shops, where political cartoons were both printed and sold.

Caricatures were popular in the Colonies, but rarely were they made by Americans. Most of the engravings sold in American print shops were copies or adaptations of British prints. Paul Revere and Benjamin Franklin were among the best known local engravers of political cartoons.

D O C U M E N T

Benjamin Franklin printed this engraving, which he may have designed himself. He sent it to leading politicians. Its message was clear: Britain had the most to lose from oppressing the colonies.

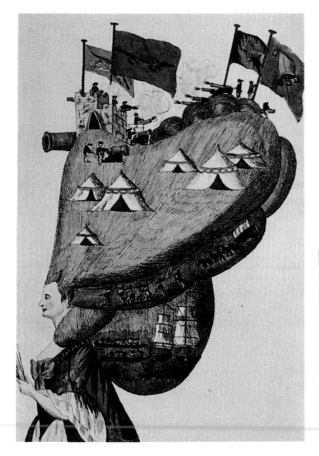

This unusual print, titled "How we are deceived," refers to the surprise occupation of Dorchester Heights by General William Howe's army and its subsequent retreat. The London engraver, Matthew Darly, specialized in caricatures of the exaggerated hair styles of his day.

CRITICAL THINKING

1. Cite techniques used by political cartoonists to convey their point of view clearly and forcefully.
2. What does the fact that many pro-American cartoons were printed in England tell about the English attitude toward freedom of expression?
3. Which cartoon, in your opinion, is the most effective in expressing its message? Explain your answer.

CHAPTER 6

INDEPENDENCE DECLARED

1774–1783

1. AN AMERICAN WOMAN WRITES OF HER ACTIVE SUPPORT OF THE REVOLUTION

The Battle of Lexington had a far-reaching effect in the colonies, as the following letter shows. The writer of the letter—C.S.—was an American woman who lived in Philadelphia. Her words make clear her patriotic sentiments.

SIR—We received a letter from you—wherein you let Mr. S. know that you had written after the battle of Lexington, particularly to me—knowing my martial spirit—that I would delight to read the exploits of heroes. Surely, my friend, you must mean the New England heroes, as they alone performed exploits worthy [of] fame—while the [British] regulars, vastly superior in numbers, were obliged to retreat. . . . You will not, I hope, take offence at any expression that, in the warmth of my heart, should escape me, when I assure you, that though we consider you as a public enemy, we regard you as a private friend; and while we detest the cause you are fighting for, we wish well to your own personal interest and safety. Thus far by way of apology. As to the martial spirit you suppose me to possess, you are greatly mistaken. I tremble at the thoughts of war; but of all wars, a civil one; our all is at stake; and we are called upon by every tie that is dear and sacred to exert the spirit that Heaven has given us in this righteous struggle for liberty.

I will tell you what I have done. My only brother I have sent to the camp with my prayers and blessings . . . I am confident he will behave with honor, and emulate the great example he has before him; and had I twenty sons and brothers they should go. I have retrenched every superfluous expense in my table and family; tea I have not drank since last Christmas, nor bought a new cap

or gown since your defeat at Lexington, and what I never did before, have learnt to knit, and am now making stockings of American wool for my servants, and this way do I throw in my mite to the public good. I know this, that as free I can die but once, but as a slave I shall not be worthy of life. I have the pleasure to assure you that these are the sentiments of all my sister Americans. They have sacrificed both assemblies, parties of pleasure, tea drinking and finery to that great spirit of patriotism, that actuates all ranks and degrees of people throughout this extensive continent. If these are the sentiments of females, what must glow in the breasts of our husbands, brothers and sons? They are as with one heart determined to die or be free. It is not a quibble in politics, a science which few understand, which we are contending for; it is this plain truth . . . that no man has a right to take their money without their consent. The supposition is ridiculous and absurd, as none but highwaymen, and robbers attempt it. Can you, my friend, reconcile it with your own good sense, that a body of men in Great Britain, who have little intercourse with America, and of course know nothing of us, nor are supposed to see or feel the misery they would inflict upon us, shall invest themselves with a power to command our lives and properties, at all times and in all cases whatsoever? You say you are no politician. Oh, sir, it requires no [political mind] to develop this, and to discover this tyranny and oppression. It is written with a sun beam. Every one will see and know it because it will make them feel, and we shall be unworthy of the blessings of Heaven, if we ever submit to it.

All ranks of men amongst us are in arms.—Nothing is heard now in our streets but the trumpet and drum; and the universal cry is "Americans to arms." . . . We have five regiments in the city and county of Philadelphia, complete in arms and uniform, and very expert at their military manoeuvers. We have companies of light-horse, light infantry, grenadiers, riflemen, and Indians, several companies of artillery, and some excellent brass cannon and field pieces. Add to this, that every county in Pennsylvania, and the Delaware government, can send two thousand men to the field. . . . We are making powder fast, and do not want for ammunition. In short, we want for nothing but ships of war to defend us, which we could procure by making alliances; but such is our attachment to Great Britain, that we sincerely wish for reconciliation, and cannot bear the thoughts of throwing off all dependence on her, which such a step would assuredly lead to. The God of mercy will, I hope, open the eyes of our king that he may see, while in seeking our destruction, he will go near to complete his own. It is my ardent prayer that the [spilling] of blood may be stopped. We hope yet to see you in this city, a friend of the liberties of America, which will give infinite satisfaction to,

> Your sincere friend,
> C.S.

Selection from *Chronicles of the American Revolution* (originally compiled by Hezekiah Niles as "Principles and Acts of the Revolution in America"), edited by Alden T. Vaughn. Published by Grosset and Dunlap, New York, copyright © 1965.

CRITICAL THINKING

1. To whom was C.S. writing? What evidence is there in her letter to support your opinion?
2. Why have C.S. and her "sister Americans" not "drank" tea since the previous Christmas?
3. Summarize C.S.'s feelings about the colonies breaking away from Great Britain.

2. ANN HULTON GIVES AN EYEWITNESS ACCOUNT OF THE BATTLE OF BUNKER HILL

The Battle of Bunker Hill was fought on June 17, 1775. Three days later, Ann Hulton, a resident of Boston and an eyewitness to the battle, wrote a letter describing what she saw and felt. The following paragraphs have been excerpted from her letter.

Boston, June 20, 1775

From the heights of this place we have a view of the whole town, the harbor and country round for a great extent, and last Saturday I was a spectator of a most awful scene my eyes ever beheld.

On the morning of the 17th it was observed that the rebels had thrown up a breastwork and were preparing to open a battery upon the heights above Charlestown, from whence they might incommode the shipping and destroy the north part of Boston. . . .

The rebels have occupied a hill about a mile from Charlestown Neck; they are very numerous, and have thrown up intrenchments, and are raising a redoubt on the higher part, whilst the ships and troops cannonade them wherever they can reach them. In the same manner, on the other side of Boston Neck, on the high ground above Roxbury . . . the rebels are intrenching and raising a battery. Such is our present situation.

In this army are many of noble family, many very respectable virtuous and amiable characters, and it grieves one that gentlemen, brave British soldiers, should fall by the hands of such despicable wretches as compose the banditti of the country; amongst whom there is not one that has the least pretension to be called a gentleman. They are a most rude, depraved, degenerate race, and it is a mortification to us that they speak English and can trace themselves from that stock.

Since Adams went to Philadelphia, one Warren, a rascally patriot and apothecary of this town, has had the lead in the Provincial Congress. He signed commissions and acted as President. This fellow happily was killed, in coming out of the trenches the other day, where he had commanded and spirited the people, etc., to defend the lines, which, he assured them, were impregnable. You may judge what the herd must be when such a one is their leader.

Selection from *The Spirit of 'Seventy-Six: The Story of the American Revolution as Told by Participants*, edited by Henry Steele Commager and Richard B. Morris. Published by Harper & Row, New York, copyright © 1958.

CRITICAL THINKING

1. What army is Ann Hulton referring to at the beginning of the second paragraph?
2. Whom does she mean by "despicable wretches" and "banditti" further on in the same paragraph?
3. Do you think C.S. (author of the previous selection) would consider Ann Hulton one of her "sister Americans?" Why?

Thomas Paine
Pushes for Common Sense and Independence

Thomas Paine failed at every occupation he tried—corset-maker, teacher, shopkeeper, tax collector, farmer, inventor—until he discovered the job for which he had been born: professional agitator. As a writer of pamphlets that excited people and stirred up their resentments against established institutions, he had no equal.

Although he was also active in England and France, Paine's greatest success came in the American colonies at the beginning of his revolutionary career. More than any other individual, Thomas Paine was responsible for the decision of Americans to forget about fighting for their rights as British subjects, and to begin fighting for independence.

Paine was born in England. He arrived in America in 1774, when the quarrel with Great Britain was well advanced. During 1775, Paine watched as the Continental Congress argued that the British Parliament had no power over them, but that Americans were still loyal to the king, George III.

This made no sense to Paine. He did not believe in monarchy—rule by a single queen or king. He believed in republics, governments in which elected representatives made the laws. In January 1776, he published these ideas setting forth the colonists' cause in a forty-seven page pamphlet called *Common Sense*.

Common Sense was an amazing success. To a population of only 2.5 million, about 150,000 copies were sold within a few months, 500,000 over five years. Every American who could read must have seen it. Many more must have heard it read to them.

Common Sense said that kings had no right to exist. It said that a whole continent, America, should not be ruled by a small island, Great Britain. It said that Americans should be independent, and their nation a place of refuge for people who fled from tyranny anywhere.

Americans did declare their independence, of course, less than six months after *Common Sense* was published. The pamphlet is one of the most effective pieces of political propaganda in the history of the world.

UNLOCKING HISTORY
KEY DOCUMENT

*T*he period of debate is closed. Arms as a last resource decide the contest; the appeal was the choice of the king, and the continent has accepted the challenge. . . .

I have heard it asserted by some, that as America hath flourished under her former connection with Great Britain, the same connection is necessary towards her future happiness, and will always have the same effect. Nothing can be more fallacious than this kind of argument. We may as well assert that because a child has thriven upon milk, that it is never to have meat, or that the first twenty years of our lives is to become a precedent for the next twenty. But even this is admitting more than is true; for I answer roundly, that America would have flourished as much, and probably much more, had no European power taken any notice of her. . . .

But she has protected us, say some. That she hath engrossed us is true, and defended the continent at our expense as well as her own is admitted; and she would have defended Turkey from the same motive, viz., for the sake of trade and dominion. . . .

France and Spain never were, nor perhaps ever will be our enemies as *Americans*, but as our being the *subjects of Great Britain*.

But Britain is the parent country, say some. Then the more shame upon her conduct. Even brutes do not devour their young, nor savages make war upon their families; wherefore, the assertion, if true, turns to her reproach; but it happens to be true. . . . Europe, and not England, is the parent country of America. This new world hath been the asylum for the persecuted lovers of civil and religious liberty from *every part* of Europe. Hither have they fled, not from the tender embraces of a mother, but from the cruelty of the monster; and it is so far true of England, that the same tyranny which drove the first emigrants from home, pursues their descendants still. . . .

Everything that is right or natural pleads for separation. The blood of the slain, the weeping voice of nature cries, 'TIS TIME TO PART. Even the distance at which the Almighty hath placed England and America is a strong and natural proof that the authority of the one over the other, was never the design of heaven. . . .

[T]here is something very absurd in supposing a continent to be perpetually governed by an island. In no instance hath nature made the satellite larger than its primary planet; and as England and America, with respect to each other, reverse the common order of nature, it is evident that they belong to different systems. England to Europe: America to itself. . . .

But where, say some, is the king of America? . . .

[I]n America THE LAW IS KING. For as in absolute governments the king is law, so in free countries the law *ought* to BE king, and there ought to be no other. But lest any ill use should afterwards arise, let the crown at the conclusion of the ceremony be demolished, and scattered among the people whose right it is.

A government of our own is our natural right; and when a man seriously reflects on the precariousness of human affairs, he will become convinced, that it is infinitely wiser and safer to form a constitution of our own in a cool deliberate manner, while we have it in our power, than to trust such an interesting event to time and chance.

Selection from Thomas Paine, *Common Sense*, 1776. Reprinted in *Great Issues in American History: From Settlement to Revolution, 1584–1776*, edited by Clarence L. Ver Steeg and Richard Hofstadter. Published by Vintage Books, a division of Random House, Inc., September 1969, copyright © 1969 by Random House, Inc. and copyright © 1958 by Richard Hofstadter.

CRITICAL THINKING

1. Which propaganda technique did Thomas Paine use to bring shame on Europe?
2. In Paine's opinion, why is law superior to monarchy?

AMOS DOOLITTLE

Amos Doolittle [1754–1832] is known for his engravings of the battle of Lexington. Born in Cheshire, Connecticut, the second eldest child in a family of 13, Doolittle learned the trade of silversmithing as a youth. But he soon turned to engraving, and earned his living by producing portraits, book illustrations, music, money, and diplomas in a shop in New Haven, Connecticut.

In the spring of 1775, when news came of a battle at Lexington, Doolittle marched to Cambridge, Massachusetts, with a volunteer military force. His services turned out not to be needed, but he was able to put the expedition to good use. Several days after the battle, he and a friend, painter Ralph Earle, returned to the scene of the fighting. Earle made sketches, using Doolittle as a model for the soldiers. Later, Doolittle translated the sketch into four copper engravings, which were advertised for sale on December 13, 1774, and became one of the most coveted engravings of the time.

As historical documents, the engravings are of questionable value. But they do provide an approximate, "eye-witness" account of what happened at the battle of Lexington.

The Doolittle-Earle engravings come close to an eyewitness report on the battle. At Concord cemetery, two British officers standing in the foreground survey their regiments. The British searched the town in vain for the colonists' supplies.

CRITICAL THINKING

1. Give reasons why the paintings might not be historically accurate.
2. Several of the structures in these paintings have survived to the present day. How does this help contemporary historians validate the accuracy of these paintings?

Militiamen hidden behind a stone wall fire upon retreating redcoats. The fighting lasted twenty hours.

At Old North Bridge near Concord were fired the shots "heard round the world." The British fell back.

3. JOHN DICKINSON'S PLEA FOR CONCILIATION

While the Battle of Bunker Hill was being fought, the Second Continental Congress was meeting in Philadelphia. Delegates could not come to unanimous agreement to declare independence from Great Britain. On July 6, 1775, the congress sent King George III A Declaration of the Cause and Necessity of Taking Up Arms, a firm but still conciliatory statement. Two days later, the following petition, written by John Dickinson, was addressed to the king. The monarch, however, was unmoved by either of these pleas, and a year later the Declaration of Independence was proclaimed throughout the colonies.

To the King's Most Excellent Majesty.

July 8, 1775

Most Gracious Sovereign: We, your Majesty's faithful subjects in the Colonies of. . . .

Attached to your Majesty's person, family, and government, with all devotion that principle and affection can inspire; connected with Great Britain by the strongest ties that can unite societies, and deploring every event that tends in any degree to weaken them, we solemnly assure your Majesty, that we not only ardently desire the former harmony between her and these Colonies may be restored, but that a concord may be established between them upon so firm a basis as to perpetuate its blessings, uninterrupted by any future dissensions to succeeding generations in both countries, and to transmit your Majesty's name to posterity, adorned with that signal and lasting glory that has attended the memory of those illustrious personages, whose virtues and abilities have extricated states from dangerous convulsions, and by securing happiness to others have erected the most noble and durable monuments to their own fame.

We therefore beseech your Majesty, that your royal authority and influence may be graciously interposed to procure us relief from our afflicting fears and jealousies, occasioned by the system before-mentioned, and to settle peace through every part of our Dominions, with all humility submitting to your Majesty's wise considerations, whether it may not be expedient, for facilitating those important purposes, that your Majesty be pleased to direct some mode, by which the united applications of your faithful Colonists to the Throne, in pursuance of their common counsels may be improved into a happy and permanent reconciliation; and that, in the meantime, measures may be taken for preventing the further destruction of the lives of your Majesty's subjects; and that such statutes as more immediately distress any of your Majesty's Colonies may be repealed.

Selection from *The Spirit of 'Seventy-Six: The Story of the American Revolution as Told by Participants*, edited by Henry Steele Commager and Richard B. Morris. Published by Harper & Row, New York, copyright © 1958.

CRITICAL THINKING

1. John Dickinson's communication to King George is often called the "Olive Branch Petition." Do you think this is appropriate? Why?
2. John Adams commented that Dickinson's petition gave Congress's activities "a silly cast." Do you agree? Why?

---

4. THE *DECLARATION OF INDEPENDENCE* IS CELEBRATED

The issuance of the Declaration of Independence resulted in enthusiastic celebrations throughout the colonies. The account of one celebration is given below.

Savannah, in Georgia, August 10, 1776

His Excellency, the President, and the Honourable the Council met in the Council chamber, and read the Declaration. They then proceeded to the square before the Assembly House, and read it likewise before a great concourse of people, when the Grenadier and Light Infantry Companies fired a general volley. After this they proceeded in the following procession to the Liberty Pole: the Grenadiers in front; the Provost-Marshall on horseback, with his sword drawn; the Secretary with the Declaration; his Excellency the President; the Honourable the Council and Gentlemen; then the Light Infantry and the rest of the Militia of the town and district of Savannah. At the Liberty Pole they were met by the Georgia Battalion who, after reading of the

Declaration, discharged their field-pieces and fired in platoons. Upon this they proceeded to the Battery at the Trustees garden, where the Declaration was read for the last time, and cannon of the Battery discharged. His Excellency and Council, Colonel Lachlan McIntosh, and other gentlemen, with the Militia, dined under the Cedar Trees, and cheerfully drank to the United Free and Independent States of America. In the evening the town was illuminated, and there was exhibited a very solemn funeral procession, attended by the Grenadier and Light Infantry Companies, and other Militia, with their drums muffled and fifes, and a greater number of people than ever appeared on any occasion before in this Province, when George III was interred before the Court-House, in the following manner:

For as much as George III, of Great Britain, hath most flagrantly violated his coronation oath and trampled upon the constitution of our country and the sacred rights of mankind, we therefore commit his political existence to the ground, corruption to corruption, tyranny to the grave, and oppression to eternal infamy, in sure and certain hope that he will never obtain a resurrection to rule again over these United States of America. But my friends and fellow-citizens, let us not be sorry as men without hope for tyrants that thus depart; rather let us remember America is free and independent; that she is, and will be, with the blessing of the Almighty, great among the nations of the earth. Let this encourage us in well-doing to fight for our rights and privileges, for our wives and children, for all that is near and dear unto us. May God give us his blessing, and let all the people say Amen!

Selection from *The Spirit of 'Seventy-Six: The Story of the American Revolution as Told by Participants*, edited by Henry Steele Commager and Richard B. Morris. Published by Harper & Row, New York, copyright © 1958.

CRITICAL THINKING

1. What does the mock burial of George III symbolize?
2. What was the mood of the participants at the ceremony?

5. ONE PATRIOT'S ATTACK ON THE TORIES

To most American patriots, the Tories, or Loyalists, were a perpetual thorn in the side. This article written by an anonymous patriot for the Pennsylvania Packet *gives some indication of the strong feelings against the Tories among American patriots during the Revolutionary War.*

June I.—Among the many errors America has been guilty of during her contest with Great Britain, few have been greater, or attended with more fatal consequences to these States, than her lenity to the Tories. . . . We can no longer be silent on this subject, and see the independence of the country, after standing every shock from without, endangered by internal enemies. Rouse, America! your danger is great—great from a quarter where you least expect it. The Tories, the Tories will yet be the ruin of you! 'Tis high time they were separated from among you. They are now busy engaged in undermining your liberties. They have a thousand ways of doing it, and they make use of them all. Who were the occasion of this war? The Tories! Who persuaded the tyrant of Britain to prosecute it in a manner before unknown to civilized nations and shocking even to barbarians? The Tories! Who prevailed on the savages of the wilderness to join the standard of the enemy? The Tories! Who have assisted the Indians in taking the scalp from the aged matron, the blooming fair one, the helpless infant, and the dying hero? The Tories! Who advised and who assisted in burning your towns . . . [and] ravaging your country? The Tories! Who are the occasion that thousands of you now mourn the loss of your dearest connections? The Tories! Who have always counteracted the endeavors of Congress to secure the liberties of this country? The Tories! . . . Who corrupt the minds of the good people of these States by every species of insidious counsel? The Tories! Who hold a traitorous correspondence with the enemy? The Tories! Who daily sends them intelligence? The Tories! Who take the oaths of allegiance to the States one day, and break them the next? The Tories! Who prevent your battalions from being filled? The Tories! Who dissuade men from entering the army? The Tories! Who persuade those who have enlisted to desert? The Tories! Who harbor those who do desert? The Tories! In short, who wish to see us conquered, to see us slaves, to see us hewers of wood and drawers of water? The Tories!

. . . Do they not insult us with their impudence? Do they not hold traitorous assemblies of their own? Do they not walk the streets at noon day, and taste the air of liberty? In short, do they not enjoy every privilege of the brave soldier who has spilt his all in our righteous cause? Yes—to our eternal shame be it spoken—they do. . . . 'Tis time to rid ourselves of these bosom vipers. An immediate separation is necessary. I dread to think of the evils every moment is big with, while a single Tory remains among us. May we not soon expect to hear of plots, assassinations, and every species of wickedness their malice and rancor can suggest? for what can restrain those who have already . . . [drenched] their hands in their country's blood? . . . For my own part, whenever I meet one in the street, or at the coffee house, my blood boils within me. Their guilt is equalled only by their impudence. They strut, and seem to bid defiance to every one. In every place, and in every company, they spread their . . . doctrines, and then laugh at . . . those who let them go unpunished. I flatter myself, however, with the hopes of soon seeing a period to their reign, and a total end to their existence in America. Awake, Americans, to a sense of your danger. No time to be lost. Instantly banish every Tory from among you. Let America be sacred alone to freemen.

Drive far from you every baneful wretch who wishes to see you fettered with the chains of tyranny. Send them . . . to the island of Britain; there let them drink the cup of slavery and eat the bread of bitterness all the days of their existence— there let them drag out a painful life, despised and accursed by those very men whose cause they have had the wickedness to espouse. Never let them return to this happy land—never let them taste the sweets of that independence which they strove to prevent. Banishment, perpetual banishment, should be their lot.

Selection from "Vengeance on the Tories! (1779)" in *American History Told by Contemporaries*, Vol. II, edited by Albert Bushnell Hart. Published by The Macmillan Company, New York, copyright © 1924.

CRITICAL THINKING

1. How well does the writer of this article support the validity of his charges against the Tories?
2. Explain why the writer thinks action should be taken against the Tories.
3. If you were writing a report on the Tories, would you use this article as a source of factual information about the activities of the Tories? Why or why not?

6. ELIAS BOUDINOT TELLS THE TALE OF BENEDICT ARNOLD'S TREACHERY

Benedict Arnold's attempt to betray the new United States is recounted here by Elias Boudinot. Boudinot was at various times President of the Continental Congress and Commissary General of American prisoners of war. He kept a journal to preserve for posterity "a great many interesting anecdotes of the Revolution." The following is from that journal. Notice that much of Boudinot's original grammar, punctuation, and spelling has been kept.

Major Andre who was Adjutant General of the British Army, having entered into a correspondence with General Benedict Arnold, who then commanded the Important post of West Point . . . which was estimated as the key to the state of New York, and indeed all the upper country, in which great part of the New England States were also greatly interested, soon ripend it into an actual communication for delivering up that Post to the British on Terms of personal emolument to Arnold. The fear of detection, led the American General to propose a personal meeting . . . at some distance below West Point & without the out posts that matters might be finally settled, and the Treason be compleated.—Andre being greatly elated with his success entered warmly into the measure, and Genl. Clinton the Commander in Chief of the British Army, received the proposal with great Expectation, and immediately provided Andre . . . with a 20 Gun ship to go up the River. . . . In the Evening the

Elias Boudinot's journal about the Revolutionary period includes an account of Benedict Arnold's betrayal of his country.

Ship came to Anchor, and after night [Andre] was landed privately on the mainland; where he met Arnold, and spent some time in planning the whole business and receiving [from] him returns of the American Army, . . . and as Genl Washington the American Commander in Chief . . . was to return in a day or two & to dine with Arnold, it was added to the rest of this iniquitous business to fix upon that day for the nefarious Act & to sieze General Washington at the same time. . . . The next Morning Andre & Arnold appeared together as old friends and such was their conduct in viewing the Works &c &c as to create some Jealousy in the Officers round the General. A Horse being furnished by the Quarter Master General Andre set off with the General's Passports. . . . Andre had passed the American out posts and finding himself as he thought out of Danger, when in a deep reverie in the Contemplation of his future Glory, he came to the cross Roads. One leading to New York [,] the other to Tarry Town. . . . It so providentially happened that the Horse on which he rode had been bred at Tarry Town, Andre lost in thought, did not attend either to his Horse or to the Road and the Horse naturally took the Road he had been used to, and Andre soon found himself challenged by a Sentinel . . . [Andre] immediately said that he was a British Officer & desired to be taken into their Post. . . . They then told him if that was the Case, he was their Prisoner for they were Americans, and therefore insisted on searching him.— Andre finding himself in this disagreeable predica-

ment, began to beg, and assuring them that he was only a Citizen of New York, who had important family business in the Country, had gone to finish it, and was returning.—That his capture could not be of service to them . . . , and if they would release him he would engage to return them, safely delivered in any private place on the lines they should name[,] any reasonable Quantity of British Goods they should desire. . . . They then told him he must be a fool . . . ; no we are Americans: and all that you are worth could not tempt us to release you; Therefore immediately submit to be searched.—Accordingly he turned out his Pockets—finding nothing material, they ordered him to pull off his Boots.—He pulled off one but said he would go no further & refused to pull off the other, on which they tripped up his heels, and on pulling off his Boot, out came all his papers.—They immediately carried him into their Post and delivered him with all the Papers to their Officer Lt Coll Jameson. . . .

The Officer was Thunder Struck on finding the Papers in the hand writing of General Arnold; and that the Plan was to deliver up the Fort with General Washington while at dinner. Andre said his name was Anderson. . . . What to do at first [the officer] did not know.—But calling a soldier he put much Confidence in, gave him a letter to General Arnold, acquainting him with the outlines of the Capture of a Mr Anderson, going into New York, and set it off according to the letter of his orders; but gave secret orders to the Soldier to lame his Horse by the way and to be detained by it, for 24 Hours. He then sent another off to ride Post & meet General Washington on his return . . . with the Papers found on Andre. The Horseman took the Road General Washington went, not knowing that he made it a rule never to go & return by the same road. By this means he missed the General, but heard of his return at a cross road and the Horseman sent to Arnold arrived at General Arnold's Quarters: a short time before General Washington, as soon as Arnold [received] the letter he sprang out of his Room, Just looked into the Room where his wife was; and told her that he must bid her farewell forever, and ran down to the fort, and got on board his barge, and ordered the Bargemen to row him down the River—General Washington arrived soon after, and enquiring at Arnold's Quarters for the Gener-

Benedict Arnold, once a respected Revolutionary War general, became the most well-known traitor in American history.

al was told that he had just gone to the Fort, General Washington rode immediately down . . . [and] found that the General was not there. . . . Arnold not appearing General Washington expressed some resentment at his not attending him and suddenly returned to his Horse, he was scarcely mounted, when the Horseman appeared with the Papers taken on Andre—As soon as he had read the letter & cast his Eye over the Papers he . . . rode to Arnold's door and called out his Aid Du Camp and drawing his Pistol from his holster solemnly declared he would blow his brains out if he did not instantly tell him where Arnold was. . . . [The aid] could tell him no more that that on receiving a Horseman from an Outpost [Arnold] had in great terror left the House & gone alone to the Fort. The General instantly ordered Coll Hamilton to ride post to the Fort . . . and order the Fort to fire on the Barge; . . . Hamilton arrived just as the fort was paying the usual Compliment to the General's Barge.— Hamilton instantly pointed the Guns, and fired on the Barge. Arnold rose and with a Pistol in each hand, swore he would put the first man to death

who should stop his oar and soon passed out of reach of the Fort.

Andre was sent to Head Quarters and put under the Care of a subaltern Officer and a strong Guard—In the night Andre acknowledged to the Officer that he was Adjutant General of the British Army. . . . The Officer was so alarmed, that he slept not a moment, but in the morning communicated this Intelligence to Head Quarters. —Coll Hamilton, who had seen Andre was sent to him, and knew him to be the man—General Washington out of respect to [Andre's] Character, instead of a more summary proceeding called a Council of General Officers, of whom La Fayette & [Von] Steuben were two, who were to enquire into the facts & the Crime of the Prisoner.— Andre finding himself unexpectedly treated with so much propriety & kindness, confessed every fact. . . . —The Council found him guilty & that he was worthy of Death. His execution was determined on, and the day fixed. [General Washington] treated Major Andre with the greatest tenderness, while he carried the Sentence of the Council into strict Execution according to the laws of War. . . . Arnold was made a Brigadier General [in the British Army] and tho' great Expectations were formed of his invitations to the American Soldiers & Citizens to Join him [against] the Rebellion of their Country, it is generally believed that scarcely a soldier ever deserted or a Citizen Joined him.—He lived dispised & disregarded, and died unlamented & unnoticed—Thus having [received] the general reward of a Traitor to his Country.

Selection adapted from Elias Boudinot, *Journal or Historical Recollections of American Events During the Revolutionary War.* Published by The New York Times & Arno Press, New York, copyright © 1968.

CRITICAL THINKING

1. If successful, what double blow would Arnold and Andre's plan have inflicted on the American revolutionary cause?
2. State a possible effect of each part of this plan.
3. What impression of George Washington do you get from Boudinot's account?

MOLDING A NATION

1783–1789

1. ALEXANDER HAMILTON CRITICIZES THE *ARTICLES OF CONFEDERATION*

In September 1780 Alexander Hamilton wrote a letter to James Duane (a member of the Confederation Congress) commenting on the weaknesses of the government set up under the Articles of Confederation. Excerpts from Hamilton's letter are reproduced below. Many of the ideas found in these excerpts were used later by Hamilton, in the numbers of the Federalist Papers *he authored, when he urged ratification of the Constitution.*

The fundamental defect is a want of power in Congress. It is hardly worth while to show in what this consists, as it seems to be universally [acknowledged], or to point out how it has happened, as the only question is how to remedy it. It may however be said that it has originated from three causes—an excess of the spirit of liberty which has made the particular states show a jealousy of all power not in their own hands; and this jealousy has led them to exercise a right of judging in the last resort of the measures recommended by Congress, and of acting according to their own opinions of their, propriety or necessity, a diffidence in Congress of their own powers, by which they have been timid and indecisive in their resolutions, constantly making concessions to the states, till they have scarcely left themselves the show of power; a want of sufficient means at their disposal to answer the public exigencies and of vigor to draw forth those means; which have occasioned them to depend on the states individually to fulfil their engagements with the army, and the consequence of which has been to ruin their influence and credit with the army. . . .

. . . [The] confederation itself is defective and requires to be altered, it is neither fit for war, nor peace. The idea of an [uncontrollable] sovereignty in each state, over its internal police, will defeat the other powers given to Congress, and make our union feeble and precarious. There are instances without number, where acts necessary for the general good, and which rise out of the powers given to Congress must interfere with the internal police of the states, and there are as many instances in which the particular states by arrangements of internal police can effectually though indirectly counteract the arrangements of Congress. . . .

The confederation gives the states individually too much influence in the affairs of the army; they should have nothing to do with it. The entire formation and disposal of our military forces ought to belong to Congress. It is an essential cement of the union; and it ought to be the policy of Congress to des(troy) all ideas of state attachments in the army. . . .It may be apprehended that this may be dangerous to liberty. But nothing appears more evident to me, than that we run much greater risk of having a weak and disunited federal government, than one which will be able to usurp upon the rights of the people. . . .

The confederation too gives the power of the purse too [entirely] to the state legislatures. It should provide perpetual funds in the disposal of Congress—by a land tax, poll tax, or the like. All imposts upon commerce ought to be laid by Congress and appropriated to their use, for without certain revenues, a government can have no power; that power, which holds the purse strings absolutely, must rule. This seems to be a medium, which without making Congress altogether independent will tend to give reality to its authority.

Another defect in our system is want of method and energy in the administration. This has partly resulted from the other defect, but in a great degree from prejudice and the want of a proper executive. Congress have kept the power too much into their own hands and have meddled too much with details of every sort. Congress is properly a deliberative corps and it forgets itself when it attempts to play the executive. It is impossible such a body, numerous as it is, constantly fluctuating, can ever act with sufficient decision, or with system. Two thirds of the members, one half the time, cannot know what has gone before them or what connection the subject in hand has to what has been transacted on former occasions. The members, who have been more permanent, will only give information, that promotes the side they espouse, in the present case, and will as often mislead as enlighten. The variety of business must distract, and the proneness of every assembly to debate must at all times delay. . . .

If a Convention is called the minds of all the states and the people ought to be prepared to receive its determinations by sensible and popular writings, which should conform to the views of Congress. There are epochs in human affairs, when *novelty* even is useful. If a general opinion prevails that the old way is bad, whether true or false, and this obstructs or relaxes the operation of the public service, a change is necessary if it be but for the sake of change. This is exactly the case now. 'Tis an universal sentiment that our present system is a bad one, and that things do not go right on this account. The measure of a Convention would revive the hopes of the people and give a new direction to their passions, which may be improved in carrying points of substantial utility. The Eastern states have already pointed out this mode to Congress; they ought to take the hint and anticipate the others. . . .

Selection from *The Papers of Alexander Hamilton*, Vol. II, edited by Harold C. Syrett and Jacob E. Cooke. Published by Columbia University Press, New York, copyright © 1961.

CRITICAL THINKING

1. According to Alexander Hamilton, who had the real political power in the United States? Why did Hamilton explain this in terms of "the power of the purse"?
2. In the last paragraph, Hamilton refers to a "Convention." What might he have expected such a convention to do?
3. In Hamilton's opinion, why was Congress inadequate when it attempted to "play the executive"?

2. THE CONFEDERATION CONGRESS SEEKS ADDITIONAL POWERS

Alexander Hamilton believed that the Confederation Congress should have the power to collect certain revenues, or taxes. In 1783, the Congress proposed that the states grant it such a taxing power, among other powers. The people of Fairfax County, Virginia, gave their representatives in the state legislature the following instructions on how to respond to the Congress's proposals.

May 30, 1783

GENTLEMEN:

We have committed to you the greatest and most sacred trust, which a free people can repose in any of their fellow-citizens; the care of our dearest and most important interests, the protection of our rights and liberty, and the power of making, on our behalf, those laws by which we are to be governed, and this commonwealth preserved in safety and prosperity. And although we confide thoroughly in your integrity and attachment to the public good, yet we judge it expedient, at this critical and important season, to communicate to you our sentiments, and to exercise our undoubted right of instructing you, as our immediate Representatives in the Legislature. . . .

We desire and instruct you strenuously to oppose all encroachments of the American Congress upon the sovereignty and jurisdiction of the separate States; and every assumption of power, not expressly vested in them, by the Articles of Confederation. If experience shall prove that further powers are necessary and safe, they can be granted only by additional articles to the Confederation, duly acceded to by all the States; for if Congress, upon the plea of necessity, or upon any pretence whatever, can arrogate powers not warranted by the Articles of Confederation, in one instance, they may in another, or in an hundred; every repetition will be strengthened and confirmed by precedents.

And in particular we desire and instruct you to oppose any attempts which may be made by Congress to obtain a perpetual revenue, or the appointment of revenue officers. Were these powers superadded to those they already possess, the

Articles of Confederation, and the Constitutions of Government in the different States would prove mere parchment bulwarks to American liberty.

We like not the language of the late address from Congress to the different States, and of the report of their committee upon the subject of revenue, published in the same pamphlet. If they are carefully and impartially examined, they will be found to exhibit strong proofs of lust of power. . . . And the present king and council of Great Britain might not improperly adopt great part of them, to prove the expediency of levying money without consent of Parliament. After having reluctantly given up part of what they found they could not maintain, they still insist that the several States shall invest *the United States in Congress assembled with the power to levy,* for the use of the United States, the following duties, &c., and that the revenue officers shall be amenable to Congress. The very style is alarming. The proposed duties may be proper, but the separate States only can safely have *the power of levying taxes.* Congress should not have even the appearance of such a power. Forms generally imply substance, and such a precedent may be applied to dangerous purposes hereafter. When the same man, or set of men, holds both the sword and the purse, there is an end of liberty. . . .

And finally we recommend it to you (for in this we will not presume to give positive instructions) to endeavor to obtain an instruction from the General Assembly to the Virginia delegates in Congress, against sending ambassadors to the courts of Europe; it being an expence which (in our present circumstances) these United States are unable to support. Such appointments can hardly fail of producing dangerous combinations, factions, and cabals, in the great council of America. And from the great distance and the difficulty of knowing and examining their conduct, there is danger, too, that some of the persons so sent, may be corrupted and pensioned by the courts where they reside. We are of opinion, that consuls to superintend our trade (at less than a tenth part of the charge of ambassadors) will be sufficient to answer every good purpose. And nature having separated us, by an immense ocean, from the European nations, the less we have to do with their quarrels or politics, the better. Having thus,

Gentlemen, given you our opinions and instructions, upon such subjects as we deem at this time most important, we remain, with sentiments of great respect and esteem, your friends and fellow-citizens.

Selection from *The Papers of George Mason, 1725–1792*, Vol. II, edited by Robert A. Rutland. Published by The University of North Carolina Press, copyright © 1970.

CRITICAL THINKING

1. Were the people of Fairfax County opposed to granting the Congress additional powers under any circumstances whatsoever? Explain.
2. What procedures would have to be followed to give further powers to the Congress?
3. Contrast Hamilton's ideas about the powers of Congress with the ideas of the people of Fairfax County.

3. BENJAMIN FRANKLIN URGES PASSAGE OF A NEW FEDERAL CONSTITUTION

By 1787 the states, recognizing the urgent need to strengthen the national government, sent delegates to Philadelphia to amend the Articles of Confederation. What the delegates in fact did was hammer out a plan for a new government—the Constitution. On the last day of the Convention, Benjamin Franklin gave his views on the new Constitution.

Monday Sepr. 17. 1787 In Convention

The Engrossed Constitution being read, Docr. Franklin rose with a speech in his hand, which he had reduced to writing for his own conveniency, and which Mr. Wilson read in the words following.

Mr. President

"I confess that there are several parts of this constitution which I do not at present approve, but I am not sure I shall never approve them: For having lived long, I have experienced many instances of being obliged by better information or fuller consideration, to change opinions even on important subjects, which I once thought right, but found to be otherwise. It is therefore that the older I grow, the more apt I am to doubt my own judgment, and to pay more respect to the judgment of others. Most men indeed as well as most sects in Religion, think themselves in possession of all truth, and that whereever others differ from them it is so far error. . . . But though many private persons think almost as highly of their own infallibility as a certain [French] lady, who in a dispute with her sister, said "I don't know how it happens, Sister but I meet with nobody but myself, that's always in the right". . . .

In these sentiments, Sir, I agree to this Constitution with all its faults, if they are such; because I think a general Government necessary for us, and there is no form of Government but what may be a blessing to the people if well administered, and believe farther that this is likely to be well administered for a course of years, and can only end in Despotism, as other forms have done before it, when the people shall become so corrupted as to need despotic Government, being incapable of any other. I doubt too whether any other Convention . . . may be able to make a better Constitution. For when you assemble a number of men to have the advantage of their joint wisdom, you inevitably assemble with those men, all their prejudices, their passions, their errors of opinion, their local interests, and their selfish views. From such an Assembly can a perfect production be expected? It therefore astonishes me, Sir, to find this system approaching so near to perfection as it does; and I think it will astonish our enemies, who are waiting with confidence to hear that our councils are confounded like those of the Builders of Babel; and that our States are on the point of separation, only to meet hereafter for the purpose of cutting one another's throats. Thus I consent, Sir, to this Constitution because I expect no better, and because I am not sure, that it is not the best. The opinions I have had of its errors, I sacrifice to the public good—I have never whispered a syllable of them abroad—Within these walls they were born, and here they shall die—If every one of us in returning to our Constituents were to report the objections he has had to it, and endeavor to gain [partisans] in support of them, we might prevent its being generally received, and thereby lose all the salutary effects & great advan-

tages resulting naturally in our favor among foreign Nations as well as among ourselves, from our real or apparent unanimity. Much of the strength & efficiency of any Government in procuring and securing happiness to the people, depends on opinion, on the general opinion of the goodness of the Government, as well as . . . of the wisdom and integrity of its Governors. I hope therefore that for our own sakes as a part of the people, and for the sake of posterity, we shall act heartily and unanimously in recommending this Constitution (if approved by Congress & confirmed by the Conventions) wherever our influence may extend, and turn our future thoughts & endeavors to the means of having it well administered.

On the whole, Sir, I cannot help expressing a wish that every member of the Convention who may still have objections to it, would with me, on this occasion doubt a little of his own infallibility —and to make manifest our unanimity, put his name to this instrument."—He then moved that the Constitution be signed by the members and offered the following as a convenient form viz. "Done in Convention, by the unanimous consent of *the States* present the 17th. of Sepr. &c—In Witness whereof we have hereunto subscribed our names."

This ambiguous form had been drawn up by Mr. G. M. in order to gain the dissenting members, and put into the hands of Docr. Franklin that it might have the better chance of success.

Selection from *The Records of the Federal Convention of 1787*, edited by Max Farrand. Published by Yale University Press, New Haven, copyright © 1966.

CRITICAL THINKING

1. What was the point of Benjamin Franklin's story about "a certain French lady?" Why did he tell it?
2. What was Franklin's main reason for agreeing to the Constitution, despite the doubts he mentions?
3. Why do you think Franklin, rather than another person, was chosen to express these ideas on the last day of the Convention?

4. PATRICK HENRY SPEAKS OUT ABOUT THE PROPOSED CONSTITUTION

After Benjamin Franklin's speech at the Convention in Philadelphia, the delegates returned to their respective states to urge ratification of the Constitution. The next three readings are excerpts from the debates at Virginia's ratification convention held in June 1788. Below are excerpts from speeches give by Patrick Henry during the ratification debates.

Mr. HENRY. . . . And here I would make this inquiry of those worthy characters who composed a part of the late federal Convention. I am sure they were fully impressed with the necessity of forming a great consolidated government, instead of a confederation. That this is a consolidated government is demonstrably clear; and the danger of such a government is, to my mind, very striking. I have the highest veneration for those gentlemen; but, sir, give me leave to demand. What right had they to say, *We, the people?* My political curiosity, exclusive of my anxious solicitude for the public welfare, leads me to ask, Who authorized them to speak the language of *We, the people*, instead of, *We, the states?* States are the characteristics and the soul of a confederation. . . . The federal Convention ought to have amended the old system; for this purpose they were solely delegated; the object of their mission extended to no other consideration. You must, therefore, forgive the solicitation of one unworthy member to know what danger could have arisen under the present Confederation, and what are the causes of this proposal to change our government. . . .

This Constitution is said to have beautiful features; but when I come to examine these features, sir, they appear to me horribly frightful. Among other deformities, it has an awful squinting; it squints towards monarchy; and does not this raise indignation in the breast of every true American?

Your President may easily become king. Your Senate is so imperfectly constructed that your dearest rights may be sacrificed by what may be a small minority; and a very small minority may continue forever unchangeably this government, although horridly defective. Where are your checks in this government? Your strongholds will be in the hands of your enemies. It is on a supposition that your American governors shall be honest, that all the good qualities of this government are founded; but its defective and imperfect construction puts it in their power to perpetrate the worst of mischiefs, should they be bad men; and, sir, would not all the world, from the eastern to the western hemisphere, blame our distracted folly in resting our rights upon the contingency of our rulers being good or bad? Show me that age and country where the rights and liberties of the people were placed on the sole chance of their rulers being good men, without a consequent loss of liberty! I say that the loss of the dearest privilege has ever followed, with absolute certainty, every such mad attempt.

If your American chief be a man of ambition and abilities, how easy is it for him to render himself absolute! The army is in his hands, and if he be a man of address, it will be attached to him, and it will be the subject of long meditation with him to seize the first auspicious moment to accomplish his design; and, sir, will the American spirit solely relieve you when this happens? I would rather infinitely—and I am sure most of this Convention are of the same opinion—have a king, lords, and commons, than a government so replete with such insupportable evils.

Selection from *The Debates in the Several State Conventions on the Adoption of the Federal Constitution*, Vol. III, edited by Jonathan Elliot. Published by J. B. Lippincott Company, Philadelphia, copyright © 1836.

CRITICAL THINKING

1. Why is Patrick Henry so concerned about the use of the words *We, the people* at the beginning of the Constitution?
2. What does Henry find objectionable in the office of the President as described in the Constitution?
3. Why does Henry think it is important to have a system of checks and balances included in the Constitution?

5. EDMUND PENDLETON SPEAKS OUT ABOUT THE PROPOSED CONSTITUTION

Edmund Pendleton, formerly one of Virginia's delegates to the Confederation Congress, was elected president of the state's ratification convention. In the following excerpt from one of his speeches at the convention, Pendleton responds to Patrick Henry and his objections to the words "We, the people."

Mr. PENDLETON. Mr. Chairman, my worthy friend (Mr. Henry) has expressed great uneasiness in his mind and informed us that a great many of our citizens are also extremely uneasy, at the proposal of changing our government; but that, a year ago, before this fatal system was thought of, the public mind was at perfect repose. It is necessary to inquire whether the public mind was at ease on the subject, and if it be since disturbed, what was the cause. What was the situation of this country before the meeting of the federal Convention? Our general government was totally inadequate to the purpose of its institution; our commerce decayed; our finances deranged; public and private credit destroyed: these and many other national evils rendered necessary the meeting of that Convention. If the public mind was then at ease, it did not result from a conviction of being in a happy and easy situation: it must have been [in] an inactive, unaccountable stupor. . . .

But an objection is made to the form: the expression, We, the people, is thought improper. Permit me to ask the gentleman who made this objection, who but the people can delegate powers? Who but the people have a right to form government? The expression is a common one, and a favorite one with me. The representatives of the people, by their authority, is a mode wholly inessential. If the objection be, that the Union ought to be not of the people, but of the state governments, then I think the choice of the former very happy and proper. What have the state governments to do with it? Were they to determine, the people would not, in that case, be the judges upon what terms it was adopted. . . .

Shall we then, sir, continue under such a government, or shall we introduce that kind of government which shall produce the real happiness and security of the people? When gentlemen say that we ought not to introduce this new government, but strengthen the hands of Congress, they ought to be explicit. In what manner shall this be done? If the union of the states be necessary, government must be equally so; for without the latter, the former cannot be effected. Government must then have its complete powers, or be ineffectual; a legislature to fix rules, impose sanctions, and point out the punishment of the transgressors of these rules; an executive to watch over officers, and bring them to punishment; a judiciary, to guard the innocent, and fix the guilty, by a fair trial. Without an executive, offenders would not be brought to punishment; without a judiciary, any man might be taken up, convicted, and punished without a trial. Hence the necessity of having these three branches. Would any gentleman in this committee agree to vest these three powers in one body—Congress? No [.] Hence the necessity of a new organization and distribution of those powers. If there be any feature in this government which is not republican, it would be exceptionable. From all the public servants responsibility is secured, by their being representatives, mediate or immediate, for short terms, and their powers defined. It is, on the whole complexion of it, a government of laws, not of men.

Selection from *The Debates in the Several State Conventions*, Vol. III, edited by Jonathan Elliott. Published by J.B. Lippincott Company, Philadelphia, copyright © 1836.

CRITICAL THINKING

1. Would you characterize the first paragraph of Edmund Pendleton's speech as sincere or sarcastic? Give reasons to explain your choice.
2. Consider Henry's and Pendleton's comments on *We, the people*. In what fundamental way do the two men differ in their ideas about the basis of governmental power?
3. How does a government of men differ from a government of law?

6. PATRICK HENRY SPEAKS OF THE NECESSITY OF A *BILL OF RIGHTS*

Inclusion of a bill of rights in the Constitution became an issue at the ratification conventions in some states. At the Virginia convention, Patrick Henry explained why many Americans believed a bill of rights was needed.

Mr. HENRY. . . . [The] necessity of a bill of rights appears to me to be greater in this government that ever it was in any government before. . . . [All] nations have adopted this construction—that all rights not expressly and unequivocally reserved to the people are . . . relinquished to rulers, as necessarily inseparable from the delegated powers. It is so in Great Britain; for every possible right, which is not reserved to the people by some express provision or compact, is within the king's prerogative. It is so in that country which is said to be in such full possession of freedom. It is so in Spain, Germany, and other parts of the world. Let us consider the sentiments which have been entertained by the people of America on this subject. At the revolution, it must be admitted that it was their sense to set down those great rights which ought, in all countries, to be held inviolable and sacred. Virginia did so, we all remember. She made a compact to reserve, expressly, certain rights. . . .

. . . It was expressly declared in our Confederation that every right was retained by the states, respectively, which was not given up to the government of the United States. But there is no such thing here [in the Constitution.]. You, therefore, by a natural and unavoidable implication, give up your rights to the general government. . . .

. . . By this Constitution, some of the best barriers of human rights are thrown away. . . .

A bill of rights may be summed up in a few words. What do they tell us?—That our rights are reserved. Why not say so? Is it because it will consume too much paper? Gentlemen's reasoning against a bill of rights does not satisfy me. Without saying which has the right side, it remains doubtful. A bill of rights is a favorite thing with the Virginians and the people of the other states likewise. It may be their prejudice, but the government ought to suit their geniuses; otherwise, its operation will be unhappy. A bill of rights, even if its necessity be doubtful, will exclude the possibility of dispute; and, with great submission, I think the best way is to have no dispute. In the present Constitution, they are restrained from issuing general warrants to search suspected places, or seize persons not named, without evidence of the commission of a fact, &c. There was certainly some celestial influence governing those who deliberated on that Constitution; for they have, with the most cautious and enlightened circumspection, guarded those indefeasible rights which ought ever to be held sacred! The officers of Congress may come upon you now, fortified with all the terrors of paramount federal authority. Excisemen [tax collectors] may come in multitudes; for the limitation of their numbers no man knows. They may, unless the general government be restrained by a bill of rights, or some similar restriction, go into your cellars and rooms, and search, ransack, and measure, every thing you eat, drink, and wear. They ought to be restrained within proper bounds. With respect to the freedom of the press, I need say nothing; for it is hoped that the gentlemen who shall compose Congress will take care to infringe as little as possible the rights of human nature. This will result from their integrity. They should, from prudence, abstain from violating the rights of their constituents.

Selection from *The Debates in the Several State Conventions,* Vol. III, edited by Jonathan Elliot. Published by J.B. Lippincott Company, Philadelphia, copyright © 1836.

CRITICAL THINKING

1. What did Patrick Henry mean by *reserved,* or *retained,* rights? What did Henry mean by *delegated* rights?
2. According to Henry, what would happen to those rights not explicitly claimed for the people in a bill of rights?

George Washington 1789–1797

James Madison 1809–1817

GILBERT STUART:

G ilbert Stuart [1755–1828] was one of the finest portrait painters in the history of American art. He painted three portraits of George Washington, as well as likenesses of the next five presidents. Many prominent Americans—other than the presidents—had their portraits painted by Stuart.

Although Stuart was born in Rhode Island, he left his native country when the Revolution broke out. In England he studied the works of Joshua Reynolds, Thomas Gainsborough, and George Romney. His first portraits were highly praised, and wealthy people began to seek him out. Fond of luxury, Stuart was often in debt because of his extravagance. Indeed, he timed his return to the United States in order to escape his European creditors.

CRITICAL THINKING

1. What are the similarities in all these portraits?
2. Compare and contrast Stuart's portraits of six American presidents to the ones that John Singleton Copley painted. (on page 59)

therefore should not attempt it had I not so much vanity as to think you will be in some measure gratified by its coming thro this chance however imperfect. . . .

[A] number of Boats with a great variety of superb Flags came up to us and dropped in our wake—Soon after we opened the Bay, General Knox and several Gentn of distinction in a large Barge presented themselves with splendid Colors, Boat after Boat & Sloop after Sloop added to our little fleet gaily dressed with every naval Armament—we began to mak[e] a most elegant appearance. Before we got to Bedlars Island a large Sloop came with full sail on our Starboard Bow, when about 20 Gentn & Ladies rose up and with excellent & melodious Voices sung an Eloquent Ode appropriate to the occasion & set to the Music of "God save the King," welcoming their Great Chief to the Seat of Government. At the conclusion we gave them our Hats, and then they with the surrounding Boats, gave three Hurra's which made the neighboring shores rebound with the Joyful acclamation. Soon after another Boat came under our Stern and threw in amongst us a number of Copies of another Ode and immediately about a dozen Gentn began to sing it in parts as we passed along. Our Worthy President was greatly affected with these tokens of profound respect & gratitude.

As we approached the Harbour Our Train increased and the Hurraing & Shouts of Joy added great vivacity to this lively scene. At this moment a shoal of porpoises came rising about the water & playing among the Boats as if desirous to know the Cause of all the Joy & Gladness.—We now discovered the Shores crowded with thousands of People. Men Women & Children. Nay I may venture to say Tens of Thousands, from the Battery to the place of Landing[.] Altho nearly half a Mile you could see little else along the Wharves in the Streets and on board the Vessels, but heads as numerous as Ears of Corn before the Harvest. The Vessels in the Harbour presented a most superb appearance draped in all the pomp of national Gaity & Elegance[ ] A Spanish Packett then lying in the Harbour in a Moment on a signal given hoisted 27 or 28 different Colors of All Nations on every part of the Rigging and paid a compliment of 13 Guns with all her Yards flying, as did another Vessel in the Harbour, displaying colors

in like manner. From the Battery we had the like compliment of 18 Pounders.

We soon arrived at the Ferry Stairs in Wall Street where many thousands of the Citizens and a chosen detachment of the Militia in Elegant Uniform, waiting with all eagerness of Expectation, welcomed this most excellent man to that Shore which he had by his Judgment, & Courageous perseverance regained from a powerful Enemy almost against Hope. We found the Stairs Covered with Carpeting, and the rails from the Water to the top of the warf hung with crimson hangings. The president being preceeded by the committee, was received by the Governor and the principal Citizens in the most brilliant and affectionate manner, he was met on the warf by many of his old and faithful companions and fellow patriots who had with him borne the heat & burthen of the day, and who like him had experienced every reverse of fortune with fortitude and patience & who now Joined the universal chorus of welcome to the Great deliverer (under providence) from all their fears[.] It was with difficulty a passage could be made by the troops through the pressing crowd, who seemed incapable of being satisfied in gazing at this man of the people. . . . The streets were lined with inhabitants as close as they could stand together, and it required all the exertions of a numerous train of City officers with their staves to make a passage for the procession. The houses were filled with Gents & Ladies elegantly dressed, and the whole distance being about half a mile & the windows to the highest stories were illuminated by the Sparkling eyes of innumerable companies of Ladies who seemed to vie with each other to show the Joy of this great occasion[.] It was full half an hour before we could finish our commission, by introducing our Charge into the house prepared by order of Congress for his reception as soon as this was done, not withstanding the presidents great fatigue both of body & mind, he had to receive the Gentlemen of Congress, & the City, the Officers of the Army and Militia, forming a very numerous body, all of whom were eagerly desirous to show their respect in the most affectionate manner[.] This duty he performed with great ease and that friendly and obliging demeanor he was so famous for—When this was finished and the people dispersed we went . . . and dined with his excellency Gov. Clinton who had provided an elegant dinner for the purpose. . . . When the president was on the wharf an officer came up politely addressing him, said he had the honor and peculiar felicity of commanding his Guard, and was ready to obey his orders[.] The president much affected answered, that as to any present arrangement he desired that it might be carried into execution agreable to orders but afterwards he hoped the officer would give himself no further trouble, as the affections of his fellow Citizens (turning to the thousands around him) were all the Guard he wanted.

Selection adapted from Elias Boudinot, *Journal or Historical Recollections of American Events During the Revolutionary War.* Published by The New York Times & Arno Press, New York, copyright © 1968.

CRITICAL THINKING

1. What reason did the people of New York have for being especially grateful to George Washington?
2. What impression of Washington's character do you get from this letter? Cite passages from the letter that give you this impression.

3. THOMAS JEFFERSON APPRAISES THE CHARACTER OF GEORGE WASHINGTON

Several years after the death of President Washington, Thomas Jefferson appraised the character of our first president in a letter to Doctor Walter Jones who was writing about Washington. Excerpts from Jefferson's letter are reproduced below.

I think I knew General Washington intimately and thoroughly; and were I called on to delineate his character, it should be in terms like these. His mind was great and powerful, without being of the very first order; his penetration strong, though not so acute as that of a Newton, Bacon, or Locke; and as far as he saw, no judgment was ever sounder. It was slow in operation, being little aided by invention or imagination, but sure in conclusion. Hence the common remark of his officers, of the advantage he derived from councils of war, where hearing all suggestions, he selected whatever was best; and certainly no General ever planned his battles more judiciously. But if deranged during the course of the action, if any member of his plan was dislocated by sudden circumstances, he was slow in re-adjustment. The consequence was, that he often failed in the field, and rarely against an enemy in station, as at Boston and York. He was incapable of fear, meeting personal dangers with the calmest unconcern. Perhaps the strongest feature in his character was prudence, never acting until every circumstance, every consideration, was maturely weighed; refraining if he saw a doubt, but, when once decided, going through with his purpose, whatever obstacles opposed. His integrity was most pure, his justice the most inflexible I have ever known, no motives of interest or consanguinity, of friendship or hatred, being able to bias his decision. He was, indeed, in every sense of the words, a wise, a good, and a great man. His temper was naturally high toned; but reflection and resolution had obtained a firm and habitual ascendency over it. If ever, however, it broke its bonds, he was most tremendous in his wrath. In his expenses he was honorable, but exact; liberal in contributions to whatever promised utility; but frowning and unyielding on all visionary projects and all unworthy calls on his charity. His heart was not warm in its affections; but he exactly calculated every man's value, and gave him a solid esteem proportioned to it. His person, you know, was fine, his stature exactly what one would wish, his deportment easy, erect and noble; the best horseman of his age, and the most graceful figure that could be seen on horseback. Although in the circle of his friends, where he might be unreserved with safety, he took a free share in conversation, his colloquial talents were not above mediocrity, possessing neither copiousness of ideas, nor fluency of words. In public, when called on for a sudden opinion, he was unready, short and embarrassed. Yet he wrote readily, rather diffusely, in an easy and correct style. This he had acquired by conversation with the world, for his education was merely reading, writing and common arithmetic, to which he added surveying at a later day. His time was employed in action chiefly, reading little, and that only in agriculture and English history. His correspondence became necessarily extensive, and, with journalizing his agricultural proceedings, occupied most of his leisure hours within doors. On the whole, his character was, in its mass, perfect, in nothing bad, in few points indifferent; and it may truly be said, that never did nature and fortune combine more perfectly to make a man great, and to place him in the same constellation with whatever worthies have merited from man an everlasting remembrance. For his was the singular destiny and merit, of leading the armies of his country successfully through an arduous war, for the establishment of its independence; of conducting its councils through the birth of a government, new in its forms and principles, until it had settled down into a quiet and orderly train; and of scrupulously obeying the laws through the whole of his career, civil and military, of which the history of the world furnishes no other example.

. . . I am satisfied the great body of republicans think of him as I do. We were, indeed, dissatisfied with him on his ratification of the British treaty. But this was short lived. We knew his honesty, the wiles with which he was encompassed, and that age had already begun to relax the firmness of his purposes; and I am convinced he is more deeply seated in the love and gratitude of the republicans, than in the Pharisaical homage of the federal monarchists. For he was no monarchist from preference of his judgment. The soundness of that gave him correct views of the rights of man, and his severe justice devoted him to them. He has often declared to me that he considered our new constitution as an experiment on the practicability of republican government, and with what dose of liberty man could be trusted for his own good; that he was determined the experiment should have a fair trial, and would lose the last drop of his blood in support of it. And these declarations he repeated to me the oftener and more pointedly, because he knew my suspicions of Colonel Hamilton's views, and probably had heard from him the same declarations which I had, to wit, "that the British constitution, with its unequal representation, corruption and other existing abuses, was the most perfect government which had ever been established on earth, and that a reformation of those abuses would make it an impracticable government." I do believe that General Washington had not a firm confidence in the durability of our government. He was naturally distrustful of men,

and inclined to gloomy apprehensions; and I was ever persuaded that a belief that we must at length end in something like a British constitution, had some weight in his adoption of the ceremonies of levees, birth-days, pompous meetings with Congress, and other forms of the same character, calculated to prepare us gradually for a change which he believed possible, and to let it come on with as little shock as might be to the public mind.

These are my opinions of General Washington, which I would vouch at the judgment seat of God, having been formed on an acquaintance of thirty years. I served with him in the Virginia legislature from 1769 to the Revolutionary war, and again, a short time in Congress, until he left us to take command of the army. During the war and after it we corresponded occasionally, and in the four years of my continuance in the office of Secretary of State, our intercourse was daily, confidential and cordial. After I retired from that office, great and malignant pains were taken by our federal monarchists, and not entirely without effect, to make him view me as a theorist, holding French principles of government, which would lead infallibly to licentiousness and anarchy. And to this he listened the more easily, from my known disapprobation of the British treaty. I never saw him afterwards, or these malignant insinuations should have been dissipated before his just judgment, as mists before the sun. I felt on his death, with my countrymen that "verily a great man hath fallen this day in Israel."

Selection from Thomas Jefferson, *The Works of Thomas Jefferson*, Vol. XI, edited by Paul Leicester Ford. Published by G. P. Putnam's Sons (The Knickerbocker Press), New York, copyright © 1905.

CRITICAL THINKING

1. What impression of Washington do you get from Jefferson's letter? In what way is this impression different from the impression you got from Boudinot's letter? Suggest a reason for the difference.
2. Why do you think Jefferson's letter may have been an accurate account of Washington's character?

GEORGE WASHINGTON
Tributes To The First President

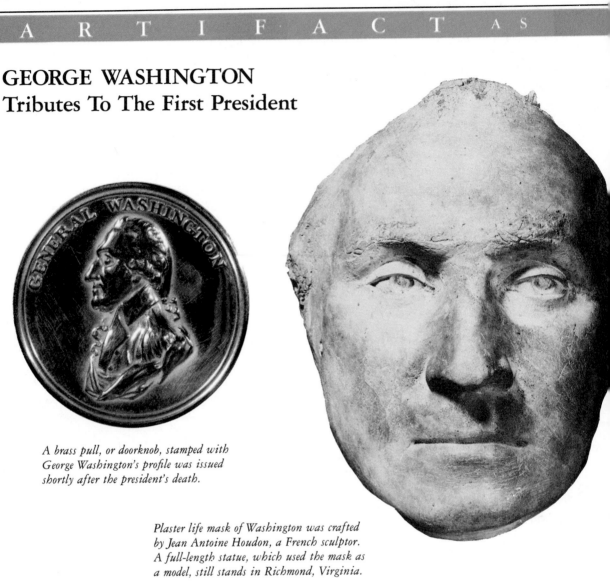

A brass pull, or doorknob, stamped with George Washington's profile was issued shortly after the president's death.

Plaster life mask of Washington was crafted by Jean Antoine Houdon, a French sculptor. A full-length statue, which used the mask as a model, still stands in Richmond, Virginia.

Americans began paying tribute to George Washington long before his death in 1799. As early as 1775, babies were christened after him. The expense accounts he kept during the Revolutionary War, while commanding the colonies' armed forces, were printed in facsimile as evidence of his frugality and efficiency. After Washington became the nation's first president, Americans honored the anniversaries of his battle victories, birthday, and inauguration with elaborate celebrations and public rituals.

Immediately following Washington's death, the grieving American public transformed Washington into an exalted figure who possessed infinite wisdom, power, and mercy. Americans' adoration of Washington achieved an almost religious fervor, and objects associated with him were commonly regarded as sacred relics.

By the middle of the nineteenth century, Washington's image was associated with character and supreme virtue. Wood cuts, engravings,

D O C U M E N T

Castiron hatchet was a souvenir commemorating the centennial of Washington's inauguration. It refers to the story of young George admitting he chopped down a cherry tree.

A cotton handkerchief, probably made in England around 1777, shows Washington surrounded by a border of cannons and crossed flags.

A tobacco company used Washington's likeness to sell tins of cut plug tobacco.

and lithographs of Washington were produced on a mass scale, and most American families displayed a likeness of him in their homes.

In the tumultuous years before the Civil War, when Americans increasingly valued the security of home and family, Washington was portrayed as a strong, stable, and comforting figure—a man who had served as father to his nation.

Since then, Washington has served as a model for nearly every American virtue.

CRITICAL THINKING

1. Compare the way current heros are treated today and the way George Washington was remembered shortly after his death.
2. Select what you think is the most significant artifact shown here and the least significant. Explain why you chose each.

4. A BROADSIDE FROM THE PRESIDENTIAL ELECTION OF 1796

President Washington declined to run for a third time in 1796. Although he had warned against the "baneful effects of the spirit of party" in his "Farewell Address," the presidential campaign of 1796 became a bitter struggle for national power between the Federalist and Democratic Republican parties. Reproduced below is a political broadside issued by the Democratic-Republican party in Pennsylvania on October 3, 1796, one month before the presidential election.

FELLOW CITIZENS!

The first concern of Freemen, calls you forth into action.—Pennsylvania was never yet found wanting when Liberty was at stake; she cannot then be indifferent when the question is, *Who shall be President of the United States?* The citizen who now holds the office of President, has publicly made known to his fellow citizens that he declines to serve in it again. Two candidates are offered to your choice, as his successor; THOMAS JEFFERSON of Virginia, and JOHN ADAMS of New England.—No other candidate is proposed, you cannot therefore mistake between them. THOMAS JEFFERSON is the man who was your late Secretary of State, and Minister of the United States to the French nation; JOHN ADAMS is the man who is now Vice President of the United States, and was late the Minister to the king of Great Britain.—THOMAS JEFFERSON is a firm REPUBLICAN,—JOHN ADAMS is an avowed MONARCHIST. . . .

Thomas Jefferson first drew the declaration of American independence;—he first framed the sacred political sentence that all men are *born* equal. *John Adams* says this is all a farce and a falsehood; that some men should be born Kings, and some should be born Nobles. Which of these, freemen of Pennsylvania, will you have for your President? Will you, by your votes, contribute to make the avowed friend of monarchy, President? or will you, by neglectfully staying at home, permit others to saddle you with Political Slavery? *Adams* has Sons who might aim to succeed their father; *Jefferson* like Washington, has no Son. *Adams* is a fond admirer of the British Constitution, and says

it is the first wonder of the world. *Jefferson* likes better our Federal Constitution, and thinks the British full of deformity, corruption and wickedness. Once more, fellow citizens! Choose ye between those two, which you will have for President, *Jefferson* or *Adams*. Remember Friday the fourth of November; attend your elections on that day; put in your tickets for fifteen good REPUBLICANS, and let the watch word be LIBERTY and INDEPENDENCE!

Selection from Martin W. Sandler, Edwin C. Rozwenc, and Edward C. Martin, *The People Make a Nation.* Published by Allyn and Bacon, Inc., Boston, copyright © 1971.

CRITICAL THINKING

1. What good points does the broadside claim for the Democratic-Republican candidate? What negative charges does the broadside make against the Federalist candidate?
2. Sometimes "broadsides" involve the use of a volley of abusive and denunciatory words. How does the above broadside fit this description?

5. FEDERALISTS SUCCEED IN PASSING FOUR *ALIEN AND SEDITION ACTS*

The election of 1796 resulted in a victory for Federalist presidential candidate John Adams. However, the battle between the Federalist and Democratic-Republican parties did not end with the election. A group of ardent Federalists brought about the passage of the anti-Republican Alien and Sedition Acts. *Excerpts from those four acts are given below.*

THE NATURALIZATION ACT
June 18, 1798

SECTION 1. *Be it enacted . . .*, that no alien shall be admitted to become a citizen of the United States, or of any state, unless . . . he shall have declared his intention to become a citizen of the United States, five years, at least, before his admission, and shall, at the time of his application to be admitted, declare and prove, to the satisfaction of the court having jurisdiction in the case, that he has resided within the United States fourteen years, at least, and within the state or territory where, or for which such court is at the time held, five years, at least, besides conforming to the other declarations, renunciations and proofs, by the said act required, any thing therein to the contrary hereof notwithstanding: *Provided*, that any alien, who was residing within the limits, and under the jurisdiction of the United States, before . . . [January 29, 1795] . . . may, within one year after the passing of this act—and any alien who shall have made the declaration of his intention to become a citizen of the United States, in conformity to the provisions of the act [of Jan. 29, 1795], may, within four years after having made the declaration aforesaid, be admitted to become a citizen, in the manner prescribed by the said act, . . . *And provided also*, that no alien, who shall be a native, citizen, denizen or subject of any nation or state with whom the United States shall be at war, at the time of his application, shall be then admitted to become a citizen of the United States.

THE ALIEN ACT
June 25, 1798

SEC. 1 *Be it enacted* . . . , That it shall be lawful for the President of the United States at any time during the continuance of this act, to *order* all such *aliens* as he shall judge dangerous to the peace and safety of the United States, or shall have reasonable grounds to suspect are concerned in any treasonable or secret machinations against the government thereof, to depart out of the territory of the United States, within such time as shall be expressed in such order, which order shall be served on such alien by delivering him a copy thereof, or leaving the same at his usual abode, and returned to the office of the Secretary of State, by the marshal or other person to whom the same shall be directed. And in case any alien, so ordered to depart, shall be found at large within the United States after the time limited in such order for his departure, and not having obtained a *license* from the President to reside therein, or having obtained such *license* shall not have conformed thereto, every such alien shall, on conviction thereof, be imprisoned for a term not exceed-

ing three years, and shall never after be admitted to become a citizen of the United States.

THE ALIEN ENEMIES ACT
July 6, 1798

SECTION 1. *Be it enacted* . . . , That whenever there shall be a declared war between the United States and any foreign nation or government, or any invasion or predatory incursion shall be perpetrated, attempted, or threatened against the territory of the United States, by any foreign nation or government, . . . all natives, citizens, denizens, or subjects of the hostile nation or government, being males of the age of fourteen years and upwards, who shall be within the United States, and not actually naturalized, shall be liable to be apprehended, restrained, secured and removed, as alien enemies.

THE SEDITION ACT
July 14, 1798

SEC. 1. *Be it enacted* . . . , That if any persons shall unlawfully combine or conspire together, with intent to oppose any measure or measures of the government of the United States, which are or shall be directed by proper authority, or to impede the operation of any law of the United States, or to intimidate or prevent any person holding a place of office in or under the government of the United States, from undertaking, performing or executing his trust or duty; and if any person or persons, with intent as aforesaid, shall counsel, advise or attempt to procure any insurrection, riot, unlawful assembly, or combination, whether such conspiracy, threatening, counsel, advice, or attempt shall have the proposed effect or not, he or they shall be deemed guilty of a high misdemeanor, and on conviction, before any court of the United States having jurisdiction thereof, shall be punished by a fine not exceeding five thousand dollars, and by imprisonment during a term not less than six months nor exceeding five years.

SEC. 2. That if any person shall write, print, utter, or publish, or shall cause or procure to be written, printed, uttered or published, or shall knowingly and willingly assist or aid in writing, printing, uttering or publishing any false, scandalous and malicious writings against the government of the United States, or either house of the Congress of the United States, or the President of

After John Adams' election to the Presidency, Federalists were able to push through passage of the Alien and Sedition Acts.

Selection excerpted from *Documents of American History*, Vol. I, edited by Henry Steele Commager. Published by Meredith Publishing Company (Appleton-Century-Crofts), New York, copyright © 1963.

CRITICAL THINKING

1. Many immigrants who came to the United States voted for Democratic-Republican candidates in elections. Which of the above acts could have deprived the Democratic-Republicans of this advantage? Explain why you think so.
2. What disadvantage would Section 2 of the Sedition Act have caused for the Democratic-Republicans while the Federalists were in office?

the United States, with intent to defame the said government, or either house of the said Congress, or the said President, or to bring them, or either of them, into contempt or disrepute; or to excite against them, or either or any of them, the hatred of the good people of the United States, or to stir up sedition within the United States, or to excite any unlawful combinations therein, for opposing or resisting any law of the United States, or any act of the President of the United States, done in pursuance of any such law, or of the powers in him vested by the constitution of the United States, or to resist, oppose, or defeat any such law or act, or to aid, encourage or abet any hostile design of any foreign nation against the United States; their people or government, then such person being thereof convicted before any court of the United States having jurisdiction thereof, shall be punished by a fine not exceeding two thousand dollars, and by imprisonment not exceeding two years.

6. STATE LEGISLATURES RESPOND TO THE ALIEN AND SEDITION ACTS

The Democratic-Republicans, recognizing the real intent of the Alien and Sedition Acts of 1798, did not take long to respond to them. By the end of that year, both the Kentucky and Virginia legislatures passed resolutions expressing strong views on the controversial acts. Two Democratic-Republicans wrote the drafts for these resolutions—Thomas Jefferson for Kentucky's and James Madison for Virginia's. Excerpts from each resolution follow.

KENTUCKY RESOLUTIONS
November 16, 1798

I *Resolved*, that the several States composing the United States of America, are not united on the principle of unlimited submission to their general government; but that by compact under the style and title of a Constitution for the United States and of amendments thereto, they constituted a general government for special purposes, delegated to that government certain definite powers, reserving each State to itself, the residuary mass of right to their own self government; and that whensoever the general government assumes undelegated powers, its acts are unauthoritative, void, and of no force . . . That the government created by this compact was not made the exclusive or final judge of the extent of the powers delegated to itself; since that would have made its discretion, and not the Constitution, the measure of its powers; but that as in all other cases of compact among parties having no common Judge, *each party has an equal right to judge for itself, as well of infractions as of the mode and measure of redress*. . . .

III. *Resolved*, that it is true as a general principle, and is also expressly declared by one of the amendments to the Constitution that "the powers not delegated to the United States by the Constitution, nor prohibited by it to the States, are reserved to the States respectively or to the people;" and that no power over the freedom of religion, freedom of speech, or freedom of the press being delegated to the United States by the Constitution, nor prohibited by it to the States, all lawful powers respecting the same did of right remain, and were reserved to the States, or to the people: That thus was manifested their determination to retain to themselves the right of judging how far the licentiousness of speech and of the press may be abridged without lessening their useful freedom. . . .

VIII. *Resolved*, that the preceding Resolution be transmitted to the Senators and Representatives in Congress from this Commonwealth, who are hereby enjoined to present the same to their respective Houses, and to use their best endeavors to procure, at the next session of Congress, a repeal of the aforesaid unconstitutional and obnoxious [Alien and Sedition] acts.

VIRGINIA RESOLUTIONS
December 24, 1798

Resolved, That the General Assembly of Virginia doth unequivocally express a firm resolution to maintain and defend the Constitution of the United States, and the Constitution of this state, against every aggression either foreign or domestic; and that they will support the Government of the United States in all measures warranted by the former. . . .

That this Assembly doth explicitly and peremptorily declare that it views the powers of the Federal Government as resulting from the com-

pact to which the states are parties, as limited by the plain sense and intention of the instrument constituting that compact; as no further valid than they are authorized by the grants enumerated in that compact; and that, in case of a deliberate, palpable, and dangerous exercise of other powers not granted by the said compact, the states, who are parties thereto, have the right and are in duty bound to interpose for arresting the progress of the evil, and for maintaining within their respective limits the authorities, rights, and liberties appertaining to them. . . .

That the General Assembly doth particularly PROTEST against the palpable and alarming infractions of the Constitution in the two late cases of the "Alien and Sedition Acts," passed at the last session of Congress; the first of which exercises a power nowhere delegated to the Federal Government, and which, by uniting legislative and judicial powers to those of {the} executive, subverts the general principles of free government, as well as the particular organization and positive provisions of the Federal Constitution: and the other of which acts exercises, in like manner, a power not delegated by the Constitution, but, on the contrary, expressly and positively forbidden by one of the amendments thereto,—a power which, more than any other, ought to produce universal alarm, because it is levelled against the right of freely examining public characters and measures, and of free communication among the people thereon, which has ever been justly deemed the only effectual guardian of every other right.

Selection excerpted from *Documents of American History*, Vol. I, edited by Henry Steele Commager. Published by Meredith Publishing Company (Appleton-Century-Crofts), New York, copyright © 1963.

CRITICAL THINKING

1. According to both resolutions, why did the states have the right to declare the Alien and Sedition Acts "unauthoritative, void, and of no force"?
2. Chief Justice Marshall made his famous ruling in *Marbury v. Madison* in 1803, five years after the two resolutions were passed in 1798. If he had made this ruling before 1798, how might history have been altered?

7. ABIGAIL ADAMS REFLECTS UPON HER EXPERIENCES AS THE FIRST, FIRST LADY TO LIVE IN THE WHITE HOUSE

John Adams was still president when Washington, D. C., officially became the capital of the United States. In this letter to her daughter, Abigail Adams —the president's wife—describes her trip to Washington and some of her experiences in setting up a home in the unfinished White House.

Abigail Adams' grandson, Charles Adams, had some of his grandmother's letters published after her death.

Washington, 21 November, 1800

I arrived here on Sunday last, and without meeting with any accident worth noticing, except losing ourselves when we left Baltimore, and going eight or nine miles on the Frederick road, by which means we were obliged to go the other eight through woods, where we wandered two hours without finding a guide, or the path. Fortunately, a straggling black came up with us, and we engaged him as a guide to extricate us out of our difficulty; but woods are all you see, from Baltimore until you reach *the city*, which is only so in name. Here and there is a small cot[tage], without a glass window, interspersed amongst the forest, through which you travel miles without seeing any human beings. In the city there are buildings enough, if they were compact and finished, to accommodate Congress and those attached to it; but as they are, and scattered as they are, I see no great comfort for them. The river, which runs up to Alexandria, is in full view of my window, and I see the vessels as they pass and repass. The house is upon a grand and superb scale, requiring about thirty servants to attend and keep the apartments in proper order, and perform the ordinary business of the house and stables; an establishment very well proportioned to the President's salary. The lighting the apartments, from the kitchen to parlours and chambers, is a tax indeed; and the fires we are obliged to keep to secure us from daily agues is another very cheering comfort. To assist us in this great castle, and render less attendance necessary, bells are wholly wanting, not one single one being hung through the whole house, and promises are all you can obtain. This is so great an inconvenience, that I know not what to do. . . . The ladies from Georgetown and in the city have many of them visited me. Yesterday I returned fifteen visits,— but such a place as Georgetown appears,—why, our Milton is beautiful. But no comparisons;—if they will put me up some bells, and let me have wood enough to keep fires, I design to be pleased. I could content myself almost anywhere three months; but, surrounded with forests, can you believe that wood is not to be had, because people cannot be found to cut and cart it! Briesler entered into a contract with a man to supply him with wood. A small part, a few cords only, has he been able to get. Most of that was expended to dry the walls of the house before we came in, and yesterday the man told him it was impossible for him to procure it to be cut and carted. He has had recourse to coals; but we cannot get grates made and set. We have, indeed, come into *a new country*.

You must keep all this to yourself, and, when asked how I like it, say that I write you the situation is beautiful, which is true. The house is made habitable, but there is not a single apartment finished, and all withinside, except the plastering, has been done since Briesler came. We have not the least fence, yard, or other convenience, without, and the great unfinished audience-room I make a drying-room of, to hang up the clothes in. The principal stairs are not up, and will not be this winter. Six chambers are made comfortable; two are occupied by the President and Mr. Shaw; two lower rooms, one for a common parlour, and one for a levee-room. Up stairs there is the oval room, which is designed for the drawingroom, and has the crimson furniture it it. It is a very handsome room now; but, when completed, it will be beautiful. If the twelve years, in which this place has been considered as the future seat of government, had been improved, as they would have been if in New England, very many of the present inconveniences would have been removed. It is a beautiful spot, capable of every improvement, and, the more I view it, the more I am delighted with it.

Selection from *American History told by Contemporaries*, Vol. III, edited by Albert Bushnell Hart. Published by The Macmillan Company, New York, copyright © 1928.

CRITICAL THINKING

1. In your own words, give the impression of Washington you formed from reading Mrs. Adams' letter.
2. Considering the date the letter was written, what does Mrs. Adams mean by "I could content myself almost anywhere three months. . . ."?

8. MANASSEH CUTLER INFORMS HIS DAUGHTER ABOUT HIS LIFE AS A CONGRESSMAN IN THE NEW CAPITAL

Manasseh Cutler, a member of Congress from Massachusetts, was among the first residents of Washington, D. C. Here, in a letter to his daughter, he describes the new city.

WASHINGTON, Dec. 21, 1801.

My Dear Betsy. . . . It shall be the subject of this letter to give you some account of my present situation and of occurrences since I left home.

The city of Washington, in point of situation, is much more delightful than I expected to find it. The ground, in general, is elevated, mostly cleared, and commands a pleasing prospect of the Potomac River. The buildings are brick, and erected in what are called large blocks, that is, from two to five or six houses joined together, and appear like one long building. There is one block of seven, another of nine, and one of twenty houses, but they are scattered over a large extent of ground. The block in which I live contains six houses, four stories high, and very handsomely furnished. It is situated east of the Capitol, on the highest ground in the city. Mr. King, our landlord, occupies the south end, only one room in front, which is our parlor for receiving company and dining, and one room back, occupied by Mr. King's family, the kitchen is below. The four chambers are appropriated to the eight gentlemen who board in the family. In each chamber are two narrow field beds and field curtains, with every necessary convenience for the boarders. Mr. Read and myself have, I think, the pleasantest room in the house, or in the whole city. It is in the third story, commanding a delightful prospect of the Capitol, of the President's house, Georgetown, all the houses in the city, a long extent of the river, and the city of Alexandria.

The air is fine, and the weather, since I have been here, remarkably pleasant. I am not much pleased with the Capitol. It is a huge pile, built, indeed, with handsome stone, very heavy in its appearance without, and not very pleasant within. The President's house is superb, well proportioned and pleasingly situated.

Selection from *American History told by Contemporaries*, Vol. III, edited by Albert Bushnell Hart. Published by the Macmillan Company, New York, copyright © 1928.

CRITICAL THINKING

1. What does Manasseh Cutler's letter reveal about the housing situation in the new city of Washington?
2. Were President and Mrs. Adams living in the "President's house" at the time Cutler wrote this letter? Explain your answer.

The Bold Republic

CHAPTER 9

THE JEFFERSONIAN REPUBLIC

1801–1824

1. PRESIDENT THOMAS JEFFERSON EXPRESSES CONCERN ABOUT FRANCE'S CONTROL OF LOUISIANA

When President Thomas Jefferson learned that France had regained control of Louisiana in 1802, he became deeply concerned. In the following letter to Robert R. Livingstone, the United States minister to France, the president explains the reasons for his concern.

WASHINGTON, Apr. 18, 1802.

The cession of Louisiana and the Floridas by Spain to France works most sorely on the U.S. On this subject the Secretary of State has written to you fully. Yet I cannot forbear recurring to it personally, so deep is the impression it makes in my mind. It compleatly reverses all the political relations of the U. S. and will form a new epoch in our political course. Of all nations of any consideration France is the one which hitherto has offered the fewest points on which we could have any conflict of right, and the most points of a communion of interests. From these causes we have ever looked to her as our *natural friend*, as one with which we never could have an occasion of difference. Her growth therefore we viewed as our own, her misfortunes ours. There is on the globe one single spot, the possessor of which is our natural and habitual enemy. It is New Orleans, through which the produce of three-eighths of our territory must pass to market, and from its fertility it will ere long yield more than half of our whole produce and contain more than half our inhabitants. France placing herself in that door assumes to us the attitude of defiance. Spain might have retained it quietly for years. Her pacific dispositions, her feeble state, would induce her to increase our facilities there, so that her possession of that place would be hardly felt by us, and it would not perhaps be very long before some circumstance might arise which might make the cession of it to us the price of something of more worth to her. Not so can it ever be in the hands of France. The impetuosity of her temper, the energy and restlessness of her character, placed in a point of eternal friction with us, and our character, which though quiet, and loving peace and the pursuit of wealth, is high-minded, despising wealth in competition with insult or injury, enterprising and energetic as any nation on earth, these circumstances render it impossible that France and the U. S. can continue long friends when they meet in so irritable a position. They as well as we must be blind if they do not see this; and we must be very improvident if we do not begin to make arrangements on that hypothesis. The day that France takes possession of N. Orleans fixes the sentence which is to restrain her forever within her low water mark. It seals the union of two nations who in conjunction can maintain exclusive possession of the ocean. From that moment we must marry ourselves to the British fleet and nation. We must turn all our attentions to a maritime force, for which our resources place us on very high grounds: and having formed and cemented together a power which may render reinforcement of her settlements here impossible to France, make the first cannon, which shall be fired in Europe the signal for tearing up any settlement she may have made, and for holding the two continents of America in sequestration for the common purposes of the united British and American nations. This is not a state of things we seek or desire. . . .

If France considers Louisiana . . . as indispensable for her views she might perhaps be willing to look about for arrangements which might reconcile it to our interests. If anything could do this it would be the ceding to us the island of New Orleans and the Floridas. This would certainly in a great degree remove the causes of jarring and irritation between us, and perhaps for such a length of time as might produce other means of making the measure permanently conciliatory to our interests and friendships. . . . Every eye in the U.S. is now fixed on this affair of Louisiana. Perhaps nothing since the revolutionary war has produced more uneasy sensations through the body of the nation. Notwithstanding temporary bickerings have taken place with France, she has still a strong hold on the affections of our citizens generally. I have thought it not amiss, by way of supplement to the letters of the Secretary of State to write you this private one to impress you with the importance we affix to this transaction.

Selection from Thomas Jefferson, *The Works of Thomas Jefferson*, Vol. IX, edited by Paul Leicester Ford. Published by G. P. Putnam's Sons (The Knickerbocker Press), New York, copyright © 1905.

CRITICAL THINKING

1. Why did Jefferson describe the "possessor" of New Orleans as the "natural and habitual enemy" of the United States?
2. What did Jefferson mean when he wrote that Spain's cession of Louisiana to France "compleatly reverses all the political relations of the U. S."?

2. NAPOLEON CONSIDERS SELLING LOUISIANA TO THE UNITED STATES

President Jefferson's concern about Louisiana might have been lessened had he known about an incident that took place in France the year after the president had expressed his concerns to Robert Livingstone about France regaining control of Louisiana. The incident is recounted in the following excerpt from the memoirs of Lucien Bonaparte, brother of Napoleon. The Joseph referred to in the memoirs was another brother of Napoleon.

"Here you are at last!" exclaimed my brother, "I was afraid you were not coming. It is a fine time to go to the theater; I come to tell you a piece of news which will not make you feel like amusing yourself." . . .

Continuing in the same tone, Joseph, replying to my question: "Do make haste and tell me what is up?" said to me:

"No, you will not believe it, and yet it is true. I give you a thousand guesses; the general (we still called Napoleon in that way), the general wishes to alienate Louisiana."

"Bah! who will buy it from him?"

"The Americans."

I was thunderstruck for a moment.

"The idea! if he could wish it, the Chambers [the French legislature] would not consent to it."

"And therefore he expects to do without their consent. That is what he replied to me when I said to him, as you do now, that the Chambers would not consent to it."

"What, he really said that to you? That is a little too much! But no, it is impossible. It is a bit of brag at your expense. . . ."

"No, no," insisted Joseph, "he spoke very seriously, and, what is more, he added to me that this sale would furnish him the first funds for war." . . .

It had become late. The plan of going to the theater was given up . . . and we separated not without having agreed that I first should go the next morning to pay a visit to the first Consul [Napoleon] . . .

The next morning . . . I betook myself to the Tuileries where I was immediately shown up to my brother [Napoleon]. . . .

. . . we had not discussed Louisiana any more than we had the year forty. I was vexed at it, but the nearer the last moment of speaking of it approached, the more I put off doing so. . . . I was about to leave the place, when Rustan scratched at the door like a cat . . .

The person for whom Rustan had broken his nails at the door . . . , was Joseph.

. . . the Consul said to Joseph:

"Well, brother, so you have not spoken to Lucien?"

"About what?" said Joseph.

"About our plan in regard to Louisiana, you know?"

"About yours, my dear brother, you mean? You cannot have forgotten that far from being mine"—

"Come, come, preacher—But I have no need of discussing that with you: you are so obstinate—With Lucien I speak more willingly of serious matters; for though he sometimes takes it into his head to oppose me, he knows how to give in to my opinion, Lucien does, when I see fit to try to make him change his." . . .

Joseph was showing annoyance at our conversation, the tone of which was more friendly than anything else, when finally he said to the Consul, rather brusquely:

In need of money to finance his war against Britain, Napoleon sold the Louisiana Territory to the United States in 1803.

"Well, you still say nothing of your great plan?"

". . . Know merely, Lucien, that I have decided to sell Louisiana to the Americans."

I thought I ought to show very moderate astonishment at this piece of news supposed to be unknown to me. Knowing very well that an opportunity would be given me to show more, I mean at his intention to dispose of it by his own will, without speaking of it to the Chambers, I contented myself with saying: "Ah! ah!" in that tone of curiosity which shows the desire to know the rest of what has been begun rather than it signifies approbation or even the contrary.

This apparent indifference made the first Consul say: "Well, Joseph, you see! Lucien does not make an outcry about that as you do. Yet he would almost have a right to do so, for his part; for after all Louisiana is his conquest. . . ."

"And then, Gentlemen, think what you please about it, but give this affair up as lost both of you; you, Lucien, on account of the sale in itself, you, Joseph, because I shall get along without the consent of anyone whomsoever, do you understand?"

. . . Joseph said to him . . .:

"And you will do well, my dear brother, not to expose your plan to parliamentary discussion, for I declare to you that I am the first one to place himself, if it is necessary, at the head of the opposition which cannot fail to be made to you." . . .

At these words, the Consul . . . said to him in a tone which I will call energetically serious and solemn:

"You will have no need to stand forth as orator of the opposition, for I repeat to you that this discussion will not take place, for the reason that the plan which is not fortunate enough to obtain your approbation, conceived by me, negotiated by me, will be ratified and executed by me all alone, do you understand? by me who snap my fingers at your opposition."

Selection from *American History told by Contemporaries*, Vol. III, edited by Albert Bushnell Hart. Published by The Macmillan Company, New York, copyright © 1928.

CRITICAL THINKING

1. Explain why President Jefferson might have felt relieved if he had known of the incident related above.
2. What impression of Napoleon's character did you get from the reading? Refer to particular passages that contributed to the formation of your impression.
3. Evaluate Lucien Napoleon's memoirs as a primary source of historical information. Support your evaluation with sound reasons.

3. THE SENATE DEBATES THE PURCHASE OF LOUISIANA FROM FRANCE

Napoleon did what he told his brothers he would do, and in May of 1803, representatives of France and the United State signed a treaty turning Louisiana over to the United States. However, according to the Constitution, all treaties must be approved by the Senate before they become binding. Reproduced below is an excerpt from the Senate debate on the Louisiana treaty.

MR. WHITE. . . I speak now . . . from mere probabilities. I wish not to be understood as predicting that the French will not cede to us the actual and quiet possession of the territory. I hope to God they may, for possession of it we must have—I mean of New Orleans, and of such other positions on the Mississippi as may be necessary to secure to us forever the complete and uninterrupted navigation of that river. This I have ever been in favor of; I think it essential to the peace of the United States, and to the prosperity of our Western country. But as to Louisiana, this new, immense, unbounded world, if it should ever be incorporated into this Union, which I have no idea can be done but by altering the Constitution, I believe it will be the greatest curse that could at present befall us; it may be productive of innumerable evils, and especially of one that I fear even to look upon. Gentlemen on all sides, with very few exceptions, agree that the settlement of this country will be highly injurious and dangerous to the United States; but as to what has been suggested of removing the Creeks and other nations of Indians from the eastern to the western banks of the Mississippi, and of making the fertile regions of Louisiana a howling wilderness, never to be trodden by the foot of civilized man, it is impracticable. The [Senator] from Tennessee . . . has shown his usual candor on this subject, and I believe with him, to use his strong language, that you had as well pretend to inhibit the fish from swimming in the sea as to prevent the population of that country after its sovereignty shall become ours. To every man acquainted with the adventurous, roving, and enterprising temper of our people, and with the manner in which our Western country has been settled, such an idea must be [unreal]. The inducements will be so strong that it will be impossible to restrain our citizens from crossing the river. Louisiana must and will become settled, if we hold it, and with the very population that would otherwise occupy part of our present territory. Thus our citizens will be removed to the immense distance of two or three thousand miles from the capital of the Union, where they will scarcely ever feel the rays of the General Government; their affections will become alienated; they will gradually begin to view us as strangers; they will form other commercial connexions, and our interests will become distinct.

These, with other causes that human wisdom may not foresee, will in time effect a separation, and I fear our bounds will be fixed nearer to our houses than the waters of the Mississippi. We have already territory enough and when I contemplate the evils that may arise to these States, from this intended incorporation of Louisiana into the Union, I would rather see it given to France, to Spain, or to any other nation of the earth, upon the mere condition that no citizen of the United States should ever settle within its limits, than to see the territory sold for an hundred millions of dollars, and we retain the sovereignty. But however dangerous the possession of Louisiana might prove to us, I do not presume to say that the retention of it would not have been very convenient to France, and we know that at the time of the mission of Mr. Monroe, our Administration had never thought of the purchase of Louisiana, and that nothing short of the fullest conviction on the part of the First Consul that he was on the very eve of a war with England; that this being the most defenceless point of his possessions, if such they could be called, was the one at which the British would first strike, and that it must inevitably fall into their hands, could ever have induced his pride and ambition to make the sale. He judged wisely, that he had better sell it for as much as he could get than lose it entirely. And I do say that under existing circumstances, even supposing that this extent of territory was a desirable acquisition, fifteen millions of dollars was a most enormous sum to give. . . .

Mr. PICKERING said, if he entertained the opinion just now expressed by the [Senator] from Delaware, . . . of the binding force of all treaties made by the President and Senate, he should think it to be his duty to vote for the bill now under consideration. "The Constitution, and the laws of the United States made in pursuance thereof, and all treaties made, or which shall be made under the authority of the United States, shall be the supreme law of the land." —But a treaty to be thus obligatory, must not contravene the Constitution, nor contain any stipulations which transcend the powers therein given to the President and Senate. The treaty between the United States and the French Republic, professing to cede Louisiana to the United States, appeared to him to contain such an exceptionable stipulation . . . which cannot be executed by any authority now existing. It is declared in the third article [of the treaty], that "the inhabitants of the ceded territory shall be incorporated in the Union of the United States." But neither the President and Senate, nor the President and Congress, are competent to such an act of incorporation. He believed that our Admin-istration admitted that this incorporation could not be effected without an amendment of the Constitution; and he conceived that this necessary amendment could not be made in the ordinary mode by the concurrence of two-thirds of both Houses of Congress, and the ratification by the Legislatures of three-fourths of the several States. He believed the assent of each individual State to be necessary for the admission of a foreign coun-try as an associate in the Union: . . . and whether the assent of every State to such an indispensable amendment were attainable was uncertain. But the articles of a treaty were necessarily related to each other; the stipulation in one article being the consideration for another. If therefore, in respect to the Louisiana Treaty, the United States fail to execute, and within a reasonable time, the engage-ment in the third article, (to incorporate that Territory into the Union,) the French Govern-ment will have a right to declare the whole treaty void. We must then abandon the country, or go to war to maintain our possession. . . .

Mr. TRACY. . . . The paragraph in the Consti-tution, which says that "new States may be admit-ted by Congress into this Union," has been quoted to justify this treaty. To this, two answers may be given, either of which are conclusive in my favor. First, if Congress have the power collectively of admitting Louisiana, it cannot be vested in the President and Senate alone. Second, Congress have no power to admit new foreign States into the Union, without the consent of the old part-ners. The article of the Constitution, if any person will take the trouble to examine it, refers to domestic States only, and not at all to foreign States; and it is unreasonable to suppose that Congress should, by a majority only, admit new foreign States, and swallow up, by it, the old partners, when two-thirds of all the members are made requisite for the least alteration in the Constitution. The words of the Constitution are completely satisfied, by a construction which shall include only the admission of domestic States, who were all parties to the Revolutionery war, and to the compact; and the spirit of the association seems to embrace no other. But I repeat it, if the Congress collectively has this power, the President and Senate cannot, of course, have it exclusively.

I think, . . . that, from a fair construction of the Constitution, and an impartial view of the nature and principles of our association, the President and Senate have not the power of thus obtruding upon us Louisiana.

Selection from *Annals of Congress*, Vol. 3. Gales and Seaton, Washington, D.C., copyright © 1852.

CRITICAL THINKING

1. What advantages and disadvantages did Mr. White see in the acquisition of Loui-siana?
2. Summarize Mr. Pickering's objections to the treaty ceding Louisiana to the United States.

4. EXPLORER WILLIAM CLARK DESCRIBES THE EVENTS OF NOVEMBER 7, 1805

In the entry from William Clark's journal reproduced below, Clark mistakenly records what he thinks is the party's first view of the Pacific Ocean. Actually, the party did not reach the shores of the Pacific for several days. Notice that most of Clark's original spelling and punctuation have been kept.

November 7th Thursday 1805

A cloudy foggey morning Some rain. we Set out early proceeded under the Stard. [right] Side under a high rugid hills with Steep assent the Shore boalt and rockey, the fog so thick we could not See across the river, two cano[e]s of Indians met and returned with us to their village, they gave us to eate Some fish, and Sold us, fish, *Wap pa to* roots three *dogs* and 2 otter skins for which we gave fish hooks principally of which they were verry fond.

Those people call themselves *War-ci-â-cum* and Speake a language different from the nativs above with whome they trade for the *Wapato* roots of which they make great use of as food. their houses differently built, raised entirely above ground eaves about 5 feet from the ground Supported and covered in the same way of those above, dores about the Same size but in the Side of the house in one corner, one fire place and that near the opposit end, around which they have their beads raised about 4 feet from the flore which is of earth, under their beads they Store away baskets of dried fish Berries & *Wappato*, over the fire they hang the fiesh as they take them and [of] which they do not make immediate use. Their Canoes are of the Same form of those above.

after delaying at this village one hour and a half we Set out piloted by an Indian dressed in a Salors dress, to the Main Chanel of the river, the tide being in we should have found much dificuelty in passing into the main Chanel from behind those islands, without a pilot, here we see a great numbers of water fowls about those Marshey Islands; here the high mountanious Countery approaches the river on the Lard [left] Side, a high Mountn. to the S.W. about 20 miles, the high mountans. countrey continue on the Stard. Side, about 14 miles below the last village we landed at a village of the same nation. it contains 7 indifferent houses built in the same form of those above, here we purchased a Dog some fish, *wap pa to*, roots and I purchased 2 beaver Skins for the purpose of makeing me a *roab*, as the robe I have is rotten and good for nothing. opposit to this village the high mountaneous contrey leave[s] the river on the Lard. Side below which the river widens into a kind of Bay & is crouded with low Islands Subject to be covered by the tides. We proceeded on about 12 miles below the Village under a high mountaneous Countrey on the Stard. Side, Shore boald and rockey and Encamped under a high hill on the Stard. Side opposit to a rock Situated half a mile from the shore, about 50 feet high and 20 Deamieter; we with dificuelty found a place clear of the tide and Sufficiently large to lie on and the only place we could get was on round stones on which we lay our mats rain continud. moderately all day & Two Indians accompanied us from the last village,

they we detected in Stealing a knife and returned,

Great joy in camp we are in *view* of the *Ocian*, this great Pacific Octean which we been so long anxious to See. and the roreing or noise made by the waves brakeing on the rockey Shores (as I suppose) may be heard disti[n]ctly

Selection from *The Journals of Lewis and Clark*, edited by Bernard Devoto. Published by Houghton Mifflin Company (The Riverside Press), Cambridge, Boston, copyright © 1953.

CRITICAL THINKING

1. Lewis and Clark left St. Louis in May, 1804. How long did it take the explorers to get to the Pacific? How long would a similar trip take by car? by jet?
2. Clark refers to an Indian pilot "in a Salors dress." What does the clothing of the Indian suggest to you?
3. Considering Clark's mistake about the Pacific, what caution should be exercised in using primary sources in researching historical information?

5. TECUMSEH SPEAKS ELOQUENTLY AGAINST THE SALE OF INDIAN LANDS

One memorable day in 1810, Tecumseh stood defiantly outside Governor Harrison's mansion in Indiana. In the eloquent words below, the Shawnee chief denounced what he saw as the unlawful sale of Indian lands to white people. Within a year, Harrison led the American force that destroyed Tecumseh's capital at Tippecanoe and drove his followers into Canada. Consequently, it came as no surprise that Tecumseh chose to fight on the British side in the War of 1812.

I am a Shawnee. My forefathers were warriors. Their son is a warrior. From them I take my only existence. From my tribe I take nothing. I have made myself what I am. And I would that I could make the red people as great as the conceptions of my own mind, when I think of the Great Spirit that rules over us all. . . . I would not then come to Governor Harrison to ask him to tear up the treaty. But I would say to him, "Brother, you have the liberty to return to your own country."

You wish to prevent the Indians from doing as we wish them, to unite and let them consider their lands as the common property of the whole. You take the tribes aside and advise them not to come into this measure. . . . You want by your distinctions of Indian tribes, in allotting to each a particular, to make them war with each other. You never

Shawnee chief Tecumseh condemned General William Henry Harrison's treaty with the Indians. At the Battle of Tippecanoe, Harrison destroyed Tecumseh's capital and drove him into exile.

see an Indian endeavor to make the white people do this. You are continually driving the red people, when at last you will drive them onto the great lake, where they can neither stand nor work.

Since my residence at Tippecanoe, we have endeavored to level all distinctions, to destroy village chiefs, by whom all mischiefs are done. It is they who sell the land to the Americans. Brother, this land that was sold, and the goods that was given for it, was only done by a few. . . . In the future we are prepared to punish those who propose to sell land to the Americans. If you continue to purchase them, it will make war among the different tribes, and at last I do not know what will be the consequences among the white people. Brother, I wish you would take pity on the red people and do as I have requested. If you will not give up the land and do cross the boundary of our present settlement, it will be very hard, and produce great trouble between us.

The way, the only way to stop this evil is for the red men to unite in claiming a common and equal right in the land, as it was at first, and should be now—for it was never divided, but belongs to all. No tribe has the right to sell, even to each other, much less to strangers. . . . *Sell a country! Why not sell the air, the great sea, as well as the earth?* Did not the Great Spirit make them all for the use of his children?

How can we have confidence in the white people?

When Jesus Christ came upon the earth you killed Him and nailed him to the cross. You thought he was dead, and you were mistaken. You have Shakers among you and you laugh and make light of their worship.

Everything I have told you is the truth. The Great Spirit has inspired me.

Selection from *I Have Spoken: American History Through the Voices of the Indians*, compiled by Virginia Irving Armstrong. Published by The Swallow Press, Inc. (Sage Books), Chicago, copyright © 1971.

CRITICAL THINKING

1. What was Tecumseh's belief about who owned the land? Did the whites have a similar or a different belief? Explain what you mean.
2. Why did Tecumseh propose to "destroy village chiefs" and "punish those who propose to sell land to the Americans"?
3. To whom was Tecumseh referring with the word *brother*? What does this suggest about his beliefs?

PAUL PETROVITCH SVININ

A rare glimpse of American life in the early nineteenth century has been preserved in the watercolors of a foreign visitor. Paul Petrovitch Svinin [1787–1839] came to the United States in 1811 as secretary to the Consul General of Russia. During the next 20 months, Svinin traveled from Maine to Virginia and recorded his impressions with color and brush. Fascinated with the rivers and countryside, he particularly admired the recently developed steamboat. He also found impressive the technical inventiveness of Americans.

Svinin thought Philadelphia the most beautiful city in the country. He appreciated its geometric plan. He pointed out that, despite the influence of the "serious" Quakers, Philadelphians wore stylish clothing and enjoyed luxurious carriages, well-furnished houses, dinner parties, and the theater.

Svinin returned to Russia in 1813. His watercolors remained there until after the Russian Revolution, when an American Red Cross worker discovered them and brought the works back to New York.

A well-dressed Philadelphia family enjoy a wintry sleigh ride. In the background is the Bank of the United States, which Svinin admired and compared to public buildings in St. Petersburg.

Svinin marveled at the luxury of the Paragon, *the Robert Fulton steamboat connecting New York and Albany. West Point can be seen in the background.*

After a night at the theater, Svinin sketched a vendor selling oysters outside Philadelphia's Chestnut Street Theater.

CRITICAL THINKING

1. How might these paintings help a theater company stage a play written about America in the early 1800s?
2. If you were considering immigration in 1814, how might seeing these paintings influence your decision?
3. Summarize the general affect or mood of these three paintings.

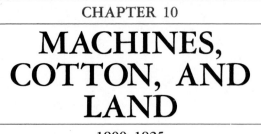

CHAPTER 10

MACHINES, COTTON, AND LAND

1800–1825

1. THE RULES AND REGULATIONS OF NEW ENGLAND MILLS

In the early 1800s, the personal lives as well as the working lives of the employees of the New England mills were strictly controlled by the mill owners as the two following documents show. The first document is a list of rules for workers who lived in a Lancaster, Massachusetts, boarding house. The second document gives the rules and regulations for employees of the Lowell Manufacturing Company.

Rules and Regulations to be attended to and followed by the Young Persons who come to Board in this House:

Rule first: Each one to enter the house without unnecessary noise or confusion, and hang up their bonnet, shawl, coat, etc., etc., in the entry.

Rule second: Each one to have their place at the table during meals, the two which have worked the greatest length of time in the Factory to sit on each side of the head of the table, so that all new hands will of course take their seats lower down, according to the length of time they have been here.

Rule third: It is expected that order and good manners will be preserved at table during meals— and at all other times either upstairs or down.

Rule fourth: There is no unnecessary dirt to be brought into the house by the Boarders, such as apple cores or peels, or nut shells, etc.

Rule fifth: Each boarder is to take her turn in making the bed and sweeping the chamber in which she sleeps.

Rule sixth: Those who have worked the longest in the Factory are to sleep in the North Chamber and the new hands will sleep in the South Chamber.

Rule seventh: As a lamp will be lighted every night upstairs and placed in a lanthorn [lantern], it is expected that no boarder will take a light into the chambers.

Rule eighth: The doors will be closed at ten o'clock at night, winter and summer, at which time each boarder will be expected to retire to bed.

Rule ninth: Sunday being appointed by our Creator as a Day of Rest and Religious Exercises, it is expected that all boarders will have sufficient discretion as to pay suitable attention to the day, and if they cannot attend to some place of Public Worship they will keep within doors and improve their time in reading, writing, and in other valuable and harmless employment.

❦

The overseers are to be punctually in their Rooms at the starting of the Mill, and not to be absent unnecessarily during working hours. They are to see that all those employed in their Rooms are in their places in due season; they may grant leave of absence to those employed under them, when there are spare hands in the Room to supply their places; otherwise they are not to grant leave of absence, except in cases of absolute necessity.

All persons in the employ of the Lowell Manufacturing Company are required to observe the Regulations of the overseer of the Room where they are employed; they are not to be absent from work without his consent, except in cases of sickness, and then they are to send him word of the cause of their absence.

They are to board in one of the Boarding-Houses belonging to the Company, and to conform to the regulations of the House where they board; they are to give information at the Counting-Room, of the place where they board, when they begin; and also give notice whenever they change their boarding-place.

The Company will not employ any one who is habitually absent from public worship on the Sabbath.

It is considered a part of the engagement that each person remains twelve months if required; and all persons intending to leave the employment of the Company are to give two weeks' notice of their intention to their Overseer, and their engagement is not considered as fulfilled unless they comply with this Regulation.

The Pay Roll will be made up to the last Saturday of every month, and the payment made to the Carpet Mill the following Saturday, and the Cotton Mill the succeeding Tuesday, when every person will be expected to pay their board.

The Company will not continue to employ any person who shall be wanting in proper respect to the females employed by the Company, or who shall smoke within the Company's premises, or be guilty of inebriety [drunkenness], or other improper conduct.

The Tenants of the Boarding-Houses are not to board or permit any part of their houses to be occupied by any person, except those in the employ of the Company.

They will be considered answerable for any improper conduct in their Houses, and are not to permit their Boarders to have company at unseasonable hours.

The doors must be closed at ten o'clock in the evening, and no person admitted after that time without some reasonable excuse.

The keeper of the Boarding-House must give an account of the number, names and employment of the Boarders when required, and report the names of such as are guilty of any improper conduct.

The Buildings, and yards about them, must be kept clean and in good order, and if they are injured otherwise than from ordinary use, all necessary repairs will be made and charged to the occupant.

It is desirable that the families of those who live in the Houses, as well as the Boarders, who have not had the Kine [cow] Pox, should be vaccinated; which will be done at the expense of the Company for such as wish it.

Some suitable chamber in the House must be reserved, and appropriated for the use of the sick, so that others may not be under the necessity of sleeping in the same room.

No one will be continued as a Tenant who shall suffer ashes to be put into any place other than the place made to receive them, or shall, by any carelessness in the use of fire, or lights, endanger the Company's property.

These regulations are considered a part of the contract with the persons entering into the employment of the Lowell Manufacturing Company.

Selections from Edith Abbott, *Women in Industry*. Published by D. Appleton and Company, New York, copyright © 1909.

CRITICAL THINKING

1. In spite of the limitations the mills placed on their freedom, New England men and women were happy to take jobs. Why do you think this was so?
2. In the second document, which of the rules and regulations do you think the Lowell Manufacturing Company had the right to make? Why?
3. Which of the Lowell rules and regulations do you think the company had no right to make? Why?

2. ELI WHITNEY INVENTS THE COTTON GIN

John C. Calhoun's dreams of an industrial South evaporated when Eli Whitney invented the cotton gin. In the letter below, Whitney explains to his father how he first got the idea for the cotton gin and what he planned to do with his idea.

NEW HAVEN, Sept. 11th, 1793.

Dear Parent,

I will give you a summary account of my southern expedition.

I went from N. York with the family of the late Major General Greene to Georgia. I went immediately with the family to their Plantation about twelve miles from Savannah with an expectation of spending four or five days and then proceed into Carolina to take [a job teaching] school as I have mentioned in former letters. During this time I heard much said of the extreme difficulty of ginning Cotton, that is, seperating it from its seed. There were a number of very respectable Gentlemen at Mrs. Greene's who all agreed that if a machine could be invented which would clean the cotton with expedition, it would be a great thing both to the Country and to the inventor. I involuntarily happened to be thinking on the subject and struck out a plan of a Machine in my mind, which I communicated to Miller, (who is agent to the Executors of Genl. Greene and resides in the family, a man of respectibility and property) he was pleased with the Plan and said if I would pursue it and try an experiment to see if it would answer, he would be at the whole expense, I should loose nothing but my time, and if I succeeded we would share the profits. Previous to this I found I was like to be disappointed in my school, that is, instead of a hundred, I found I could get only fifty Guineas a year. I however held the refusal of the school until I tried some experiments. In about ten Days I made a little model, for which I was offered, if I would give up all right and title to it, a Hundred Guineas. I concluded to relinquish my school and turn my attention to perfecting the Machine. I made one before I came away which required the labor of one man to turn it and with which one man will clean ten times as much cotton as he can in any other way before known and also cleanse it much better than in the usual mode. This machine may be turned by water or, with a horse, with the greatest ease, and one man and a horse will do more than fifty men with the old machines. It makes the labor fifty times less, without throwing any class of People out of business.

I returned to the Northward for the purpose of having a machine made on a large scale and obtaining a Patent for the invintion. I went to Philadelphia soon after I arrived, made myself acquainted with the steps necessary to obtain a Patent, took several of the steps and the Secretary of State Mr. Jefferson agreed to send the Pattent to me as soon it could be made out—so that I apprehended no difficulty in obtaining the Patent. . . . I am certain I can obtain a patent in England. As soon as I have got a Patent in America I shall go with the machine which I am now making, to Georgia, where I shall stay a few weeks to see it at work. From thence I expect to go to England, where I shall probably continue two or three years. How advantageous this business will eventually prove to me, I cannot say. It is generally said by those who know anything about it, that I shall make a Fortune by it. I have no expectation that I shall make an independent fortune by it, but think I had better pursue it than any other business into which I can enter. Something which cannot be foreseen may frustrate my expectations and defeat my Plan; but I am now so sure of success that ten thousand dollars, if I saw the money counted out to me, would not tempt me to give up my right and relinquish the object. I wish you, sir, not to show this letter nor communicate anything of its contents to anybody except My Brothers and Sisters, *enjoining* it on them to keep the whole a *profound secret.*

Selection from *The American Historical Review*, Vol. III (October 1897 to July 1898). Published by The Macmillan Company, New York, copyright © 1898.

CRITICAL THINKING

1. Why do you think Whitney immediately wanted to get a patent for his cotton gin and to keep the matter a secret?
2. From what your textbook says about Whitney's financial success with the machine, do you think his caution and secrecy were effective? Explain your thinking.

3. ELIJAH ILES RECALLS HIS MOVE TO ILLINOIS IN 1821

The excerpt below is from an account written by Elijah Iles of his move to Springfield in the "new" state of Illinois, when Iles was 25. The experiences he describes took place in 1821. Iles's account shows that he was a very enterprising and determined young man. It also shows a real need for the kind of internal improvements that Henry Clay advocated for tying the sections of the United Sates together.

I hunted around and found the stake that had been stuck for the beginning of a town named Springfield [Illinois], and then bargained for the erection of a store house, to be set near the stake, eighteen feet square, with sheds on the sides for shelter. The house was to be of hewn logs, covered with boards, with heavy poles laid on to keep the boards from blowing off. . . .

I bought my goods at St. Louis, mostly at auction at very low prices, as many goods were then being forced to sale, but to complete the assortment had to buy some at private sale. I then chartered a boat . . . on which to ship my goods up the Illinois river to the mouth of the Sangamon, one hundred and fifty miles above St. Louis and within fifty miles of Springfield. The boat was towed up the river by five men walking on shore and pulling a tow line about three hundred feet long. One man on the boat acting as steersman, with myself as supercargo, completed the crew.

Just below the mouth of the Missouri river, where the current was very strong, a large cotton-wood tree had fallen into the water, and the boat had to be steered out so as to clear it. As it struck the current, the bow was forced under the water. I calmly folded my arms with the thought that if it went down I would go too, as it held all that I had so far struggled for, together with four hundred dollars belonging to each of my brothers, William and Washington Iles, which my father had given me to invest for them; but, as the hatches were closed, only a few barrels of water got into the boat, and the bow soon raised and we pursued our upward course rejoicing—at least I did. The first house we came to above the mouth of the Missouri was the ferryman's, now the city of Alton. The next was at the mouth of the Illinois river. The next was a vacant cabin, with doors and windows cut out, but without shutters. This was at the mouth of the Sangamon river. . . .

At the vacant cabin the boatmen landed my goods on the beach and started down the river on their return to St. Louis. I took my seat on the head of a . . . barrel, . . . and watched the boat until it got out of sight, and I thought and thought. But as thinking would do no good, I went to the top of the bank and examined the cabin, and found a few household goods and farming utensils stowed in it. The articles had been brought there by emigrants in what were called dug-outs. I believe the boat bringing my goods was the first boat that ever ascended the river, other than Indian-trading boats. . . .

. . . I met two teams going to the river; and as neither of them would have full loads, I turned back and made up their loads. . . . Upon my arrival at Springfield I employed teams to haul the goods. As there were about twenty-five tons of them, it took more than a month to do this, but it was finally accomplished without having the first thing disturbed or missing. . . .

. . . I found my store house was not quite ready, for the want of nails, and you may believe it was a rough concern; but it answered my purpose. This was the first store house erected in Springfield or in the county, and I was the first one to sell goods in Springfield. For some time my sales were about as much to Indians as to the whites. For the

first two years I had no competition, and my customers were widely and thinly scattered.

Selection from *The American Reader: From Columbus to Today*, edited by Paul M. Angle. Published by Rand McNally & Company, New York, copyright © 1958.

CRITICAL THINKING

1. What kind of river transportation was used to bring Iles's goods from St. Louis to the mouth of the Sangamon River near Springfield? According to Iles, what was unusual about this?
2. Verify the following statement by referring to specific parts of Iles's account: The successful opening of the American West was due, above all, to the spirit and determination of individual men and women.

4. JOHN FITCH DESCRIBES A DEMONSTRATION OF HIS STEAMBOAT

Steamboats played a crucial role in making rivers like the Mississippi and Missouri important American highways for transportation. In the reading below, John Fitch describes a demonstration of his first steamboat in 1787.

When we had got the alterations made, we found ourselves more imbarrassed than ever. We found our Engine to work exceedingly well, and plenty of steam, but not to go fast enough to answer a valuable purpose on the Delaware. Which threw me into the greatest consternation. We found that we must have a greater force than we had supposed. . . . We were convinced that we had got the whole of our force from a 12 Inch cylinder, and the cylinder must be inlarged, consequently [also] the whole of our [vessel], which was like begining the whole [vessel] anew. This Disaster could never have been overcome had it not been for the interference of Mr. Wells, Dr.[,] Say Mr. Stockton and some others. But after some deliberations on the matter, it was resolved by the Company that I should be ordered to procure an 18 inch cylinder, instead of a 12 inch, which we then had.

I might have observed befor this, that I got several of the principal characters in the city to take a sail with us, in order to take an opinion of our [vessel], some of which I shall here relate. I invited Dr. Johnson a member of the Continental Convention then sitting in Philadelphia, who invited a number of other gentlemen with him. . . . The next day Dr. Johnson favoured me with the following Note:

Dr. Johnson presents his compliments to Mr. Fitch, and assures him that the Exhibition yesterday gave the Gentlemen present much satisfaction. He himself, and he doubts not the other gentlemen will allways be happy to give him every continance & encouragement in their Power, which his Ingenuity and industry entitles him to.

Thursday Afternoon, 23 August 1787.

There was very few of the convention but called to see it, and [I] do not know whether I may except any but General Washington himself. The reasons he omitted if I do not pretend to say. Governour Randolph with several if not all of the Virginia members were pleased to give it every countinance they could. But as the season was so far advanced . . . the scheme became in a very tottering situation. And altho I had Mr. Wells and others to surport me, in order to set the scheme afloat again . . . the Task was too great for me.

Selection from *The Autobiography of John Fitch*, edited by Frank D. Prager. Published by The American Philosophical Society, Philadelphia, copyright © 1976.

CRITICAL THINKING

1. What was the purpose of the convention meeting in Philadelphia at the time of John Fitch's steamboat demonstration?
2. What changes were necessary if Fitch's steamboat was to serve a valuable purpose on the Delaware River?
3. How would you describe Fitch's frame of mind after the demonstration?

5. ROBERT FULTON DESCRIBES HIS FIRST SUCCESSFUL STEAMBOAT VOYAGE FROM NEW YORK TO ALBANY

Twenty years after Fitch's demonstration voyage, in 1807, Robert Fulton took his Clermont *on a famous voyage on the Hudson River. In the reading below, a letter to a friend, Fulton describes the voyage.*

My steamboat voyage to Albany has turned out rather more favorably than I had calculated. The distance from New York to Albany is one hundred and fifty miles. I ran it up in thirty-two hours, and down in thirty. I had a light breeze against me the whole way, both going and coming, and the voyage has been performed wholly by the power of steam. I overtook many sloops and schooners beating to windward and parted with them as if they had been at anchor. The power of propelling boats by steam is now fully proved. The morning I left New York there were not, perhaps, thirty persons in the city who believed that the boat would ever move one mile an hour, or be of the least utility, and while we were putting off from the wharf, which was crowded with spectators, I heard a number of sarcastic remarks. . . .

Having employed much time, money, and zeal in accomplishing this work, it gives me, as it will you, great pleasure to see it fully answer my expectations. It will give a cheap and quick conveyance to the merchants on the Mississippi, the Missouri, and other great rivers which are now laying open their treasures to the enterprise of our country; and although the prospect of personal emolument has been some inducement to me, yet I feel infinitely more pleasure in reflecting on the numerous advantages that my country will derive from the invention.

Selection from Charles Burr Todd, *Life and Letters of Joel Barlow*. Published by Da Capo Press, New York, copyright © 1970.

CRITICAL THINKING

1. What adverse wind condition served to prove the *Clermont's* worth? How?
2. How might comments about Fulton differ before and after this voyage?

6. THOMAS WOODCOCK'S ACCOUNT OF A TRIP THROUGH THE ERIE CANAL

The Erie Canal was not a part of Henry Clay's American System. It was built with private funds. In the reading below, Thomas S. Woodcock describes a trip as a passenger on one of the boats that traveled the canal.

May 25th. Left Albany [New York] at 9 'O Clock by the Railway for Schenectady, a distance of 17 Miles, for which 62½ cents is charged. we were drawn by Horses about 2 Miles, being a steep ascent. we then found a Steam Engine waiting for us (built by Stephenson and called the John Bull). . . . we at length stop to have our carriages attached to a stationary Engine which lets us down an inclined plane, from the top of which we have a fine view of Schenectady and part of the Valley of the Mohawk. it is chiefly built of Bricks and is in a low flat situation, and I think a place of no great importance. we arrived at this place at ½ past 10. from the cars we proceeded to enter our names for the Packet Boat. these boats are about 70 feet long, and with the exception of the Kitchen and bar, is occupied as a Cabin. the forward part being the ladies Cabin, is seperated by a curtain, but at meal times this obstruction is removed, and the table is set the whole length of the boat. the table is supplied with everything that is necessary and of the best quality with many of the luxuries of life. on finding we had so many passengers, I was at a loss to know how we should be accomodated with berths, as I saw no convenience for anything of the kind, but the Yankees ever awake to contrivances have managed to stow more in so small a space than I thought them capable of doing. the way they proceed is as follows—The Settees [couches] that go the whole length of the Boat on each side unfold and form a cot bed. the space between this bed and the ceiling is so divided as to make room for two more. the upper berths are merely frames with sacking bottoms, one side of which has two projecting pins, which fit into sockets in the side of the boat. the other side has two cords attached one to each corner. these are suspended from hooks in the ceiling. the bedding is then placed upon them, the space between the berths being barely sufficient

for a man to crawl in, and presenting the appearance of so many shelves. much apprehension is always entertained by passengers when first seeing them, lest the cords should break. such fears are however groundless. the berths are allotted according to the way bill the first on the list having his first choice and in changing boats the old passengers have the preference. the first Night I tried an upper berth, but the air was so foul that I found myself sick when I awoke. afterwards I choose an under berth and found no ill effects from the air. these Boats have *three* Horses, go at quicker rate and have the preference in going through the locks, carry no freight, are built extremely light, and have quite Genteel Men for their Captains, and use *silver* plate. the distance between Schenectady and Utica is 80 Miles the passage is $3.50 which includes board. . . . The Bridges on the Canal are very low, particularly the old ones, indeed they are so low as to scarcely allow the baggage to clear, and in some cases actually rubbing against it. every Bridge makes us bend double if seated on anything, and in many cases you have to lie on your back. the Man at the helm gives the Word to the Passengers. "Bridge" "*very* low Bridge" "the lowest in the Canal" as the case may be. some serious accidents have happened for want of caution. a young English Woman met with her death a short time since, she having fallen asleep with her head upon a box had her head crushed to pieces. such things however do not often occur, and in general it affords amusement to the passengers who soon immatate the cry, and vary it with a command, such as "All Jackson men bow down." after such commands we find few Aristocrats.

Selection from *New York to Niagara, 1836: The Journal of Thomas S. Woodcock*, edited by Deoch Fulton. Published by The New York Public Library, New York, copyright © 1938.

CRITICAL THINKING

1. In your own words, describe the example of Yankee ingenuity given by Woodcock.
2. What do you find most surprising in Woodcock's narrative? Why?
3. Would this account most likely be classified as factual or fictional? Give reasons for your choice?

IRON: The History Of An American Industry, 1800–1825

By the 1850s, factories like the one above made finished iron products and shipped them by rail to other parts of the country.

After the Revolutionary War, the American iron industry went into a serious decline. It was exhausted from the war effort and technologically behind the times. The greatest impediment to rebuilding the industry, however, was the abundance of cheap English iron flooding the American market. English fleets were dumping shiploads of iron and iron products at American ports, and selling the goods at prices below the cost of domestic production.

Relief didn't come to American ironworks until the embargo of 1808, and the War of 1812, when United States ports were closed. During that brief period iron manufacturers flourished, but then the deflation following the war ruined many of them.

From 1813–1833, a movement began to protect the "infant industries." Although British imports continued to rise steadily, they were subject to higher import duties.

By the 1820s, the first American iron factories went into production. Because the population was still predominantly agricultural, the factories specialized in the production of farm machinery and tools. Hundreds of factories were turning out plows, hay rakes, cultivators, reapers, and a variety of other agricultural equipment.

Other early iron products were the "pot-bellied" stove and the nail. In 1810, there were already 410 naileries producing 16 million nails. By 1925, the Patent Office had recognized 120 different nailmaking machines.

Despite the successful exploitation of new technologies in England, American iron producers clung to traditional methods and fuels until the middle of the nineteenth century. Real expansion of the iron industry occurred with the introduction of the Bessamer converter in the 1850s.

D O C U M E N T

Before the advent of mass production transformed the iron industry, workers in the smithy above can be seen individually crafting agricultural tools. At right, cast-iron cannon stoves, named for their round shapes, became popular because they gave more heat and used less wood. The worker below is cutting nails from an iron plate. This was the chief method of nailmaking until the later 19th century when nails began to be produced from wire.

CRITICAL THINKING

1. What do you know about transportation and air pollution from observing the details in one of these illustrations?
2. Which of these pictures clearly shows a technological advance over handmade iron products?

7. CHARLES FENNO HOFFMAN DESCRIBES TRAVEL ON HENRY CLAY'S NATIONAL ROAD

In winter, ice clogged the canals and many of the rivers. At this time of year, travelers between East and West were glad for the country's roads—even those like Henry Clay's National Road, described below. The description was written by Charles Fenno Hoffman, an American novelist and newspaperman, who traveled on horseback through much of what was the American West in 1833.

About thirty miles from Wheeling we first struck the national road. It appears to have been originally constructed of large round stones, thrown without much arrangement on the surface of the soil, after the road was first levelled. These are now being ploughed up, and a thin layer of broken stones is in many places spread over the renovated surface. I hope the roadmakers have not the conscience to call this Macadamizing. It yields like snow-drift to the heavy wheels which traverse it, and the very best parts of the road that I saw are not to be compared with a Long Island turnpike. Two-thirds indeed of the extent traversed were worse than any artificial road I ever travelled, except perhaps the log causeways among the new settlements in northern New York. The ruts are worn so broad and deep by heavy travel, that an army of pigmies might march into the bosom of the country under the cover they would afford. . . .

There is one feature, however, in this national work which is truly fine,—I allude to the massive stone bridges which form a part of it. They occur, as the road crosses a winding creek, a dozen times within twice as many miles. They consist either of one, two, or three arches; the centre arch being sprung a foot or two higher than those on either side. Their thick walls projecting above the road, their round stone buttresses, and carved keystones combine to give them an air of Roman solidity and strength. They are monuments of taste and power that will speak well for the country when the brick towns they bind together shall have crumbled in the dust. . . .

Apropos of pedestrians, though your true western man generally journeys on horseback, yet one meets numbers of the former on this side [the western side] of the Alleghanies. They generally have a tow-cloth knapsack, or light leathern valise, hung across their backs, and are often very decently dressed in a blue coat, gray trousers, and round hat. They travel about forty miles a day.

The horsemen almost invariably wear a drab great-coat, fur cap, and green cloth leggins; and in addition to a pair of well-filled saddle-bags, very often have strapped to their crupper a convenience the last you would expect to find in the wardrobe of a backwoodsman, . . . an umbrella. The females of every rank, in this mountainous country, ride in short dresses. They are generally wholly unattended, and sometimes in large parties of their own sex. The saddles and housings of their horses are very gay; and I have repeatedly seen a party of four or five buxom damsels, mounted on sorry-looking beasts, whose rough hides, unconscious of a currycomb, contrasted oddly enough with saddles of purple velvet, reposing on scarlet saddle-cloths, worked with orange-coloured borders. I have examined the manufacture of these gorgeous trappings at the saddleries in some of the towns in passing. They much resemble those which are prepared in New-York for the South American market, and are of a much cheaper make, and far less durable, than those which a plainer taste would prefer. Still the effect of these gay colours, as you catch a glimpse of them afar off, fluttering through the woods, is by no means bad. They would show well in a picture, and be readily seized by a painter in relieving the shadows of a sombre landscape.

But by the far the greatest portion of travellers one meets with, not to mention the ordinary stage-coach passengers, consists of teamsters and the emigrants. The former generally drive six horses before their enormous wagons—stout, heavy-looking beasts, descended, it is said, from the famous draught horses of Normandy. They go about twenty miles a day. The leading horses are often ornamented with a number of bells suspended from a square raised frame-work over their collars, originally adopted to warn these lumbering machines of each other's approach, and prevent their being brought up all standing in the narrow parts of the road.

As for the emigrants, it would astonish you to witness how they get along. A covered one-horse wagon generally contains the whole worldly substance of a family consisting not unfrequently of a dozen members. The tolls are so high along this western turnpike, and horses are comparatively so cheap in the region whither the emigrant is bound, that he rarely provides more than one miserable [animal] to transport his whole family to the far west. The strength of the poor animal is of course half the time unequal to the demand upon it, and you will, therefore, unless it be raining very hard, rarely see anyone in the wagon, except perhaps some child overtaken by sickness, or a mother nursing a young infant. The head of the family walks by the horse, cheering and encouraging him on his way. The good woman, when not engaged as hinted above, either trudges along with her husband, or, leading some weary little traveller by the hand far behind, endeavours to keep the rest of her charge from loitering by the wayside. . . .

The hardships of such a tour must form no bad preparatory school for the arduous life which the new settler has afterward to enter upon. Their horses, of course, frequently give out on the road; and in companies so numerous, sickness must frequently overtake some of the members. Nor should I wonder at serious accidents often occurring with those crank conveyances among the precipices and ravines of the mountains. At one place I saw a horse, but recently dead, lying beneath a steep, along the top of which the road led; and a little farther in advance, I picked up a pocketbook with some loose leaves floating near the edge of the precipice.

Selection from *The American Reader: From Columbus to Today*, edited by Paul M. Angle. Published by Rand McNally & Company, New York, copyright © 1958.

CRITICAL THINKING

1. How does Hoffman help his readers to picture the ruts on the National Road?
2. What do you think was carried in the six-horse wagons Hoffman encountered? What modern equivalents of these wagons would you see on the country's east-west interstate highways today?
3. What was the destination of the emigrants Hoffman met? What did he mean by saying that the National Road was "no bad preparatory school" for them?

CHAPTER 11
THE AGE OF THE COMMON PERSON
1824–1844

1. PRESIDENTIAL CANDIDATE ANDREW JACKSON IS ACCUSED OF SERIOUS CRIMES

The presidential campaign of 1828 was bitter. The two candidates were the targets of accusations of all kinds. The so-called Coffin Handbill, released by the Adams faction, accused Andrew Jackson of extremely serious crimes—responsibility for the deaths of more than 30 people. Copies of this handbill were distributed widely during the campaign. As election day neared, it was reproduced again in Our Country *in Hagerstown, Maryland. Some of the remarks that introduced the handbill appear below. Also reproduced is a list of rewards, outlining Jackson's alleged crimes and challenging his supporters to prove that their candidate was innocent of these crimes.*

October 18, 1828.

We lay this far-famed handbill before our readers to-day. We have two reasons for doing so. Many of them have never yet seen it—this is one reason. The other is, that the Jacksonites call it an infamous bill, and pronounce all its statements false. It is neither infamous nor false. If there be any infamy connected with it, that infamy should attach to General Jackson—for, however black—however appalling this bill may appear, it presents but an inadequate representation of the still blacker and still more appalling acts of this violent and vindictive man. . . .

No man living would be more rejoiced than we would, to be satisfied that the charges contained in this bill against Gen. Jackson were not well founded. At least one ground of our objection to him would then be removed. As an inducement for his friends to attempt their removal, we hereby offer $20 for such evidence as will satisfy the public that the six militia men were not shot by Gen.

Jackson's order, after their time had expired, and contrary to law.

$20 for any evidence by which we can convince the public that the eight regulars were not unnecessarily shot, by order of Gen. Jackson, near Nashville.

$20 for any evidence by which we can convince the humane and the merciful that the gallant but unfortunate youth, John Woods, was not cruelly and unnecessarily put to death by order of General Jackson.

$20 for the pointing out of any mistake in Gen. Jackson's own account of the massacre of the sixteen Indians, and the murder of the Prophet and his countrymen.

$20 for any evidence that may enable us to convince the public that Gen. Jackson did not run his cane sword through Samuel Jackson.

$20 for any testimony showing that General Jackson and his bullies did not make the attack on Col. Benton and his Brother, an account of which the Colonel gives in his letter. And

$20 for such facts as will satisfy the public that the Jackson party have not been misrepresenting those bills with a view of deceiving the people as to the real character and temper of their Farmer Hero.

If our offer be not taken, the correctness of the charges must be considered as admitted by the Heroe's friends. And if all these charges be true—if all these black and horrid deeds have been done or sanctioned by Gen. Jackson, where the impropriety?—where the infamy?—where the falsehood of the bill? There is neither impropriety —infamy—nor falsehood, in the business. But, on the contrary, there is a virtue in proclaiming the deep-dark-cold-chilling-damning facts, that this bill sets forth against this aspirant for a situation, for which every consideration of prudence, of justice and of patriotism, proclaims him unfit and undeserving. And, "if it should be the last act of our life", and subject us to the penalties of the "second section", if possessed of the means, we would spread this black bill—this true picture of wrong—oppression—and tyranny—through every district—city—town—village and neighborhood, that no living soul in the land, entitled to the right of suffrage, should be ignorant of its contents, when he deposits his vote in the ballot box at the next election.

Selection from *Correspondence of Andrew Jackson*, Vol. III, edited by John Spencer Bassett. Published by The Carnegie Institution of Washington, Washington, D. C., copyright © 1928.

CRITICAL THINKING

1. The Coffin Handbill had been circulated widely almost from the beginning of the 1828 presidential campaign. Suggest a motive for yet another appearance of this handbill in *Our Country* on October 18.
2. Twenty dollars was a great amount of money in 1828. Do you think offering rewards of this amount indicates that Jackson's accusers were certain of the truth of their charges against him, or did they merely use this as a propaganda technique? Explain your thinking.

2. PRESIDENT ANDREW JACKSON'S INAUGURAL CELEBRATION GETS OUT OF HAND

When President Jackson was elected in 1828, many Americans feared his democratic ideas. The worst fears of these people must have seemed realized on the day in 1829 when Jackson was inaugurated. Margaret Bayard Smith, a well-known American writer and prominent resident of Washington, D. C., recorded what she saw that day in a letter to a friend.

[Washington] March 11th, Sunday [1829.] Thursday morning. I left the rest of this sheet for an account of the inauguration. It was not a thing of detail of a succession of small incidents. No. it was one grand whole. . . . Thousands and thousands of people, without distinction of rank, collected in an immense mass round the Capitol, silent, orderly and tranquil, with their eyes fixed on the front of that edifice, waiting the appearance of the President in the portico. The door from the Rotunda opens, preceded by the marshals, surrounded by the Judges of the Supreme Court, the old man with his grey locks, that crown of glory, advances, bows to the people, who greet him with a shout that rends the air. . . . After reading his speech, the oath was administered to him by the Chief Justice. The Marshal presented the Bible.

The President took it from his hands, pressed his lips to it, laid it reverently down, then bowed again to the people—Yes, to the people in all their majesty. . . . At the moment the General entered the Portico and advanced to the table, the shout that rent the air, still resounds in my ears. When the speech was over, and the President made his parting bow, the barrier that had separated the people from him was broken down and they rushed up the steps all eager to shake hands with him. It was with difficulty he made his way through the Capitol and down the hill to the gateway that opens on the avenue. Here for a moment he was stopped. The living mass was impenetrable. After a while a passage was opened, and he mounted his horse which had been provided for his return (for he had walked to the Capitol) then such a cortege as followed him! Country men, farmers, gentlemen, mounted and dismounted, boys, women and children, black and white. Carriages, wagons and carts all pursuing him to the President's house. . . . The day was delightful, the scene animating, so we walked backward and forward at every turn meeting some new acquaintance and stopping to talk and shake hands. . . . We continued promenading here, until near three, returned home unable to stand and threw ourselves on the sopha. Some one came and informed us the crowd before the President's house, was so far lessen'd, that they thought we might enter. This time we effected our purpose. But what a scene did we witness! The *Majesty of the People* had disappeared, and a rabble, a mob, of boys, negros, women, children, scrambling fighting, romping. What a pity what a pity! No arrangements had been made no police officers placed on duty and the whole house had been inundated by the rabble mob. We came too late. The President, after having been *literally* nearly pressed to death and almost suffocated and torn to pieces by the people in their eagerness to shake hands with Old Hickory, had retreated through the back way or south front and had escaped to his lodgings at Gadsby's. Cut glass and china to the amount of several thousand dollars had been broken in the struggle to get the refreshments, punch and other articles had been carried out in tubs and buckets, but had it been in hogsheads it would have been insufficient, ice-creams, and cake and lemonade, for 20,000 people, for it is said that number were

there, tho' I think the estimate exaggerated. Ladies fainted, men were seen with bloody noses and such a scene of confusion took place as is impossible to describe,—those who got in could not get out by the door again, but had to scramble out of windows. At one time, the President who had retreated and retreated until he was pressed against the wall, could only be secured by a number of gentlemen forming round him and making a kind of barrier of their own bodies, and the pressure was so great that Col Bomford who was one said that at one time he was afraid they should have been pushed down, or on the President. It was then the windows were thrown open, and the torrent found an outlet, which otherwise might have proved fatal.

This concourse had not been anticipated and therefore not provided against. Ladies and gentlemen, only had been expected at this Levee, not the people en masse. But it was the People's day, and the People's President and the People would rule. God grant that one day or other, the People, do not put down all rule and rulers. I fear, enlightened Freemen as they are, they will be found, as they have been found in all ages and countries where they get the Power in their hands, that of all tyrants, they are the most ferocious, cruel and despotic.

Selection from Mrs. Samuel Harrison Smith (Margaret Bayard), *The First Forty Years of Washington Society*, edited by Gaillard Hunt. Published by Charles Scribner's Sons, New York, copyright © 1906.

CRITICAL THINKING

1. Mrs. Margaret Bayard Smith said that "the people en masse" were not expected at the White House on Inauguration Day. Why do you think ordinary people felt they had the right to join in the celebration there?
2. What attitude toward "the people," "the enlightened Freemen," do you detect in Mrs. Smith's letter to her friend? Support your answer with references to particular parts of her letter that supply clues to her thinking.

President Andrew Jackson Champions Opportunity for Individuals and Argues for a Strong National Government

Very few people have been so symbolic of the era in which they lived as Andrew Jackson. Jackson's followers in the Democratic party idolized him because he was a person who began life poor and earned great wealth and position because of his own efforts. He was the symbol of opportunity for the "common man." His success showed that, in America, anyone could rise from the bottom to the top.

Indeed, Jackson preached the importance of preserving opportunities for other ordinary people to succeed when he vetoed a law of Congress that gave fifteen more years of life to the Bank of the United States. The "Monster Bank," as Jackson called it, was controlled by wealthy individuals who used their power over the nation's money supply to prevent others from improving the quality of their lives. A majority of Americans agreed with Jackson. In 1832, they reelected him to the presidency by a landslide.

Nationalists, people who believed that the federal government should be more powerful than the state governments, found a hero in Jackson. When South Carolina tried to nullify a law of Congress that placed a high tax (or tariff) on goods imported into the country, Jackson threatened to lead an army into South Carolina.

Jackson never put his threat into practice. The crisis between the federal government and South Carolina was settled by compromise. But in his strong statement on behalf of national over state power, "Old Hickory" again symbolized the spirit of his age.

UNLOCKING HISTORY
KEY DOCUMENT

President Jackson Vetoes the Bank Bill

WASHINGTON, *July 10, 1832.*

To the Senate:

The bill "to modify and continue" the act entitled "An act to incorporate the subscribers to the Bank of the United States" was presented to me on the 4th July instant. Having . . . come to the conclusion that it ought not to become a law, I herewith return it to the Senate, in which it originated, with my objections. . . .

The present corporate body . . . enjoys an exclusive privilege of banking under the authority of the General Government, a monopoly of its favor and support, and, as a necessary consequence, almost a monopoly of the foreign and domestic exchange. . . .

[But every] monopoly and all exclusive privileges are granted at the expense of the public, which ought to receive a fair equivalent. The many millions which this act proposes to bestow on the stockholders of the existing bank must come directly or indirectly out of the earnings of the American people. . . .

It is not conceivable how the present stockholders can have any claim to the special favor of the Government. The present corporation has enjoyed its monopoly during the period stipulated in the original contract. If we must have such a corporation, why should not the Government sell out the whole stock and thus secure to the people the full market value of the privileges granted? Why should not Congress create and sell twenty-eight millions of stock, incorporating the purchasers with all the powers and privileges secured in this act and putting the premium upon the sales into the Treasury? . . .

There are no necessary evils in government. Its evils exist only in its abuses. If it would confine itself to equal protection, it would be an unqualified blessing. In the act before me there seems to be a wide and unnecessary departure from these just principles. . . .

President Jackson Argues for a Strong National Government

December 10, 1832

A small majority of the citizens of one State in the Union have elected delegates to a State convention; that convention has ordained that all the revenue laws of the United States must be repealed, or that they are no longer a member of the Union. The governor of that State has recommended to the legislature the raising of an army to carry the secession into effect, and that he may be empowered to give clearances to vessels in the name of the State. No act of violent opposition to the laws has yet been committed, but such a state of things is hourly apprehended. And it is the intent of this instrument to *proclaim*, not only that the duty imposed on me by the Constitution "to take care that the laws be faithfully executed" shall be performed to the extent of the powers already vested in me by law, or of such others as the wisdom of Congress shall devise and intrust to me for that purpose, but to warn the citizens of South Carolina who have been deluded into an opposition to the laws of the danger they will incur by obedience to the illegal and disorganizing ordinance of the convention; to exhort those who have refused to support it to persevere in their determination to uphold the Constitution and laws of their country; and to point out to all the perilous situation into which the good people of that State have been led.

Both selections from James D. Richardson, editor, *A Compilation of the Messages and Papers of the Presidents*, Prepared under the Direction of the Joint Committee on Printing of the House and Senate, 52nd Congress, New York: Bureau of National Literature, 1897–1917, Volume II, page 576 ff. [Bank Bill]; page 640 ff. [government].

CRITICAL THINKING

1. In what ways did Jackson's veto reflect the thinking of average Americans?
2. Why did Jackson believe South Carolina's action constituted "a crisis?"

P I C T U R E A S

THE RIGHT TO VOTE
The Spread Of Democracy In America

In an 1815 election, Philadelphia voters line up outside the State House and hand their ballots in through the windows.

At the time of the American Revolution, democracy had not yet become a popular concept. Many of the statesmen who drafted the Constitution felt antagonistic to rule by the people. Even Thomas Jefferson, who advocated a government "of the people", feared that majority rule had the potential to be as oppressive as a dictatorship.

But the Revolution had brought multitudes of people into the political arena. Those who could not vote or hold office had still boycotted British goods and fought in the War of Independence. Now they wanted to gain an effective means of expressing their political views.

After the establishment of the new federal government, local, state and national elections further stimulated interest in public issues. Speeches were made and published, and political newspapers, books, pamphlets, and leaflets multiplied.

This mass political awakening naturally led to the idea of democracy. Because the Declaration of Independence had declared all men equal, it followed that all men had the right to vote and to hold office.

Postrevolutionary paintings of political gatherings provide a visual record of political campaigns and voting practices of that time, which in certain ways differed from modern methods. The artists who painted these pictures give modern viewers a second gift: an insight into painting styles of the period.

D O C U M E N T

Citizens listen attentively to campaign oratory as a candidate delivers a "stump" speech from a makeshift platform.

In the 1850s, politics was a popular form of entertainment. The painting below shows election day in Catonsville, Maryland.

Two men argue current events in an oyster house, in this 1848 depiction of American politics by Richard Caton Woodville.

CRITICAL THINKING

1. From these pictures and what you know about modern political campaigns, compare ways in which early political campaigns and today's campaigns are similar. In which ways are they different?
2. Look closely at the paintings. What is one critical difference between voters today and those of the 1800s?

3. SENATOR DANIEL WEBSTER RESPONDS TO PRESIDENT JACKSON'S VETO OF THE BANK BILL

Senator Daniel Webster had sided with Nicholas Biddle and Henry Clay on the bank issue. The day after President Jackson sent his veto message to the Senate, Daniel Webster made a speech in that legislative body responding to the President's message. Parts of Webster's speech follow.

MR. PRESIDENT, no one will deny the high importance of the subject now before us. Congress, after full deliberation and discussion, has passed a bill, by decisive majorities, in both houses, for extending the duration of the Bank of the United States. It has not adopted this measure until its attention had been called to the subject, in three successive annual messages of the President. The bill having been thus passed by both houses, and having been duly presented to the President, instead of signing and approving it, he has returned it with objections. These objections go against the whole substance of the law originally creating the bank. They deny, in effect, that the bank is constitutional; they deny that it is expedient; they deny that it is necessary for the public service. . . .

But . . . it is not the local interest of the West, nor the particular interest of Pennsylvania, or any other State, which has influenced Congress in passing this bill. It has been governed by a wise foresight, and by a desire to avoid embarrassment in the pecuniary concerns of the country, to secure the safe collection and convenient transmission of public moneys, to maintain the circulation of the country, sound and safe as it now happily is, against the possible effects of a wild spirit of speculation. Finding the bank highly useful, Congress has thought fit to provide for its continuance. . . .

Before proceeding to the constitutional question, there are some other topics, treated in the message, which ought to be noticed. It commences by an inflamed statement of what it calls the "favor" bestowed upon the original bank by the government, or, indeed, as it is phrased, the "monopoly of its favor and support"; and through the whole message all possible changes are rung

on the "gratuity," the "exclusive privileges," and "monopoly," of the bank charter. Now . . . the truth is, that the powers conferred on the bank are such, and no others, as are usually conferred on similar institutions. They constitute no monopoly, although some of them are of necessity, and with propriety, exclusive privileges. "The original act," says the message, "operated as a gratuity of many millions to the stockholders." What fair foundation is there for this remark? The stockholders received their charter, not gratuitously, but for a valuable consideration in money, prescribed by Congress, and actually paid. . . . The message proceeds to declare, that the present act proposes another donation, another gratuity, to the same men, of at least seven millions more. It seems to me that this is an extraordinary statement, and an extraordinary style of argument, for such a subject and on such an occasion. In the first place, the facts are all assumed; they are taken for true without evidence. There are no proofs that any benefit to that amount will accrue to the stockholders, nor any experience to justify the expectation of it. It rests on random estimates, or mere conjecture. But suppose the continuance of the charter should prove beneficial to the stockholders; do they not pay for it? . . .

But . . . there is a larger and a much more just view of this subject. The bill was not passed for the purpose of benefiting the present stockholders. Their benefit, if any, is incidental. . . . Congress passed the bill, not as a bounty or a favor to the present stockholders, nor to comply with any demand of right on their part; but to promote great public interests, for great public objects. Every bank must have some stockholders, unless it be such a bank as the President has recommended, and in regard to which he seems not likely to find much concurrence of other men's opinions; and if the stockholders, whoever they may be, conduct the affairs of the bank prudently, the expectation is always, of course, that they will make it profitable to themselves, as well as useful to the public. If a bank charter is not to be granted, because, to some extent, it may be profitable to the stockholders, no charter can be granted. The objection lies against all banks. . . .

. . . Following up the impulses of the same spirit, the message goes on gravely to allege, that the act, as passed by Congress, proposes to make a *present* of some millions of dollars to foreigners, because a portion of the stock is held by foreigners. . . .

From the commencement of the government, it has been thought desirable to invite, rather than to repel, the introduction of foreign capital. Our stocks have all been open to foreign subscriptions; and the State banks, in like manner, are free to foreign ownership. Whatever State has created a debt has been willing that foreigners should become purchasers, and desirous of it. . . . It is easy to say that there is danger to liberty, danger to independence, in a bank open to foreign stockholders, because it is easy to say any thing. But neither reason nor experience proves any such danger. The foreign stockholder cannot be a director. He has no voice even in the choice of directors. His money is placed entirely in the management of the directors appointed by the President and Senate and by the American stockholders. . . . He has parted with the control over his own property. . . .

. . . We have arrived at a new epoch. We are entering on experiments, with the government and the Constitution of the country, hitherto untried, and of fearful and appalling aspect. This message calls us to the contemplation of a future which little resembles the past. Its principles are at war with all that public opinion has sustained, and all which the experience of the government has sanctioned. It denies first principles; it contradicts truths, heretofore received as indisputable. It denies to the judiciary the interpretation of law, and claims to divide with Congress the power of originating statues. It extends the grasp of executive pretension over every power of the government. But this is not all. It presents the chief magistrate of the Union in the attitude of arguing away the powers of that government over which he has been chosen to preside. . . . It appeals to every prejudice which may betray men into a mistaken view of their own interests, and to every passion which may lead them to disobey the impulses of their understanding. It urges all the specious topics of State rights and national encroachment against that which a great majority of the States have affirmed to be rightful, and in which all of them have acquiesced. It sows, in an unsparing manner, the seeds of jealousy and ill-will against that government of which its author is

the official head. It raises a cry, that liberty is in danger, at the very moment when it puts forth claims to powers heretofore unknown and unheard of. It affects alarm for the public freedom, when nothing endangers that freedom so much as its own unparalleled pretences. This, even, is not all. It manifestly seeks to inflame the poor against the rich; it wantonly attacks whole classes of the people, for the purpose of turning against them the prejudices and the resentments of other classes. It is a state paper which finds no topic too exciting for its use, no passion too inflammable for its address and its solicitation.

Selection from *The Works of Daniel Webster*, Vol. III. Published by Little, Brown and Company, Boston, copyright © 1854.

CRITICAL THINKING

1. Which of Webster's arguments do you find most convincing? Summarize this argument.
2. Webster charges that President Jackson attempted "to inflame the poor against the rich." Do you think this was the President's intention? Give reasons for your answer.

4. A BAPTIST MISSIONARY TELLS OF THE "TRAIL OF TEARS"

Many Americans were outraged by the decisions that led the Cherokees of Georgia on the infamous "Trail of Tears." Among these Americans were missionaries who lived and worked among the ill-fated Indian nation. One such missionary for the Baptist Church was a certain Mr. Jones. An excerpt from one of his letters concerning the "Trail of Tears" appears below.

May 21, [1838]. Our minds have, of late, been in a state of intense anxiety and agitation. The 24th of May is rapidly approaching. The major-general has arrived, and issued his summons, declaring that every man, woman and child of the Cherokees must be on their way to the west before another moon shall pass. The troops, by thousands, are assembling around the devoted victims. The Cherokees, in the mean time, apprized of all that is doing, wait the result of these terrific preparations, with feelings not to be described. . . .

Camp Hetzel, near Cleveland, June 16. The Cherokees are nearly all prisoners. They have been dragged from their houses, and encamped at the forts and military posts, all over the nation. In Georgia, especially, multitudes were allowed no time to take any thing with them, except the clothes they had on. Well-furnished houses were left a prey to plunderers, who like hungry wolves, follow in the train of the captors. These wretches rifle the houses, and strip the helpless, unoffending owners of all they have on earth. Females, who have been habituated to comforts and comparative affluence, are driven on foot before the bayonets of brutal men. Their feelings are mortified by vulgar and profane vociferations. It is a painful sight. The property of many has been taken, and sold before their eyes for almost nothing—the sellers and buyers, in many cases, being combined to cheat the poor Indians. These things are done at the instant of arrest and consternation; the soldiers standing by, with their arms in hand, impatient to go on with their work, could give little time to transact business. The poor captive, in a state of distressing agitation, his weeping wife almost frantic with terror, surrounded by a group of crying, terrified children, without a friend to speak a consoling word, is in a poor condition to make a good disposition of his property, and is in most cases stripped of the whole, at one blow. Many of the Cherokees, who, a few days ago, were in comfortable circumstances, are now victims of abject poverty. Some, who have been allowed to return home, under passport, to inquire after their property, have found their cattle, horses, swine, farming-tools, and house-furniture all gone. And this is not a description of extreme cases. It is altogether a faint representation of the work which has been perpetrated on the unoffending, unarmed and unresisting Cherokees. . . .

It is due to justice to say, that, at this station, (and I learn the same is true of some others,) the officer in command treats his prisoners with great respect and indulgence. But fault rests somewhere. They are prisoners, without a crime to justify the fact. . . .

The principal Cherokees have sent a petition to Gen. Scott, begging most earnestly that they may not be sent off to the west till the sickly season is over. They have not received any answer yet. The agent is shipping them off by multitudes from Ross's Landing. Nine hundred in one detachment, and seven hundred in another, were driven into boats, and it will be a miracle of mercy if one-fourth escape the exposure to that sickly climate. They were exceedingly depressed, and almost in despair.

[July] 11. . . . as soon as General Scott agreed to suspend the transportation of the prisoners till autumn, I accompanied brother Bushy-head, who by permission of the General carried a message from the chiefs to those Cherokees who had evaded the troops by flight to the mountains. We had no difficulty in finding them. They all agreed to come in, on our advice, and surrender themselves to the forces of the United States; though, with the whole nation, they are still as strenuously opposed to the treaty as ever. Their submission, therefore, is not to be viewed as an acquiescence in the principles or the terms of the treaty; but merely as yielding to the physical force of the U. States.

Selection from "Cherokees, Extracts from Letters of Mr. Jones," in *The Baptist Missionary Magazine*, Vol. XVIII. Published by John Putnam, Boston, copyright © 1838.

CRITICAL THINKING

1. What key words in the first paragraph of the selection set the tone of Mr. Jones' letter? Is that tone sustained throughout the letter?
2. List the events that Mr. Jones described in chronological order.
3. What is the main message that the missionary wanted his readers to remember about the "trail of tears"?
4. Speculate about what events might have taken place if the Cherokees had chosen not to surrender to the United States troops.

CHAPTER 12

AMERICAN REFORM MOVEMENTS

1815–1850

1. TRANSCENDENTALIST AMY REED WRITES OF HER EXPERIENCES AT BROOK FARM

The New England Transcendentalists founded several utopian communities, the most famous of which was Brook Farm in Massachusetts. Amy Reed, the writer of the letters below, joined the Transcendentalist community in 1844 and remained there until it disbanded in 1847.

BROOK FARM, Sunday, April 14, '44.
DEAR BROTHER FRANK,

Now my business is as follows (but perhaps liable to frequent change): I wait on the breakfast table (½ hour), help M. A. Ripley clear away breakfast things, etc. (1½ hours), go into the dormitory group till eleven o'clock,—dress for dinner—then over to the Eyrie and sew till dinner time,—half past twelve. Then from half past one or two o'clock until ½ past five, I teach drawing in Pilgrim Hall and sew in the Eyrie. At ½ past five go down to the Hive, to help set the tea table, and afterwards I wash tea cups, etc., till about ½ past seven. Thus I make out a long day of it, but alternation of work and pleasant company and chats make it pleasant. I am about entering a flower garden group and assisting Miss Russell in doing up muslins. I have one very pleasant drawing class, consisting of the young ladies and the young men, José, Martin Cushing, etc. The other class is composed of the children in the regular school. We enjoy ourselves here very well, and I can't but think that after some weeks I shall become perfectly attached to the place—I have felt perfectly at home from the first. We need more leisure, or rather, we should like it. There are so many, and so few women to do the work, that we have to be nearly all the time about it. I can't find time to write till it comes evening, and then we generally assemble in little bands somewhere for a little talk or amusement.

BROOK FARM, Dec. 14, '44.
DEAREST ANNA,

Have I told you about our retrenchment? . . . You know it is one of our rules not to incur any debt, but to pay as we go along—well, we found that we could not be sure of commanding ready money this winter sufficient to pay our expenses, so we agreed to retrench in our table fare, in order to make a saving and come within the means we can command. It was really cheering to see how readily this measure was adopted. We now set one of the long tables in our old style for boarders, scholars and visitors,—and a *few associates* who feel that their *health* requires (!) the use of meat, tea, etc. At the other tables we have no meat, no tea, nor butter, nor sugar. This "retrenchment" has afforded us no little amusement. We are not at a loss for something to eat,—have good potatoes, turnips, squashes, etc., etc., and puddings. At our breakfast table I counted nine different articles this morning; so we can't complain of want of variety.

BROOK FARM, Sunday, Dec. 7, 1845.
MY DEAR ANNA,

You speak of a crisis,—this is one of the things I can't write fully about, and whatever I may say will be confidential. We have reached, I believe, our severest crisis. If we survive it, we shall probably go on safely and not be obliged to struggle thro' another. I think here lies the difficulty,—we have not had business men to conduct our affairs—we have had *no* strictly business transactions from the beginning, and those among us who have some business talents, see this error, and feel that we cannot go on as we have done. They are ready to give up if matters cannot be otherwise managed, for they have no hope of success here under the past and present government. All important matters have been done up in council of one or two or three individuals, and everybody else kept in the dark (perhaps I exaggerated somewhat) and now it must be so no longer;—our young men have started "enquiry meetings," and it must be a sad state of things that calls for such measures. We are perplexed by debts, by want of capital to carry on any business to advantage,—by want of our Phalanstery [the building where members of the community would live] or the means to finish it. From want of wisdom we have failed to profit by some advantages we have had. And then Brisbane is vague and unsteady; the help he promised us from his efforts comes not—but on the contrary, he and other friends to the cause in New York, instead of trying to concentrate all efforts upon Brook Farm as they promised, have wandered off,—have taken up a vast plan of getting $100,000 and starting anew, so they are for disposing of us in the shortest manner,—would set their foot upon us, as it were, and divert what capital might come to us. . . .

My hopes are here; our council seems to be awake and ready for action; if we get the money, we will finish the buildings,—then we will enlarge our school, which should bring us in a handsome income. Our sash and blind business is very profitable, and may be greatly enlarged in the spring, the tailor's business is good, the tin block, and why do I forget the printing, and the Farm? Also we shall have together a better set of people than ever before. Heaven help us, and make us wise, for the failure of Brook Farm must defer the cause a long time. This place as it is (take it all in all) is the best place under the sky; why can't people see this, and look upon it hopefully and encouragingly?

Selection from *The American Reader: From Columbus to Today*, edited by Paul M. Angle. Published by Rand McNally & Company, New York, copyright © 1958.

CRITICAL THINKING

1. In the letter to her brother Frank, Amy Reed describes in some detail her daily routine at Brook Farm. How would you enjoy living in such a community?
2. Does Amy Reed's second letter indicate any strife among the members of the Brook Farm community? Explain what you mean.
3. Brook Farm failed in 1847. What reasons for this failure are suggested in the third letter?

2. PHILOSOPHER HENRY DAVID THOREAU ADDRESSES THE QUESTION OF CIVIL DISOBEDIENCE

In his famous essay "Civil Disobedience," Henry David Thoreau wrote that citizens have a duty to disobey unjust laws of their governments. The ideas expressed in Thoreau's essay had great influence on the actions of such individuals and groups as Gandhi in India, Martin Luther King, Jr., and the civil rights activists in the United States, and anti-nuclear protesters in many countries. In the excerpts from "Civil Disobedience," below, Thoreau describes how he applied his ideas and what happened as a result.

I HEARTILY accept the motto,—"That government is best which governs least"; and I should like to see it acted up to more rapidly and systematically. Carried out, it finally amounts to this, which also I believe,—"That government is best which governs not at all". . . .

This American government,—what is it but a tradition, though a recent one, endeavoring to transmit itself unimpaired to posterity, but each instant losing some of its integrity? It has not the vitality and force of a single living man; for a single man can bend it to his will. . . . this government never of itself furthered any enterprise, but by the alacrity [speed] with which it got out of its way. *It* does not keep the country free. *It* does not settle the West. *It* does not educate. The character inherent in the American people has done all that has been accomplished; and it would have done somewhat more, if the government had not sometimes got in its way. . . .

I have paid no poll-tax for six years. I was put into a jail once on this account, for one night; and, as I stood considering the walls of solid stone, two or three feet thick, the door of wood and iron, a foot thick, and the iron grating which strained the light, I could not help being struck with the foolishness of that institution which treated me as if I were mere flesh and blood and bones, to be locked up. . . . I did not for a moment feel confined, and the walls seemed a great waste of stone and mortar. I felt as if I alone of all my townsmen had paid my tax. They plainly did not know how to treat me, but behaved like persons who are underbred. . . . I saw that the State was halfwitted, that it was timid as a lone-woman with her silver spoons, and that it did not know its friends from its foes, and I lost all my remaining respect for it, and pitied it.

Thus the State never intentionally confronts a man's sense, intellectual or moral, but only his body, his senses. It is not armed with superior wit or honesty, but with superior physical strength. . . .

The night in prison was novel and interesting enough[.] The prisoners in their shirt-sleeves were enjoying a chat and the evening air in the doorway, when I entered. But the jailer said, "Come, boys, it is time to lock up"; and so they dispersed, and I heard the sound of their steps returning into the hollow apartments. My room-mate was introduced to me by the jailer, as "a first-rate fellow and a clever man." When the door was locked, he showed me where to hang my hat, and how he managed matters there. The rooms were whitewashed once a month; and this one, at least, was the whitest, most simply furnished, and probably the neatest apartment in the town. He naturally wanted to know where I came from, and what brought me there; and, when I had told him, I asked him in my turn how he came there, presuming him to be an honest man of course; and, as the world goes, I believe he was. "Why," said he, "they accuse me of burning a barn; but I never did it." As near as I could discover, he had probably gone to bed in a barn when drunk, and smoked his pipe there; and so a barn was burnt. He had the reputation of being a clever man, had been there some three months waiting for his trial to come on, and would have to wait as much longer; but he was quite domesticated and con-tented, since he got his board for nothing, and thought that he was well treated.

He occupied one window, and I the other; and I saw, that, if one stayed here long, his principal business would be to look out the window. . . .

When I came out of prison,—for some one interfered, and paid that tax,—I did not perceive that great changes had taken place on the com-mon, such as he observed who went in a youth, and emerged a tottering and gray-headed man; and yet a change had to my eyes come over the scene,—the town, and State, and country,—greater than any that mere time could effect. I saw yet more distinctly the State in which I lived. I saw

to what extent the people among whom I lived could be trusted as good neighbors and friends; that their friendship was for summer weather only; that they did not greatly propose to do right; that they were a distinct race from me by their prejudices and superstitions, as the Chinamen and Malays are; that, in their sacrifices to humanity, they ran no risks, not even to their property; that, after all, they were not so noble but they treated the thief as he had treated them, and hoped, by a certain outward observance and a few prayers, and by walking in a particular straight though useless path from time to time, to save their souls. This may be to judge my neighbors harshly; for I believe that many of them are not aware that they have such an institution as the jail in their village. . . .

The authority of government, even such as I am willing to submit to,—for I will cheerfully obey those who know and can do better than I, and in many things even those who neither know nor can do so well,—is still an impure one: to be strictly just, it must have the sanction and consent of the governed. It can have no pure right over my person and property but what I concede to it. The progress from an absolute to a limited monarchy, from a limited monarchy to a democracy, is a progress toward a true respect for the individual. Even the Chinese philosopher was wise enough to regard the individual as the basis of the empire. Is a democracy, such as we know it, the last improve-ment possible in government? Is it not possible to take a step further towards recognizing and orga-nizing the rights of man? There will never be a really free and enlightened State, until the State comes to recognize the individual as a higher and independent power, from which all its own power and authority are derived, and treats him accord-ingly. I please myself with imagining a State at last which can afford to be just to all men, and to treat the individual with respect as a neighbor; which even would not think it inconsistent with its own repose, if a few were to live aloof from it, not meddling with it, nor embraced by it, who fulfilled all the duties of neighbors and fellow-men. A State which bore this kind of fruit, and suffered it to drop off as fast as it ripened, would prepare the way for a still more perfect and glorious State, which also I have imagined, but not yet anywhere seen.

Selection from Henry D. Thoreau, "Civil Disobedience" in *A Yankee in Canada, with Anti-slavery and Reform Papers.* Published by Greenwood Press, Publishers, New York, copyright © 1969.

Dorthea Dix spent her life fighting for better treatment of the mentally ill.

CRITICAL THINKING

1. How did Henry Thoreau apply his ideas on civil disobedience in his own life and what was the result? Do you think Thoreau's action was effective? Why or why not?
2. When they were being tried for war crimes after World War II, Nazi leaders defended themselves by saying they were following the orders of their government. How would Thoreau have responded to this defense?

3. DORTHEA DIX PLEADS THE PLIGHT OF THE MENTALLY ILL

Dorothea Dix was one of the most effective of the evangelical reformers of the nineteenth century. In 1843, at a time when women were discouraged from playing roles in public life, she had the courage to go before the Massachusetts legislature to plead the plight of the mentally ill. Parts of her address are given below.

Gentlemen,—I respectfully ask to present this Memorial, believing that the *cause*, which actuates to and sanctions so unusual a movement, presents no equivocal claim to public consideration and sympathy. Surrendering to calm and deep convictions of duty my habitual views of what is womanly and becoming, I proceed briefly to explain what has conducted me before you unsolicited and unsustained, trusting, while I do so, that the memorialist will be speedily forgotten in the memorial.

About two years since leisure afforded opportunity and duty prompted me to visit several prisons and almshouses in the vicinity of this metropolis. I found, near Boston, in the jails and asylums for the poor, a numerous class brought into unsuitable connection with criminals and the general mass of paupers. I refer to idiots and insane persons, dwelling in circumstances not only adverse to their own physical and moral improvement, but productive of extreme disadvantages to all other persons brought into association with them. I applied myself diligently to trace the causes of these evils, and sought to supply remedies. . . . I shall be obliged to speak with great plainness, and to reveal many things revolting to the taste. . . . But truth is the highest consideration. *I tell what I have seen*—painful and shocking as the details often are—that from them you may feel more deeply the imperative obligation which lies upon you to prevent the possibility of a repetition or continuance of such outrages upon humanity. . . .

I come to present the strong claims of suffering humanity. . . . I come as the advocate of helpless, forgotten, insane, and idiotic men and women. . . .

I proceed, gentlemen, briefly to call your attention to the *present* state of insane persons confined within this Commonwealth, in *cages, closets, cellars, stalls, pens! Chained, naked, beaten with rods,* and *lashed* into obedience. . . .

. . . I would speak as kindly as possible of all wardens, keepers, and other responsible officers, believing that *most* of these have erred not through hardness of heart and wilful cruelty so much as want of skill and knowledge, and want of consideration. . . .

Springfield. In the jail, one lunatic woman, furiously mad, a State pauper, improperly situated, both in regard to the prisoners, the keepers, and herself. It is a case of extreme self-forgetfulness and oblivion to all the decencies of life, to describe which would be to repeat only the grossest scenes. She is much worse since leaving Worcester. In the almshouse of the same town is a woman apparently only needing judicious care, and some well-chosen employment, to make it unnecessary to confine her in solitude, in a dreary unfurnished room. Her appeals for employment and companionship are most touching, but the mistress replied "she had no time to attend to her."

Northampton. In the jail, quite lately, was a young man violently mad, who had not, as I was informed at the prison, come under medical care, and not been returned from any hospital. In the almshouse the cases of insanity are now unmarked by abuse, and afford evidence of judicious care by the keepers.

Williamsburg. The almshouse has several insane, not under suitable treatment. No apparent intentional abuse. . . .

Burlington. A woman, declared to be very insane; decent room and bed; but not allowed to rise oftener, the mistress said, "than every other day: it is too much trouble." . . .

Lincoln. A woman in a cage. *Medford.* One idiotic subject chained, and one in a close stall for seventeen years. *Pepperell.* One often doubly chained, hand and foot; another violent; several peaceable now. *Brookfield.* One man caged, comfortable. *Granville.* One often closely confined; now losing the use of his limbs from want of exercise. . . .

Besides the above, I have seen many who, part of the year, are chained or caged. The use of cages all but universal. Hardly a town but can refer to some not distant period of using them; chains are less common; negligences frequent; wilful abuse less frequent than sufferings proceeding from ignorance, or want of consideration. I encountered during the last three months many poor creatures wandering reckless and unprotected through the country. . . .

Men of Massachusetts, I beg, I implore, I demand pity and protection for these. . . . Fathers, husbands, brothers, I would supplicate you for this boon; but what do I say? I dishonor you, divest you at once of Christianity and humanity, does this appeal imply distrust. If it comes burdened with a doubt of your righteousness in this legislation, then blot it out; while I declare confidence in your honor, not less than your humanity. Here you will put away the cold, calculating spirit of selfishness and self-seeking; lay off the armor of local strife and political opposition; here and now, for once, forgetful of the earthly and perishable, come up to these halls and consecrate them with one heart and one mind to works of righteousness and just judgment. Become the benefactors of your race, and just guardians of the solemn rights you hold in trust. Raise up the fallen, succor the desolate, restore the outcast, defend the helpless, and for your eternal and great reward receive the benediction, "Well done, good and faithful servants, become rulers over many things!" . . .

It is not few, but many, it is not a part, but the whole, who bear unqualified testimony to this evil. A voice strong and deep comes up from every almshouse and prison in Massachusetts where the insane are or have been protesting against such evils as have been illustrated in the preceding pages.

Gentlemen, I commit to you this sacred cause. Your action upon this subject will affect the present and future condition of hundreds and of thousands.

In this legislation, as in all things, may you exercise that "wisdom which is the breath of the power of God."

Respectfully submitted,

D. L. DIX.

85 MT. VERNON STREET, BOSTON.
January, 1843.

Selection excerpted from Old South Leaflet No. 148, in *Old South Leaflets*, Vol. VI. Published by Directors of the Old South Work, Old South Meeting House, Boston, undated.

CRITICAL THINKING

1. Judging from Dorthea Dix's testimony, what attitude does she seem to be exhibiting toward the mentally ill? Toward the persons responsible for their care?
2. In what way was Dix's appearance before the Massachusetts legislature unusual?

4. ABRAHAM LINCOLN EXPRESSES HIS OPINION ABOUT THE "KNOW-NOTHINGS"

Abraham Lincoln's political star was on the rise at the time the Know-Nothings were preaching opposition to Irish and other Catholic immigrants. Lincoln's feelings about the Know-Nothings are clearly expressed in a letter he wrote to an old friend, Joshua Speed, in 1855. Part of that letter is reproduced here.

I am not a Know-Nothing. That is certain. How could I be? How can any one who abhors the oppression of negroes, be in favor of degrading classes of white people? Our progress in degeneracy appears to me to be pretty rapid. As a nation, we began by declaring that "*all men are created equal.*" We now practically read it "all men are created equal, *except negroes.*" When the Know-Nothings get control, it will read "all men are created equal, except negroes, and *foreigners, and catholics.*" When it comes to this I should prefer emigrating to some country where they make no pretence of loving liberty—to Russia, for instance, where despotism can be taken pure, and without the base alloy of hypocracy.

Mary [Lincoln] will probably pass a day or two in Louisville in October. My kindest regards to Mrs. Speed. On the leading subject of this letter, I have more of her sympathy than I have of yours.

And yet let [me] say I am   Your friend forever

A. Lincoln—

Selection from *The Collected Works of Abraham Lincoln*, Vol. II, edited by Roy P. Basler. Published by Rutgers University Press, New Brunswick, New Jersey, copyright © 1953.

CRITICAL THINKING

1. What American document is Abraham Lincoln quoting from in the sentence beginning "As a nation . . ."?
2. What "hypocracy" (hypocrisy) does Lincoln see in the position of the Know-Nothings?
3. How do you interpret Lincoln's statements about negroes?

5. SARAH GRIMKE SUGGESTS REASONS FOR THE SITUATION WOMEN FOUND THEMSELVES IN DURING THE 1800s

The Seneca Falls Convention of 1848 was not an isolated event. It was a culmination of years of public discussion about the need to improve the position of women who lived in the first half of the 1800s. For example, a Boston newspaper reprinted a letter written in 1837 by Sarah Grimke to her sister Angelina. Both women were deeply involved not only in the women's movement but also in the antislavery movement. In the excerpts from her letter that follow, Sarah Grimke suggests reasons why the minds of many women of her time were "crushed" and their reasoning powers almost "wholly uncultivated."

LETTER X.
INTALLECT OF WOMAN.

Brookline, 8th Mo. 1837.

MY DEAR SISTER,—It will scarcely be denied, I presume, that, as a general rule, men do not desire the improvement of women. There are few . . . men . . . magnamimous enough to be entirely willing that women should know more than themselves, on any subjects except dress and cookery; and, indeed, this necessarily flows from their assumption of superiority. As *they* have determined that Jehovah has placed woman on a lower platform than man, they of course wish to keep her there; and hence the noble faculties of our minds are crushed, and our reasoning powers are almost wholly uncultivated.

A writer in the time of Charles I. [King of England] says—'She that knoweth how to compound a pudding, is more desirable than she who skilfully compounded a poem. A female poet I mislike at all times.' Within the last century, it has been gravely asserted that, 'chemistry enough to keep the pot boiling, and geography enough to know the location of the different rooms in her house, is learning sufficient for a woman.' Byron [an English poet] who was too sensual to conceive of a pure and perfect companionship between the sexes, would limit a woman's library to a Bible and cookery book. I have myself heard men, who knew for themselves the value of intellectual culture, say they cared very little for a wife who could not make a pudding, and smile with contempt at the ardent thirst for knowledge exhibited by some women.

But all this is miserable wit and worse philosophy. It exhibits that passion for the gratification of a pampered appetite, which is beneath those who claim to be so far above us, and may justly be placed on a par with the policy of the slaveholder, who says that men will be better slaves, if they are not permitted to learn to read.

In spite, however, of the obstacles which impede the progress of women towards that state of high mental cultivation for which her Creator prepared her, the tendency towards the universal dissemination of knowledge has had its influence on their destinies; and in all ages, a few have surmounted every hindrance, and proved, beyond dispute, that they have talents equal to their brethren. . . .

Woman, in all ages and countries, has been the scoff and jest of her lordly master. If she attempted, like him, to improve her mind, she was ridiculed as pedantic, and driven from the temple of science and liturature by coarse attacks and vulgar sarcasms. . . .

. . . This reminds me of a remark made by my brother, Thomas S. Grimke, when speaking of the importance of women being well educated, that 'educated men would never make educated women, but educated women would make educated men.' I believe the sentiment is correct, because if the wealth of latent intellect among women was fully evolved and improved, they would rejoice to communicate to their sons all their own knowledge, and inspire them with desires to drink from the fountain of literature.

I pass over many interesting proofs of the intellectual powers of women; but I must not omit glancing at the age of chivalry, which has been compared to a golden thread running through the dark ages. During this remarkable era, women who, before this period, had been subject to every species of oppression and neglect, were suddenly elevated into deities, and worshipped with a mad fanaticism. It is not improbable, however, that even the absurdities of chivalry were beneficial to women, as it raised them from that extreme degradation to which they had been condemned, and prepared the way for them to be permitted to enjoy some scattered rays from the sun of science

and literature. As the age of knight-errantry declined. . . . Women preached in public, supported controversies, published and defended theses, filled the chairs of philosophy and law, harangued the popes in Latin, wrote Greek and read Hebrew. Nuns wrote poetry, women of rank became divines, and young girls publicly exhorted Christian princes to take up arms for the recovery of the holy sepulchre. . . . in England the names of many women, from Lady Jane Gray down to Harriet Martineau, are familiar to every reader in history. Of the last mentioned authoress, Lord Brougham said that her writings on political economy were doing more good than those of any man in England. . . . France has produced many distinguished women, whose names are familiar to every lover of literature. And I believe it is conceded universally, that Madame de Stael was intellectually the greatest woman that ever lived. The United States have produced several female writers, some of whom have talents of the highest order. But women, even in this free republic, do not enjoy *all* the intellectual advantages of men, although there is a perceptible improvement within the last ten or twenty years; and I trust there is a desire awakened in my sisters for solid acquirements, which will elevate them to their 'appropriate sphere,' . . .

Thine in the bonds of womanhood,

SARAH M. GRIMKE.

Selection from *The Liberator*, January 26, 1838.

CRITICAL THINKING

1. What reason does Sarah Grimke offer as the chief reason for the intellectual state of the woman of her time? Support your answer with references to parts of her letter.
2. What comparison does Grimke make between the position of slaves and the position of women?
3. Name some of the present-day successors to Grimke and other early leaders of the women's movement. What ideas have these present-day leaders brought up for public discussion, and with what results?

JOHN JAMES AUDUBON

John James Audubon [1785–1851] came to Philadelphia from France when he was 18 and became one of the first American naturalists. Following his early passion for sketching birds and nature, Audubon trekked through the woods of America drawing wildlife.

In 1820, leaving Kentucky and setting off on a flatboat down the Mississippi, he began to concentrate on birds in their natural surroundings. His later work as a taxidermist at the Western Museum in Cincinnati, Ohio, helped him render bird species with accurate detail. He also hunted birds and used the specimens for study.

Audubon intended to publish a collection of his watercolors and call it *Birds of America*. By the time he was 42, he had drawn over 400 paintings of birds. Some ornithologists have criticized the exaggerated configurations of his birds. Art lovers, however, appreciated the work's drama and design. Many colored engravings of the watercolors were made in England to satisfy the demand of Audubon's enthusiastic followers.

Passenger pigeons once numbered in the millions. They were killed for sport and for food. The last passenger pigeon died in a zoo in 1914 and the specie became extinct. Their beauty is preserved in this Audubon painting.

Audubon painted this nesting pair of barn swallows. He paid close attention to the appearance and construction of the swallows' nest.

Behind the Snowy Heron, painted by Audubon, is a South Carolina rice plantation drawn by a Swiss artist who traveled through the South with Audubon in 1831. Audubon sometimes hired assistants to finish the painting of his watercolors.

CRITICAL THINKING

1. Why was Audubon's contribution to natural science so important?
2. From the richly-colored picture of the barn swallow where do you think the nest is located and what do you think it is made of?
3. Comprise a list of skills, other than painting, that might have helped Audubon with his work.

143

Division and Reunion

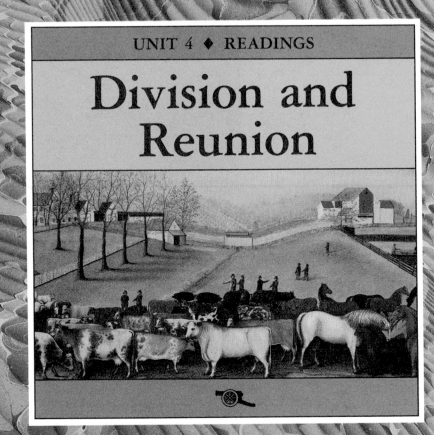

CHAPTER 13

THE SOUTH AND SLAVERY

1820–1860

1. FORMER SLAVE SOLOMON NORTHUP TELLS HIS STORY

In spite of claims to the contrary, some slaves led extremely difficult lives with very few bright spots. In the excerpts from his book below, Solomon Northup gives his recollections of life in bondage. For Northup, being a slave was especially hard. He was a free black who was kidnapped from his home in New York in 1841 and sold into slavery in the South. After 12 years he was eventually returned to freedom. The excerpts reveal the deep mark that life as a slave left on the man.

In the latter part of August begins the cotton picking season. At this time each slave is presented with a sack. A strap is fastened to it, which goes over the neck, holding the mouth of the sack breast high, while the bottom reaches nearly to the ground. Each one is also presented with a large basket that will hold about two barrels. This is to put the cotton in when the sack is filled. The baskets are carried to the field and placed at the beginning of the rows.

When a new hand, one unaccustomed to the business, is sent for the first time into the field, he is whipped up smartly, and made for that day to pick as fast as he can possibly. At night it is weighed, so that his capability in cotton picking is known. He must bring in the same weight each night following. If it falls short, it is considered evidence that he has been laggard, and a greater or less number of lashes is the penalty.

An ordinary day's work is considered two hundred pounds. A slave who is accustomed to picking, is punished, if he or she brings in a less quantity than that. There is a great difference among them as regards this kind of labor. Some of them seem to have a natural knack, or quickness, which enables them to pick with great celerity, and with both hands, while others, with whatever practice or industry, are utterly unable to come up

to the ordinary standard. Such hands are taken from the cotton field and employed in other business. . . .

The hands are required to be in the cotton fields as soon as it is light in the morning, and, with the exception of ten or fifteen minutes, which is given them at noon to swallow their allowance of cold bacon, they are not permitted to be a moment idle until it is too dark to see, and when the moon is full, they often times labor till the middle of the night. They do not dare to stop even at dinner time, nor return to the quarters, however late it be, until the order to halt is given by the driver.

The day's work over in the field, the baskets are "toted," or in other words, carried to the gin-house, where the cotton is weighed. No matter how fatigued and weary he may be—no matter how much he longs for sleep and rest—a slave never approaches the gin-house with his basket of cotton but with fear. If it falls short in weight—if he has not performed the full task appointed him, he knows that he must suffer. . . . After weighing, follow the whippings; and then the baskets are carried to the cotton house, and their contents stored away like hay, all hands being sent in to tramp it down. . . .

This done, the labor of the day is not yet ended, by any means. Each one must then attend to his respective chores. One feeds the mules, another the swine—another cuts the wood, and so forth; besides, the packing is all done by candle light. Finally, at a late hour, they reach the quarters, sleepy and overcome with the long day's toil. Then a fire must be kindled in the cabin, the corn ground in the small hand-mill, and supper, and dinner for the next day in the field, prepared. All that is allowed them is corn and bacon, which is given out at the corncrib and smoke-house every Sunday morning. Each one receives, as his weekly allowance, three and a half pounds of bacon, and corn enough to make a peck of meal. That is all—no tea, coffee, sugar, and with the exception of a very scanty sprinkling now and then, no salt. . . . Master Epps' hogs were fed on *shelled* corn—it was thrown out to his "niggers" in the ear. The [hogs] he thought, would fatten faster by shelling, and soaking it in the water—the [slaves], perhaps, if treated in the same manner, might grow too fat to labor. . . .

When the corn is ground, and fire is made, the

bacon is taken down from the nail on which it hangs, a slice cut off and thrown upon the coals to broil. The majority of slaves have no knife, much less a fork. They cut their bacon with the axe at the woodpile. The corn meal is mixed with a little water, placed in the fire, and baked. When it is "done brown," the ashes are scraped off, and being placed upon a chip, which answers for a table, the tenant of the slave hut is ready to sit down upon the ground to supper. By this time it is usually midnight. The same fear of punishment with which they approach the gin-house, possesses them again on lying down to get a snatch of rest. It is the fear of oversleeping in the morning. Such an offence would certainly be attended with not less than twenty lashes. With a prayer that he may be on his feet and wide awake at the first sound of the horn, he sinks to his slumbers nightly.

The softest couches in the world are not to be found in the log mansion of the slave. The one whereon I reclined year after year, was a plank twelve inches wide and ten feet long. My pillow was a stick of wood. The bedding was a coarse blanket, and not a rag or shred beside. Moss might be used, were it not that it directly breeds a swarm of fleas.

The cabin is constructed of logs, without floor or window. The latter is altogether unnecessary, the crevices between the logs admitting sufficient light. In stormy weather the rain drives through them, rendering it comfortless and extremely disagreeable. The rude door hangs on great wooden hinges. In one end is constructed an awkward fire-place.

An hour before day light the horn is blown. Then the slaves arouse, prepare their breakfast, fill a gourd with water, in another deposit their dinner of cold bacon and corn cake, and hurry to the field again. It is an offence invariably followed by a flogging, to be found at the quarters after day-break. . . .

Ploughing, planting, picking cotton, gathering the corn, and pulling and burning stalks, occupies the whole of the four seasons of the year. Drawing and cutting wood, pressing cotton, fattening and killing hogs, are but incidental labors. . . .

It was rarely that a day passed by without one or more whippings. This occurred at the time the cotton was weighed. The delinquent, whose weight had fallen short, was taken out, stripped, made to lie upon the ground, face downwards, when he received a punishment proportioned to his offense. It is the literal, unvarnished truth, that the crack of the lash, and the shrieking of the slaves, can be heard from dark till bed time, on Epps' plantation, any day almost during the entire period of the cotton-picking season.

The number of lashes is graduated according to the nature of the case. Twenty-five are deemed a mere brush, inflicted, for instance, when a dry leaf or piece of boll is found in the cotton, or when a branch is broken in the field; fifty is the ordinary penalty following all delinquencies of the next higher grade; one hundred is called severe; it is the punishment inflicted for the serious offence of standing idle in the field; from one hundred and fifty to two hundred is bestowed upon him who quarrels with his cabin-mates, and five hundred, well laid on, besides the mangling of the dogs, perhaps is certain to consign the poor, unpitied runaway to weeks of pain and agony. . . .

The only respite from constant labor the slave has through the whole year, is during the Christmas holidays. Epps allowed us three—others allow four, five and six days, according to the measure of their generosity. It is the only time to which they look forward with any interest or pleasure. They are glad when night comes, not only because it brings them a few hours repose, but because it brings them one day nearer Christmas. . . . It is the time of feasting, and frolicking, and fiddling— the carnival season with the children of bondage. They are the only days when they are allowed a little restricted liberty, and heartily indeed do they enjoy it.

It is the custom for one planter to give a "Christmas supper," inviting the slaves from neighboring plantations to join his own on the occasion; for instance, one year it is given by Epps, the next by Marshall, the next by Hawkins, and so on. Usually from three to five hundred are assembled, coming together on foot, in carts, on horseback, on mules, riding double and triple, sometimes a boy and girls, at others a girl and two boys, and at others again a boy, a girl and an old woman. . . .

The table is spread in the open air, and loaded with varieties of meat and piles of vegetables. Bacon and corn meal at such times are dispensed with. Sometimes the cooking is performed in the kitchen on the plantation, at others in the shade of wide branching trees. In the latter case, a ditch is dug in the ground, and wood laid in and burned until it is filled with glowing coals, over which chickens, ducks, turkeys, pigs, and not unfrequently the entire body of a wild ox are roasted. They are furnished also with flour, of which biscuits are made, and often with peach and other preserves, with tarts, and every manner and description of pies, except the mince, that being an article of pastry as yet unknown among them. Only the slave who has lived all the years on his scanty allowance of meal and bacon, can appreciate such suppers. White people in great numbers assemble to witness the gastronomical enjoyments.

They seat themselves at the rustic table—the males on one side, the females on the other. The two between whom there may have been an exchange of tenderness, invariably manage to sit opposite; for the omnipresent Cupid disdains not to hurl his arrows into the simple hearts of slaves. Unalloyed and exulting happiness lights up the dark faces of them all. The ivory teeth, contrasting with their black complexions, exhibit two long, white streaks the whole extent of the table. All round the bountiful board a multitude of eyes roll in ecstacy. Giggling and laughter and the clattering of cutlery and crockery succeed . . . and so the fun and merriment flow on.

When the viands have disappeared, and the hungry maws of the children of toil are satisfied, then, next in the order of amusement, is the Christmas dance. My business on these gala days always was to play on the violin. . . .

During the remaining holidays succeeding Christmas, they are provided with passes, and permitted to go where they please within a limited distance, or they may remain and labor on the plantation, in which case they are paid for it. It is very rarely, however, that the latter alternative is accepted. . . . Such is "southern life as it is," *three days in the year*, as I found it—the other three hundred and sixty-two being days of weariness, and fear, and suffering, and unremitting labor.

Selection from Solomon Northup, *Twelve Years a Slave*, edited by Sue Eakin and Joseph Logsdon. Published by Louisiana State University Press, Baton Rouge, Louisiana, copyright © 1968.

CRITICAL THINKING

1. According to Solomon Northup, what emotion dominated his life as a slave? Do you think this emotion was justified? Why or why not?
2. In describing his memories of Epps, what picture of "masters" or slaveowners does Northrup present? What is the predominant tone of his recollections?
3. Which part of Northup's narrative touched you most? Why?

2. JOSIAH HENSON RECALLS THE DAY HIS FAMILY WAS SOLD

Josiah Henson was a slave who escaped from Kentucky to freedom in Canada in 1830. After his escape, Henson became a preacher, a community leader, and worker in the Underground Railroad. He also wrote a book describing his experiences as a slave. Excerpts from his book appear below. A preface by Harriet Beecher Stowe was written for the first edition of Henson's book. Indeed, Mrs. Stowe is said to have based Uncle Tom, the main character of her famous novel, on some of Henson's experience.

" A nigger [Henson's father] has struck a white man;" that is enough to set a whole county on fire; no question is asked about the provocation. The authorities were soon in pursuit of my father. . . . And the penalty followed: one hundred lashes on the bare back, and to have the right ear nailed to the whipping-post, and then severed from the body. For a time my father kept out of the way, hiding in the woods, and at night venturing into some cabin in search of food. But at length the strict watch set baffled all his efforts. His supplies cut off, he was fairly starved out, and compelled by hunger to come back and give himself up.

The day for the execution of the penalty was appointed. The negroes from the neighboring plantations were summoned, for their moral improvement, to witness the scene. A powerful blacksmith named Hewes laid on the stripes. Fifty were given, during which the cries of my father might be heard a mile, and then a pause ensued.

True, he had struck a white man, but as valuable property he must not be damaged. Judicious men felt his pulse. Oh! he could stand the whole. Again and again the thong fell on his lacerated back. His cries grew fainter and fainter, till a feeble groan was the only response to the final blows. His head was then thrust against the post, and his right ear fastened to it with a tack; a swift pass of a knife, and the bleeding member was left sticking to the place. Then came a hurra from the degraded crowd, and the exclamation, "That's what he's got for striking a white man." A few said, "it's a [great] shame;" but the majority regarded it as but a proper tribute. . . .

For two or three years my mother and her young family of six children had resided on this estate; and we had been in the main very happy. She was a good mother to us . . . .

Our term of happy union as one family was now, alas! at an end. Mournful as was the [master's] death to his friends it was a far greater calamity to us. The estate and the slaves must be sold and the proceeds divided among the heirs. We were but property. . . .

Common as are slave-auctions in the southern states, and naturally as a slave may look forward to the time when he will be put up on the block, still the full misery of the event . . . is never understood till the actual experience comes. The first sad announcement that the sale is to be; the knowledge that all ties of the past are to be sundered; the frantic terror at the idea of being sent "down south;" the almost certainty that one member of a family will be torn from another; the anxious scanning of purchasers' faces; the agony at parting, often forever, with husband, wife, child— these must be seen and felt to be fully understood. . . . The crowd collected around the stand, the huddling group of negroes, the examination of muscle, teeth, the exhibition of agility, the look of the auctioneer, the agony of my mother—I can shut my eyes and see them all.

My brothers and sisters were bid off first and one by one, while my mother, paralyzed by grief, held me by the hand. Her turn came, and she was bought by Isaac Riley of Montgomery county. Then I was offered to the assembled purchasers. My mother, half distracted with the thought of parting forever from all her children, pushed through the crowd, while the bidding for me was going on, to the spot where Riley was standing. She fell at his feet, and clung to his knees, entreating him in tones that a mother only could command, to buy her *baby* as well as herself and spare to her one, at least, of her little ones. Will it, can it be believed that this man, thus appealed to, was capable not merely of turning a deaf ear to her supplication, but of disengaging himself from her with such violent blows and kicks, as to reduce her to the necessity of creeping out of his reach, and mingling the groan of bodily suffering with the sob of a breaking heart? . . . I must have been then between five and six years old. . . .

I was bought by a stranger named Robb, and truly a robber he was to me. He took me to his home, about forty miles distant, and put me into his negro quarters with about forty others, of all ages, colors, and conditions, all strangers to me. Of course nobody cared for me. The slaves were brutalized by this degradation, and had no sympathy for me. I soon fell sick, and lay for some days almost dead on the ground. Sometimes a slave would give me a piece of corn bread or a bit of herring. Finally I became so feeble that I could not move. This, however, was fortunate for me; for in the course of a few weeks Robb met Riley, who had bought my mother, and offered to sell me to him cheap. Riley said he was afraid "the little devil would die," and he did not want to buy a "dead nigger;" but he agreed, finally, to pay a small sum for me in horse-shoeing if I lived, and nothing if I died. Robb was a tavern keeper, and owned a line of stages with the horses, and lived near Montgomery court-house; Riley carried on blacksmithing about five miles from the place. This clenched the bargain, and I was soon sent to my mother. A blessed change it was. I had been lying on a lot of rags thrown on a dirt floor. All day long I had been left alone, crying for water, crying for mother; the slaves, who all left at daylight, when they returned caring nothing for me. Now, I was once more with my best friend on earth, and under her care; destitute as she was of the proper means of nursing me, I recovered my health and grew to be an uncommonly vigorous boy and man. . . .

Selection from Josiah Henson, *Truth Stranger Than Fiction: Father Henson's Story of His Own Life*. Published by John P. Jewett and Company, Boston, copyright © 1858. Reprinted by Corinth Books, New York, copyright © 1962.

CRITICAL THINKING

1. Comment on the punishment Josiah Henson's father received for striking a white man. Why do you think southern whites imposed such a penalty for blacks who committed this act?
2. If you were a northern abolitionist, how would Henson's account of the slave auction affect you? Would it move you to action? Explain what you mean.

3. UNDERGROUND RAILROADMAN WILLIAM STILL REMEMBERS THE COURAGE OF HARRIET TUBMAN

William Still worked for 14 years at one of the stations of the Underground Railroad in Philadelphia. During that time, he kept a complete record of the runaway slaves that passed through his station. In one of the accounts in his record, he reveals that one of the fleeing slaves he helped was his own brother, from whom he was separated since they both were children. In the account below, Still reminisces about a meeting with Harriet Tubman when she brought six runaways to his station.

Harriet Tubman had been . . . "Moses" [to six runaway slaves she brought to Still]. . . . She had faithfully gone down into Egypt, and had delivered these six bondmen by her own heroism. Harriet was a woman of no pretensions, indeed, a more ordinary specimen of humanity could hardly be found among the most unfortunate-looking farm hands of the South. Yet, in point of courage, shrewdness and disinterested exertions to rescue her fellow-men, by making personal visits to Maryland among the slaves, she was without her equal.

Her success was wonderful. Time and again she made successful visits to Maryland on the Underground Rail Road, and would be absent for weeks at a time, running daily risks while making preparations for herself and passengers. Great fears were entertained for her safety, but she seemed wholly devoid of personal fear. The idea of being captured by slave-hunters or slave-holders, seemed never to enter her mind. She was apparently proof against all adversaries. While she thus manifested such utter personal indifference, she was much more watchful with regard to those she was piloting. Half of her time, she had the appearance of one asleep, and would actually sit down by the road-side and go fast asleep when on her errands of mercy through the South, yet, she would not suffer one of her party to whimper once, about "giving out and going back," however wearied they might be from hard travel day and night. She had a very short and pointed rule or law of her own, which implied death to any who talked of giving out and going back. Thus, in an emergency she would give all to understand that "times were very critical and therefore no foolishness would be indulged in on the road." That several who were rather weak-kneed and faint-hearted were greatly invigorated by Harriet's blunt and positive manner and threat of extreme measures, there could be no doubt.

After having once enlisted, "they had to go through or die." Of course Harriet was supreme, and her followers generally had full faith in her, and would back up any word she might utter. So when she said to them that "a live runaway could do great harm by going back, but that a dead one could tell no secrets," she was sure to have obedience. Therefore, none had to die as traitors on the "middle passage." It is obvious enough, however, that her success in going into Maryland as she did, was attributable to her adventurous spirit and utter disregard of consequences. Her like it is probable was never known before or since.

Selection from William Still, *The Underground Railroad*. Published by Porter & Coates, Philadelphia, 1872. (Reprinted by Arno Press and The New York Times), New York, copyright © 1968.

CRITICAL THINKING

1. William Still describes Harriet Tubman as a very "ordinary specimen of humanity." Do you think her appearance was an advantage in doing her work? Explain what you mean.
2. How did Harriet Tubman keep the runaways moving in times of danger or when they became fainthearted? Explain your reaction to the method she used.

WILLIAM SIDNEY MOUNT

William Sidney Mount [1807–1868] painted scenes of American life in the years between 1835 and 1860, when the United States was still largely a land of farmers. His paintings show the citizens of a hardworking nation enjoying the prosperity and optimism of their new democracy.

Mount's paintings echo the values of the Age of Jackson. Painted scenes of everyday rural life become popular sources for magazine illustrations, which were also bought by the rapidly growing middle class.

Later in the century, with the growth of industry and the emergence of cities, factories and cities replace rural America as the center of American life. But in Mount's paintings, country people are seen enjoying their homemade amusements of music, dance, and conversation. The trauma of the War had not yet forced them to connect with the national crisis beyond their communities.

Mount is particularly interesting for his warm and dignified portrayal of black Americans. He shows blacks who are a part of the rural world but who are not totally included. Although the comment is subtle, it is possible to see it as a foreshadowing of the conflict that would nearly destroy the young country and bring an end to its innocence.

William Mount's painting, "Long Island Farmer Husking Corn," epitomizes the independent, prosperous American of the nineteenth century. Haymakers (below) are celebrating the harvest with an energetic and simple dance.

Mount often included portraits of blacks in his scenes of rural life before the Civil War. His painting, "Eel Spearing at Setauket," is based on one of his own childhood experiences.

CRITICAL THINKING

1. Mount's painting, "Long Island Farmer Husking Corn," appeared on engraved currency in ten different states. Cite reasons why this image of the American farmer might have been chosen.
2. The industrial revolution began in the mid 1800s. As documents, why are these paintings important?
3. Why do you think that harvest time was depicted as a joyous celebration?

William Lloyd Garrison
Attacks Slavery Through *The Liberator*

Before 1830, most debates about slavery were relatively calm and cautious. Both supporters of slavery and those who opposed it usually discussed the *wisdom* of slavery rather than its *morality*. That is, they asked whether it was a good idea to own slaves, rather than whether slavery was right or wrong. Even blacks who wanted slavery abolished, such as the astronomer and mathematician, Benjamin Banneker, expressed their point of view in cool, logical terms.

Then, in 1831, a new kind of newspaper began publishing anti-slavery articles. Using borrowed money and a borrowed printing press, William Lloyd Garrison launched *The Liberator*. The newspaper was devoted to collecting stories of horrible cruelty towards slaves, fierce attacks on the immorality of slavery, and—this was an important new development—personal attacks on individual slaveowners. To Garrison, any person who owned slaves, no matter how fair and kind he

tried to be, was so evil that there could be no calm argument with him. Each slaveowner was the enemy, to be attacked relentlessly by moral people.

Many white southerners, even those who disliked the institution of slavery, protested that Garrison wanted to start a slave rebellion that would bathe the South in blood. *The Liberator* was banned from the South. Some states offered a reward for anyone who could bring Garrison to trial. Just as Garrison refused to discuss the issue of slavery with any slaveowners, many southern whites now refused to listen to any critics, including moderates.

Garrison was not popular in the North either. In fact, a Boston mob nearly hanged him. Nevertheless, by keeping up his attacks, Garrison strengthened those people who were against slavery and probably helped the anti-slavery movement to grow. He was also a supporter of equal rights for women, temperance in the drinking of alcohol, and pacifism.

*D*uring my recent tour for the purpose of exciting the minds of the people by a series of discourses on the subject of slavery, every place that I visited gave fresh evidence of the fact, that a greater revolution in public sentiment was to be effected in the free states—*and particularly in New-England*—than at the south. I found contempt more bitter, opposition more active, detraction more relentless, prejudice more stubborn, and apathy more frozen, than among the slave owners themselves. Of course there were individual exceptions to the contrary.

This state of things afflicted, but did not dishearten me. I determined, at every hazard, to lift up the standard of emancipation in the eyes of the nation, *within sight of Bunker Hill and in the birth place of liberty*. That standard is now unfurled; and long may it float, unhurt by the spoliations of time or the missiles of a desperate foe—yea, till every chain be broken, and every bondman set free! Let southern oppressors tremble—let their secret abettors tremble—let their northern apologists tremble —let all the enemies of the persecuted blacks tremble. . . .

I am aware that many object to the severity of my language; but is there not cause for severity? I *will be* as harsh as truth, and as uncompromising as justice. On this subject, I do not wish to think, or speak, or write, with moderation. No! no! Tell a man whose house is on fire, to give a moderate alarm; . . . tell the mother to gradually extricate her babe from the fire into which it has fallen;—but urge me not to use moderation in a cause like the present. I am in earnest—I will not equivocate—I will not

excuse—I will not retreat a single inch—AND I WILL BE HEARD. . . .

And here I close with this fresh dedication:
"Oppression! I have seen thee, face to face,
And met thy cruel eye and cloudy brow;
But thy soul-withering glance I fear not now—
For dread to prouder feelings doth give place
Of deep abhorrence! Scorning the disgrace
Of slavish knees that at thy footstool bow,
I also kneel—but with far other bow
Do hail thee and thy herd of hirelings base:—
I swear, while life-blood warms my throbbing veins,
Still to oppose and thwart, with heart and hand,
Thy brutalizing sway—'till Afric's chains
Are burst, and Freedom rules the rescued land,—
Trampling Oppression and his iron rod:
Such is the vow I take—SO HELP ME GOD!"

Selection from William Lloyd Garrison, *The Liberator*, January 1, 1831 issue. Reprinted in *American Primer*, edited by Daniel Boorstin. Published by University of Chicago Press, Chicago, copyright © 1966.

CRITICAL THINKING

1. Why are William Lloyd Garrison's examples of the actions of homeowner and a mother appropriate to the issue of slavery?
2. How did Garrison push his readers to take a position on the morality of owning a slave?
3. What was the probable effect of Garrison's newspaper on the debates over slavery?

CHAPTER 14

EXPANSION AND DIVISION

1835–1860

1. SAM HOUSTON SPEAKS OUT IN SUPPORT OF TEXAS JOINING THE UNION

Interest in the possible annexation of the Republic of Texas was high among Americans in 1845. So during that year when Sam Houston, former president of the Lone Star Republic, spoke in New Orleans on a tour of the United States, people thronged the hall where he appeared. Excerpts from his speech appear below.

From the New Orleans Bulletin, May 29. [1845]

The announcement that General Houston would address the public on the subject of Texas and annexation, drew together last evening an overflowing meeting. . . .

General Houston . . . adverted to the fact, that it was in that hall that the first meeting had been held in behalf of the Texans when struggling for their independence, and the first means derived from their assistance, and expressed his gratitude and that of the country, for the manifold favors they had received from the people of the United States, and especially from this city. He then gave a succinct and accurate outline of the history of Texas, as a department of the Mexican confederacy, and of the circumstances and causes that led to its separation from that government, showing that no people had ever evinced a more loyal disposition, or a more sincere and patient compliance with their obligations, than the Texans, and that it was the . . . repeated attempts to subject them to an absolute and self-appointed despotism, that finally drove the people of Texas to arms. The charge so frequently alleged against the people of Texas, that they had emigrated thither for the purpose of robbing Mexico of her dominions, and had refused to comply with the engagements which they had entered into with Mexico, he rejected as a false and unjust imputation on the American name. . . .

In conclusion, General H. spoke of the subject of annexation, stating that he had shown his partiality for the measure by voting for it in 1836, and dispatching, immediately on his accession to the presidency in that year, a special envoy to bring the subject before the cabinet at Washington. The subject remained before the cabinet, he continued, until 1838, when it was thought to be contrary to true policy and to the dignity of Texas further to importune, and the proposition was withdrawn. The subject then slumbered until he was again chosen to the presidency, in 1841, when he instructed Mr. Riley, who was minister at Washington, to bring the subject again before our government. Again, he said, Texas was treated cavalierly, and the proposition was not pressed, until Mr. Van Zandt became the Texan resident in the United States, when he solicited instructions on the subject of annexation, and he was . . . [given] directions to open negotiations, should a favorable opportunity occur.

With this statement of facts, General H. said, he would leave the public to infer whether he was opposed to, or in favor of, annexation. It was true, he said, that he had [flirted] a little with G. Britain, and made the United States as jealous of that power as he possibly could; and had it not been, he said, for the eagerness of the Texan congress in passing and sending to this country a declaration, that nine-tenths of the people of Texas were in favor of the measure, he would have so operated on the fears of the American senate that the prize would slip through their grasp, as to have secured the ratification of the treaty last spring. . . .

He then stated, that there exists but one sentiment in Texas, and that is in favor of annexation; that he is perfectly sure the Texan executive, as far as he can do it, will carry out the measure in good faith; that when the congress meets, they will give their assent to the measure, as the president has already given his, and that, when the special deputies of the people meet in convention, in pursuance of the president's proclamation, they will ratify the act with every solemnity, and then the country will present [a united] front. He said, there was no opposition among the people; he was sure the president would not, nor would he himself, interpose one breath in its way.

General H. then alluded, in very graceful terms, to the object of his present tour, which is

Samuel Houston led the fight for Texas's independence from Mexico and later became president of the new Republic of Texas.

once more to have an interview with General Jackson, before the death of that illustrious citizen. He then sat down amid the general cheers of the house.

Selection from *Niles' National Register*, Vol. LXVIII, June 14, 1845.

CRITICAL THINKING

1. Texas was admitted to the Union on December 29, 1845. When did Sam Houston first request annexation? What caused the long delay?
2. Houston claimed that Americans in Texas had complied with all the agreements (engagements) they had entered into with Mexico. Would Mexican leaders have agreed with this claim? Explain what you mean.
3. What was Houston's purpose in "flirting" with Great Britain?

2. JOHN O'SULLIVAN PROCLAIMS AMERICA'S "MANIFEST DESTINY"

By 1846, many Americans were talking ardently of the "manifest destiny" of the United States to bring within its borders all the lands of North America. The phrase "manifest destiny" was first used by writer John L. O'Sullivan in his article "Annexation" which appeared a few months before Texas became the twenty-eighth state in the Union. Passages from O'Sullivan's article are reproduced below.

IT IS TIME now for opposition to the Annexation of Texas to cease. . . .

Texas is now ours. Already, before these words are written, her Convention has undoubtedly ratified the acceptance, by her Congress, of our proffered invitation into the Union; and made the requisite changes in her already republican form of constitution to adopt it to its future federal relations. Her star and her stripe may already be said to have taken their place in the glorious blazon of our common nationality; and the sweep of our eagle's wing already includes within its circuit the wide extent of her fair and fertile land. She is no longer to us a mere geographical space— a certain combination of coast, plain, mountain, valley, forest and stream. She is no longer to us a mere country on the map. She comes within the dear and sacred designation of Our Country. . . .

. . . [The reason for annexing Texas] surely is to be found, found abundantly, in the manner in which other nations have undertaken to intrude . . . in a spirit of hostile interference against us, for the avowed object of thwarting our policy and hampering our power, limiting our greatness and checking the fulfilment of our manifest destiny to overspread the continent allotted by Providence for the free development of our yearly multiplying millions. . . .

It is wholly untrue . . . that the Annexation has been a measure . . . of military conquest under forms of peace and law—of territorial aggrandizement at the expense of justice. . . . This view of the question is wholly unfounded. . . . The independence of Texas was complete and absolute. It was an independence, not only in fact but of right. No obligation of duty towards Mexico tended in the least degree to restrain our right to effect the desired recovery of the fair province once our own. . . . If Texas became peopled with an American population, it was by no contrivance of our government, but on the express invitation of . . . Mexico. . . .

Nor is there any just foundation for the charge that Annexation is a great pro-slavery measure—calculated to increase and perpetuate that institution. Slavery had nothing to do with it. . . . Texas has been absorbed into the Union in the inevitable fulfilment of the general law which is rolling our population westward; the connexion of which with that ratio of growth in population which is destined within a hundred years to swell our numbers to the enormous population of *two hundred and fifty millions* (if not more), is too evident to leave us in doubt of the manifest design of Providence in regard to the occupation of this continent. . . .

California will, probably, next fall away from the loose adhesion which, in such a country as Mexico, holds a remote province in a slight equivocal kind of dependence on the metropolis. Imbecile and distracted, Mexico never can exert any real governmental authority over such a country . . . tyranny may retain a military dominion which is no government in the legitimate sense of the term. In the case of California this is now impossible. The Anglo-Saxon foot is already on its borders. Already the advance guard of the irresistible army of Anglo-Saxon emigration has begun to pour down upon it, armed with the plough and the rifle, and marking its trail with schools and colleges, courts and representative halls, mills and meeting-houses. A population will soon be in actual occupation of California, over which it will be idle for Mexico to dream of dominion. They will necessarily become independent. All this without agency of our government, without responsibility of our people. . . . they will have a right to independence—to self-government—to the possession of the homes conquered from the wilderness by their own labors and dangers, sufferings and sacrifices—a better and a truer right than the artificial title of sovereignty in Mexico a thousand miles distant, inheriting from Spain a title good only against those who have none better. . . . there can be no doubt that the population now fast streaming down upon California will both assert and maintain that independence. Whether they will then attach themselves to our Union or not, is not to be predicted with any certainty. Unless the projected rail-road across the continent to the Pacific be carried into effect, perhaps they may not; though even in that case, the day is not distant when the Empires of the Atlantic and Pacific would again flow together into one, as soon as their inland border should approach each other. . . .

Away, then, with all idle . . . talk of *balances of power* on the American Continent. There is no growth in Spanish America! Whatever progress of population there may be in the British Canadas, is only for their own early severance of their present colonial relation to the little island three thousand miles across the Atlantic; soon to be followed by Annexation, and destined to swell the still accumulating momentum of our progress.

Selection from *The Shaping of the American Tradition*, edited by Louis M. Hacker and Helene S. Zahler. Published by Columbia University Press, New York, copyright © 1947.

CRITICAL THINKING

1. State in your own words what John O'Sullivan meant by the phrase "manifest destiny."
2. One American Congressman said he would agree with the supporters of "manifest destiny" when they showed him the clause in "Father Adam's will" that left the North American continent to the United States. What did he mean?
3. O'Sullivan advocates westward expansion. In your own words, cite possible objections to manifest destiny.

3. RUNAWAY SLAVE ANTHONY BURNS IS ARRESTED IN BOSTON

Belief in "manifest destiny" led to American westward expansion. Proslavery and antislavery forces struggled for control of the western territories that would become states. When California applied for statehood, talk of southern secession was heard. To head off such an eventuality, the Compromise of 1850 was passed by Congress. The Fugitive Slave Act, a *part of the Compromise, was bitterly opposed by northern abolitionists. The following reading tells what happened in 1854 when federal marshals enforced the* Fugitive Slave Act *by arresting runaway slave Anthony Burns in Boston.*

In the evening of the twenty-fourth of May, 1854, Anthony Burns was arrested as a fugitive slave in the heart of Boston. He had been employed, during the day, in a clothing store situated in Brattle street, and belonging to Coffin Pitts, a respectable colored trader. . . . Burns had passed exactly one month of quiet freedom, spent in honest industry, when the sudden interruption of his happiness took place. . . .

The arrest was made under a warrant issued on the same day, by Edward G. Loring, a United States Commissioner. The person charged with its immediate execution was a man who had already become infamous by making the hunting of fugitive slaves his special vocation. The name of this man was Asa O. Butman. . . .

The news of Burns's arrest quickly spread through the city. . . . Whenever a slaveholder arrived in the city, he was watched [by the Committee of Vigilance] and the object of his visit inquired into. If he had come in the pursuit of ordinary business, he was left alone, but the slightest indication that he was in pursuit of a slave, sufficed to place him under a surveillance that never ceased while he remained in the city. . . .

By this Committee of Vigilance, the case of Burns was now taken in hand. Early in the afternoon of the day following his arrest, a full meeting for the purpose was secretly convened. On the main point there was but one voice; all agreed that, be the Commissioner's decision what it might, Burns should never be taken back to Virginia, if it were in their power to prevent. But there were two opinions as to the method by which they should proceed to effect their purpose. One party counselled an attack on the Court House, and a forcible rescue of the prisoner. The other party were in favor of a less violent course. They proposed to await the Commissioner's decision; then, if it were adverse to the prisoner, they would crowd the streets when he was brought forth, present an impassable living barrier to the progress of the escort, and see to it that, in the

melee which would inevitably follow, Burns made good his escape. . . . Their weapons of attack were various; some were armed with revolvers, some carried axes, and some butcher's cleavers that had just been purchased and were left in their paper coverings for better concealment. In a passage-way hard by, a large stick of timber had been secretly deposited to serve as a battering-ram. Soon after nine o'clock, everything was ready for the assault. It was at this juncture that the alarm had been given to the meeting in Faneuil Hall.

Scarcely had the crowd from the Hall begun to pour into the Square when the assault [on the Court House] was commenced. The lamps that lighted the Square had already been extinguished, so that under cover of darkness the assailants might more easily escape detection. . . .

In the City Hall, hard by, the Mayor, with several officers of the municipal government, happened to be present at the same hour. Notified by the Chief of Police of the state of affairs, he at once ordered out two companies of artillery. Both arrived on the ground before midnight, and were stationed, the one in the Court House, the other in the City Hall. At the same time, the Marshal dispatched his deputy to procure a body of United States troops. Proceeding to East Boston, the deputy there chartered a steamer, directed his course with all speed to Fort Warren, and took on board a corps of marines under command of Maj. S. C. Ridgley. In six hours after, they were quartered within the walls of the Court House. Another company of marines was dispatched from the Navy Yard in Charlestown, on the requisition of the Marshal, and was also quartered in the same building. . . .

At eleven o'clock, [on June 2, 1854] Court Square presented a spectacle that became indelibly engraved upon the memories of men. The people had been swept out of the Square, and stood crowded together in Court street, presenting to the eye a solid rampart of living beings. At the eastern door of the Court House, stood the cannon, loaded, and with its mouth pointed full upon the compact mass. By its side stood the officer commanding the detachment of United States troops, gazing with steady composure in the same direction. It was the first time that the armed power of the United States had ever been arrayed against the people of Massachusetts. Men who witnessed the sight, and reflected upon its cause, were made painfully to recognize the fact, before unfelt, that they were the subjects of two governments. . . .

One o'clock had arrived, and yet the movement of the *cortege* was delayed. Meanwhile, Gen. Edmands had from time to time dashed into the Square, and, dismounting, held hurried conferences with the Marshal in the building. A bystander who heard their conversation, learned that the delay was caused by the General's inability to clear the streets, and his fear of being unable to accomplish the task he had undertaken.

At length, about two o'clock, the column was formed in the Square. First came a detachment of United States Artillery, followed by a platoon of United States Marines. After these followed the armed civil posse of the Marshal, to which succeeded two platoons of Marines. The cannon, guarded by another platoon of Marines, brought up the rear. When this arrangement was completed, Burns, accompanied by a officer on each side with arms interlocked, was conducted from his prison through a passage lined with soldiers, and placed in the centre of the armed posse. Immediately after the decision, Mr. Dana and Mr. Grimes had asked permission to walk with Burns' arm in arm, from the Court House to the vessel at the wharf; and the Marshal had given them his consent. At the last moment, he sought them out and requested that they would not insist upon the performance of his promise, because, in the opinion of some of the military officers, such a spectacle would add to the excitement. . . .

. . . Accordingly, without a single friend at his side, and hemmed in by a thickset hedge of gleaming blades, Burns took his departure.

The route from the Court House to the wharf had by this time become thronged with a countless multitude. It seemed as if the whole population of the city had been concentrated upon this narrow space. . . .

At the end of the wharf lay a small steamer which had been chartered by the United States Government. On board this vessel Burns was conducted by the Marshal, and immediately withdrawn from the sight of the gazing thousands into the cabin below. The United States troops followed, and, after an hour's delay, the cannon was

also shipped. At twenty minutes past three o'clock, the steamer left the wharf, and went down the harbor.

Selection from Charles Emery Stevens, *Anthony Burns: A History*. Published by John P. Jewett and Company, Boston, 1856. Reprinted by Arno Press and The New York Times, copyright © 1969.

CRITICAL THINKING

1. Do you think Boston was an appropriate setting for the actions described above? Give reasons for your answer.
2. How do you think Henry Thoreau might have reacted to the actions taken by the people of Boston? What do you think of their actions?

4. ENGLISH TRAVELER THOMAS H. GLADSTONE WITNESSES THE SACK OF LAWRENCE, KANSAS

Violence over slavery between proslavery southerners and antislavery northerners increased. It erupted in a particularly shocking way when it came time for the people in Kansas Territory to decide whether they would enter the Union as a free state or a slave state. In the excerpts below, an English traveler, Thomas H. Gladstone, describes what he witnessed in "bleeding Kansas" 1855–1856.

The autumn of 1854 witnessed the erection of the first log-huts of Lawrence by a few families of New England settlers. During the year 1855 its population increased rapidly, chiefly by the arrival of emigrants from the Northern States. Its log-hut existence gave way to a more advanced stage, in which buildings of brick and stone were introduced; and the growing prosperity of the "Yankee town" early began to excite the jealousy of the abettors of slavery. Viewed as the stronghold of the Free-state party, it was made the point of attack during what was called "the Wakarusa war" in the winter of 1855. Before the termination of this its first siege, . . . the inhabitants of Lawrence proceeded to fortify their town by the erection of four or five circular earthworks, thrown up about seven feet in height, and measuring a hundred feet in diameter. These were connected with long lines of earthwork entrench-ments, rifle-pits, and other means of fortification. . . . The inhabitants were also placed under arms, formed into companies, with their respective com-manders, under the generalship of Robinson and Lane. . . .

The pacification which followed the Wakarusa campaign in December, 1855, afforded only a temporary lull. . . . The Missourians did not con-ceal that they were organizing another invasion, which should effectually "wipe out Lawrence," and win Kansas for slavery, "though they should wade to the knees in blood to obtain it." The Southern states were being appealed to far and wide, to aid by men and money in the extirpation of every Northern settler. . . .

The month of May [1866] arrived. . . . The pro-slavery, or, as it was commonly termed, the border-ruffian army, had . . . gained strength by large reinforcements . . . from Alabama, . . . from Florida, . . . from South Carolina and Geor-gia, all of whom had sworn to fight the battles of the South in Kansas. The President [Buchanan], too, through his Secretary-at-War, had placed the federal troops at the command of Governor Shan-non, and the Chief Justice Lecompte had declared, in a notable charge to a grand jury, that all who resisted the laws made by the fraudulently elected Legislature were to be found guilty of high treason. . . .

Meanwhile, Sheriff Jones rode about the coun-try with a "posse" of United States troops, arrest-ing whomsoever he pleased. . . . Governor Rob-inson and several other men of influence in the Free-state cause were . . . seized and held as pris-oners; Free-state men were daily molested in the highway, some robbed, and others killed; and a constantly increasing army was encamping right and left of Lawrence, pressing daily more closely around it, and openly declaring that their inten-tion was to "wipe out the traitorous city, and not to leave an abolitionist alive in the territory." . . .

The newspaper offices were the first objects of attack. First that of the *Free State*, then that of the *Herald of Freedom*, underwent a thorough demoli-tion. The presses were in each case broken to pieces, and the offending type carried away to the river. The papers and books were treated in like manner, until the soldiers became weary of carry-ing them to the Kaw, when they thrust them in

piles into the street, and burnt, tore, or otherwise destroyed them.

From the printing offices they went to the hotel. . . .

As orders were given to remove the furniture, the wild mob threw the articles out of the win-dows, but shortly found more congenial employ-ment in emptying the cellars. By this time four cannon had been brought opposite the hotel, and . . . they commenced to batter down the building. In this however, they failed. . . . They then placed kegs of gunpowder in the lower parts of the building, and attempted to blow it up. The only result was, the shattering of some of the windows and other limited damage. At length, to complete the work which their own clumsiness or [drunkenness] had rendered difficult hitherto, or-ders were given to fire the building in a number of places, and, as a consequence, it was soon encir-cled in a mass of flames. . . .

The firing of the cannon had been the signal for most of the women and children in Lawrence to leave the city. This they did, not knowing whither to turn their steps. The male portion of its citizens watched, without offering resistance, the destruc-tion of the buildings named, and next had to see their own houses made the objects of unscrupu-lous plunder.

The sack of Lawrence occupied the remainder of the afternoon. . . .

Selection adapted from "Civil War in Kansas," in *American History told by Contemporaries*, Vol. IV, edited by Albert Bushnell Hart. Published by The Macmillan Company, New York, copyright © 1924.

CRITICAL THINKING

1. Would you say that what happened in Lawrence, Kansas, was the first battle of the American Civil War? Give reasons to support your answer.
2. What position did President Buchanan and the federal government take with regard to the incidents in Lawrence?
3. How would you evaluate the above ex-cerpt as a primary source of historical information? Why?

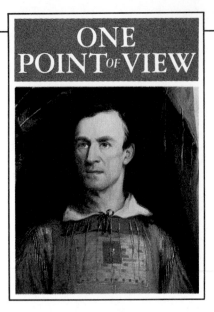

This woman, named "The Fire Bug That Creeps," belonged to the Assiniboin tribe. In the 1830s, her husband was part of a delegation visiting Washington, D.C. When he returned and described steamships and railroads, his disbelieving fellow tribesmen killed him for telling lies.

GEORGE CATLIN

In 1830, the American frontier still reached only as far as the Mississippi River. The paintings of George Catlin [1796–1872] are one of the most important sources of knowledge we have about the Native American civilizations that existed beyond this boundary.

George Catlin was trained as a lawyer in Connecticut and began to practice law in 1820. Dissatisfied, he sold his lawbooks in 1821 and started a new career as a portrait painter in Philadelphia, where he first saw American Indians. The Indians Catlin saw were traveling in a delegation from the wilderness. Catlin was so impressed by these people that he vowed to spend the rest of his life documenting their way of life.

In 1830, he went to St. Louis where he made the acquaintance of General William Clark, the famous explorer of the Northwest. With Clark's help, he began to meet and sketch Indians. Inspired by his contact with the people he so admired, Catlin began a series of journeys that for the next six years would carry him to the Great Plains where he lived and painted among the tribes. In the winter months he returned from the wilderness to work on his paintings in his studio, only to go back to the plains in the warmer seasons.

CRITICAL THINKING

1. List things in these paintings that had ceased to exist by the turn of the century. Which ones were nearly destroyed?
2. Identify items shown in these paintings that are still used by people today.
3. From the details in this painting, deduce techniques used by Plain Indians to hunt buffalo.
4. How was Catlin's admiration of Indians reflected in his portraits of them?

When Catlin wanted to paint a Mandan chief, the fearful tribal council met to discuss whether it might be dangerous. Plains Indians (below) are shown hunting buffalo in deep snow.

5. A POPULAR SONG CELEBRATES JOHN BROWN'S RAID ON HARPER'S FERRY

John Brown's raid on Harper's Ferry in 1859 widened the gap between North and South. While many southerners viewed Brown's action with horror, many northerners saw the raid as an act of heroism. "The John Brown Song" (sung to the same music as The Battle Hymn of the Republic) *was extremely popular among the opponents of slavery. Several versions of the song appeared. The version below, written by Reverend William Patton, gained popularity in 1861, after the Civil War had begun.*

JOHN BROWN

Old John Brown's body lies moldering in the grave,
While weep the sons of bondage whom he ventured all to save;
But tho he lost his life while struggling for the slave,
   His soul is marching on.
     Glory, glory hallelujah!

John Brown was a hero, undaunted, true and brave,
And Kansas knows his valor when he fought her rights to save;
Now, tho the grass grows green above his grave,
   His soul is marching on.
     Glory, hallelujah!

He captured Harper's Ferry, with his nineteen men so few,
And frightened "Old Virginny" till she trembled thru and thru;
They hung him for a traitor, themselves a traitor crew,
   But his soul is marching on.
     Glory, hallelujah!

John Brown was John the Baptist of the Christ we are to see,
Christ who of the bondmen shall the Liberator be,
And soon thruout the Sunny South the slaves shall all be free,
   For his soul is marching on.
     Glory, hallelujah!

The conflict that he heralded he looks from heaven to view,
On the army of the Union with its flag red, white and blue,
And heaven shall ring with anthems o'er the deed they mean to do,
   For his soul is marching on.
     Glory, hallelujah!

Ye soldiers of Freedom, then strike, while strike ye may,
The death blow of oppression in a better time and way,
For the dawn of old John Brown has brightened into day,
   And his soul is marching on.
     Glory, hallelujah!

CRITICAL THINKING

1. How does Reverend Patton depict John Brown in this song? Cite specific parts of the song to support your answer.
2. Which verses of the song do you think southerners would find most offensive? Why?

6. ABRAHAM LINCOLN SPEAKS ABOUT THE INCIDENT AT HARPER'S FERRY

Southerners blamed the new Republican party for extreme antislavery actions like John Brown's. Abraham Lincoln defended the Republicans in a speech he made in New York on February 27, 1860, a few months before he became the Republicans' presidential nominee. In the excerpts from that speech below, Lincoln addresses southerners and members of his own party.

Consider . . . whether your [southerners'] claim of conservatism for yourselves, and your charge of destructiveness against us, are based on the most clear and stable foundations.

. . . you say we [the Republicans] have made the slavery question more prominent than it formerly was. We deny it. We admit that it is more prominent, but we deny that we made it so. It was not we, but you, who discarded the old policy of the fathers [Founding Fathers]. We resisted, and still resist, your innovation; and thence comes the greater prominence of the question. Would you have that question reduced to its former proportions? Go back to that old policy. What has been will be again, under the same conditions. If you would have the peace of the old times, readopt the precepts and policy of the old times.

You charge that we stir up insurrections among your slaves. We deny it; and what is your proof? Harper's Ferry! John Brown!! John Brown was no Republican; and you have failed to implicate a single Republican in his Harper's Ferry enterprise. If any member of our party is guilty in that matter, you know it or you do not know it. If you do know it, you are inexcusable for not designating the man and proving the fact. If you do not know it, you are inexcusable for asserting it, and especially for persisting in the assertion after you have tried and failed to make the proof. You need not be told that persisting in a charge which one does not know to be true, is simply malicious slander. . . .

Some of you admit that no Republican designedly aided or encouraged the Harper's Ferry affair; but still insist that our doctrines and declarations necessarily lead to such results. We do not believe it. We know we hold to no doctrine, and make no declaration, which were not held to and made by "our fathers who framed the Government under which we live." . . . Republican doctrines and declarations are accompanied with a continual protest against any interference whatever with your slaves, or with you about your slaves. Surely, this does not encourage them to revolt. True, we do, in common with "our fathers, who framed the Government under which we live," declare our belief that slavery is wrong. . . .

Slave insurrections are no more common now than they were before the Republican party was organized. What induced the Southampton insurrection, twenty-eight years ago, in which, at least, three times as many lives were lost as at Harper's Ferry? You can scarcely stretch your very elastic fancy to the conclusion that Southampton was "got up by Black Republicanism." . . .

John Brown's effort was peculiar. It was not a slave insurrection. It was an attempt by white men to get up a revolt among slaves, in which the slaves refused to participate. In fact, it was so absurd that the slaves, with all their ignorance, saw plainly enough it could not succeed. . . .

And how much would it avail you, if you could, by the use of John Brown, Helper's Book, and the like, break up the Republican organization? Human action can be modified to some extent, but human nature cannot be changed. There is a judgment and a feeling against slavery in this nation, which cast at least a million and a half of votes. You cannot destroy that judgment and feeling—that sentiment—by breaking up the political organization which rallies around it. You can scarcely scatter and disperse an army which has been formed into order in the face of your heaviest fire; but if you could, how much would you gain by forcing the sentiment which created it out of the peaceful channel of the ballot-box, into some other channel? What would that other channel probably be? Would the number of John Browns be lessened or enlarged by the operation? . . .

A few words now to Republicans. *It is exceedingly desirable that all parts of this great Confederacy shall be at peace, and in harmony, one with another. Let us Republicans do our part to have it so. Even though much provoked, let us do nothing through passion and ill temper. Even though the southern people will not so much as listen to us, let us calmly consider their demands, and yield to them if, in our deliberate view of our duty, we possibly can. Judging by all they say and do, and by the subject and nature of their controversy with us, let us determine, if we can, what will satisfy them.*

Selection from *The Collected Works of Abraham Lincoln*, Vol. III, edited by Roy P. Basler. Published by Rutgers University Press, New Brunswick, New Jersey, copyright © 1953.

CRITICAL THINKING

1. Abraham Lincoln said that, even if the Republican party were destroyed, opposition to slavery would continue. How does he support this statement?
2. Do you think the position Lincoln took in this speech was extremist? Refer to specific parts of the speech that support your answer.

CHAPTER 15
THE CIVIL WAR
1861–1865

1. SOUTHERNER MARY BOYKIN CHESNUT DESCRIBES THE ATTACK ON FORT SUMTER

The excerpts below are taken from the diary of Mary Boykin Chesnut, the wife of James Chesnut, Jr., who was the Senator from South Carolina until the start of the Civil War. In these diary entries, Mrs. Chesnut gives her impressions of the Confederate firing on Fort Sumter, the incident that began the fighting between North and South.

April 18th. . . . There was no placidity to-day, with cannon bursting and Allen on the Island. No sleep for anybody last night. The streets were alive with soldiers, men shouting, marching, singing. . . . My husband has been made an aide-de-camp to General Beauregard.

Three hours ago we were quickly packing to go home. The Convention [which framed the Confederate Constitution] has adjourned. Now he tells me the attack on Fort Sumter may begin to-night; depends upon Anderson and the fleet outside. The Herald says that this show of war outside of the bar is intended for Texas. John Manning came in with his sword and red sash, pleased as a boy to be on Beauregard's staff, while the row goes on. He has gone with Wigfall to Captain Hartstein with instructions. Mr. Chesnut is finishing a report he had to make to the Convention. . . .

To-day at dinner there was no allusion to things as they stand in Charleston Harbor. There was an undercurrent of intense excitement. There could not have been a more brilliant circle. In addition to our usual quartette (Judge Withers, Langdon Cheves, and Trescott), our two ex-Governors dined with us, Means and Manning. These men all talked so delightfully. For once in my life I listened. That over, business began in earnest. Governor Means had rummaged a sword and red sash from somewhere and brought it for Colonel

Chesnut, who had gone to demand the surrender of Fort Sumter. And now patience—we must wait.

Why did that green goose Anderson go into Fort Sumter? Then everything began to go wrong. Now they have intercepted a letter from him urging them to let him surrender. He paints the horrors likely to ensue if they will not. He ought to have thought of all that before he put his head in the hole.

April 12th.—Anderson will not capitulate. Yesterday's was the merriest, maddest dinner we have had yet. Men were audaciously wise and witty. We had an unspoken foreboding that it was to be our last pleasant meeting. Mr. Miles dined with us to-day. Mrs. Henry King rushed in saying, "The news, I come for the latest news. All the men of the King family are on the Island," of which fact she seemed proud.

While she was here our peace negotiator, or envoy, came in—that is, Mr. Chesnut returned. His interview with Colonel Anderson had been deeply interesting, but Mr. Chesnut was not inclined to be communicative. He wanted his dinner. He felt for Anderson and had telegraphed to President Davis for instructions—what answer to give Anderson, etc. He has now gone back to Fort Sumter with additional instructions. When they were about to leave the wharf A. H. Boykin sprang into the boat in great excitement. He thought himself ill-used, with a likelihood of fighting and he to be left behind!

I do not pretend to go to sleep. How can I? If Anderson does not accept terms at four, the orders are, he shall be fired upon. I count four, St. Michael's bells chime out and I begin to hope. At half-past four the heavy booming of a cannon. I sprang out of bed, and on my knees prostrate I prayed as I never prayed before.

There was a sound of stir all over the house, pattering of feet in the corridors. All seemed hurrying one way. I put on my double-gown and a shawl and went, too. It was to the housetop. The shells were bursting. In the dark I heard a man say, "Waste of ammunition." I knew my husband was rowing about in a boat somewhere in that dark bay, and that the shells were roofing it over, bursting toward the fort. If Anderson was obstinate, Colonel Chesnut was to order the fort on one side to open fire. Certainly fire had begun. The regular roar of the cannon, there it was. And who could tell what each volley accomplished of death and destruction?

The women were wild there on the housetop. Prayers came from the women and imprecations from the men. And then a shell would light up the scene. To-night they say the forces are to attempt to land. We watched up there, and everybody wondered that Fort Sumter did not fire a shot. . . .

. . . we hear nothing, can listen to nothing; boom, boom goes the cannon all the time. The nervous strain is awful, alone in this darkened room. . . .

April 13th.—Nobody has been hurt after all. How gay we were last night. Reaction after the dread of all the slaughter we thought those dreadful cannon were making. Not even a battery the worse for wear. Fort Sumter has been on fire. Anderson has not yet silenced any of our guns. So the aides, still with swords and red sashes by way of uniform, tell us. But the sound of those guns makes regular meals impossible. None of us go to table. Tea-trays pervade the corridors going everywhere. Some of the anxious hearts lie on their beds and moan in solitary misery. Mrs. Wigfall and I solace ourselves with tea in my room. These women have all a satisfying faith. "God is on our side," they say. When we are shut in Mrs. Wigfall and I ask "Why?" "Of course, He hates the Yankees, we are told. You'll think that well of Him."

April 15th.—I did not know that one could live such days of excitement. Some one called: "Come out! There is a crowd coming." A mob it was, indeed, but it was headed by Colonels Chesnut and Manning. The crowd was shouting and showing these two as messengers of good news. They were escorted to Beauregard's headquarters. Fort Sumter had surrendered! Those upon the housetops shouted to us "The fort is on fire." That had been the story once or twice before.

When we had calmed down, Colonel Chesnut, who had taken it all quietly enough, if anything more unruffled than usual in his serenity, told us how the surrender came about. Wigfall was with them on Morris Island when they saw the fire in the fort; he jumped in a little boat, and with his handkerchief as a white flag, rowed over. Wigfall went in through a porthole. When Colonel Chesnut arrived shortly after, and was received at the regular entrance, Colonel Anderson told him he

The Civil War diary kept by the aristocratic Southerner, Mary Boykin Chesnut, is one of the most revealing documents of the period.

had need to pick his way warily, for the place was all mined. As far as I can make out the fort surrendered to Wigfall. But it is all confusion. Our flag is flying there. Fire-engines have been sent for to put out the fire. Everybody tells you half of something and then rushes off to tell something else or to hear the last news.

In the afternoon, Mrs. Preston, Mrs. Joe Heyward, and I drove around the Battery. We were in an open carriage. What a changed scene—the very liveliest crowd I think I ever saw, everybody talking at once. All glasses were still turned on the grim old fort.

Selection from Mary Boykin Chesnut, *A Diary from Dixie.* Published by D. Appleton and Company, 1905. Reprinted by Peter Smith, Gloucester, Massachusetts, copyright © 1961.

CRITICAL THINKING

1. As you were reading the diary entries, what attitude towards their cause did you detect in the southerners Mrs. Chesnut mentions? Refer to specific parts of the entries that reveal this attitude.
2. Of what value are the diary entries as primary sources of information about the firing on Fort Sumter?

CIVIL WAR PHOTOGRAPHERS
The New Documentors

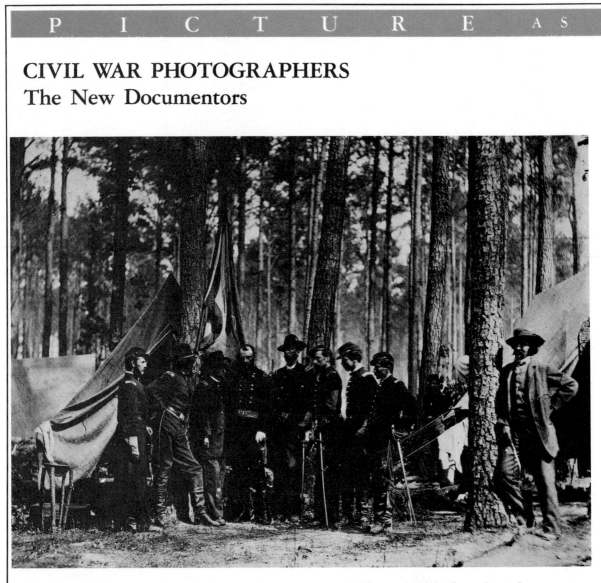

Matthew Brady, at the extreme right, leans against a tree before an 1864 battle. In his right hand, he is thought to be holding a device to set off a pre-set "automatic camera."

The lives of field photographers during the Civil War were not easy. They had to carry cameras, darkrooms, and· supplies with them onto the battlefield.

Taking a single picture was a tedious and lengthy operation. First, a glass plate had to be carefully coated with collodion and sensitized in the "darkroom"—a buggy with a black hood. Then, the "wet plate" had to be rushed to the camera, exposed for 10 to 30 seconds, and rushed back to the darkroom for developing. A moment of delay could result in a loss of brilliancy or depth in the negative.

Because of the long exposure time, it was practically impossible to photograph live action. Battle scenes were restricted to events that occurred after the actual fighting had ended. But Civil War photographers, such as Matthew B. Brady, gave the American public vivid and objective impressions of the war.

D O C U M E N T

This picture of General William Sherman's men tearing up a railroad track in Atlanta, Georgia, was shot by George M. Barnard, who was one of the few official photographers for the Union Army.

Matthew Brady used horsedrawn, portable darkrooms to develop his negatives behind the lines. Many pictures were ruined because exploding shells and gunfire frightened the horses.

The importance of Brady's photographs at Bull Run, Virginia, one of the earliest battles of the war, was described by a contemporary writer: "His are the only reliable records at Bull's Run. The correspondents of the Rebel newspapers are sheer falsifiers; the correspondents of the Northern journals are not to be depended on, and the correspondents of the English press are altogether worse than either; but Brady never misrepresents."

CRITICAL THINKING

1. Compare the possible responses of Union supporters and Confederate supporters as they viewed these photographs.
2. Until the Civil War, battles were documented by artists. How might photographs differ from paintings?

2. PRESIDENT ABRAHAM LINCOLN OFFERS EMANCIPATION AMENDMENTS TO THE CONSTITUTION

President Abraham Lincoln issued a preliminary form of the Emancipation Proclamation *in September, 1862. In December of the same year, in his annual message to Congress, Lincoln suggested drafts for three Constitutional amendments, designed to implement the freeing of the slaves. The proposed amendments and Lincoln's comments about them appear below.*

I recommend the adoption of the following resolution and articles amendatory to the Constitution of the United States:

"Resolved by the Senate and House of Representatives of the United States of America in Congress assembled (two-thirds of both houses concurring), That the following articles be proposed to the legislatures (or conventions) of the several States as amendments to the Constitution of the United States, all or any of which articles when ratified by three fourths of the said legislatures (or conventions) to be valid as part or parts of the said Constitution, viz.:

"ARTICLE—.

"Every State wherein slavery now exists which shall abolish the same therein at any time or times before the first day of January in the year of our Lord one thousand and nine hundred, shall receive compensation from the United States as follows, to wit:

"The President of the United States shall deliver to every such State bonds of the United States, bearing interest at the rate of _____ per cent. per annum, to an amount equal to the aggregate sum of ___, for each slave shown to have been therein by the eighth census of the United States, said bonds to be delivered to such State by instalments, or in one parcel at the completion of the abolishment, accordingly as the same shall have been gradual or at one time within such State; and interest shall begin to run upon any such bond only from the proper time of its delivery as aforesaid. Any State having received bonds as aforesaid, and afterward reintroducing or tolerating slavery therein, shall refund to the United States the bonds so received, or the value thereof, and all interest paid thereon.

"ARTICLE—.

"All slaves who shall have enjoyed actual freedom by the chances of the war at any time before the end of the rebellion, shall be forever free; but all owners of such who shall not have been disloyal shall be compensated for them at the same rates as are provided for States adopting abolishment of slavery, but in such way that no slave shall be twice accounted for.

"ARTICLE—.

"Congress may appropriate money and otherwise provide for colonizing free colored persons, with their own consent, at any place or places without the United States."

I beg indulgence to discuss these proposed articles at some length. Without slavery the rebellion could never have existed; without slavery it could not continue.

Among the friends of the Union there is great diversity of sentiment and of policy in regard to slavery and the African race amongst us. Some would perpetuate slavery; some would abolish it suddenly, and without compensation; some would abolish it gradually, and with compensation; some would remove the freed people from us, and some would retain them with us; and there are yet other minor diversities. Because of these diversities we waste much strength in struggles among ourselves. By mutual concession we should harmonize and act together. This would be compromise; but it would be compromise among the friends, and not with the enemies, of the Union. These articles are intended to embody a plan of such mutual concessions. If the plan shall be adopted, it is assumed that emancipation will follow at least in several of the States.

Selection from *Abraham Lincoln: Complete Works*, Vol. II, edited by John G. Nicolay and John Hay. Published by The Century Company, New York, copyright © 1894.

CRITICAL THINKING

1. Summarize the content of each of President Lincoln's proposed amendments.
2. What group or groups would you say each proposed amendment was meant to mollify? Explain your thinking.

3. CITING THE *EMANCIPATION PROCLAMATION*, A SLAVE SERVING IN THE CONFEDERATE ARMY FREES HIMSELF

Although, technically, the Emancipation Proclamation *freed no slaves, after its issuance, many slaves interpreted it as a license to free themselves and took responsibility for their lives into their own hands. The story of such a self-emancipated slave, John the runaway, is given below. It originally appeared in a book by William Wells Brown, a fugitive slave who is regarded as the first black novelist in the United States.*

On Thursday . . . our [guards caught sight of] a solitary horseman, with a bucket on his arm, jogging soberly towards them. He proved to be a dark mulatto, of about thirty-five. As he approached, they ordered a halt.

"Where are you from?"

"Southern Army, cap'n," giving the military salute.

"Where are you going?"

"Coming to yous all."

"What do you want?"

"Protection, boss. You won't send me back, will you?"

"No: come in. Whose servant are you?"

"Cap'n Rhett's of South Carliny: you's heard of Mr. Barnwell Rhett, editor of 'The Charleston Mercury'? His brother commands a battery."

"How did you get away?"

"Cap'n gove me fifteen dollars this morning, and said, 'John, go out, and forage for butter and eggs.' So you see, boss (with a broad grin), I'se out foraging! I pulled my hat over my eyes, and jogged along on the cap'n's horse (see the brand S.C. on him?) with this basket on my arm, right by our guards. . . . They never challenged me once. If they had, though, I brought the cap'n's pass." And the new comer produced this document from his pocket-book, written in pencil, and carefully folded. . . .

Pass my servant, John, on horseback, anywhere between Winchester and Martinsburg, in search of butter, &c., &c.

"A. BURNETT RHETT, *Capt. Light Artillery, Lee's Battalion.*"

"Are there many negroes in the rebel corps?"

"Heaps, boss."

"Would the most of them come to us if they could?"

"All of them, cap'n. There isn't a little pickanniny so high (waving his hand two feet from the ground) that wouldn't."

"Why did *you* expect protection?"

"Heard so in Maryland, before the Proclamation."

"Where did you hear about the Proclamation?"

"Read it, sir, in a Richmond paper."

"What is it?"

"That every slave is to be emancipated on and after the thirteenth day of January. I can't state it, boss."

"Something like it. When did you learn to read?"

"In '49, sir. I was head waiter at Mrs. Nevitt's boarding-house in Savannah, and Miss Walcott, a New York lady, who was stopping there, taught me." . . .

"Were you at Antietam?"

"Yes, boss. Mighty hard battle!"

"Who whipped?"

"Yous all, massa. They say you didn't; but I saw it, and know. If you had fought us that next day,—Thurday,—you would have captured our whole army. They say so themselves."

"Who?"

"Our officers, sir."

"Did you ever hear of old John Brown?"

"Hear of *him*? Lord bless you, yes, boss: I've read his life, and have it now in my trunk in Charleston; sent to New York . . . and got it. I've read it to heaps of the colored folks. Lord, they think John Brown was almost a god. Just say you was a friend of his, and any slave will almost kiss your feet, if you let him. They say, if he was only alive now, he would be king. How it did frighten the white folks when he raised the insurrection! It was Sunday when we heard of it. They wouldn't let a negro go into the streets. I was waiter at the Mills House in Charleston. There was a lady from Massachusetts, who came down to breakfast that morning at my table. 'John,' she says, 'I want to see a negro church; where is the principal one?' 'Not any open today, mistress,' I told her. 'Why not?' 'Because a Mr. John Brown has raised an insurrection in Virginny.' 'Ah!' she says; 'well, they'd better look out, or they'll get the white churches shut up in that way some of these days, too!' Mrs. Nicholson, one of the proprietors, was listening from the office to hear what she said. Wasn't that lady watched after that? I have a History of San Domingo, too, and a Life of Fred. Douglass, in my trunk, that I got in the same way."

"What do the slaves think about the war?"

"Well, boss, they all wish the Yankee army would come. The white folks tell them all sorts of bad stories about you all; but they don't believe them."

John was taken to Gen. McClellan, to whom he gave all the information he possessed about the position, numbers, and organization of the rebel army. His knowledge was full and valuable, and is corroborated by all the facts we have learned from other sources. . . . At the close of the interview, he asked anxiously,

"General, you won't send me back, will you?"

"Yes," replied the general, with a smile, "I believe I will."

"I hope you won't, general. If you say so, I know I will have to go; but I come to yous all for protection and I hope you won't."

"Well, then, I suppose we will not. No, John, you are at liberty to go where you please. Stay with the army, if you like. No one can ever take you against your will."

Selection from William Wells Brown, *The Negro in the American Rebellion: His heroism and his fidelity.* Published by Lee & Shepard, Boston, 1867. Reprinted by Johnson Reprint Corporation, New York, copyright © 1968.

CRITICAL THINKING

1. With which army did John, the runaway, make contact in this story? Did he deliberately seek contact? Explain.
2. In what way do you consider John unusual?
3. What information beyond that presented in the textbook did you learn from reading the story above?

4. "JOHNNY REB" ENCOUNTERS "BILLY YANK"

The Civil War was the bloodiest war the United States has ever fought. Yet, diaries, journals, and letters of the fighting men describe many friendly encounters between Rebel and Yankee "foes." Alexander Hunter, a young Confederate soldier, describes one of these meetings.

It was the latter part of August [1863]; orders were given to be prepared to go on [guard] early in the morning; and until a late hour the men were busy cooking rations and cleaning equipments.

Before the mists had been chased by the rising sun, the company in close column of fours marched down the road. Men and animals were in perfect condition, brimful of mettle and in buoyant spirits.

The route lay along the banks of the river, upon the winding course of which, after several hours' riding, the regiment reached its destination and relieved the various [guards]. A sergeant and squad of men were left at each post, the company being spread out several miles on the river banks . . . to watch the enemy on the other side of the Rappahannock.

The next day our squad, Sergeant Joe Reid in command, sauntered down the bank, but seeing no one we lay at length under the spreading trees. . . .

The Rappahannock, which was at this place about two hundred yards wide, flowing slowly oceanward, its bosom reflecting the roseate-hued morn, was as lovely a body of water as the sun ever shone upon. The sound of the gentle ripple of its waves upon the sand was broken by a faint "halloo" which came from the other side.

"Johnny Reb; I say, J-o-h-n-n-y R-e-b, don't shoot!"

Joe Reid shouted back, "All right!"

"What command are you?"

The spoken words floated clear and distinct across the water, "The Black Horse Cavalry. Who are you?"

"The Second Michigan Cavalry."

"Come out on the bank," said our spokesman, "and show yourselves; we won't fire."

"On your honor, Johnny Reb?"

"On our honor, Billy Yank."

In a second a large squad of blue-coats across the way advanced to the water's brink. The Southerners did the same; then the former put the query.

"Have you any tobacco?"

"Plenty of it," went out our reply.

"Any sugar and coffee?" they questioned.

"Not a taste nor a smell."

"Let's trade," was shouted with eagerness.

"Very well," was the reply. "We have not much with us, but we will send to Fredericksburg for more, so meet us here this evening."

"All right," they answered; then added, "Say, Johnny, want some newspapers?"

"Y-e-s!"

"Then look out, we are going to send you some."

"How are you going to do it?"

"Wait and see."

The Rebs watched the group upon the other side curiously, wondering how even Yankee ingenuity could devise a way for sending a batch of papers across the river two hundred yards wide, and in the meantime each man had his own opinion.

"They will shoot arrows over," said Martin.

"Arrows, the devil!" replied the sergeant; "there never was a bow bent which could cast an arrow across this river."

"Maybe they will wrap them around a cannon ball and shoot them across; we'd better get away from here," hastily answered a tall, slim six-footer, who was rather afraid of big shots.

A roar of laughter followed this suggestion, but the originator was too intent on his own awakened fears to let the slightest movement of the enemy pass unscanned. Eagerly he watched while the others were having all the fun at his expense. Presently he shouted:

"Here they come!" and then in a tone of intense admiration, "I'll be doggoned if these Yanks are not the smartest people in the world."

On the other side were several miniature boats and ships—such as school-boys delight in—with sails set; the gentle breeze impelled the little crafts across the river, each freighted with a couple of newspapers. Slowly, but surely, they headed for the opposite bank as if some spirit Oberon or

Puck sat at the tiller; and in a few minutes had accomplished their voyage and were drawn up to await a favorable wind to waft them back.

Drawing lots, Joe Boteler, who found luck against him, started to town, with a muttered curse, to buy tobacco, leaving his comrades to seek some shady spot, and . . . sink deep in the latest war news from the enemy's standpoint, always interesting reading.

It was a cloudless day,—a day to dream,—and with a lazy . . . manner and half-shut eyes, enjoy to the soul the deep loveliness of the scene which lay around us like some fair creation of the fancy, listening the while to the thrills of the blue-bird which sat on the top of a lofty tree industriously practicing his notes like a prima donna getting a new opera by heart.

Joe returned in the evening with a box of plug tobacco about a foot square; but how to get it across was the question. The miniature boats could not carry it, and we shouted over to the Yanks that we had about twenty pounds of cut plug, and asked them what we must do? They hallooed back to let one of us swim across, and declared that it was perfectly safe. We held a council of war, and it was found that none of the Black Horse could swim beyond a few rods. Then I volunteered. Having lived on the banks of the Potomac most of my life, I was necessarily a swimmer.

Sergeant Reid went to a house not far off and borrowed a bread trough, and placing it on a plank, the box of tobacco was shipped, and disrobing I started, pushing my queer craft in front of me. As I approached the shore the news of my coming had reached camp, and nearly all the Second Michigan were lined up along the bank.

I felt a little queer, but I had perfect faith in their promise and kept on without missing a stroke until my miniature scow grounded on the beach. The blue-coats crowded around me and gave me a hearty welcome, and relieving the trough of its load, heaped the craft with offerings of sugar, coffee, lemons, and even candy, till I cried out that they would sink my transport. I am sure they would have filled a rowboat to the gunwhale had I brought one.

There was no chaffing or banter, only roistering welcomes.

Bidding my friends the enemy good-by, I swam

back with the precious cargo, and we had a feast that night.

Selection from *The Blue and the Gray: The Story of the Civil War as Told by Participants*, Vol. I, edited by Henry Steele Commager. Published by The Bobbs-Merrill Company, Indianapolis, copyright © 1950.

CRITICAL THINKING

1. Does the writer of the above account seem like a hardened professional warrior to you? Refer to specific parts of his account to back up your answer.
2. Give examples of the warmth and respect these "enemies" felt for each other. What is your reaction to this behavior?
3. Confederate and Yankee soldiers like those above might, at a later meeting, kill or wound each other in fierce fighting. How do you account for this?

5. GENERAL ULYSSES S. GRANT RECOUNTS THE SURRENDER OF THE ARMY OF NORTHERN VIRGINIA AT APPOMATTOX COURTHOUSE

The destructive din of the Civil War came to a quiet and dignified conclusion at Appomattox Courthouse, Virginia. There, in the house of Mr. Wilmer McLean, the two commanding generals of the opposing armies met to find a way to stop the fighting and end the costly war. General Ulysses S. Grant's recollections of that historic meeting are below.

The white flag was put out by Lee. . . . I was . . . moving towards Appomattox Court House. . . . Lee . . . sent a flag to the rear to advise Meade and one to the front to Sheridan, saying that he had sent a message to me for the purpose of having a meeting to consult about the surrender of his army, and asked for a suspension of hostilities until I could be communicated with . . . both of these commanders hesitated very considerably about suspending hostilities at all. They were afraid it was not in good faith, and we had the Army of Northern Virginia where it could not escape except by some deception. They, however, finally consented to a suspension of hostili-

ties for two hours to give an opportunity of communicating with me in that time, if possible. . . .

. . . But I had no doubt about the good faith of Lee, and pretty soon was conducted to where he was. I found him at the house of a Mr. [Wilmer] McLean, at Appomattox Court House, with Colonel [Charles] Marshall, one of his staff officers, awaiting my arrival. . . .

General Lee was dressed in a full uniform which was entirely new, and was wearing a sword of considerable value, very likely the sword which had been presented by the State of Virginia. . . . In my rough traveling suit, the uniform of a private with the straps of a lieutenant-general, I must have contrasted very strangely with a man so handsomely dressed, six feet high and of faultless form. But this was not a matter that I thought of until afterwards.

We soon fell into a conversation about old army times. He remarked that he remembered me very well in the old army; and I told him that as a matter of course I remembered him perfectly. . . . Our conversation grew so pleasant that I almost forgot the object of our meeting. After the conversation had run on in this style for some time, General Lee called my attention to the object of our meeting, and said that he had asked for his interview for the purpose of getting from me the terms I proposed to give his army. I said that I meant merely that his army should lay down their arms, not to take them up again during the continuance of the war unless duly and properly exchanged. He said that he had so understood my letter.

Then we gradually fell off again into conversation about matters foreign to the subject which had brought us together. This continued for some little time, when General Lee again interrupted the course of the conversation by suggesting that the terms I proposed to give his army ought to be written out. I called to General [Ely S.] Parker, secretary on my staff, for writing materials, and commenced writing out the following terms:

Appomattox C. H., Va.,
Ap'l 9th, 1865

GEN. R. E. LEE, Comd'g C. S. A.

GEN.: In accordance with the substance of my letter to you of the 8th inst., I propose to receive the surrender of the Army of N. Va. on the following terms, to wit: Rolls of all the officers and men to be made in duplicate. One copy to be given to an officer designated by me, the other to be retained by such officer or officers as you may designate. The officers to give their individual paroles [promises] not to take up arms against the Government of the United States until properly exchanged, and each company or regimental commander sign a like parole for the men of their commands. The arms, artillery and public property to be parked and stacked, and turned over to the officer appointed by me to receive them. This will not embrace the side-arms of the officers, nor their private horses or baggage. This done, each officer and man will be allowed to return to their homes, not to be disturbed by United States authority so long as they observe their paroles and the laws in force where they may reside.

Very respectfully,
U.S. Grant,
Lt.-Gen.

. . . As I wrote on, the thought occurred to me that the officers had their own private horses and effects, which were important to them, but of no value to us; also that it would be an unnecessary humiliation to call upon them to deliver their side arms.

No conversation, not one word, passed between General Lee and myself, either about private property, side arms, or kindred subjects. . . . When he read over that part of the terms about side arms, horses and private property of the officers, he remarked, with some feeling, I thought, that this would have a happy effect upon his army.

Then . . . General Lee remarked to me again that their army was organized a little differently from the army of the United States (still maintaining by implication that we were two countries); that in their army the cavalrymen and artillerists owned their own horses; and he asked if he was to understand that the men who so owned their horses were to be permitted to retain them. . . .

I then said to him that I thought this would be about the last battle of the war—I sincerely hoped so; and I said further I took it that most of the men in the ranks were small farmers. The whole country had been so raided by the two armies that it was doubtful whether they would be able to put in a crop to carry themselves and their families

through the next winter without the aid of the horses they were then riding. The United States did not want them and I would, therefore, instruct the officers I left behind to receive the paroles of his troops to let every man of the Confederate army who claimed to own a horse or mule take the animal to his home. Lee remarked again that this would have a happy effect. . . .

The much talked of surrendering of Lee's sword and my handing it back, this and much more that has been said about it is the purest romance. The word sword or side arms was not mentioned by either of us until I wrote it in the terms. . . .

General Lee, . . . before taking his leave, remarked that his army was in a very bad condition for want of food, and that they were without forage; that his men had been living for some days on parched corn exclusively, and that he would have to ask me for rations and forage. I told him "certainly," and asked for how many men he wanted rations. His answer was "about twenty five thousand": and I authorized him to send his own commissary and quartermaster to Appomattox Station, two or three miles away, where he could have, out of the trains we had stopped, all the provisions wanted. As for forage, we had ourselves depended almost entirely upon the country for that. . . .

Lee and I then separated as cordially as we had met.

Selection from *Personal Memoirs of U. S. Grant*, edited by E. B. Long. Published by The World Publishing Company, New York, 1952. Universal Library Edition, Grosset and Dunlap, New York, copyright © 1962.

CRITICAL THINKING

1. Contrast General Ulysses S. Grant, the wager of the war of attrition, with General Grant, the victor depicted in his account.
2. Give examples of Grant's consideration for the physical and emotional needs of the defeated Confederate leaders and men.
3. In writing this account, is it possible that Grant was attempting to make himself look good? How could you check the accuracy of what he reports?

CHAPTER 16

RECONSTRUCTING THE UNION

1865–1877

1. NORTHERN NEWSPAPER CORRESPONDENT SIDNEY ANDREWS DISPATCHES REPORTS FROM POSTWAR SOUTH CAROLINA

In September, October, and November of 1865, Sidney Andrews traveled through three states of the defeated Confederacy as the correspondent for the Boston Advertiser *and the* Chicago Tribune. *The following excerpts from his dispatches give his impressions of postwar Charleston and Columbia in the state of South Carolina.*

CHARLESTON, September 4, 1865.

A city of ruins, of desolation, of vacant houses, of widowed women, of rotting wharves, of deserted warehouses, of weed-wild gardens, of miles of grass-grown streets, of acres of pitiful and voiceful barrenness,—that is Charleston, wherein Rebellion loftily reared its head five years ago, on whose beautiful promenade the fairest of cultured women gathered with passionate hearts to applaud the assault of ten thousand upon the little garrison of Fort Sumter! . . .

Mothers yet teach their children hate of the North, I judge; for when I asked a bright-eyed girl of half a dozen years, with whom I walked on a back street for a block or two, whose girl she was, she promptly answered, "A Rebel mother's girl." Patience, good people who love liberty, patience; this petty woman's spite will bite itself to death in time. . . .

COLUMBIA, September 12, 1865.
. . . We rode over the road where [Sherman's] army marched. . . .

There is a great scarcity of stock of all kinds. What was left by the Rebel conscription officers was freely appropriated by Sherman's army, and the people really find considerable difficulty not less in living than in travelling. Milk, formerly an article much in use, can only be had now in limited quantities: even at the hotels we have more meals without than with it. There are more mules than horses, apparently; and the animals, whether mules or horses, are all in ill condition and give evidence of severe overwork.

Columbia was doubtless once the gem of the State. It is as regularly laid out as a checker-board, —the squares being of uniform length and breadth and the streets of uniform width. What with its broad streets, beautiful shade-trees, handsome lawns, extensive gardens, luxuriant shrubbery, and wealth of flowers, I can easily see that it must have been a delightful place of residence. No South-Carolinian with whom I have spoken hesitates an instant in declaring that it was the most beautiful city on the continent; and, as already mentioned, they charge its destruction directly to General Sherman.

It is now a wilderness of ruins. Its heart is but a mass of blackened chimneys and crumbling walls. Two thirds of the buildings in the place were burned, including, without exception, everything in the business portion. Not a store, office, or shop escaped; and for a distance of three fourths of a mile on each of twelve streets there was not a building left. "They destroyed everything which the most infernal Yankee ingenuity could devise means to destroy," said one gentleman to me. . . .

Every public building was destroyed, except the new and unfinished state-house. This is situated on the summit of tableland whereon the city is built, and commands an extensive view of the surrounding country, and must have been the first building seen by the victorious and on-marching Union army. From the summit of the ridge, on the opposite side of the river, a mile and a half away, a few shells were thrown at it, apparently by way of reminder, three or four of which struck it, without doing any particular damage. With this exception, it was unharmed, though the workshops, in which were stored many of the architraves, caps, sills, &c., were burned,—the fire, of course, destroying or seriously damaging their contents. The poverty of this people is so deep that there is no probability that it can be finished, according to the original design, during this generation at least.

The ruin here is neither half so eloquent nor touching as that at Charleston. This is but the work of flame, and might have mostly been brought about in time of peace. Those ghostly and crumbling walls and those long-deserted and grass-grown streets show the prostration of a community,—such prostration as only war could bring.

I find a commendable spirit of enterprise, though, of course, it is enterprise on a small scale, and the enterprise of stern necessity. The work of clearing away the ruins is going on, not rapidly or extensively, to be sure, but something is doing, and many small houses of the cheaper sort are going up. Yet, at the best, this generation will not ever again see the beautiful city of a year ago. Old men and despondent men say it can never be rebuilt. "We shall have to give it up to the Yankees, I reckon," said one of two gentlemen conversing near me this morning. "Give it up!" said the other; "they've already moved in and taken possession without asking our leave." I guess the remark is true. I find some Northern men already here, and I hear of more who are coming. . . .

The women who consider it essential to salvation to snub or insult Union officers and soldiers at every possible opportunity do not seem as numerous as they appeared to be in Charleston; and indeed marriages between soldiers and women of the middle class are not by any means the most uncommon things in the world; while I notice, in a quiet, unobservant manner, as even the dullest traveller may, that at least several very elegant ladies do not seem at all averse to the attentions of the gentlemen of shoulder straps. Can these things be, and not overcome the latent fire of Rebellion.

Selection from Sidney Andrews, *The South Since the War.* Published by Arno Press and the New York Times, New York, copyright © 1969.

CRITICAL THINKING

1. Give examples of anti-northern feelings among southerners Andrews met in both Charleston and Columbia. Do you think such a feeling was justified? Explain.
2. Do Andrews dispatches suggest that the South will recover and lose its bitterness toward the North? Using the text, support your answer.

2. PRESIDENT ANDREW JOHNSON EXTENDS AMNESTY TO MOST SOUTHERNERS

On May 29, 1865, as a part of his Reconstruction plan, President Andrew Johnson issued an amnesty proclamation, parts of which are given below. As a condition for receiving amnesty, southerners had to take the oath that appears first in the following excerpt. Several classes of southerners, however, were not permitted to take the oath until they followed certain steps.

MAY 29, 1865

BY THE PRESIDENT OF THE UNITED STATES OF AMERICA.

A PROCLAMATION.

I——— ———, do solemnly swear (or affirm), in presence of Almighty God, that I will henceforth faithfully support, protect, and defend the Constitution of the United States and the Union of the States thereunder, and that I will in like manner abide by and faithfully support all laws and proclamations which have been made during the existing rebellion with reference to the emancipation of slaves. So help me God.

The following classes of persons are excepted from the benefits of this proclamation:

First. All who are or shall have been pretended civil or diplomatic officers or otherwise domestic or foreign agents of the pretended Confederate government.

Second. All who left judicial stations under the United States to aid the rebellion.

Third. All who shall have been military or naval officers of said pretended Confederate government above the rank of colonel in the army or lieutenant in the navy.

Fourth. All who left seats in the Congress of the United States to aid the rebellion.

Fifth. All who resigned or tendered resignations of their commissions in the Army or Navy of the United States to evade duty in resisting the rebellion.

Sixth. All who have engaged in any way in treating otherwise than lawfully as prisoners of war persons found in the United States service as officers, soldiers, seamen, or in other capacities.

President Andrew Johnson's unpopularity after the Civil War led to an historic impeachment trial, but he was acquitted and finished his term.

Seventh. All persons who have been or are absentees from the United States for the purpose of aiding the rebellion.

Eighth. All military and naval officers in the rebel service who were educated by the Government in the Military Academy at West Point or the United States Naval Academy.

Ninth. All persons who held the pretended offices of governors of States in insurrection against the United States.

Tenth. All persons who left their homes within the jurisdiction and protection of the United States and passed beyond the Federal military lines into the pretended Confederate States for the purpose of aiding the rebellion.

Eleventh. All persons who have been engaged in the destruction of the commerce of the United States upon the high seas and all persons who have made raids into the United States from Canada or been engaged in destroying the commerce of the United States upon the lakes and rivers that separate the British Provinces from the United States.

Twelfth. All persons who, at the time when they seek to obtain the benefits hereof by taking the oath herein prescribed, are in military, naval, or civil confinement or custody, or under bonds of the civil, military, or naval authorities or agents of the United States as prisoners of war, or persons detained for offenses of any kind, either before or after conviction.

Thirteenth. All persons who have voluntarily participated in said rebellion and the estimated value of whose taxable property is over $20,000.

Fourteenth. All persons who have taken the oath of amnesty as prescribed in the President's proclamation of December 8, A.D. 1863, or an oath of allegiance to the Government of the United States since the date of said proclamation and who have not thenceforward kept and maintained the same inviolate.

Provided, That special application may be made to the President for pardon by any person belonging to the excepted classes, and such clemency will be liberally extended as may be consistent with the facts of the case and the peace and dignity of the United States.

The Secretary of State will establish rules and regulations for administering and recording the said amnesty oath, so as to insure its benefit to the people and guard the Government against fraud.

Selection from *Documents of American History*, edited by Henry Steele Commager. Published by Appleton-Century-Crofts (Division of Meredith Publishing Company), New York, copyright © 1963.

CRITICAL THINKING

1. Where in the structure of southern society would you place the persons listed as "excepted" from the benefits of President Johnson's proclamation? Why do you think these persons were excepted?
2. Many of the excepted persons became officials in southern state government. How was this possible? Refer to a specific part of Johnson's proclamation in your answer.
3. To which part of the proclamation do you think Congress most objected? Why?

3. WILLIAM H. CROOK'S EYEWITNESS ACCOUNT OF THE SENATE'S IMPEACHMENT PROCEEDINGS AGAINST PRESIDENT ANDREW JOHNSON

The clash over Reconstruction policies between Andrew Johnson and the Radical Republicans led to the first and only impeachment of a President of the United States. A bodyguard of the President— William H. Crook—was present at the impeachment proceedings and left this record of what he witnessed.

On the 23d of March, . . . the actual trial began. . . . When, from my seat in the gallery, I looked down on the Senate chamber, I had a moment of almost terror. It was not because of the great assemblage; it was rather in the thought that one could feel in the mind of every man and woman there that for the first time in the history of the United States a President was on trial for more than his life—his place in the judgment of his countrymen and of history.

There was a painful silence when the counsel for the President filed in and took their places. They were seated under the desk of the presiding officer . . . Chief-Justice Chase—on the right-hand side of the Senate chamber. The managers for the prosecution were already in their seats. Every seat in the gallery was occupied.

. . . Manager Butler arose to make the opening address for the prosecution. . . .

His speech was a violent attack upon the President. It was clever. Actually blameless incidents were made to seem traitorous. The address was so bitter, and yet so almost theatrical, that it seemed unreal. I wondered at the time why it so impressed me. In Butler's later action—to which I shall hereafter refer—came a possible explanation of this impression.

The trial lasted three weeks. The President, of course, never appeared. In that particular the proceedings lacked a spectacular interest they might have had. Every day the President had a consultation with his lawyers. For the rest, he attended to the routine work of his position. He was absolutely calm through it all. . . .

As the trial proceeded, the conviction grew with me—I think it did with every one—that the weight of evidence and of constitutional principle lay with the defence. There were several clever lawyers on the prosecution, and Butler had his legal precedents skilfully marshalled, but the greater part of the proceedings showed personal feeling and prejudice rather than proof. Every appeal that could be made to the passions of the time was utilized. . . .

In comparison, the calm, ordered, masterly reasoning of the defence must have inspired every one with a conviction of the truth of their cause. . . .

But the legal struggle . . . was hardly the contest that counted. The debate was for the benefit of the country at large; while the legal lights argued, the enemies of the President were working in other ways. The Senate was thoroughly canvassed, personal argument and influence were in constant use. Every personal motive, good or bad, was played upon. Long before the final ballot, it became known how most of the men would probably vote. Toward the end the doubtful ones had narrowed down to one man—Senator Ross, of Kansas. Kansas, which had been the fighting-ground of rebel guerilla and Northern abolitionist, was to have, in all probability, the determining vote in this contest.

Kansas was, from inception and history, abolitionist, radical. It would have been supposed that Senator Ross would vote with the Radicals. He had taken the place of James H. Lane, who had shot himself. Lane was a friend of the President, and, had he lived, in all probability would have supported him. But Ross had no such motive. It became known that he was doubtful. . . .

Then the cohorts of the Senate and the House bore down upon the Senator from Kansas. Party discipline was brought to bear, and then ridicule. Either from uncertainty, or policy, or a desire to keep his associates in uncertainty, Ross refused to make an announcement of his policy. In all probability, he was honestly trying to convince himself. . . .

On May 16th the vote was taken.

Every one who by any possible means could get a ticket of admission to the Senate chamber produced it early that morning at the Capitol. The floor and galleries were crowded.

The journal was read; the House of Representatives was notified that the Senate, "sitting for the trial of the President upon the articles of impeachment," was ready to receive the other House in the Senate chamber. . . .

The tension grew. There was a weary number of names before that of Ross was reached. When the clerk called it, and Ross stood forth, the crowd held its breath.

"Not guilty," called the Senator from Kansas.

It was like the bubbling over of a caldron. The Radical Senators, who had been laboring with Ross only a short time before, turned to him in rage; all over the house people began to stir. The rest of the roll-call was listened to with lessened interest, although there was still the chance for a surprise. When it was over, and the result—thirty-five to nineteen—was announced, there was a wild outburst, chiefly groans of anger and disappointment, for the friends of the President were in the minority. . . .

I ran all the way from the Capitol to the White House. I was young and strong in those days, and I made good time. When I burst into the library, where the President sat with Secretary Welles and two other men whom I cannot remember, they were quietly talking. Mr. Johnson was seated at a little table on which luncheon had been spread in the rounding southern end of the room. There were no signs of excitement.

"Mr. President," I shouted, too crazy with delight to restrain myself, "you are acquitted!"

All rose. I made my way to the President and got hold of his hand. The other men surrounded him, and began to shake his hand. The President responded to their congratulations calmly enough for a moment, and then I saw that tears were rolling down his face.

Selection from *The American Reader: From Columbus to Today*, edited by Paul M. Angle. Published by Rand McNally & Company, New York, 1958.

CRITICAL THINKING

1. Explain how the position of William H. Crook might have affected the validity of his eyewitness record as a primary source of historical information.
2. Why was Senator Ross's vote so important?
3. What does Ross's vote suggest to you about the man? Explain what you mean.

4. *KU KLUX KLAN* MEMBER ROBERT HAYES MITCHELL IS TRIED ON A CHARGE OF MURDER

Following are excerpts from the record of a case, tried before the Circuit Court of the United States, at Columbia, South Carolina. In the trial, Robert Hayes Mitchell, a member of the Ku Klux Klan, *was tried on a charge related to the lynching of Jim Williams, a black man. This was one of several "Ku Klux Klan Cases" tried in South Carolina in 1871.*

COLUMBIA, December 12, 1871. The indictment, charging Robert Hayes Mitchell, was read in the hearing of the prisoner.

Mr. Corbin [the prosecutor]. . . . The defendant who is now called before you is charged with having entered into a conspiracy for the purpose of preventing and restraining divers male citizens of the United States, of African descent, and qualified to vote, from exercising the right of voting.

We shall first show you that he entered into a general conspiracy, existing in the County of York, for the purpose of preventing colored voters of that County from exercising the right to vote.

We shall prove the existence of an organization, perfect in all its details, armed and disguised; that this organization was bound together by a terrible oath, the penalty for breaking of which was declared to be the doom of a traitor—death! death!! death!!! We shall show that this organization had a constitution and by-laws, regulating, in detail, all the duties of its members; that it prevaded the whole County, or a large portion of it; that it was inaugurated in 1868; that its active operations were somewhat suspended during the years '69 and '70, but that in '71, particularly, it became very active; that great numbers of colored citizens, who were entitled, by law, to vote, in that County, were visited by the Klan, and whipped, and many of them murdered. In this case, we shall show to you that this organization deliberately planned and executed the murder of Jim Williams, whose name you will find in this indictment, in pursuance of the purpose of the organization. We shall prove to you, gentlemen, that the defendant was present, aided and assisted in carrying out the purpose of the organization; and was present at the execution of Jim Williams. . . .

We shall endeavor to show that this attack upon Jim Williams was, not only for the purpose of preventing his voting in 1872, but because he had exercised the right and privilege of voting in 1870. . . .

TESTIMONY OF MRS. ROSY WILLIAMS.

Mrs. Rosy Williams, a witness for the prosecution, being duly sworn, testified as follows:

Direct Examination by Mr. Corbin.

Q. Are you the wife of Jim Williams?

A. Yes, sir.

Q. Where do you live? Where did you live when Jim Williams was living?

A. On Bratton's place.

Q. In what County? York County?

A. Yes sir.

Q. When was Jim Williams killed—your husband?

A. The 7th of March.

Q. Tell the court and jury all about it—all you know about it?

A. They came to my house about 2 o'clock in the night; came in the house and called him.

Q. Who came?

A. Disguised men. I can't tell who it was. I don't know any of them.

Q. What do you call them?

A. I call them Ku Klux.

Q. How many came?

A. I don't know how many there was.

Q. How many do you think?

A. I reckon about nine or ten came into the house, as nigh as I can guess it?

Q. What did they do?

A. He went under the house before they came, and after they came in he came up in the house and gave them the guns. There were but two in the house, and then they asked him for the others, and cussed, and told him to come out. He told them he had never had any of the guns. He went with them, and after they had took him outdoors they came in the house after me, and said there were some guns hid. I told them there was not, and after I told them that they went out, and after

they had went out there, I heard him make a fuss like he was strangling.

Q. Who?

A. Williams. Then I went to the door and pulled the door open, and allowed to go down and beg them not to hurt him. They told me not to go out there. Well, I didn't go out. Then they told me to shut the door, and take my children and go to bed. I shut the door, but didn't go to bed. I looked out of the crack after them until they got under the shadows of the trees. I couldn't see them then.

Q. Did they take Jim Williams?

A. Yes, sir; but I couldn't tell him from the rest.

Q. Was that the last time you ever saw him alive?

A. Yes, sir.

Q. Or did you see him again?

A. No, sir. The next morning I went and looked for him, but I didn't find him. I was scared too. Then I went for my people, to get some one to go help me look for him; and I met an old man who told me they had found him, and said he was dead. They had hung him; but I didn't go out there until 12 o'clock.

Q. Did you go out there then? Did you see him?

A. Yes, sir.

Q. What was his condition?

A. He was hung on a pine tree.

Q. With a rope around his neck?

A. Yes, sir.

Q. Dead?

A. Yes, sir; he was dead.

Selection from *Proceedings in the Ku Klux Trials, at Columbia, S.C. in the United States Circuit Court, November Term, 1871.* Reprinted by Negro Universities Press, a Division of Greenwood Publishing Corporation, New York, copyright © 1969. Originally published by Republican Printing Company, State Printers, 1872.

CRITICAL THINKING

1. What charge was brought against Robert Mitchell? What law of the United States made his action a crime?
2. What effects did actions like the lynching of Jim Williams have on the place of free blacks in southern society? Explain why you think they had these effects.

WASHINGTON, D.C.
Home Of The
Nation's Government

The Capitol was extended with a massive new dome and two enormous wings, after Congress decided to appropriate funds for construction of large-scale public works in 1849. Additions to the building were seen as an expression of faith in the permanence of the United States.

On November 17, 1800, the Federal Government officially moved from Philadelphia to its new home in Washington, D.C. But the Washington that greeted 106 legislators and 32 senators on that day was nothing more than a few buildings and roughly-paved roads along the Potomac River.

President John Adams and his wife Abigail moved into an "executive palace" that was unplastered and unfurnished. The muddy grounds outside the mansion were landscaped with old kilns from brick-making, water-filled pits, stonecutters' shacks, and supply sheds.

Over at the "Congress house" the situation was little better. Congressmen complained of cramped quarters and of the city's dreariness

D O C U M E N T

An early view of Washington, D.C., was painted by George Cooke in 1833. Today it is on display in the Oval Office of the White House.

A watercolor of a Washington street was painted by Baroness Hyde de Neuville, the wife of the French ambassador, in 1817.

and inconvenience. Many legislators lived in Washington only while Congress was in session, and for several years, debate raged about whether the government could remain in "The Capital of Miserable Huts."

Not until the end of the nineteenth century did the capital city assume the grace, dignity, and beauty its forefathers had envisioned.

CRITICAL THINKING

1. How does the drawing of a Washington, D.C. Street (above) depict life in America in 1817?
2. Identify the buildings in the 1833 painting of Washington, D.C.

The Transformation of America

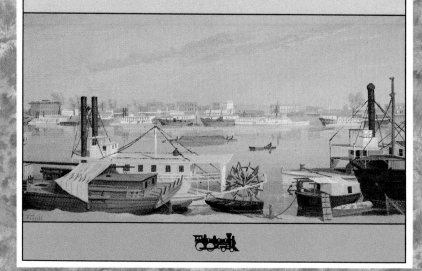

CHAPTER 17

AN INDUSTRIAL NATION

1865–1900

1. RAILWAY WORKER ALEXANDER TOPONCE REMEMBERS THE DAY THE TRANSCONTINENTAL RAILROAD WAS FINISHED

For seven years, workers of the Central Pacific and Union Pacific railroads labored to lay track between Iowa and California. On May 10, 1869, two engines —the Union Pacific Jupiter and the Central Pacific No. 119—met at Promontory Point, Utah, and the effort was completed. A number of years later, one witness, Alexander Toponce, described what he had seen that day.

On the last day, only about 100 feet [of track] were laid, and everybody tried to have a hand in the work. I took a shovel . . . and threw a shovel full of dirt on the ties just to tell about it afterward.

A special train from the west brought Sidney Dillon, General Dodge, T. C. Durant, John R. Duff, S. A. Seymour, [and] a lot of newspaper men. . . .

Another train made up at Ogden carried the band from Fort Douglas [and] the leading men of Utah Territory. . . .

California furnished the Golden Spike. Governor Tuttle of Nevada furnished one of silver. General Stanford . . . presented one of gold, silver, and iron from Arizona. The last tie was of California laurel.

When they came to drive the last spike, Governor Stanford, president of the Central Pacific, took the sledge, and the first time he struck he missed the spike and hit the rail.

What a howl went up! Irish, Chinese, Mexicans, and everybody yelled with delight. "He missed it. Yee." The engineers blew the whistles and rang their bells. Then Stanford tried it again and tapped the spike . . . [The] telegraph operators had fixed their instruments so that the tap was reported in all the offices east and west, and set bells to tapping in hundreds of towns and cities. . . .Then Vice President T. C. Durant of the Union Pacific took up the sledge and he missed the spike the first time. Then everybody slapped everybody else again and yelled, "He missed it too, yow!"

It was a great occasion, every one carried off souvenirs and there are enough splinters of the last tie in museums to make a good bonfire.

When the connection was finally made the Union Pacific and the Central Pacific engineers ran their engines up until the pilots touched. Then the engineers shook hands and had their pictures taken.

Selection from "Reminiscences of Alexander Toponce, Pioneer," in *A Treasury of Railroad Folklore* edited by B. A. Botkin and Alvin F. Harlow. Published by Bonanza Books, New York, copyright © 1953.

CRITICAL THINKING

1. What was the general mood of the crowd as the two railroad lines were joined?
2. In what ways did people show that they believed that the event was of great importance?

2. SIMON STERNE CRITICIZES THE RAILROADS

As time went on, not all Americans were as enthusiastic about the development of the great railroads as the people at Promontory Point in 1869. Many critics spoke out against what they saw as the unfair profits, business practices, and political power of the railroads. One such critic was Simon Sterne, a New York attorney and social reformer. This passage comes from an entry Sterne wrote about monopolies for a nineteenth-century encyclopedia of political science and economics.

That enterprises such as railways have a tendency to become monopolies, although their building is quite free in the United States, arises from the nature of such enterprises. The proportion of fixed charges to mere operating expenses . . . is so great in the railway, that [after it has been constructed] it may almost indefinitely increase its business without at all in proportion increasing its expenses. . . . The existing line can, therefore, almost always outbid a competitor for business. . . . As the service is consumed at the spot where it is created, and is rendered without a relative increase of expenditure . . . there is in such a case . . . a monopoly created which demands the constant exercise of legal restraint. Although railways may be increased in number from given points . . . the number of those railways will necessarily be so few that their interest to combine, as against their tendency to compete, will outweigh competition, and combination becomes the general result of almost all competitive railway building. After combination has been effected, the community is confronted with the fact that its service is no cheaper than it was before; that its business is done by two or three lines instead of one which previously rendered the service; that one line would have sufficed to have done the whole business, and that there is a loss of capital to the community represented by the building of the second or third line. This capital is lost because the community has failed to do its duty to limit the charges of these transporting corporations, which are enabled to earn extravagant rates of charge by the growth of the community . . . ; and so large is the income . . . that new capital is tempted into the same field for the purpose of dividing the business with the existing line, not because there is any necessity for the rival line . . . but simply because of the profit made by the existing line. . . . No service is done to the community by the building of the new line between two given points, if prices remain the same to the community, and the business is subsequently divided between the two roads, but the ten millions of capital are diverted from other employments. If in consequence of competition between the two lines the price . . . is reduced, the community is the gainer . . . but if, after the new line is built, a combination is made between the two roads to maintain prices so that both may earn dividends upon their capital, the community has lost for other purposes the ten millions unnecessarily invested—a very serious loss indeed. This has so frequently been the case that it is no longer a hypothetical illustration, but one taken from facts within the knowledge of every man who has observed the course of railway construction and railway wars and railway combinations in the United States; and while it is true that a competing line does touch, at intermediate points, territory which is not touched by the line previously existing, and thus incidental benefits are conferred, those incidental benefits by no means outweigh the enormous waste of capital which has been occasioned by railway construction for mere purposes of dividing business, with combination as to rates.

Selection from Simon Sterne, "Monopolies," in *Cyclopedia of Political Science, Political Economy, and of the Political History of the United States*, Vol. II, edited by John J. Lalor. Published by Melbert B. Cary & Company, Chicago, copyright © 1883.

CRITICAL THINKING

1. According to Sterne, why did existing railway lines tend to get more business than new lines?
2. What reasons did Sterne give for believing that American railways tended to become monopolies?
3. What policy did Sterne seem to be recommending in regard to railways?

---

3. JOURNALIST HENRY D. LLOYD WARNS AGAINST AN "AGE OF COMBINATION"

The growing power of corporations, monopolies, and other combinations of power alarmed many Americans. Among them was Henry D. Lloyd, a journalist known for his articles about John D. Rockefeller's Standard Oil Company. In 1884, Lloyd wrote "Lords of Industry," an article warning of the dangers of what he called the coming "age of combination."

On the theory of "too much of everything" our industries, from railroads to workingmen, are being organized to prevent milk, nails, lumber, freights, labor, soothing syrup, and all these other things, from becoming too cheap. The majority have never yet been able to buy enough of anything. The minority have too much of everything to sell. Seeds of social trouble germinate fast in such conditions. Society is letting these combinations become institutions without compelling them to adjust their charges to the cost of production, which used to be the universal rule of price. Our laws and commissions to regulate the railroads are but toddling steps in a path in which we need to walk like men. The change from competition to combination is nothing less than one of those revolutions which march through history with giant strides. It is not likely that this revolution will go backward. . . .

Man, the only animal which forgets, has already in a century or two forgotten that the freedom, . . . which he has enjoyed for a brief interval, has been unknown in most of the history of our race, and in all the history of most races. . . .

. . . We have had an era of material inventions. We now need a renaissance of moral inventions, contrivances to tap the vast currents of moral magnetism flowing uncaught over the face of society. Morals and values rise and fall together. If our combinations have no morals, they can have no values. If the tendency to combination is irresistible, control of it is imperative. Monopoly and anti-monopoly . . . represent the two great tendencies of our time: monopoly, the tendency to combination; anti-monopoly, the demand for social control of it. As the man is bent toward business or patriotism, he will negotiate combinations or agitate for laws to regulate them. The first is capitalistic, the second is social. The first, industrial; the second, moral. The first promotes wealth; the second, citizenship. . . . Our young men can no longer go west; they must go up or down. Not new land, but new virtue must be the outlet for the future. . . . We cannot hereafter, as in the past, recover freedom by going to the prairies; we must find it in the society of the good. In the presence of great combinations, in all departments of life, the moralist and patriot have work to do of a significance never before approached.

Selection from Henry D. Lloyd, "Lords of Industry," *North American Review*, CXXXVIII (June, 1884).

CRITICAL THINKING

1. What dangers did Lloyd see for Americans in "the age of combinations"?
2. Why was the closing of the frontier such an important part of this?

4. JOHN D. ROCKEFELLER DEFENDS HIS BUSINESS PRACTICES

For decades, the name John D. Rockefeller {1839–1937} was almost synonymous with wealth, power, and busines practices of American capitalism. The son of a peddler, Rockefeller began as a clerk. By the time he was 31, he had transformed a highly successful produce business into the Standard Oil Company, the largest refining company in the world. By 1882, the Standard Oil Trust controlled nearly all oil refining and distribution in America. In 1899, Rockefeller made this statement to a government commission.

Q*uestion.* To what advantages, or favors, or methods of management do you ascribe chiefly the success of the Standard Oil Company?

Answer. I ascribe the success of the Standard to its consistent policy to make the volume of its business large through the merits and cheapness of its products. It has spared no expense in finding, securing, and utilizing the best and cheapest methods of manufacture. It has sought the best superintendents and workmen and paid the best wages. It has not hesitated to sacrifice old machinery and old plants for new and better ones. It has placed its [factories] at the points where they could supply markets at the least expense. It has not only sought markets for its principal products, but for all possible by-products. . . . It has not hesitated to invest millions of dollars in methods of cheapening the gathering and distribution of oils by pipe lines, special cars, tank steamers, and tank wagons. It has erected tank stations at every important railroad station to cheapen the storage and delivery of its products. It has spared no expense in forcing its products into the markets of the world. . . .

Question. What are . . . the chief advantages [of] industrial combinations . . .?

Answer. All the advantages which can be derived from a cooperation of persons and aggregation of capital. . . .

It is too late to argue about advantages of industrial combinations. They are a necessity. And if Americans are to have the privilege of extending their business in all the states of the Union, and into foreign countries as well, they are a necessity on a large scale, and require the agency of more than one corporation. Their chief advantages are:

(1) Command of necessary capital.
(2) Extension of limits of business.
(3) Increase of number of persons interested in business.
(4) Economy in the business.
(5) Improvements and economies which are derived from knowledge of many interested persons of wide experience.
(6) Power to give the public improved products at less prices and still make a profit for stockholders.
(7) Permanent work and good wages for laborers.

I speak from my experience. . . . Our first combination was a partnership and afterwards a corporation in Ohio. That was sufficient for a local refining business. But dependent solely upon local business we should have failed years ago. We were forced to extend our markets and to seek for export trade. This . . . made the seaboard cities a necessary place of business. . . .

We soon discovered as the business grew that the primary method of transporting oil in barrels could not last. . . . Hence[,] we . . . adopted the pipe-line system, and found capital for pipe-line construction. . . .

To operate pipelines required franchises from the States in which they were located, and consequently corporations in those States. . . . To perfect the pipe-line system . . . required in the neighborhood of fifty millions of capital. This could not be obtained or maintained without industrial combination. . . .

The pipeline system required other improvements, such as tank cars upon railways, and finally the tank steamer. Capital had to be furnished for them and corporations created to own and operate them.

Every step taken was necessary in the business if it was to be properly developed, and only through such successive steps and by such an industrial combination is America to-day enabled to utilize the bounty which its land pours forth, and to furnish the world with the best and cheapest light ever known.

Selection adapted from J. D. Rockefeller, testimony, December 30, 1899, *Report of the United States Industrial Commission*, I., in Thomas G. Manning and David M. Potter, *Government and the American Economy, 1870–Present*, Published by Henry Holt and Company, New York, copyright © 1950.

CRITICAL THINKING

1. Summarize the advantages Rockefeller saw for industrial combinations and corporations.
2. What steps did Rockefeller say he took to gain complete control of the refining and distribution of oil?
3. What justifications for this did he offer?

5. RUSSELL HERMAN CONWELL'S SPEECH CAPTURES THE SPIRIT OF HIS AGE

The ambition that spurred entrepreneurs to build railroads and found oil fortunes was not limited to men like John D. Rockefeller. The anyone-can-get-rich attitude was perhaps best summed up in this 1870 speech by Russell Herman Conwell, a Baptist minister and popular lecturer. His oration is aptly titled "Acres of Diamonds."

I say to you that you have "acres of diamonds" in Philadelphia right where you now live. "Oh," but you will say, "you cannot know much about your city if you think there are any 'acres of diamonds' here." . . .

Now then, I say again that the opportunity to get rich, to attain unto great wealth, is here in Philadelphia now, within the reach of almost every man and woman who hears me speak to-night, and I mean just what I say. I have not come to this platform even under these circumstances to recite something to you. I have come to tell you what in God's sight I believe to be the truth, and if the years of life have any value to me in the attainment of common sense, I know I am right; that the men and women sitting here, who found it difficult perhaps to buy a ticket to this lecture or gathering to-night, have within their reach "acres of diamonds," opportunities to get largely wealthy. There never was a place on earth more adapted than the city of Philadelphia to-day, and never in the history of the world did a poor man without capital have such an opportunity to get rich quickly and honestly as he has now in our city. I say it is the truth, and I want you to accept it as such; for if you think I have come to simply recite something, then I would better not be here. I have no time to waste in any such talk, but to say the things I believe, and unless some of you get richer for what I am saying to-night my time is wasted.

I say that you ought to get rich, and it is your duty to get rich. How many of my pious brethren say to me, "Do you, a Christian minister, spend your time going up and down the country advising young people to get rich, to get money?" "Yes, of course I do." They say, "Isn't that awful! Why don't you preach the gospel instead of preaching about man's making money?" "Because to make money honestly is to preach the gospel." That is the reason. The men who get rich may be the most honest men you find in the community. . . .

There are some . . . people who think if you take any profit on anything you sell that you are an unrighteous man. On the contrary, you would be a criminal to sell goods for less than they cost. You have no right to do that. You cannot trust a man with your money who cannot take care of his own. You cannot trust a man in your family that is not true to his own wife. You cannot trust a man in the world that does not begin with his own heart, his own character, and his own life. It would have been my duty to have furnished a jack-knife to the third man, or the second, and to have sold it to him and actually profited myself. I have no more right to sell goods without making a profit on them than I have to overcharge him dishonestly beyond what they are worth. But I should so sell each bill of goods that the person to whom I sell shall make as much as I make.

To live and let live is the principle of the gospel, and the principle of every-day common sense. Oh, young man, hear me; live as you go along. Do not wait until you have reached my years before you begin to enjoy anything of this life. If I had the millions back, or fifty cents of it, which I have tried to earn in these years, it would not do me anything like the good that it does me now in this almost sacred presence to-night. Oh, yes, I am paid over and over a hundredfold to-night for dividing as I have tried to do in some measure as I went along through the years. I ought not speak that way, it sounds egotistic, but I am old enough now to be excused for that. I should have helped my fellow-men, which I have tried to do, and every one should try to do, and get the happiness of it. The man who goes home with the sense that

Clergyman Russell Herman Conwell delivered his "Acres of Diamonds" lecture over 6,000 times.

he has stolen a dollar that day, that he has robbed a man of what was his honest due, is not going to sweet rest. He arises tired in the morning, and goes with an unclean conscience to his work the next day. He is not a successful man at all, although he may have laid up millions. But the man who has gone through life dividing always with his fellow-men, making and demanding his own rights and his own profits, and giving to every other man his rights and profits, lives every day, and not only that, but it is the royal road to great wealth. The history of the thousands of millionaires shows that to be the case.

Selection from *American Forum: Speeches on Historic Issues, 1788–1900*, edited by Ernest J. Wrage and Barnet Baskerville. Published by Harper & Row, New York, copyright © 1960.

CRITICAL THINKING

1. Explain what Conwell means by "acres of diamonds in Philadelphia."
2. Conwell states that "it is your duty to get rich." List the arguments he makes to support his statement.
3. How does the author compare the principle of the gospel and common sense?

P I C T U R E A S

THE PHILADELPHIA CENTENNIAL
America Demonstrates Its New Industrial Power

On opening day, large crowds gathered at the Centennial Exhibition's major buildings: the Main Hall, Horticultural Building, Agricultural Hall, Machinery Hall, and Memorial Hall which is the only building still standing.

Originally conceived as a gift from France to the U.S. in honor of the Centennial, the Statue of Liberty was completed in 1884 and not unveiled until 1886. The torch, however, was ready in time for display at the Expo.

To celebrate the 100th anniversary of American independence, an international exposition of arts, manufactures, and products was held in Philadelphia, Pennsylvania, in 1876. Thirty-five nations and twenty-six states participated in the Centennial Exhibition, which was housed in more than 200 buildings, spread over 236 acres.

Among the biggest attractions at this world's fair were working models of numerous new machines and recent inventions, many of them on display for the first time. Included on display were the typewriter, telephone, refrigerator car, air brake and first mechanical computer.

As a showcase for American industry and products, the Exhibition greatly enhanced the

D O C U M E N T

Up-to-date technology was admired by visitors who witnessed a demonstration of the latest technique in newspaper printing: the Web Press.

President Grant and Brazilian Emperor Dom Pedro II started the Corliss steam engine, which powered all machinery at this exhibition.

In the Women's Pavilion, teachers demonstrated a new idea in pre-school education: the Kindergarten.

United States' prestige. It drew nearly 10 million people, including many foreign visitors, whose admiration did much to revise previous European opinion of the United States as a second-rank country. The Philadelphia Centennial marked the beginning of worldwide recognition of the United States as a powerful industrial nation.

CRITICAL THINKING

1. Cite specific pictures to support your conclusions about public support of the Centennial.
2. What ideas, shown in these pictures, are recognizable as early forms of something we use today?

ONE POINT OF VIEW

THOMAS EAKINS

Thomas Eakins [1844–1916] painted in the last quarter of the nineteenth century. The machine age had arrived and the scientific age was just beginning.

Eakins portrayed this new America in his paintings. While many other American artists followed European fashion by painting pictures of exotic, faraway places, Thomas Eakins painted baseball games, medical operations, and portraits of uncompromising honesty. "If America is to produce great painters," he wrote, "and if young art students wish to assume a place in the history of the art of their country, their first desire should be to remain in America, to peer deeper into the art of American life."

Eakins was a painter of facts who often avoided the pretty gracefulness sought by his contemporaries. He was a master of perspective and anatomy who created three dimensional models in his studio in order to study the composition and light in his paintings. He used his skill as a photographer to make paintings which were scientifically true to life. Both the way he painted and the subjects he chose to paint reflect Eakins' belief in a rational world, a belief that was central to the development of industrial America.

In the surgical amphitheater of Philadelphia's Jefferson Medical College, Dr. Samuel Gross directed medical operations. All observers and participants appear unemotional in the service of science, except for one figure, possibly the patient's mother, who recoils in horror.

CRITICAL THINKING

1. Eakins was known for painting "not what ought to be, but what is." How is this style of painting useful to students of history?
2. Eakins used photography as a tool to help him paint more realistically. What elements in these pictures display his commitment to realism?

In 1871, Thomas Eakins painted this domestic scene in his own comfortable Philadelphia home. *Home Scene* shows a stylishly dressed woman occupied at the piano while her child plays on the richly carpeted floor. This is a picture of an increasingly comfortable America.

"Max Schmidt in a Single Scull" is among the earliest paintings in which we see Eakin's scientific and mechanical approach to both his subject and his method of painting. His reliance on perspective is evident here.

CHAPTER 18

POLITICS AND POLITICIANS

1868–1896

1. SOCIOLOGIST WILLIAM GRAHAM SUMNER DESCRIBES THE HEALTH OF AMERICAN POLITICS IN 1876

As many commentators noted, the state of American politics in the years following the Civil War was far from good. In some areas, bribery and corruption were the rule; in many others, the political process seemed to have become virtually a "business." William Graham Sumner, who was to become one of the country's most famous sociologists, wrote this description of the state of American politics in 1876.

It seems to me that, taking the whole community through, the tone is rising and the standard is advancing, and that this is one great reason why the system seems to be degenerating. Existing legislation nourishes and produces some startling scandals, which have great effect on people's minds. The same legislation has demoralized the people, and perverted their ideas of the functions of government even in the details of town and ward interests. The political machinery also has been refined and perfected until it totally defeats the popular will, and has produced a kind of despair in regard to any effort to recover that of which the people have been robbed; but I think that it would be a great mistake to suppose that there are not, behind all this, quite as high political standards and as sound a public will as ever before. An obvious distinction must be made here between the administration of the government, or the methods of party politics, and the general political morale of the people. Great scandals are quickly forgotten, and there are only too many of them throughout our history. Party methods have certainly become worse and worse. The public service has certainly deteriorated; but I should judge that the political will of the nation never was purer than it is to-day. That will needs instruction and guidance. It is instructed only slowly and by great effort . . . because it has learned distrust. . . . [B]ut there are some public signs of it, which are the best encouragement we have to-day.

Selection from William Graham Sumner, "Politics in America, 1776–1876," *The North American Review*, Vol. 122, January, 1876.

CRITICAL THINKING

1. What flaws did William Sumner find in American political life?
2. What evidence did Sumner give for being hopeful about the future of American politics?

---

2. PRESIDENT RUTHERFORD B. HAYES FAVORS CIVIL SERVICE REFORM

Rutherford B. Hayes, who succeeded Ulysses S. Grant as President in 1876, was a leading advocate of governmental reform. In his inaugural address he declared his support of civil service reform—a view that helped lead the way toward the passage of the Pendleton Act, in 1883.

I ask the attention of the public to the paramount necessity of reform in our civil service —a reform not merely as to certain abuses and practices of so-called official patronage which have come to have the sanction of usage in the several Departments of our Government, but a change in the system of appointment itself; a reform that shall be thorough, radical, and complete; a return to the principles and practices of the founders of the Government. They neither expected nor desired from public officers any partisan service. They meant that public officers should owe their whole service to the Government and to the people. They meant that the officer should be secure in his tenure as long as his personal character remained untarnished and the performance of his duties satisfactory. They held that appointments to office were not to be made nor expected merely as rewards for partisan services. . . .

The President of the United States of necessity

owes his election to office to the suffrage and zealous labors of a political party, the members of which cherish with ardor and regard as of essential importance the principles of their party organization; but he should strive to be always mindful of the fact that he serves his party best who serves the country best.

Selection from *Inaugural Addresses of the Presidents of the United States*. Published by U.S. Government Printing Office, Washington, D.C., 1969.

CRITICAL THINKING

1. What reasons might President Hayes have had for declaring that the use of political patronage for government offices was not intended by the founders of the country?
2. Explain . . . "he serves his party best who serves the country best."

---

3. ROBERT INGERSOLL WAVES A "BLOODY SHIRT"

During this period, many Republican politicians practiced what was called "waving the bloody shirt." The following speech, which Robert G. Ingersoll gave in Maine during the campaign of 1880, shows how these politicians stirred up sentiment against the South and the Democratic party by reminding Northern voters of the Civil War.

Ladies and gentlemen: This is in my opinion the grandest and best country in the world. . . . And when I speak of "Our country" I mean the North, East, and West. There are parts of this country that are not yet civilized. There are parts of this country in which the people do not believe in the great principle of self-government. . . .

I want you to know that every man that thinks the State is greater than the Union, is a Democrat. Every man that declared [in favor of] slavery was a Democrat. Every man that signed an ordinance [declaration] of secession was a Democrat. Every man that lowered our flag from the skies was a Democrat. Every man that bred bloodhounds was a Democrat. Every preacher that said that slavery was a divine institution was a Democrat. Recollect it! Every man that shot a Union soldier was a Democrat. Every wound borne by you Union soldiers is a souvenir of a Democrat. You got your crutches from Democrats. Every man that starved a Union soldier was a Democrat. . . . The keepers of Andersonville and Libby [camps for Union prisoners of war], those two wings that will bear the Confederacy to eternal infamy, were all Democrats. . . . The men who attempted to spread yellow fever in our Northern cities were all Democrats. The men who proposed to give our Northern cities to the flames were all Democrats! . . . The men who wanted to assassinate Northern Governors were Democrats.

Now all I ask you to do is what you believe to be right. If you really think liberty of speech, the ballot box, [and] the revenue are safer with the South than with the North, then vote the Democratic ticket early and often. If you believe it is better to trust the men who fought against the country than the men who fought to preserve it . . . then vote the Democratic ticket. . . .

. . . The Democrats now have both houses of Congress. If they get the Executive they'll have the whole; they'll annul the legislation of the war. They'll make Unionism disreputable. They'd make a Union soldier ashamed to say he lost a leg on the field of glory and make him say he lost it in a thrashing machine. . . . I don't want to see them have that pleasure. The Rebel possessions and claims don't amount to anything in dollars and cents. Liberty is cheap at any price. . . . I want my government to be proud and free. Liberty is a thing wherein extravagance is economy.

Selection from Robert G. Ingersoll, "Speech at Lewiston, Maine," (1880) in *Words that Made American History*, edited by Richard N. Current, *et. al*. Published by Little Brown, Boston, copyright © 1972.

CRITICAL THINKING

1. What emotions was Robert Ingersoll appealing to in this speech?
2. According to Ingersoll, what values and principles were being jeopardized by Southerners and Democrats?
3. What arguments or evidence did Ingersoll offer to support his claim that the Democrats were dangerous to the Union?

THOMAS NAST

N ever before or since has the work of a cartoonist had a more powerful influence on American politics than the cariacatures of Thomas Nast [1840–1902].

Nast was a German immigrant who received little schooling. At 15, he began working as an illustrator for a weekly newspaper. By the time he was 25, his drawings of the Civil War had brought him success and recognition. But it is for his cartoons of "Boss" William Tweed that Nast is best remembered.

Nast's cartoons led to public indignation against Tweed, who controlled the government of New York City. Investigations into corruption eventually resulted in the arrest of Tweed and many members of his "Ring."

It was Nast's drawings that proved Tweed's final undoing: after a year in prison, Tweed tried to flee the country, but he was soon caught—by policemen who recognized him from a Nast cartoon!

Thomas Nast's drawings of "Boss Tweed" became the stereotype image of all corrupt political bosses and, indeed, a "type" to represent any kind of civic corruption. Later cartoonists' depictions of other corrupt political bosses, along with greedy heads of large organizations, were clearly modeled on Nast's original Tweed drawings.

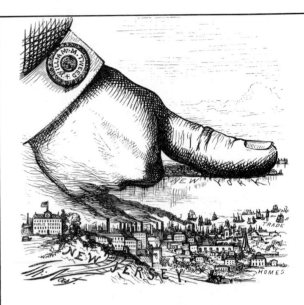

Nast saw New York City being crushed by the corrupt thumb of Boss Tweed. The vitriolic cartoon below shows Tweed and his "Ring" as vultures gloating over their victims' bones.

The Republican elephant made its first appearance in November, 1874, in the above cartoon. Nast also was the first to use the donkey as a symbol of the Democratic Party. In the cartoon at the left, Nast reveals that he understood the considerable power of his pen. He portrays himself perched on a printing press that is pulverizing corrupt politicians.

CRITICAL THINKING

1. Why did Nast's cartoons become powerful political influences?
2. What do present-day cartoonists owe to Nast and his critical approach to politics?
3. Cite two kinds of background information viewers would need before they could understand these political cartoons.
4. In what ways do political cartoons differ from other kinds of cartoons?

4. EDITOR RICHARD WATSON GILDER DEFINES A NEW TYPE OF PATRIOTISM

The corruption of politics in the late 1800s helped to undermine the respect that most people once placed in political parties. The editor of the Century *magazine, Richard Watson Gilder, suggests in his speech, "The New Patriotism," that politicians and statesmen must develop new attitudes toward courage.*

What seems to be the most needed patriotism in our day and country? In the first place, we ought as a nation to cultivate peace with all other nations. This was good patriotism in the days of George Washington; it ought to be good patriotism in our day. The new patriotism, therefore, aims at a condition of peace with all the world; it believes that Christianity is mocked by the spectacle of Christian nations in arms against each other. It believes that if America is ever to lift the sword against a foreign foe, it must not only be a righteous cause, but with a pure heart; that he who takes up his sword to enforce his will upon another must see that his own will is right and that his own hands are clean.

But the new patriotism has other duties than those of armed conflict; duties less splendid, but no less onerous, and requiring no less bravery; requiring bravery of a rarer order than that which shown upon a hundred battlefields of our Civil War. The roll of cowards among those who wore either the blue or gray is insignificant indeed. And there was scarcely a single act of treachery among the combatants on either side. Yes, most men will march for country and honor's sake straight into the jaws of death.

But how many men in our day, when put to the test of civic courage, have we beheld turn cowards and recreants? How many political careers have we seen blighted by conscienceless compromise or base surrender?

We have also seen the tremendous power of wise and disinterested effort in the domain of public affairs. We have seen brave men do notable deeds for the betterment of our country and our communities. But there must be more such men, or the evil forces will, for a while, at least, triumph in a republic, whose fortunate destiny must not be

Richard Watson Gilder, an eminent editor of the late nineteenth century, was associated with magazines like Scribner's and Century.

weakly taken for granted by those who passionately love their country. We must have more leaders, and we must have more followers of the right. Men who will resist civic temptation, who will refuse to take the easy path of compliance, and who will fight for honesty and purity in public affairs.

Selection from *The Best American Orations of To-Day*, edited by Harriet Blackstone. Published by Hinds, Noble & Eldredge, New York, copyright © 1903.

CRITICAL THINKING

1. Summarize what Gilder says are the two great needs of patriotism for his day.
2. How does Gilder compare courage in the Civil War to civic courage in his own day?

CHAPTER 19

GROWING PAINS

1865–1900

1. AMERICAN CAPITALIST ANDREW CARNEGIE RECALLS RECEIVING HIS FIRST DIVIDEND CHECK

Andrew Carnegie, whose Carnegie Steel Corporation at one time produced over one-fourth of the steel manufactured in America, firmly believed that social and financial success came to those individuals who earned and deserved it. In this passage from his book, The Gospel of Wealth, *he describes some of his own first steps toward wealth and power. The passage begins with Carnegie describing his reaction to the dividend check he received from his purchase of ten shares of Adams Express Company.*

Adams Express stock then paid monthly dividends of one per cent, and the first check for five dollars arrived. I can see it now, and I well remember the signature of "J. C. Babcock, Cashier". . . .

The next day being Sunday, we boys—myself and my ever-constant companions—took our usual Sunday afternoon stroll in the country, and sitting down in the woods, I showed them this check, saying, "Eureka! We have found it."

Here was something new to all of us, for none of us had ever received anything but from toil. A return from capital was something strange and new.

How money could make money, how, without any attention from me, this mysterious golden visitor should come, led to much speculation upon the part of the young fellows, and I was for the first time hailed as a "capitalist."

You see, I was beginning to serve my apprenticeship as a business man in a very satisfactory manner.

A very important incident in my life occurred when, one day in a train, a nice, farmer-looking gentleman approached me, saying that the conductor had told him I was connected with the Pennsylvania Railroad, and he would like to show me something. He pulled from a small green bag the model of the first sleeping-car. This was Mr. Woodruff, the inventor.

Its value struck me like a flash. I asked him to come to Altoona the following week, and he did so. Mr. Scott, with his usual quickness, grasped the idea. A contract was made with Mr. Woodruff to put two trial cars on the Pennsylvania Railroad. Before leaving Altoona, Mr. Woodruff came and offered me an interest in the venture, which I promptly accepted. But how I was to make my payments rather troubled me, for the cars were to be paid for in monthly installments after delivery, and my first monthly payment was to be two hundred and seventeen dollars and a half.

I had not the money, and I did not see any way of getting it. But I finally decided to visit the local banker and ask him for a loan, pledging myself to repay at the rate of fifteen dollars per month. He promptly granted it. Never shall I forget his putting his arm over my shoulder, saying, "Oh, yes, Andy; you are all right!"

I then and there signed my first note. Proud day this; and surely now no one will dispute that I was becoming a "business man." I had signed my first note, and, most important of all,—for any fellow can sign a note,—I had found a banker willing to take it as "good."

My subsequent payments were made by the receipts from the sleeping-cars, and I really made my first considerable sum from this investment in the Woodruff Sleeping-car Company, which was afterward absorbed by Mr. Pullman—a remarkable man whose name is now known over all the world.

Shortly after this I was appointed superintendent of the Pittsburg division. . . . Wooden bridges were then used exclusively upon the railways, and the Pennsylvania Railroad was experimenting with a bridge built of cast-iron. I saw that wooden bridges would not do for the future, and organized a company in Pittsburgh to build iron bridges.

Here again I had recourse to the bank, because my share of the capital was twelve hundred and fifty dollars, and I had not the money; but the bank lent it to me, and we began the Keystone Bridge Works, which proved a great success. . . .

This was my beginning in manufacturing; and from that start all our other works have grown, the profits of one building the other. My "apprenticeship" as a business man soon ended, for I resigned my position as an officer of the Pennsylvania Railroad Company to give exclusive attention to business.

Selection from Kenneth S. Lynn, *The American Society*. Published by George Braziller, New York, copyright © 1963.

CRITICAL THINKING

1. How did Andrew Carnegie view the idea of making money from money, rather than toil?
2. What ethical questions might be raised about Carnegie's investments in railroad-related industries while still working for the Pennsylvania Railroad?

2. ITALIAN DRAMATIST GIUSEPPE GIACOSA OFFERS HIS ASSESSMENT OF AMERICAN SLAUGHTERHOUSES

During the late nineteenth century, more and more people noticed the often shocking conditions under which many Americans worked. To some, however, these conditions were justified by the prosperity that industry brought, both to the individual workers and to the country as a whole. In 1898, Giuseppe Giacosa, an Italian playwright, visited the United States. Among the sights he reported on was the Chicago slaughterhouses, which, just a few years later, would be the subject of Upton Sinclair's famous exposé, The Jungle. *To Giacosa, however, the scene pointed out some of the basic complexities and contradictions of American life.*

The slaughterhouses of Chicago are famous even among [Europeans]. They are famous and fabulous because everyone thinks them more organized, polished, and mechanically perfect than in reality they are. To me they seemed the nastiest pits the human mind could imagine. It is enough to say that these immense places are entirely made of wood—floors, columns, stairs, and all—although in certain months of the year close to 60,000 head of cattle are slaughtered, bled, skinned, quartered, and packed there daily. The vapors of blood impregnate the pores of the walls, dribble down from the ceiling in rivulets of blood, soaking into the vats, the benches, the pillars, and the tables. On the floor the blood forms into a dark, pestiferous, glutinous, slippery mud; frequent washings cannot mop it out, only cause it to penetrate more deeply into the fibers of the wood. In addition, these places are low and crowded; the workers trample upon each other; and the visitors suffer loathsome contacts. The vapors that escape from the boiling water and from the palpitating meat render still more uncertain the uncertain light that penetrates from the little windows into those dark walls.

Hundreds of laborers move about in such quarters, each one fixed to a special job and constrained to furious and uninterrupted labor by a mechanical routine of a succession of operations. These unfortunate men have neither the face nor the body of humans. Their features are contracted by an overwhelming disgust and by an irritating intoxication from the blood around them. Their eyes are constantly strained by the necessity for distinguishing through the penumbra the precise point at which to strike. The greasy matter, reddish and shiny, that stains their foreheads and cheeks, the encrusted blood hardened on beards and hair, the abrupt and rapid movements by which they throw severed pieces to neighboring workers—all that amidst the smoke, the moldly smell, and the moans and gurgling cries—gives them an appearance altogether inhuman, and rather like the savage animals they destroy with so much dispatch. And the clothing! The shirts and trousers are so hard with dried blood that the men are forced to walk with long stiff strides. Stained from tip to toe, lined with blood and flowing with blood, the bottoms of their trousers drag in the bloody mud, so that every step makes a splash, and the feet, detached from the soles by force give forth a sucking sound and leave a bubble that seems like a live tumor.

Flee from this pit of horrors and the nausea will pursue you for a long time, will follow you through the streets and into the gardens; the sounds will continue to disturb you; and for several days any non-vegetable food will be disgusting. But should your mind allow you to spy at the exit of this intricate parcel of streets, alleys, buildings, huts, and viaducts . . . the sight that would greet you at the end of the working day would give you a more just conception of the complexity of American life.

Hazardous conditions in Chicago slaughterhouses drew the ire of reformers. Turn-of-the-century European visitors, like playwright Giuseppe Giacosa (right), were equally revolted.

A half hour after the end of work there come forth from the enclosure a lordly collection of gentlemen whom one of our courtly ladies would take as models of sporty elegance. They are often young, tall and blond, with well-trimmed mustaches and polished shoes. They wear handsome ties, plaid jackets in the English style, and little hard hats. The more mature men are clad in dignified black and in derbys. All are solemn and sober; you would think they were leaving an aristocratic club or a classical concert. . . .

Who would recognize amidst such refinement the butchers and slaughterers of a while ago? Having taken off their filthy clothes, scrubbed their hands, arms, and faces, they are now disposed to enjoy politely the money they earned in the blood and mud. These men undertake the most loathsome and most fatiguing work, but they do not thereby renounce the good things of life, food in plenty, and curtain homes. . . . Born of a nation which knows no ease, the Americans accept the inequality of labor in order to attain a relative equality of goods.

Selection from Oscar Handlin, *This Was America*. Published by Harper Torchbooks, New York, copyright © 1964.

CRITICAL THINKING

1. What "complexity" did Giuseppe Giacosa see in American life?
2. Why might Giacosa have emphasized the contradiction in the workers' lives?

3. JOSEPH KIRKLAND TELLS OF WORKING CONDITIONS IN MANUFACTURING "SWEATSHOPS"

Conditions in the clothing industry often were among the worst of any manufacturing business. In cities like New York and Chicago, much of the work was done in "sweatshops," with the labor done mostly by women and children. Joseph Kirkland wrote the following description of a sweatshop.

The *sweat-shop* is a place where, separate from the tailor-shop or clothing-warehouse, a "sweater" (middleman) assembles journeymen tailors and needle-women, to work under his supervision. He takes a cheap room outside the dear [expensive] and crowded business center, and within the neighborhood where the work-people live. Thus is rent saved to the employer, and time and travel to the employed. The men can do work more hours than was possible under the centralized system, and their wives and children can help, especially when, as is often done, the garments are taken home to "finish." (Even the very young can pull out basting-threads.) This "finishing" is what remains undone after the machine has done its work, and consists in "felling" [turning down and sewing seams] the waist and leg-ends of trousers (paid at one and one-half cent a pair), and, in short, all the "felling" necessary on every garment of any kind. For this service, at the prices paid, they cannot earn more than from twenty-five to forty cents a day, and the work is largely done by Italian, Polish, and Bohemian women and girls. . . .

Girls, hand-sewers, earn nothing for the first month, then as unskilled workers they get $1 to $1.50 a week, $3 a week, and (as skilled workers) $6 a week. The first-named class constitutes fifty per cent of all, the second thirty per cent, and the last twenty per cent. In the general work men are only employed to do button-holing and pressing, and their earnings are as follows: "Pressers," $8 to $12 a week; "underpressers," $4 to $7. Cloak operators earn $8 to $12 a week. Four-fifths of the sewing-machines are furnished by the "sweaters" (middlemen); also needles, thread, and wax.

The "sweat-shop" day is ten hours; but many take work home to get in overtime; and occasionally the shops themselves are kept open for extra work, from which the hardest and ablest workers sometimes make from $14 to $16 a week. On the other hand, the regular work-season for the cloak-making is but seven months, and for other branches nine months, in the year. The average weekly living expenses of a man and wife, with two children, as estimated by a self-educated workman named Bisno, are as follows: Rent (three or four small rooms), $2; food, fuel, and light, $4; clothing, $2, and beer and spirits, $1. . . .

. . . A city ordinance enacts that rooms provided for workmen shall contain space equal to five hundred cubic feet of air for each person employed; but in the average "sweat-shop" only about a tenth of that quantity is to be found. In one such place there were fifteen men and women

in one room, which contained also a pile of mattresses on which some of the men sleep at night. The closets were disgraceful. In an adjoining room were piles of clothing, made and unmade, on the same table with the food of the family. Two dirty little children were playing about the floor. . . .

The "sweating system" has been in operation about twelve years, during which time some firms have failed, while others have increased their production tenfold. Meantime certain "sweaters" have grown rich; two having built from their gains tenement-houses for rent to the poor workers. The wholesale clothing business of Chicago is about $20,000,000 a year.

Selection from Joseph Kirkland, "Among the Poor of Chicago," in *The Poor in Great Cities.* Published by Charles Scribner's Sons, New York, copyright © 1895.

CRITICAL THINKING

1. According to Joseph Kirkland, what was the main reason for the use of the "sweating system"?
2. What evidence did Kirkland offer to gain the readers' sympathies for the conditions endured by the workers?

---

4. THE *KNIGHTS OF LABOR* LISTS ITS AIMS

Like many early organizations of American workers, the Knights of Labor demanded improvements in both wages and working conditions in American factories. The following statement of the goals of the Knights of Labor comes from Terence Powderly's Thirty Years of Labor, *written several years after he became Grand Master of the organization.*

Preamble.

The recent alarming development and aggression of aggregated wealth, which, unless checked, will inevitably lead to the pauperization and hopeless degradation of the toiling masses, render it imperative, if we desire to enjoy the

After Terence Powderly became Grand Master of the Knights of Labor, the once-secret lodge waged successful strikes against the railroads.

blessings of life, that a check should be placed upon its power and upon unjust accumulation, and a system adopted which will secure to the laborer the fruits of his toil; and as this much-desired object can only be accomplished by the thorough unification of labor, . . . we have formed the*****with a view of securing the organization and direction, by cooperative effort, of the power of the industrial [working] classes; and we submit to the world the objects sought to be accomplished by our organization, calling upon all who believe in securing "the greatest good to the greatest number" to aid and assist us:

I. To bring within the folds of organization every department of productive industry, making knowledge a standpoint for action, and industrial and moral worth, not wealth, the true standard of individual and national greatness.

II. To secure to the toilers a proper share of the wealth that they create. . . .

III. To . . . [demand] from the various govern-ments the establishment of Bureaus of Labor Statistics.

IV. The establishment of co-operative institutions, productive and distributive.

V. The reserving of the public lands . . . for the actual settler. . . .

VI. The abrogation [repeal] of all laws that do not bear equally upon capital and labor, the removal of unjust technicalities, delays, and discriminations in the administration of justice, and the adopting of measures providing for the health and safety of those engaged in mining, manufacturing, or building pursuits.

VII. The enactment of laws to compel chartered corporations to pay their employees weekly. . . .

VIII. The enactment of laws giving mechanics and laborers a first lien on their work for their full wages.

IX. The abolishment of the contract system on national, State, and municipal work.

X. The substitution of arbitration for strikes. . . .

XI. The prohibition of the employment of children in workshops, mines, and factories before attaining their fourteenth year.

XII. To abolish the system of letting out by contract the labor of convicts. . . .

XIII. To secure for both sexes equal pay for equal work.

XIV. The reduction of the hours of labor to eight per day. . . .

XV. To prevail upon governments to establish a purely national circulation [money], based upon the faith and resources of the nation, and issued directly to the people, without the intervention of any system of banking corporations. . . .

Selection from Terence V. Powderly, *Thirty Years of Labor.* Published by Augustus M. Kelley, New York, copyright © 1967.

CRITICAL THINKING

1. What dangers did the Knights of Labor see in the development of American capitalism?
2. Summarize the major demands and goals set forth in this document.

Jacob Riis Tells Americans About Their Slums

In 1870, a young man from Denmark decided to emigrate to the United States. There was nothing unusual in this. In 1870, almost 31,000 people left Denmark and the other Scandinavian countries for the land of opportunity.

But Jacob August Riis was a very unusual person. Unlike many immigrants, he had had the opportunity to receive formal education. He was also very good at languages. He learned English so well that, by 1877, he was writing professionally, as a newspaper reporter in New York City.

Riis' reporter's beat was the police department. He accompanied officers on their rounds, witnessed arrests, and helped out in investigations. In return, he often got "scoops," stories that his newspaper printed before any of its competitors. To Riis, however, the biggest story was not crime, but one of the causes of it: poverty. He roamed the horrible slums of New York City, the home of thousands of poor people, including dozens of the immigrant groups that, after 1880, came to the United States from China and almost every country of Europe.

Jacob Riis believed that once they knew about it, wealthy and middle-class Americans would do something about the poverty and squalor. The trouble was, they did not know about it. Well-to-do New Yorkers rarely visited the city's poorer areas. Riis developed the idea of writing a book that was like a tour of New York's slums. To give his book life, he learned to use the bulky cameras of the time and carried one with him everywhere, capturing heart-rending scenes of misery.

How the Other Half Lives was published in 1890. It was an instant "best-seller." It made Jacob Riis famous and provided him with the influence to work for reform. He supported movements to purify drinking water in big cities, thus reducing disease; to build parks and playgrounds in the worst parts of the city; and to organize clubs for poor boys and girls to get them away from the bad influences of the streets.

Most important, *How the Other Half Lives* shocked hundreds of thousands of Americans. Riis was right. Decent people living comfortable lives simply did not know such horrors as Riis described existed in the United States. In many ways, *How the Other Half Lives* was the first shot in the great surge of reform known as the Progressive Movement. It is also important as a document in what is called "journalism of exposure." Jacob Riis *exposed* social evils in order to begin the process of curing them. He was followed by dozens of journalists called "muckrakers" who wrote about similar ills and what they saw as abuses in the use of power by some large corporations.

How the Other Half Lives profoundly influenced young Theodore Roosevelt. When he became New York City's chief commissioner of police in 1895, he asked Riis to show him the things about which he had read. The two men became fast friends. Teddy Roosevelt called the immigrant, Riis, "the best American I ever knew." In return, Riis became a strong supporter of Roosevelt when he was governor and, later, as president. No doubt he took satisfaction in the fact that Roosevelt was considered one of the nation's leading reformers. Jacob Riis helped make him one.

*B*e a little careful, please! The hall is dark and you might stumble over the children pitching pennies back there. Not that it would hurt them; kicks and cuffs are their daily diet. They have little else. Here where the hall turns and dives into utter darkness is a step, and another, another. A flight of stairs. You can feel your way, if you cannot see it. Close? Yes! What would you have? All the fresh air that ever enters these stairs comes from the hall-door that is forever slamming, and from the windows of dark bedrooms that in turn receive from the stairs their sole supply of the elements God meant to be free, but man deals out with such an ungenerous hand. That was a woman filling her pail by the hydrant you just bumped against. The sinks are in the hallway, that all the tenants may have access—and all be poisoned alike by their summer stenches. Hear the pump squeak! It is the lullaby of tenement-house babes. In summer, when a thousand thirsty throats pant for a cooling drink in this block, it is worked in vain. But the saloon, whose open door you passed in the hall, is always there. The smell of it has followed you up. Here is a door. Listen! That short hacking cough, that tiny, helpless wail—what do they mean? They mean that the soiled bow of white you saw on the door downstairs will have another story to tell—Oh! a sadly familiar story—before the day is at an end. The child is dying with measles. With half a chance it might have lived; but it had none. That dark bedroom killed it.

"It was took all of a suddint," says the mother, smoothing the throbbing little body with trembling hands. There is no unkindness in the rough voice of the man in the jumper, who sits by the window grimly smoking a clay pipe, with the little life ebbing out in his sight, bitter as his words sound: "Hush, Mary! If we cannot keep the baby, need we complain—such as we?"

Such as we! What if the words ring in your ears as we grope our way up the stairs and down from floor to floor, listening to the sounds behind the closed doors—some of quarrelling, some of coarse songs, more of profanity. They are true. When the summer heats come with their suffering they have meaning more terrible than words can tell. Come over here. Step carefully over this baby—it is a baby, spite of its rags and dirt—under these iron bridges called fire-escapes, but loaded down, despite the incessant watchfulness of the firemen, with broken household goods, with wash-tubs and barrels, over which no man could climb from a fire. This gap between dingy brick-walls is the yard. That strip of smoke-colored sky up there is the heaven of these people. . . . That baby's parents live in the rear tenement here. She is at least as clean as the steps we are now climbing. There are plenty of houses with half a hundred such in. The tenement is much like the one in front we just left, only fouler, closer, darker—we will not say more cheerless. The word is a mockery. A hundred thousand people lived in rear tenements in New York last year.

Selection adapted from Jacob Riis, *How the Other Half Lives: Studies Among the Tenements of New York*. Published by Charles Scribner's Sons, New York, copyright © 1890.

CRITICAL THINKING

1. Which part of Jacob Riis's article did you find to be most effective in informing well-to-do people about poverty?
2. Why was this book such an effective tool in bringing about needed social reform?

JACOB RIIS

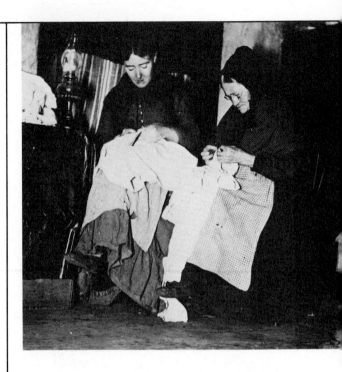

When "piecework" began, people brought outside work into the home. Because working conditions could not be regulated, the quality of life for workers deteriorated. Riis used flash powder to light the dark interior of a tenement room filled with lodgers (below.)

F ew people have been as instrumental in improving the living conditions of their fellow citizens as Jacob Riis [1849–1914]. His influential book, *How the Other Half Lives*, published in 1890, perhaps more than any other single work, roused the American public to the problems of the urban poor.

Riis, a Danish immigrant, became a newspaper reporter in 1877. Assigned to New York City's poorest neighborhood as a police reporter, he was appalled by the terrible living conditions he saw—the filthy, airless, unheated, and unsafe tenement buildings. He believed that environment—not solely the poor themselves —was responsible for poverty and crime.

Through his newspaper articles, Riis attempted to arouse sympathy for the poor and to stir his audience to work for reform. In 1887, he began using a camera to *show* his readers the conditions he described.

Riis' vivid photographs and his sympathetic writing were responsible for new laws and for the formation of social organizations to combat the problems of poverty—thus helping to pave the way for the dramatic social reforms of the twentieth century.

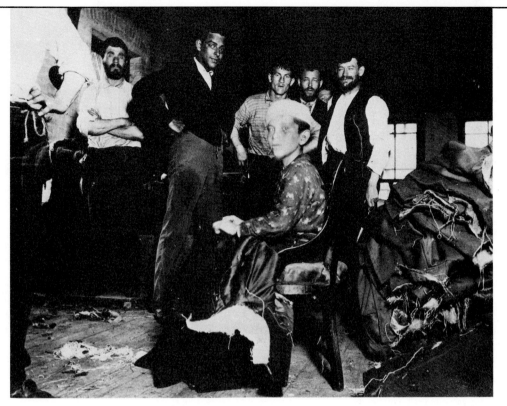

Riis was especially concerned about the appalling working conditions for young children. They were forced to work long hours at even lower wages than the poorly-paid adults.

Riis took this picture of New York City schoolchildren practicing voting. He was largely responsible for getting legislation passed requiring newly-built schools in New York to have playgrounds.

CRITICAL THINKING

1. Why might Riis' photographs have been more persuasive than newspaper articles about tenement living?
2. What difficulties did Riis probably have to overcome to take these photographs?
3. Riis believed that there was a direct connection between peoples' poor living and working conditions and crime, health, and morals. What point did he try to make by publishing these photographs? Was he successful? Explain.

5. IMMIGRANT MARY ANTIN ARRIVES IN AMERICA—"THE PROMISED LAND"

For many immigrants, arrival in America meant a complete change in their lives—perhaps even their names. Mary Antin was born in 1881 in the Russian town of Polotzk and emigrated to the United States in the 1890s. She described her first days in America in her book The Promised Land.

My father found occasion to instruct or correct us [about America] even on the way from the pier to Wall Street, which journey we made crowded together in a rickety cab. He told us not to lean out of the windows, not to point, and explained the word "greenhorn." We did not want to be "greenhorns," and gave the strictest attention to my father's instructions. . . .

The first meal was an object lesson of much variety. My father produced several kinds of food, ready to eat, without any cooking, from little tin cans that had printing all over them. He attempted to introduce us to a queer, slippery kind of fruit, which he called "banana," but had to give it up for the time being. After the meal, he had better luck with a curious piece of furniture on runners, which he called "rocking-chair." There were five of us newcomers, and we found five different ways of getting into the American machine of perpetual motion, and as many ways of getting out of it. . . . We laughed immoderately over our various experiments with the novelty, which was a wholesome way of letting off steam after the unusual excitement of the day.

In our flat . . . [t]here was no bathtub. So in the evening of the first day my father conducted us to the public baths. As we moved along in a little procession, I was delighted with the illumination of the streets. So many lamps, and they burned until morning, my father said, and so people did not need to carry lanterns. In America, then, everything was free, as we had heard in Russia. Light was free. . . . Music was free; we had been serenaded, to our gaping delight, by a brass band of many pieces, soon after our installation on Union Place.

Education was free. That subject my father had written about repeatedly, as comprising his chief hope for us children, the essence of American opportunity, the treasure that no thief could touch, not even misfortune or poverty. It was the one thing that he was able to promise us when he sent for us; surer, safer than bread or shelter. On our second day I was thrilled with the realization of what this freedom of education meant. A little girl from across the alley came and offered to conduct us to school. My father was out, but we five between us had a few words of English by this time. We knew the word school. We understood. This child, who had never seen us till yesterday, who could not pronounce our names, who was not much better dressed than we, was able to offer us the freedom of the schools of Boston! No application made, no questions asked, no examinations, . . . no fees. The doors stood open for every one of us. The smallest child could show us the way.

This incident impressed me more than anything I had heard in advance of the freedom of education in America. It was a concrete proof—almost the thing itself. . . .

[As time went on] we had to visit the stores and be dressed from head to foot in American clothing; we had to learn the mysteries of the iron stove, the washboard, and the speaking-tube; we had to learn to trade with the fruit peddler through the window, and not to be afraid of the policeman; and, above all, we had to learn English. . . .

With our despised immigrant clothing we shed also our impossible . . . names. A committee of our friends, several years ahead of us in American experience, put their heads together and concocted American names for us all. Those of our real names that had no pleasing American equivalents they ruthlessly discarded, content if they retained the initials. My mother, possessing a name that was not easily translatable, was punished with the undignified nickname of Annie. Fetchke, Joseph, and Deborah issued as Frieda, Joseph, and Dora, respectively. As for poor me, I was simply cheated. The name they gave me was hardly new. My Hebrew name being Maryashe in full, Mashke for short, Russianized into Marya (*Mar-ya*), my friends said that it would hold good in English as *Mary*; which was very disappointing, as I longed to possess a strange-sounding American name like the others.

Selection from Mary Antin, *The Promised Land*. Published by Houghton Mifflin, Boston, copyright © 1912.

6. PRESIDENT GROVER CLEVELAND VETOES A BILL PROPOSING LITERACY TESTS FOR IMMIGRANTS

Prejudice against new groups of immigrants from Russia and Italy, who were mostly illiterate, led to efforts that would restrict immigration. In 1891, Senator Henry Cabot Lodge of Massachusetts proposed legislation that would have required newcomers to pass a literacy test. By 1897, the bill had gotten through Congress but it was vetoed by President Grover Cleveland two days before his term expired.

I herewith return, without approval, House Bill No. 7864, entitled "An act to amend the immigration laws of the United States."

By the first section of this bill it is proposed to amend Section 1 of the act of March 3, 1891, relating to immigration, "by adding to the classes of aliens thereby excluded from admission to the United States the following: all persons physically capable and over sixteen years of age who cannot read and write the English language or some other language; but a person not so able to read and write who is over fifty years of age and is the parent or grandparent of a qualified immigrant over twenty-one years of age and capable of supporting such parent or grandparent may accompany such immigrant, or such a parent or grandparent may be sent for and come to join the family of a child or grandchild over twenty-one years of age, similarly qualified and capable, and a wife or minor child not so able to read and write may accompany or be sent for and come and join the husband or parent similarly quailified and capable."

A radical departure from our national policy relating to immigration is here presented. Heretofore, we have welcomed all who came to us from other lands, except for those whose moral or physical condition or history threatened danger to our national welfare and safety. Relying upon the jealous watchfulness of our people to prevent injury to our political and social fabric, we have encouraged those coming from foreign countries to cast their lot with us and join in the development of our vast domain, securing in return a share in the blessings of American citizenship.

A century's stupendous growth, largely due to the assimilation and thrift of millions of sturdy and patriotic adopted citizens, attests to the success of this generous and freehanded policy, which, while guarding the people's interests, exacts from our immigrants only physical and moral soundness and willingness and ability to work.

A contemplation of the grand results of this policy cannot fail to arouse a sentiment in its defense; for however it might have been regarded as an original proposition and viewed as an experiment, its accomplishments are such that if it is to be uprooted at this late day its disadvantages should be plainly apparent and the substitute adopted should be just and adequate, free from uncertainties and guarded against difficult or oppressive administration.

It is not claimed, I believe, that the time has come for the further restriction of immigrants on the ground that an excess of population overcrowds our land.

It is said, however, that the quality of the recent immigration is undesirable. The time is quite within recent memory when the same thing was said of our immigrants who with their descendants are now numbered among our best citizens.

It is said that too many immigrants settle in our cities, thus dangerously increasing their idle and vicious population. This is certainly a disadvantage. It cannot be shown, however, that it affects all our cities, nor that it is permanent; nor does it appear that this condition, where it exists, demands as its remedy the reversal of our present immigration policy.

The claim is also made that the influx of foreign laborers deprives of the opportunity to work those who are better entitled than they to the privilege of earning their livelihood by daily toil. An unfortunate condition is certainly presented when any who are willing to labor are unemployed. But so far as this condition now exists among our people, it must be conceded to be a result of phenomenal business depression and the stagnation of all enterprises of which labor is a factor. With the advent of settled and wholesome financial and economic governmental policies and consequent encouragement of the activity of capital, the misfortunes of unemployed labor should, to a great extent at least, be remedied. If it continues, its natural consequences must be to check the further immigration to our cities of foreign laborers and to deplete the ranks of those already here. In the meantime, those most willing and best entitled ought to be able to secure the advantages of such work as there is to do.

It is proposed by the bill under consideration to meet the alleged difficulties of the situation by establishing an educational test by which the right of a foreigner to make his home with us shall be determined. Its general scheme is to prohibit from admission to our country all immigrants "physically capable and over sixteen years of age who cannot read and write the English language or some other language"; and it is provided that this test shall be applied by requiring immigrants seeking admission to read and afterwards to write not less than twenty nor more than twenty-five words of the Constitution of the United States in some language, and that any immigrant failing in this shall not be admitted, but shall be returned to the country from whence he came at the expense of the steamship or railroad company which brought him.

The best reason that could be given for this radical restriction of immigration is the necessity of protecting our population against degeneration and saving our national peace and quiet from imported turbulence and disorder.

I cannot believe that we would be protected against these evils by limiting immigration to those who can read and write in any language twenty-five words of our Constitution. In my opinion it is infinitely more safe to admit a hundred thousand immigrants who, though unable to read and write, seek among us only a home and opportunity to work, than to admit one of those

unruly agitators and enemies of governmental control, who cannot only read and write, but delights in arousing by inflammatory speech the illiterate and peacefully inclined to discontent and tumult. Violence and disorder do not originate with illiterate laborers. They are rather the victims of the educated agitator. The ability to read and write as required in this bill, in and of itself, affords, in my opinion, a misleading test of contented industry and supplies an unsatisfactory evidence of desirable citizenship or a proper apprehension of the benefits of our institutions. If any particular element of our illiterate immigration is to be feared for other causes than illiteracy, these cause should be dealt with directly instead of by making illiteracy the pretext for exclusion, to the detriment of other illiterate immigrants against whom the real cause of complaint cannot be alleged.

The provisions intended to rid that part of the proposed legislation already referred to from obvious hardship appears to me to be indefinite and inadequate. . . .

A careful examination of this bill has convinced me that for the reasons given, and others not specifically stated, its provisions are unnecessarily harsh and oppressive, and that its defects in construction would cause vexation and its operation would result in harm to our citizens.

Selection from *Makers of America—Natives and Aliens, 1891–1903.* Published by Encyclopaedia Britannica Educational Corporation, copyright © 1971.

CRITICAL THINKING

1. Describe the literacy qualifications included in the immigration bill proposed by Senator Lodge.
2. What argument does President Grover Cleveland use to refute the charge that illiterate immigrants from Italy and Russia threatened America's national peace and quiet?
3. From the above reading, what can you conclude about President Cleveland's attitude toward the latest wave of immigrants?

7. SUFFRAGIST SUSAN B. ANTHONY AND SENATOR JOSEPH BROWN TAKE SIDES ON A WOMAN SUFFRAGE AMENDMENT

Notable American women such as Jane Addams were leading important reform movements, but 40 years after the Seneca Falls Declaration on women's rights, they still could not vote. In the first selection, Susan B. Anthony testifies before a Senate committee in 1884. In the second, Georgia Senator Joseph Brown puts on record his opposition to a woman suffrage amendment in 1887.

SUSAN BROWNELL ANTHONY

Mr. Chairman and Gentlemen: Mrs. Spencer said that I would make an argument. I do not propose to do so, because I take it for granted that the members of this committee understand that we have all the argument on our side, and such an argument would be simply a series of platitudes and maxims of government. The theory of this Government from the beginning has been perfect equality to all the people. That is shown by every one of the fundamental principles, which I need not stop to repeat. Such being theory, the application would be, of course, that all persons not having forfeited their right to representation in the Government should be possessed of it at the age of twenty-one. But instead of adopting a practice in conformity with the theory of our Government, we began first by saying that all men of property were the people of the nation upon whom the Constitution conferred equality of rights. The next step was that all white men were the people to whom should be practically applied the fundamental theories. There we halt to-day and stand at a deadlock, so far as the application of our theory may go. We women have been standing before the American republic for thirty years, asking the men to take yet one step further and extend the practical application of the theory of equality of rights to all the people to the other half of the people—the women. That is all that I stand here to-day to attempt to demand. . . .

I voted in the State of New York in 1872 under the construction of those amendments, which we felt to be the true one, that all persons born in the United States, or any State thereof, and under the jurisdiction of the United States, were citizens, and entitled to equality of rights, and that no State could deprive them of their equality of rights. I found three young men, inspectors of election, who were simple enough to read the Constitution and understand it in accordance with what was the letter and what should have been its spirit. Then, as you will remember, I was prosecuted by the officers of the Federal court, and the cause was carried through the different courts in the State of New York, in the northern district, and at last I was brought to trial at Canandaigua.

When Mr. Justice Hunt was brought from the supreme bench to sit upon that trial, he wrested my case from the hands of the jury altogether, after having listened three days to testimony, and brought in a verdict himself of guilty, denying to my counsel even the poor privilege of having the jury polled. Through all that trial when I, as a citizen of the United States, as a citizen of the State of New York and city of Rochester, as a person who had done something at least that might have entitled her to a voice in speaking for herself and for her class, in all that trial I not only was denied my right to testify as to whether I voted or not, but there was not one single woman's voice to be heard nor to be considered, except as witnesses, save when it came to the judge asking, "Has the prisoner anything to say why sentence shall not be pronounced?" Neither as judge, nor as attorney, nor as jury was I allowed any person who could be legitimately called by peer to speak for me.

Then, as you will remember, Mr. Justice Hunt not only pronounced the verdict of guilty, but a sentence of $100 fine and costs of prosecution. I said to him, "May it please your honor, I do not propose to pay it"; and I never have paid it, and I never shall. . . .

Let me remind you that in the case of all other classes of citizens under the shadow of our flag you have been true to the theory that taxation and representation are inseparable. Indians not taxed are not counted in the basis of representation, and are not allowed to vote; but the minute that your Indians are counted in the basis of representation and are allowed to vote they are taxed. . . .

. . . When the fourteenth and fifteenth amendments were attached to the Constitution they carried to the black man of Connecticut the boon of the ballot as well as the burden of taxation, whereas they carried to the black woman of Connecticut the burden of taxation, but no ballot by which to protect her property. . . .

Then you ask why we do not get suffrage by the popular-vote method, State by State? I answer, because there is no reason why I, for instance, should desire the women of one State of this nation to vote any more than the women of another State. I have no more interest as regards the women of New York than I have as regards the women of Indiana, Iowa, or any of the States represented by the women who have come up here. The reason why I do not wish to get this right by what you call the popular-vote method, the State vote, is because I believe there is a United States citizenship. I believe that this is a nation, and to be a citizen of this nation should be a guaranty to every citizen of the right to express my opinion. You deny to me my liberty, my freedom, if you say that I shall have no voice whatever in making, shaping, or controlling the conditions of society in which I live. . . .

. . . The franchise to you men is not secure. You hold it to-day, to be sure, by the common consent of white men, but if at any time, on your principle of government, the majority of any of the States should choose to amend the State constitution so as to disfranchise this or that portion of the white men by making this or that condition, by all the decisions of the Supreme Court and by the legislation thus far there is nothing to hinder them.

Therefore the women demand a sixteenth amendment to bring to women the right to vote, or if you please to confer upon women their right to vote, to protect them in it, and to secure men in their right, because you are not secure. . . .

. . . The amendment which has been presented before you reads:

ARTICLE XVI.

SECTION 1. The right of suffrage in the United States shall be based on citizenship, and the right of citizens of the United States to vote shall not be denied or abridged by the United States, or by any State, on account of sex, or for any reason not equally applicable to all citizens of the United States.

SECTION 2. Congress shall have power to enforce this article by appropriate legislation.

. . . We were all born into the idea that the proper sphere of women is subjection, and it takes education and thought and culture to lift us out of it. Therefore when men go to the ballot-box they all vote "no," unless they have actual argument on it. . . . It is a question that the unthinking masses never have thought upon. They do not care about it one way or the other, only they have an instinctive feeling that because women never did vote therefore it is wrong that they ever should vote.

JOSEPH EMERSON BROWN

Mr. President: The joint resolution introduced by my friend, the Senator from New Hampshire [Mr. Blair], proposing an amendment to the Constitution of the United States, conferring the right to vote upon the women of the United States, is one of paramount importance. . . .

I believe that the Creator intended that the sphere of the males and females of our race should be different, and that their duties and obligations, while they differ materially, are equally important and equally honorable, and that each sex is equally well qualified by natural endowments for the discharge of the important duties which pertain to each, and that each sex is equally competent to discharge those duties.

Man, by reason of physical strength, and his other endowments and faculties, is qualified for the discharge of those duties that require strength and ability to combat with the sterner realities and difficulties of life. The different classes of outdoor labor which require physical strength and endurance are by nature assigned to man, the head of the family, as part of his task. He discharges such labors as require greater physical endurance and strength than the female sex are usually found to possess.

It is not only his duty to provide for and protect the family, but as a member of the community it is also his duty to discharge the laborious and responsible obligations which the family owe to the State, and which obligations must be discharged by the head of the family, until the male members of the family have grown up to manhood and are able to aid in the discharge of those obligations, when it becomes their duty each in his turn to take charge of and rear a family, for which he is responsible.

Among other duties which the head of the family owes to the State, is military duty in time of war, which he, when able-bodied, is able to discharge, and which the female members of the family are unable to discharge. . . .

On the other hand, the Creator has assigned to woman very laborious and responsible duties, by no means less important than those imposed upon the male sex, though entirely different in their character. In the family, she is a queen. She alone is fitted for the discharge of the sacred trust of wife and the endearing relation of mother. . . .

Mr. President, it is no part of my purpose in any manner whatever to speak disrespectfully of the large number of intelligent ladies, sometimes called strong-minded, who are constantly going before the public, agitating this question of female suffrage. While some of them may, as if frequently charged, be courting notoriety, I have no doubt they are generally engaged in a work which, in their opinion, would better their condition and would do no injury to society.

In all this, however, I believe they are mistaken.

I think the mental and physical structure of the sexes, of itself, sufficiently demonstrates the fact that the sterner, more laborious, and more difficult duties of society are to be performed by the male sex; while the more delicate duties of life, which require less physical strength, and the proper training of youth, with the proper discharge of domestic duties, belong to the female sex. Nature has so arranged it that the male sex can not attend properly to the duties assigned by the law of nature to the female sex, and that the female sex can not discharge the more rigorous duties required of the male sex.

This movement is an attempt to reverse the very laws of our being, and to drag woman into an arena for which she is not suited, and to devolve upon her onerous duties which the Creator never intended that she should perform.

While the husband discharges the laborious and fatiguing duties of important official positions, and conducts political campaigns, and discharges the duties connected with the ballot-box, or while he bears arms in time of war, or discharges executive or judicial duties, or the duties of juryman, requiring close confinement and many times great mental fatigue; or while the husband in a different sphere of life discharges the laborious duties of the plantation, the workshop, or the machine ship, it devolves upon the wife to attend to the duties connected with home life, to care for infant children, and to train carefully and properly those who in the youthful period are further advanced towards maturity.

The woman with the infant at the breast is in no condition to plow on the farm, labor hard in the workshop, discharge the duties of a juryman, conduct causes as an advocate in court, preside in important cases as a judge, command armies as a general, or bear arms as a private. These duties, and others of like character, belong to the male sex; while the more important duties of home, to which I have already referred, devolve upon the female sex. We can neither reverse the physical nor the moral laws of our nature, and as this movement is an attempt to reverse these laws, and to devolve upon the female sex important and laborious duties for which they are not by nature physically competent, I am not prepared to support this bill.

My opinion is that a very large majority of the American people, yes, a large majority of the female sex, oppose it, and that they act wisely in doing so. I therefore protest against its passage.

Selection from *American Forum: Speeches on Historic Issues, 1788–1900*, edited by Ernest J. Wrage and Barnet Baskerville. Published by Harper & Row, New York, copyright © 1960.

CRITICAL THINKING

1. Contrast the arguments of Susan B. Anthony and Joseph Brown on the issue of women's suffrage.
2. What can you infer about the character of Susan B. Anthony from this reading?
3. Joseph Brown describes the ballot box duties as "laborious and fatiguing," and thus part of man's sphere. Evaluate this argument.

ELLIS ISLAND
Gateway To America

Steerage passengers, toting their possessions, are seen hurrying toward the reception area at Ellis Island. There they will be admitted, detained, or deported.

Almost 16 million immigrants entered America at the port of New York between 1890 and 1930. The great majority passed through the immigration center at Ellis Island, an experience that provoked both awe and anxiety in them.

Many immigrants had left their families, sold all their possessions, and endured miserable ocean voyages to come to America. Now, one 45-minute "test" would determine whether they would be admitted to the promised land— or sent back to their native countries.

The first part of the "test" was a medical examination. Each immigrant was inspected by a team of doctors for physical or mental defects, or any signs of disease. Next, a registration

D O C U M E N T

Immigrant children play while waiting for their parents to pass medical examinations.

Most dreaded is the eye test. Half of those detained have contagious eye inflammations.

New arrivals are tagged with identification cards and ushered into a hall called "The Pen."

Individuals who could not pass intelligence tests were detained for further examination.

official would question the immigrant to determine his or her character, political beliefs, financial status, and prospects for work.

The small percentage who failed the examination could be detained. Some of those were deported. But the vast majority were handed cards that read "admitted"—their precious tickets into the land of freedom, hope, and opportunity.

CRITICAL THINKING

1. Study these photographs and list some of the emotions these immigrants might be feeling.
2. Note details in the picture on page 212 and write several sentences to describe two of the immigrants.

The Closing of the Frontier

CHAPTER 20

THE WEST

1865–1900

1. OGALALA SIOUX CHIEF STANDING BEAR ANALYZES THE INDIAN WAY OF LIFE

Government policy toward the country's native American population changed several times during the late nineteenth century, but few of these policies seemed to meet with much success. One view of the reasons for this failure was taken by Chief Luther Standing Bear {1863–1939}, an Ogalala Sioux chief, who wrote several books about the history of his people and the injustice of their treatment by white America.

The feathered and blanketed figure of the American Indian has come to symbolize the American continent. He is the man who through centuries has been moulded and sculped by the same hand that shaped its mountains, forests, and plains, and marked the course of its rivers.

The American Indian is of the soil, whether it be the region of forests, plains, pueblos, or mesas. He fits into the landscape, for the hand that fashioned the continent also fashioned the man for his surroundings. He once grew as naturally as the wild sunflowers; he belongs just as the buffalo belonged.

With a physique that fitted, the man developed fitting skills—crafts which today are called American. And the body had a soul, also formed and moulded by the same master hand of harmony. Out of the Indian approach to existence there came great freedom—an intense and absorbing love for nature; a respect for life; enriching faith in a Supreme Power; and principles of truth, honesty, generosity, equity, and brotherhood as a guide to mundane relations. . . .

The white man does not understand the Indian for the reason that he does not understand America. He is too far removed from its formative process. The roots of the tree of his life have not yet grasped the rock and soil. The white man is still troubled with primitive fears; he still has in his consciousness the perils of this frontier continent, some of its fastnesses not yet having yielded to his questing footsteps and inquiring eyes. He shudders still with the memory of the loss of his forefathers upon its scorching deserts and forbidding mountain-tops. The man from Europe is still a foreigner and an alien. And he still hates the man who questioned his path across the continent.

But in the Indian the spirit of the land is still vested; it will be until other men are able to divine and meet its rhythm. Men must be born and reborn to belong. Their bodies must be formed of the dust of their forefathers' bones.

The attempted transformation of the Indian by the white man and the chaos that has resulted are but the fruits of the white man's disobedience of a fundamental and spiritual law. . . . Tyranny, stupidity, and lack of vision have brought the situation now alluded to as the "Indian Problem."

There is, I insist, no Indian problem as created by the Indian himself. Every problem that exists today in regard to the native population is due to the white man's cast of mind, which is unable, at least reluctant, to seek understanding and achieve adjustment in a new and a significant environment into which it has so recently come. . . .

True, the white man brought great change. But the varied fruits of his civilization, though highly colored and inviting, are sickening and deadening. And if it be the part of civilization to maim, rob, and thwart, then what is progress?

I am going to venture that the man who sat on the ground in his tipi [tepee] meditating on life and its meaning, accepting the kinship of all creatures, and acknowledging unity with the universe of things was infusing into his being the true essence of civilization. And when native man left off this form of development, his humanization was retarded in growth.

Selection from C Merton Babcock, *The American Frontier: A Social and Literary Record.* Published by Holt, Rinehart and Winston, New York, copyright © 1965.

CRITICAL THINKING

1. What evidence did Luther Standing Bear give to back his opinion that white Americans caused the "Indian Problem"?
2. What contrasts did he seem to see between Native American and White American attitudes and ways of life?

2. SIOUX CHIEF RED CLOUD SPEAKS SADLY ABOUT OLD WRONGS

Red Cloud, chief of a large Sioux tribe, was an influential Indian leader who sought peace with the United States government. At the same time, however, he persistently criticized its policies toward the Indians. In 1870, during a visit to New York City, Chief Red Cloud spoke at a reception given in his honor.

My brethren and my friends who are here before me this day, God Almighty has made us all, and He is here to bless what I have to say to you today. The Good Spirit made us both. He gave you lands and He gave us lands; He gave us these lands; you came in here, and we respected you as brothers. God Almighty made you but made you all white and clothed you; when He made us He made us with red skins and poor; now you have come.

When you first came we were very many, and you were few; now you are many, and we are getting very few, and we are poor. You do not know who appears before you today to speak. I am a representative of the original American race, the first people of this continent. We are good and not bad. The reports that you hear concerning us are all on one side. We are always well disposed to them. You are here told that we are traders and thieves, and it is not so. We have given you nearly all our lands, and if we had any more land to give we would be very glad to give it. We have nothing more. We are driven into a very little land, and we want you now, as our dear friends, to help us with the government of the United States.

The Great Father made us poor and ignorant—made you rich and wise and more skillful in these things that we know nothing about. The Great Father, the Good Father in heaven, made you all to eat tame food—made us to eat wild food—gives us the wild food. You ask anybody who has gone through our country to California; ask those who have settled there and in Utah, and you will find that we have treated them always well. You have children; we have children. You want to raise your children and make them happy and prosperous; we want to raise and make them happy and prosperous. We ask you to help us to do it.

At the mouth of the Horse Creek, in 1852, the Great Father made a treaty with us by which be agreed to let all that country open for fifty-five years for the transit of those who were going through. We kept this treaty; we never treated any man wrong; we never committed any murder or depredation until afterward the troops were sent into that country, and the troops killed our people and ill-treated them, and thus war and trouble arose; before the troops were sent there we were quiet and peaceable, and there was no disturbance. Since that time there have been various goods sent from time to time to us, the only ones that ever reached us, and then after they reached us (very soon after) the government took them away. You, as good men, ought to help us to these goods.

Colonel Fitzpatrick of the government said we must all go to farm, and some of the people went to Fort Laramie and were badly treated. I only want to do that which is peaceful, and the Great Fathers know it, and also the Great Father who made us both. I came to Washington to see the Great Father in order to have peace and in order to have peace continue. That is all we want, and that is the reason why we are here now.

In 1868 men came out and brought papers. We are ignorant and do not read papers, and they did not tell us right what was in these papers. We wanted them to take away their forts, leave our country, would not make war, and give our traders something. They said we had bound ourselves to trade on the Missouri, and we said, no, we did not want that. The interpreters deceived us. When I went to Washington I saw the Great Father. The Great Father showed me what the treaties were; he showed me all these points and showed me that the interpreters had deceived me and did not let me know what the right side of the treaty was. All I want is right and justice. . . . I represent the Sioux Nation; they will be governed by what I say and what I represent. . . .

Look at me. I am poor and naked, but I am the Chief of the Nation. We do not want riches, we do not ask for riches, but we want our children properly trained and brought up. We look to you for your sympathy. Our riches will . . . do us no good; we cannot take away into the other world anything we have—we want to have love and peace. . . . We would like to know why commissioners are sent out there to do nothing but rob

[us] and get the riches of this world away from us?

I was brought up among the traders and those who came out there in those early times. I had a good time for they treated us nicely and well. They taught me how to wear clothes and use tobacco, and to use firearms and ammunition, and all went on very well until the Great Father sent out another kind of men—men who drank whiskey. He sent out whiskeymen, men who drank and quarreled, men who were so bad that he could not keep them at home, and so he sent them out there.

I have sent a great many words to the Great Father, but I don't know that they ever reach the Great Father. They were drowned on the way, therefore I was a little offended with it. The words I told the Great Father lately would never come to him, so I thought I would come and tell you myself.

And I am going to leave you today, and I am going back to my home. I want to tell the people that we cannot trust his agents and superintendents. I don't want strange people that we know nothing about. I am very glad that you belong to us. I am very glad that we have come here and found you and that we can understand one another. I don't want any more such men sent out there, who are so poor that when they come out there their first thoughts are how they can fill their own pockets.

Selection from *Makers of America—Seekers After Freedom, 1849–1870*. Published by Encyclopaedia Britannica Educational Corporation, Chicago, copyright © 1971.

CRITICAL THINKING

1. Cite several examples from the selection to support the statement "The lives of the Sioux changed with the arrival of white settlers."
2. Chief Red Cloud's concern is for peace. Summarize the obstacles to this goal as told by Red Cloud, and analyze the effect of each.
3. Interpret Red Cloud's statement "I am poor and naked, but I am the chief of the Nation," based on your reading of the selection.

3. COWHAND JAMES H. COOK REMINISCES ABOUT THE ADVENTURES OF A "LONG DRIVE"

The giant cattle drives along routes like the Chisholm Trail were a dramatic—and often romantic—part of the "Wild West." This cowhand's description of the first few days of a drive gives a picture of life on a "Long Drive." It also suggests the kind of adventure that lured many young people to the West.

When Mr. Roberts informed me that I was to be one of his trail waddies, I immediately moved all my personal belongings over to his camp. I was allowed to take five of the best saddle horses which I had been riding, to be used on the trail. Roberts's trail crew consisted of twelve riders and the cook, beside himself. We were most fortunate in having with us on that trip a man who was one of the best ox drivers or bull-whackers, as well as cooks, that ever popped a bull whip over a cattle trail. The men who usually did this work were veterans on the frontier, who had seen long service with wagon trains drawn by oxen. Too much praise cannot be given to those old-time trail cooks who were numbered among the good ones. A camp cook could do more toward making life pleasant for those about him than any other man in an outfit, especially on those trail trips.

On the morning when we were to start up the trail, all was in readiness. About a dozen extra men were to help us for a few days while we were breaking in the herd to accustom them to being held by riders both night and day (for we should have no more corrals). They were also to help us out of the brush country to the open plains. After reaching this open country the extra men would turn back.

On the trail we were each allowed to take a pair of bed blankets and a sack containing a little extra clothing. No more load than was considered actually necessary was to be allowed on the wagon, for there would be no wagon road over most of the country which we were to traverse, and there was plenty of rough country, with creeks and steep-banked rivers to be crossed. We had no tents or shelter of any sort other than our blankets. Our food and cooking utensils were the same as those used in cow camps of the brush country. No provision was made for the care of men in case of accident. Should anyone become injured, wounded, or sick, he would be strictly "out of luck." A quick recovery and a sudden death were the only desirable alternatives in such cases, for much of the time the outfit would be far from the settlements and from medical or surgical aid.

On the first day I was told to help drive the saddle horses and to keep them with the wagon. The wagon started, and we followed with the horses, the cattle herd following us in the trail made by the oxen and wagon. Roberts [the trail boss] pointed out the course which he desired the outfit to follow, and then rode on ahead to select our first camp ground. After going a few miles he found a place with water and some fairly open ground upon which to bed the cattle down for the night. Returning to us, he told us where to go and where the wagon was to be located, so that it would not be too close to the herd.

After the first night we divided the night-herding into two watches, half of the entire outfit being on guard at a time. When we were out of the brush country the extra help turned back, and as the cattle were now pretty well broken to being night-herded, we divided the watch into three tricks, three men going on guard with the cattle at a time and one man on each watch over the horses.

One night we were camped on a little creek that ran into the Llano River at its head. Throughout that day we had seen a lot of fresh Indian signs. I was on the first watch with the horses. Roberts had arranged for me to be on guard with the horse herd during the early part of each evening and also just at the break of day, those hours being the Indian's favorite times for deviltry. I was known to be the best shot in that outfit, and I was expected to score straight bull's-eyes . . . no matter how plentiful, hideous, or dangerously close the human targets. . . .

I started for camp again and, riding up to the campfire, swung down off my horse, with my rifle in my hand—for I had been carrying it, ready to shoot at a moment's notice, all the evening.

Just as my foot touched the ground I heard a couple of dozen shots in quick succession. I turned my head and could see the flash from the guns. I fired one shot in the direction of the flashes. My horse had also turned his head when the shots were fired. A bullet struck him in the forehead, and he went down at my feet. I jumped away from that campfire as quickly as possible and crawled under a big cedar tree, the branches of which came very close to the ground. The next moment most of the horse herd came tearing right through camp. We had ropes stretched from the wagon wheels to some trees to make a corral . . . and the horses ran against the ropes, upsetting the wagon.

Every man in the camp ran for his life into the thicket. The horses ran into the cattle herd, and away went the cattle into a big cedar brake containing many old dead trees. There was a smashing and crashing and about as great an uproar as any cowboy ever heard. The men with the cattle did not dare yell at the animals or sing to them, lest Indians locate and slip an arrow into somebody.

I lay quite still under the tree. After a time I heard Roberts's voice calling out: "Don't let them get away with the horses, boys! Stay with 'em!" One by one I could hear the boys answer him. I did not like to get out from beneath that tree, but I did not care to be called a coward, so I joined him, although I thought it the most foolish thing we could possibly do. It was so dark that an Indian could slip up within three foot of a man and not be seen.

Frank Dennis not appearing, I made up my mind that he had been killed. We went and searched, but could find no trace of the missing cowboy. We then wandered about until daylight.

About sunrise Frank Dennis came into camp. He was a little pale, but quite cheerful. He said, "Well, fellers, good morning; we had a very pleasant night of it, didn't we?" When he swung down from his horse I saw that there was blood on his clothes, and that his hand was tied up in his handkerchief, which was soaked with blood.

Selection adapted from James H. Cook, *Fifty Years on the Old Frontier.* Published by Yale University Press, New Haven, copyright © 1923.

CRITICAL THINKING

1. Why do you think people like James Cook were anxious to sign up for the hardships of this kind of cattle drive?
2. Why do you think cowhands felt that a good trail cook was so important?

4. CATTLEMAN JOHN CLAY RECALLS THE END OF THE OPEN RANGE

During 1886 and 1887, a combination of harsh winters, severe drought, and over-population of the grazing range brought on an economic disaster that led to a major change in the cattle industry. Within a few years, fenced-in ranches replaced the romantic West of the "open range" and the long "cattle drives." One witness, John Clay, described some of the causes of what happened during 1886 and 1887.

Fenced-in ranches became common sights as the open range began to vanish in the 1880s.

May was dry, June did not bring the usual rains, and by July 4th it looked so bad that we finally decided to do nothing. By August it was hot, dry, dusty and grass closely cropped. Every day made it apparent that even with the best of winters cattle would have a hard time. . . .

. . . Our neighbors kept piling cattle onto the bone-dry range. The Continental Cattle Company drove up to 32,000 head of steers. The Worsham Cattle Company, with no former holdings, turned loose 5,000 head or threreabouts. Major Smith, who had failed to sell 5,500 Southern three-year-old steers, was forced to drive them to his range on Willow Creek near to Stoneville, now Alzada, Montana. The Dickey Cattle Company had brought up 6,000 mixed cattle from the Cheyenne and Arapahoe country. . . . Thousands of other cattle were spread over the Western and North-western country in the most reckless way—no thought for the morrow. Even with the best of winters it would have been a case of suicide. As things turned out it was simple murder, at least for the Texas cattle. Winter came early and it stayed long. The owners were mostly absent, and even those who remained could not move about or size up the situation.

It was not till the spring roundups that the real truth was discovered, and then it was only mentioned in a whisper. Bobby Robinson, acute judge of conditions, estimated the loss among . . . [those] cattle at less than 50 per cent. It turned out to be a total loss among this class of cattle, and the wintered herds suffered from 30 to 60 per cent. . . . It was simply appalling, and the cowmen could not realize their position. From southern Colorado to the Canadian line, from the one-hundredth meridian almost to the Pacific slope it was a catastrophe which the cowmen of today . . . can never understand. Three great streams of ill-luck, mismanagement, greed, met together—in other words, recklessness, want of foresight, and the weather, which no man can control. The buffalo had probably gone through similar winters with enormous losses, and thus natural conditions were evened up in the countless years they had grazed the prairie; and in the survival of the fittest their constitutions had been built up to stand the rigors of winter and the drought of summer. . . .

The cowmen of the West and Northwest were flat broke. Many of them never recovered. They had not the heart to face another debacle such as they had gone through, and consequently they disappeared from the scene. Most of the Eastern men and the Britishers said "enough" and went away.

Selection from John Clay, *My Life on the Range.* Published by University of Oklahoma Press, Norman, Okla., copyright © 1962.

CRITICAL THINKING

1. According to John Clay, how had greed and mismanagement helped contribute to the disaster that overtook the cattle industry?
2. In what ways did Clay indicate that his sympathies were not wholly with the "cowmen" who went broke during this period?

5. MARK TWAIN SPINS A YARN ABOUT TARANTULAS IN CARSON CITY

At the age of 26, Samuel Clemens arrived in the Territory of Nevada, where his older brother had been appointed acting governor and secretary. There Clemens began his literary career as a newspaper reporter and adopted his famous pseudonym, "Mark Twain." The following adventure, from Roughing It, *occurred shortly after he and his brother arrived in Carson City, following a long stagecoach trip from St. Joseph, Missouri.*

By and by Carson City was pointed out to us. It nestled in the edge of a great plain and was a sufficient number of miles away to look like an assemblage of mere white spots in the shadow of a grim range of mountains overlooking it, whose summits seemed lifted clear out of companionship and consciousness of earthly things.

We arrived, disembarked, and the stage went on. It was a "wooden" town; its population two thousand souls. . . .

We found the state palace of the Governor of Nevada Territory to consist of a white frame one-story house with two small rooms in it and a stanchion supported shed in front—for grandeur —it compelled the respect of the citizen and inspired the Indians with awe. The newly-arrived Chief and Associate Justices of the Territory, and other machinery of the government, were domiciled with less splendor. They were boarding around privately, and had their offices in their bedrooms.

The Secretary and I took quarters in the "ranch" of a worthy French lady by the name of Bridget O'Flannigan. . . . Our room was on the lower floor, facing the plaza; and when we had got our bed, a small table, two chairs, the government fireproof safe, and the Unabridged Dictionary into it, there was still room enough left for a visitor— maybe two, but not without straining the walls. . . . We had a carpet and a genuine queen's-ware washbowl. Consequently we were hated without reserve by the other tenants of the O'Flannigan "ranch." When we added a painted oilcloth window curtain, we simply took our lives into our own hands. To prevent bloodshed I removed upstairs and took up quarters with the untitled plebians in one of the fourteen white pine cot-bedsteads that stood in two long ranks in the one sole room of which the second story consisted.

It was a jolly company, the fourteen. They were principally voluntary camp-followers of the Governor, who had joined his retinue by their own election at New York and San Francisco, and came along, feeling that in the scuffle for little territorial crumbs and offices they could not make their condition more precarious than it was, and might reasonably expect to make it better. They were popularly known as the "Irish Brigade," though there were only four or five Irishmen among all the Governor's retainers. His good-natured Excellency was much annoyed at the gossip his henchmen created—especially when there arose a rumor that they were paid assassins of his, brought along to quietly reduce the democratic vote when desirable!

Mrs. O'Flannigan was boarding and lodging them at ten dollars a week apiece, and they were cheerfully giving their notes for it. They were perfectly satisfied, but Bridget presently found that notes that could not be discounted were but a feeble constitution for a Carson boarding-house. So she began to harry the Governor to find employment for the "Brigade." Her importunities and theirs together drove him to a gentle desperation at last, and he finally summoned the Brigade to the presence. Then, said he:

"Gentlemen, I have planned a lucrative and useful service for you—a service which will provide you with recreation amid noble landscapes, and afford you never-ceasing opportunities for enriching your minds by observation and study. I want you to survey a railroad from Carson City westward to a certain point! When the legislature meets I will have the necessary bill passed and the remuneration arranged."

"What, a railroad over the Sierra Nevada Mountains?"

"Well, then, survey it eastward to a certain point!"

He converted them into surveyors, chain-bearers, and so on, and turned them loose in the desert. It was "recreation" with a vengeance! Recreation on foot, lugging chains through sand and sage-brush, under a sultry sun and among cattle bones, coyotes, and tarantulas. "Romantic adventure" could go no further. They surveyed very slowly, very deliberately, very carefully. They returned every night during the first week, dusty, footsore, tired, and hungry, but very jolly. The brought in great store of prodigious hairy spiders—tarantulas—and imprisoned them in covered tumblers upstairs in the "ranch." . . .

Some of these spiders could straddle over a common saucer with their hairy, muscular legs, and when their feelings were hurt, or their dignity offended, they were the wickedest-looking desperadoes the animal world can furnish. If their glass prison-houses were touched ever so lightly they were up and spoiling for a fight in a minute. . . . In the midst of the turmoil, Bob H—— sprung up out of a sound sleep, and knocked down a shelf with his head. Instantly he shouted:

"Turn out, boys—the tarantulas is loose!"

No warning ever sounded so dreadful. Nobody tried, any longer, to leave the room, lest he might step on a tarantula. Every man groped for a trunk or a bed, and jumped on it. Then followed the strangest silence—a silence of grisly suspense it was, too—waiting, expectancy, fear. It was as dark as pitch, and one had to imagine the spectacle of those fourteen scant-clad men roosting gingerly on trunks and beds, for not a thing could be seen. Then came occasional little interruptions of the silence, and one could recognize a man and tell his locality by his voice, or locate any other sound a sufferer made by his gropings or changes of position. The occasional voices were not given to much speaking—you simply heard a gentle ejaculation of "Ow!" followed by a solid thump, and you knew the gentleman had felt a hairy blanket or something touch his bare skin and had skipped from a bed to the floor. Another silence. Presently you would hear a gasping voice say:

"Su-su-something's crawling on the back of my neck!"

Every now and then you could hear a little subdued scramble and a sorrowful "O Lord!" and then you knew that somebody was getting away from something he took for a tarantula, and not losing any time about it, either. Directly a voice in the corner rang out wild and clear:

"I've got him! I've got him!" (Pause, and probable change of circumstances.) "No, he's got me! Oh, ain't they *never* going to fetch a lantern!"

The lantern came at that moment, in the hands of Mrs. O'Flannigan, whose anxiety to know the

amount of damage done by the assaulting roof had not prevented her waiting a judicious interval, after getting out of bed and lighting up, to see if the wind was done, now, upstairs, or had a larger contract.

The landscape presented when the lantern flashed into the room was picturesque, and might have been funny to some people, but was not to us. Although we were perched so strangely upon boxes, trunks and beds, and so strangely attired, too, we were too earnestly distressed and too genuinely miserable to see any fun about it, and there was not the semblance of a smile anywhere visible. I know I am not capable of suffering more than I did during those few minutes of suspense in the dark, surrounded by those creeping, bloody-minded tarantulas. I had skipped from bed to bed and from box to box in a cold agony, and every time I touched anything that was fuzzy I fancied I felt the fangs. I had rather go to war than live that episode over again. Nobody was hurt. The man who thought a tarantula had "got him" was mistaken—only a crack in a box had caught his finger. Not one of those escaped tarantulas was ever seen again. There were ten or twelve of them. We took candles and hunted the place high and low for them, but with no success. Did we go back to bed then? We did nothing of the kind. Money could not have persuaded us to do it. We sat up the rest of the night playing cribbage and keeping a sharp lookout for the enemy.

Selection from *Mark Twain, A Laurel Reader*, edited by Edmund Fuller. Published by Dell Publishing Co., New York, copyright © 1958.

CRITICAL THINKING

1. Summarize Twain's discovery of how the various levels of the political scene in Carson City were distinguished from each other.
2. What can you conclude about the relationship between the Governor and his camp-followers?
3. Twain describes the tarantulas as "the enemy." Cite several examples of how Twain created humor in the episode concerning their escape.

P I C T U R E AS

CUSTER'S LAST STAND
A Romantic Subject For Illustration

Indians were the only living survivors of the Battle of Little Big Horn. They recalled the bloody fight in a number of drawings and watercolors. Kicking Bear demonstrates the Indians' sense of victory in his drawing above.

General George Armstrong Custer's doomed battle at Little Big Horn is one of the most illustrated events in American history. Artists have produced more than 1300 pictures of the 1876 fight, and recent depictions of the episode have appeared on bubblegum cards, jigsaw puzzles, milk-bottle caps, and cereal boxes.

Much of the art is an attempt to explain what might have happened. Not one of Custer's troops—including Custer himself—lived to tell the tale of the dramatic ambush in what is now the state of South Dakota. Artists were intrigued by the flamboyant "boy general." At the time of his death at Little Big Horn, Custer was widely considered the most daring and courageous cavalry officer in the Army.

The woodcut by W. M. Cary, shown on page 223, was made just 13 days after the earliest telegraphed reports of the battle. In this woodcut, Custer is seen as a soldier of heroic propor-

D O C U M E N T

The first known picture of Custer's Last Stand was a woodcut in the New York Graphic and Illustrated Evening Newspaper *dated July 19, 1876. The woodcut was crude, and obviously done quickly, but it set the tone for many future engravings of the fight.*

tion, ready to battle to the end.

Indians who fought in the battle of Little Big Horn produced numerous drawings of what happened from their point of view. In a drawing by White Bull, the old Sioux warrior who killed Custer, the Indian is shown striking the general with a riding whip. Other Indian artists, such as Kicking Bear, celebrated the victory in watercolors done on muslin, deerskin, buffalo hide, and torn paper.

CRITICAL THINKING

1. Which illustration portrays the massacre emotionally and romantically? List details to support your answers.

2. List details in the drawing by Kicking Bear that help the viewer understand the artist's point of view. How does it differ from W. M. Cary's?

Fabulous accounts of life in Virginia City, Nevada, one of the silver-mining towns that grew up in the area of the Comstock Lode, became part of the legendary American West.

6. ARTEMUS WARD PENS A DUBIOUS ACCOUNT OF THE SILVER-MINING TOWNS OF NEVADA

Another account of Carson City, Nevada, was written by Artemus Ward (Charles Farrar Browne). Life in the Territory's mining towns provided a rich lode of raw material for humorous writers such as Browne and Clemens.

We reach Carson City about nine o'clock in the morning. It is the capital of the Silver-producing territory of Nevada.

They shoot folks here somewhat. . . .

I visit the territorial Prison, and the Warden points out the prominent convicts to me, thus:

"This man's crime was horse-stealing. He is here for life.

"This man is in for murder. He is here for three years."

But shooting isn't as popular in Nevada as it once was. A few years since they used to have a dead man for breakfast every morning. A reformed desperado told me that he supposed he had killed men enough to stock a grave-yard. "A feeling of remorse," he said, "sometimes comes over me! But I'm an altered man now. I hain't killed a man for over two weeks! What'll yer poison yourself with?" he added, dealing a resonant blow on the bar.

There used to live near Carson City a notorious desperado, who never visited town without killing somebody. He would call for liquor at some drinking-house, and if anybody declined joining him he would at once commence shooting. But one day he shot a man too many. Going into the St. Nicholas drinking-house he asked the company present to join him in a North American drink. One individual was rash enough to refuse. With a look of sorrow rather than of anger the desperado revealed his revolver, and said, "Good God! *Must*I kill a man every time I come to Carson?" and so saying he fired and killed the individual on the spot. But this was the last murder the bloodthirsty miscreant ever committed, for the aroused citizens pursued him with rifles and shot him down in his own dooryard.

I lecture in the theatre at Carson, which opens out of a drinking and gambling house. On each side of the door where my ticket-taker stands there are montè-boards and sweat-cloths, but they are deserted to-night, the gamblers being evidently of a literary turn of mind.

Five years ago there was only a pony-path over the precipitous hills on which now stands the marvellous city of Virginia, with its population of twelve thousand persons, and perhaps more. Virginia, with its stately warehouses and gay shops; its splendid streets, paved with silver ore; its banking houses and faro-banks; its attractive coffee-houses and elegant theatre; its music halls and its three daily newspapers.

Virginia is very wild, but I believe it is now pretty generally believed that a mining city must go through with a certain amount of unadulterated cussedness before it can settle down and behave itself in a conservative and seemly manner. Virginia has grown up in the heart of the richest silver regions in the world, the El Dorado of the hour; and of the immense numbers who are swarming thither not more than half carry their mother's Bible or any settled religion with them. The gambler and the strange . . . [individual] as naturally seek the new sensational town as ducks take to that element which is so useful for making cocktails and bathing one's feet; and these people make the new town rather warm for awhile. But by-and-by the earnest and honest citizens get tired of this ungodly nonsense and organize a Vigilance Committee, which hangs the more vicious of the pestiferous crowd to a sour apple-tree; and then come good municipal laws, ministers, meeting-houses, and a tolerably sober police in blue coats with brass buttons. About five thousand able-bodied men are in the mines underground, here; some as far down as five hundred feet. The Gould & Curry Mine employs nine hundred men, and annually turns out about twenty million dollars' worth of "demnition gold and silver." as Mr. Mantalini might express it—though silver chiefly.

❧

There are many other mines here and at Gold-Hill (another startling silver city, a mile from here), all of which do nearly as well. The silver is melted down into bricks of the size of common house bricks; then it is loaded into huge wagons, each drawn by eight and twelve mules, and sent off to San Francisco. To a young person fresh from the land of greenbacks this careless manner of carting off solid silver is rather of a startler. It is related that a young man who came Overland from New Hampshire a few months before my arrival became so excited about it that he fell in a fit, with the name of his Uncle Amos on his lips! The hardy miners supposed he wanted his uncle there to see the great sight, and faint with him. But this was pure conjecture, after all.

I visit several of the adjacent mining towns, but I do not go to Aurora. No, I think not. A lecturer on psychology was killed there the other night by the playful discharge of a horse-pistol. . . . This circumstance, and a rumor that the citizens are *agin* literature, induce me to go back to Virginia.

❧

I had pointed out to me at a Restaurant a man who had killed four men in street broils, and who had that very day cut his own brother's breast open in a dangerous manner with a small supper knife. He was a gentleman, however. I heard him tell some men so. He admitted it himself. And I don't think he would lie about a little thing like that.

The theatre at Virginia will attract the attention of the stranger, because it is an unusually elegant affair of the kind, and would be so regarded anywhere. It was built, of course, by Mr. Thomas Maguire, the Napoleonic manager of the Pacific, and who has built over twenty theatres in his time and will perhaps build as many more, unless somebody stops him—which, by the way, will not be a remarkably easy thing to do.

As soon as a mining camp begins to assume the proportions of a city; at about the time the whiskey-vender draws his cork or the gambler spreads his green cloth, Maguire opens a theatre, and with the hastily-organized "Vigilance Committee" of actors, commences to execute Shakspeare.

Selection from Charles Farrar Browne, *Artemus Ward: His Travels*. Published by Carleton Publisher, New York, copyright © 1865.

CRITICAL THINKING

1. Explain why, according to Ward, a new mining city is "very wild" at first.
2. What can you infer about the establishment of law and order in Carson City, based on Ward's theory of the "wild town"?
3. Cite an example of Ward's use of humor in portraying the reception of intellectuals in mining towns.

7. A COLORFUL MEMOIR OF LIFE IN VIRGINIA CITY, NEVADA, IN ITS HEYDAY

The life of the miners, shopkeepers, and others who inhabited the gold-and silver-rush communities of the West could be even more colorful than the life of the cowhands. The following account of life in Virginia City, Nevada, the site of the Comstock silver strike, comes from a reminiscence written in 1889.

The Comstock, for a number of years, was the most productive mining district that the world has ever known. Several years ago . . . a careful estimate was made of the dimensions of the pile, supposing all the bullion taken out of the mines up to that time had been concentrated in one solid block. I found it would make a cubicle brick . . . twenty-six feet in height. . . .

In the palmiest days it was not an unusual circumstance for a million of dollars to be taken out of a single mine as a result of a month's labor. Those who lived directly over the mines at the time did not seem to have a full realizing sense of their wonderful richness or of the excitement the reports of the ore product was producing throughout the civilized world. One day I asked . . . for a good piece of ore to send as a specimen to friends in the East. [The mine superintendent] picked up a piece of rock weighing five or six pounds which assayed 30,000 to the ton. The mass seemed to be almost solid silver and likewise carried about 40 per cent of gold.

The men who worked in the mines . . . were [a] happy-go-easy set of fellows, fond of good living, and not particularly interested in religious affairs. . . .

. . . As regarded deportment, everyone was a law unto himself. Perhaps one reason for the laxity in the observance of the Sabbath was the fact that work in the mines went on uninterruptedly during the whole 365 days of the year. Another demoralizing circumstance was that most of the men employed in the mines were unmarried and enjoyed none of the refining, humanizing influences of home life. They boarded at a restaurant, slept in a lodging-house, and, as a general rule, spent their leisure time on the street or at the gambling-tables.

During the flush times as many as twenty-five faro games were in full blast night and day. When sporting men, as for example, Joe Stewart, Cross and Bill Gibson, sat down of an evening to a friendly game of poker it was no uncommon occurrence for five or six thousand dollars to change hands at a single sitting. Some idea of the amount of money in circulation may be inferred from the fact that every working-man's wages amounted to at least 120 dollars per month.

From what has already been written there is no desire to convey the impression that a low standard of morality was the rule in the Comstock mining district. Men quarreled at times and fire-arms were discharged with but slight provocation. Nevertheless they all had an acute instinct of right and wrong, a high sense of honor, and a chivalrous feeling of respect for the gentler sex. A woman unattended could pass along the streets of Virginia and Gold Hill without the slightest danger of insult or annoyance.

One of the most prominent traits of character as regarded the miners was their generous response to any worthy object. If a man of family lost his life in the mines thousands of dollars would be contributed to those dependent upon him. Each miner contributed regularly one or two days' wages for benevolent purposes. An annual fair given in aid of an orphan school under the charge of the Sisters of Charity, even in dull times, usually netted from 10,000 dollars to 12,000 dollars. . . .

When a man died he was given "a good send-off." A band of music headed the funeral procession, and if the officiating clergyman could not think of anything redeeming in the character of the deceased he carefully refrained from saying anything ill.

Selection from *The Mining Frontier: Contemporary Accounts from the American West in the Nineteenth Century*, edited by Marvin Lewis. Published by University of Oklahoma Press, Norman, Okla., copyright © 1967.

CRITICAL THINKING

1. Summarize the writer's view of the miners' character and habits.
2. What evidence is there that the writer was romanticizing the miners?

CHAPTER 21
THE REVOLT OF THE FARMERS
1873–1896

1. WRITER HAMLIN GARLAND FICTIONALIZES THE MIDWESTERN FARMER

Hamlin Garland {1860–1940} was born near West Salem, Wisconsin, and spent his youth in the Middle West. His novels and nonfiction writings gave Americans a close, personal look at the life of the farms and farmers of that region. This passage from Other Main-Travelled Roads *gives a fictionalized view of how one person viewed farm life—and how he thought it could be reformed.*

P oor fellows," sighed Lily, almost unconsciously. "I hate to see them working there in the dirt and hot sun. It seems a hopeless sort of life, doesn't it?"

"Oh, but this is the most beautiful part of the year," said Radbourn. "Think of them in the mud, in the sleet; think of them husking corn in the snow, a bitter wind blowing; think of them a month later in the harvest; think of them imprisoned here in winter!"

"Yes, it's dreadful! But I never felt it so keenly before. You have opened my eyes to it. Of course, I've been on a farm, but not to live there."

"Writers and orators have lied so long about "the idyllic" in farm life, and said so much about the "independent American farmer," that he himself has remained blind to the fact that he's one of the hardest-working and poorest-paid men in America. See the houses they live in—hovels."

"Yes, yes, I know," said Lily. . . . "And the fate of the poor women, oh, the fate of the women—"

"Yes, it's a matter of statistics," went on Radbourn pitilessly, "that the wives of the American farmers [fill] our insane asylums. See what a life they lead, most of them; no music, no books. Seventeen hours a day, a couple of rooms—dens. Now there is Sim Burns! What a travesty of a home! Yet there are a dozen just as bad in sight. He works like a fiend, as does his wife—and what is their reward? Simply a hole to hibernate in and to sleep and eat in in summer. A dreary present and a well-nigh hopeless future. . . . "

"I know Mrs. Burns," Lily said, after a pause; "she sends several children to my school. Poor, pathetic little things, half-clad and wistful-eyed. They make my heart ache; they are so hungry for love, and so quick to learn." . . .

. . . Radbourn let the reins fall slack as he talked on. He did not look at the girl; his eyebrows were drawn into a look of gloomy pain.

"It isn't so much the grime that I abhor, nor the labor that crooks their backs and makes their hands bludgeons. It's the horrible waste of life involved in it all. I don't believe God intended a man to be bent to plough-handles like that, but that isn't the worst of it. The worst of it is, these people live lives approaching automata. They become machines to serve others more lucky or more unscrupulous than themselves. What is the world of art, of music, of literature, to these poor devils—to Sim Burns and his wife there, for example? Or even to the best of these farmers?"

The girl looked away over the shimmering lake of yellow-green corn. A choking came into her throat. Her gloved hand trembled.

Hamlin Garland's writings about Midwestern farm life were notable for their realism.

"What is such a life worth? It's all very comfortable for us to say, 'They don't feel it.' How do we know what they feel? What do we know of their capacity for enjoyment of art and music? They never have leisure or opportunity. The master is very glad to be taught by preacher, and lawyer, and novelist, that his slaves are contented and never feel any longings for a higher life. These people live lives but little higher than their cattle —are *forced* to live so. Their hopes and aspirations are crushed out, their souls are twisted and deformed just as toil twists and deforms their bodies. They are on the same level as the city laborer. . . ."

"What can we do?" murmured the girl.

"Do? Rouse these people for one thing; preach *discontent*, a noble discontent."

"It will only make them unhappy."

"No, it won't; not if you show them the way out. If it does, it's better to be unhappy striving for higher things, like a man, than to be content to wallow like swine."

"But what *is* the way out?"

This was sufficient to set Radbourn upon his hobby horse. He outlined his plan of action: the abolition of all indirect taxes, the state control of all privileges, the private ownership of which interfered with the equal rights of all. He would utterly destroy speculative holdings of the earth. He would have land everywhere brought to its best use, by appropriating all ground rents to the use of the state, etc., etc.

Selection from Hamlin Garland, *Other Main-Travelled Roads.* Published by Harper & Brothers, New York, copyright © 1910.

CRITICAL THINKING

1. What did Hamlin Garland seem to believe were the emotional and psychological effects of farm life?
2. How might Radbourn's reforms have changed the farmers' existence?
3. What evidence did Radbourn offer to support his idea that farmers were not even aware of how difficult and unfair their lot was?

2. THE POPULIST PARTY DRAFTS A CONTROVERSIAL PLATFORM IN 1892

The platform drafted by the Populists in 1892 was one of the most hotly debated documents of the period. The following passages from that platform show what the Populists' policies and demands were—and suggest why these might have been resisted so strongly.

We have witnessed for more than a quarter of a century the struggles of the two great political parties for power and plunder, while grievous wrongs have been inflicted upon the suffering people. We charge that the controlling influence[s] dominating both these parties have permitted the existing dreadful conditions to develop without serious effort to prevent or restrain them. Neither do they now promise us any substantial reform. . . .

. . . We believe that the power of government —in other words, of the people—should be expanded (as in the case of the postal service) as rapidly and as far as the good sense of an intelligent people and the teachings of experience shall justify, to the end that oppression, injustice and poverty, shall eventually cease in the land. . . .

CURRENCY. We demand free and unlimited coinage of silver and gold at the present legal ratio of 16 to 1.

We demand that the amount of circulating medium [money] be speedily increased to not less than $50 per capita.

We demand that postal savings banks be established by the government for the safe deposit of the earnings of the people and to facilitate exchange.

TRANSPORTATION. Transportation being a means of exchange and a public necessity, the government should own and operate the railroads in the interest of the people. The telegraph and telephone, like the post office system, being a necessity for the transmission of news, should be owned and operated by the government in the interest of the people.

LAND. The land, including all the natural sources of wealth, is the heritage of the people, and should not be monopolized for speculative purposes, and alien [foreign] ownership of land should be prohibited. All land now held by railroads and other corporations in excess of their actual needs, and all lands now owned by aliens, should be reclaimed by the government and held for actual settlers only.

Selection from *National Party Conventions 1831–1976*. Published by *Congressional Quarterly*, Washington, D.C., copyright © 1979.

CRITICAL THINKING

1. Summaraize the Populist's demands for currency reforms.
2. Why might the Populists have been concerned with "alien" ownership of American land?

In 1894, President Grover Cleveland sent federal troops to break the Pullman Strike.

3. PRESIDENT GROVER CLEVELAND UPHOLDS THE DIGNITY OF LABOR

Before his first term as president, Grover Cleveland's views appeared to be sympathetic toward the rights of workingpeople. The excerpt below is from his 1884 acceptance of the presidential nomination. During the labor wars of the 1890s, however, Cleveland responded by sending federal troops to Chicago, to break a strike of railway workers against the Pullman Co.

ALBANY, N.Y., August 18, 1884.

GENTLEMEN:

I have received your communication, dated July 28, 1884, informing me of my nomination to the office of President of the United States by the National Democratic Convention, lately assembled at Chicago. I accept the nomination with a grateful appreciation of the supreme honor conferred and a solemn sense of the responsibility, which, in its acceptance, I assume. . . .

A true American sentiment recognizes the dignity of labor and the fact that honor lies in honest toil. Contented labor is an element of national prosperity. Ability to work constitutes the capital and the wage of labor the income of a vast number of our population, and this interest should be jealously protected. Our workingmen are not asking unreasonable indulgence. . . .

In a letter accepting the nomination to the office of Governor [of New York], nearly two years ago, I made the following statement, to which I have steadily adhered:

The laboring classes constitute the main part of our population. They should be protected in their efforts peaceably to assert their rights when endangered by aggregated capital, and all statutes on this subject should recognize the care of the State for honest toil, and be framed with a view of improving the condition of the workingman.

Selection from *The Writings and Speeches of Grover Cleveland*, edited by George F. Parker. Published by Cassell Publishing Co., New York, copyright © 1892. Reprinted by Kraus Reprint Co., New York, 1970.

CRITICAL THINKING

1. What traditional American views of work was Grover Cleveland upholding?
2. What clue to Cleveland's actions in the Pullman Strike can be found in his statement on labor as Governor of New York?

229

P I C T U R E AS

PIONEER HOUSING
American Ingenuity Turns Logs, Sod, And Adobe Into Homes

At first, settlers often lived in tents. Later on, neighbors might pitch in to build houses.

With bricks and boards rarely available, building a home for most early settlers necessarily became the art of improvisation. How their houses were built depended upon the materials that existed on the land where they lived, and this differed from region to region.

In forested areas, such as the Pacific Northwest, cabins were constructed from logs, which had been chopped down, stacked on top of one another, and then interlocked by notches at each corner of the structure. Doors and windows were cut out of the walls, and the spaces between the logs were filled with mud.

On the Great Plains, where there were few trees, settlers built dugouts and sod houses. Dugouts were dwellings crudely hollowed out of hillsides with a shovel. If there were no hills, sod houses were constructed using blocks of earth, cut from the tough grassland. These chunks of "prairie marble" were set on top of

D O C U M E N T

It took an acre of prairie sod to construct a one-room house measuirng 16 by 20 feet.

Sturdy walls provided warmth during the prairie's bitter winters and coolness in summer.

The typical log cabin was one small room, perhaps with a loft for sleeping or storage.

Cool, insulated adobe houses were well-suited to the hot, dry climate of the Southwest.

one another to form walls, with wooden frames set into the mud and serving for the doors and the windows.

In much of the Southwest, where there was neither timber nor sod, settlers built houses of "adobe" (mud bricks). They mixed sandy soil or clay with water and a small amount of straw, shaped it into bricks, and baked the bricks in the sun for several weeks, before assembling their homes.

CRITICAL THINKING

1. The design and construction of a pioneer house was dependent on several factors. Describe the construction materials and method of construction.
2. Study the top right photograph. How did these settlers make their house comfortable?

CHAPTER 6

AMERICAN EXPANSION

1896–1903

1. ADMIRAL ALFRED T. MAHAN ANALYZES THE INFLUENCE OF SEA POWER ON INTERNATIONAL POLITICS

Born in 1840, at West Point, New York, Alfred Thayer Mahan was a naval officer who gained fame as a historian of sea power. During the late nineteenth and early twentieth centuries, his arguments for strengthening the United States Navy influenced many of the country's leaders. The following passage comes from an essay entitled "Navies as International Factors."

More almost than armies, which in these changes [in territory among European nations] were the instruments of forcible yet beneficent adjustments, navies are instruments of international relations. They are so more purely, because a navy, as has long been recognized, can very rarely be used to oppress the people of its country in their domestic conditions, as armies often have been. While thus more strictly international, the scope of navies is also far wider. They can be felt where the national armies cannot go, except under naval protection. Just here it becomes necessary to point out a further distinction, which closely affects the United States and shows more clearly how entirely the navy, and consequently the numbers and constitution of the navy, is a matter to be determined by international considerations, and not merely by those which are domestic and internal to the country. Exactly as a navy cannot be used as an instrument of domestic oppression, so in international affairs it is less effective for aggression than armies are; yet to a state whose frontiers are maritime, and to the external interests of such a state, it is more effective as a defensive force for protection, because of its mobility. The United States has neither the tradition nor the design to act aggressively beyond seas, but she has very important

transmarine interests which need protection, as well as two home coasts separated by a great intervening space and open to attack.

The quesiton for the United States, as regards the size of its navy, is not so much what it desires to accomplish as what it is willing or not willing to concede. For instance, we have shown plainly that we are unwilling to concede anything as regards the control of the Panama Canal, even to discuss the right to fortify it. The Monroe Doctrine, too, is only a claim to maintain security for that which we possess. In no sense does it propose to add to our holdings. How far is the country prepared to be obliged to concede on these points, because unready to maintain them by organized force?

Selection from A. T. Mahan, *Armaments and Arbitration, Or, The Place of Force in the International Relations of States.* Published by Harper & Brothers, New York, copyright © 1912.

CRITICAL THINKING

1. What role did Alfred Mahan believe navies played in a nation's policy?
2. What did he believe the United States needed to consider in deciding what kind and how large a navy it would have?

---

2. PRESIDENT WILLIAM McKINLEY DECIDES TO ANNEX THE PHILIPPINES

In April 1898, the United States Congress passed the Teller Amendment, which declared that the United States would not take any Cuban territory gained in the war with Spain. However, when the final peace treaty was signed in December, 1898, the United States took at least temporary control of Cuba, Puerto Rico, and Guam. It also took over Spain's claims to the Philippines for a sum of $20 million. President William McKinley's description of how he reached a decision on the Philippines follows.

When next I realized that the Philippines had dropped into our laps I confess I did not know what to do with them. I sought counsel from all sides—Democrats as well as Republicans—but got little help. I thought first we would take only Manila; then Luzon; then other islands perhaps also. I walked the floor of the White House night after night until midnight; and I am not ashamed to tell you, gentlemen, that I went down on my knees and prayed Almighty God for light and guidance more than one night. And one night late it came to me this way—I don't know how it was, but it came: (1) That we could not give them back to Spain—that would be cowardly and dishonorable; (2) that we could not turn them over to France or Germany—our commercial rivals in the Orient—that would be bad business and discreditable; (3) that we could not leave them for themselves—they were unfit for self-government—and they would soon have anarchy and misrule worse than Spain's was; and (4) that there was nothing left for us to do but take them all, and to educate the Filipinos, and uplift and civilize and Christianize them . . . as our fellow-men for whom Christ also died. And then I went to bed, and went to sleep, and slept soundly, and the next morning I sent for the chief engineer of the War Department (our map-maker), and I told him to put the Philippines on the map of the United States . . . and there they are, and there they will stay while I am President!

Selection adapted from *History of U.S. Political Parties*, Vol. 3, edited by Arthur M. Schlesinger, Jr. Published by Chelsea House Publishers, New York, copyright © 1973.

CRITICAL THINKING

1. What arguments did President McKinley give for justifying his decision?
2. What role did McKinley foresee for the United States in the Philippines?

3. INDIANA SENATOR ALBERT J. BEVERIDGE ENVISIONS THE "MARCH OF AMERICA'S FLAG"

Few political leaders were as outspoken in their expansionist views as Albert Beveridge. Born in 1862 in Ohio, he served as a Senator from Indiana from 1899 to 1911. The following speech, which became famous as a Republican campaign document in the Middle West, was made in Indianapolis during the election campaign of 1898.

It is a noble land that God has given us; a land that can feed and clothe the world; a land whose coastlines would inclose half the countries of Europe; a land set like a sentinel between the two imperial oceans of the globe; a greater England with a nobler destiny.

It is a mighty people that He has planted on this soil; a people sprung from the most masterful blood of history; a people perpetually revitalized by the virile, man-producing working-folk of all the earth; a people imperial by virtue of their power, by right of their institutions, by authority of their Heaven-directed purposes—the propagandists and not the misers of liberty.

It is a glorious history our God has bestowed upon His chosen people; a history heroic with faith in our mission and our future; a history of statesmen who flung the boundaries of the Republic out into unexplored lands and savage wilderness; a history of soldiers who carried the flag across blazing deserts and through the ranks of hostile mountains, even to the gates of sunset; a history of a multiplying people who overran a continent in half a century. . . .

Therefore, in this campaign, the question is larger than a party question. It is an American question. It is a world question. Shall the American people continue their march toward the commercial supremacy of the world? Shall free institutions broaden their blessed reign as the children of liberty wax in strength, until the empire of our principles is established over the hearts of all mankind?

Have we no mission to perform, no duty to discharge to our fellow-man? Has God endowed us with gifts beyond our deserts and marked us as the people of His peculiar favor, merely to rot in our own selfishness, as men and nations must, who take cowardice for their companion and self for their deity—as China has, as India has, as Egypt has?

. . . shall we reap the reward that waits on our discharge of our high duty; shall we occupy new markets for what our farmers raise, our factories make, our merchants sell—aye, and please God, new markets for what our ships shall carry?

Hawaii is ours; Puerto Rico is to be ours; at the prayer of her people Cuba finally will be ours; in the islands of the East, even to the gates of Asia, coaling stations are to be ours at the very least; the flag of a liberal government is to float over the Philippines, and may it be the banner that [General Zachary] Taylor unfurled in Texas [in the Mexican-American War, 1846–1848] and Fremont carried to the coast [during the California revolt against Mexico in 1846].

The Opposition tells us that we ought not to govern a people without their consent. I answer, The rule of liberty that all just government derives its authority from the consent of the governed, applies only to those who are capable of self-government. We govern the Indians without their consent, we govern our territories without their consent, we govern our children without their consent. How do they know that our government would be without their consent? Would not the people of the Philippines prefer the just, humane, civilizing government of this Republic to the savage, bloody rule of pillage and extortion from which we have rescued them?

And, regardless of this formula of words made only for enlightened, self-governing people, do we owe no duty to the world? Shall we turn these people back to the reeking lands from which we have taken them? Shall we abandon them, with Germany, England, Japan, hungering for them? Shall we save them from those nations to give them a self-rule of tragedy?

They ask us how we shall govern these new possessions. I answer: Out of local conditions and the necessities of the case[,] methods of government will grow. If England can govern foreign lands, so can America. If Germany can govern foreign lands, so can America. . . . Why is it more difficult to administer Hawaii than New Mexico or California? Both had a savage and an alien population; both were more remote from the seat of government when they came under our dominion that the Philippines are to-day.

Will you say by your vote that American ability to govern has decayed, that a century's experience in self-rule has failed of a result? Will you affirm by your vote that you are an infidel to American power and practical sense? Or will you say that ours is the blood of government; ours the heart of dominion; ours the brain and genius of administration? Will you remember that we do but what our fathers did, we but pitch the tents of liberty farther westward, farther southward—we only continue the march of the flag?

Selection from *History of U.S. Political Parties*, Vol. III, edited by Arthur M. Schlesinger, Jr. Published by Chelsea House, New York, copyright © 1973.

CRITICAL THINKING

1. What arguments did Albert Beveridge offer against the idea that Americans should not govern other people without their consent?
2. What reasons did Beveridge give for the need to expand beyond America's present borders?

4. MISSOURI SENATOR CARL SCHURZ QUESTIONS AMERICAN MILITARY EXPANSION

Not all Americans were in favor of America's new policy of expansion and world power. Carl Schurz was a Republican who served as a Senator from Missouri and as Secretary of the Department of the Interior. In this passage from his writings, he argued that the growth of military power threatened consitutional democracy in the United States.

No candid observer of current events will deny that even to-day the spirit of the new policy awakened by the victories and conquests achieved in the Spanish war, and by the occurrences in the Philippines, has moved even otherwise sober-minded persons to speak of the Constitutional limitations of governmental power with a levity which a year ago would have provoked serious alarm and stern rebuke. We are loudly told by the advocates of the new policy that the Constitution no longer fits our present conditions and aspirations as a great and active world Power, and should not be permitted to stand in our way. . . .

Such usurpations [of constitutional authority] are most apt to be acquiesced in when, in time of war, they appeal to popular feeling in the name of military necessity, or of the honor of the flag, or of National glory. In a democracy acting through universal suffrage . . . every influence is unhealthy that prevents men from calm reasoning. And nothing is more calculated to do that than martial excitements which stir the blood. . . .

History shows that military glory is the most unwholesome food that democracies can feed upon. War withdraws, more than anything else, the popular attention from those problems and interests which are, in the long run, of the greatest consequence. It produces a strange moral and political color-blindness. It creates false ideals of patriotism and civic virtue. . . .

You will have observed that I have treated the matter of militarism in the United States in intimate connection with our warlike enterprises, as if they were substantially the same thing. I have done so purposely. As I endeavored to set forth, the development of militarism in European states can be explained on the theory that each Power may think the largest possible armaments necessary for the protection of its safety among its neighbors, and for the preservation of peace. With us such a motive cannot exist. Not needing large armaments for our safety—for this Republic, if it maintained its old traditional policy, would be perfectly safe without them—we can need them only in the service of warlike adventure undertaken at our own pleasure, for whatever purpose. And here I may remark, by the way, that in my opinion, although such a course of warlike adventure may have begun with a desire to liberate and civilize certain foreign populations, it will be likely to develop itself, unless soon checked, into a downright and reckless policy of conquest with all the "criminal aggression" and savagery such a policy implies. At any rate, that policy of warlike adventure and militarism will, with us, go together as essentially identical. Without the policy of warlike adventure large standing armaments would, with us, have no excuse and would not be tolerated. If we continue that policy, militarism with its characteristic evils will be inevitable. If we wish to escape those evils and to protect this democracy against their dangerous effects, the policy of warlike adventure must be given up, for the two things are inseparable.

Selection from *Speeches, Correspondence, and Political Papers of Carl Schurz* Vol. VI edited by Frederic Bancroft. Published by G. P. Putnam's, New York, copyright © 1913. Reprinted by Negro Universities Press, New York.

> ## CRITICAL THINKING
>
> 1. What did Senator Carl Schurz believe would be the long-term effects of the new American foreign policy?
> 2. Later in this same essay, Senator Schurz wrote that the United States should "restrict [its] standing armaments to the lowest practicable limits." What arguments did he offer here for this view?
> 3. In what ways did Schurz see American actions in the Spanish-American War as an illustration of his idea that militarism was unhealthy for democracies?

5. HAWAII'S QUEEN LILIUOKALANI CALLS ON AMERICANS TO NOT ANNEX HAWAII

One of the most eloquent voices raised in opposition to the American expansionist policy was that of Queen Liliuokalani of Hawaii. The following passage from Hawaii's Story By Hawaii's Queen *was written while the United States debated whether or not to annex the islands.*

Will it . . . be thought strange that education and knowledge of the world have enabled us [the people of Hawaii] to perceive that as a race we have some special mental and physical requirements not shared by the other races which have come among us? That certain habits and modes of living are better for our health and happiness than others? And that a separate nationality, and a particular form of government, as well as special laws, are, at least for the present, best for us? And these things remained to us, until the pitiless and tireless "annexation policy" was effectively backed by the naval power of the United States.

To other usurpations of authority on the part of those whose love for the institutions of their native land we could understand and forgive we had submitted. We had allowed them virtually to give us a constitution, and control the offices of state. Not without protest, indeed; for the usurpation was unrighteous, and cost us much humiliation and distress. But we did not resist it by force. It had not entered into our hearts to believe that these friends and allies from the United States, even with all their foreign affinities, would ever go so far as to absolutely overthrow our form of government, seize our nation by the throat, and pass it over to an alien power.

And while we sought by peaceful political means to maintain the dignity of the throne, and to advance national feeling among the native people, we never sought to rob any citizen, wherever born, of either property, franchise, or social standing.

Perhaps there is a kind of right, depending upon the precedents of all ages, and known as the "Right of Conquest," under which robbers and marauders may establish themselves in possession of whatsoever they are strong enough to ravish from their fellows. I will not pretend to decide how far civilization and Christian enlightenment have outlawed it. But we have known for many years that our Island monarchy has relied upon the protection always extended to us by the policy and the assured friendship of the great American republic.

If we have nourished in our bosom those who have sought our ruin, it has been because they were of the people whom we believed to be our dearest friends and allies. If we did not by force resist their final outrage, it was because we could not do so without striking at the military force of the United States. Whatever constraint the executive of [the United States] may be under to recognize the present government at Honolulu has been forced upon it by no act of ours, but by the unlawful acts of its own agents. Attempts to repudiate those acts are vain. . . .

It is not for me to consider this matter from the American point of view; although the pending question of annexation involves nothing less than a departure from the established policy of that country, and an ominous change in its foreign relations. It is enough that I am able to say, and with absolute authority, that the native people of Hawaii are entirely faithful to their own chiefs, and are deeply attached to their own customs and mode of government; that they either do not understand, or bitterly oppose, the scheme of annexation. . . .

Oh, honest Americans . . . hear me for my down-trodden people! Their form of government is as dear to them as yours is precious to you.

Queen Liliuokalani protested unsuccessfully against the U.S. annexation of Hawaii in 1898.

Quite as warmly as you love your country, so they love theirs. With all your goodly possessions, covering a territory so immense that there yet remain parts unexplored . . . do not covet the little vineyard of Naboth's, so far from your shores, lest the punishment of Ahab fall upon you, if not in your day, in that of your children, for "be not deceived, God is not mocked."

Selection from Liliuokalani, *Hawaii's Story by Hawaii's Queen.* Published by Lothrop, Lee & Shepard Co.:Boston, copyright © 1898.

CRITICAL THINKING

1. What arguments did Queen Liliuokalani use to support her position that annexation of Hawaii was unfair?
2. What reasons might Liliuokalani have had for declaring that the Hawaiians had always depended upon the friendship of America?
3. What contrast did Liliuokalani see between the actions of the Hawaiians and the actions of the Americans living in Hawaii?

6. WILLIAM RANDOLPH HEARST—YOUNG, BRASH, AND AMBITIOUS—SEEKS HIS OWN NEWSPAPER

Newspapers such as William Randolph Hearst's New York Journal *used almost every opportunity to push the country toward war with Spain. Sensational stories and headlines reminded readers to "Remember the Maine." This style of writing, known as "yellow," was partly the invention of Hearst. This letter to his multi-millionaire father, who owned the San Francisco* Examiner, *explains Hearst's views on newspaper publishing when he was only 22 and had yet to embark on a career.*

1885 [Washington]

DEAR FATHER:

I have begun to have a strange fondness for our little paper [the San Francisco *Examiner*] —a tenderness like unto that which a mother feels for a puny or deformed offspring, and I should hate to see it die now after it had battled so long and so nobly for existence; in fact, to tell the truth, I am possessed of the weakness, which at some time or other of their lives, pervades most men; I am convinced that I could run a newspaper successfully.

Now if you should make over to me the *Examiner*—with enough money to carry out my schemes—I'll tell you what I would do!

In the first place I would change the general appearance of the paper and make seven wide columns where we now have nine narrow ones, then I would have the type spaced more, and these two changes would give the pages a much cleaner and neater appearance.

Secondly, it would be well to make the paper as far as possible original, to clip only when absolutely necessary and to imitate only some such leading journal as the New York *World* which is undoubtedly the best paper of that class to which the *Examiner* belongs—that class which appeals to the people and which depends for its success upon enterprise, energy and a certain startling originality and not upon the wisdom of its political opinions or the lofty style of its editorials: And to accomplish this we must have—as the *World* has—active, intelligent and energetic young men; we must have men who come out West in the hopeful

buoyancy of youth for the purpose of making their fortunes and not a worthless scum that has been carried there by the eddies of repeated failures.

Thirdly, we must advertise the paper from Oregon to New Mexico and must also increase our number of advertisements if we have to lower our rates to do it, thus we can put on the first page that our circulation is such and our advertisements so and so and constantly increasing.

And now having spoken of the three great essential points let us turn to details. The illustrations are a detail, though a very important one. Illustrations embellish a page; illustrations attract the eye and stimulate the imagination of the masses and materially aid the comprehension of an unaccustomed reader and thus are of particular importance to that class of people which the *Examiner* claims to address. Such illustrations, however, as have heretofore appeared in the paper, nauseate rather than stimulate the imagination and certainly do anything but embellish a page.

Another detail of questionable importance is that we actually or apparently establish some connection between ourselves and the New York *World*, and obtain a certain prestige in bearing some relation to that paper. We might contract to have important private telegrams forwarded or something of that sort, but understand that the principal advantage we are to derive is from the attention such a connection would excite and from the advertisement we could make of it. Whether the *World* would consent to such an arrangement for any reasonable sum is very doubtful, for its net profit is over one thousand dollars a day and four years ago it belonged to Jay Gould and was losing money rapidly.

And now to close with a suggestion of great consequence, namely, that all these changes be made not by degrees but at once so that the improvement will be very marked and noticeable and will attract universal attention and comment.

There is little to be said about my studies. I am getting on in all of them well enough to be able to spend considerably time in outside reading and in Journalistic investigation. There is, moreover, very little to be said about Washington, for Congress is as stupid as it is possible to conceive of and has been enlivened only once during our stay and that the other day when Wise of Virginia sat on

Boutelle of Maine for attempting to revive the dissensions of the war. So heavily, indeed, did Mr. Wise sit on Boutelle that I fear the latter gentlemen has not even yet recovered his characteristic rotundity of form.

Well, good-by. I have given up all hope of having you write to me, so I suppose I must just scratch along and trust to hearing of you through the newspapers. By the way, I heard you had bought 2000 acres of land the other day and I hope some of it was the land adjoining our ranch tht I begged you to buy in my last letter.

Your affectionate son,

W.R.Hearst

Selection from *A Treasury of The World's Great Letters*, edited by M. Lincoln Schuster. Published by Simon and Schuster, New York, copyright © 1940.

CRITICAL THINKING

1. What conclusions can you draw about Hearst's ability to express his thoughts?
2. List two ways Hearst used to structure his argument concerning the *Examiner*.
3. Summarize Hearst's approach to increasing the newspaper's circulation by appealing to its particular audience.

7. WILLIAM DEAN HOWELLS VISITS A SPANISH PRISONER-OF-WAR CAMP IN NEW HAMPSHIRE

For many people, the Spanish-American War was too brief and too far away to make much of an impact on their daily lives. An unexpected memoir of the war is supplied by William Dean Howells, novelist and later editor of the Atlantic Monthly *magazine. This selection is a speech in which he recalled visiting an internment camp for Spanish prisoners of war, in New Hampshire.*

Certain summers ago our cruisers, the *St. Louis* and the *Harvard*, arrived at Portsmouth, New Hampshire, with sixteen or seventeen hundred Spanish prisoners from Santiago de Cuba. They were partly soldiers of the land forces picked up by our troops in the fights before the city, but

William Dean Howells ranked with Henry James and Mark Twain as one of the three most influential American novelists of his era.

by far the greater part were sailors and marines from Cervera's ill-fated fleet.

It was an afternoon of the brilliancy known only to an afternoon of the American summer, and the water of the swift Piscataqua River glittered in the sun with a really incomparable brilliancy. But nothing could light up the great monster of a ship, painted the dismal lead-color which our White-Squadrons put on with the outbreak of the war, and she lay sullen in the stream with a look of ponderous repose, to which the activities of the coaling-barges at her side and of the sailors washing her decks, seemed quite unrelated. A long gun forward and a long gun aft threatened the fleet of launches, tugs, dories, and cat-boats which fluttered about her, but the *Harvard* looked tired and bored, and seemed as if asleep. She had, in fact, finished her mission. The captives whom death had released had been carried out and sunk in the sea; those who survived to a further imprisonment had all been taken to the pretty island a mile farther up the river, where the tide rushes back and forth through the Narrows like a torrent. Its defiant rapidity has won it there the graphic name of Pull-and-be-Damned; and we could only hope to reach the island by a series of skilful tacks, which should humor both the wind and the tide, both dead against us. Our boatman, one of those shore New Englanders who are born with a knowledge of sailing, was easily master of the art of this, but it took time.

We drew nearer and nearer their prison isle, and it opened its knotty points and little ravines, overrun with sweet-fern, blueberry-bushes, and low blackberry-vines, and rigidly traversed with a high stockade of yellow pine boards. Six or eight long, low, wooden barracks stretched side by side across the general slope, with the captive officers quarters, sheathed in weather-proof black paper, at one end of them. About their doors swarmed the common prisoners, spilling out over the steps and on the grass, where some of them lounged, smoking.

The prisoners were already filing out of their quarters at a rapid trot towards the benches where the great wash-boilers of coffee were set. Each man had a soup plate and a bowl of enamelled tin, and each in his turn received a quarter of a loaf of fresh bread and a big ladleful of steaming coffee, which he made off with to his place at one of the long tables under a shed at the side of the stockade. One young fellow tried to get a place not his own in the shade, and our officer when he came back explained that he was a *guerrillero*, and rather unruly. We heard that eight of the prisoners were in irons, by sentence of their own officers, for misconduct, but all save this *guerrillero* here were docile and obedient enough, and seemed only too glad to get peacefully at their bread and coffee.

First among them came the men of the *Cristóbal Colón*, and these were the best looking of all the captives. From their pretty fair average the others varied to worse and worse, till a very scrub lot, said to be ex-convicts, brought up the rear. They were nearly all little fellows, and very dark, though here and there a six-footer towered up, or a blond showed among them. They were joking and laughing together, harmlessly enough, but I must own that they looked a crew of rather sorry jail-birds; though whether any kind of humanity clad in misfits of our navy blue and white, and other chance garments, with close-shaven heads, and sometimes bare feet, would have looked much less like jail-birds I am not sure. Still they were not prepossessing, and though some of them were pathetically young, they had none of the charm of boyhood. No doubt they did not do themselves justice, and to be herded together like cattle did not improve their chances of making a favorable impression on the observer. At a certain bugle-call they dispersed, when they had finished their bread and coffee, and scattered about over the grass, or returned to their barracks. We were told that these children of the sun dreaded its heat, and kept out of it whenever they could, even in its decline; but they seemed not so much to withdraw and hide themselves from that, as to vanish into the history of "old, unhappy, far-off" times, where prisoners of war properly belong. I roused myself with a start as if I had lost them in the past.

The whole thing was very American in the perfect decorum and the utter absence of ceremony. Our good fellows were in the clothes they wore through the fights of Santiago, and they could not have put on much splendor if they had wished, but apparently they did not wish. They were simple, straightforward and adequate. There was some dry joking about the superiority of the prisoners' rations and lodgings, and our officers ironically professed his intention of messing with the Spanish officers. But there was no grudge, and not a shadow of ill-will, or of that stupid and atrocious hate toward the public enemy which abominable newspapers and politicians had tried to breed in the popular mind. There was nothing manifest but a sort of cheerful purpose to live up to that military ideal of duty which is so much nobler than the civil ideal of self-interest. Perhaps duty will year become the civil ideal, when the peoples shall have learned to live for the common good, and are as united for the operation of the industries as they now are for the hostilities.

Selection from *The Best American Orations of To-Day*, edited by Harriet Blackstone. Published by Hinds, Noble & Eldredge, New York, copyright © 1903.

CRITICAL THINKING

1. What conclusion can you draw about Howells' attitude toward the newspapers' treatment of the war.
2. Cite the quality that Howells found most impressive in the Americans' attitude toward the prisoners.
3. Summarize Howells' impressions of the prisoners.

William Jennings Bryan
Exhorts the Democratic Party Not to "Crucify Mankind Upon a Cross of Gold"

Before the days of movies, radio and television, amusement parks, regular vacations, recorded music, and all the other forms of entertainment so familiar to us, Americans expected their political leaders to be good orators—public speakers. Political speeches were not only a source of information about government, they were also a form of entertainment and mental stimulation.

Particularly people who led very isolated lives liked speeches that went on much longer than would ever be tolerated today. They liked speakers who quoted from the Bible or made reference to familiar religious ideas. They liked to hear quotations from the ancient Greek and Roman philosophers and poets, from great works of literature like the plays of Shakespeare. They liked speakers who were actors, who spoke dramatically and emphasized their points with grand, sweeping gestures and exaggerated "body language."

William Jennings Bryan was probably the greatest orator of his day. Born in Illinois, a resident of Nebraska when he became famous in 1896, Bryan had a booming voice that could be heard for a hundred yards. He used all the tricks of a stage actor in getting his points across—long pauses, walking nervously around the platform, raising and lowering his voice as his speech required. Deeply religious, Bryan would often quote from the Bible with great conviction.

And, like all good entertainers, Bryan worked at his skills. Before he gave his "Cross of Gold" speech at the Democratic convention in 1896, he had rehearsed it dozens of times at county fairs and political meetings in rural America. Although he was almost unknown in Chicago, where the convention was held, Bryan was already a hero to farm people who believed, as he said, that their serious problems were a result of special interests whose supporters dwelled in the city.

The Cross of Gold speech was such a masterpiece that the delegates at the convention exploded in enthusiasm for the young politician. (He was only 36 years of age at the time.) On the following day, he was nominated to run for president over more prominent candidates.

Bryan lost the election of 1896 to the Republican nominee, William McKinley. But his power as a speaker was so strong that for thirty years he remained a hero to Democrats, particularly those who lived in the rural South and Midwest. They made him their presidential nominee three times.

UNLOCKING HISTORY
KEY DOCUMENT

*W*OULD be presumptuous, indeed, to present myself against the distinguished gentlemen to whom you have listened if this were a mere measuring of abilities; but this is not a contest between persons. The humblest citizen in all the land, when clad in the armor of a righteous cause, is stronger than all the hosts of error. I come to speak to you in defense of a cause as holy as the cause of liberty—the cause of humanity.

When this debate is concluded, a motion will be made to lay upon the table the resolution offered in commendation of the administration, and also the resolution offered in condemnation of the administration. We object to bringing this question down to the level of persons. The individual is but an atom; he is born, he acts, he dies; but principles are eternal; and this has been a contest over a principle. . . .

The sympathies of the Democratic party, . . . are on the side of the struggling masses who have ever been the foundation of the Democratic party. There are two ideas of government. There are those who believe that, if you will only legislate to make the well-to-do prosperous, their prosperity will leak through on those below. The Democratic idea, however, has been that if you legislate to make the masses prosperous, their prosperity will find its way up through every class which rests upon them.

You come to us and tell us that the great cities are in favor of the gold standard; we reply that the great cities rest upon our broad and fertile prairies. Burn down your cities and leave our farms, and your cities will spring up again as if by magic; but destroy our farms and the grass will grow in the streets of every city in the country.

My friends, we declare that this nation is able to legislate for its own people on every question . . . It is the issue of 1776 over again.

Our ancestors, when but three millions in number, had the courage to declare their political independence of every other nation; shall we, their descendants, when we have grown to seventy millions, declare that we are less independent that our forefathers? No, my friends, that will never be the verdict of our people. Therefore, we care not upon what lines the battle is fought. If they say bimetallism is good, but that we cannot have it until other nations help us, we reply that, instead of having a gold standard because England has, we will restore bimetallism, and then let England have bimetallism because the United States has it. If they dare to come out in the open field and defend the gold standard as a good thing, we will fight them to the uttermost. Having behind us the producing masses of this nation and the world, supported by the commercial interests, the laboring interests, and the toilers everywhere, we will answer their demand for a gold standard by saying to them: You shall not press down upon the brow of labor this crown of thorns, you shall not crucify mankind upon a cross of gold.

Selection from William Jennings Bryan, Speech at the Democratic Convention, 1896. Published in William Jennings Bryan, *The First Battle*. Published by W. B. Conkey Company, Chicago, copyright © 1896, page 199 ff. Reprinted in *American Primer*, edited by Daniel Boorstin, published by New American Library, copyright © 1968, pages 595, 601–2.

CRITICAL THINKING

1. Explain or restate William Jennings Bryan's argument about the comparative strength of rural America over the big cities. What point was he trying to make to his listeners?
2. How did Bryan imply that adopting the gold standard would affect people?

8. FREDERIC HASKIN PROUDLY RECOUNTS THE CUTTING OF THE PANAMA CANAL

In the early years of the century, Americans regarded the building of the Panama Canal as a stupendous engineering achievement. They were as proud of the feat as later generations would be of putting a human on the moon. The feeling of intense national pride is perfectly captured in journalist Frederic Haskin's essay, "Culebra Cut."

CULEBRA CUT! Here the barrier of the continental divide resisted to the utmost the attacks of the canal army; here disturbed and outraged Nature conspired with gross mountain mass to make the defense stronger and stronger; here was the mountain that must be moved. Here came the French, jauntily confident, to dig a narrow channel that would let their ships go through. The mountain was the victor. And then here came the Americans, confident but not jaunty. They weighed that mass, laid out the lines of a wider ditch, arranged complicated transportation systems to take away the half hundred million cubic yards of earth and rocks that they had measured. Nature came to the aid of the beleaguered mountain. The volcanic rocks were piled helter-skelter and when the ditch deepened the softer strata underneath refused to bear the burden and the slides, slowly and like glaciers, crept out into the ditch, burying shovels and sweeping aside the railway tracks. Even the bottom of the canal bulged up under the added stress of the heavier strata above.

Grim, now, but still confident, the attackers fought on. The mountain was defeated.

Now stretches a man-made canyon across the backbone of the continent; now lies a channel for ships through the barrier; now is found what Columbus sought in vain—the gate through the West to the East. Men call it Culebra Cut.

Nine miles long, it has an average depth of 120 feet. At places its sides tower nearly 500 feet above its channel bottom, which in nowhere narrower than 300 feet.

It is the greatest single trophy of the triumph of man over the terrestrial arrangement of his world. Compared to it, the scooping out of the sand levels of Suez seems but child's play—. . . the sport of boys. It is majestic. It is awful. It is the Canal.

When estimates for digging the canal were made it was calculated that 53,000,000 cubic yards of material would have to be removed from the cut, and that under the most favorable conditions it would require eight and a half years to complete the work. But at that time no one had the remotest idea of the actual difficulties that would beset the canal builders; no one dreamed of the avalanches of material that would slide into the cut. . . .

No less than 26 slides and breaks were encountered in the construction of Culebra Cut, their total area being 225 acres. The largest covered 75, and another 47 acres. When the slides, which were more like earthen glaciers than avalanches, began to flow into the big ditch, sometimes steam shovels were buried, sometimes railroad tracks were caught beneath the débris, and sometimes even the bottom of the cut itself began to bulge and disarrange the entire transportation system, at the same time interfering with the compressed air and water supplies. But with all these trials and tribulations, the army that was trying to conquer the eternal hills that had refused passage to the ships of the world for so many centuries, kept up its courage and renewed its attack. The result is that ships sail through Culebra and that engineers everywhere have new records of efficiency to inspire them. . . .

To remove the 105,000,000 cubic yards of earth from the backbone of the Americas required about 6,000,000 pounds of high-grade dynamite each year to break up the material, so that it might be successfully attacked by the steam shovels. To prepare the holes for placing the explosives required the services of 150 wet drills, 230 tripod rock drills, and a large corps of hand drillers. Altogether they drilled nearly a thousand miles of holes annually. During every working day in the year about 600 holes were fired. They had an average depth of about 19 feet. In addition to this a hundred toe holes were fired each day, and as many more "dobe" blasts placed on top of large boulders to break them up into loadable sizes. So carefully was the dynamite handled that during a period of three years, in which time some 19,000,000 pounds were exploded in Culebra Cut, only eight men were killed. . . .

The major portion of the material excavated

The Panama Canal, completed in 1914, was regarded as a great feat of modern engineering.

from the canal had to be hauled out and dumped where it was of no further use. From the Central Division alone, which includes Culebra Cut, upward of a hundred million cubic yards of material was hauled away and dumped as useless. At Tabernilla one dump contained nearly 17,000,000 cubic yards. A great deal of spoil, however, was used to excellent advantage. Wherever there was swampy ground contiguous to the permanent settlements it was covered over with material from the cut and brought up above the water level. Many hundreds of acres were thus converted from malaria-breeding grounds into high and dry lands.

During the last stages of the work in Culebra Cut it was found that some of the slides were so bad that they were breaking back of the crest of the hills that border the cut. Therefore it was found to be feasible to attack the problem by sluicing the material down the side of the hills into the valley beyond. To this end a big hydraulic plant which had been used on the Pacific end of the canal was brought up and installed beyond the east bank of the cut. A reservoir of water was impounded and tremendous pumps installed. They pumped a stream of water 40 inches in diameter. This was gradually tapered down to a number of 4-inch nozzles, and out of these spouted streams of water with a pressure of 80 pounds to the square inch. These streams ate away the dirt at a rapid rate.

The slides did not hold up the completion of the canal a minute, at least to the point of usability. The day that the lock gates were ready there was water enough in the canal to carry the entire American navy from ocean to ocean. That day the big dredges from the Atlantic and Pacific were brought into the cut, and with them putting the finishing touches on the slides at the bottom, and the hydraulic excavators attacking them at the top, the problem of the slides was solved.

Today Culebra Mountain bows its lofty head to the genius of the American engineer and to the courage of the canal army. Through its vitals there runs a great artificial canyon nearly 9 miles long, 300 feet wide at its bottom, in places as much as a half mile at its top and nearly 500 feet deep at the deepest point. Out of it there were taken 105,000,000 cubic yards of material, and at places it cost as much as $15,000,000 a mile to make the excavations. Through it now extends a great ribbon of water broad enough to permit the largest vessels afloat to pass one another under their own power and deep enough to carry a ship with a draft beyond anything in the minds of naval constructors today. With towering hills lining it on either side, with banks that are precipitous here and far flung there, with great and deep recesses at one place and another telling of the gigantic breaks and slides with which the men who built it had to contend, going through Culebra Cut gives to the human heart a thrill such as the sight of no other work of the human hand can give. Its magnitude, its awe-inspiring aspect as one navigates the channel between the two great hills which stand like sentinels above it, and the memory of the thousands of tons of dynamite, the hundreds of millions of money and the vast investment of brain and brawn required in its digging, all conspire to make the wonder greater. It is the mightiest deed the hand of man has done.

Selection from *Modern Essays of Various Types*, edited by Charles A. Cockayne. Published by Charles E. Merrill Co., New York, copyright © 1927.

CRITICAL THINKING

1. What can you conclude about the failure of the French to dig the canal, as compared with the American success?
2. Cite the biggest problem the builders had to cope with in digging the canal.
3. Explain why the canal was valuable apart from its practical use in shipping.

FREDERIC
REMINGTON

T he paintings and sculptures of Frederic Remington [1861–1909], with their Indians and bronco-busting cowboys, convey the spirit of the American frontier. Born in Canton, New York, Remington began to sketch at 15 after seeing some drawings done by a friend. His favorite subjects were horses and soldiers.

At the age of 20, after briefly studying art at Yale University, he worked in a government office in Albany, where he often sketched his associates. Soon tiring of office work and curious about the West, he moved to Kansas where he herded sheep for a short time. Fascinated with cowboys, cacti, ponies, Indians, cavalrymen, and Mexicans, he sketched with pen and ink and also took photos to record details. He sold his sketches to *Harper's Weekly, Harper's Monthly, Century,* and *Scribner's Magazine.* By 1886, Remington was earning $75.00–$125.00 per page for his illustrations.

Concerned with the possible disappearance of the Indian, the trapper, and the cowboy, he began to paint these subjects with simple color in bright light. His action-filled illustrations and paintings had enormous appeal for those eager to know about the frontier, which already was changing and beginning to vanish.

Remington carefully researched all the details for "A Dash for the Timber," a painting that recreates a battle between cowboys and native Americans on the frontier. He collected hats, boots, and chaps in order to correctly present the vigorous assault.

CRITICAL THINKING

1. Compare the paintings in the spread. What is the mood in these paintings? How did Remington use color to set mood? What feelings did he hope the viewer would have?
2. Remington was aware of the disappearance of the frontier. What was Remington trying to preserve in his paintings that could not as easily be expressed in writing?

Remington's last painting, shadowy figures around a campfire, was left unfinished when he was stricken with appendicitis and died.

The painting below, "Under Which King," was made during Remington's brief visit to Cuba in 1896, during the Spanish-American war.

The Progressive Era

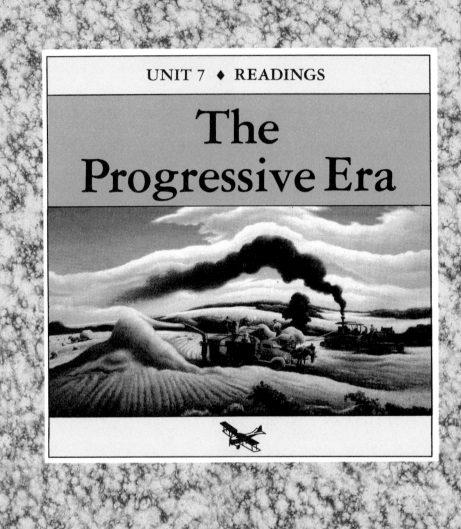

CHAPTER 23

THE GOOD OLD DAYS

1890–1910

1. FRENCH NEWSPAPER CORRESPONDENT CHARLES BOURGET REPORTS HIS OBSERVATIONS OF AN AMERICAN COLLEGE FOOTBALL GAME IN THE AUTUMN OF 1894

A French writer, Charles Joseph Paul Bourget, visited the United States in 1894. During that time, he wrote articles for the New York Herald *about his impressions of the country. These articles, which were published in France as a book, sparked a great deal of controversy. In the following passage, Bourget commented on the American love of football.*

No sport has become more fashionable for the past few years than football. Last autumn, in the peaceful city of Cambridge, [Massachusetts] I was present at a game between the Harvard team and that of the University of Pennsylvania. . . . The electric cars, following one another at intervals of a minute, were filled with passengers, seated, standing, or hanging on the steps crowding, pushing, crushing one another. Although November is cruelly cold under a Massachusetts sky, the contest was held as were Roman gladiatorial combats, in a sort of open-air enclosure. A stone's throw away from Memorial Hall wooden stands were erected, on which were perhaps fifteen-thousand spectators. In the immense quadrilateral hemmed in by the stands the two teams of eleven youths each waited for the signal to begin.

What a tremor in that crowd, composed not of the lower classes but of well-to-do people, and how the excitement increased as time went on. Although a feverish thrill ran through this crowd, it was of itself not enough for the enthusiasts of the game. Propagators of enthusiasm, students with unbearded, deeply lined faces, passed between the benches and still further increased the

ardor of the public by uttering the war-cry of the University, the "rah! rah! rah!" thrice repeated, which terminates in the frenzied call, "Haaarvard." The partisans of "Pennsy" replied with a similar cry. . . .

The signal is given and the play begins. It is a fearful game . . . a game of young bulldogs trained to bite, to rush upon the quarry, the game of a race made for wild attack, for violent defense, for implacable conquests, and desperate struggles. With their leather vests and sleeves of cloth, so soon to be torn, with leather gaiters to protect their shins, with their great shoes, and with long hair floating around their pale and flushed faces, these schoolboy athletes are admirable and frightful to the sight when once the demon of the contest enters into them. The entire object of the game is to throw an enormous leather ball, which each side holds in turn. All the excitement of this ferocious amusement is concentrated in waiting for this throw. He who holds the ball is there, bent forward. His companions and his adversaries likewise bend down around him in the attitude of beasts of prey about to spring. All of a sudden he runs to throw the ball or else with a wildly rapid movement hands it to another, who rushes off with it. All depends on stopping him.

The roughness with which the opposing players seize the bearer of the ball is impossible to imagine. He is grasped by the middle of the body, by the head, by the legs, by the feet. He rolls over and his assailants roll with him. As they fight for the ball, the two sides come to the rescue, and fall into a heap of twenty-two bodies tumbling on top of one another, like an inextricable knot of serpents with human heads. This heap writhes on the ground and tugs at itself. One sees faces, hair, backs, or legs appearing in a monstrous and agitated melee. Then this murderous knot unravels itself and the ball, thrown by the most agile, bounds away and is again followed with the same fury.

Often, after one of those frenzied entanglements, one of the combatants remains on the field motionless, incapable of rising, so hard has he been hit, pressed, crushed, thumped. . . .

If the roughness of this terrible sport was for the spectators only the occasion of a few hours of nervous excitement, the young athletes would not indulge in it with the enthusiasm that makes them accept the most painful, sometimes the most dangerous, training. "The feats of the champions keep the game fashionable," explained one of the Harvard professors; "hence all the small boys in the remotest parts of America take up this exercise, and thus athletes are formed." He was putting into abstract form the instinct of the American crowd. . . .

No sooner are such matches announced than the portraits of the various players are in all the papers. The incidents of the game are described in detail, with graphic pictures, so that the movements of the ball may better be followed. Conquerors and conquered are alike interviewed.

Selection from Oscar Handlin, *This Was America*. Published by Harper Torchbooks, New York, copyright © 1964.

CRITICAL THINKING

1. Judging from this article, why might Charles Bourget's essays on America have been so controversial?
2. Bourget frequently described football in terms of combat and warfare. Why might he have done this?
3. What did Bourget think the love of football implied about Americans' character and personality?

2. A GLIMPSE OF THE RICH AT PLAY, IN SARATOGA

One result of the affluence of the late nineteenth century was the rise of resorts, where people of wealth and position could play—and be seen playing. One of the most important of these aristocratic resorts was Saratoga, New York, which became famous both for the "cure" offered by its mineral springs and for the society that gathered there.

If Newport [Rhode Island] occupies first place for ocean bathing in the United States, Saratoga must take the palm for its mineral waters. Two powerful attractions draw the Americans, particularly those in high life, to the latter town. On the one hand there is the therapeutic value of its springs, which were secretly used even by the Indians, who venerated them as gifts of the Great Spirit; on the other there is the splendor and richness of its hotels and the irresistible fascination of the enchantress we call fashion. . . .

Every night the United States Hotel . . . presents an impressive spectacle. The spacious interior garden, adorned with trees and fountains and lighted by electricity, is crammed with the flower of aristocratic society—three-fourths, women elegantly dressed—who listen to the music played in the center. Part of the crowd stroll in the aisles among the blossoms; part is seated on chairs around the numerous tables scattered here and there, and engages in lively and jolly conversation. In the piazzas is the same luxury, the same happiness, the same movement. From the open doors of the parlors, and from the other regally furnished rooms, pour streams of light. There is dancing in the ballroom. There I tried the "Boston," which seemed to be a kind of waltz embellished with a graceful circular motion. Apparently, however, the American aristocracy do not consider it altogether dignified to indulge in this diversion; I was told that even at the evening garden parties, in which they dance on a platform built over the garden, only a very few men participate.

Walking through the halls, the garden, the piazzas, I had the opportunity to study high society. . . . And I could particularly note the difference in character between the two sexes, a difference so great that one might suppose them members of two different races.

The men have a rigid temperament; they speak little; and all, whatever their title—senator, governor, colonel—dress always in morning clothes [formal dress], except for a white cravat [necktie] which they wear everywhere. In the salon the American male is a fish out of water; not one of them will deny that his true place is the office, the countinghouse, or the political meeting.

The women, on the other hand, are full of spirit, chatter freely and coquettishly, yet do not go too far. They seem in their natural element. The alpha and omega [beginning and end] of their daily routine is to rise, to eat, to talk, to change their costumes three or four times, and to sleep. When they come back in the morning from the mineral waters they have a substantial breakfast at about ten; then sit on the rocking chairs on the piazzas until it begins to be warm; then go to their rooms to change for lunch, which is at two. At the end of that meal they again retire to their chambers, and steal a nap on the sofa. At about six they reappear in traveling clothes, and ride in a carriage to Lake Saratoga, some seven kilometers away by a beautiful road lined with trees. There they may have an ice before they come back in time for supper. At nine they dress for the evening, almost always in gowns. . . . After an hour they descend to the piazza by the steps, a journey which reveals to best advantage their elegant shoes, on which there are often buttons or buckles made of diamonds.

It is then that the life of the hotels really begins. The elegant people who live in the United States Hotel go to the gardens, the parlors, and the piazzas of the Grand Union and the Congress hotels, while in return those who live in the latter two come to the United States Hotel. Thus the women give each other an opportunity to observe and criticize the clothes and jewels of their rivals and to make full show of their own.

Selection from Oscar Handlin, *This Was America*. Published by Harper Torchbooks, New York, copyright © 1964.

CRITICAL THINKING

1. What was the writer's attitude toward the men and women of American society he encountered?
2. How did the writer emphasize the difference in manner and attitude between American men and women?

3. MUCKRAKER LINCOLN STEFFENS QUESTIONS THE PRACTICE OF RUNNING THE GOVERNMENT LIKE A BUSINESS

One of the most famous of the "muckrakers" who exposed corruption in American business and politics was Lincoln Steffens. The Shame of the Cities, published at the beginning of this century, described the corrupt practices that existed in many American cities. In his introduction, Steffens argued that "business" methods had actually increased political corruption in American life and he proposed a "businesslike" solution to the political reform.

Politics is business. That's what's the matter with it. . . . Make politics a sport, as they do in England, or a profession, as they do in Germany, and we'll have—well, something else than we have now. . . . But don't try to reform politics with the banker, the lawyer, and the dry-goods merchant, for these are business men and there are two great hindrances to their achievement of reform: one is that they are different from, but no better than, the politicians; the other is that politics is not "their line." . . . The politician is a business man with a specialty. When a business man of some other line learns the business of politics, he is a politician, and there is not much reform left in him. Consider the United States Senate, and believe me.

The commercial spirit is the spirit of profit, not patriotism; of credit, not honor; of individual gain, not national prosperity; of trade and dickering, not principle. "My business is sacred," says the business man in his heart. "Whatever prospers my business, is good; it must be. Whatever hinders it, is wrong; it must be. A bribe is bad, that is, it is a bad thing to take; but it is not so bad to give one, not if it is necessary to my business." "Business is business" is not a political sentiment, but our politician has caught it. He takes essentially the same view of the bribe, only he saves his self-respect by piling all his contempt upon the bribe-giver. . . .

But there is hope, not alone despair, in the commercialism of our politics. If our political leaders are to be always a lot of political merchants, they will supply any demand we may create. All we have to do is to establish a steady demand for good government. The bosses have us split up into parties. To him parties are nothing but means to his corrupt ends. He "bolts" his party, but we must not; the bribe-giver changes his party, from one election to another, from one country to another, from one city to another, but the honest voter must not. Why? Because if the honest voter cared no more for his party than the politician and the grafter, then the honest vote would govern, and that would be bad—for graft. It is idiotic, this devotion to a machine that is used to take our sovereignty from us. If we would leave parties to the politicians, and would not vote for the party, not even for men, but for the city, and the State, and the nation, we should rule parties, and cities, and States, and nation. If we would vote in mass on the more promising ticket, or, if the two were equally bad, would throw out the party that is in, and wait till the next election and then throw out the other party that is in—then, I say, the commercial politician would feel a demand for good government and he would supply it. That process would take a generation or more to complete, for the politicians now really do not know what good government is. But it has taken as long to develop bad government, and the politicians know what that is. If it would not "go," they would offer something else, and, if the demand were steady, they, being so commercial, would "deliver the goods."

But do the people want good government? Tammany [the New York City political machine] says they don't. Are the people honest? Are the people better than Tammany? Are they better than the merchant and the politician? Isn't our corrupt government, after all, representative?

President Roosevelt has been sneered at for going about the country preaching, as a cure for our American evils, good conduct in the individual, simple honesty, courage, and efficiency. "Platitudes!"the sophisticated say. Platitudes? If my observations have been true, the literal adoption of Mr. Roosevelt's reform scheme would result in a revolution, more radical and terrible to existing institutions, from the Congress to the Church, from the bank to the ward organization, than socialism or even than anarchy. Why, that would change all of us—not alone our neighbors, not alone the grafters, but you and me.

Selection from Lincoln Steffens, *The Shame of the Cities.* Published by Sagamore Press, New York, copyright © 1957.

CRITICAL THINKING

1. What reasons did Lincoln Steffens offer to support his view that business people do not help reform government in America?
2. In *The Shame of the Cities* what was Steffens' suggestion for how Americans could use business practices to bring about good government?

4. WISCONSIN GOVERNOR ROBERT LA FOLLETTE ARGUES IN FAVOR OF PRIMARY ELECTIONS

In most states, candidates for office were chosen by party conventions, a practice that meant political bosses could select slates of candidates who would, if elected, work for special rather than public interests. The Progressive leader, Robert M. La Follette, believed that primary elections should be the preferred method of nominating candidates for public office. Choosing a candidate was, he said, as much a citizen's sacred right as casting a ballot.

WE BELIEVE with the President [Theodore Roosevelt], as recognized by him in daily speech, that these great monopolies constitute the foremost of national questions. We uphold his hands in his effort to curb these trusts by the enforcement of laws now upon the statute books. There is probably not an important trust in the United States which does not have the assistance of railroads in destroying its competitors in business. The limitation and control of these public-service corporations in the legitimate field, as common carriers, are an important element in the practical solution of the problem with which we have to deal.

In accepting renomination for the office of governor [of Wisconsin] at the hands of the Republican party, I said:

"The greatest danger menacing public institutions today is the overbalancing control of city, state, and national legislatures by the wealth and power of public-service corporations."

I made this statement advisedly then. I repeat it now. Not is a spirit of hostility to any interest, but deeply impressed with its profound significance to republican institutions and its ultimate influence upon all citizens and all citizenship.

The idea is not new. It is not peculiar to Wisconsin.

The responsibility it brings cannot be shirked or pushed aside or postponed. The national government, every state government—particularly that of every rich and prosperous state—every city government—particularly that of every large city—has this problem to solve; not at some other time, but now.

The question of primary elections is one of government for the people and by the people.

Under our system of government by political parties, two elements, equal in importance, are involved in the exercise of suffrage; one, the making of the ballot; the other, the casting of the ballot. The right to cast the ballot is regarded as sacred. The right to make the ballot is equally sacred. No man would be willing to delegate his power to vote the ballot at general elections. No man shall be compelled to delegate his power to make his ballot. Boss Tweed said: "You may elect whichever candidates you please to office, if you will allow me to select the candidates." The boss can always afford to say, "You may vote any ticket you please so long as I make all the tickets." The character of the men nominated and the influences to which they owe their nomination determine the character of government.

The result and the only result sought by a primary election is to give every man an equal voice in the selection of all candidates; to lodge in the people the absolute right to say who their candidates for office shall be; to root out forever the power of the political boss to control the selection of officials through the manipulation of caucuses and conventions. A primary election should provide the same safeguards for nominating candidates as for electing them. It should fix the day, name the hour, use the same polling places, have the same election officers, provide the Australian ballot, containing the names of all the candidates to be voted upon at the election. It should be an election, possessing all the legal sanctions of an election.

It is needless to trace the evolution of the political machine, its combination with aggregate wealth and corporate power, making the interests of the citizen and the state subservient to their selfish ends. The names of the great bosses today are better known than the great statesmen. The tendency to monopolization of political control by a few men in each party, county, city, state, and community has operated, except in cases of profound interest, excitement, and tremendous effort, to disfranchise the great majority of citizens in so far as participating in the caucus and convention is concerned.

The day that Chief Justice Ryan prophesied would come is here. The issue he said would arise is pending.

"Which shall rule—wealth or man; which shall lead—money or intellect; who shall fill public stations—educated and patriotic freemen, or the feudal servants of corporate power?"

If the chosen representative does not represent the citizen, his voice is stifled; is denied any part in government. If majority decision as determined by the law of the land is ignored and reversed, if the expressed will of the people is scorned and scorned again—then the popular government fails, then government of the people, by the people, and for the people is at an end. Its forms may be observed—you may have the mockery of "elections," and the force of "representation," but a government based upon the will of the people has perished from the earth.

Selection from Charles Hurd, *A Treasury of Great American Speeches*. Published by Hawthorn Books, New York, copyright © 1959.

CRITICAL THINKING

1. Contrast Boss Tweed and La Follette's views on primary elections.
2. What can you infer from this reading about La Follette's political philosophy?

5. FREDERIC HOWE SHOWS DEMOCRACY WORKS IN WISCONSIN

Wisconsin was one state where the efforts of reformers and "good government movements" seemed to lead to success. Frederic C. Howe studied what happened in that state during the Progressive era and reported on how the state government worked—and how the reforms had been accomplished. In the conclusion to Wisconsin: An Experiment in Democracy, *Howe summarized what he saw as the lesson of reform in that state.*

What is the explanation of Wisconsin? Why has it been able to eliminate corruption, machine politics, and rid itself of the boss? . . . Why has Wisconsin succeeded where other states have uniformly failed?

I think the explanation is simple. It is also perfectly natural. It is traceable to democracy, to the political freedom which had its beginning in the direct primary law, and which has been continuously strengthened by later laws. Without it the subsequent achievements of the state would have been impossible. . . .

We have been taught to believe that the trouble with our politics is traceable to our people, to political indolence, to our absorption in money getting, to extreme partisanship. These are the causes usually assigned for our failures. We have assumed that our evils are personal, ethical, in some way traceable to the political incapacity of our people. . . .

I believe we are the wisest people, politically, in the world; I believe we know more about the wrongs of politics than do the voters of any country. And I think we are individually as intolerant of abuses.

The explanation of our cities and states is not personal or ethical at all. It is institutional and economic. We have made representative government almost impossible by the complicated machinery of nominations and elections, by the distribution of powers and responsibility among so many officials, by the rigidity of our written constitutions. In addition, we have lured business into politics by privileges of colossal value. We have minimized the sovereignty of the community and exalted the sovereignty of private property.

. . . In no country is the machinery of government so complex in its provisions or so intricate in its workings. State and federal constitutions add to the difficulty. They increase the apathy of the people. They have been a citadel of strength to privileged interests. . . .

Wisconsin assumed that the trouble with our politics is not with our people, but with the machinery with which the people work. And Wisconsin has taken the kinks, the angles, the circumlocution out of government. . . .

The achievements of Wisconsin came through freedom, through freedom in thought as well as in action. There was an end of fear. Men dared to stand for ideas. Freedom of speech and of research were preserved in the university. The by-products of political freedom were greater than the direct political gains which followed. . . .

It is impossible to measure the psychological

Political scientist Frederic C. Howe investigated Wisconsin's experiments in reform government during the Progressive period.

effect of freedom on the mind of a state. It is obvious, however, that Wisconsin could not have entered on its policy of corporation control under the old system. It is equally obvious that the far-reaching industrial programme of workmen's compensation and state insurance, would have been well-nigh impossible. A widening of political power carried with it a widening of the idea of political service: Equal opportunity for all, rather than special privileges for the few, became the motive of legislation. . . .

Democracy, too, began to use its powers to serve, to serve people as well as business, to serve humanity as well as property. Democracy has begun a war on poverty, on ignorance, on disease, on human waste. The state is using its collective will to promote a programme of human welfare.

Wisconsin is dispelling the fears of those who distrusted democracy. It is demonstrating the possibility of using the state as an instrument for the well-being of all people. It is laying the foundations for a commonwealth whose ideal it is to serve.

Selection from Frederic C. Howe, *Wisconsin: An Experiment in Democracy*. Published by Charles Scribner's Sons, New York, copyright © 1912.

CRITICAL THINKING

1. What evidence did Frederic Howe provide that the problem with American government lay with political institutions, not with people?
2. What reasons did Howe give for believing that more freedom, rather than less, was necessary to reform American government?

6. MUCKRAKER UPTON SINCLAIR'S *THE JUNGLE* EXPOSES THE MEAT-PACKING INDUSTRY

Foremost among the muckrakers was writer Upton Sinclair, whose book The Jungle *described sickening conditions in Chicago's slaughterhouses and meat-processing plants. The 1906 book provoked government investigation and was largely responsible for passage of the Pure Food and Drug Act.*

"Bubbly Creek" is an arm of the Chicago River, and forms the southern boundary of the yards; all the drainage of the square mile of packing houses empties into it, so that it is really a great open sewer a hundred or two feet wide. One long arm of it is blind, and the filth stays there forever and a day. The grease and chemicals that are poured into it undergo all sorts of strange transformations, which are the cause of its name; it is constantly in motion, as if huge fish were feeding in it, or great leviathans disporting themselves in its depths. Bubbles of carbonic acid gas will rise to the surface and burst, and make rings two or three feet wide. Here and there the grease and filth have caked solid, and the creek looks like a bed of lava; chickens walk about on it, feeding, and many times an unwary stranger has started to stroll across, and vanished temporarily. The packers used to leave the creek that way, till every now and then the surface would catch on fire and burn furiously, and the fire department would have to come and put it out. Once, however, an ingenious stranger came and started to gather this filth in scows, to make lard out of; then the packers took the cue, and got out an injunction to stop him, and afterward gathered it themselves. The banks of "Bubbly Creek" are plastered thick with hairs, and this also the packers gather and clean.

And there were things ever stranger than this, according to the gossip of the men. The packers had secret mains, through which they stole billions of gallons of the city's water. The newspapers had been full of this scandal—once there had even been an investigation, and an actual uncovering of the pipes; but nobody had been punished, and the thing went right on. And then there was the condemned meat industry, with its endless horrors. The people of Chicago saw the government inspectors in Packingtown, and they all took that to mean that that they were protected from diseased meat; they did not understand that these hundred and sixty-three inspectors had been appointed at the request of the packers, and that they were paid by the United States government to certify that all the diseased meat was kept in the state. They had no authority beyond that; for the inspection of meat to be sold in the city and state the whole force in Packingtown consisted of three henchmen of the local political machine! And shortly afterward one of these, a physician, made the discovery that the carcasses of steers which had been condemned as tubercular by the government inspectors, and which therefore contained ptomaines, which are deadly poisons, were left upon an open platform and carted away to be sold in the city; and so he insisted that these carcasses be treated with an injection of kerosene—and was ordered to resign the same week! So indignant were the packers that they went farther, and compelled the mayor to abolish the whole bureau of inspection; so that since then there has not been even a pretense of any interference with the graft. There was said to be two thousand dollars a week hush money from the tubercular steers alone; and as much again from the hogs which had died of cholera on the trains, and which you might see any day being loaded into boxcars and hauled away to a place called Globe, in Indiana, where they make a fancy grade of lard.

Jurgis heard of these things little by little, in the gossip of those who were obliged to perpetrate them. It seemed as if every time you met a person from a new department, you heard of new swindles and new crimes. There was, for instance, a Lithuanian who was a cattle butcher for the plant where Marija had worked, which killed meat for canning only; and to hear this man describe the animals which came to this place would have been worth while for a Dante or a Zola. It seemed that they must have agencies all over the country, to hunt out old and crippled and diseased cattle to be canned. There were cattle which had been fed on "whiskey-malt," the refuse of the breweries, and had become what the men called "steerly"—which means covered with boils. It was a nasty job killing these, for when you plunged your knife into them they would burst and splash foul-smelling stuff into your face; and when a man's sleeves were smeared with blood, and his hands steeped in it, how was he ever to wipe his face, or to clear his eyes so that he could see? It was stuff such as this that made the "embalmed beef" that had killed several times as many United States soldiers as all the bullets of the Spaniards; only the army beef, besides, was not fresh canned, it was old stuff that had been lying for years in the cellars.

Then one Sunday evening, Jurgis sat puffing his pipe by the kitchen stove, and talking with an old fellow whom Jonas had introduced, and who worked in the canning rooms at Durham's; and so Jurgis learned a few things about the great and only Durham canned goods, which had become a national institution. They were regular alchemists at Durham's; they advertised a mushroom-catsup, and the men who made it did not know what a mushroom looked like. They advertised "potted chicken,"—and it was like the boardinghouse soup of the comic papers, through which a chicken had walked with rubbers on. Perhaps they had a secret process for making chickens chemically—who knows? said Jurgis' friend; the things that went into the mixture were tripe, and the fat of pork, and beef suet, and hearts of beef, and finally the waste ends of veal, when they had any. They put these up in several grades, and sold them at several prices; but the contents of the cans all came out of the same hopper. And then there was "potted game" and "potted grouse," "potted ham," and "deviled ham"—de-vyled, as the men called it. "De-vyled" ham was made out of the waste ends of smoked beef that were too small to be sliced by the machines; and also tripe, dyed with chemicals so that it would not show white; and trimmings of hams and corned beef; and potatoes, skins and all; and finally the hard cartilaginous gullets of beef, after the tongues had been cut out. All this

ingenious mixture was ground up and flavored with spices to make it taste like something. Anybody who could invent a new imitation had been sure of a fortune from old Durham, said Jurgis' informant; but it was hard to think of anything new in a place where so many sharp wits had been at work for so long; where men welcomed tuberculosis in the cattle they were feeding, because it made them fatten more quickly; and where they bought up all the old rancid butter left over in the grocery stores of a continent, and "oxidized" it by a forced-air process, to take away the odor, rechurned it with skim milk, and sold it in bricks in the cities! Up to a year or two ago it had been the custom to kill horses in the yards—ostensibly for fertilizer; but after long agitation the newspapers had been able to make the public realize that the horses were being canned. Now it is against the law to kill horses in Packingtown, and the law was really complied with—for the present, at any rate. Any day, however, one might see sharp-horned and shaggy-haired creatures running with the sheep—and yet what a job you would have to get the public to believe that a good part of what it buys for lamb and mutton is really goat's flesh!

There was another interesting set of statistics that a person might have gathered in Packingtown —those of the various afflictions of the workers. When Jurgis had first inspected the packing plants with Szedvilas, he had marveled while he listened to the tale of all the things that were made out of the carcasses of animals, and of all the lesser industries that were maintained there; now he found that each one of these lesser industries was a separate little inferno, in its way as horrible as the killing beds, the source and fountain of them all. The workers in each of them had their own peculiar diseases. And the wandering visitor might be skeptical about all the swindles, but he could not be skeptical about these, for the worker bore the evidence of them about on his own person— generally he had only to hold out his hand.

There were the men in the pickle rooms, for instance, where old Antanas had gotten his death; scarce a one of these that had not some spot of horror on his person. Let a man so much as scrape his finger pushing a truck in the pickle rooms, and he might have a sore that would put him out of the world; all the joints in his fingers might be eaten by the acid, one by one. Of the butchers and floorsmen, the beef-boners and trimmers, and all those who used knives, you could scarcely find a person who had the use of his thumb; time and time again the base of it had been slashed, till it was a mere lump of flesh against which the man pressed the knife to hold it. The hands of these men would be criss-crossed with cuts, until you could no longer pretend to count them or trace them. They would have no nails,—they had worn them off pulling hides; their knuckles were swollen so that their fingers spread out like a fan. There were men who worked in the cooking rooms, in the midst of steam and sickening odors, by artificial light; in these rooms the germs of tuberculosis might live for two years, but the supply was renewed every hour. There were the beef-luggers, who carried two-hundred-pound quarters into the refridgerator-cars; a fearful kind of work, that began at four o'clock in the morning, and that wore out the most powerful men in a few years. There were those who worked in the chilling rooms, and whose special disease was rheumatism; the time limit that a man could work in the chilling rooms was said to be five years. There were the wool-pluckers, whose hands went to pieces even sooner than the hands of the pickle men; for the pelts of the sheep had to be painted with acid to loosen the wool, and then the pluckers had to pull out this wool with their bare hands, till the acid had eaten their fingers off. There were those who made the tins for the canned meat; and their hands, too, were a maze of cuts, and each cut represented a chance for blood poisoning. Some worked at the stamping machines, and it was very seldom that one could work long there at the pace that was set, and not give out and forget himself, and have a part of his hand chopped off. There were the "hoisters," as they were called, whose task it was to press the lever which lifted the dead cattle off the floor. They ran along upon a rafter, peering down through the damp and steam; and as old Durham's architects had not built the killing room for the convenience of the hoisters, at every few feet they would have to stoop under a beam, say four feet above the one they ran on; which got them into the habit of stooping, so that in a few years they would be walking like chimpanzees. Worst of any, however, were the fertilizer men, and those who served in the cooking rooms. These people could not be shown to the visitor,—

Upton Sinclair, best known as a fiction writer, later ran for political office.

for the odor of a fertilizer man would scare an ordinary visitor at a hundred yards, and as for the other men, who worked in tank rooms full of steam, and in some of which there were open vats near the level of the floor, their peculiar trouble was that they fell into the vats; and when they were fished out, there was never enough of them left to be worth exhibiting,—sometimes they would be overlooked for days, till all but the bones of them had gone out to the world as Durham's Pure Leaf Lard!

Selection from Upton Sinclair, *The Jungle.* Published by Robert Bentley, Inc., Cambridge, Mass., copyright © 1905, 1906.

CRITICAL THINKING

1. What is Upton Sinclair's point of view on the meat packing industry? Give reasons for your answer.
2. Do you think Sinclair's piece is an example of straightforward reporting? How can you tell?
3. Cite evidence for the statement: "They were regular alchemists at Durham's."

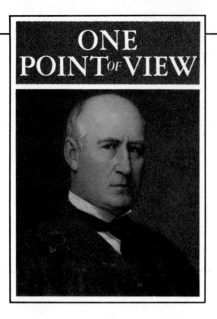

CHARLES DANA GIBSON

Charles Dana Gibson [1867–1944] was the most successful illustrator of his day. His career began at 19, when he sold his first sketch to *Life*, and he continued to draw until his death. But the height of his popularity was from 1890 to about 1910.

Appearing mostly in popular magazines, Gibson's sharply drawn, gently satirical, pen and ink drawings recorded and commented upon the activities and foibles of the upper and middle class American family. The member of that family that established Gibson's fame was the "Gibson Girl." Among his other characters, however, was the "Gibson Man"—tall, handsome, clean-shaven, and, more often than not, gazing adoringly at the Gibson Girl.

At first, the Gibson Girl was simply a single idealized reflection of reality—Gibson's conception of the beautiful American woman. But soon life began to imitate art. A generation of young women modeled their looks and manners on the Gibson Girl, who became a symbol of fashion and style for the decade of the 1890s.

The Gibson Girl was not merely beautiful. She also was a healthy young woman who enjoyed playing golf, riding a bicycle, and swimming.

Gibson was also known for his gently satiric portrayals of social rituals practiced by the comfortable middle class, who could afford to employ butlers. The Gibson Girl profile (left) became so popular that it was eventually immortalized on china, pillow covers, wallpaper, matchboxes, and souvenir spoons.

CRITICAL THINKING

1. How might Gibson's drawings be considered a statement of the changing times and economy?
2. The term "Gibson-girl hairdo" and "Gibson-girl look" have survived in today's fashion terminology. From these pictures describe the hairstyle and the look that Gibson preserved.

CHAPTER 24

THE PROGRESSIVES IN POWER

1901–1916

1. PROGRESSIVE WRITER AMOS PINCHOT RELATES A PERSONAL STORY ABOUT THE FAMOUS "TR" STYLE

Perhaps no one symbolized the activity and energy of the Progressivge era more than Theodore Roosevelt. From his days in the West to his government service in New York and Washington, D.C., he struck a style that appealed to millions of Americans. Amos Pinchot, who gained prominence as a Progressive writer, wrote the following memoir of a meeting with "TR"—as Teddy Roosevelt was affectionately called.

I was never a friend of Roosevelt's. My association with him came about through his close friendship with my brother [Gifford Pinchot, the conservationist and Chief U.S. Forester]. My role was that of an admiring but relatively remote satellite, to whom he would occasionally entrust small commissions. . . . I talked with him frequently in those Progressive days, on political and economic matters. I do not flatter myself that he ever took my advice on any subject whatever, or was even in the slightest degree influenced by anything I ever said. But I certainly was always flattered by his notice of me. And a rare invitation to the White House or Sagamore Hill, a walk with his tennis cabinet through Rock Creek Park, or to the war college, was to me a great event.

Roosevelt was a kindly man. Lustily as he hated, his anger never lasted for long; and never did he harbor malice. He was always bubbling with the most infectious enthusiasms. The steam was always up, and the engine loudly chuffing. One's hopes were kindled by his certainty that he was doing big things. Even in his days of fading fame, ocean breezes seemed to sweep the stuffy *Outlook*

office [a progressive political magazine] when the Colonel came in. And the "jolly" he royally dispensed to intimate friend and mere acquaintance indifferently, though overlavish and, eventually, largely mechanical, was enough to put heart in the most timorous of his followers.

I remember especially, as an example of the Colonel's methods in his later phase, a visit to his office in the early autumn of 1912. After a rather long talk on the subject of the switch some of us had made to him, after La Follette's breakdown at the Publishers Dinner at Philadelphia [during the campaign of 1912], I descended in the elevator, only to discover that it was pouring with rain, and that I had left my umbrella in the Colonel's room. Taking an upgoing car, and landing, I think, on the seventh floor, I proceeded along the hall, when the Colonel, doubling the corner at breakneck speed, spied me and seized me by the hand. The conversation we had just had, momentous as it had seemed to me, had evidently entirely faded from his memory under stress of more important matters, as had also the trifling fact that he had said good-by to me but three minutes before. He greeted me as a newcomer, wrung my hand, beat me on the shoulder with his clenched fist, and asked with great effusiveness what he could do for me. "Why nothing, thanks," I replied, a little dismayed. "I was just going back to your office to get my umbrella. It's raining."

"Bully!" cried the Colonel, "Bully! Splendid! Bully! Come in and see me again any time." And at every word he showed his powerful teeth, snapped his muscular jaws, and continued to thump me, until, wheeling suddenly, he hurtled off with a triumphant upward wave of the hand.

Selection from Amos R. E. Pinchot, *History of the Progressive Party, 1912–1916.* Published by New York University Press, New York, copyright © 1958.

CRITICAL THINKING

1. What effect did this meeting with Theodore Roosevelt have on Amos Pinchot?
2. What elements of what Pinchot saw as Roosevelt's "style" can be seen in this anecdote?

2. PRESIDENT THEODORE ROOSEVELT NAMES THE VIRTUES NEEDED BY A PRACTICAL POLITICIAN

Action was not simply a matter of style with President Theodore Roosevelt; it was a part of his deepest political and social principles. In a famous essay entitled "The Manly Virtues and Practical Politics," Roosevelt outlined the qualities he believed were needed in those entering public service.

The first requisite in the citizen who wishes to share the work of our public life, whether he wishes himself to hold office or merely to do his plain duty as an American by taking part in the management of our political machinery, is that he shall act disinterestedly and with a sincere purpose to serve the commonwealth.

But disinterestedness and honesty and unselfish desire to do what is right are not enough in themselves. A man must not only be disinterested, but he must be efficient. If he goes into politics he must go into practical politics, in order to make his influence felt. Practical politics must not be construed to mean dirty politics. On the contrary, in the long run the politics of fraud and treachery and foulness are unpractical politics, and the most practical of all politicians is the politician who is clean and decent and upright. But a man who goes into the actual battles of the political world must prepare himself much as he would for the struggle in any other branch of our life. He must be prepared to meet men of far lower ideals than his own, and to face things, not as he would wish them, but as they are. He must not lose his own high ideal, and yet he must face the fact that the majority of the men with whom he must work have lower ideals. He must stand firmly for what he believes, and yet he must realize that political action, to be effective, must be the joint action of many men, and that he must sacrifice somewhat of his own opinions to those of his associates if he ever hopes to see his desires take practical shape.

The prime thing that every man who takes an interest in politics should remember is that he must act, and not merely criticise the actions of others. It is not the man who sits by his fireside reading his evening paper, and saying how bad our politics and politicians are, who will ever do anything to save us; it is the man who goes out into the rough hurly-burly of the caucus, the primary, and the political meeting, and there faces his fellows on equal terms. The real service is rendered, not by the critic who stands aloof from the contest, but by the man who enters into it and bears his part as a man should, undeterred by the blood and the sweat. It is a pleasant but a dangerous thing to associate merely with cultivated, refined men of high ideals and sincere purpose to do right, and to think that one has done all one's duty by discussing politics with such associates. It is a good thing to meet men of this stamp; . . . but if we associate with such men exclusively we can accomplish nothing. The actual battle must be fought out on other and less pleasant fields. The actual advance must be made in the field of practical politics among the men who represent or guide or control the mass of the voters, the men who are sometimes rough and coarse, who sometimes have lower ideals than they should, but who are capable, masterful, and efficient. It is only by mingling on equal terms with such men, by showing them that one is able to give and to receive heavy punishment without flinching, and that one can master the details of political management as well as they can, that it is possible for a man to establish a standing that will be useful to him in fighting for a great reform. Every man who wishes well to his country is in honor bound to take an active part in political life. . . He will have the satisfaction of knowing that the salvation of the country ultimately lies . . . in the hands of those who, however imperfectly, actually do the work of the nation.

Selection from Theodore Roosevelt, *American Ideals.* Published by G.P. Putnam's Sons, New York, copyright © 1920.

CRITICAL THINKING

1. What arguments did President Roosevelt give in support of his idea that it is more important to enter into practical politics than it is to offer idealistic criticism?
2. In what ways are Roosevelt's belief in action and enthusiasm a part of his views in this passage?

A R T I F A C T AS

"TR" MEMORABILIA
A Popular President Is Remembered

Souvenirs of Teddy Roosevelt's 1912 campaign (pictured at left) include two Bull Moose pins. Although he declared that he felt "as fit as a bull moose," he lost the election to Woodrow Wilson. An earlier campaign item (above) is a colorful serving tray showing Roosevelt as a Rough Rider. It, too, has now become a valuable collector's item.

Few American political figures have generated more memorabilia than did Theodore Roosevelt. Perhaps as a consequence of the twenty-sixth president's colorful personality and career, the items tend to be whimsical or humorous. They include: campaign buttons, bandannas, banners, posters, flasks, cologne bottles, commemorative medals, marbles, busts, paperweights, pens, plates, cigar boxes, post-

cards, hats, tapestries, pipes, jugs, serving trays, toy banks, straight razors, and even whistles in the shape of Roosevelt's teeth. Board games on Rough Rider and safari themes were inspired by his exploits in the Spanish-American War and as a big game hunter in Africa.

Most of these artifacts have faded from the public eye into the obscurity of museums or private collections. One item, however, is still

D O C U M E N T

Cartoonist Clifford Berryman showed Roosevelt refusing to shoot a cub during a 1902 bear hunt, thus starting a toy bear craze.

Inspired by Berryman's cartoon, toy companies began to make stuffed animal bears in the early 1900s and called them "Teddy Bears."

Red, white, and black campaign bandanna is adorned by some of the symbols associated with Roosevelt—moose, big sticks, glasses.

being manufactured today and is more popular than ever. It began with a 1902 newspaper cartoon, which showed the President refusing to shoot a trapped bear. This gave a Brooklyn, New York, candystore owner an idea. He and his wife made—and put on sale—a small, brown, plush stuffed animal. Displaying the cartoon with it, they attached to the toy a label that read "Teddy's Bear."

CRITICAL THINKING

1. Examine the campaign bandanna and identify the symbols. Why were they associated with TR?
2. Study the memorabilia of Teddy Roosevelt on these two pages. From the collection, how do you think the public felt about TR?

3. AMERICAN CONSERVATIONIST GIFFORD PINCHOT PUTS FORTH THREE PRINCIPLES OF CONSERVATION

Teddy Roosevelt's love of nature was as famous as his love of action, sports, and exercise. Conservation became one of his—and other Progressives'—major concerns. Gifford Pinchot, one of the most famous of the progressive conservationists, expressed this concern in a speech given to the First National Conservation Congress, in 1909, later revised and printed in his book, The Fight for Conservation.

Gifford Pinchot believed that government should help manage the nation's natural resources.

The first great fact about conservation is that it stands for development. There has been a fundamental misconception that conservation means nothing but the husbanding of resources for future generations. There could be no more serious mistake. Conservation does mean provision for the future, but it means also and first of all the recognition of the right of the present generation to the fullest necessary use of all the resources with which this country is so abundantly blessed. Conservation demands the welfare of this generation first, and afterward the welfare of the generations to follow.

The first principle of conservation is development, the use of the natural resources now existing on this continent for the benefit of the people who live here now. There may be just as much waste in neglecting the development and use of certain natural resources as there is in their destruction. We have a limited supply of coal, and only a limited supply. Whether it is to last for a hundred or a hundred and fifty or a thousand years, the coal is limited in amount, unless through geological changes which we shall not live to see, there will never be any more of it than there is now. But coal is in a sense the vital essence of our civilization. If it can be preserved, if the life of the mines can be extended, if by preventing waste there can be more coal left in this country after we of this generation have made every needed use of this source of power, then we shall have deserved well of our descendants. . . .

In every case and in every direction the conservation movement has development for its first principle, and at the very beginning of its work. The development of our natural resources and the fullest use of them for the present generation is the first duty of this generation. . . .

In the second place conservation stands for the prevention of waste. There has come gradually in this country an understanding that waste is not a good thing and that the attack on waste is an industrial necessity. I recall very well indeed how, in the early days of forest fires, they were considered simply and solely as acts of God, against which any opposition was hopeless and any attempt to control them not merely hopeless but childish. It was assumed that they came in the natural order of things, as inevitably as the seasons or the rising and setting of the sun. To-day we understand that forest fires are wholly within the control of men. So we are coming in like manner to understand that the prevention of waste in other directions is a simple matter of good business. The first duty of the human race is to control the earth it lives upon. . . .

In addition to the principles of development and preservation of our resources there is a third principle. It is this: The natural resources must be developed and preserved for the benefit of the many, and not merely for the profit of the few.

Selection from Gifford Pinchot, *The Fight for Conservation.* Published by University of Washington Press, Seattle, copyright © 1910.

4. PRESIDENT THEODORE ROOSEVELT SPEAKS ON THE RELATIONSHIP BETWEEN BIG BUSINESS AND GOVERNMENT

Anti-trust activity was another area in which Theodore Roosevelt—and other Progressives—gained fame. In his early days as President, however, Roosevelt's actual views were more conservative. In his first congressional message as President, he outlined his reasons for caution in dealing with businesses and corporations.

During the last five years business confidence has been restored, and the nation is to be congratulated because of its present abounding prosperity. Such prosperity can never be created by law alone, although it is easy enough to destroy it by mischievous laws. . . . Fundamentally the welfare of each citizen, and therefore the welfare of the aggregate of citizens which makes the nation, must rest upon individual thrift and energy, resolution, and intelligence. Nothing can take the place of this individual capacity; but wise legislation and honest and intelligent administration can give it the fullest scope, the largest opportunity to work to good effect.

The tremendous and highly complex industrial development which went on with ever accelerated rapidity during the latter half of the nineteenth century brings us face to face, at the beginning of the twentieth, with very serious social problems. The old laws, and the old customs which had al-

most the binding force of law, were once quite sufficient to regulate the accumulation and distribution of wealth. Since the industrial changes which have so enormously increased the productive power of mankind, they are no longer sufficient.

The growth of cities has gone on beyond comparison faster than the growth of the country, and the upbuilding of the great industrial centers has meant a startling increase, not merely in the aggregate of wealth, but in the number of very large individual, and especially of very large corporate, fortunes. The creation of these great corporate fortunes has not been due to the tariff nor to any other governmental action, but to natural causes in the business world, operating in other countries as they operate in our own.

The process has aroused much antagonism, a great part of which is wholly without warrant. . . . There have been abuses connected with the accumulation of wealth; yet it remains true that a fortune accumulated in legitimate business can be accumulated by the person specially benefited only on condition of conferring immense incidental benefits upon others. Successful enterprise, of the type which benefits all mankind, can only exist if the conditions are such as to offer great prizes as the rewards of success.

The captains of industry who have driven the railway systems across this continent, who have built up our commerce, who have developed our manufactures, have on the whole done great good to our people. Without them the material development of which we are so justly proud could never have taken place. . . .

An additional reason for caution in dealing with corporations is to be found in the international commercial conditions of to-day. The same business conditions which have produced the great aggregations of corporate and individual wealth have made them very potent factors in international commercial competition. . . . America has only just begun to assume that commanding position in the international business world which we believe will more and more be hers. It is of the utmost importance that this position be not jeoparded, especially at a time when the overflowing abundance of our own natural resources and the skill, business evergy, and mechanical aptitude of our people make foreign markets essential. Under such conditions it would be most unwise to cramp or to fetter the youthful strength of our Nation. . . .

The mechanism of modern business is so delicate that extreme care must be taken not to interfere with it in a spirit of rashness or ignorance. Many of those who have made it their vocation to denounce the great industrial combinations which are popularly, although with technical inaccuracy, known as "trusts," appeal especially to hatred and fear. These are precisely the two emotions, particularly when combined with ignorance, which unfit men for the exercise of cool and steady judgment. In facing new industrial conditions, the whole history of the world shows that legislation will generally be both unwise and ineffective unless undertaken after calm inquiry and with sober self-restraint. . . . In dealing with business interests, for the Government to undertake by crude and ill-considered legislation to do what may turn out to be bad, would be to incur the risk of such far-reaching national disaster that it would be preferable to undertake nothing at all. . . .

There is a widespread conviction in the minds of the American people that the great corporations known as trusts are in certain of their features and tendencies hurtful to the general welfare. This springs from no spirit of envy or uncharitableness, nor lack of pride in the great industrial achievements that have placed this country at the head of the nations struggling for commercial supremacy. . . . It is based upon sincere conviction that combination and concentration should be, not prohibited, but supervised and within reasonable limits controlled; and in my judgment this conviction is right. . . .

Corporations engaged in interstate commerce should be regulated if they are found to exercise a license working to the public injury. It should be as much the aim of those who seek for social betterment to rid the business world of crimes of cunning as to rid the entire body politic of crimes of violence. Great corporations exist only because they are created and safeguarded by our institutions; and it is therefore our right and our duty to see that they work in harmony with these institutions.

Selection from James Richardson, *A Compilation of the Messages and Papers of the Presidents*, Vol. XV. Published by Bureau of National Literature, New York, copyright © 1908.

5. PRESIDENTIAL CANDIDATE THEODORE ROOSEVELT CAMPAIGNS FOR THE "SQUARE DEAL"

In the 1912 presidential election, Theodore Roosevelt ran as the Progressive Party candidate. The following statements about the role played by special business interests in the governing of the nation were made in a campaign speech given in Kansas during that presidential campaign.

I stand for the square deal. But when I say that I am for a square deal, I mean not merely that I stand for fair play under the present rules of the game, but that I stand for having the rules changed so as to work for a more substantial equality of opportunity and of reward for equally good service. One word of warning, which, I think, is hardly necessary in Kansas. When I say I want a square deal for the poor man, I do not mean that I want a square deal for the man who remains poor because he has not the energy to work for himself. If a man who has had a chance will not make good, then he has got to quit. . . .

Now, this means that our government, national and state, must be freed from the sinister influence or control of special interests. Exactly as the special interests of cotton and slavery threatened our political integrity before the Civil War, so now the great special business interests too often control and corrupt the men and methods of government for their own profit. We must drive the special interests out of politics. That is one of our tasks to-day. Every special interest is entitled to justice—full, fair and complete. . . . but not one is entitled to a vote in Congress, to a voice on the bench, or to representation in any public office. The Constitution guarantees protection to property, and we must make that promise good. But it does not give the right of suffrage to any corporation.

The true friend of property, the true conservative, is he who insists that property shall be the servant and not the master of the commonwealth; who insists that the creature of man's making shall be the servant and not the master of the man who made it. The citizens of the United States must effectively control the mighty commercial forces which they have themselves called into being.

There can be no effective control of corporations while their political activity remains. To put an end to it will be neither a short nor an easy task, but it can be done.

Selection from Theodore Roosevelt, *The New Nationalism.* Published by Prentice Hall, Englewood Cliffs, N.J., copyright © 1961.

CRITICAL THINKING

1. What kind of government regulation or control of corporations did President Roosevelt seem to support in this speech?
2. What dangers did he seem to believe corporate political power posed to the country?

6. PRESIDENT WILLIAM HOWARD TAFT SENDS A MESSAGE TO CONGRESS CONCERNING SEAL HUNTING

One of the issues that helped to kill President William Howard Taft politically was conservation. During the friction between Gifford Pinchot and Richard Ballinger, President Taft disappointed those who expected more forceful support from him. In 1913, he further displeased the conservationists by sending to Congress this special message on the destruction of seals.

At the last session of Congress an act was adopted to give effect to the fur-seal treaty of July 7, 1911, between Great Britain, Japan, Russia, and the United States, in which act was incorporated a provision establishing a five-year period during which the killing of seals upon the Pribilof Islands is prohibited. Prior to the passage of this act, I pointed out in my message to Congress, on August 14 last, the inadvisability of adopting legislation the effect of which was to require this government to suspend the killing of surplus male seals on land before it was actually proved by the test of experience and scientific investigation that such suspension of killing was necessary for the protection and preservation of the seal herd. I also pointed out in that message that the other Governments, interested might justly complain if this Government by prohibiting all land killing should deprive them of their expected share of the skins taken on land, unless we can show by satisfactory evidence that this course was adopted as the result of changed conditions justifying a change in our previous attitude on the subject. As was then anticipated, the other parties interested have now objected to the suspension thus imposed on the ground that it is contrary to the spirit, if not the letter, of the treaty, inasmuch as under existing conditions a substantial number of male seals not required for breeding purposes can be killed annually without detriment to the reproductive capacity of the herd. . . .

It now appears that under the operation of te fur-seal convention during the past year the condition and size of the herd has improved to an extent which seems to indicate that there is now no necessity, and therefore no justification, for the suspension of all land killing of male seals, as required by the act under consideration.

Last season's reports from the officials in charge on the Pribilof Islands show that the herd which the year before contained at the highest estimate not more than 140,000 seals, now numbers upward of 215,000 by actual count, showing in one season an increase of at least 75,000 seals. This increase is largely due to the protection afforded by the treaty to the breeding female seals, which last summer numbered 82,000, many thousands of which, except for the treaty, would have been slaughtered by pelagic sealers, and as every breeding female adds one pup to the herd each year, over 81,000 new pups were added last season. Moreover, instead of losing 10,000 or 15,000 of these pups through starvation as heretofore on account of the slaughter of the nursing mothers by

265

pelagic sealers, this summer by actual count the number of dead pups found on the rockeries was only 1,060.

It is evident from these reports that there has been a very remarkable increase in the size of the herd in one season under the opeation of this convention and that a large part of this increase consists of female seals, upon which the future increase of the herd depends.

The present condition of the herd shows that there will be about 100,000 breeding female seals in the herd next summer, each one of which will produce one pup, and in the following year the female pups born last summer, amounting in accordance with the laws of nature to one-half of the total number of the year's pups, will pass into the breeding class, subject to losses from natural mortality, thus adding a possible 40,000 more, which would bring the total up in the neighborhood of 140,000 breeding female seals; and so on from year to year the reproductive strength of the herd will increase in almost geometrical progression, so that we can confidently count on having the present size of the herd doubled and trebled within a very short period.

All that is required to fulfill these expectations is to protect absolutely the female seals and set aside an adequate number of male seals for breeding purposes. The protection and preservation of the herd does not require the protection and preservation of the surplus male seals not needed from breeding purposes. Owing to the polygamous habits of the seals, the increase in the number of these surplus bachelor seals can in no conceivable way increase the birth rate or the reproductive capacity of the herd. Seals of this class contribute nothing to the welfare of the herd, and in some ways they are a distinct detriment as a disturbing element on the rookeries and as consumers of food, which is bound to become scarcer as the size of the herd increases. These nonbreeding males, therefore, are of no value as members of the herd except to furnish skins for the market in place of those heretofore taken by pelagic sealers, and in this connection it should be noted that the value of their skins for commercial purposes diminishes after they are 4 years old and ceases altogether after the age of 5 or 6. . . .

It is right and necessary that the killing of all seals in the herd other than the non-breeding males should be absolutely prohibited not only for five years but forever. Land killing . . . must be strictly limited by law to male seals. . .

The question of how many male seals should be reserved each year for breeding purposes can readily be determined. In the act under consideration, as it passed the House and before it was amended in the Senate, there was a provision that hereafter only 3-year-old males shall be killed, and that there shall be reserved from among the finest and most perfect seals of that age not fewer than 2,000 in 1913, 2,500 in 1914, 3,000 in 1915, 3,500 in 1916, and 4,000 each year from 1917 to 1921, inclusive, and 5,000 each year thereafter during the continuance of the convention. These figures were arrived at after full and careful investigation by the House Committee on Foreign Affairs and it appears from the committee reports accompanying this act that these figures were intended to be and were regarded as large enough to be on the safe side. . . .

In view of the present condition of the herd and the very marked increase in its size and particularly in the number of female seals, which has resulted from the operation of this convention during a single year, and which, as above shown, is to be attributed almost wholly to the protection afforded by the prohibition against pelagic sealing, I recommend to Congress the immediate consideration of whether or not the complete suspension of land killing imposed by this act is now necessary for the protection and preservation of the herd, and for increasing its number within the meaning and for the purposes of the convention. If no actual necessity is found for such suspension then it is not justified under the convention, and the act should be amended accordingly.

Selection from *A Compilation of the Messages and Papers of the Presidents*, Vol. XVI. Published by Bureau of National Literature, Inc., New York, copyright © 1917.

CRITICAL THINKING

1. List the arguments Taft uses to justify killing excess male seals.
2. Is Taft persuasive in his arguments? Explain your answers.

7. PRESIDENTIAL CANDIDATE WOODROW WILSON SEES AMERICA CHANGING

Theodore Roosevelt was not the only candidate advocating major changes in national policy and attitudes in 1912. The winner of that election, Woodrow Wilson, though in many ways more conservative than Roosevelt, called for important changes of direction in American goals and government. The following statements come from The New Freedom, *a book based on Wilson's speeches.*

We are in the presence of a new organization of society. Our life has broken away from the past. The life of America is not the life that it was twenty years ago. . . . We have changed our economic conditions, absolutely, from top to bottom; and, with our economic society, the organization of our life. The old political formulas do not fit the present problems; they read now like documents taken out of a forgotten age. The older cries sound as if they belonged to a past age which men have almost forgotten. Things which used to be put into the party platforms of ten years ago would sound antiquated if put into a platform now. We are facing the necessity of fitting a new social organization, as we did once fit the old organization, to the happiness and prosperity of the great body of citizens; for we are conscious that the new order of society has not been made to fit and provide the convenience or prosperity of the average man. The life of the nation has grown infinitely varied. It does not center now upon questions of governmental structure or of the distribution of governmental powers. It centers upon questions of the very structure and operation of society itself, of which government is only the instrument. Our development has run so fast and so far along the lines sketched in the earlier day of constitutional definition, has so crossed and interlaced those lines, has piled upon them such novel structures of trust and combination, has elaborated within them a life so manifold, so full of forces which transcend the boundaries of the country itself and fill the eyes of the world, that a new nation seems to have been created which the old formulas do not fit or afford a vital interpretation of. . . .

What this country needs above everything else is a body of laws which will look after the men who are on the make rather than the men who are already made. Because the men who are already made are not going to live indefinitely, and they are not always kind enough to leave sons as able and as honest as they are.

The originative part of America, the part of America that makes new enterprises, the part into which the ambitious and gifted workingman makes his way up, the class that saves, that plans, that organizes, that presently spreads its enterprises until they have a national scope and character, —that middle class is being more and more squeezed out by the processes which we have been taught to call processes of prosperity. Its members are sharing prosperity, no doubt; but what alarms me is that they are not *originating* prosperity. . . . The treasury of America does not lie in the brains of the small body of men now in control of the great enterprises that have been concentrated under the direction of a very small number of persons. The treasury of America lies in those ambitions, those energies, that cannot be restricted to a special favored class. It depends upon the inventions of unknown men, upon the originations of unknown men, upon the ambitions of unknown men. Every country is renewed out of the ranks of the unknown, not out of the ranks of those already famous and powerful and in control.

We are in a new world, struggling under old laws. As we go inspecting our lives to-day, surveying this new scene of centralized and complex society, we shall find many more things out of joint.

Selection from Woodrow Wilson, "The New Freedom," in *Words That Made American History*, edited by Richard N. Current, *et. al.* Published by Little, Brown, Boston, copyright © 1965.

CRITICAL THINKING

1. What was Woodrow Wilson's attitude toward those middle class people who, he said, were "on the make rather than . . . already made"?
2. What kinds of changes did Wilson see going on in the United States at the time?
3. What response did he believe that government should make to these changes?

CHAPTER 25

AMERICA GOES TO WAR

1914–1920

1. NEBRASKA SENATOR GEORGE NORRIS OPPOSES UNITED STATES INVOLVEMENT IN WORLD WAR I

Although public opinion generally supported the Allies—and American entry into the war on the side of Britain, France, and Italy—many Americans were opposed to their country's involvement. Among them was Senator George Norris of Nebraska, who served in Congress from 1903 to 1913 and in the Senate from 1914 to 1943. These passages, from a speech Norris gave on April 4, 1917, right after President Wilson's War Message, was one of his most eloquent statements against the war.

There are a great many American citizens who feel that we owe it as a duty to humanity to take part in this war. Many instances of cruelty and inhumanity can be found on both sides. Men are often biased in their judgment on account of their sympathy and their interests. To my mind, what we ought to have maintained from the beginning was the strictest neutrality. If we had done this I do not believe we would have been on the verge of war at the present time. We had a right as a nation, if we desired, to cease at any time to be neutral. We had a technical right to respect the English war zone and to disregard the German war zone, but we could not do that and be neutral. I have no quarrel to find with the man who does not desire our country to remain neutral. While many such people are moved by selfish motives and hopes of gain, I have no doubt but that in a great many instances, through what I believe to be a misunderstanding of the real condition, there are many honest, patriotic citizens who think we ought to engage in this war and who are behind the President in his demand that we should declare war against Germany. I think such people err in judgment and to a great extent have been misled as to the real history and the true facts by the almost unanimous demand of the great combination of wealth that has a direct financial interest in our participation in the war. We have loaned many hundreds of millions of dollars to the allies in this controversy. While such action was legal and countenanced by international law, there is no doubt in my mind but the enormous amount of money loaned to the allies in this country has been instrumental in bringing about a public sentiment in favor of our country taking a course that would make every bond worth a hundred cents on the dollar and making the payment of every debt certain and sure. . . . It is now demanded that the American citizens shall be used as insurance policies to guarantee the safe delivery of munitions of war to belligerent nations. The enormous profits of munition manufacturers, stockbrokers, and bond dealers must be still further increased by our entrance into the war. This has brought us to the present moment, when Congress, urged by the President and backed by the artificial sentiment, is about to declare war and engulf our country in the greatest holocaust that the world has ever known. . . .

To whom does war bring prosperity? Not to the soldier who for the munificent compensation of $16 per month shoulders his musket and goes into the trench, there to shed his blood and to die if necessary; not to the broken-hearted widow who waits for the return of the mangled body of her husband; not to the mother who weeps at the death of her brave boy; not to the little children who shiver with cold; not to the babe who suffers from hunger; nor to the millions of mothers and daughters who carry broken hearts to their graves. War brings no prosperity to the great mass of common and patriotic citizens. It increases the cost of living of those who toil and those who already must strain every effort to keep soul and body together. War brings prosperity to the stock gambler on Wall Street—to those who are already in possession of more wealth than can be realized or enjoyed. . . .

We are taking a step to-day that is fraught with untold danger. We are going into war upon the command of gold. We are going to run the risk of sacrificing millions of our countrymen's lives in order that other countrymen may coin their life-blood into money. And even if we do not cross the

Atlantic and go into the trenches, we are going to pile up a debt that the toiling masses that shall come many generations after us will have to pay. Unborn millions will bend their backs in toil in order to pay for the terrible step we are now about to take. We are about to do the bidding of wealth's terrible mandate. By our act we will make millions of our countrymen suffer, and the consequences of it may well be that millions of our brethren must shed their lifeblood, millions of broken-hearted women must weep, millions of children must suffer with cold, and millions of babes must die from hunger, and all because we want to preserve the commercial right of American citizens to deliver munitions of war to belligerent nations.

Selection from speech by Senator George Norris, April 4, 1917, *Congressional Record*, Vol. LV. Published by United States Government Printing Office, Washington, D.C., copyright © 1917.

Theodore Roosevelt's youngest son, Quentin, was killed during World War I, at the age of 21.

CRITICAL THINKING

1. What reasons did Senator Norris give for believing that various financial interests were responsible for American entry into the war?
2. What specific appeals to sentiment did Norris make during his speech?

2. FORMER PRESIDENT THEODORE ROOSEVELT WRITES A LETTER ABOUT THE WAR IN EUROPE

When the Lusitania was sunk by a German submarine in 1915, former president Theodore Roosevelt denounced the Germans and called upon his countrymen to avenge the tragedy. Critical of President Woodrow Wilson's administration, he urged preparedness for the coming war. In this letter to a noted editor, Mrs. William Brown Meloney, he prescribed a regimen of Spartan living for the United States in the days ahead.

August 5, 1916

DEAR MRS. MELONEY:

There are a good many things that America needs, if Santa Claus could only give them!

Here are a few of them.

1. That every molly-coddle, professional pacifist, and man who is "too proud to fight" when the nation's quarrel is just, should be exiled to those out of the way parts . . . where the spirit of manliness has not yet penetrated.

2. That every decent young man should have a family, a job, and the military training which will enable him to help keep this country out of war by making it dangerous for any ruthless military people to attack us.

3. That every youngster may have a good and wise mother; and every good woman a child for her arms.

4. That we may all of us become an efficient, patriotic, and nobly proud people—too proud either to inflict wrong or to endure it.

Good luck, Always yours

Theodore Roosevelt

Selection from *A Second Treasury of the World's Great Letters*, edited by Wallace Brockway and Bart Keith Winer. Published by Simon and Schuster, New York, copyright © 1941.

CRITICAL THINKING

1. Wilson was the man who was "too proud to fight." From this selection, what can you infer was Roosevelt's view of Wilson?
2. Assess Roosevelt's views of America's needs. Does he present an objective assessment?

WORLD WAR I POSTERS
Building Public Support

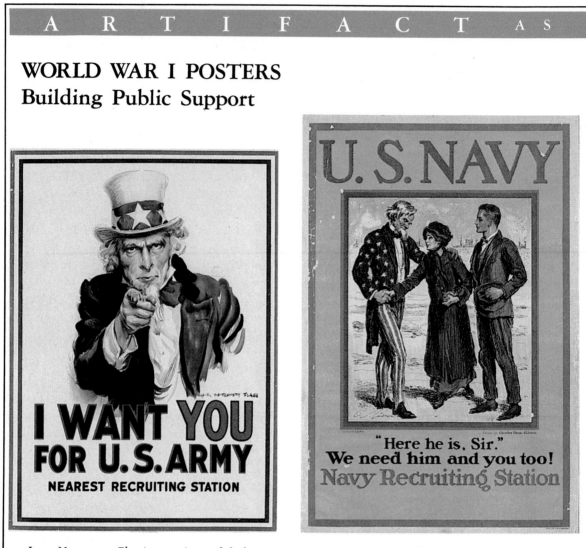

James Montgomery Flagg's poster is one of the best known—and most widely reproduced—in history. Nearly 5 million copies were printed during the two world wars.

War posters portrayed American women as compassionate and virtuous individuals ready to make sacrifices.

When the United States declared war on Germany in 1917, there was an immediate need for wide public support, as well as for workers and soldiers. One quick way of communicating these needs to the public was through poster campaigns. A federal Department of Pictorial Publicity was created to recruit artists, design graphics, and produce posters. Orders for posters were taken from governmental departments, then translated into poster themes and assigned to individual artists by chairman Charles Dana Gibson.

At the beginning of the war, posters were used mainly to recruit soldiers and to raise war funds. Posters supporting the five Liberty Loans helped the government raise nearly $22 billion for the war effort. Later, poster campaigns were aimed at maintaining the morale of the public

DOCUMENT

The first phase of war poster themes was the call for investment of private funds, urging the people to support the war with purchases of war savings stamps and war bonds.

During the war, an increasing shortage of supplies led to a need to conserve at home.

and America's fighting forces. Citizens were urged to provide comfort to the troops, to aid war victims and refugees, to sacrifice at home, and to save vital materials.

By the end of the war, the Department of Pictorial Publicity had produced a staggering 700 posters. All of the creative ideas and designs for the posters were contributed by patriotic American artists, free-of-charge.

CRITICAL THINKING

1. Propaganda is an idea or fact used to deliberately aid or damage a cause. What was the purpose of these propaganda posters?
2. Examine the posters and tell how the symbol of "Uncle Sam" was used to get the government's message to the people.

271

3. AN AMERICAN SOLDIER IN FRANCE WRITES HOME FROM "THE FRONT"

To Americans, whose knowledge of the war came from the various media that attempted to bolster the country's "fighting spirit," The Great War—as World War I was referred to—of a battle between "civilization" and "barbarism." For those taking part and those in touch with them, however, the war often had simpler, more direct meanings. On July 8, 1918, Eldon Canright wrote the following letter from "Somewhere in France."

MY DEAR FOLKS: I believe I have told you in another letter that because of the fine record we have made since we have been at the front we have been chosen for "shock troops." Well, we sure are being *shocked!*

Try and picture the very worst thunderstorm you have ever seen: then multiply it by about ten thousand and you will get some idea of the battle that has been and still is raging along this front and in which we are taking a very active part! The battle started shortly after midnight a few days ago and has been raging ever since! It started with a very heavy bombardment all along the front. . . . The first night a shell struck an ammunition dump and rockets went shooting in every direction; it lasted for several minutes and was very thrilling!

Of course every little while the "gentle Hun" sends over gas, so that we have to be constantly on the alert for it and wear our gas clothes most of the time and carry our gas masks all the time!

We all have cotton in our ears, but, nevertheless, the concussion of the guns has made some of us temporarily deaf. We have not taken off any of our clothes or gone to bed since the battle started. When it slows up a little we just lie down on the ground, right by the guns, and get what little rest and sleep we can. Our meals are brought to us, as we may not leave the position long enough to go and get them!

The first day they brought down an observation balloon right near us. An aviator attacked it and hit it with an incendiary bullet from his machine gun. The balloon came down in flames, but the observer jumped and came down in a parachute! However, about a minute later, and even before the observer had struck the ground another airplane had rushed up after the machine that "got" the balloon. It was partly cloudy that morning and he was trying to get away and hide behind the clouds, but the aviator brought him down and he came tumbling out of the clouds with his machine a mass of flames. That happened three days ago, and the burned and broken airplane is still lying there, and so are the two aviators!

Selection from Eldon J. Canright, "Some War-Time Letters," *Wisconsin Magazine of History*, Vol. V, 1921–1922.

CRITICAL THINKING

1. What were the general conditions at the front near Eldon Canright's position?
2. What was Canright's attitude toward the war and the conditions?

---

4. AMERICAN AMBULANCE DRIVER GUY EMERSON BOWERMAN, JR. RECORDS HIS EXPERIENCES IN THE FINAL DAYS OF WORLD WAR I

Guy Emerson Bowerman, Jr., was among the Americans who served as ambulance drivers during the war. Some, like the writers e.e. cummings and Ernest Hemingway, went to France before United States entry into the war; others, like Bowerman, served after America joined the conflict. The following entries give Bowerman's personal account of the last days of the war.

Thurs. Oct. 31. The attack started early this morning with two French divisions on the flanks and one American at the center. The Americans went too fast and got ahead of their barrage which was put up by the French artillery so that there are many wounded and their ambulances don't seem to be able to handle them. At Zult this morning a young Frenchman walked a quarter of a kilometer holding his entrails in with his hands. After being bandaged he asked for a cigarette and when we put him into a car he was smiling as if nothing had happened. I don't suppose he will live but he surely had unlimited nerve. A little later I drove a captain up to an advanced poste[,] a little thatched cottage at the end of a lane. While I was waiting outside I heard a terrible scream from within. I rushed inside but was too late to see the cause of the scream—an amputation without ether of a young Boche's [German's] leg. Never in my life have I seen anything which could compare to the pain and anguish in the face and every muscle of the body of that German. . . .

Mon. Nov. 4. The attack has been very successful and is at last terminated. The Americans added additional glory to their record in France and one may count numbers of khaki bodies lying half concealed by the [beet] tops of Belgian farms. . . . The Germans surely did retreat in a hurry tho in good order. . . .

Tues. Nov. 5. Section moves from Noker[e] to Vive St. Eloi. On our way over we were greatly surprised to be bombed by a German airplane which was flying so high that we never imagined he would try to hit us. We were not only surprised to have him throw his bombs at us but we were utterly astounded when he succeeded in wounding an American officer. . . .

I have a bad cold and I feel like a dog. I hope it's not the Spanish grippe [influenza].

Wed. Nov. 6. Not feeling any better today and since we are now on reserve and awaiting orders I can remain in my bunk.

Frid. Nov. 8. Every one is positive that two German generals came across the lines today with a white flag to demand an armistice. Foch [the French commander-in-chief who became commander of the unified command in April, 1918] has given them 72 hours to accept or refuse his terms and meanwhile preparations for another big attack are being made in this sector. . . .

Sun. Nov. 10. 10 P.M. LA PAIX EST SIGNÉE [the peace is signed]. All the sky is lighted up with Verey Lights and gun flashes. All the Frenchmen are shouting and shooting and we're so plain . . . happy we don't know where we are. All the Section is out.

LA GUERRE EST FINIE!

[Undated entry beginning at top of page 55 of recopied diary; (equivalent entry in original diary dated Nov. 17):] Really the entry for Nov. 10 should end on page 54. The make up of the bottom of that page portrays exactly our, or should I say my? feelings but those few lines were written while the daze had not left me. Then all

was supreme gladness, un-adulterated, supreme, ecstatic joy. Joy, pure joy, but thoughtless joy. The entry under Nov. 10 does not explain why our joy was insane nor why, a little later when the spasm had spent itself, we drew within ourselves and went quietly back to our bunks where some of us laid till almost morning, silent, but wide awake. I remember how Rouget the French sergeant threw up his arms and fell limply into his cot exclaiming "Bon Dieu, it is the end of a bad dream." And so it was but like the awakening from a bad dream we were troubled to assure ourselves that the dream had ended, that now we were awake safe from the hideous thing which pursued us in our slumbers. . . . We had heard so many rumors that we [thought] this but the fabled cry of "wolf." We had hoped so long and passionately for this hour to come and had been so long disappointed that our minds could not grasp the meaning of it when it was here. As I have said before, after our first few months in the war we had so far identified with war that we were as men who have had a lapse of memory. The old life was gone forever and each succeeding day and each succeeding horror drove the peaceful part farther behind us till at last it was gone completely from our ken. Here we were, men made for war, men born to war, men whose life is filled from beginning to end with war and we felt secretly in our hearts that there could be no other life. Then to those of us who had been enough in war to lose our peace identity completely were suddenly, precipitately and unwarned flung into another life, a life of peace. We could have been no more awed, no more bewildered than would the men of Mars could they suddenly find themselves on this planet. Then gradually we came to realize what it all meant though we walked warily like men fearing ambush[,] fearful of having this new-found joy snatched from our grasp. Even, when after a week the guns were still [quiet,] though we outwardly were jovial and carefree, certain of seeing home again[,] yet within ourselves we questioned, doubted nor were we ever sure deep down within us till we got our final pay, took off our uniforms and again sat at our family table.

Selection from Guy Emerson Bowerman, Jr., *The Compensations of War: The Diary of an Ambulance Driver during the Great War*, edited by Mark C. Carnes. Published by University of Texas Press, Austin, copyright © 1983.

5. MASSACHUSETTS SENATOR HENRY CABOT LODGE DEMANDS HARSH PEACE TERMS

Even while the war was going on, the debate over the peace terms began. In August, 1918, Senator Henry Cabot Lodge, Chairman of the foreign affairs committee and one of the more influential Republican leaders, argued in favor of a peace based upon Germany's unconditional surrender. After listing the various territorial concessions that Germany, Austria-Hungary, and the Ottoman Empire would have to make, he described his attitude toward what the peace terms should represent.

These [concessions and compensations] are the principal conditions which alone will give us a victory worth having, and when we talk about a complete peace and a just and righteous peace, let it be known to all the world that this is what we mean. It is idle to talk about our annihilating the German people. Nobody, of course, has any such idea. It could not be done even if we wished to do it. We are not engaged in this war to try to arrange a government for Germany. The German people must do that themselves, and they will get precisely the government which they desire and deserve —just as they now have the government they prefer, whose purposes and ambitions and barbarism they share and sustain. Our part and our business is to put Germany in a position where she can do no more harm in the future to the rest of the world. Unless we achieve this we shall have fought in vain. Congress and the President had no right to declare war unless they meant to do precisely this thing. Nothing less should justify our action. We are pouring out the best blood of the country, the blood of our chosen youth, upon the altar of patriotism. We are making every sort of pecuniary [monetary] sacrifice. We are bearing an immense burden of taxation. We are mortgaging with our loans the future of coming generations. We have set aside for the time being the Constitution under which individual liberty has been preserved and the country has grown and prospered. . . . It is our intention to return, as our laws show, to the old restrictions, protections, and rights of the ordered freedom of the Constitution. We are taking these vast risks, we are bearing these huge burdens, we are making these unspeakable sacrifices of life with a brave and cheerful spirit; but we have no right to do all these things unless we win the prize and reach the goal which alone can warrant and justify them. . . . The only peace for us is one that rests on hard physical facts, the peace of unconditional surrender. No peace that satisfies Germany in any degree can ever satisfy us. It can not be a negotiated peace. It must be a dictated peace, and we and our allies must dictate it. The victory bringing such a peace must be won inside, not outside, the German frontier. It must be won finally and thoroughly in German territory, and can be so won nowhere else.

Selection from Henry Cabot Lodge speech, August 23, 1918, in *History of U.S. Political Parties*, Vol. III, edited by Arthur M. Schlesinger. Published by Chelsea House, New York, copyright © 1973.

6. SUFFRAGIST CARRIE CHAPMAN CATT TELLS WHY THE LEAGUE OF WOMEN VOTERS WAS FORMED

The final struggle for the enfranchisement of women was led by Carrie Chapman Catt, an Iowa-born newspaperwoman and teacher. In 1919, she organized the League of Women Voters, whose immediate goal was to finish the fight for the vote. After that had been achieved, the League planned an ambitious program of literacy and political education for all voting citizens, regardless of their sex.

A half-century ago the Legislature of the Territory of Wyoming granted women the same political privileges as the men of the Territory enjoyed. This was the first commonwealth in the world to give women the ballot on equal terms with men. It stood, therefore, as the working model of a new ideal in democracy.

In the same year that Wyoming gave equal rights to women—1869—the National and the American Woman Suffrage Associations were formed for the purpose of gaining equal political rights for women throughout the country. Twenty years later these two associations were merged into the National American Woman Suffrage Association.

For fifty years the National American Woman Suffrage Association and its two predecsesors have been seeking to persuade the National and State Governments to follow the example of Wyoming and incorporate justice to women in their constitutions. . . .

Women have learned much in these fifty years of effort. They have learned, for example, some of the blind spots in our democracy. They know where, and, to some extent, to what influences the electorate is vulnerable. They have found out, at great cost to themselves, how votes may be manipulated and ignorant men, unconsciously to themselves, made to thwart the freedom of their sisters and wives. . . .

Therefore, as women, vitally concerned with the honor of the nation and with the welfare of the race, those suffragists who met at St. Louis [on March 24-29, 1919] had . . . an object facing toward the future. This was the formation of the League of Women Voters, whose main aim is to catch up and use to the full the newly gained political freedom of millions of women. . . .

Having whole-heartedly worked for their political freedom, as no men had ever worked for it, having proved by their loyalty to American institutions that they are worthy to be counted among those whose patriotism is tried and proved, the women of the voting States, united in this League of Women Voters, determined that their first collective act should be to raise the standards of citizenship for both sexes. . . .

This League of Voters is an effort to make into a working reality those dreams of a free America which have been potent in the long fight women

Carrie Chapman Catt played a leading role in winning ratification of the 19th Amendment and founded the League of Women Voters.

have made for the ballot. They have for so long declared that democracy is something worth giving a lifetime to obtain that they will not rest until an All-American democracy comes up to their dreams of it.

Selection from Carrie Chapman Catt, "Women Voters at the Crossroads," *The Public: A Journal of Democracy*, Vol. 22, May 31, 1919.

CRITICAL THINKING

1. Might there have been other reasons for the League's formation besides sharing the lessons women had learned during their fight for enfranchisement?

2. How did World War I impede women's suffrage? Advance it?

President Woodrow Wilson
Proposes a Fourteen Point Peace Plan

Woodrow Wilson was the son of a minister and the grandson of two ministers. His deeply religious background affected almost everything he ever did, including, when he was president between 1913 and 1921, his foreign policy.

When, early in his first term, a dictatorial general, Victoriano Huerta, seized power in Mexico by assassinating the elected president, Francisco Madero, Wilson refused to recognize the new government. The United States, he said, would never exchange ambassadors with a murderer.

When Europe went to war in 1914, Wilson did his best to keep the United States out of it. As far as he was concerned, the war was the result of secret alliances among the great European nations. Wilson believed that it was immoral as well as dangerous to make secret agreements. When other prominent Americans argued that it was in the best interest of the United States to join the war on the side of the British and French, Wilson replied: "There is such a thing as a man being too proud to fight. There is such a thing as a nation being so right that it does not need to convince others by force that it is right."

Wilson changed his mind. In 1917, he led the United States into World War I. He decided on this action, he said, because the German government had shown itself to be immoral.

Using a cruel weapon, the submarine, the Germans struck at defenseless merchant ships, including the ships of neutral nations like the United States. Such a nation, Wilson told Congress, must be defeated. Its influence must not be allowed to spread.

The President's belief that relations among nations should be moral and just was expressed in the "Fourteen Points" which he hoped would be the basis of the treaty that ended World War I. Among the Fourteen Points were opposition to secret treaties and support for the principle of nationalism: people who spoke the same language and shared the same culture should live in their own nation. One of the Fourteen Points provided for freedom of the seas. Wilson believed a *League of Nations*, Point Fourteen, would solve problems between nations fairly.

Wilson's moral approach to foreign policy has had many critics. Believers in *Realpolitik*, or "realistic politics," argue that morality has no place in foreign relations. Adherents to this political philosophy believe that a country should follow the policy that is best for its own interests, no matter that this sometimes means doing things that would be regarded as immoral when done by an individual. Wilson's policy was ultimately a failure and he retired from the presidency a broken and bitter man. National self-interest, and not moral principles, remained the basis of foreign policy.

UNLOCKING HISTORY
KEY DOCUMENT

President Wilson's "Fourteen Points"

I. Open covenants of peace, openly arrived at, after which there shall be no private international understandings of any kind . . .

II. Absolute freedom of navigation upon the seas, outside territorial waters, alike in peace and in war . . .

III. The removal, so far as possible, of all economic barriers and the establishment of an equality of trade conditions . . .

IV. Adequate guarantees given and taken that national armaments will be reduced to the lowest point consistent with domestic safety.

V. A free, open-minded, and absolutely impartial adjustment of all colonial claims . . .

VI. The evacuation of all Russian territory and such a settlement of all questions affecting Russia as will secure the best and freest cooperation of the other nations of the world in obtaining for her an unhampered and unembarrassed opportunity for the independent determination of her own political development and national policy and assure her of a sincere welcome into the society of free nations under institutions of her own choosing; and, more than a welcome, assistance also of every kind that she may need and may herself desire . . .

VII. Belgium, the whole world will agree, must be evacuated and restored, without any attempt to limit the sovereignty which she enjoys in common with all other free nations. . . .

VIII. All French territory should be freed and the invaded portions restored, and the wrong done to France by Prussia in 1871 in the matter of Alsace-Lorraine, which has unsettled the peace of the world for nearly fifty years, should be righted, in order that peace may once more be made secure in the interest of all.

IX. A readjustment of the frontiers of Italy should be effected along clearly recognizable lines of nationality.

X. The peoples of Austria-Hungary, whose place among the nations we wish to see safe-guarded and assured should be accorded the freest opportunity of autonomous development.

XI. Rumania, Serbia, and Montenegro should be evacuated; occupied territories restored; Serbia accorded free and secure access to the sea; and the relations of the several Balkan states to one another determined by friendly counsel along historically established lines of allegiance and nationality . . .

XII. The Turkish portions of the present Ottoman Empire should be assured a secure sovereignty, but the other nationalities which are now under Turkish rule should be assured . . . opportunity of autonomous development . . .

XIII. An independent Polish state should be erected which should include the territories inhabited by indisputably Polish populations, which should be assured a free and secure access to the sea, and whose political and economic independence and territorial integrity should be guaranteed by international covenant.

XIV. A general association of nations must be formed under specific covenants for the purpose of affording mutual guarantees of political independence and territorial integrity to great and small states alike.

Selection from *The American Primer*, Daniel Boorstin, editor. Published by New American Library, New York, copyright © 1968, pages 802–803.

CRITICAL THINKING

1. President Wilson strongly opposed America's entrance into the war. Why did he change his mind?
2. Briefly summarize the main ideas in the "Fourteen Points."
3. Do you think Wilson's moral approach to foreign policy would appeal to many Americans today? Why or why not?

UNIT 8 ◆ READINGS

Good Times, Bad Times

CHANGES IN POSTWAR AMERICA

1920–1929

1. GERMAN TOURIST COUNT FELIX GRAF VON LUCKNER OBSERVES THE EFFECTS OF PROHIBITION

Prohibition was one of the major factors of life in the 1920s. The attempt to prohibit the sale and purchase of alcoholic beverages produced a wave of illegal activities that ranged from individual citizens' refusal to take the law seriously to the notorious activities of the famous gangsters of the Twenties. The way in which Prohibition was treated in many areas was described in the 1920s by a German aristocrat, Count Felix graf von Luckner, who visited America during the period, lectured, and later wrote a book about his travels.

I suppose I should set forth my investigations into the subject of prohibition. Here is a new experience, at a club's celebration. Each man appears with an impressive portfolio. Each receives his glass of pure water; above the table the law reigns supreme. The brief cases rest under the chairs. Soon they are drawn out, the merry noise of popping corks is heard, and the guzzling begins.

Or, I come to a banquet in a hotel dining room. On the table are the finest wines. I ask, "how come?" Answer: "Well, two of our members lived in the hotel for eight days and every day brought in cargoes of this costly stuff in their suitcases." My informant was madly overjoyed at this cunning. . . .

In time, I learned that not everything in America was what it seemed to be. I discovered, for instance, that a spare tire could be filled with substances other than air, that one must not look too deeply into certain binoculars, and that the Teddy Bears that suddenly acquired tremendous popularity among the ladies very often had hollow metal stomachs.

"But," it might be asked, "where do all these people get the liquor?" Very simple. Prohibition has created a new, a universally respected, a well-beloved, and a very profitable occupation, that of the bootlegger who takes care of the importation of the forbidden liquor. Everyone knows this, even the powers of government. But this profession is beloved because it is essential, and it is respected because its pursuit is clothed with an element of danger and with a sporting risk. Now and then one is caught, that must happen *pro forma* and then he must do time or, if he is wealthy enough, get someone to do time for him.

Yet it is undeniable that prohibition has in some respects been signally [notably] successful. The filthy saloons, the gin mills which formerly flourished on every corner and in which the laborer once drank off half his wages, have disappeared. But, on the other hand, a great deal of poison and methyl alcohol has taken the place of the good old pure whiskey. The number of crimes and misdemeanors that originated in drunkenness has declined. But by contrast, a large part of the population has become accustomed to disregard and to violate the law without thinking. The worst is, that precisely as a consequence of the law, the taste for alcohol has spread ever more widely among the youth. The sporting attraction of the forbidden and the dangerous leads to violations.

Selection from Oscar Handlin, *This Was America*. Published by Harper Torchbooks, New York, copyright © 1964.

CRITICAL THINKING

1. What was Count Felix graf von Luckner's view of the American prohibition experiment?
2. What evidence did von Luckner present in the above selection to support this view of prohibition?
3. How might an advocate of prohibition have responded to Count von Luckner's view?

THE TWENTIES
Taking Time
For Fun and Games

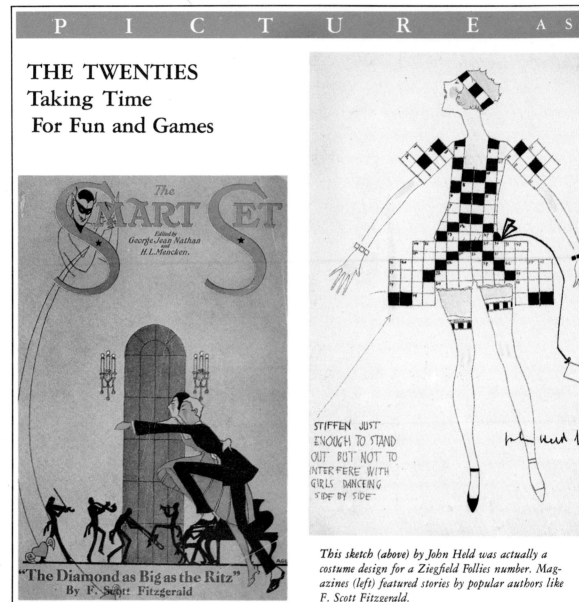

STIFFEN JUST
ENOUGH TO STAND
OUT BUT NOT TO
INTERFERE WITH
GIRLS DANCING
SIDE BY SIDE

This sketch (above) by John Held was actually a costume design for a Ziegfeld Follies number. Magazines (left) featured stories by popular authors like F. Scott Fitzgerald.

During the 1920s, a number of fads swept the nation. Some of the biggest crazes were mah-jongg, crossword puzzles, and dance marathons; but flagpole-sitting, goldfish swallowing, and outdoor pajama-wearing also had their day.

Americans embraced these fads with a passion that resembled mass mania. Frederick Lewis Allen, in his chronicle of the Twenties, *Only Yesterday*, described public reaction to the Chinese tile game of mah-jongg. "The wealthy bought five-hundred-dollar sets; dozens of manufacturers leaped into the business. A Mah Jong League of America was formed . . . and the correct dinner party wound up with every one setting up ivory and bamboo tiles on green baize tables."

After mah-jongg, Americans went mad for crossword puzzles. The first crossword puzzle book, brought out by the young publishing team of Simon and Schuster, immediately became a national best-seller. According to Allen, the crossword craze created innumerable cross-

D O C U M E N T

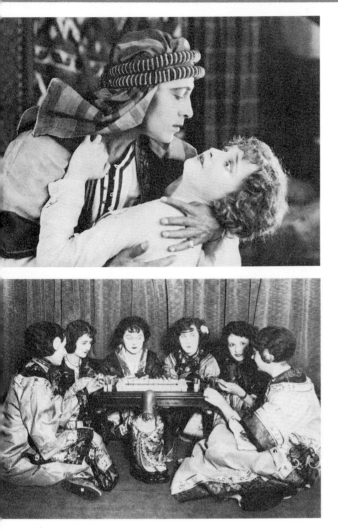

Rudolph Valentino (left) was the great romantic idol of the "silver screen." In a scene from The Sheik, *Valentino romances screen star Agnes Ayres.*

During the mah-jongg craze, people adorned themselves in the Oriental manner.

In this picture, the Miss America of 1926 is getting a free hair "permanent."

word addicts. Sales of dictionaries soared; a man was jailed for refusing to leave a restaurant after working on a puzzle for four hours; a Chicago woman became a "crossword widow" when her husband's devotion to puzzles left him no time to support her; and the Baltimore and Ohio Railroad placed dictionaries on its main line trains.

Most of the fads died out as quickly as they had cropped up, but crossword puzzles remains a daily feature in most newspapers.

CRITICAL THINKING

1. Judging from the pictures, in what ways are the pastimes of today similar to the pastimes of the 20s?
2. One picture is from a poster advertising a movie. List ways in which movies might be valuable as primary source documents. How might movies not be good primary sources?

 281

2. HISTORIAN FREDERICK LEWIS ALLEN REPORTS HOW THE YOUNGER GENERATION RAN WILD

After the war, a revolution in manners and morals rocked the country's youth and eventually spread to older age groups. As this piece, by popular historian Frederick Lewis Allen indicates, there were striking changes in dress and behavior. The selection is taken from Allen's classic work, Only Yesterday.

A FIRST-CLASS revolt against the accepted American order was certainly taking place during those early years of the Post-war Decade, but it was one with which Nikolai Lenin had nothing whatever to do. The shock troops of the rebellion were not alien agitators, but the sons and daughters of well-to-do American families, who knew little about Bolshevism and cared distinctly less, and their defiance was expressed not in obscure radical publications or in soap-box speeches, but right across the family breakfast table into the horrified ears of conservative fathers and mothers. Men and women were still shivering at the Red Menace when they awoke to the no less alarming Problem of the Younger Generation, and realized that if the Constitution were not in danger, the moral code of the country certainly was.

This code, as it currently concerned young people, might have been roughly summarized as follows: Women were the guardians of morality; they were made of finer stuff than men and were expected to act accordingly. Young girls must look forward in innocence (tempered perhaps with a modicum of physiological instruction) to a romantic love match which would lead them to the alter and to living-happily-ever-after; and until the "right man" came along they must allow no male to kiss them. . . . Boys and girls were permitted large freedom to work and play together, with decreasing and well-nigh nominal chaperonage, but only because the code worked so well on the whole that a sort of honor system was supplanting supervision by their elders; it was taken for granted that if they had been well brought up they would never take advantage of this freedom. And although the attitude toward smoking and drinking by girls differed widely in different strata of society and different parts of the country, majority opinion held that it was morally wrong for them to smoke and could hardly imagine them showing the effects of alcohol.

The war had not long been over when cries of alarm from parents, teachers, and moral preceptors began to rend the air. For the boys and girls just growing out of adolescence were making mincemeat of this code.

The dresses that the girls—and for that matter most of the older women—were wearing seemed alarming enough. In July, 1920, a fashion-writer reported in the *New York Times* that "the American woman . . . has lifted her skirts far beyond any modest limitation," which was another way of saying that the hem was now all of nine inches above the ground. It was freely predicted that skirts would come down again in the winter of 1920–21, but instead they climbed a few scandalous inches farther. The flappers wore thin dresses, short-sleeved and occasionally (in the evening) sleeveless; some of the wilder young things rolled their stockings below their knees, revealing to the shocked eyes of virtue a fleeting glance of shinbones and knee-cap; and many of them were visibly using cosmetics. "The intoxication of rouge," earnestly explained Dorothy Speare in *Dancers in the Dark*, "is an insidious vintage known to more girls than mere man can ever believe." Useless for frantic parents to insist that no lady did such things; the answer was that the daughters of ladies were doing it, and even retouching their masterpieces in public. Some of them, furthermore, were abandoning their corsets. "The men won't dance with you if you wear a corset," they were quoted as saying.

The current mode of dancing created still more consternation. Not the romantic violin but the barbaric saxophone now dominated the orchestra, and to its passionate crooning and wailing the fox-trotters moved in what the editor of the Hobart College *Herald* disgustedly called a "syncopated embrace." No longer did even an inch of space separate them; they danced as if glued together, body to body, cheek to cheek.

Supposedly "nice" girls were smoking cigarettes—openly and defiantly, if often rather awkwardly and self-consciously. They were drinking—somewhat less openly but often all too efficaciously. There were stories of daughters of the most exemplary parents getting drunk—

"blotto," as their companions cheerfully put it—on the contents of the hip-flasks of the new prohibition régime, and going out joyriding with men at four in the morning. . . .

It was not until F. Scott Fitzgerald, who had hardly graduated from Princeton and ought to know what his generation was doing, brought out *This Side of Paradise* in April, 1920, that fathers and mothers realized fully what was afoot . . . .

It was incredible. It was abominable. What did it all mean? Was every decent standard being thrown over? . . . But in due course other books appeared to substantiate the findings of Mr. Fitzgerald: *Dancing in the Dark, The Plastic Age, Flaming Youth.* Magazine and newspaper reiterated the scandals. To be sure, there were plenty of communities where nice girls did not, in actual fact, "behave like that"; and even in the more sophisticated urban centers there were plenty of girls who did not. Nevertheless, there was enough fire beneath the smoke of these sensational revelations to make the Problem of the Younger Generation a topic of anxious discussion from coast to coast.

The forces of morality rallied to the attack. Dr. Francis E. Clark, the founder and president of the Christian Endeavor Society, declared that the modern "indecent dance" was "an offense against womanly purity, the very fountainhead of our family and civil life." The new style of dancing was denounced in religious journals as "impure, polluting, corrupting, debasing, destroying spirituality, increasing carnality," and the mothers and sisters and church members of the land were called upon to admonish and instruct and raise the spiritual tone of these dreadful young people. President Murphree of the University of Florida cried out with true Southern warmth, "The low-cut gowns, the rolled hose and short skirts are born of the Devil and his angels, and are carrying the present and future generations to chaos and destruction." A group of Episcopal church-women in New York, speaking with the authority of wealth and social position (for they included Mrs. J. Pierpoint Morgan, Mrs. Borden Harriman, Mrs. Henry Phipps, Mrs. James Roosevelt, and Mrs. E.H. Harriman), proposed an organization to discourage fashions involving an "excess of nudity" and "improper ways of dancing." The Y.W.C.A. conducted a national campaign against immodest

dress among high school girls, supplying newspapers with printed matter carrying headlines such as "Working Girls Responsive to Modesty Appeal" and "High Heels Losing Ground Even in France." In Philadelphia a Dress Reform Committee of prominent citizens sent a questionnaire to over a thousand clergymen to ask them what would be there idea of a proper dress, and although the gentlemen of the cloth showed a distressing variety of opinion, the committee proceeded to design a "moral gown" which was endorsed by ministers of fifteen denominations. The distinguishing characteristics of this moral gown were that it was very loose-fitting, that the sleeves reached just below the elbows, and that the hem came within seven and a half inches of the floor.

Not content with example and reproof, legislators in several states introduced bills to reform feminine dress once and for all. The *New York American* reported in 1921 that a bill was pending in Utah providing fine and imprisonment for those who wore on the streets "skirts higher than three inches above the ankle." A bill was laid before the Virginia legislature which would forbid any woman from wearing shirtwaists or evening gowns which displayed "more than three inches of her throat." In Ohio the proposed limit of decolletage was two inches; the bill introduced in the Ohio legislature aimed also to prevent the sale of any "garment which unduly displays or accentuates the lines of the female figure," and to prohibit any "female over fourteen years of age" from wearing "a skirt which does not reach to that part of the foot known as the instep."

Meanwhile innumerable families were torn with dissension over cigarettes and gin and all-night automobile rides. Fathers and mothers lay awake asking themselves whether their children were not utterly lost; sons and daughters evaded questions, lied miserably and unhappily, or flared up to reply rudely that at least they were not dirty-minded hypocrites, that they saw no harm in what they were doing and proposed to go right on doing it. From those liberal clergymen and teachers who prided themselves on keeping step with all that was new, came a chorus of reassurance: these young people were at least franker and more honest than their elders had been; having experimented from themselves, would they not soon find out which standards were outworn and which represented the accumulated moral wisdom of the race? Hearing such hopeful words, many good people took heart again. Perhaps this flare-up of youthful passion was a flash in the pan, after all. Perhaps in another year or two the boys and girls would come to their senses and everything would be all right again.

They were wrong, however. For the revolt of the younger generation was only the beginning of a revolution in manners and morals that was already beginning to affect men and women of every age in every part of the country.

Selection from Frederick Lewis Allen, *Only Yesterday: An Informal History of the Nineteen-Twenties.* Harper & Brothers, New York, copyright © 1931.

CRITICAL THINKING

1. Cite evidence for the statement that "the moral code" of the country for young women was in danger.
2. What is Allen's point of view on the changes of the 1920s?
3. Contrast the two responses to change in the 1920s as Allen describes them.

---

3. LANGSTON HUGHES REMEMBERS HARLEM IN THE TWENTIES

In his memoir The Big Sea, *noted writer Langston Hughes described what it was like during the 1920s, when Harlem became fashionable. As the following passage suggests, Hughes recognized that the sudden popularity of Harlem would be short-lived.*

White people began to come to Harlem in droves. For several years they packed the expensive Cotton Club on Lenox Avenue. But I was never there, because the Cotton Club was a Jim Crow club for gangsters and monied whites. They were not cordial to Negro patronage, unless you were a celebrity like Bojangles. So Harlem Negroes did not like the Cotton Club and never appreciated its Jim Crow policy in the very heart of their . . . community. Nor did ordinary Negroes like the growing influx of whites toward Harlem after sundown, finding the little cabarets and bars where formerly only colored people laughed and sang, and where now the strangers were given the best ringside tables to sit and stare at the Negro customers—like amusing animals in a zoo. . . .

All of us know that the gay and sparkling life of the so-called Negro Renaissance of the '20's was not so gay and sparkling beneath the surface as it looked. . . .

It was a period when, at almost every Harlem uppercrust dance or party, one would be introduced to various distinguished white celebrities there as guests. . . . It was a period when local and visiting royalty were not at all uncommon in Harlem. . . . It was a period when every season there was at least one hit play on Broadway acted by a Negro cast. And when books by Negro authors were being published with much greater frequency and much more publicly than ever before. . . . It was a period when white writers wrote about Negroes more successfully (commercially speaking) than Negroes did about themselves. . . . It was the period when the Negro was in vogue.

I was there. I had a swell time while it lasted. But I thought it wouldn't last long. . . . But some Harlemites thought the millennium had come. They thought the race problem had at last been solved. . . .

Selection from Langston Hughes, *The Big Sea*. Published by Hill and Wang, New York, copyright © 1940.

CRITICAL THINKING

1. What evidence did Langston Hughes offer to support his idea that the sudden popularity of Harlem did not indicate any deep changes about white attitudes toward black Americans?
2. What was Hughes's attitude toward the whites who made Harlem an "in" spot?

4. MORDECAI JOHNSON SPEAKS OUT ON THE TESTING OF BLACK FAITH

In contrast to the so-called Harlem Renaissance described by Langston Hughes, there was another reality for Black Americans in the Twenties: migration to the cities of the North, poverty and unemployment, the revival of the Ku Klux Klan. In 1922, a Baptist minister from Charleston, West Virginia, Mordecai Wyatt Johnson, addressed the June graduates at Harvard University. His speech pointed out that Blacks were losing faith in the principles of democracy.

Since there emancipation from slavery the masses of American Negroes have lived by the strength of a simple but deeply moving faith. They have believed in the love and providence of a just and holy God; they have believed in the principles of democracy and in the righteous purpose of the Federal Government; and they have believed in the disposition of the American people as a whole and in the long run to be fair in all their dealings.

In spite of disfranchisement and peonage, mob violence and public contempt, they have kept this faith and have allowed themselves to hope with the optimism of Booker T. Washington that in proportion as they grew in intelligence, wealth, and self-respect they should win the confidence and esteem of their fellow white Americans, and should gradually acquire the responsibilities and privileges of full American citizenship.

In recent years, and especially since the Great War, this simple faith has suffered a widespread disintegration. When the United States Government set forth its war aims, called upon Negro soldiers to stand by the colors and Negro civilians, men, women, and children, to devote their labor and earnings to the cause, and when the war shortage of labor permitted a quarter million Negroes to leave the former slave States for the better conditions of the North, the entire Negro people experienced a profound sense of spiritual release. For the first time since emancipation they found themselves comparatively free to sell their labor on the open market for a living wage, found themselves launched on a great world enterprise with a chance to vote in a real and decisive way, and, best of all, in the heat of the struggle they found themselves bound with other Americans in the spiritual fellowship of a common cause.

When they stood on the height of this exalted experience and looked down on their pre-war poverty, impotence, and spiritual isolation, they realized as never before the depth of the harm they had suffered, and there arose in them a mighty hope that in some way the war would work a change in their situation. For a time indeed it seemed that their hope would be realized as never before the depth of the harm they had suffered, and there arose in them a mighty hope that in some way the war would work a change in their situation. For a time indeed it seemed that their hope would be realized. For when the former slave States saw their labor leaving for the North, they began to reflect upon the treatment they had been accustomed to give the Negro, and they decided that it was radically wrong. Newspapers and public orators everywhere expressed this change of sentiment, set forth the wrongs in detail, and urged immediate improvement. And immediate improvement came. Better educational facilities were provided here and there, words of appreciation for the worth and spirit of the Negro as a citizen began to be uttered, and public committees arose to inquire into his grievances and to lay out programs for setting these grievances right. The colored people in these States had never experienced such collective good-will, and many of them were so grateful and happy that they actually prayed for the prolongation of the war.

At the close of the war, however, the Negro's hope were suddenly dashed to the ground. Southern newspapers began at once to tell the Negro soldiers that the war was over and the sooner they forgot it the better. "Pull off your uniform," they said, "find the place you had before the war, and stay in it." "Act like a Negro should act," said one newspaper, "work like a Negro should work, talk like a Negro should talk, study like a Negro should study. Dismiss all ideas of independency or of being lifted up to the plane of the white man. Understand the necessity of keeping a Negro's place." In connection with such admonitions there came the great collective attacks on Negro life and property in Washington, Chicago, Omaha, Elaine, and Tulsa. There came also the increasing boldness of lynchers who advertised their purposes in advance and had their photographs taken around the burning bodies of their victims. There came vain appeals by the colored people to the President of the United States and to the houses of Congress. And finally there came the reorganization and rapid growth of the Ku Klux Klan.

The swift succession and frank brutality of all this was more than the Negro people could bear. Their simple faith and hope broke down. Multitudes took weapons into their own hands and fought back violence with bloody resistance. "If we must die," they said, "it is well that we die fighting." And the Negro American world, looking on their deed with no light of hope to see by, said: "It is self-defense; it is the law of nature, of man, and of God; and it is well."

From those terrible days until this day the Negro's faith in the righteous purpose of the Federal Government has sagged. Some have laid the blame on the parties in power. Some have laid it elsewhere. But all the colored people, in every section of the United States, believe that there is something wrong, and not accidentally wrong, at the very heart of the Government.

Some of our young men are giving up the Christian religion, thinking that their fathers were fools to have believed so long. One group among us repudiates entirely the simple faith of former days. It would put no trust in God, no trust in democracy, and would entertain no hope for betterment under the present form of government. It believes that the United States Government is through and through controlled by selfish capitalists who have no fundamental good-will for Negroes or for any sort of laborers whatever. In their publications and on the platform the members of this group urge the colored man to seek his salvation by alliance with the revolutionary labor movement of America and the world.

Another and larger group among us believes in religion and believes in the principles of democracy, but not in the white man's religion and not in the white man's democracy. It believes that the creed of the former slave States is the tacit creed of the whole nation, and that the Negro may never expect to acquire economic, political, and spiritual liberty in America. This group has held congresses with representatives from the entire Negro world, to lay the foundations of a black empire, a black religion, and a black culture; it has organized the provisional Republic of Africa, set going a multitude of economic enterprises, instituted branches of its organization wherever Negroes are to be found, and binds them together with a newspaper ably edited in two languages.

Whatever one may think of these radical movements and their destiny, one thing is certain: they are home-grown fruits, with roots deep sprung in a world of black American suffering. Their power lies in the appeal which they make to the Negro to find a way out of his trouble by new and self-reliant paths. The larger masses of the colored people do not belong to these more radical movements. They retain their belief in the Christian God, they love their country, and hope to work out their salvation within its bounds. But they are completely disillusioned. They see themselves surrounded on every hand by a sentiment of antagonism which does not intend to be fair. They see themselves partly reduced to peonage, shut out from labor unions, forced to an inferior status before the courts, made subjects of public contempt, lynched and mobbed with impunity, and deprived of the ballot, their only means of social defense. They see this antagonistic sentiment consolidated in the places of power in the former slave States and growing by leaps and bounds in the North and West. They know that it is gradually reducing them to an economic, political, and social caste. And they are now no longer able to believe with Dr. Booker T. Washington, or with any other man, that their own efforts after intelligence, wealth, and self-respect can in any way wise avail to deliver them from these conditions unless they have the protection of a just and beneficent public policy in keeping with American ideals. With one voice, therefore, from pulpit and from press, and from the humblest walks of life, they are sending up a cry of pain and petition such as is heard today among the citizens of no other civilized nation in the world. They are asking for the protection of life, for the security of property, for the liberation of their peons, for the freedom to sell their labor on the open market, for a human being's chance in the courts, for a better system of public education, and for the boon of the ballot. They ask, in short, for public equality under the protection of the Federal Government.

Their request is sustained by every sentiment of humanity and by every holy ideal for which this nation stands. The time has come when the elemental justice called for in this petition should be embodied in a public policy initiated by the Federal Government and continuously supervised by a commission of that Government representing the faith and will of the whole American people.

The Negro people of America have been with us here for three hundred years. They have cut our forests, tilled our fields, built our railroads, fought our battles, and in all of their trials until now they have manifested a simple faith, a grateful heart, a cheerful spirit, and an undivided loyalty to the nation that has been a thing of beauty to behold. Now they have come to the place where their faith can no longer feed on the bread of repression and violence. They ask for the bread of liberty, of public equality, and public responsibility. It must not be denied them.

Selection from Carter G. Woodson, *Negro Orators and Their Orations*. Published by Russell & Russell, New York, copyright © 1925, 1969.

David Walsh, U.S. Senator from Massachusetts, argued against the use of immigration quotas.

CRITICAL THINKING

1. List the benefits of World War I for blacks, according to Johnson.
2. Compare and contrast the reaction of different groups of blacks toward the persecution that followed World War I.

5. MASSACHUSETTS SENATOR DAVID I. WALSH OPPOSES THE NEW IMMIGRATION QUOTAS OF 1924

Not all Americans supported the effort to restrict and regulate the origins of immigrants. The following plea for an end to what he saw as prejudice was made by Massachusetts Senator David Ignatius Walsh in the Senate, on April 15, 1924.

What is the real driving force behind the movement of basing the quota on the census of 1890? The peoples of the world will attribute it to our belief that the "Nordic" is a superior race. The world will assume that our Government considers the Italians, Greeks, Jews, Poles, and the Slavs inferior to the Nordics, congenitally as well as culturally. It is a dangerous

assumption. Millions of people here in America will resent this slur upon their racial character. . . .

The history of this country records that from the beginning the dominant groups in control of its affairs have regarded each group of newer strangers as more or less the "enemy" to be feared and, if possible, controlled. Even as early as the year 1700 . . . when the Dutch came and settled in great numbers in what is now New York City[,] the English and Scotch colonists thought them an inferior and an unwholesome contribution to the population of the colonies. But within a few years these people intermarried and the storm against the previously unwelcome Dutch subsided . . . .

Thus, all down the years, history records this haughty spirit asserting itself again and again whenever a new race of people dared to seek peace and protection in America, but happily this attempted caste control based on the accident of birth, wealth, or privilege has never made any great progress, for such unholy and inhuman prejudices can never prevail in this democracy. . . .

What are the nationalities whose coming to America is chiefly curtailed by this arbitrary resort to the 1890 census? The Greeks, to whom civilization owes so much in the fields of literature, science, art, and government. The Italians, who from the day of early Roman history have contributed immensely to civilization along the lines of government, literature, art, music, and navigation, including the gift of the discoverer of America. The liberty-loving Poles, whose sacrifices and struggles for freedom have arrested the admiration of mankind. . . . The Jews, who contributed to the world literature, religion, standards of righteous conduct that can not be overvalued. . . .

Have we learned nothing from the earlier generations' mistaken notions about the Dutch, the French, the Irish, the Germans, and the Scandinavians . . .? They were condemned and criticized by the earlier settlers, just as we are now undertaking to condemn the races from southern Europe. . . .

Read the names . . . in the American military cemeteries in France. Go there, you who are saying that certain races are undesirable, and read the names upon the graves of the poor lads. . . . Read the names of these dead; read the names of those over whom the poppies now grow, practically all of them foreign born—Poles, Italians, Greeks, and Slavs. . . .

Stop, I urge you, before you announce not only to Americans who are descendants of all the races . . . but to the peoples of the world that certain races are ineligible to enjoy American citizenship.

"Keep America American." Yes; but do not keep out of America through discriminatory immigration laws any lover of liberty, whatever his accident of birth may be, if he is willing to live in America, accept its ideals, and die, if necessary, for the preservation of American institutions.

Selection from speech by David I. Walsh, April 15, 1924, *Congressional Record*, Vol. LXV—Part 7. Published by Government Printing Office, Washington, D.C., copyright © 1924.

CRITICAL THINKING

1. What evidence did David Walsh offer to support his theory that there was a pattern of prejudice against the most recent immigrants?
2. What arguments did he offer against limiting immigration in the proposed way?

6. SOCIOLOGISTS ROBERT AND HELEN LYND STUDY "MIDDLETOWN"

The everyday lives of people living in a Midwestern community during the 1920s was the subject of a classic work, Middletown, *by Robert S. Lynd and Helen Merrell Lynd. They applied the methods of anthropology to an in-depth examination of a small city, which was actually Muncie, Indiana. This selection deals with the ways in which Middletowners earned a living.*

A stranger unfamiliar with the ways of Middletown, dropped down into the city, as was the field staff in January, 1924, would be a lonely person. He would find people intently engaged day after day in some largely routinized, specialized occupation. Only the infants, the totteringly old, and a fringe of women would seem to be available to answer his endless questions.

In a word—

43 people out of every 100 in Middletown are primarily occupied with getting the living of the entire group.

23 of every 100 are engaged in making the homes of the bulk of the city.

19 of every 100 are receiving day after day the training required of the young

15 of every 100, the remainder, are chiefly those under six year, and the very old.

Not only do those engaged in getting the living of the group predominate numerically, but as the study progressed it became more and more apparent that the money medium of exchange and the cluster of activities associated with its acquisition drastically condition the other activities of the people. Rivers begins his study of the Todas with an account of the ritual of the buffalo dairy, because "the ideas borrowed from the ritual of the dairy so pervade the whole of Toda ceremonial." A similar situation leads to the treatment of the activities of Middletown concerned with getting a living first among the six groups of activities to be described. The extent of the dominance of this sector in the lives of the people will appear as the study progresses.

At first glance it is difficult to see any semblance of pattern in the workaday life of a community exhibiting a crazy-quilt array of nearly four hundred ways of getting a living—such diverse things as being abstractors, accountants, auditors, bank cashiers, bank tellers, bookkeepers, cashiers, checkers, core makers, crane operators, craters, crushers, cupola tenders, dye-workers, efficiency engineers, electricians, electrical engineers, embalmers, entomologists, estimating engineers, illuminating engineers, linotypists, mechanical engineers, metallurgists, meteorologists, riggers, riveters, rivet makers, and so on indefinitely. On closer scrutiny, however, this welter may be resolved into two kinds of activities. The people who engage in them will be referred to throughout the report as the Working Class and the Business Class. Members of the first group, by and large, address their activities in getting their living primarily to *things*, utilizing material tools in the making of things and the performance of services, while the members of the second group address their activities predominantly to *people* in the selling or promotion of things, services, and ideas. This second group supplies to Middletown the multitude of non-material institutional activities such as "credit," "legal contract," "education," "sale for a price," "management," and "city government" by which Middletown people negotiate with each other in converting the narrowly specialized product of their workaday lives into "a comfortable evening at home," "a Sunday afternoon out in the car," "fire protection," "a new go-cart for the baby," and all the other things that constitute living in Middletown. If the Federal Census distribution of those gainfully employed in Middletown in 1920 is reclassified according to this grouping we find that there are two and one-half times as many in the working class as in the business class—seventy-one in each 100 as against twenty-nine.

No such classification is entirely satisfactory. The aerial photographer inevitably sacrifices minor contours as he ascends high enough to view a total terrain. Within these two major groups there is an infinite number of gradations—all the way from the roughest day laborer to the foreman, the foundry molder, and the linotype operator in the one group, and from the retail clerk and cashier to the factory owner and professional man in the other. There is naturally, too, a twilight belt in which some members of the two groups overlap or merge.

Were a minute structural diagram the aim of this study, it would be necessary to decipher in much greater detail the multitude of overlapping groupings observable in Middletown. Since what is sought, however, is an understanding of the major functional characteristics of this changing culture, it is important that significant outlines be not lost in detail, and the groups in the city which exhibit the dominant characteristics most clearly must, therefore, form the foci of the report. While an effort will be made to make clear at certain points variant behavior within these two groups, it is after all this division into working class and business class that constitutes the outstanding cleavage in Middletown. The mere fact of being born upon one or the other side of the watershed roughly formed by these two groups is the most significant single cultural factor tending to influence what one does all day long throughout one's life; whom one marries; when one gets up in the morning; whether one belongs to the Holy Roller or the Presbyterian church; or drives a Ford or a Buick; whether or not one's daughter makes the desirable high school Violet Club; or one's wife meets with the Sew We Do Club or with the Art Students' League; whether one belongs to the Odd Fellows or to the Masonic Shrine; whether one sits about evenings with one's necktie off; and so on indefinitely throughout the daily comings and goings of a Middletown man, woman, or child.

Wherever throughout the report either Middletown or any group within the city is referred to as a unit, such a mode of expression must be regarded as simply a shorthand symbol. Any discussions of characteristics of groups are of necessity approximations only and the fact that the behavior of individuals is the basis of social behavior must never be lost sight of.

Selection from Robert S. Lynd and Helen Merrell Lynd, *Middletown: A Study in American Culture.* Published by Harcourt, Brace and Co., New York, copyright © 1929.

CRITICAL THINKING

1. Using the Lynds' categories, classify the following occupations: rigger, welder, salesman, electrician, advertising writer.
2. Explain the effect belonging to the business or working class has on a person.

CHAPTER 27

PROSPERITY AND CRASH

1923–1929

1. EDWARD EARLE PURINTON OFFERS A TRIBUTE TO THE BUSINESS GAME

For many Americans during the 1920s, the business of America, as President Calvin Coolidge put it, "was business." Business—and business people—were treated, in many quarters, with an admiration and regard not seen before in America. The following statements about business come from an article published in 1921.

The finest game is business. The rewards are for everybody, and all can win. There are no favorites—Providence always crowns the career of the man who is worthy. And in this game there is no "luck"—you have the fun of taking chances but the sobriety of guaranteeing certainties. The speed and size of your winnings are for you alone to determine; you needn't wait for the other fellow in the game—it is always your move. . . . The great sportsmen of the world are the great business men.

The soundest science is business. All investigation is reduced to action, and by action proved or disproved. The idealistic motive animates the materialistic method. . . .

The fullest education is business. A proper blend of study, work, and life is essential to advancement. . . .

The sanest religion is business. Any relationship that forces a man to follow the Golden Rule rightfully belongs amid the ceremonials of the church. A great business enterprise includes and presupposes this relationship. . . .

The future work of the business man is to teach the teacher, preach to the preacher, admonish the parent, advise the doctor, justify the lawyer, superintend the statesman, fructify the farmer, stabi-

lize the banker, harness the dreamer, and reform the reformer.

Selection from Edward Earle Purinton, "Big Ideas from Big Business," *The Independent*, April 16, 1921.

CRITICAL THINKING

1. What evidence did Edward Purinton offer to justify giving business people such an important role?
2. What attitude did Purinton seem to have toward those who were not involved in business?

2. WISCONSIN SENATOR AND 1924 PROGRESSIVE PARTY PRESIDENTIAL CANDIDATE ROBERT LA FOLLETTE SPEAKS OUT AGAINST MONOPOLISTIC POWER

Despite general prosperity—and popular enthusiasm for business and the stock market—the spirit of reform remained alive in much of America. In 1924, Senator Robert La Follette of Wisconsin, who had tried for the nomination in 1912, became the presidential candidate of the Progressive Party. These passages from La Follette's announcement of his candidacy on July 3, 1924, suggest that the Progressive era's concerns were still a part of the American scene.

After long experience in public life and painstaking consideration of the present state of public affairs, I am convinced that the time has come for a militant political movement, independent of the two old party organizations, and responsive to the needs and sentiments of the common people. . . .

The necessity for an independent Progressive movement lies in the failure of the two old parties to purge themselves of the influences which have caused their administrations repeatedly to betray the American people. . . .

The rank and file of the membership of both old parties is Progressive. But through a vicious and undemocratic convention system and under the evil influences which have been permitted to thrive at Washington, both party organizations have fallen under the domination and control of corrupt wealth, devoting the powers of government exclusively to selfish political interests. . . .

To break the combined power of the private monopoly system over the political and economic life of the American people is the one paramount issue of the 1924 campaign.

If the Progressives will but unite with a single purpose to meet this issue fearlessly and squarely they may rely with entire confidence upon the support of the plain people who are the victims of the present system and who have the right and the power, through the ballot, to control their own government.

Selection from *History of U.S. Political Parties*, Vol. III, edited by Arthur M. Schlesinger, Jr. Published by Chelsea House, New York, copyright © 1973.

CRITICAL THINKING

1. What element of the electorate was Senator La Follette counting on for his presidential bid?
2. Why might the voters have rejected the platform of the Progressive Party?

3. PRESIDENT CALVIN COOLIDGE VETOES A REFORM BILL

The prevailing attitude toward government in the 1920s was not one of reform. Instead, people seemed to look toward their leaders to do as little as possible to interfere with the workings of the American economic and social system. It was precisely this view that President Calvin Coolidge voiced in his veto of the McNary-Haugen Bill, an attempt to stabilize agricultural income and prices.

A bureaucratic tyranny of unprecedented proportions would be let down upon the backs of the farm industry and its distributors throughout the Nation in connection with the enforcement of this measure. Thousands of contracts involving scores of different grades, quantities, and varieties of products would have to be signed by the board with the 4,400 millers, the 1,200 meat-packing plants, the 3,000 or more cotton and woolen mills, and the 2,700 canners. If this bill had been in operation in 1925, it would have involved collections upon an aggregate of over 16,000,000,000 units of wheat, corn, and cotton.

The bill undertakes to provide insurance against loss, but presumably only against unreasonable and unavoidable loss. Just what this might be would involve judgment on the part of Government employees upon tens of thousands of transactions running into billions of dollars. This is bureaucracy gone mad. Cooperative associations, flour mills, packing plants, and grain elevators will cease to be private and become public agencies.

Swarms of inspectors, auditors, disbursers, accountants, and regulatory officers would be let loose throughout the land to enforce the terms of these contracts and to curb the inevitable attempts at evasion of the equalization fee. This plague of petty officialdom would set up an intolerable tyranny over the daily lives and operations of farmers and of every individual and firm engaged in the distribution of farm products, intruding into every detail of their affairs, setting up thousands of prohibitory restrictions and obnoxious inspections.

Such autocratic domination over our major industry, its dependent trades, and the everyday activities of hundreds of thousands of our citizens would indeed be profoundly repugnant to every instinct of our institutions. It would undermine individual initiative, place a premium upon evasion and dishonesty, and poison the very wellsprings of our national spirit of providing abundant rewards for thrift and for open competitive effort.

Selection from "Calvin Coolidge McNary-Haugen Bill Veto Message, May 23, 1928," *History of U.S. Political Parties*, Vol. III, edited by Arthur M. Schlesinger, Jr. Published by Chelsea House, New York, copyright © 1973.

CRITICAL THINKING

1. Summarize President Coolidge's objections to the bill.
2. What techniques did Coolidge use to emphasize what he saw as the dangers of the bill?

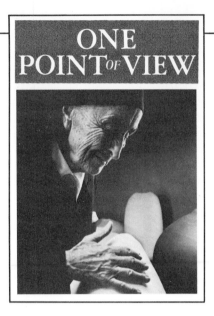

ONE POINT OF VIEW

GEORGIA O'KEEFFE

T he 1920s was a decade of exuberant confidence in the future.

Georgia O'Keeffe [born in 1887] is a major figure in the development of American abstract art. She studied in the best art schools of Chicago and New York, where she learned about the traditional art of the past and also the new European art movements. O'Keeffe worked as a commercial artist and a public school teacher while practising her painting. By 1915 she had gained the skill and understanding she needed to create her own style, one which is simplified, uncluttered, and revealing of her personal vision.

O'Keeffe believes that nature and art can be interwoven and even compliment one another. In her art she imposes abstract design on natural forms. She arranges plants, rocks, bones, clouds, flowers, and a variety of other natural shapes in well-ordered compositions. Her paintings affirm her faith that the progress of the modern world will be orderly and life-affirming.

With its dense skyline of tall buildings and smokestacks, "The East River from the Shelton" is modern, yet true to O'Keeffe's feelings for nature.

"Ranchos Church 1" is the first in a series of paintings of an eighteenth century adobe church. The simplicity and spare elegance of O'Keeffe's abstract style emphasize the shapes of the old church's massive architecture.

Georgia O'Keeffe lived in New York and New Mexico. The grey weatherbeaten barns of the East inspired this massive building that could be compared to the natural stone structures of the West.

"Black Hollyhock, Blue Larkspur" evokes a weightless feeling. Isolated from surroundings, the flowers assume a new significance.

CRITICAL THINKING

1. O'Keeffe is known for optimistic, positive statements in her art. What symbols in these paintings express this optimism?
2. Compare and contrast two aspects of Georgia O'Keeffe's paintings. First, deal with her painting style. Is it consistent? Next, discuss the subject matter she chose.

4. PRESIDENT CALVIN COOLIDGE DEFENDS AMERICAN INTERVENTION IN NICARAGUA

Nicaragua was one of the Latin American countries where American business investors had substantial investments. In 1927, when political disturbances in Nicaragua seemed to threaten United States business interests, President Calvin Coolidge sent a special message to Congress explaining why it was necessary to send marines there to preserve order.

It is well known that in 1912 the United States intervened in Nicaragua with a large force and put down a revolution, and that from that time to 1925 a legation guard of American marines was, with the consent of the Nicaraguan Government, kept in Managua to protect American lives and property. In 1923 representatives of the five Central American countries, namely Costa Rica, Guatemala, Honduras, Nicaragua, and Salvador, at the invitation of the United States, met in Washington and entered into a series of treaties. These treaties dealt with limitation of armament, a Central American tribunal for arbitration, and the general subject of peace and amity. The treaty last referred to specifically provides . . . that the Governments of the contracting parties will not recognize any other government which may come into power in any of the five Republics through a coup d'état, or revolution, and disqualifies the leaders of such coup d'etat, or revolution, from assuming the presidency or vice presidency . . .

The United States was not a party to this treaty, but it was made in Washington under the auspices of the Secretary of State, and this Government has felt a moral obligation to apply its principles in order to encourage the Central American States in their efforts to prevent revolution and disorder.

. . . The Nicaraguan constitution provides in article 106 that in the absence of the President and Vice President the Congress shall designate one of its members to complete the unexpired term of President . . . the action of Congress in designating Senor Diaz was perfectly legal and in accordance with the constitution. Therefore the United States Government on November 17 extended recognition to Senor Diaz. . . .

Immediately following the inauguration of President Diaz and frequently since that date he has appealed to the United States for support, has informed this Goverment of the aid which Mexico is giving to the revolutionists, and has stated that he is unable solely because of the aid given by Mexico to the revolutionists to protect the lives and property of American citizens and other foreigners. When negotiations leading up to the Corinto conferences began, I immediately placed an embargo on the shipment of arms and ammunition to Nicaragua. . . .

At the end of November, after spending some time in Mexico City, Doctor Sacasa went back to Nicaragua, landing at Puerto Cabezas, near Bragmans Bluff. He immediately placed himself at the head of the insurrection and declared himself President of Nicaragua. He has never been recognized by any of the Central American Republics nor by any other government, with the exception of Mexico, which recognized him immediately. As arms and munitions in large quantities were reaching the revolutionists, I deemed it unfair to prevent the recognized government from purchasing arms abroad, and, accordingly, the Secretary of State has notified the Diaz Government that licenses would be issued for the export of arms and munitions purchased in this country. It would be thoroughly inconsistent for this country not to support the government recognized by it while the revolutionists were receiving arms and munitions from abroad. . . .

For many years numerous Americans have been living in Nicaragua, developing its industries and carrying on business. At the present time there are large investments in lumbering, mining, coffee growing, banana culture, shipping, and also in general mercantile and other collateral business.

In addition to these industries now in existence, the Government of Nicaragua, by a treaty entered into on the 5th day of August, 1914, granted in perpetuity to the United States the exclusive proprietary rights necessary and convenient for the construction, operation, and maintenance of an oceanic canal. . . .

There is no question that if the revolution continues American investments and business interests in Nicaragua will be very seriously affected, if not destroyed.

Manifestly the relation of this Government to the Nicaraguan situation and its policy in the existing emergency, are determined by the facts which I have described. The proprietary rights of the United States in the Nicaraguan canal route, with the necessary implications growing out of it affecting the Panama Canal, together with the obligations flowing from the investments of all classes of our citizens in Nicaragua, place us in a position of peculiar responsibility. I am sure it is not the desire of the United States to intervene in the internal affairs of Nicaragua or of any other Central American Republic. Nevertheless it must be said that we have a very definite and special interest in the maintenance of order and good government in Nicaragua at the present time, and that the stability, prosperity, and independence of all Central American countries can never be a matter of indifference to us. The United States can not, therefore, fail to view with deep concern any serious threat to stability and constitutional government in Nicaragua tending toward anarchy and jeopardizing American interests, especially if such state of affairs is contributed to or brought about by outside influences or by any foreign power. It has always been and remains the policy of the United States in such cicumstances to take the steps that may be necessary for the preservation and protection of the lives, the property, and the interests of its citizens and of this Government itself. In this respect I propose to follow the path of my predecessors.

Consequently, I have deemed it my duty to use the powers committed to me to insure the adequate protection of all American interests in Nicaragua, whether then by endangered by internal strife or by outside interference in the affairs of that Republic.

Selection from *Documents of American History*, edited by Henry Steele Commager. Published by Appleton»Century-Crofts, Inc., New York, copyright © 1958.

CRITICAL THINKING

1. List in chronological order the major events mentioned by Coolidge from the time the U.S. first intervened in Nicaragua in 1912.
2. Summarize Coolidge's arguments for the need to intervene in Nicaragua.

THE DEPRESSION AND THE NEW DEAL
1929–1937

1. IOWA LAWYER REMLEY GLASS REFLECTS ON THE HARDSHIPS FACING FARMERS IN THE CORN BELT DURING THE GREAT DEPRESSION

Few Americans were prepared for the extent—and duration—of the economic crisis set off by the stock-market crash of 1929. People quickly learned that no one was immune to the effects of the Great Depression. The following comments, taken from an article written by Remley Glass, an Iowa attorney, show some of the effects the Depression had on farmers in one of Iowa's more prosperous farming communities.

Men who had sunk every dollar they possessed in the purchase, upkeep, and improvement of their home places were turned out with small amounts of personal property as their only assets. Landowners who had regarded farm land as the ultimate in safety, after using their outside resources in vain attempts to hold their lands, saw these assets go under the sheriff's hammer [at bankruptcy auctions] on the courthouse steps.

During the two-year period of 1931–1932, in this formerly prosperous Iowa county, twelve and a half per cent of the farms went under the hammer, and almost twenty-five percent of the mortgaged farm real estate was foreclosed. And the conditions in my home county have been substantially duplicated in every one of the ninety-nine counties of Iowa and in those of the surrounding States.

We lawyers of the Corn Belt have had to develop a new type of practice, for in pre-war days foreclosure litigation amounted to but a small part

 295

of the general practice. In these years of the depression almost one-third of the cases filed have to do with this situation. Our courts are clogged with such matters. . . .

Men and women who have lived industrious, comfortable, and contented lives have faced bravely the loss of luxuries and comforts, but there is a decided change in their attitude toward the financial and economic powers that be when conditions take away their homes and imperil the continued existence of their families.

Selection from Remley Glass, "Gentlemen, the Corn Belt," *Harper's Monthly Magazine*, July, 1933.

CRITICAL THINKING

1. What was Remley Glass's attitude toward the farmers of the area?
2. What changes were taking place in Corn Belt people's attitudes because of the Depression?

2. WRITER JAMES AGEE BRINGS TO LIFE THE PLIGHT OF THE SHARECROPPER

One of the most evocative accounts of the Great Depression and what it meant for rural America was written by James Agee in 1941. His Let Us Now Praise Famous Men *was illustrated with Walker Evans' photographs of sharecroppers.*

WOODS and Ricketts work for Michael and T. Hudson Margraves, two brother, in partnership, who live in Cookstown. Gudger worked for the Margraves for three years; he now (1936) works for Chester Boles, who lives two miles south of Cookstown. . . .

Gudger has no home, no land, no mule; none of the more important farming implements. He must get all these of his landlord. Boles, for his share of the corn and cotton, also advances him rations money during four months of the year, March through June, and his fertilizer.

Gudger pays him back with his labor and with the labor of his family.

At the end of the season he pays him back further; with half his corn; with half his cotton;

with half his cottonseed. Out of his own half of these crops he also pays him back the rations money, plus interest, and his share of the fertilizer, plus interest, and such other debts, plus interest, as he may have incurred.

What is left, once doctor's bills and other debts have been deducted, is his year's earnings.

Gudger is a straight half-cropper, or sharecropper.

Woods and Ricketts own no home and no land, but Woods owns one mule and Ricketts owns two, and they own their farming implements. Since they do not have to rent these tools and animals, they work under slightly different arrangement. They give over to the landlord only a third of their cotton and a fourth of their corn. Out of their own parts of the crop, however, they owe him the price of two thirds of their cotton fertilizer and three fourths of their corn fertilizer, plus interest; and, plus interest, the same debts or rations money.

Woods and Ricketts are tenants: they work on third and fourth.

A very few tenants pay cash rent: but these two types of arrangement, with local variants (company stores; food instead of rations money; slightly different divisions of the crops) are basic to cotton tenantry all over the South.

From March through June, while the cotton is being cultivated, they live on the rations money.

From July through to late August, while the cotton is making, they live however they can.

From late August through October or into November, during the picking and ginning season, they live on the money from their share of the cottonseed.

From then on until March, they live on whatever they have earned in the year; or however the can.

During six to seven months of each year, then—that is, during exactly such time as their labor with the cotton is of absolute necessity to the landlord—they can be sure of whatever living is possible in rations advances and in cottonseed money.

During five to six months of the year, of which three are the hardest months of any year, with the worst of weather, the least adequacy of shelter, the worst and least of food, the worst of health, quite normal and inevitable, they can count on nothing except that they may hope least of all for any help from their landlords.

Gudger—a family of six—lives on ten dollars a month rations money during four months of the year. He has lived on eight, and on six. Woods—a family of six—until this year was unable to get better than eight a month during the same period; this year he managed to get it up to ten. Ricketts—a family of nine—lives on ten dollars a month during this spring and early summer period.

This debt is paid back in the fall at eight per cent interest. Eight per cent is charged also on the fertilizer and on all other debts which tenants incur in this vicinity.

At the normal price, a half-sharing tenant gets about six dollars a bale from his share of the cottonseed. A one-mule, half-sharing tenant makes on the average three bales. This half-cropper, then, Gudger, can count on eighteen dollars, more or less, to live on during the picking and ginning: though he gets nothing until his first bale is ginned.

Working on third and fourth, a tenant gets the money from two thirds of the cottonseed of each bale. Woods, with a mule, makes three bales, and gets twenty-seven dollars. Ricketts, with two mules, makes and gets twice that, to live on during the late summer and fall.

What is earned at the end of a given year is never to be depended on and, even late in a season, is never predictable. It can be enough to tide through the dead months of the winter, sometimes even better: it can be enough, spread very thin, to take through two months, and a sickness, or six weeks, or a month: it can be little enough to be completely meaningless: it can be nothing: it can be enough less than nothing to insure a tenant only of an equally hopeless lack of money at the end of his next year's work: and whatever one year may bring in the way of good luck, there is never any reason to hope that that luck will be repeated in the next year or the year after that.

The best that Woods has ever cleared was $1300 during a war year. During the teens and twenties he fairly often cleared as much as $300; he fairly often cleared $50 and less; two or three times he ended the year in debt. During the depression years he has more often cleared $50 and less; last year he cleared $150, but serious illness during the winter ate it up rapidly.

The best that Gudger has ever cleared is $125. That was in the plow-under year. He felt exceedingly hopeful and bought a mule: but when his landlord warned him of how he was coming out the next year, he sold it. Most years he has not made more then $25 to $30; and about one year in three he has ended in debt. Year before last he wound up $80 in debt; last year, $12; of Boles, his new landlord, the first thing he had to do was borrow $15 to get through the winter until rations advances should begin.

Years ago the Ricketts were, relatively speaking, almost prosperous. Besides their cotton farming they had ten cows and sold the milk, and they lived near a good stream and had all the fish they wanted. Ricketts went $400 into debt on a fine young pair of mules. One of the mules died before it had made its first crop; the other died the year after; against his fear, amounting to full horror, of sinking to the half-crop level where nothing is owned, Ricketts went into debt for other, inferior mules: his cows went one by one into debts and desperate exchanges and by sickness; he got congestive chills; his wife got pellagra; a number of his children died; he got appendicitis and lay for days on end under the ice cap; his wife's pellagra got into her brain; for ten consecutive years now, though they have lived on so little rations money, and have turned nearly all their cottonseed money toward their debts, they have not cleared or had any hope of clearing a cent at the end of the year.

It is not often, then, at the end of the season, that a tenant clears enough money to tide him through the winter, or even an appreciable part of it. More generally he can count on it that, during most of the four months between settlement time in the fall and the beginning of work and the resumption of rations advances in the early spring, he will have no money and can expect none, nor any help, from his landlord: and of having no money during the six midsummer weeks of laying by, he can be still more sure. Four to six months of each year, in other words, he is much more likely than not to have nothing whatever, and during these months he must take care of himself: he is no responsibility of the landlord's. All he can hope to do is find work. This is hard, because there are a good many chronically unemployed in the towns, and they are more convenient to most openings for work and can at all times be counted on if they are needed; also there is no increase, during these two dead farming seasons, of other kinds of work to do. And so, with no more jobs open than at any other time of year, and with plenty of men already convenient to take them, the whole tenant population, hundreds and thousands in any locality, are desperately in need of work.

A landlord saves up certain odd jobs for these times of year: they go, at less than he would have to pay others, in those of his tenants who happen to live nearest or to those of his tenants who he thinks best of; and even at best they don't amount to much.

When there is wooded land on the farm, a landlord ordinarily permits a tenant to cut and sell firewood for what he can get. About the best a tenant gets of this is a dollar a load, but more often (for the market is glutted, so many are trying to sell wood) he can get no better than half that and less, and often enough, at the end of a hard day's peddling, miles from home, he will let it go for a quarter or fifteen cents rather than haul it all the way home again: so it doesn't amount to much. Then, too, by no means everyone has wood to cut and sell; in the whole southern half of the county we were working mainly in, there was so little wood that the negroes, during the hard winter of 1935–36, were burning parts of their fences, outbuildings, furniture and houses, and were dying off in great and not seriously counted numbers, of pnemonia and other afflictions of the lungs.

WPA work is available to very few tenants: they are, technically, employed, and thus have no right to it: and if by chance they manage to get it, landlords are more likely than not to intervene. They feel it spoils a tenant to be paid wages, even for a little while. A tenant who so much as tries to get such work is under disapproval.

There is not enough direct relief even for the widows and the old of the country.

Gudger and Ricketts, during this year, were exceedingly lucky. After they, and Woods, had been turned away from government work, they found work in a sawmill. They were given the work on condition that they stay with it until the mill was moved, and subject strictly to their landlords' permission: and their employer wouldn't so much as hint how long the work might last. Their landlords quite grudgingly gave them

permission, on condition that they pay for whatever help was needed in their absence during the picking season. Gudger hired a hand, at eight dollars a month and board. Ricketts did not need to: his family is large enough. They go a dollar and a quarter a day five days a week and seventy-five cents on Saturday, seven dollars a week, ten hours' work a day. Woods did not even try for this work: he was too old and too sick.

Selection from James Agee and Walker Evans, *Let Us Now Praise Famous Men*. Published by Ballantine Books, New York, copyright © 1941.

CRITICAL THINKING

1. Compare and contrast the condition of a sharecropper with that of a tenant farmer.
2. Explain why very few tenant farmers were able to take WPA work.
3. Cite evidence for the statement, "Gudger and Ricketts, during this year, were extremely lucky."

---

3. PRESIDENT HERBERT HOOVER REJECTS MAJOR GOVERNMENTAL CONTROLS OF THE ECONOMIC SYSTEM AS A CURE FOR THE GREAT DEPRESSION

The policies undertaken by the Hoover Administration seemed to have little effect on the economic crises set off by the stock-market crash of 1929. As the Depression worsened, more and more Americans lost confidence in President Herbert Hoover and his policies. The President, however, was firm in his convictions about the need for "rugged individualism" and the avoidance of major intervention by the federal government. The following remarks were made as part of Hoover's acceptance speech during the Republican National Convention of 1932.

The last three years have been a time of unparalleled economic calamity. They have been years of greater suffering and hardship than any which have come to the American people since the aftermath of the Civil War. . . .

If we look back over the disasters of these three years, we find that three quarters of the population of the globe has suffered from the flames of revolution. Many nations have been subject to constant change and vacillation of government. Others have resorted to dictatorship or tyranny in desperate attempts to preserve some sort of social order. . . .

In a large sense the test of success of our program is simple. Our people, while suffering great hardships, have been and will be cared for. In the long view our institutions have been sustained intact and are now functioning with increasing confidence of the future. As a nation we are undefeated and unafraid. Government by the people has not been defiled. . . .

Before I enter upon a discussion of [our] policies I wish to say something of my conception of the relation of our Government to the people and of the responsibilities of both, particularly as applied to these times. The spirit and devising of this Government by the people was to sustain a dual purpose—on the one hand to protect our people among nations and in domestic emergencies by great national power, and on the other to preserve individual liberty and freedom through local government.

The function of the Federal Government in these times is to use its reserve powers and its strength for the protection of citizens and local governments by supporting our institutions against forces beyond their control. It is not the function of the Government to relieve individuals of their responsibilities to their neighbors or to relieve private institutions of their responsibilities to the public, or of local government to the States, or of State governments to the Federal Government. In giving that protection and that aid the Federal Government must insist that all of them exert their responsibilities in full. It is vital that the programs of the Government shall not compete with or replace any of them but shall add to their initiative and their strength. It is vital that by the use of public revenues and public credit in emergency the Nation shall be strengthened and not weakened.

And in all these emergencies and crises, and in all our future policies, we must also preserve the fundamental principles of our social and economic system. That system is founded upon a conception of ordered freedom. The test of that freedom is that there should be maintained equality of opportunity to every individual so that he may achieve for himself the best to which his character, ability, and ambition entitle him. It is only by this release of initiative, this insistence upon individual responsibility, that we accrue the great sums of individual accomplishment which carry this Nation forward. . . .

The solution of our many problems which arise from the shifting scene of national life is not to be found in haphazard experimentation or by revolution. It must be through organic development of our national life under these ideals. It must secure that cooperative action which builds initiative and strength outside of government. It does not follow because our difficulties are stupendous, because there are some souls timorous enough to doubt the validity and effectiveness of our ideals and our system, that we must turn to a State-controlled or State-directed social or economic system in order to cure our troubles. That is not liberalism; it is tyranny. It is the regimentation of men under autocratic bureaucracy with all its extinction of liberty, of hope, and of opportunity. Of course, no man of understanding says that our system works perfectly. It does not. The human race is not perfect. Nevertheless, the movement of a true civilization is toward freedom rather than regimentation. This is our ideal.

Selection from Herbert C. Hoover, "Acceptance Speech," August 11, 1932, in *Campaign Speeches of American Presidential Candidates: 1928–1972*. Published by Frederick Ungar, New York, copyright © 1976.

CRITICAL THINKING

1. What arguments did Herbert Hoover use to support his view that the federal government should not become the major force in combatting the Depression?
2. What political and social goals did Hoover have for the United States?
3. What dangers did he see in increased government activity during the economic crisis?

UNLOCKING HISTORY
COMMENTARY

President Franklin D. Roosevelt and the Great Depression

By the fall of 1932, the United States seemed to be paralyzed by the Great Depression. For three years, the values of shares on the stock market had sunk to record low levels. Because banks had loaned so much money to people who were buying stocks, many loans were unpaid and banks went bankrupt, closing their doors. This wiped out the small savings accounts of ordinary middle class and working people.

With money hard to come by, manufacturers found that the markets for their goods had disappeared. Employers had to reduce their employees' pay and the number of hours they could work. Other employers simply laid off many of their workers and some factories closed down completely. When unemployed city dwellers were forced to cut back on their own purchases, including even food, farmers suffered. Homeowners could not pay their mortgages. Farmers could not pay back loans they had made. Hundreds of thousands of property-owners lost their homes and their land.

Single men rode freight trains looking for work. Families wandered the country in decrepit, Model T Fords. In the cities, unemployed workers sat on park benches, their heads in their hands. Homeless women and children slept in doorways or moved into *Hoovervilles*. Hoovervilles were clusters of shacks made out of junk wood and discarded cardboard and sheet metal. They were named after Republican President Herbert Hoover. It was a way to tell Hoover that many Americans blamed him for the economic disaster.

President Hoover was not responsible for the Great Depression. However, he seemed helpless in his efforts to fight it. To many people, it seemed as if he sat in the White House doing nothing. Hoover, never known for having an exciting personality, now seemed like a messenger of gloom and doom on the few occasions he appeared in public. In fact, Hoover was handicapped in his attempts to fight the Depression by a strict belief that government should not interfere too much in the workings of the economy.

His Democratic Party opponent in the election of 1932, Governor Franklin D. Roosevelt of New York, had no more of a plan to fight the Depression than Hoover did. However, Roosevelt did believe that government had a duty to help the people who were suffering the most from the economic disaster.

Perhaps more important, "FDR" (as he was affectionately called) had a cheerful, outgoing, and charming personality. If he had no specific plan, he did have confidence in himself and the ability of the American people to overcome their difficulties. He was a pragmatic leader— willing to try anything that might work, discard it if it failed, and try something else.

More than anything else, it was because of FDR's self-confidence and willingness to take action that Americans elected him president in November 1932. In his Inaugural Address, delivered on March 4, 1933, he issued a ringing proclamation of faith in the future. That the sun broke through the wintry gray clouds when he began to speak, seemed symbolically hopeful.

It would be a long, hard fight before the Depression was over. But to a majority of voters, hope was possible because at least the government was doing something. Never while he lived would a majority of American voters fail to support Franklin D. Roosevelt as their leader. He was elected four times, the only person ever to be elected president more than twice.

UNLOCKING HISTORY
KEY DOCUMENT

*T*his is a day of national consecration, and I am certain that my fellow-Americans expect that on my induction into the Presidency I will address them with a candor and a decision which the present situation of our nation impels.

This is pre-eminently the time to speak the truth, the whole truth, frankly and boldly. Nor need we shrink from honestly facing conditions in our country today. This great nation will endure as it has endured, will revive and will prosper.

So first of all let me assert my firm belief that the only thing we have to fear is fear itself—nameless, unreasoning, unjustified terror which paralyzes needed efforts to convert retreat into advance.

In every dark hour of our national life a leadership of frankness and vigor has met with that understanding and support of the people themselves which is essential to victory. I am convinced that you will again give that support to leadership in these critical days.

In such a spirit on my part and on yours we face our common difficulties. They concern, thank God, only material things. Values have shrunken to fantastic levels; taxes have risen; our ability to pay has fallen, government of all kinds is faced by serious curtailment of income; the means of exchange are frozen in the currents of trade; the withered leaves of industrial enterprise lie on every side; farmers find no markets for their produce; the savings of many years in thousands of families are gone.

More important, a host of unemployed citizens face the grim problem of existence, and an equally great number toil with little return. Only a foolish optimist can deny the dark realities of the moment.

Yet our distress comes from no failure of substance. We are stricken by no plague of locusts. Compared with the perils which our forefathers conquered because they believed and were not afraid, we have still much to be thankful for. Nature still offers her bounty and human efforts have multiplied it. Plenty is at our doorstep, but a generous use of it languishes in the very sight of the supply.

Happiness lies not in the mere possession of money; it lies in the joy of achievement, in the thrill of creative effort.

The joy and moral stimulation of work no longer must be forgotten in the mad chase of evanescent profits. These dark days will be worth all they cost us if they teach us that our true destiny is not to be ministered unto but to minister to ourselves and to our fellow-men.

Recognition of the falsity of material wealth as the standard of success goes hand in hand with the abandonment of the false belief that public office and high political position are to be valued only by the standards of pride of place and personal profit; and there must be an end to a conduct in banking and in business which too often has given to a sacred trust the likeness of callous and selfish wrongdoing.

Small wonder that confidence languishes, for it thrives only on honesty, on honor, on the sacredness of obligations, on faithful protection, on unselfish performance. Without them it cannot live.

Restoration calls, however, not for changes in ethics alone. This nation asks for action, and action now.

Selection from *Public Papers and Addresses of Franklin D. Roosevelt*, Vol. II, 1933. Published by Random House, New York, 1937.

CRITICAL THINKING

1. In President Roosevelt's Inaugural Address, why do you think he deliberately used words such as "fear" and "terror"?
2. Define what Roosevelt meant by "happiness."
3. Compare the personal styles of presidents Hoover and Roosevelt.

MARGARET BOURKE-WHITE

Bourke-White's photograph of Montana's Fort Peck Dam (above) appeared on LIFE's *first cover. An interior view is shown below.*

Margaret Bourke-White [1906–1971] was a premier photojournalist of her time. Early in her career, her ground-breaking images of American industry illustrated the pages of the business magazine, *Fortune*. In 1936, when *Fortune*'s publishers founded *Life*, she became one of the magazine's first staff photographers. A Bourke-White photograph appeared on the cover of the first issue of *Life*.

In the 1930s and 1940s, Bourke-White's assignments ranged from Germany and Russia, to the Canadian Arctic, and America's "Dust Bowl." Her work included taking portraits of important world leaders, such as Winston Churchill, Joseph Stalin, and Mohandas Gandhi. During World War II, she was one of very few female war correspondents. Beside the routine danger of accompanying bombing raids, she once escaped from a torpedoed troop ship on a lifeboat. She covered the Italian and North African fronts, as well as the release of concentration camp prisoners in Germany. Stories she photographed after the war included India's independence struggle, the Korean war, and racial and labor unrest in South Africa.

CRITICAL THINKING

1. How did Bourke-White's photojournalism differ from that of Jacob Riis? (page 204)
2. Why do you think Bourke-White's photographs engaged imaginations?

Starting her career as a war correspondent, Bourke-White personally witnessed the beginning of the war, in 1941, between Germany and Russia and recorded the German bombing of Moscow.

Mohandas K. Gandhi was photographed at his spinning wheel in April, 1946. Bourke-White covered Indian independence in 1947 and stayed in the country long enough to witness Gandhi's tragic death.

4. PRESIDENTIAL ADVISOR RAYMOND MOLEY REMINISCES ON THE "FIRST HUNDRED DAYS" OF FDR'S ADMINISTRATION

The first hundred days of President Franklin Delano Roosevelt's administration were dramatic, with both the Congress and the Administration taking action after action to do something—anything—to restore American confidence and economic vitality. Raymond Moley, one of President Roosevelt's original "Brain Trust" advisors, described some of the spirit and atmosphere of that time in the following interview.

During the whole '33 one-hundred days' Congress, people didn't know what was going on, the public. Couldn't understand these things that were being passed so fast. They knew something was happening, something good for them. They began investing and working and hoping again.

People don't realize that Roosevelt chose a conservative banker as Secretary of Treasury [William H. Woodin] and a conservative from Tennessee as Secretary of State [Cordell Hull]. Most of the reforms that were put through might have been agreeable to Hoover, if he had the political power to put them over. They were all latent in Hoover's thinking, especially the bank rescue. The rescue was done not by Roosevelt—he signed the papers—but by Hoover leftovers in the Administration. They knew what to do.

The bank rescue of 1933 was probably the turning point of the Depression. When people were able to survive the shock of having all the banks closed, and then see the banks open up, with their money protected, there began to be confidence. Good times were coming. Most of the legislation that came after didn't really help the public. The public helped itself, after it got confidence.

It marked the revival of hope. The people were scared for a little while—a week. Then, Congress passed the bill, and the banks were opened. Roosevelt appealed to them on Sunday night, after the week of the closing. It was his very first fireside chat. They put their money back in the banks, the people were so relieved.

A Depression is much like a run on a bank. It's a crisis of confidence. People panic and grab their money. There's a story I like to tell: In my home town, when I was a little boy, [a man] came up from the quarry where he was working, went into the bank, and said, "If my money's here, I don't want it. If it's not here, I want it."

The guarantee of bank deposits was put through by Vice President Garner, Jesse Jones (a Texas banker), and Senator Vandenburg—three conservatives. They rammed it down Roosevelt's throat, and he took credit for it ever after. If you can quiet the little fellows, the big fellows pretty much take care of themselves. If you can cover it up to $10,000, all the little fellows are guaranteed.
. . .

Now that wouldn't be agreed to by some liberals. But, after all, I was never a real liberal. I was an old-fashioned Democrat. I was a believer in our industrial system. It didn't need a complete rehauling. I thought if we could get it back into operation and [if] normal conditions return[ed], we'd be all right. This happened.

Selection from Studs Terkel, *Hard Times.* Published by Pantheon Books, New York, copyright © 1970.

CRITICAL THINKING

1. What reasons did Raymond Moley give for believing the bank crisis of 1933 was a turning point in the Depression?
2. Moley later left the Roosevelt administration because of differences over government policy. What signs of these differences can be seen in his statements here?

5. *NEW DEAL* PROGRAMS ARE CREATED TO HELP THE TRANSIENT UNEMPLOYED

The New Deal established hundreds of agencies to help the unemployed and get the economy in motion. One of these groups dealt with the transient unemployed—the Americans who, during the Depression, were moving from place to place and from job to whatever other job they could find. The following comes from a report written by John Webb, one of the Roosevelt Administration's leading experts on the problem. It shows both how the New Deal handled the situation and the extent of its efforts.

The transient relief population consisted of unattached individuals and family groups who were not legal residents of the community in which they applied for relief. Because non-residents were ineligible for relief from existing public agencies, special provision for their care was included in the Federal Emergency Relief Act of May, 1933. In the administration of relief under this provision, transients were defined as unattached persons or family groups that had not resided for one continuous year or longer within the boundaries of the State at the time of application for relief.

Early in the depression there were indications of an increase in the number of needy non-residents. During the fall and winter of 1930, municipal lodging houses, missions, and shelters in metropolitan areas reported that, in comparison with previous years, the number of homeless men seeking assistance was increasing rapidly. At about the same time, States in the South and West became alarmed at the influx of needy non-residents.

Because these depression migrants were constantly on the move, it was impossible to determine the number of different individuals included. During the Congressional hearings on relief legislation, the number of transients was estimated to be between one and one-half and five million persons. These estimates proved to be greatly in excess of the number of transients who received care under the Transient Relief Program. . . .

Even after the inauguration of the Transient Relief Program, it was impossible to determine with any degree of accuracy the size of this relief group. Actually, the transient population was not a definite and fixed group in the total relief population, but one that changed its membership constantly and was never the same on any two days in any one place. . . .

Total monthly registrations included duplications resulting from the rapid movement of part of the population; while the number under care on one full day a month did not include those en route. Therefore, the size of the population during any month was somewhere between the number registered during the month and the number under care on one day during that month. Careful estimates place the maximum size during the operation of the Transient Relief Program at 200,000 unattached persons and 50,000 family groups. But because the transient relief population was constantly undergoing a change of membership, it seems probable that the number of individuals and family groups that *at some time* received assistance from transient bureaus was two to three times these estimates.

Selection from John N. Webb, *The Transient Unemployed: A Description and Analysis of the Transient Relief Population.* Research Monograph published by Works Progress Administration, U.S. Government, Washington, D.C., copyright © 1935.

CRITICAL THINKING

1. What does the tone of this report indicate about how the New Deal tried to deal with the enormous problems of the Depression?
2. Judging from John Webb's description of the size and make-up of the transient unemployed population, what sorts of problems most likely arose in administering relief to these people?

---

6. NEW YORK GOVERNOR ALFRED E. SMITH TALKS PLAINLY ABOUT HIS CATHOLICISM

In 1928 Alfred E. Smith, Governor of New York, became the first Roman Catholic nominated for president of the United States by a major party. Campaigning against Herbert Hoover in Oklahoma City, the "Happy Warrior" squarely brought into the open the subject of his religion.

I FEEL that I owe it to the Democratic party to talk out plainly. If I had listened to the counselors that advised political expediency I would probably keep quiet, but I'm not by nature a quiet man.

I never keep anything to myself. I talk it out. And I feel I owe it, not only to the party, but I sincerely believe that I owe it to the country itself to drag this un-American propoganda out into the open.

Because this country, to my way of thinking, cannot be successful if it ever divides on sectarian lines. If there are any considerable number of our people that are going to listen to appeals to their passions and to their prejudice, if bigotry and intolerance and their sister vices are going to succeed, it is dangerous for the future life of the Republic, and the best way to kill anything un-American is to drag it out into the open; because anything un-American cannot live in the sunlight. . . .

Prior to the convention the grand dragon of the Realm of Arkansas wrote to one of the delegates from Arkansas, and in the letter he advised the delegate that he not vote for me in the national convention, and he put it on the ground of upholding American ideals against institutions as established by our forefathers. Now, can you think of any man or any group of men banded together in what they call the Ku Klux Klan, who profess to be 100 per cent Americans, and forget the great principle that Jefferson stood for the equality of man, and forget that our forefathers in their wisdom, foreseeing probably such a sight as we look at today, wrote into the fundamental law of the country that at no time was religion to be regarded as a qualification for public office.

Just think of a man breathing the spirit of hatred against millions of his fellow citizens, proclaiming and subscribing at the same time to the doctrine of Jefferson, of Lincoln, of Roosevelt and of Wilson. Why, there is no greater mockery in this world today than the burning of the cross, the emblem of faith, the emblem of salvation, the place upon which Christ Himself made the great sacrifice for all of mankind, by these people who are spreading this propaganda, while the Christ they are supposed to adore, love and venerate, during all of His lifetime on earth, taught the holy, sacred writ of brotherly love. . . .

Let me make myself perfectly clear. I do not want any Catholic in the United States of America to vote for me on the 6th of November because I am a Catholic. If any Catholic in this country believes that the welfare, the well-being, the prosperity, the growth and the expansion of the United States is best conserved and best promoted by the election of Hoover, I want him to vote for Hoover and not for me.

But on the other hand, I have the right to say that any citizen of this country that believes I can promote its welfare, that I am capable of steering the ship of state safely through the next four years and then votes against me because of my religion, he is not a real, pure, genuine American.

Selection from *A Treasury of Great American Speeches*, edited by Charles Hurd. Published by Hawthorn Books, New York, copyright © 1959.

CRITICAL THINKING

1. List the reasons Smith gives for bringing the religion issue into the open.
2. What can you infer about Smith's character from this reading?

---

7. A MINER'S SON TALKS ABOUT GROWING UP IN THE HARD TIMES OF THE *GREAT DEPRESSION*

The Depression affected most Americans in almost every imaginable way—it changed their living and spending habits and even the way they thought about themselves and their society. The following reminiscence of the period is by Edward Santander, an administrator at a midwestern college, and comes from Studs Terkel's oral history of the Depression, Hard Times.

My first real memories come about '31. It was simply a gut issue then: eating or not eating, living or not living. My father was a coal miner, outside a small town in Illinois. My dad, my grandfather and my uncle worked in this same mine. He had taken a cut in wages, but we were still doing pretty well. We were sitting in a '27 Hudson [automobile], when I saw a line of men waiting near the I.C. [Illinois Central] tracks. I asked him what was the trouble. They were waiting to get something to eat.

When the mine temporarily closed down in the early Thirties, my dad had to hunt work elsewhere. He went around the state, he'd paint barns, anything.

I went to an old, country-style schoolhouse. . . . One building that had eight rows in it, one for each grade. Seven rows were quiet, while the eighth row recited. The woman teacher got the munificent sum of $30 a month. She played the organ, an old pump organ with pedals, she taught every subject, and all eight grades. This was 1929, '30, '31. . . . At the back corner was a great pot-bellied stove that kept the place warm. It has about an acre of ground, a playground with no equipment. Out there were the toilets. . . . You'd be surprised at the number of people in rural areas that didn't have much in this way [toilet facilities], as late as the Thirties.

One of the greatest contributions of the WPA [Works Progress Administration, which provided work for the needy unemployed] was the standardized outdoor toilet, with modern plumbing. (Laughs.) They built thousands of them around here. You can still see some of 'em standing. PWA [Public Works Administration, which lent money to state and local governments to construct public buildings, bridges, and roads] built new schools and the City Hall in this town. I remember NYA [National Youth Administration, which provided training for unemployed youths]. I learned a good deal of carpentry in this.

Roosevelt was idolized in that area. The county had been solidly Republican from the Civil War on. And then was Democratic till the end of Truman's time. F.D.R. was held in awe by most people. . . . The newspaper in the area hated Roosevelt, just hated him. (Laughs)

Almost everybody was in the same boat, pretty poorly off. . . .

People in the Thirties did feel a bit different [than now]. When the pig-killing [when farmers would kill pigs rather than "sell" them at a loss] was going on, the farmers would kill the pigs well enough, but they'd tell the people where they buried them, and they'd go dig 'em up and take 'em home. The farmers couldn't sell the pigs anyway, so they weren't out anything.

It isn't true that people who have very little won't share. When everybody is in the same position, they haven't anything to hide from one another. So they share. But when prosperity comes around. . . .

The Depression was such a shock to some people that when World War II was over—you'd hear men in the army say it: "When I get back, I'm going to get a good job, a house and a car, some

Studs Terkel is known for his use of oral history techniques—recounting historical events by taping interviews with participants. His book Hard Times chronicles the Depression.

money in the bank, and I'm never going to worry again." These people have passed this on to their kids. . . .

I never heard anyone who expressed feeling that the United States Government, as it existed, was done for. It was quite the opposite. The desire to restore the country to the affluence it had. This was uppermost in people's minds.

Selection from Studs Terkel, *Hard Times.* Published by Pantheon Books, New York, copyright © 1970.

CRITICAL THINKING

1. What was the attitude of the people in Edward Santander's area during the Depression?
2. What psychological effects did the Depression seem to have on them?
3. How did they react to the government's efforts at restoring the economy?

FSA PHOTOGRAPHERS
Recorders Of The
New Deal Programs

*In the 1930s, some Americans had funds to pur-
chase household goods. Marion P. Walcott's photo of
a West Virginia family contrasts with the Arthur
Rothstein picture of a less-fortunate woman living
in Washington, D.C.*

The Farm Security Administration (FSA) was one of the small federal agencies that grew out of President Franklin Roosevelt's New Deal programs. Its aim was to assist farmers who did not own land but who worked as share-croppers, tenants, hired hands, and migrant workers.

The FSA established a special publicity section devoted to publicizing its programs, in an effort to gain broad public approval for them. Called the Historical Section and headed by Roy Stryker, the FSA publicity section em-ployed relatively unknown photographers such as Walker Evans, Dorothea Lange, Russell Lee, Arthur Rothstein, and Ben Shahn. Stryker as-signed the FSA's staff of photographers the task of recording the FSA's efforts in bringing relief to the rural poor. The photographers photo-graphed Americans against the backgrounds of farms, small towns, and cities. Ultimately, the FSA amassed a photographic record of Ameri-can life in the 1930s, and the photographers went to to build distinguished careers based on their FSA work.

In 1938, many migrant families on their way to California were forced to abandon overfarmed land. They camped out, often near public highways. Dorothea Lange's photograph points up the difference between their lifestyle and that of people who could travel in comfort.

By the end of the decade, the photographers of the FSA had become a respected force in American photography. Featured in national magazines, their pictures brought to the attention of the world the daily struggle for survival experienced by millions of Americans. *Now Let Us Praise Famous Men* by James Agee and *Twelve Million Black Voices* by Richard Wright are literary classics of the Depression that used the work of FSA photographers as illustrations. Today, the photography of the FSA can be found in numerous museums.

CRITICAL THINKING

1. Which photograph makes a visual statement about differing American lifestyles? How?
2. Examine these photographs and cite reasons why they were effective then, and are important now.
3. Compare the way the family sitting at home spent their leisure time with people today.

America in a Turbulent World

CHAPTER 29

THE WORLD IN CONFLICT

1930–1945

1. PRESIDENT FRANKLIN DELANO ROOSEVELT ADDRESSES CONGRESS ON THE PROBLEMS OF AMERICAN NEUTRALITY

The neutrality that President Roosevelt tried to maintain during the early stages of the war in Europe was a precarious one. As this January, 1939, message to Congress shows, Roosevelt hoped to keep the United States out of direct involvement as long as possible while, at the same time, making it clear that the United States disapproved of the actions of Germany, Italy, and Japan.

There comes a time in the affairs of men when they must prepare to defend not their homes alone but the tenets of faith and humanity on which their churches, their governments, and their very civilization are founded. The defense of religion, of democracy, and of good faith among nations is all the same fight. To save one we must now make up our minds to save all.

We know what might happen to us of the United States if the new philosophies of force were to encompass the other continents and invade our own. We, no more than other nations, can afford to be surrounded by the enemies of our faith and our humanity. Fortunate it is, therefore, that in this Western Hemisphere we have, under a common ideal of democratic government, a rich diversity of resources and of peoples functioning together in mutual respect and peace. . . .

But the world has grown so small and weapons of attack so swift that no nation can be safe in its will to peace so long as any other single powerful nation refuses to settle its grievances at the council table.

For if any government bristling with implements of war insists on policies of force, weapons of defense give the only safety. . . .

We have learned that God-fearing democracies of the world which observe the sanctity of treaties and good faith in their dealings with other nations cannot safely be indifferent to international lawlessness anywhere. They cannot forever let pass, without effective protest, acts of aggression against sister nations—acts which automatically undermine all of us.

Obviously they must proceed along practical, peaceful lines. But the mere fact that we rightly decline to intervene with arms to prevent acts of aggression does not mean that we must act as if there were no aggression at all. Words may be futile, but war is not the only means of commanding a decent respect for the opinions of mankind. There are many methods short of war, but stronger and more effective than mere words, of bringing home to aggressor governments the aggregate sentiments of our own people.

At the very least, we can and should avoid any action, or any lack of action, which will encourage, assist, or build up an aggressor. We have learned that when we deliberately try to legislate neutrality, our neutrality laws may operate unevenly and unfairly—may actually give aid to an aggressor and deny it to the victim. The instinct of self-preservation should warn us that we ought not to let that happen any more.

And we have learned something else—the old, old lesson that probability of attack is mightily decreased by the assurance of an ever-ready defense. Since 1931 world events of thunderous import have moved with lightning speed. During these 8 years many of our people clung to the hope that the innate decency of mankind would protect the unprepared who showed their innate trust in mankind. Today we are all wiser—and sadder.

Selection from "Message of the President of the United States," January 4, 1939, *Congressional Record*, Vol. 84, Part 1. Published by United States Government Printing Office, Washington, D.C., copyright © 1939.

CRITICAL THINKING

1. What general international policy was President Roosevelt recommending?
2. What arguments did he use to support his plan?
3. What principles did Roosevelt declare were at stake?

2. PRESIDENT FRANKLIN ROOSEVELT CALLS DECEMBER 7, 1941, A DATE OF INFAMY

Japan and the United States were working toward a peaceful solution of their differences over problems in the Far East when, on December 7, 1941, Japan attacked Pearl Harbor in Hawaii. (On September 27, 1940, Japan had signed a pact with Germany and Italy, bringing it into the Axis coalition.) The next day, President Franklin Roosevelt went to Congress with the special message reprinted below and asked for a declaration of war against Japan.

YESTERDAY, DECEMBER 7, 1941—a date which will live in infamy—the United States of America was suddenly and deliberately attacked by naval and air forces of the Empire of Japan.

The United States was at peace with that nation, and, at the solicitation of Japan, was still in conversation with its government and its emperor looking toward the maintenance of peace in the Pacific. Indeed, one hour after Japanese air squadrons had commenced bombing in Oahu, the Japanese ambassador to the United States and his colleague delivered to the secretary of state a formal reply to a recent American message. While this reply stated that it seemed useless to continue the existing diplomatic negotiations, it contained no threat or hint of war or armed attack.

It will be recorded that the distance of Hawaii from Japan makes it obvious that the attack was deliberately planned many days or even weeks ago. During the intervening time the Japanese government has deliberately sought to deceive the United States by false statements and expressions of hope for continued peace.

The attack yesterday on the Hawaiian Islands has caused severe damage to American naval and military forces. Very many American lives have been lost. In addition, American ships have been reported torpedoed on the high seas between San Francisco and Honolulu.

Yesterday the Japanese government also launched an attack against Malaya.

Last night Japanese forces attacked Guam.

Last night Japanese forces attacked the Philippine Islands.

Last night the Japanese attacked Wake Island.

This morning the Japanese attacked Midway Island.

Japan has, therefore, undertaken a surprise offensive extending throughout the Pacific area. The facts of yesterday speak for themselves. The people of the United States have already formed their opinions and well understand the implications to the very life and safety of our nation.

As commander in chief of the Army and Navy I have directed that all measures be taken for our defense.

Always will we remember the character of the onslaught against us. No matter how long it may take us to overcome this premeditated invasion, the American people, in their righteous might, will win through to absolute victory. I believe I interpret the will of the Congress and of the people when I assert that we will not only defend ourselves to the uttermost but will make very certain that this form of treachery shall never endanger us again.

Hostilities exist. There is no blinking at the fact that our people, our territory, and our interests are in grave danger.

With confidence in our armed forces—with the unbounded determination of our people—we will gain the inevitable triumph—so help us God.

I ask that the Congress declare that since the unprovoked and dastardly attack by Japan on Sunday, December 7, a state of war has existed between the United States and the Japanese Empire.

Selection from *The Annals of America, 1940–1949*, Vol. 16. Published by Encyclopaedia Britannica, Inc., Chicago, copyright © 1968.

CRITICAL THINKING

1. Why does President Roosevelt conclude that the attack was planned many days or even weeks ago?
2. List three predictions Roosevelt makes in his speech.
3. What details does Roosevelt give that help you infer his personal reaction to the Japanese attack?

3. PRESIDENT FRANKLIN ROOSEVELT BROADCASTS A FIRESIDE CHAT ABOUT WAR

The day after President Franklin Roosevelt asked for a declaration of war, on December 9, 1941, he spoke to the nation by radio, describing the events that had led to war. Of all his so-called "Fireside Chats," this may be the saddest.

The sudden criminal attacks perpetrated by the Japanese in the Pacific provide the climax of a decade of international immorality.

Powerful and resourceful gangsters have banded together to make war upon the whole human race. Their challenge has now been flung at the United States of America. The Japanese have treacherously violated the long-standing peace between us. Many American soldiers and sailors have been killed by enemy action. American ships have been sunk, American airplanes destroyed.

The Congress and the people of the United States have accepted that challenge.

Together with other free peoples, we are now fighting to maintain our right to live among our world neighbors in freedom and in common decency, without fear of assault. . . .

We are now in this war. We are all in it — all the way. Every single man, woman, and child is a partner in the most tremendous undertaking of our American history. We must share together the bad news and the good news, the defeats and the victories — the changing fortunes of war.

So far, the news has all been bad. We have suffered a serious setback in Hawaii. Our forces in the Philippines, which include the brave people of that commonwealth, are taking punishment, but are defending themselves vigorously. The reports from Guam and Wake and Midway islands are still confused, but we must be prepared for the announcement that all these three outposts have been seized.

The casualty lists of these first few days will undoubtedly be large. I deeply feel the anxiety of all families of the men in our armed forces and the relatives of people in cities which have been bombed. I can only give them my solemn promise that they will get news just as quickly as possible.

Most earnestly I urge my countrymen to reject all rumors. These ugly little hints of complete disaster fly thick and fast in wartime. They have to be examined and appraised. As an example, I can tell you frankly that until further surveys are made, I have not sufficient information to state the exact damage which has been done to our naval vessels at Pearl Harbor. Admittedly the damage is serious. But no one can say how serious until we know how much of this damage can be repaired and how quickly the necessary repairs can be made.

I cite as another example a statement made on Sunday night that a Japanese carrier had been located and sunk off the Canal Zone. And when you hear statements that are attributed to what they call "an authoritative source," you can be reasonably sure that under these war circumstances the "authoritative source" was not any person in authority.

Many rumors and reports which we now hear originate with enemy sources. For instance, today the Japanese are claiming that as a result of their one action against Hawaii they have gained naval supremacy in the Pacific. This is an old trick of propaganda which had been used innumerable times by the Nazis. The purposes of such fantastic claims are, of course, to spread fear and confusion among us and to goad us into revealing military information which our enemies are desperately anxious to obtain. Our government will not be caught in this obvious trap—and neither will our people.

It must be remembered by each and every one of us that our free and rapid communication must be greatly restricted in wartime. It is not possible to receive full, speedy, accurate reports from distant areas of combat. That is particularly true where naval operations are concerned. For in these days of the marvels of radio it is often impossible for the commanders of various units to report their activities by radio, for the very simple reason that this information would become available to the enemy, and would disclose their position and their plan of defense or attack.

Of necessity there will be delays in officially confirming or denying reports of operations, but we will not hide facts from the country if we know the facts and if the enemy will not be aided by their disclosure.

To all newspapers and radio stations—all those who reach the eyes and ears of the American people—I say this: You have a most grave responsibility to the nation now and for the duration of this war. If you feel that your government is not disclosing enough of the truth, you have every right to say so. But—in the absence of all the facts, as revealed by official sources—you have no right to deal out unconfirmed reports in such a way as to make people believe they are gospel truth.

Every citizen, in every walk of life, shares this same responsibility. The lives of our soldiers and sailors—the whole future of the nation—depend upon the manner in which each and every one of us fulfills his obligation to our country.

Now a word about the recent past—and the future. A year and a half has elapsed since the fall of France, when the whole world first realized the mechanical might which the Axis nations had been building for so many years. America has used that year and a half to great advantage. Knowing that the attack might reach us in all too short a time, we immediately began greatly to increase our industrial strength and our capacity to meet the demands of modern warfare.

Precious months were gained by sending vast quantities of our war materials to the nations of the world still able to resist Axis aggression. Our policy rested on the fundamental truth that the defense of any country resisting Hitler or Japan was in the long run the defense of our own country. That policy has been justified. It has given us time, invaluable time, to build our American assembly lines of production. Assembly lines are now in operation. Others are being rushed to completion. A steady stream of tanks and planes, of guns and ships, of shells and equipment—that is what these eighteen months have given us.

But it is only a beginning of what has to be done. We must be set to face a long war against crafty and powerful bandits. The attack at Pearl Harbor can be repeated at any one of many points in both oceans and along both our coastlines and against all the rest of the hemisphere.

It will not be only be a long war, it will be a hard war. That is the basis on which we now lay our plans. That is the yardstick by which we measure what we shall need and demand—money, materials, doubled and quadrupled production, ever increasing. The production must be not only for our own Army and Navy and air forces. It must reinforce the other armies and navies and air forces fighting the Nazis and the war lords of Japan throughout the Americas and the world.

I have been working today on the subject of production. Your government has decided on two broad policies. The first is to speed up all existing production by working on a seven-day-week basis in every war industry, including the production of essential raw materials. The second policy, now being put into form, is to rush additions to the capacity of production by building more new plants, by adding to old plants, and by using the many smaller plants for war needs.

Over the hard road of the past months we have at times met obstacles and difficulties, divisions and disputes, indifference and callousness. That is now all past and, I am sure, forgotten. The fact is that the country now has an organization in Washington built around men and women who are recognized experts in their own fields. I think the country knows that the people who are actually responsible in each and every one of these many fields are pulling together with a teamwork that has never before been excelled.

On the road ahead there lies hard work—gruelling work—day and night, every hour and every minute. I was about to add that ahead there lies sacrifice for all of us. But it is not correct to use that word. The United States does not consider it a sacrifice to do all one can, to give one's best to our nation when the nation is fighting for its existence and its future life.

It is not a sacrifice for any man, old or young, to be in the Army or the Navy of the United States. Rather it is a privilege. It is not a sacrifice for the industrialist or the wage earner, the farmer or the shopkeeper, the trainman or the doctor to pay more taxes, to buy more bonds, to forego extra profits, to work longer or harder at the task for which he is best fitted. Rather it is a privilege. It is not a sacrifice to do without many things to which we are accustomed if the national defense calls for doing without.

A review this morning leads me to the conclusion that at present we shall not have to curtail the normal articles of food. There is enough food for all of us and enough left over to send to those who are fighting on the same side with us. There will be a clear and definite shortage of metals of many kinds for civilian use for the very good reason that in our increased program we shall need for war purposes more than half of that portion of the principal metals which during the past year have gone into articles for civilian use. We shall have to give up many things entirely.

I am sure that the people in every part of the nation are prepared in their individual living to win this war. I am sure they will cheerfully help to pay a large part of its financial cost while it goes on. I am sure they will cheerfully give up those material things they are asked to give up. I am sure that they will retain all those great spiritual things without which we cannot win through.

I repeat that the United States can accept no result save victory, final and complete. Not only must the shame of Japanese treachery be wiped out but the sources of international brutality, wherever they exist, must be absolutely and finally broken.

In my message to the Congress yesterday I said that we "will make very certain that this form of treachery shall never endanger us again." In order to achieve that certainty, we must begin the great task that is before us by abandoning once and for all the illusion that we can ever again isolate ourselves from the rest of humanity.

In these past few years—and, most violently, in the past few days—we have learned a terrible lesson. It is our obligation to our dead—it is our sacred obligation to their children and our children—that we must never forget what we have learned.

And what we all have learned is this: There is no such thing as security for any nation—or any individual—in a world ruled by the principles of gangsterism. There is no such thing as impregnable defense against powerful aggressors who sneak up in the dark and strike without warning. We have learned that our ocean-girt hemisphere is not immune from severe attack—that we cannot measure our safety in terms of miles on any map.

We may acknowledge that our enemies have performed a brilliant feat of deception, perfectly timed and executed with great skill. It was a thoroughly dishonorable deed, but we must face the fact that modern warfare as conducted in the Nazi manner is a dirty business. We don't like it—we didn't want to get in it—but we are in it and we're going to fight it with everything we've got.

I do not think any American has any doubt of our ability to administer proper punishment to the perpetrators of these crimes. Your government knows that for weeks Germany has been telling Japan that if Japan did not attack the United States, Japan would not share in dividing the spoils with Germany when peace came. She was promised by Germany that if she came in she would receive the complete and perpetual control of the whole of the Pacific area—and that means not only the Far East, not only all of the islands in the Pacific but also a stranglehold on the west coast of North, Central, and South America. We also know that Germany and Japan are conducting their military and naval operation in accordance with a joint plan. That plan considers all peoples and nations which are not helping the Axis Powers as common enemies of each and every one of the Axis Powers.

That is their simple and obvious grand strategy. That is why the American people must realize that it can be matched only with similar grand strategy. We must realize, for example, that Japanese successes against the United States in the Pacific are helpful to German operations in Libya; that any German success against the Caucasus is inevitably an assistance to Japan in her operations against the Dutch East Indies; that a German attack against Algiers or Morocco opens the way to a German attack against South America. On the other side of the picture, we must learn to know that guerrilla warfare against the Germans in Serbia helps us; that a successful Russian offensive against the Germans in Serbia helps us; that British successes on land or sea in any part of the world strengthen our hands.

Remember always that Germany and Italy, regardless of any formal declaration of war, consider themselves at war with the United States at this moment just as much as they consider themselves at war with Britain and Russia. And Germany puts all the other republics of the Americas into the category of enemies. The people of the hemisphere can be honored by that.

The true goal we seek is far above and beyond the ugly field of battle. When we resort to force, as now we must, we are determined that this force shall be directed toward ultimate good as well as against immediate evil. We Americans are not destroyers; we are builders.

We are now in the midst of a war, not for

conquest, not for vengeance, but for a world in which this nation and all that this nation represents will be safe for our children. We expect to eliminate the danger from Japan, but it would serve us ill if we accomplished that and found that the rest of the world was dominated by Hitler and Mussolini.

We are going to win the war, and we are going to win the peace that follows.

And in the dark hours of this day—and through dark days that may be yet to come—we will know that the vast majority of the members of the human race are on our side. Many of them are fighting with us. All of them are praying for us. For, in representing our cause, we represent theirs as well—our hope and their hope for liberty under God.

Selection from *The Annals of America, 1940–1949*, Vol. 16. Published by Encyclopaedia Britannica, Inc., Chicago, copyright © 1968.

CRITICAL THINKING

1. Roosevelt begins, "The sudden criminal attacks . . ." List other phrases in the speech designed to arouse emotions against Japan and Germany.
2. How does Roosevelt persuade listeners that the work ahead is not a sacrifice?
3. Summarize what Roosevelt says the U.S. has learned from Nazi aggression and the Japanese attack at Pearl Harbor.

4. AMERICAN NOVELIST JOHN STEINBECK REPORTS ON THE JOB OF A WAR-CORRESPONDENT

Once the United States joined the conflict, Americans learned what the new style of war was like—both first hand and from the correspondents who reported on the war for newspapers, magazines, and newsreels. Among the many distinguished correspondents was novelist John Steinbeck, whose book The Grapes of Wrath *had given Americans one of their most dramatic images of the Depression. Steinbeck wrote the following about his experiences as a war-correspondent in the Mediterranean theater.*

You can't see much of a battle. Those paintings reproduced in history books which show long lines of advancing troops are either idealized or else times and battles have changed. The account in the morning papers of the battle of yesterday was not seen by the correspondent, but was put together from reports.

What the correspondent really saw was dust and the nasty burst of shells, low bushes and slit trenches. He lay on his stomach, if he had any sense, and watched ants crawling among the little sticks on the sand dune, and his nose was so close to the ants that their progress was interfered with by it.

Then he saw an advance. Not straight lines of men marching into cannon fire, but little groups scuttling like crabs from bits of cover to other cover, while the high chatter of machine guns sounded, and the deep proom of shellfire.

Perhaps the correspondent scuttled with them and hit the ground again. His report will be of battle plan and tactics, of taken ground or lost terrain, of attack and counter-attack. But these are some of the things he probably saw:

He might have seen the splash of dirt and dust that is a shell burst, and a small Italian girl in the street with her stomach blown out, and he might have seen an American soldier standing over a twitching body, crying. He probably saw many dead mules, lying on their sides, reduced to pulp. He saw the wreckage of houses, with torn beds hanging like shreds out of the spilled hole in a plaster wall. There were red carts and the stalled vehicles of refugees who did not get away.

The stretcher-bearers come back from the lines, walking in off step, so that the burden will not be jounced too much, and the blood dripping from the canvas, brother and enemy in the stretchers, so long as they are hurt. And the walking wounded coming back with shattered arms and bandaged heads, the walking wounded struggling painfully to the rear.

He would have smelled the sharp cordite in the air and the hot reek of blood if the going has been rough. The burning odor of dust will be in his nose and the stench of men and animals killed yesterday and the day before. . . . When his throat is dry he will drink the warm water from his canteen, which tastes of disinfectant.

While the correspondent is writing for you of

advances and retreats, his skin will be raw from the woolen clothes he has not taken off for three days, and his feet will be hot and dirty and swollen from not having taken off his shoes for days. He will itch from last night's mosquito bites and from today's sand-fly bites. Perhaps he will have a little sand-fly fever, so that his head pulses and a red rim comes into his vision. . . .

"The 5th Army advanced two kilometers," he will write, while the lines of trucks churn the road to deep dust and truck drivers hunch over their wheels. And off to the right the burial squads are scooping slits in the sandy earth. Their charges lie huddled on the ground and before they are laid in the sand, the second of the two dog tags is detached so that you know that that man with that Army serial number is dead and out of it.

These are the things he sees while he writes of tactics and strategy and names generals and in print decorates heroes. . . .

. . . The correspondent will get the communiqué and will write your morning dispatch on his creaking, dust-filled portable: "General Clark's 5th Army advanced two kilometers against heavy artillery fire yesterday."

Selection from John Steinbeck, *Once There Was a War.* Published by Viking Press, New York, copyright © 1958.

CRITICAL THINKING

1. Why might John Steinbeck have chosen to emphasize the difference between what a correspondent wrote and what he or she might actually have seen?
2. What contrast did Steinbeck see between the traditional image of war and what he saw during the fighting in Italy?

5. WAR-CORRESPONDENT ERNIE PYLE SENDS HOME A REPORT ON THE BRAVERY AND SPIRIT OF AMERICAN SOLDIERS

One of the most famous war-correspondents was Ernie Pyle, whose popular reports on the life and experiences of the "GI" brought him both fame and the affection of American soldiers. This is part of the report he made from Normandy, shortly after the landings.

Beach landings are always planned to a schedule that is set far ahead of time. They all have to be timed, in order for everything to mesh and for the following waves of troops to be standing off the beach and ready to land at the right moment. . . .

I have always been amazed at the speed called for in these plans. Schedules will call for engineers to land at H-hour plus 2 minutes, and service troops at H-hour plus 30 minutes, and even for press censors to land at H-hour plus 75 minutes. But in the attack on my special portion of the beach—the toughest spot of all, incidentally—the schedule didn't hold.

Our men simply could not get past the beach. They were pinned down right on the water's edge by an inhuman wall of fire from the bluff. Our first waves were on that beach for hours, instead of a few minutes, before they could begin working inland. . . .

Medical corpsmen attended the wounded as best they could. Men were killed as they stepped out of landing craft. An officer whom I knew got a bullet through the head just as the door of his landing craft was let down. Some men were drowned.

The first crack in the beach defenses was finally accomplished by terrific and wonderful naval gunfire, which knocked out the big emplacements. Epic stories have been told of destroyers that ran right up into shallow water and had it out point-blank with the big guns in those concrete emplacements ashore.

When the heavy fire stopped, our men were organized by their officers and pushed off the sand, circling machine-gun nests and taking them from the rear.

As one officer said, the only way to take a beach is to face it and keep going. It is costly at first, but it's the only way. If the men are pinned down on the beach, dug in and out of action, they might as well not be there at all. They hold up the waves behind them, and nothing is being gained.

Our men were pinned down for a while, but finally they stood up and went through, and so we took that beach and accomplished our landing. In the light of a couple of days of retrospection, we sat and talked and called it a miracle that our men ever got on at all or were able to stay on.

They suffered casualties. And yet considering

the entire beachhead assault, including other units that had a much easier time, our total casualties in driving that wedge into the Continent of Europe were remarkably low—only a fraction, in fact, of what our commanders had been prepared to accept.

And those units that were so battered and went through such hell pushed on inland without rest, their spirits high, their egotism in victory almost reaching the smart-alecky stage.

Their tails were up. "We've done it again," they said. They figured that the rest of the Army wasn't needed at all. Which proves that, while their judgment in this respect was bad, they certainly had the spirit that wins battles, and eventually wars.

Selection from Ernie Pyle, *Brave Men*. Published by Henry Holt and Company, New York, copyright © 1944.

CRITICAL THINKING

1. Ernie Pyle was considered by many Americans to be the "common soldier's correspondent." What do you see in this report that earned him this distinction?
2. What kind of spirit did Pyle see in the American troops? Why did he consider it so important for victory?

---

6. DEFENSE WORKER RACHEL WRAY REMINISCES ABOUT HER WARTIME EXPERIENCES AS A RIVETER

On the home front, American women assumed a major role in the industrial activity necessary to build and maintain the country's war effort. The following reminiscence comes from Rachel Wray, who was born on a farm in Oklahoma and who became a defense worker after her husband left to serve in the Pacific.

I was one of the first women hired at Convair [aircraft factory] . . . Convair had a motto on their plant which said that anything short of right was wrong, and that stuck with me. I went to work in the riveting group in metal bench assembly. The mechanics would bring us the jobs they had

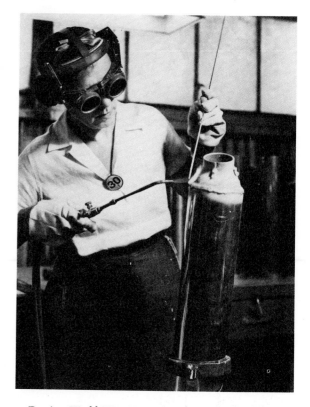

During World War II, women learned new skills, such as soldering in aircraft factories.

put together, and we would take the blueprints and rivet what they brought us. . . .

I tackled everything. I had a daring mother who was afraid of nothing, horses, farm implements, anything, so maybe I inherited a little bit of that from her. I remember my brother, who was in the air force at the time, and his friends laughed at me one day, thinking I couldn't learn this mechanical stuff. I can still see them, but it only made me more determined. I think it probably hurt their pride a little bit that I was capable of doing this.

Pretty soon I was promoted to bench mechanic work, which was detailed hand riveting. Then I was given a bench with nothing to do but repair what other people had ruined. I visited a man recently who's seventy-four years old, and he said to my daughter, "All we had to do was foul up a job and take it to her and she'd fix it."

I loved working at Convair. I loved the challenge of getting dirty and getting into the work. I did one special riveting job, hand riveting that could not be done by machine. I worked on that job for three months, ten hours a day, six days a week, and slapped three-eights-or three-quarter-inch rivets by hand that no one else would do. I didn't have that kind of confidence as a kid growing up, because I didn't have that opportunity. Convair was the first time in my life that I had the chance to prove that I could do something, and I did. They finally made me a group leader to help break the new women in.

Selection from Mark Jonathan Harris, et. al., *The Homefront: America During World War II.* Published by G.P. Putnam's Sons, New York, copyright © 1984.

CRITICAL THINKING

1. How did Rachel Wray react to defense work?
2. What special opportunities did this work seem to give her?

---

7. MARGARET TAKAHASHI DESCRIBES THE INTERNMENT OF JAPANESE-AMERICANS AFTER THE JAPANESE ATTACK AT PEARL HARBOR

The homefront was not the same for all Americans. For Japanese-Americans, the situation was particularly difficult. The following description comes from Margaret Takahashi, who ran a landscape nursery in Los Angeles with her husband. After several months in an internment camp, the family found refuge on a farmhouse in the famous Boys' Town facility.

After Pearl Harbor we [Japanese-Americans] started to get worried because the newspapers were agitating and printing all those stories all the time. And people were getting angrier. You kept hearing awful rumors. You heard that people were getting their houses burned down and we were afraid that those things might happen to us. . . . You didn't know when the blow was going to fall, or what was going to happen. You didn't quite feel that you could settle down to anything. Your whole future seemed in question. The longer the war dragged on, the worse the feeling got.

When the evacuation order finally came I was relieved. Lots of people were relieved, because you were taken care of. You wouldn't have all this worry. . . .

You could only take one suitcase apiece, but people who had gone to camp before us were able to tell us what to bring, so we were a little better off than others. My husband bought foot lockers, so our luggage was pretty big and we took sheets and things that the other people hadn't taken. . . .

The day we were taken to camp we had to go to a special designated place to get the bus. This friend of ours took me and the baby so that we wouldn't have to walk. Most people just walked. We got on the bus and everybody was just sitting there, and I was thinking, Gee, everybody's so brave, nobody's crying, and I wasn't going to cry either, because Japanese frown on weakness, so I wouldn't look at anybody. And then [a woman] came up and looked in the bus window and she said, "Oh, look at the poor thing, she has a tiny baby." And then I started to bawl, and I bawled the whole way to camp. I felt like a fool, because nobody else cried. They didn't even cry when I cried. . . .

When I think back to the internment camp, I want to call it a concentration camp, but it wasn't. We have a neighbor who escaped from Auschwitz during the war, and there's no comparison. In our life it was only four months, and that's not long.

But the evacuation did change our philosophy. It made you feel that you knew what it was to die, to go somewhere you couldn't take anything but what you had inside you. And so it strengthened you. I think from then on we were very strong. I don't think anything could get us down now.

Selection from Mark Jonathan Harris, et. al., *The Homefront: America During World War II.* Published by G.P. Putnam's Sons, New York, copyright © 1984.

CRITICAL THINKING

1. How did the family react to the general uncertainty before the internment order came?
2. How did Margaret Takahashi react to leaving for the camp?
3. What was her final judgment about the experience?

P I C T U R E AS

LIFE MAGAZINE GOES TO WAR
A PHOTOGRAPHIC RECORD

An exhausted U.S. soldier, weary from fighting Germans, eats his first hot meal in fifteen days. Heroic GIs fought in this German forest for weeks in the winter of 1945.

Despite heavy German bombing of central London in 1940, the civilian population continued to work. Here a flower vendor warms her hands over the ruins of an incendiary bomb.

*L*IFE magazine sent more photographers and artists to cover World War II than all the newspapers in the United States combined. In 1938, *LIFE's* editors had stated their case for presenting Americans with the most horrific images of war ever seen: "The love of peace has no meaning unless it is based in a knowledge of war's terrors. Dead men have died in vain if live men refuse to look at them."

The *LIFE* photographers who covered the war were among the finest photographers of their generations: Robert Capa, W. Eugene Smith, Margaret Bourke-White, George Strock, Ralph Morse, and Alfred Eisenstadt. Most were exposed to extreme danger in the course of their journalistic duties. Although no photographer was ever killed in action, five were wounded, two sailed aboard ships that were torpe-

D O C U M E N T

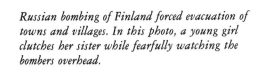

Russian bombing of Finland forced evacuation of towns and villages. In this photo, a young girl clutches her sister while fearfully watching the bombers overhead.

Battles in jungles of New Guinea were often nightmares of hand-to-hand combat. In this historic photo, an aborigine helps an Australian soldier blinded by an exploding shell.

Attacked by dive-bombers, American soldiers take refuge in a foxhole. Officers concerned with troop performance often asked to see pictures taken by LIFE photographers.

doed, and two were shot down.

The commitment of some photographers extended beyond merely reporting the war. Two German-Americans, covertly joined Fascist organizations and helped expose the destructive activities of Nazis in North America. After Fritz Goro's story about the Canadian Nazis appeared in *LIFE,* the group virtually disbanded.

CRITICAL THINKING

1. Defend the cliche "one picture is worth a thousand words" based on these examples of photojournalism.
2. Photojournalism is sometimes criticized as an invasion of privacy. Why might some of these pictures be viewed in this way?

PRESIDENT HARRY TRUMAN FACES THE AWESOME DECISION OF WHETHER OR NOT TO DROP THE ATOMIC BOMB

The most important fact of life in the world today is nuclear weaponry. Many nations have the capacity to destroy others with nuclear bombs. The United States and the Soviet Union have the capacity to destroy the world several times over.

This Nuclear Age began quietly on August 2, 1939 when the brilliant physicist, Albert Einstein, wrote a personal letter to President Franklin D. Roosevelt. In his own handwriting, to emphasize the importance of his message, Einstein explained that it was possible to build "extremely powerful bombs of a new type"—nuclear reaction bombs capable of destroying an entire city.

Einstein was a refugee from totalitarianism in Europe. He was a Jew who fled Germany because of the Nazi takeover. The scientists Enrico Fermi (an Italian) and Leo Szilard (a Hungarian), on whose discoveries Einstein's letter was based, had also fled the tyranny of the Fascists. All three men were worried because there were signs that the Germans were already researching the possibility of making an atomic bomb. There is no doubt that when Roosevelt approved an American nuclear bomb project, it was Germany he had in mind as a target. Given the criminal nature of the Nazi state, it was vitally important to build the A-Bomb before Hitler did.

But Germany surrendered in the spring of 1945, before the American bomb was ready for testing. However, Japan was fighting on and within days after he succeeded Roosevelt as president, Harry S. Truman was faced with an awesome decision: should the atomic bomb be used against Japan, which was not a criminal state in the sense Nazi Germany was, which had never even begun research in nuclear weaponry, and which was nearly defeated by massive American military superiority?

Einstein and Szilard said no. The bomb was a horrible creation. The only excuse for making one was the even more horrible threat of the Nazis. Most of Truman's military advisers, however, said that if the United States invaded Japan using conventional weapons only, there would be a million casualties, more than the two bombs in existence would kill.

Other advisers, however, like Admiral William Leahy, insisted that the bomb was unnecessary and it would be morally wrong of the United States to use such an inhumane weapon.

Historians have never agreed on exactly why the bomb was dropped. Some say that the motive was simply to end the war as quickly as possible. Surprise was necessary and it was a bad idea to "demonstrate" the bomb in an uninhabited area because it might not work. Then the Japanese would be encouraged to fight on.

Some historians have argued that the real target was not Japan but America's ally, the Soviet Union. Hiroshima and Nagasaki were bombed, they say, to warn the Soviets not to push too hard in the international discussions that would follow the war—or an atomic bomb might be dropped on Russia.

Regardless of the motives held by the various participants in the decision-making process, one person had to ultimately decide whether or not to drop the world's first atomic bomb. President Truman's account of that awesome decision follows.

$\mathcal{A}$t noon [April 25] I saw Secretary of War Stimson . . .

Stimson was one of the very few men responsible for the setting up of the atomic bomb project. He had taken a keen and active interest in every stage of its development. He said he wanted specifically to talk to me today about the effect the atomic bomb might likely have on our future foreign relations. . . .

I listened with absorbed interest, for Stimson was a man of great wisdom and foresight. He went into considerable detail in describing the nature and power of the projected weapon. If expectations were to be realized, he told me, the atomic bomb would be certain to have a decisive influence on our relations with other countries. And if it worked, the bomb, in all probability, would shorten the war.

[Secretary of State] Byrnes had already told me that the weapon might be so powerful as to be potentially capable of wiping out entire cities and killing people on an unprecedented scale. And he had added that in his belief the bomb might well put us in a position to dictate our own terms at the end of the war. Stimson, on the other hand, seemed at least as much concerned with the role of the atomic bomb in the shaping of history as in its capacity to shorten this war. . . . He also suggested that I designate a committee to study and advise me of the implications of this new force. . . . [June I] The conclusions reached by these men, both in the advisory committee of scientists and in the larger committee, were brought to me by Secretary Stimson on June I.

It was their recommendation that the bomb be used against the enemy as soon as it could be done. They recommended further that it should be used without specific warning and against a target that would clearly show its devastating strength. I had realized, of course, that an atomic bomb explosion would inflict damage and casualties beyond imagination. On the other hand, the scientific advisers of the committee reported, "We can propose no technical demonstration likely to bring an end to the war; we see no acceptable alternative to direct military use." It was their conclusion that no technical demonstration they might propose, such as over a deserted island, would be likely to bring the war to an end. It had to be used against an enemy target.

The final decision of where and when to use the atomic bomb was up to me. Let there be no mistake about it. I regarded the bomb as a military weapon and never had any doubt that it should be used. The top military advisers to the President recommended its use, and when I talked to Churchill he unhesitatingly told me that he favored the use of the atomic bomb if it might aid to end the war.

In deciding to use this bomb I wanted to make sure that it would be used as a weapon of war in the manner prescribed by the laws of war. That meant that I wanted it dropped on a military target. I had told Stimson that the bomb should be dropped as nearly as possible upon a war production center of prime military importance. . . . Four cities were finally recommended as targets: Hiroshima, Kokura, Niigata, and Nagasaki. . . .

Selection from *Memoirs of Harry S. Truman: year of Decisions*, Published by Doubleday & Co., New York, 1955. Reprinted in Paul M. Angle, *The American Reader*, by Rand McNally, Chicago, 1958, pages 632–633.

CRITICAL THINKING

1. What reasons did President Truman offer to justify his decision on the use of the atomic bomb?
2. Summarize Truman's alternatives to bombing Hiroshima and Nagasaki.
3. Truman foresaw that nuclear weapons might affect the country's future foreign relations. In what ways did this prove true in the post-war years?

President Harry S. Truman announced that an atomic bomb had been dropped on Hiroshima.

8. PRESIDENT HARRY S. TRUMAN REVEALS THE DROPPING OF AN ATOMIC BOMB ON HIROSHIMA

The first atomic bomb was dropped on Hiroshima on the morning of August 6, 1945. It destroyed more than four square miles of the city and killed or injured some 135,000 residents. On that same morning, President Harry S. Truman announced to the nation that America's secret bomb had been used.

Sixteen hours ago an American airplane dropped one bomb on Hiroshima, an important Japanese Army base. That bomb had more power than 20,000 tons of TNT. It had more than 2,000 times the blast power of the British "Grand Slam," which is the largest bomb ever yet used in the history of warfare.

The Japanese began the war from the air at Pearl Harbor. They have been repaid manyfold. And the end is not yet. With this bomb we have now added a new and revolutionary increase in destruction to supplement the growing power of our armed forces. In their present form these bombs are now in production, and even more powerful forms are in development.

It is an atomic bomb. It is a harnessing of the basic power of the universe. The force from which the sun draws its power has been loosed against those who brought war to the Far East.

Before 1939, it was the accepted belief of scientists that it was theoretically possible to release atomic energy. But no one knew any practical method of doing it. By 1942, however, we knew that the Germans were working feverishly to find a way to add atomic energy to the other engines of war with which they hoped to enslave the world. But they failed. We may be grateful to Providence that the Germans got the V-1's and V-2's late and in limited quantities and even more grateful that they did not get the atomic bomb at all.

The battle of the laboratories held fateful risks for us as well as the battles of the air, land, and sea, and we have now won the battle of the laboratories as we have won the other battles.

Beginning in 1940, before Pearl Harbor, scientific knowledge useful in war was pooled between the United States and Great Britain, and many priceless helps to our victories have come from that arrangement. Under that general policy the research on the atomic bomb was begun. With American and British scientists working together we entered the race of discovery against the Germans.

The United States had available the large number of scientists of distinction in the many needed areas of knowledge. It had the tremendous industrial and financial resources necessary for the project, and they could be devoted to it without undue impairment of other vital war work. In the United States the laboratory work and the production plants, on which a substantial start had already been made, would be out of reach of enemy bombing, while at that time Britain was exposed to constant air attack and was still threatened with the possibility of invasion. For these reasons Prime Minister Churchill and President Roosevelt agreed that it was wise to carry on the project here.

We now have two great plants and many lesser works devoted to the production of atomic power. Employment during peak construction numbered 125,000 and over 65,000 individuals are even now engaged in operating the plants. Many have worked there for two and a half years. Few know what they have been producing. They see great quantities of material going in and they see nothing coming out of these plants, for the physical size of the explosive charge is exceedingly small. We have spent $2 billion on the greatest scientific gamble in history—and won.

But the greatest marvel is not the size of the enterprise, its secrecy, nor its cost, but the achievement of scientific brains in putting together infinitely complex pieces of knowledge held by many men in different fields of science into a workable plan. And hardly less marvelous has been the capacity of industry to design, and of labor to operate, the machines and methods to do things never done before so that the brainchild of many minds came forth in physical shape and performed as it was supposed to do. Both science and industry worked under the direction of the United States Army, which achieved a unique success in managing so diverse a problem in the advancement of knowledge in an amazingly short time. It is doubtful if such another combination could be got together in the world. What has been done is the greatest achievement of organized science in history. It was done under high pressure and without failure.

We are now prepared to obliterate more rapidly and completely every productive enterprise the Japanese have above ground in any city. We shall destroy their docks, their factories, and their communications. Let there be no mistake; we shall completely destroy Japan's power to make war.

It was to spare the Japanese people from utter destruction that the ultimatum of July 26 was issued at Potsdam. Their leaders promptly rejected that ultimatum. If they do not now accept our terms they may expect a rain of ruin from the air, the like of which has never been seen on this earth. Behind this air attack will follow sea and land forces in such numbers and power as they have not yet seen and with the fighting skill of which they are already well aware.

The secretary of war, who has kept in personal touch with all phases of the project, will immediately make public a statement giving further details.

His statement will give facts concerning the sites at Oak Ridge near Knoxville, Tennessee, and at Richland near Pasco, Washington, and an installation near Sante Fe, New Mexico. Although the workers at the sites have been making materials to be used in producing the greatest destructive force in history, they have not themselves been in danger beyond that of many other occupations, for the utmost care has been taken of their safety.

The fact that we can release atomic energy ushers in a new era in man's understanding of nature's forces. Atomic energy may in the future supplement the power that now comes from coal, oil, and falling water, but at present it cannot be produced on a basis to compete with them commercially. Before that comes there must be a long period of intensive research.

It has never been the habit of the scientists of this country or the policy of this government to withhold from the world scientific knowledge. Normally, therefore, everything about the work with atomic energy would be made public.

But under present circumstances it is not intended to divulge the technical processes of production or all the military applications, pending further examination of possible methods of protecting us and the rest of the world from the danger of sudden destruction.

I shall recommend that the Congress of the United States consider promptly the establishment of an appropriate commission to control the production and use of atomic power within the United States. I shall give further consideration and make further recommendations to the Congress as to how atomic power can become a powerful and forceful influence towards the maintenance of world peace.

Selection from *The Annals of America, 1940–1949*, Vol. 16. Published by Encyclopaedia Britannica, Inc., Chicago, copyright © 1968.

CRITICAL THINKING

1. Explain what Truman means by "the battle of the laboratories."
2. List the reasons why the atomic bomb development project was carried on in the United States instead of Britain.
3. What can you infer was the ultimatum issued at Potsdam?

ONE POINT OF VIEW

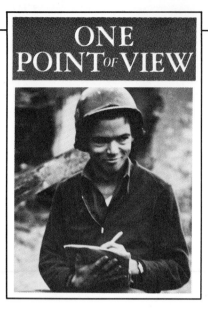

BILL MAULDIN

"Hit th' dirt, boys!"

Two of the most famous characters to come out of World War II were Willie and Joe—a pair of grimy, combat-weary "dogfaces" whose cartoon adventures and gripes entertained both soldiers and civilians. They were the creation of Bill Mauldin [born in 1921], a young infantryman who drew them for the Army's newspaper, *Stars and Stripes*. His realistic portrayal of frontline soldiers and their hardships made his cartoons widely popular.

Mauldin saw action on the Italian front and was obliged to do his work under the most challenging conditions. He was wounded and received the Purple Heart.

While a few in the Army's upper echelons objected that the bedraggled Willie and Joe gave a bad impression of U.S. soldiers, most of the Army hierarchy saw Mauldin's cartoons as a positive way of allowing soldiers to blow off steam by having their complaints aired harmlessly.

Before entering the Army, Mauldin, who had studied at the Chicago Academy of Art, had met with little success in getting his cartoons published. Willie and Joe, however, brought him the recognition he sought. In 1945 he won a Pulitzer Prize.

Keeping a sense of humor under stress characterized Mauldin's cartoons. Tired GIs were his main target but occasionally he satirized the officers. He received a Purple Heart medal covering the war in Italy, but could not refrain from poking fun at other medal winners.

CRITICAL THINKING

1. How do Bill Mauldin's cartoons differ from those of Thomas Nast?
2. Choose two of the cartoons on these pages and explain what the humor is in each one.
3. How might Army officers' feelings toward Mauldin's cartoons differ from those of the enlisted men? Which cartoon demonstrates this?

"Yer lucky. Yer learnin' a trade."

"Just gimme th' aspirin. I already got a Purple Heart."

"Beautiful view! Is there one for the enlisted men?"

"Able Fox Five to Able Fox. I got a target, but ya gotta be patient."

9. A DESCRIPTION OF THE CITY OF HIROSHIMA AFTER THE DROPPING OF A SINGLE ATOMIC BOMB

The atomic bomb that was dropped on Hiroshima ended World War II—and ushered in a new age in world affairs. This contemporary account by Clark Lee detailed some of the effects of the bomb.

A total of 53,000 of Hiroshima's pre-atomic bomb population is dead.

Thirty-three thousand are known to have died almost immediately in that awful flash at 8:18 a.m., when man first proved to himself that it is in his power to destory all living things, and the death toll has been rising daily since that day.

At least 5,000 persons now are dying of radioactive burns . . . and it is expected that the dead will total more than 80,000.

The death rate is still about 100 persons daily.

A Japanese provincial official furnished us with these . . . figures . . .

On Aug. 20—33,000 dead; 30,000 missing and probably dead; 14,000 seriously injured; 43,500 less seriously injured.

On Sept. 1, known dead had mounted to 53,000.

But no casualty figures could possibly describe the four and one half miles of terrifying desolation —an area where the fear of death will bar permanent residents for years to come.

Street cars are running and a few people are walking through the ruins of Hiroshima but there is nothing standing above the ground except a dozen reinforced concrete buildings—all of which are burned.

Every Japanese-style building in the stricken area has been blasted or burned flat and all that remains in the streets are piles of scattered tiles and black, dead trees.

Gravestones, too, and some concrete bridges and fences withstood the blast.

There is no city in the world so terribly destroyed—not Berlin, Hamburg or any other.

Selection from Clark Lee, "A Kid Thought the Moon Had Fallen," in *This Was Your War*, edited by Frank Brookhouser. Published by Doubleday, Garden City, N.Y., copyright © 1960.

10. WRITER DWIGHT MACDONALD PRESENTS A PACIFIST'S VIEW OF THE A-BOMB

Controversy about the dropping of two atomic bombs that destroyed Hiroshima and Nagasaki began almost immediately. Advocates of the bombings insisted that they had prevented untold casualties, both military and civilian. Among those opposed to the bombings was Dwight MacDonald, a political writer and pacifist who brought up the moral responsibility of the scientists who had contributed to the bomb.

It seems fitting that The Bomb was not developed by any of the totalitarian powers, where the political atmosphere might at first glance seem to be more suited to it, but by the two "democracies," the last major powers to continue to pay at least ideological respect to the humanitarian-democratic tradition. It also seems fitting that the heads of these governments, by the time The Bomb exploded, were not Roosevelt and Churchill, figures of a certain historical and personal stature, but Attlee and Truman, both colorless mediocrities, Average Men elevated to their positions by the mechanisms of the system. All this emphasizes that perfect automation, that absolute lack of human consciousness or aims which our society is rapidly achieving. As a uranium "pile," once the elements have been brought together, inexorably runs through a series of "chain reactions" until the final explosion takes place, so the elements of our society act and react, regardless of ideologies or personalities, until The Bomb explodes over Hiroshima. The more commonplace the personalities and senseless the institutions, the more grandious the destruction. It is *Götterdämme-rung* without the gods.

The scientists themselves whose brain-work produced The Bomb appear not as creators but as raw material to be hauled about and exploited like uranium ore. Thus, Dr. Otto Hahn, the German scientist who in 1939 first split the uranium atom and who did his best to present Hitler with an atom bomb, has been brought over to this country to pool his knowledge with our atomic "team" (which includes several Jewish refugees who were kicked out of Germany by Hitler). Thus Professor Kaputza, Russia's leading experimenter with uranium, was decoyed from Cambridge University in the thirties back to his native land, and, once there, refused permission to return. Thus a recent report from Yugoslavia tells of some eminent native atom-splitter being highjacked by the Red Army (just like a valuable machine tool) and rushed by plane to Moscow.

Insofar as there is any moral responsibility assignable for The Bomb, it rests with those scientists who developed it and those political and military leaders who employed it. Since the rest of us Americans did not even know what was being done in our name—let alone have the slightest possibility of stopping it—The Bomb becomes the most dramatic illustration to date of the fallacy of "The Responsibility of Peoples."

Yet how can even those immediately concerned be held responsible? . . . What, then, can a man do *now*? How can he escape playing his part in the ghastly process?

Quite simply by not playing it. Many eminent scientists, for example, worked on The Bomb: Fermi of Italy, Bohr of Denmark, Chadwick of England, Oppenheimer, Urey and Compton of USA. It is fair to expect such men, of great knowledge and intelligence, to be aware of the consequences of their actions. And they seem to have been so. Dr. Smyth observes: "Initially, many scientists could and did hope that some principle would emerge which would prove that atomic bombs were inherently impossible. The hope has faded gradually. . . ." Yet they all accepted the "assignment," and produced The Bomb. Why? Because they thought of themselves as specialists, technicians, and not as complete men. Specialists in the sense that the process of scientific discovery is considered to be morally neutral, so

that the scientist may deplore the uses to which his discoveries are put by the generals and politicians but may not refuse to make them for that reason; and specialists also in that they reacted in the war as partisans of one side, whose function was the narrow one of defeating the Axis governments even if it meant sacrificing their broader responsibility as human beings.

But, fortunately for the honor of science, a number of scientists refused to take part in the project. I have heard of several individual cases over here, and Sir James Chadwick has revealed "that some of his colleagues refused to work on the atomic bomb for fear they might be creating a planet-destroying monster." These scientists reacted as whole men, not as special-ists or partisans. Today the tendency is to think of peoples as responsible and individuals as irresponsible. The reversal of both these conceptions is the first condition of escaping the present decline to barbarism. The more each individual thinks and behaves as a whole Man (hence responsibly) rather than as a specialized part of some nation or profession (hence irresponsibly), the better hope for the future. To insist on acting as a responsible individual in a society which reduces the individual to impotence may be foolish, reckless, and ineffectual; or it may be wise, prudent, and effective. But whichever it is, only thus is there a chance of changing our present tragic destiny. All honor then to the as yet anonymous British and American scientists—Men, I would rather say—who were so wisely foolish as to refuse their cooperation on The Bomb! This is "resistance," this is "negativism," and in it lies our best hope.

Selection from Dwight MacDonald, *Memoirs of a Revolutionist: Essays in Political Criticism.* Published by Meridian Books, Inc., New York, copyright © 1957.

CRITICAL THINKING

1. How does MacDonald compare the chain reaction of an atomic bomb to democratic society?
2. List some examples of scientists being treated as raw material.
3. Explain why MacDonald praises scientists who refuse to work on the atomic bomb.

CHAPTER 30

COLD WAR TENSIONS

1945–1952

1. THE *TRUMAN DOCTRINE* IS ESTABLISHED TO HALT THE SPREAD OF COMMUNISM

In 1945, various Greek political groups, including Communists, formed a coalition government that was pledged to rebuild Greece. Their effort was threatened, in 1947, by an economic crisis in Great Britain that forced Britain to suspend its military and economic aid to Greece. Fearing that the Communists would use this as an opportunity to take control of the Greek government, American leaders proposed a program of massive United States aid for both Greece and Turkey. President Truman's announcement of this proposal, on March 12, 1947, illustrates the ideas and programs that would become the Truman Doctrine, *which sought to contain Communism by aiding anti-Communist governments.*

One of the primary objectives of the foreign policy of the United States is the creation of conditions in which we and other nations will be able to work out a way of life free from coercion. This was a fundamental issue in the war with Germany and Japan. Our victory was won over countries which sought to impose their will, and their way of life, upon other nations.

To insure the peaceful development of nations, free from coercion, the United States has taken a leading part in establishing the United Nations. The United Nations is designed to make possible lasting freedom and independence for all its members. We shall not realize our objectives, however, unless we are willing to help free peoples to maintain their free institutions and their national integrity against aggressive movements that seek to impose upon them totalitarian regimes. . . .

The peoples of a number of countries of the world have recently had totalitarian regimes forced upon them against their will. The Government of the United States has made frequent protests against coercion and intimidation, in violation of the Yalta agreement, in Poland, Rumania, and Bulgaria. I must also state that in a number of other countries there have been similar developments.

At the present moment in world history nearly every nation must choose between alternative ways of life. The choice is too often not a free one.

One way of life is based upon the will of the majority, and is distinguished by free institutions, representative governments, free elections, guaranties of individual liberty, freedom of speech and religion, and freedom from political oppression.

The second way of life is based upon the will of a minority forcibly imposed upon the majority. It relies upon terror and oppression, a controlled press and radio, fixed elections, and the suppression of personal freedoms.

I believe that it must be the policy of the United States to support free peoples who are resisting attempted subjugation by armed minorities or by outside pressures.

I believe that we must assist free peoples to work out their own destinies in their own way.

I believe that our help should be primarily through economic and financial aid, which is essential to economic stability and orderly political processes.

The world is not static and the status quo is not sacred. But we cannot allow changes in the status quo in violation of the Charter of the United Nations by such methods as coercion, or by such subterfuges as political infiltration. . . .

I therefore ask the Congress to provide authority for assistance to Greece and Turkey in the amount of $400,000,000 for the period ending June 30, 1948. . . .

The United States contributed $341,000,000,000 toward winning World War II. This is an investment in world freedom and world peace.

The assistance that I am recommending for Greece and Turkey amounts to little more than one-tenth of 1 percent of this investment. It is only common sense that we should safeguard this investment and make sure that it was not in vain.

The seeds of totalitarian regimes are nurtured by misery and want. They spread and grow in the evil soil of poverty and strife. They reach their full growth when the hope of a people for a better life has died.

We must keep that hope alive.

Selection from address by President Harry S. Truman, March 12, 1947, *Congressional Record*, Vol. 93—Part 2. Published by United States Government Printing Office, Washington, D.C., copyright © 1947.

CRITICAL THINKING

1. What reasons did President Truman give for the aid to Greece and Turkey?
2. In his address, Truman saw nations as facing a choice between two major systems. What did he see as the major differences between those systems?
3. What role did Truman outline for the United States in world affairs?

2. SECRETARY OF STATE GEORGE MARSHALL DEVISES A PLAN TO REBUILD EUROPE

In the same year, 1947, that the Truman Doctrine was stated, Secretary of State George Marshall proposed a program of economic aid for Europe, including the Soviet Union and the nations of Eastern Europe. (The Soviets rejected the offer.) In the following speech, Marshall outlines what came to be known as the Marshall Plan.

In considering the requirements for the rehabilitation of Europe the physical loss of life, the visible destruction of cities, factories, mines and railroads was correctly estimated, but it has become obvious during recent months that this visible destruction was probably less serious than the dislocation of the entire fabric of European economy. For the past ten years conditions have been highly abnormal.

The feverish preparation for war and the more feverish maintenance of the war effort engulfed all aspects of national economies. Machinery has fallen into disrepair or is entirely obsolete. Under the arbitrary and destructive Nazi rule, virtually every possible enterprise was geared into the German war machine. Longstanding commercial ties, private institutions, banks, insurance companies and shipping companies disappeared, through loss of capital, absorption through nationalization or by simple destruction.

In many countries, confidence in the local currency has been severely shaken. The breakdown of the business structure of Europe during the war was complete. Recovery has been seriously retarded by the fact that two years after the close of hostilities a peace settlement with Germany and Austria has not been agreed upon. But even given a more prompt solution of these difficult problems, the rehabilitation of the economic structure of Europe quite evidently will require a much longer time and greater effort than had been foreseen. . . .

The truth of the matter is that Europe's requirements for the next three or four years of foreign food and other essential products—principally from America—are so much greater than her present ability to pay that she must have substantial additional help, or face economic, social and political deterioration of a very grave character.

The remedy lies in breaking the vicious circle and restoring the confidence of the European people in the economic future of their own countries and of Europe as a whole. The manufacturer and the farmer throughout wide areas must be able and willing to exchange their products for currencies, the continuing value of which is not open to question.

Aside from the demoralizing effect on the world at large and the possibilities of disturbances arising as a result of the desperation of the people concerned, the consequences to the economy of the United States should be apparent to all. It is logical that the United States should do whatever it is able to do to assist in the return of normal economic health in the world, without which there health in the world, without which there can be no political stability and no assured peace.

Our policy is directed not against any country or doctrine but against hunger, poverty, desperation and chaos. Its purposes should be the revival of a working economy in the world so as to permit the emergence of political and social conditions in which free institutions can exist. Such assistance, I am convinced, must not be on a piecemeal basis as various crises develop. Any assistance that this Government may render in the future should provide a cure rather than a mere palliative. . . .

It is already evident that, before the United States Government can proceed much further in its efforts to alleviate the situation and help start the European world on its way to recovery, there must be some agreement among the countries of Europe as to the requirements of the situation and the part those countries themselves will take in order to give proper effect to whatever action might be undertaken by this Government. It would be neither fitting nor efficacious for this Government to undertake to draw up unilaterally a program designed to place Europe on its feet economically. This is the business of the Europeans. The initiative, I think, must come from Europe. The role of this country should consist of friendly aid in the drafting of the European program so far as it may be practical for us to do so. The program should be a joint one, agreed to by a number, if not all European nations.

Selection from *Documents of American History,* edited by Henry Steele Commager. Published by Appleton-Century-Crofts, Inc., New York, copyright © 1958.

CRITICAL THINKING

1. List the economic effects Marshall says resulted from preparation for war and maintenance of the war effort.
2. Summarize Marshall's reasons for urging the United States to aid the countries of Europe.

---

3. PRESIDENT HARRY TRUMAN SPEAKS PLAINLY ABOUT CIVIL RIGHTS

President Harry Truman's support of civil rights legislation surprised many politicians, especially in the South. Behind the President's efforts, at desegregating the armed forces and forcing an end to discrimination in both the federal government and companies doing business with the government, was his personal belief in civil rights. His views come through in an interview from Merle Miller's oral biography of President Truman, Plain Speaking. *Miller began the discussion by quoting a speech Truman made in 1940.*

In 1940 in Sedalia, Missouri, before an audience mostly of farmers, many of them ex-Ku Kluxers, and not a black face anywhere, Harry Truman spoke out on civil rights. . . .

"I believe in the brotherhood of man, not merely the brotherhood of white men but the brotherhood of all men before law.

"I believe in the Constitution and the Declaration of Independence. In giving Negroes the rights which are theirs we are only acting in accord with our own ideals of a true democracy.

"If any class or race can be permanently set apart from, or pushed down below the rest in political and civil rights, so may any other class or race when it shall incur the displeasure of its more powerful associates, and we may say farewell to the principles on which we count our safety. . . ."

Mr. President, when I came across that speech. . . . last night, I found it surprising. It seems to me to have been very courageous.

"I don't know why. That sort of thing, whether what I was saying was courageous or not, never did occur to me. And you have to understand what I said out there at Sedalia wasn't anything *new* for me to say. All those Southern fellas were very much surprised by my program for civil rights in 1948. What they didn't understand was that I'd been for things like that all the time I was in politics. I believe in the Constitution, and if you do that, then everybody's got to have their rights, and that means *everybody,* doesn't matter . . . who they are or what color they are.

The minute you start making exceptions, you might as well not have a Constitution. So that's the reason I felt the way I did, and if a lot of folks were surprised to find out where I stood on [civil rights], well, that's because they didn't know me."

Selection from Merle Miller, *Plain Speaking: An Oral Biography of Harry S. Truman.* Published by Berkley Publishing Corp., New York, copyright © 1973.

CRITICAL THINKING

1. What reasons did President Truman give for his support of civil rights legislation?
2. What was Truman's attitude toward those opposed to his civil rights policies?

---

4. VICTOR NAVASKY TALLIES UP THE COSTS OF "McCARTHYISM"

The Cold War period saw the rise of supposed professional informers who testified to their fellow Americans' Un-Americanism. In the Senate, Joseph McCarthy took subversive activities as his mandate for action; in the lower house, it was the House on Un-American Activities (HUAC). Author Victor Navasky attempts to add up the costs of McCarthyism.

THE SOCIAL COSTS of what came to be called McCarthyism have yet to be computed. By conferring its prestige on the red hunt, the state did more than bring misery to the lives of hundreds of thousands of Communists, former Communists, fellow travelers, and unlucky liberals. It weakened American culture and it weakened itself.

Unlike the Palmer Raids of the early 1920s, which were violent hit-and-run affairs that had no long-term effect, the vigilante spirit [Joseph] McCarthy respresented still lives on in legislation accepted as a part of the American political way. The morale of the United States' newly reliable and devoted civil service was savagely undermined in the 1950s, and the purge of the Foreign Service contributed to our disastrous miscalculations in Southeast Asia in the 1960s and the consequent human wreckage. The congressional investigations of the 1940s and 1950s fueled the anti-Communist hysteria which eventually led to the investment of thousands of billions of dollars in a nuclear arsenal, with risks that boggle the minds of even those who specialize in "thinking about the unthinkable." Unable to tolerate a little subversion (however one defines it)—if that is the price of freedom, dignity, and experimentation—we lost our edge, our distinctiveness. McCarthyism decimated its target—the American Communist Party, whose membership fell from about seventy-five thousand just after World War II to less than ten thousand in 1957 (probably a high percentage of these lost were FBI informants)—but the real casualties of that assault were the walking wounded of the liberal left and the already impaired momentum of the New Deal. No wonder a new general of radical idealists came up through the peace and civil-rights movements rather than the Democratic Party.

The damage was compounded by the state's chosen instruments of destruction, the professional informers—those ex-Communists whom the sociologist Edward Shils described in 1956 as a host of frustrated, previously anonymous failures, . . .

It is no easier to measure the impact of McCarthyism on culture than on politics, although emblems of the terror were ever on display. In the literary community, for example, generally thought to be more permissive than the mass media . . . the distinguished editor-in-chief of the distinguished publisher Little, Brown & Co. was forced to resign because he refused to repudiate his progressive politics and he became unemployable. Such liberal publications as the *New York Post* and the *New Republic* refused to accept ads for the *transcript* of the trial of Julius and Ethel Rosenberg. Albert Maltz's short story "The Happiest Man on Earth," which had won the O'Henry Memorial Short Story Award in 1938 and been republished seventy-six times in magazines, newspapers, and anthologies, didn't get reprinted again from the time he entered prison in 1950 until 1963. Ring Lardner, Jr., had to go to England to find a publisher for his critically acclaimed novel *The Ecstasy of Owen Muir.* . . . The FBI had a permanent motion-picture crew stationed across the street from the Four Continents Bookstore in New York, which specialized in literature sympathetic to the Soviet Union's brand of Marxism. How to measure a thousand such pollutions of the cultural environment?

Selection from Victor S. Navasky, *Naming Names.* Published by the Viking Press, New York, copyright © 1980.

CRITICAL THINKING

1. Victor Navasky believes that "a little subversion" may be the price a country must pay for its freedom and its right to experiment. Do you agree or disagree?
2. What examples does Navasky give to support his charge that McCarthyism polluted American culture?

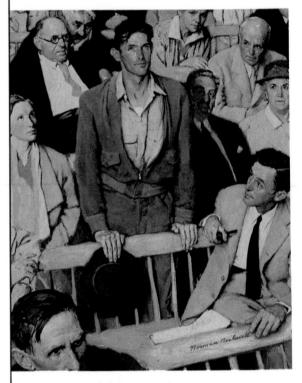

"The Town Meeting" is one of Norman Rockwell's paintings celebrating the Four Freedoms that are the foundation of American democracy. A strong, intelligent citizen speaking easily to an assembly of his townfolk symbolizes the Freedom of Speech.

NORMAN ROCKWELL

Norman Rockwell [1894–1978] began painting in the 1920s and he reached the height of his popularity as an illustrator in the 1950s. His cover illustrations for the weekly magazine, *The Saturday Evening Post*, appealed to the national taste by telling humorous stories and presenting scenes of small town life. An America of harmonious towns with traditional values came to life in his paintings.

Rockwell's work celebrated the ideals of democracy, and reflected the positive side of the country and its people. His pictures show the festivals of American public and private life, the heartwarming struggles of young families as they build their lives, the political rituals of government, and, often, the good-natured amusement with which Americans handled the new technology and changing social life of the Fifties.

Rockwell used traditional painting techniques and a realistic style, taking great pains to be certain his details were accurate and his characters appropriate to his stories. He represented the tastes and values of small town America. His paintings were the artistic opposite of the new abstract art being created by a growing number of modern artists living in America's urban centers.

CRITICAL THINKING

1. The emerging art form of Rockwell's time was abstract. Did Rockwell's illustrations conform to this movement? How do his pictures document American life in a different way than abstract expressionism does?
2. Cite details from these pictures to show why they had mass appeal.

The occupant of this old house probably welcomed his first radio with the same enthusiasm with which he greets his first television. Rockwell's painting, "The New Television Set," shows that the very new can be grafted to the enduring old.

CHAPTER 31

DOMESTIC AND FOREIGN CHALLENGES

1952–1960

1. THE SUPREME COURT'S DECISION ON *BROWN v. BOARD OF EDUCATION OF TOPEKA* BEGINS THE PROCESS OF SCHOOL DESEGREGATION

In 1954, the United States Supreme Court handed down its landmark decision on school desegregation, Brown v. Board of Education of Topeka. *Reversing the decisions of 75 years earlier, which had accepted the existence of "separate but equal" facilities for races, the decision set in motion the beginning of desegregation in schools throughout America. This passage from the Court decision reveals part of the reasoning behind the Court's ruling.*

In approaching this problem [of segregation], we cannot turn the clock back to 1868 when the [Fourteenth] Amendment was adopted, or even to 1896 when Plessy v. Ferguson [the decision allowing "separate but equal" facilities] was written. We must consider public education in the light of its full development and its present place in American life throughout the Nation. Only in this way can it be determined if segregation in public schools deprives these plaintiffs of the equal protection of the laws.

Today, education is perhaps the most important function of state and local governments. Compulsory school attendance laws and the great expenditures for education both demonstrate our recognition of the importance of education to our democratic society. It is required in the performance of our most basic public responsibilities, even service in the armed forces. It is the very foundation of good citizenship. Today it is a

principal instrument in awakening the child to cultural values, in preparing him for later professional training, and in helping him to adjust normally to his environment. In these days, it is doubtful that any child may reasonably be expected to succeed in life if he is denied the opportunity of an education. Such an opportunity, where the state has undertaken to provide it, is a right which must be made available to all on equal terms.

We come then to the question presented: Does segregation of children in public schools solely on the basis of race, even though the physical facilities and other "tangible" factors may be equal, deprive the children of the minority group of equal educational opportunities? We believe that it does.

In Sweatt v. Painter . . . in finding that a segregated law school for Negroes could not provide them equal educational opportunities, this Court relied in large part on "those qualities which are incapable of objective measurement but which make for greatness in a law school." In McLaurin v. Oklahoma State Regents . . . the Court, in requiring that a Negro admitted to a white graduate school be treated like all other students, again resorted to intangible considerations:" . . . his ability to study, to engage in discussions and exchange views with other students, and, in general, to learn his profession." Such considerations apply with added force to children in grade and high schools. To separate them from others of similar age and qualifications solely because of their race generates a feeling of inferiority as to their status in the community that may affect their hearts and minds in a way unlikely ever to be undone. . . .

We conclude that in the field of public education the doctrine of "separate but equal" has no place. Separate educational facilities are inherently unequal. Therefore, we hold that the plaintiffs and others similarly situated . . . are, by reason of the segregation complained of, deprived of the equal protection of the laws guaranteed by the Fourteenth Amendment.

Selection from *Cases Argued and Decided in the Supreme Court of the United States, October Term,* in *U.S. Reports,* Vol. 347. Published by the Lawyers Cooperative Publishing Company, Rochester, N.Y., copyright © 1954.

CRITICAL THINKING

1. What reasons are cited for rejecting the notion of "separate but equal" educational facilities for blacks and whites?
2. What changes in American life did the Court suggest was responsible for a decision different from the earlier Plessy v. Ferguson decision?

2. ROSA PARKS REFUSES TO GIVE UP HER SEAT ON THE BUS

In December, 1955, an incident took place that gave added impetus to the young civil rights movement. Mrs. Rosa Parks, a black woman from Montgomery, Alabama, refused to give up her seat on a Montgomery city bus to accomodate white passengers. Her arrest led black religious and civic leaders to organize a boycott of the city's bus system. One of the leaders of that boycott was Reverend Martin Luther King, Jr., whose role in the crisis during the following weeks brought him to national attention. In his book Stride Toward Freedom, *King described what he believed to have been Mrs. Parks' motives.*

Tried for refusing to move from her seat on a Montgomery bus, Rosa Parks was fined $14.

On December 1, 1955, an attractive Negro seamstress, Mrs. Rosa Parks, boarded the Cleveland Avenue Bus in downtown Montgomery. She was returning home after her regular day's work in the Montgomery Fair—a leading department store. Tired from long hours on her feet, Mrs. Parks sat down in the first seat behind the section reserved for whites. Not long after she took her seat, the bus operator ordered her, along with three other Negro passengers, to move back in order to accomodate boarding white passengers. By this time every seat in the bus was taken. This meant that if Mrs. Parks followed the driver's command she would have to stand while a white male passenger, who had just boarded the bus, would sit. The other three Negro passengers immediately complied with the driver's request. But Mrs. Parks quietly refused. The result was her arrest.

There was to be much speculation about why Mrs. Parks did not obey the driver. Many people in the white community argued that she had been "planted" by the NAACP [National Association for the Advancement of Colored People] in order to lay the groundwork for a test case, and at first glance that explanation seemed plausible, since she was a former secretary of the local branch of the NAACP. So persistent and persuasive was this argument that it convinced many reporters from all over the country. Later on, when I was having press conferences three times a week—in order to accommodate the reporters and journalists who came to Montgomery from all over the world—the invariable first question was: "Did the NAACP start the bus boycott?"

But the accusation was totally unwarranted, as the testimony of both Mrs. Parks and the officials of the NAACP revealed. Actually, no one can understand the action of Mrs. Parks unless he realizes that eventually the cup of endurance runs over, and the human personality cries out, "I can take it no longer." Mrs. Parks' refusal to move back was her intrepid affirmation that she had had enough. It was an individual expression of a timeless longing for human dignity and freedom. She was not "planted" there by the NAACP, or any other organization; she was planted there by her personal sense of dignity and self-respect. She was anchored to that seat by the accumulated indignities of days gone by and the boundless aspirations of generations yet unborn. She was a victim of both the forces of history and the forces of destiny. She had been tracked down by the *Zeitgeist*—the spirit of the time.

Selection from Martin Luther King, Jr., *Stride Toward Freedom: The Montgomery Story*. Published by Harper & Row, New York, copyright © 1958.

CRITICAL THINKING

1. What did Martin Luther King see as the main reason behind Rosa Parks' action on the bus?
2. Why might Mrs. Parks' attitude have provided an important example for the people struggling to overcome racial segregation laws?
3. Why might King have gone to such lengths in this passage to deny that the incident was planned by the NAACP?

---

3. PRESIDENT DWIGHT EISENHOWER WRITES ABOUT THE SPUTNIK SATELLITE

In October, 1957, the Soviet Union launched the first satellite into orbit. Sputnik, which means "traveling companion," came as an unwelcome shock to the United States and the countries of Western Europe, who had downgraded Soviet technology. The resulting hysteria is recounted by President Dwight D. Eisenhower in his book, Waging Peace.

In the weeks and months after Sputnik many Americans seemed to be seized not only with a sudden worry that our defenses had crumbled, but also with an equally unjustified alarm that our entire educational system was defective. The Soviets, some suspected, would soon surpass us intellectually, if indeed they had not already done so.

Acting on such an assumption, many argued for a broad-gauge crash federal outlay to finance higher education. In answer to such suggestions, I could only remind people to think the problem through: "There are very grave dangers that would accompany any initiation of a *general* federal support for these institutions," I wrote to one educator. "In this statement I do not mean, of course, to be opposed to support . . . in special areas to meet special and pressing needs of the government." But I was convinced that my objections to the concept of generalized and direct federal help for all higher education were sound. . . .

Other persons recommended astronomical amounts of direct defense spending. Again and again I reiterated my philosophy on the defense budget: Excessive spending helps cause deficits, which cause inflation, which in turn cuts the amount of equipment and manpower the defense dollar can buy. The process is circular and self-defeating.

Every addition to defense expenditures does not automatically increase military security. Because security is based upon moral and economic, as well as purely military strength, a point can be reached at which additional funds for arms, far from bolstering security, weaken it. . . .

I had made as strong a case for confidence and sane direction as I could. I was hampered, of course, by the fact that I could not reveal secrets which in themselves would have reassured our people. For example, shortly before this address Foster Dulles, in a meeting with Allen Dulles, General Goodpaster, and me, had asked, "Should we disclose tonight that the United States has the capability of photographing the Soviet Union from very high altitudes without interference?"

Reluctantly, I decided I could not make such a revelation. It was not to become public for another two and a half years when an airplane called the U-2 fell in Soviet territory.

Six days later I flew to Oklahoma City and spoke again of deterrent and defense. I included short discussions on scientific education and greater concentration on research. We had tough choices to make, I said. Some civilian programs were desirable but not essential. Some savings would be squeezed out through the wringer. "And pressure groups will wail in anguish," I said. But we would not sacrifice security to worship a balanced bud-

President Dwight Eisenhower (left) did not agree with those who favored increased defense spending or a "space race" after the Soviet Union had launched its Sputnik satellite (right) in 1957.

get. We would never be an aggressor—we wanted adequate security—we wanted no more than adequacy. But we would accept nothing less.

This was a period of anxiety. Sputnik had revealed the psychological vulnerability of our people. The Communists were steadily fomenting trouble and rattling sabers; our economy was sputtering somewhat, and the ceaseless and usually healthy self-criticism in which we of the United States indulge had brought a measure of genuine self-doubt. Added to these and other factors was the failure of our first satellite launching attempt in the full glare of publicity, and the alleged missile "gaps" which political observers claimed they had detected. There was ample stimulus for public uncertainty.

The Soviet satellites were a genuine technological triumph, but this was exceeded by their propaganda value. To uninformed peoples in the world, Soviet success in one area led to the belief that Soviet Communism was surging ahead in all types of activity.

One beneficial effect to us was that the Soviet achievement jarred us out of what might have been a gradually solidifying complacency in technology. It caused us to give increased attention to scientific education in this country and ultimately to all phases of education.

Their most harmful effects were to cause our people who had manifold reasons to be proud to be temporarily fearful, and to add to the fire of

demand for larger appropriations as the answer to everything.

The older I grow, the more I come to respect balance—not only in budgets but in people.

As we began to overcome the psychological crisis, I felt a degree of satisfaction. I could not know then that Sputnik would color events of the next three years, including the 1960 election, or that the third confidence speech on which I was working would never be delivered. Another blow had come—a personal one, just one week away—involved a sudden illness, my third in three years. As I wrote a friend on November 18:

"Since July 25th of 1956, when Nasser announced the nationalization of the Suez, I cannot remember a day that has not brought its major or minor crisis." Crisis had now become "normalcy."

Selection from Dwight D. Eisenhower, *Waging Peace, 1956–1961*. Published by Doubleday & Co., Garden City, N.Y., copyright © 1965.

CRITICAL THINKING

1. List Eisenhower's reasons for opposing "astronomical amounts of direct defense spending."
2. Contrast what Eisenhower says were the beneficial and harmful effects of Sputnik.

FREEDOM RIDES
The Quest For Racial Integration And Equality

Birmingham, May 9. Jay Davis, student, Rev. B. Eusden, professor, Rev. William Coffin, professor, and Mrs. Coffin attend a rally at a Black church.

Anniston, May 15. A man blocks path of Freedom Rider bus. Later, the bus was stopped by a flat tire and burned. The passengers got off without serious injury.

The Congress of Racial Equality (CORE) was founded in 1942 by black and white citizens who wanted to bring about an end to racial segregation through the use of nonviolent action. In 1961, CORE decided to test local segregation laws in interstate transportation facilities by sponsoring "freedom rides" throughout the South. Although recent Supreme Court decisions had specifically prohibited racial discrimination in interstate buses and bus stations, facilities in many parts of the South were still segregated.

On May 16, 1961, a multi-racial group of "freedom riders" left Washington, D.C., en-route to New Orleans. The group, led by CORE director James Farmer, included such distinguished clergymen as the Reverend William Sloane Coffin, Jr. of Yale University.

Throughout Alabama and Mississippi, the buses were met by violent mobs. Many of the riders were beaten, and some buses were bombed and burned. It took 2 battalions of National Guard, 22 cars of highway patrolmen, 3 Army reconnaissance planes, and a helicopter to escort a busload of freedom riders and 17 reporters from Montgomery, Alabama, to the Mississippi state line.

Within a month after the Freedom Rides had

D O C U M E N T

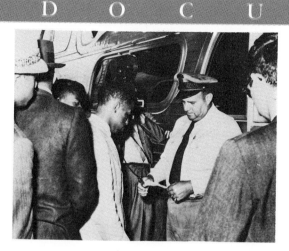

Birmingham, May 20. Bus to Montgomery held for 20 hours to thwart Freedom Riders.

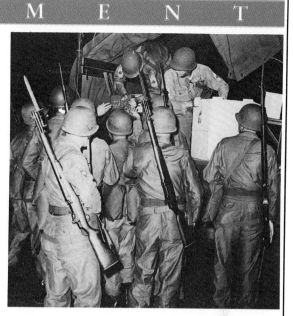

Mongtomery, May 21. National Guard troops enforce martial-law after an outbreak of racial violence. Soliders patrol near a Black church with an integration rally in progress.

Jackson, May 25. Police officers take names of Freedom Riders, 27 of whom were arrested for not heeding police orders in a bus station.

begun, more than 200 people had been fined and jailed—including many Freedom Riders, who were arrested for disturbing the peace.

The violent consequences of the Freedom Rides sent shock waves throughout the world. But in September, 1961, the Interstate Commerce Commission prescribed new rules prohibiting discrimination in interstate buses and bus stations. It ordered buses crossing state lines to display signs that read: SEATING ABOARD THIS VEHICLE IS WITHOUT REGARD TO RACE, COLOR, CREED OR NATIONAL ORIGIN BY ORDER OF THE INTERSTATE COMMERCE COMMISSION.

CRITICAL THINKING

1. Note the dates of each of these photographs and list the incidents portrayed in chronological order. Then write a short paragraph summarizing the events pictured.
2. Cite evidence from several pictures to support the claim that these photographs are primary-source documents and an accurate reflections of the civil rights movement during the times indicated.

New American Frontiers

CHAPTER 32

THE VIGOROUS SIXTIES

1960–1968

1. MASSACHUSETTS SENATOR JOHN F. KENNEDY CALLS ON AMERICANS TO BE NEW PIONEERS ON THE "NEW FRONTIER"

During his campaign for the Presidency, Massachusetts Senator John Fitzgerald Kennedy repeatedly focused on the need for strong leadership to restore a sense of purpose to American life. In his acceptance speech at the Democratic National Convention, July 15, 1960, he outlined some of the challenges facing the United States and called on Americans to meet the "New Frontier."

We are not merely running against Mr. Nixon. Our task is not merely one of itemizing Republican failures. Nor is that wholly necessary. For the families forced from the farm will know how to vote without our telling them. The unemployed miners and textile workers will know how to vote. The old people without medical care—the families without a decent home—the parents of children without adequate food or schools—they all know that it's time for a change. . . .

Today our concern must be with the future. For the world is changing. The old era is ending. The old ways will not do.

Abroad, the balance of power is shifting. There are new and more terrible weapons—new and uncertain nations—new pressures of population and deprivation. One-third of the world . . . may be free—but one-third is the victim of cruel repression—and the other one-third is rocked by pangs of poverty, hunger, and envy. More energy is released by the awakening of these new nations than by the fission of the atom itself. . . .

Here at home, the changing fact of the future is equally revolutionary. . . .

A technological revolution on the farm has led to an output explosion—but we have not yet learned to harness that explosion usefully, while protecting our farmers' right to full parity income.

An urban population revolution has overcrowded our schools, cluttered up our suburbs, and increased the squalor of our slums.

A peaceful revolution for human rights—demanding an end to racial discrimination in all parts of our community life—has strained at the leashes imposed by timid Executive leadership.

A medical revolution has extended the life of our elder citizens without providing the dignity and security those later years deserve. And a revolution of automation finds machines replacing men in the mines and mills of America, without replacing their income or their training or their need to pay the family doctor, grocer, and landlord.

There [has] also been a change—a slippage—in our intellectual and moral strength. Seven lean years of drought and famine have withered the fields of ideas. Blight has descended on our regulatory agencies—and a dry rot, beginning in Washington, is seeping into every corner of America—in the payola mentality, the expense account way of life, the confusion between what is legal and what is right. Too many Americans have lost their way, their will, and their sense of historic purpose.

It is time, in short, for a new generation of leadership—new men to cope with new problems and new opportunities. . . .

I tell you the New Frontier is here, whether we seek it or not. Beyond that frontier are uncharted areas of science and space, unsolved problems of peace and war, unconquered pockets of ignorance and prejudice, unanswered questions of poverty and surplus . . .

I believe the times demand invention, innovation, imagination, decision. I am asking each of you to be new pioneers on that New Frontier. My call is to the young in heart, regardless of age—to the stout in spirit, regardless of party—to all who respond to the . . .call: "Be strong and of good courage; be not afraid, neither be thou dismayed."

Selection from Arthur M. Schlesinger, Jr., *History of U.S. Political Parties*, Vol. IV. Published by Chelsea House, New York, copyright © 1973.

2. POET ROBERT FROST RECITES AT PRESIDENT JOHN F. KENNEDY'S INAUGURATION

Millions of Americans remember Robert Frost reading this poem, "The Gift Outright," at the inauguration of John F. Kennedy in January, 1961. Frost recited it from memory because the glare from the sun and snow was so bright he could not see the words on the paper. First published in 1942, the poem captured for many the spirit of the Kennedy years.

The land was ours before we were the land's.
She was our land more than a hundred years
Before we were her people. She was ours
In Massachusetts, in Virginia,
But we were England's, still colonials,
Possessing what we still were unpossessed by,
Possessed by what we now no more possessed.
Something we were withholding made us weak
Until we found out that it was ourselves
We were withholding from our land of living,
And forthwith found salvation in surrender.
Such as we were we gave ourselves outright
(The deed of gift was many deeds of war)
To the land vaguely realizing westward,
But still unstoried, artless, unenhanced,
Such as she was, such as she would become.

Selection from *The Annals of America*, Vol. 16. Published by Encyclopaedia Britannica, Inc., Chicago, copyright © 1968.

At John F. Kennedy's inauguration, Poet Robert Frost recited from his work. Standing at his side is Vice President Lyndon Johnson.

3. PRESIDENT LYNDON B. JOHNSON OFFERS AMERICANS HIS VISION OF A "GREAT SOCIETY"

In his first years in office, President Lyndon Baines Johnson launched a wave of social legislation aimed at building what he called the "Great Society." In an address given at Ann Arbor, Michigan, in May, 1964, President Johnson outlined the goals of these programs.

The Great Society is a place where every child can find knowledge to enrich his mind and to enlarge his talents. It is a place where leisure is a welcome chance to build and reflect, not a feared cause of boredom and restlessness. It is a place where the city of man serves not only the needs of the body and the demands of commerce but the desire for beauty and the hunger for community.

It is a place where man can renew contact with nature. It is a place which honors creation for its own sake and for what it adds to the understanding of the race. It is a place where men are more concerned with the quality of their goals than the quantity of their goods.

But most of all, the Great Society is not a safe harbor, a resting place, a final objective, a finished work. It is a challenge constantly renewed, beckoning us toward a destiny where the meaning of our lives matches the marvelous products of our labor. . . .

Many of you will live to see the day, perhaps 50 years from now, when there will be 400 million Americans—four-fifths of them in urban areas. In the remainder of this century urban population will double, city land will double, and we will have to build homes, highways, and facilities equal to all those built since this country was first settled. So in the next 40 years we must rebuild the entire urban United States. . . .

A second place where we begin to build the Great Society is in our countryside. We have always prided ourselves on being not only America the strong and America the free, but America the beautiful. Today that beauty is in danger. The water we drink, the food we eat, the very air that we breathe, are threatened with pollution. Our parks are overcrowded, our seashores overburdened. Green fields and dense forests are disappearing. . . .

A third place to build the Great Society is in the classrooms of America. There your children's lives will be shaped. Our society will not be great until every young mind is set free to scan the farthest reaches of thought and imagination. We are still far from that goal. . . .

These are three of the central issues of the Great Society. While our Government has many programs directed at those issues, I do not pretend that we have the full answer to those problems.

But I do promise this: We are going to assemble the best thought and the broadest knowledge from all over the world to find those answers for America. . . .

The solution to these problems does not rest on a massive program in Washington, nor can it rely solely on the strained resources of local authority. They require us to create new concepts of cooperation, a creative federalism, between the National Capital and the leaders of local communities.

In 1964, President Lyndon Baines Johnson outlined a program of liberal domestic legislation, which he called the Great Society.

Selection from Arthur M. Schlesinger, Jr., *History of U.S. Political Parties*, Vol. IV. Published by Chelsea House, New York, copyright © 1973.

CRITICAL THINKING

1. What goals did President Johnson set for the Great Society?
2. What type of governmental action did he think would be necessary to achieve his goals?

UNLOCKING HISTORY
COMMENTARY

Reverend Martin Luther King, Jr.'s Dream For America

In 1954, the southeastern states were segregated by race. That is, blacks and whites went to separate schools. They used separate waiting rooms in railway stations and airports and separate seating arrangements on buses. The "color line," which blacks were forbidden to cross, was drawn in many other areas of daily life.

In 1954, the Supreme Court ruled that segregation was unconstitutional because it treated blacks and whites unequally. This is forbidden by the Fourteenth Amendment. In 1955, while blacks waited for this decision to be put into practice, they found a leader for their Civil Rights Movement in Montgomery, Alabama. Boycotting city buses because they were required to give up certain seats when white people demanded them, the blacks of Montgomery were inspired and electrified by the sermons of a young Baptist minister in the city, Martin Luther King, Jr. Soon, because of television, the eloquent King was known to the entire nation.

Martin Luther King, Jr., had deep roots in the southern black religious tradition. He was, in his own words, "the son, the grandson, and the great grandson of preachers." This tradition placed great value on a minister's talent for giving sermons in richly cadenced rhythms.

King was a master in the pulpit. But he went further than this tradition in what he said. In graduate school, he studied Henry David Thoreau and the leader of the independence movement in India, Mohandas "Mahatma" Gandhi. From them, King concluded that in fighting injustice, such as the segregation laws, it was essential that protesters not respond to the violence of unjust authorities with violence of their own. King urged blacks and their white supporters to disobey segregation laws. But when they were arrested or even beaten by police, they were to "turn the other cheek," and submit non-violently.

There was plenty of violence in the years of the Civil Rights Movement. King's home in Montgomery was bombed. His supporters elsewhere in the South were whipped, tortured with electric cattle prods, stunned by high-pressure fire hoses, and even murdered.

Still, King preached his faith in the moral power of non-violence and his example brought many whites from the South and the North to his cause. No person did more than King did to win passage of the landmark Civil Rights Acts of 1964 and 1965. His greatest speech—or, rather, sermon—was delivered in front of the Lincoln Memorial in August 1963. A quarter of a million supporters of Civil Rights had marched there to hear him describe his dream for an America that was just to all. It is one of the greatest public statements in our history.

UNLOCKING HISTORY
KEY DOCUMENT

I am not unmindful that some of you have come here out of great trials and tribulations. Some of you have come fresh from narrow jail cells. Some of you have come from areas where your quest for freedom left you battered by the storms of persecution and staggered by the winds of police brutality. You have been the veterans of creative suffering. Continue to work with the faith that unearned suffering is redemptive.

Go back to Mississippi, go back to Alabama, go back to South Carolina, go back to Georgia, go back to Louisiana, go back to the slums and ghettos of our northern cities, knowing that somehow this situation can and will be changed. Let us not wallow in the valley of despair.

I say to you today, my friends, even though we face the difficulties of today and tomorrow, I still have a dream. It is a dream deeply rooted in the American dream.

I have a dream that one day this nation will rise up and live out the true meaning of its creed: "We hold these truths to be self-evident; that all men are created equal."

I have a dream that one day on the red hills of Georgia the sons of former slaves and the sons of former slaveowners will be able to sit down together at the table of brotherhood.

I have a dream that one day even the state of Mississippi, a state sweltering with the heat of injustice, sweltering with the heat of oppression, will be transformed into an oasis of freedom and justice.

I have a dream that my four little children will one day live in a nation where they will not be judged by the color of their skin but by the content of their character. . . .

And if America is to be a great nation this must become true. So let freedom ring from the prodigious hilltops of New Hampshire. Let freedom ring from the mighty mountains of New York. Let freedom ring from the heightening Alleghenies of Pennsylvania!

Let freedom ring from the snowcapped Rockies of Colorado!

Let freedom ring from the curvacious slopes of California!

But not only that; let freedom ring from Stone Mountain of Georgia!

Let freedom ring from Lookout Mountain of Tennessee.

Let freedom ring from every hill and mole hill of Mississippi. From every mountainside, let freedom ring, and when this happens, when we allow freedom to ring, when we let it ring from every village and every hamlet, from every state and every city, we will be able to speed up that day when all of God's children, black men and white men, Jews and Gentiles, Protestants and Catholics, will be able to join hands and sing in the words of the old Negro spiritual, "Free at last! Free at last! Thank God almighty, we are free at last!"

Selection from Reverend Martin Luther King, Jr., Speech at the Lincoln Memorial, Washington, D.C., August 1963. Published in Robert D. Marcus and David Burner, *America Personified: Portraits from History*, published by St. Martin's Press, New York, copyright © 1974, pages 397–399.

CRITICAL THINKING

1. What particular language in Reverend Martin Luther King, Jr.'s, speech makes it strong and memorable?
2. Give evidence from the speech to support the following statement: Reverend King was optimistic in his belief that equality could occur for the next generation of Americans.

4. STOKELY CARMICHAEL AND CHARLES HAMILTON DISCUSS "BLACK POWER"

During the 1960s, the demand for racial equality was voiced both in the South—where the traditional segregation system was directly challenged by nonviolent protest—and in other areas of the country, where discrimination was present but less visible. In the following selection, two of the most famous advocates of "black power" discuss the importance of black-oriented language to the image and political power of black people.

During an address at a Third World conference in Texas, activist Stokely Carmichael quoted from a book written by Malcolm X.

Today, the American educational system continues to reinforce the entrenched values of the society through the use of words. Few people in this country question that this is "the land of the free and the home of the brave." They have had these words drummed into them from childhood. Few people question that this is the "Great Society" or that this country is fighting "Communist aggression" around the world. We mouth these things over and over, and they become truisms not to be questioned. In a similar way, black people have been saddled with epithets. . . .

Black people must redefine themselves, and only *they* can do that. Throughout this country, vast segments of the black communities are beginning to recognize the need to assert their own definitions, to reclaim their history, their culture; to create their own sense of community and togetherness. There is a growing resentment of the word "Negro," for example, because this term is the invention of our oppressor; it is *his* image of us that he describes. Many blacks are now calling themselves African-Americans, Afro-Americans or black people because that is *our* image of ourselves. When we begin to define our own image, the stereotypes—that is, lies—that our oppressor has developed will begin in the white community and end there. The black community will have a positive image of itself that *it* has created. This means we will no longer call ourselves lazy, apathetic, dumb, good-timers, shiftless, etc. Those are words used by white America to define us. If we accept these adjectives, as some of us have in the past, then we see ourselves only in a negative way, precisely the way white America wants us to see ourselves. Our incentive is broken

and our will to fight is surrendered. From now on we shall view ourselves as African-Americans and as black people who are in fact energetic, determined, intelligent, beautiful, and peace-loving. . . .

More and more black Americans are developing this feeling. They are becoming aware that they have a history which pre-dates their forced introduction to this country. African-American history means a long history beginning on the continent of Africa, a history not taught in the standard textbooks of this country. It is absolutely essential that black people know this history, that they know their roots, that they develop an awareness of their cultural heritage. . . .

Only when black people fully develop this sense of community, of themselves, can they begin to deal effectively with the problems of racism in *this* country. This is what we mean by a new consciousness; this is the vital first step.

Selection from Stokely Carmichael and Charles V. Hamilton, *Black Power: The Politics of Liberation in America*. Published by Vintage Books, New York, copyright © 1967.

1. What reasons did Stokely Carmichael and Charles Hamilton give for the widespread rejection of the term "Negro"?
2. What reasons did they give for believing that a strong sense of black identity was necessary in order to solve the problems of racism in America?

5. ARKANSAS SENATOR J. WILLIAM FULBRIGHT OPPOSES AMERICAN MILITARY INVOLVEMENT IN THE VIETNAM WAR

As early as 1965 and 1966, opposition to American involvement in the fighting in Vietnam was growing. One of the first—and best-known—opponents of United States foreign policy was Senator J. William Fulbright of Arkansas, Chairman of the Senate Foreign Relations Committee. The following passage is from his book The Arrogance of Power, *published in 1966.*

The United States is now involved in a sizable and "open-ended" war against communism in the only country in the world which won freedom from colonial rule under communist leadership. In South Vietnam as in North Vietnam, the communists remain today the only solidly organized political force. That fact is both the measure of our failure and the key to its possible redemption.

So-called "wars of national liberation" are political wars, whose outcomes depend on a combination of political and military factors. The communist guerillas in Malaya could not have been beaten without hard fighting, but neither, in all probability, could they have been beaten had Malaya not been given its independence. . . . The major reason for the success of the Viet Cong in South Vietnam has not been aid from the North but the absence of a cohesive alternative nationalist movement in the South. Both the success of the communists in South Vietnam and their failure in India, Burma, Malaya, Indonesia, and the Philippines strongly suggest that "wars of national liberation" depend for their success more on the weakness of the regime under attack than on the strength of support from outside.

Our search for a solution to the Vietnamese war must begin with the general fact that nationalism is the strongest single political force in the world today and the specific fact . . . that in Vietnam the most effective nationalist movement is communist-controlled. We are compelled, therefore, once again to choose between opposition to communism and support of nationalism. I strongly recommend that for once we give priority to the latter. . . . I strongly recommend . . . that we seek to come to terms with both Hanoi and the Viet Cong, not, to be sure, by "turning tail and running," as the saying goes, but by conceding the Viet Cong a part in the government of South Vietnam.

Selection from J. William Fulbright, *The Arrogance of Power.* Published by Random House, New York, copyright © 1966.

Senator J. William Fulbright was an active opponent of American involvement in Vietnam.

1. What reasons did Senator Fulbright give for believing that the Viet Cong should be included in a South Vietnamese government?
2. What evidence did he offer to support his view that the current policy could not succeed?

6. PRESIDENT LYNDON JOHNSON REAFFIRMS HIS ADMINISTRATION'S FOREIGN POLICY GOALS

On March 31, 1968, President Lyndon Johnson surprised Americans by announcing that he would not seek reelection. That announcement came at the end of an address that reaffirmed his administration's goals and policies in the fighting in Vietnam.

Our objective in South Vietnam has never been the annihilation of the enemy. It has been to bring about a recognition in Hanoi that its objective—taking over the South by force—could not be achieved. . . .

So tonight I reaffirm the pledge that we made at Manila: that we are prepared to withdraw our forces from South Vietnam as the other side withdraws its forces to the North, stops the infiltration, and the level of violence thus subsides. . . .

One day, my fellow citizens, there will be peace in Southeast Asia. It will come because the people of Southeast Asia want it—those whose armies are at war tonight; those who, though threatened, have thus far been spared.

Peace will come because Asians were willing to work for it and to sacrifice for it—and to die by the thousands for it.

But let it never be forgotten: peace will come also because America sent her sons to help secure it.

It has not been easy—far from it. During the past four and a half years, it has been my fate and my responsibility to be Commander in Chief. I have lived daily and nightly with the cost of this war. I know the pain that it has inflicted. I know perhaps better than anyone the misgivings it has aroused.

And throughout this entire long period I have been sustained by a single principle: that what we are doing now in Vietnam is vital not only to the security of Southeast Asia but . . . [also] to the security of every American.

Surely, we have treaties which we must respect. Surely, we have commitments that we are going to keep. . . .

But the heart of our involvement in South Vietnam under three different Presidents, three separate Administrations, has always been America's own security.

And the larger purpose of our involvement has always been to help the nations of Southeast Asia become independent, and stand alone self-sustaining as members of a great world community, at peace with themselves, at peace with all others. And with such a nation our country—and the world—will be far more secure than it is tonight.

I believe that a peaceful Asia is far nearer to reality because of what America has done in Vietnam. I believe that the men who endure the dangers of battle there, fighting there for us tonight, are helping the entire world avoid far greater conflicts, far wider wars, far more destruction, than this one.

Selection from Arthur M. Schlesinger, Jr., *History of U.S. Political Parties*, Vol. IV. Published by Chelsea House, New York, copyright © 1973.

CRITICAL THINKING

1. What did President Johnson cite as the goals of America's involvement in Vietnam?
2. What reasons did he give for believing American involvement was helping world peace?

---

7. ESSAYIST DAVE DELLINGER VISITS NORTH VIETNAM

Opposition to American involvement in the war increased throughout the 1960s and early 1970s. Much of this opposition was fueled by reports from both North and South Vietnam of just what the war was like. The following report was made by Dave Dellinger, a pacifist and anti-war spokesperson, after a visit to North Vietnam.

I hope that I may be forgiven for beginning this report by saying that I recoil from the prospect of writing it, because of the difficulties of communication involved. The problem is partly the superficiality of our most cherished words and concepts before the abrupt finality of premature, man-made death and the lingering horror of dismembered or faceless survivors. . . .

What words are there with which to talk to any young mother who tearfully hands one a snapshot of her three dead children? But what does an American say to a young Vietnamese mother who hands him such a snapshot and says: "We Vietnamese do not go to the United States to fight your people. Why have they come over here to kill my children?"

What can one say to a twenty-year-old girl, swathed in bandages and still in a state of shock because her mother, father, three brothers and sisters were all killed at their noonday meal when American bombers attacked the primitive agricultural village in which they lived? She herself was pulled unconscious and severely burned from the straw hut in which the rest of the family perished.

"Ask your President Johnson," she said to me, "if our straw huts were made of steel and concrete" (a reference to the President's claim that our targets in North Vietnam are military structures of steel and concrete). "Ask him if our Catholic Church that they destroyed was a military target. . . . Tell him that we will continue our life and struggle no matter what future bombings there will be, because we know that without independence and freedom nothing is worthwhile." . . .

Meanwhile an American mother mourns the death of her son, drafted into the armed forces and shot down on a bombing raid over Vietnam. In the United States we are told that he was defending the Vietnamese people against Chinese aggression, but there are no Chinese soldiers in Vietnam. In fact, the Vietnamese will tell you that the last Chinese soldiers to invade Vietnam were 180,000 U.S.-supported Chiang Kai-shek troops, in the winter of 1945–46. They helped the Allies suppress the Vietnamese independence which the United States had promised Vietnam when we needed her help during World War II. Earlier, when the Vietnamese first declared their independence, on September 2, 1945, the Allies hastily rearmed 90,000 Japanese soldiers who had been waiting shipment back to Japan. During the next nine years, the United States supplied eighty percent of the cost of the unsuccessful "French" war to preserve Western colonialism in Indochina. President Eisenhower's refusal, in 1956, to allow democratic elections and reunification of Vietnam, as promised in the Geneva Accords, was not our

Ex-seminarian Dave Dellinger was a leader of the anti-Vietnam war protesters in the 1960s.

first flagrant betrayal of Vietnamese independence. Most Americans are ignorant of these facts, or dimly aware of them as unfortunate mistakes committed in a confused and distant past, but there is hardly a Vietnamese family that does not measure America's broken promises in terms of the death of one or more loved ones.

Selection from Dave Dellinger, *Revolutionary Nonviolence*. Published by Bobbs-Merrill, Indianapolis, copyright © 1970.

CRITICAL THINKING

1. What evidence did Dave Dellinger cite to support his view that the United States had consistently attempted to deny Vietnam its independence?
2. Why might he have insisted on using the words "our" and "we" when referring to American actions in Vietnam?

AMERICAN SPACE PROGRAM
A Success Story

In May 1969, the crew of Apollo 10 photographed the far side of the moon. Photos taken of the crater-covered landscape helped NASA decide on the landing location for the crew of Apollo 11.

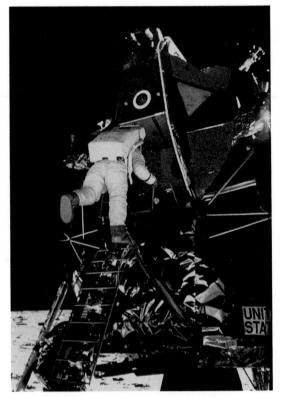

Edwin "Buzz" Aldrin followed Neil Armstrong down the ladder of the Lunar Module, Eagle. Aldrin and Armstrong set up scientific experiments ·and walked on the moon's surface for two hours and twenty minutes.

After John Glenn orbited the earth in 1962, each mission in space brought the United States space program closer to the moment when a human would walk on the moon.

On the morning of July 16, 1969, an estimated 125 million Americans watched a Saturn V rocket power astronauts Neil Armstrong, Edwin Aldrin, and Michael Collins into space.

Apollo XI was heading for the moon. Three days later, the spacecraft began its lunar orbit. As it neared the moon's surface, Armstrong and Aldrin entered the lunar module *Eagle* and descended toward the region known as the Sea of Tranquillity. With Armstrong at the manual controls, the landing craft gently settled on the moon. At 4:17 P.M. (E.D.T.) on July 20, he

D O C U M E N T

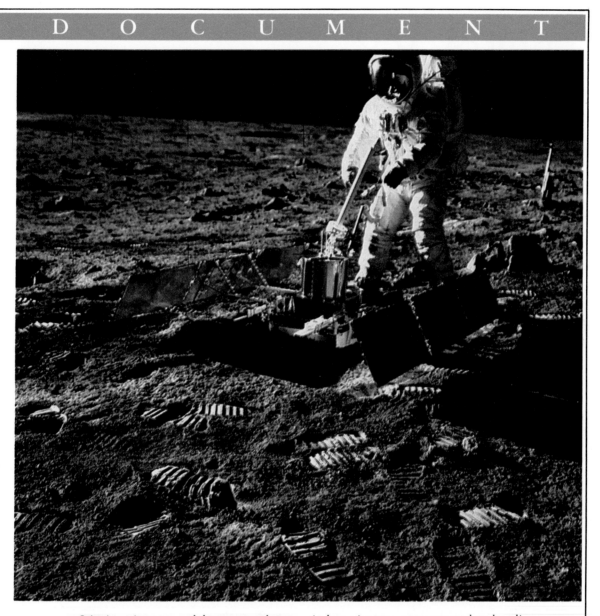

Seismic equipment recorded tremors on the moon. At least nine more astronauts conducted studies and left bootprints on the lunar soil before the last Apollo mission in 1972 ended.

announced: "Tranquillity Base here. The Eagle has landed."

A few hours later Armstrong stepped down the ladder and planted his foot on the lunar surface—the first human to touch the moon. He called back to the waiting world: "That's one small step for man, one giant leap for mankind."

CRITICAL THINKING

1. What responses might these photos have evoked when they appeared?
2. Suggest a new name for "The Sea of Tranquility" and cite photographic evidence for your choice.

CHAPTER 33

DIPLOMACY, DETENTE, AND CRISIS

1968–1976

1. THE AMERICAN SPACE PROGRAM PROVES SUCCESSFUL

Despite the continuing fighting in Vietnam—and the conflict in cities and on campuses at home— Americans found special reason to celebrate in the summer of 1969. On July 20, 1969, Edwin Aldrin and Neil Armstrong achieved the goal that had been set by the Kennedy Administration—to land Americans on the moon by the end of the 1960s. In the following selection, astronauts Aldrin, Armstrong, and Michael Collins described the first moments Aldrin and Armstrong spent on the moon's surface in this way.

The first message from Tranquility Base [the name for the lunar module, Eagle, while on the moon's surface] was perhaps the understatement of the flight. The voice was Neil Armstrong's: "I tell you, we're going to be busy for a minute." When Charlie Duke responded, "You are STAY," he was not yet in a position to know for how long; Eagle had to be checked out, and the men in Mission Control had to be satisfied with the data on their consoles. If a serious malfunction should be detected, either by the men in Eagle or by the men on the ground, an immediate liftoff could be ordered and certainly would be ordered. But the checking and evaluation had to be done at breakneck speed, because the most suitable abort points were three minutes and twelve minutes after touchdown. In that brief time, "STAYS" would be measured in minutes. After passing the twelve-minute abort point, Eagle would have to remain where it was until Columbia [the command module] had gone behind the moon and come around again. . . .

EAGLE (Armstrong): Houston, that may have seemed like a very long final phase. The AUTO targeting was taking us right into a football field-sized crater, with a large number of big boulders and rocks for about one or two crater diameters around us.

HOUSTON (Duke): Roger, we copy. It was beautiful from here, Tranquility. Over.

EAGLE (Aldrin): We'll get to details of what's around here, but it looks like a collection of just every variety of shapes, angularities, granularities, every variety of rock you could find. The colors vary pretty much depending on how you're looking relative to the zero phase point. There doesn't appear to be too much of a general color at all. However, it looks as though some of the rocks and boulders, of which there are quite a few in the near area—it looks as though they are going to have some interesting colors to them. Over.

HOUSTON (Duke): Roger, copy. Sounds good to us, Tranquility. . . . Be advised there are lots of smiling faces in this room, and all over the world.

EAGLE (Aldrin): There are two of them up here.

COLUMBIA (Collins): And don't forget one in the command module.

Selection from Neil Armstrong, Michael Collins, Edwin E. Aldrin, Jr. et. al., *First on the Moon.* Published by Little, Brown and Company, Boston, copyright © 1970.

CRITICAL THINKING

1. How did the pair of astronauts at Tranquility Base react to landing on the moon?
2. At the time, some critics charged that sending people to the moon was basically a "gimmick"—they said that satellites operating solely with instruments were just as able to get scientific information and were less expensive and less dangerous. What evidence is there to the contrary in the astronauts' own recollected description of the landing?

2. SECRETARY OF STATE HENRY KISSINGER EXPLAINS THE MEANING OF *DETENTE*

Throughout the Nixon Administration, Secretary of State Henry Kissinger worked to reestablish what he saw as the balance of power between the major world powers. In his memoirs, Years of Upheaval, *Kissinger described the situation that prevailed after he had succeeded in negotiating a cease-fire for the Arab-Israeli war of 1973 and discussed what the policy of* detente *meant for America.*

We were making progress, if slowly and painfully, toward peace in the Middle East. But we could not forget that our ultimate task was to strengthen peace in the world. The American people expected it from their leaders; the nuclear age imposed it as a moral and practical necessity. . . . We could resist aggressive policies best from a platform of peace; men and women of goodwill and decency could be enlisted only in support of a policy of positive aspirations. . . .

In the light of America's historical experience, relations with the Soviets were a difficult challenge. . . . [To the] American perception of international affairs . . . [relations] among states are either peaceful or warlike—there is no comfortable position in between. Periods of peace call for goodwill, negotiation, arbitration. . . . In war the attitude must be one of unremitting hostility. Conflict is perceived as "unnatural"; it is caused by evil men or motives and can thus be ended only by the extirpation [removal] of the offenders.

Americans traditionally have seen foreign policy less as a seamless web than as a series of episodic events or discrete self-contained problems each of which could be dealt with by the application of common sense and the commitment of resources. . . . This belief derived in part from our geographic remoteness from the center of world affairs, which enables us to shift to other countries the burden of maintaining the global balance of power. The perception would thus have become impossible to sustain in any event when the growth of Soviet power ended our invulnerability and forced us to abandon isolationism. . . .

The Soviet Union is a tyranny and an ideological adversary, thus fulfilling our traditional image of irreconcilable conflict between good and evil. But Soviet ideological hostility translates itself into geopolitical rivalry in the manner of a traditional great power, seeking gains any one of which might be marginal but whose accumulation will upset the global equilibrium. Emotionally committed to facing an overall moral challenge in an apocalyptic confrontation, we thus run the risk of floundering [in regard to] more ambiguous Soviet attempts to nibble away at the balance of power. At the same time, the postwar world was nuclear; statesmen now no longer risked their armies but their societies and all of mankind. . . .

The most important task of the second Nixon Administration was therefore psychological: to educate the American public in the complexity of the world we would have to manage. The United States as the leader of the democracies had a responsibility to defend global security even against ambiguous and seemingly marginal assaults. We would have to do this while simultaneously exploring the limits of coexistence with a morally repugnant ideology. We would have to learn that there would be no final answers. I was convinced then—and remain so—that we cannot find our goals either in an apocalyptic showdown or in a final reconciliation. Rather, we must nurture the fortitude to meet the Soviet challenge over an historical epoch at times by resistance, at times by negotiation.

Selection from Henry Kissinger, *Years of Upheaval*. Published by Little, Brown and Company, Boston, copyright © 1982.

CRITICAL THINKING

1. What reasons did Henry Kissinger give to support his belief that relations between the United States and the Soviet Union would end in a series of conflicts and negotiations rather than an allout war or a final friendship?
2. What attitude toward world affairs did Kissinger want the American people to have?
3. What role did he see for the United States in world affairs?

3. PRESIDENT RICHARD NIXON ESTABLISHES DIPLOMATIC AND ECONOMIC RELATIONS WITH THE PEOPLE'S REPUBLIC OF CHINA

One result of Secretary of State Henry Kissinger's and President Richard Nixon's policies in world affairs was the establishment of diplomatic and economic relations with the People's Republic of China. President Nixon wrote the following about his visit to China in 1972.

Our joint statement, issued from Shanghai at the end of the trip, has become known as the Shanghai Communique.

Following the formula Kissinger had worked out during Polo II [an earlier trip by the Secretary of State], the communiqué broke diplomatic ground by stating frankly the significant differences between the two sides on major issues rather than smoothing them over. . . .

The first substantive section begins: "The U.S. side stated" and then details our positions on each of the major issues discussed. This is followed by a section that begins: "The Chinese side stated" and then covers the same ground in counterpoint. . . .

Perhaps the most vitally important section of the Shanghai Communiqué was the provision that neither nation "should seek hegemony [domination] in the Asia Pacific region and each is opposed to efforts by any other country or group of countries to establish such hegemony." By agreeing to this provision both the P.R.C. [People's Republic of China] and the United States were imposing restraints on themselves. But far more important, particularly as far as the Chinese were concerned, was that the provision subtly but unmistakably made it clear that we both would oppose efforts by the U.S.S.R. or any other major power to dominate Asia.

As I look back on that week in China two impressions stand out most vividly. One is the awesome sight of the disciplined but wildly—almost fanatically—enthusiastic audience at the gymnastic exhibition in Peking, confirming my belief that we must cultivate China during the next few decades while it is still learning to develop its national strength and potential. Otherwise we will one day be confronted with the most formidable enemy that has ever existed in the history of the world.

My other most vivid memory of the trip is the unique personality of Chou En-lai. My meeting with Mao Tse-tung was too brief and too formal to have given me much more than a superficial personal impression. But many hours of formal talks and social conversation with Chou made me appreciate his brilliance and dynamism.

Unlike many world leaders and statesmen who are completely absorbed in one particular cause or issue. Chou En-lai was able to talk in broad terms about men and history. Even though his perspective .was badly distorted by his rigid ideological frame of reference the extent of his knowledge was impressive.

After one of the banquets in Peking, I made notes of our conversation.

Diary

It was interesting to note the remarkable knowledge of history that Chou En-lai displays, and, also, how his historical perspective is shaped by his ideology. For example, he sees the French intervention in the Revolutionary War as being by volunteers . . . and not by the French government.

Chou also sees Lincoln [as one] who "after many defeats," as he put it, finally prevailed because he had the people on his side.

Selection from *RN: The Memoirs of Richard Nixon*, Vol. 2. Published by Warner Books, New York, copyright © 1978.

CRITICAL THINKING

1. What reasons did Richard Nixon give for believing that it was necessary for the United States to "cultivate China" during the next decades?
2. What was President Nixon's personal assessment of the Chinese leaders—Mao Tse-tung and Chou En-lai—and what evidence did he offer to support his view of the two men?

4. POLITICAL WRITER ELIZABETH DREW RECOUNTS THE VOTE TO IMPEACH PRESIDENT RICHARD NIXON

The events included under the general title of "Watergate"—break-ins, political "dirty tricks," cover-ups, attempts to halt investigations, and so on—eventually brought about the political downfall of President Nixon. Political writer Elizabeth Drew wrote about the dramatic scene as the House Judiciary Committee voted to impeach the President for his conduct during the scandal, a matter of days before the President resigned.

At seven o'clock, the roll is called on whether or not the House Judiciary Committee will recommend to the House that the President be impeached. Technically, the vote is on whether the Sarbanes substitute article should be adopted, but it is in effect the definitive vote. And, no matter how seemingly inevitable this vote has been for some time now, no matter how well we know the outcome, there has been no way of preparing ourselves for this moment. More than any of the several other moments when the emotional reverberations outran the intellectual anticipation, this one has stolen up on us, taken over, leaves us sitting here feeling stunned, drained, almost disbelieving as the clerk calls the roll and the members cast their votes. The room is utterly still except for the call of the roll and the sound of cameras clicking. The moment has taken over the members; they know what they are doing, and they are physically, mentally, and emotionally spent. They have been through a long period of strain. No other group in the Congress has ever had to go through anything like this. One can barely hear the members as they respond to the clerk.

First the Democrats. Even those for whom this is not a difficult vote are somber as they respond "Aye"—perhaps in part because they know they should be. Mann, for whom this has not been easy, stares into space as he says "Aye." His voice is all but inaudible. Again there appear to be tears in his eyes. Father Drinan, his long, thin face looking stern and sober, ever more like an El Greco painting, quietly says "Aye." Barbara Jordan, usually of full voice, also responds quietly. Ray Thornton looks at the ceiling, closes his eyes, and says, softly, "Aye." They are impeaching Richard Nixon. They are setting loose an unimaginable course of events, and they know it.

The first vote cast with a loud certitude is Hutchinson's "No." Hutchinson smiles—the only one who does. . . .

Rodino, who casts his vote last, undramatically says "Aye." The clerk announces, "Twenty-seven members have voted aye, eleven members have voted no." All twenty-one Democrats—including three Southerners—and six Republicans have voted to impeach the President for the cover-up.

The vote on the article as amended is a ceremonial vote now, but it must be taken, and again it is taken solemnly. This time, Rodino's voice cracks as he speaks the final "Aye." The room is utterly silent, and then, at a few minutes after seven, Rodino announces, "Article I . . . is adopted and will be reported to the House."

Hamilton Fish comes out of the committee room holding his wife's hand. Some members are being interviewed on television. Barbara Jordan, preparing to be interviewed, is having difficulty composing herself. Some members—Rodino included—went into the anteroom behind the committee room and wept. There is a small group of observers, dressed in casual summer clothes, standing quietly outside the Rayburn [Congressional Office] Building. When Barbara Jordan comes out of the Rayburn Building, several in the group applaud. She smiles and waves vaguely. Reporters have gone back to the pressrooms to file their stories. It is good to have something that must be done.

The Capitol grounds are very quiet tonight. Across the way is the Supreme Court Building. Could it really have been only three days ago that the Court ruled against the President? The committee members have taken the first step—the hardest step, making it easier for those who will follow. They didn't walk away from it; they became the definers. But there doesn't seem to be much of a sense of triumph on anyone's part tonight. Perhaps this will be written of in the future as a moment of triumph—"the system worked"—but that is not how it feels now. There

UNIT 10

is a feeling of sadness, and exhaustion, at what everyone has been through. A feeling, too, of foreboding about those unimaginable next steps. It is a drained feeling. When history records events, it tends to leave out this kind of human emotion.

Selection from Elizabeth Drew, *Washington Journal: The Events of 1973–1974*. Published by Random House, New York, copyright © 1975.

CRITICAL THINKING

1. What evidence is there that, as Elizabeth Drew wrote, "the moment had taken over the members" of the committee?
2. How did she suggest that the vote proved that "the system worked"?

---

5. WRITER SEYMOUR HERSH DISSECTS THE HENRY KISSINGER–RICHARD NIXON TEAM

In 1973, as President Richard Nixon became increasingly preoccupied with the Watergate scandal, he appointed Henry Kissinger to be Secretary of State, replacing William P. Rogers. Writer Seymour Hersh examines Nixon's collapse and the end of his active collaboration with Kissinger. He asks: what price did each man pay for his use—or misuse—of power?

Kissinger's long-sought appointment as Secretary of State was inevitable by the fall of 1973. He was again threatening to resign, according to the private journal kept by one of his office staff, and such a threat amidst Watergate carried weight. The President treated Kissinger shoddily in the weeks before announcing the nomination. It was clear to those on the inside that he was naming Kissinger only as part of his Watergate defense. In early August, according to the second volume of Kissinger's memoirs, Nixon told Haig that he would make the appointment, "provided he did not have to dismiss Rogers personally." Haig then sought Rogers' resignation but got nowhere. It took a week for Nixon to get around to meeting with Rogers, who—much to Nixon's

(and Kissinger's) relief—at once offered his letter of resignation. "And still Nixon said nothing to me," Kissinger complained in his memoirs, adding that he was not officially told about his nomination until less than a day before it was announced.

Richard Nixon understood, as few did in the government, the full price Kissinger had paid to remain in power. In the end, it was Kissinger who survived and Richard Nixon who did not. Kissinger would lose little of his immense public standing as he careened from crisis to crisis—many of them self-inflicted—as Secretary of State. There would be serious misjudgments in Cyprus, Portugal, and Angola, many of them well reported but none that undermined Kissinger's basic credibility. South Vietnam would finally fall, in the face of the long-awaited attack by North Vietnam, and America would watch on the nightly news as its Ambassador was helicoptered from the beseiged American Embassy in Saigon hours before the end. There would be few television reports about the fall of the Lon Nol government in Phnom Penh to the ragtag and crazed troops of the Khmer Rouge, whose leader, Pol Pot, would seal Cambodia's borders and begin a program of retribution and genocide whose final death toll reached into the millions.

Kissinger would demonstrate how little he had learned within a few days after Saigon's collapse. On May 12, 1975, Cambodian gunboats forcibly seized the S.S. *Mayaguez*, an American merchant ship, in international waters sixty miles south of Cambodia. The crew of forty was taken to Koh Tang island, also under Cambodian control and closer to the mainland. The Ford Administration viewed the ship's seizure as an arbitrary act of defiance, although the new government in Phnom Penh had repeatedly proclaimed that its territorial waters extended ninety miles offshore and had been detaining vessels in the area for the past ten days. Kissinger argued for immediate retaliation— air strikes against the mainland and a Marine invasion to free the *Mayaguez* crew. He got his way, as he usually did with President Ford. The invasion was a slaughter: Eighteen Marines were killed and fifty more wounded out of an assault force of 110; twenty-three Air Force men also died in an offshore crash. The Marines, in their desperate evacuation, detonated a 15,000-ton bomb on the island, the largest nonnuclear weap-

358

on in the U.S. arsenal. Heightening the tragedy was the fact that the *Mayaguez* crew members were no longer on the island; they had been set free by the Cambodians hours before. Later congressional investigations revealed that Ford and Kissinger had behaved during the crisis just as Nixon and Kissinger would have. They had waited ten hours after learning of the *Mayaguez*'s seizure before making an effort to reach the Cambodian government to arrange a diplomatic solution. They had failed to act after learning of a Cambodian broadcast announcing the release of the *Mayaguez* crew, a broadcast that reached the White House just as the Marine invasion was beginning. They had ignored a confidential communication delivered fourteen hours before the U.S. assault in which a foreign government revealed that it was intervening in Cambodia and expected an early release of the ship and crew. And, finally, they chose to publicly celebrate the crew's release as an American victory—the result of their use of force.

Kissinger and Nixon would repeatedly claim that the failures in South Vietnam and Cambodia were not their responsibility but the fault of Congress, which had cut off funding for the war. . . . America proved a sore loser in Vietnam, and quickly turned its back not only on its policies but also on its young men who had fought, suffered, and died there.

In the end, as in the beginning, Nixon and Kissinger remained blind to the human costs of their actions—a further price of power. The dead and maimed in Vietnam and Cambodia—as in Chile, Bangladesh, Biafra, and the Middle East—seemed not to count as the President and his national security adviser battled the Soviet Union, their misconceptions, their political enemies, and each other.

Richard Nixon paid a high price for his misuse of power. On August 9, 1974, after the House of Representatives Committee on Impeachment had recommended impeachment proceedings, and ten days before the full House was to open debate, the thirty-seventh President of the United States resigned. He was the first President to do so. On September 8, 1974, Nixon was spared the possibility of an extended criminal trial by a jury of citizens when President Gerald Ford, his successor, granted him a "full, free and absolute pardon"

for any offenses against the United States from January 20, 1969, his first inaugural, through the date of his resignation. Ford himself had become Vice President the preceding December, after financial scandals forced Spiro Agnew to resign and, later, to plead no contest to an income tax evasion charge. The pardon to Nixon embraced not only Watergate offenses but all the Nixon-Kissinger foreign policy activities, including those known at the time, such as the illegal B-52 bombing of Cambodia, and those still secret, such as the CIA operations against Salvador Allende. After years of self-imposed isolation in California, New York, and Saddle River, New Jersey, Nixon began to be active in public affairs once again in the early 1980s; he was received as a former President, Republican elder statesman, author, and expert on international relations. . . .

Henry Kissinger served as Secretary of State under Nixon and then under Ford. When Carter took office, Kissinger began a new career as an international consultant, writer, speech maker, and part-time university lecturer. He was a personal consultant to the Shah of Iran after his exile, and is associated with many prominent firms, as an advisor or consultant, including Goldman Sachs & Co., an investment house, and the Rockefellers' Chase Manhattan Bank. He is also a consultant for many foreign firms, including the General Electric Company of Britain. Kissinger is constantly portrayed by the news media as an advisor and consultant on foreign policy issues to the Reagan Administration, but as of spring 1983, he had not rejoined the government.

Selection from Seymour M. Hersh, *The Price of Power: Kissinger in the Nixon White House.* Published by Summit Books, New York, copyright © 1983.

CRITICAL THINKING

1. Give evidence for Seymour Hersh's statement, "Kissinger would demonstrate how little he had learned."
2. What is Seymour Hersh's point of view toward the policy of Nixon and Kissinger? Cite examples.
3. List the offenses Ford's pardon of Nixon covered, according to Hersh.

AMERICA'S BICENTENNIAL
1776–1976

On the eve of the Fourth, President Gerald Ford urged Americans to "break out the flag, strike up the band and light up the sky." In Charleston, New Hampshire drummers dressed in Revolutionary War garb entertained the local population.

On July 4, 1976, the United States celebrated its two hundredth anniversary with one of the biggest birthday parties in history. The festivities officially began at dawn, on top of Mars Hill Mountain in Maine, where the rays of the rising sun first strike U.S. soil. At 4:31 AM, an American flag was hoisted and National Guardsmen fired a 50-gun salute, kicking off parties, parades, and a variety of bicentennial celebrations in towns and cities across the nation.

In Philadelphia, at least one million people showed up for a re-enactment of the signing of the Declaration of Independence. The cracked Liberty Bell was struck softly with a mallet, and Queen Elizabeth of England presented her nation's birthday gift to America—a six-ton bell cast at the same foundry that made the original Liberty Bell.

In Washington, D.C., people waited for hours to catch a glimpse of the original Declaration of Independence. Thomas Jefferson's parchment document was on display for 76 hours at the Capitol. On the grounds of the

D O C U M E N T

Patriotism was expressed uniquely. A red Rolls Royce headed a parade in Grafton, Vermont.

The Bicentennial engaged the imagination of Americans across the country. Ventura, California had a colorful birthday party.

In New York City, parades launched the sailing of "tall ships". About seven million people took part in New York City's festivities.

Washington Monument, 33½ tons of fireworks were detonated in what must have been the largest display of pyrotechnics that day.

But perhaps the most spectacular display was the regatta of 212 sailing ships from 34 nations that gathered in New York's harbor. Six million people watched from the shore as the flotilla, which included 16 of the world's largest ships, lifted anchor and sailed up the Hudson River. The majestic procession sailed to dozens of cities including Boston, Miami, Chicago, and Los Angeles.

CRITICAL THINKING

1. Examine the photographs of bicentennial celebrations and summarize their general tone, citing details from each picture.
2. Using only the photographs as a guide, how could a viewer deduce what event is being celebrated? Which picture most clearly states the event?

6. BETTY FRIEDAN LOOKS AT "THE FEMININE MYSTIQUE"

By the time women finally won the vote in 1919, the feminist movement had very nearly exhausted itself. Feminism resurfaced in the 1960s as the women's liberation movement, and the event that sparked its rebirth was the publication of Betty Friedan's controversial book, The Feminine Mystique. *Modern women, Friedan argued, were being shortchanged by the widespread belief that the only conceivable role for a female was that of housewife-mother.*

And so the feminine mystique began to spread through the land, grafted onto old prejudices and comfortable conventions which so easily give the past a stranglehold on the future. Behind the new mystique were concepts and theories deceptive in their sophistication and their assumption of accepted truth. These theories were supposedly so complex that they were inaccessible to all but a few initiates, and therefore irrefutable. It will be necessary to break through this wall of mystery and look more closely at these complex concepts, these accepted truths, to understand fully what has happened to American women.

The feminine mystique says that the highest value and the only commitment for women is the fulfillment of their own femininity. It says that the great mistake of Western culture, through most of its history, has been the undervaluation of this femininity. It says this femininity is so mysterious and intuitive and close to the creation and origin of life that man-made science may never be able to understand it. But however special and different, it is in no way inferior to the nature of man; it may even in certain respects be superior. The mistake, says the mystique, the root of women's troubles in the past is that women envied men, women tried to be like men, instead of accepting their own nature, which can find fulfillment only in . . . passivity, male domination, and nurturing maternal love.

But the new image this mystique gives to American women is the old image: "Occupation: housewife." The new mystique makes the housewife-mother, who never had a chance to be anything else, the model for all women; it presupposes that history has reached a final and glorious end in the here and now, as far as women are concerned. Beneath the sophisticated trappings, it simply makes certain concrete, finite, domestic aspects of feminine existence—as it was lived by women whose lives were confined, by necessity, to cooking, cleaning, washing, bearing children—into a religion, a pattern by which all women must now live or deny their femininity.

Fulfillment as a woman had only one definition for American women after 1949—the housewife-mother. As swiftly as in a dream, the image of the American woman as a changing, growing individual in a changing world was shattered. Her solo flight to find her own identity was forgotten in the rush for the security of togetherness. Her limitless world shrunk to the cozy walls of home. . . .

The material details of life, the daily burden of cooking and cleaning, of taking care of the physical needs of husband and children—these did indeed define a woman's world a century ago when Americans were pioneers, and the American frontier lay in conquering the land. But the women who went west with the wagon trains also shared the pioneering purpose. Now the American frontiers are of the mind, and of the spirit. Love and children and home are good, but they are not the whole world. . . . Why should women accept this picture of a half-life, instead of a share in the whole of human destiny? Why should women try to make housework "something more," instead of moving on the frontiers of their own time as American women moved beside their husbands on the old frontiers?

A baked potato is not as big as the world, and vacuuming the living room floor—with or without makeup—is not work that takes enough thought or energy to challenge any woman's full capacity. Women are human beings, not stuffed dolls.

Selection from Betty Friedan, *The Feminine Mystique*. Published by W.W. Norton & Company, New York, copyright © 1963.

CRITICAL THINKING

1. According to Betty Friedan, what consequences did the feminine mystique have for American women after 1949?
2. Why do you imagine *The Feminine Mystique* became so controversial a book?

AMERICA'S THIRD CENTURY BEGINS

1976–PRESENT

1. FIRST LADY ROSALYNN CARTER RECALLS PRESIDENT CARTER'S ENERGY PROGRAM

One of the first priorities of President Jimmy Carter's new administration was dealing with America's energy crisis. In her memoirs of her time in the White House, Rosalynn Carter described both the personal and public side of that energy program.

Jimmy knew that . . . the oil supplies of the world were exhaustible, and we had to develop an energy program for the United States to ensure against a disastrous future. We had done our best to set an example in the Governor's Mansion [in Georgia]. We had turned off lights, decorated at Christmas with natural, old-fashioned decorations. . . . We switched from big, gas-guzzling state cars to smaller ones. . . .

When we arrived at the White House, Jimmy informed me that we were going to set an example again. He said that in his first address on national television, which would be a fireside chat, he was going to ask the American people to turn down their thermostats to 65 degrees during the day, 55 at night. He had already ordered all the thermostats in the White House turned down, including those in our living quarters. I couldn't believe it; I had been freezing ever since we moved in. My offices were so cold I couldn't concentrate, and my staff was typing with gloves on. . . . Every time I turned on the news since we moved to Washington, there were stories about its being one of the coldest winters on record, and I believed it. Now it was going to be colder . . .

In Jimmy's first address to the people as Presi-

dent, he wore a sweater and sat in front of a real fire in the Library on the ground floor. He wanted it to be an informal talk, but his message on energy was sobering when he pointed out that "the United States is the only major industrial country . . . without a comprehensive, long-range energy policy."

Two months later, in April 1977, he submitted his energy program to Congress, calling the effort to make the United States energy-independent "the moral equivalent of war."

We knew from the beginning that Jimmy's energy campaign was politically risky. People want to believe that everything is going to be fine, that they are not going to have to make any sacrifices, that the future is always going to be better than the present. They don't want to hear about crises or problems, but without an aroused public, Jimmy knew he would never be able to prevail over the powerful oil companies and other lobbyists to develop an effective energy policy. There was no natural constituency for his program, parts of which were unpopular with everyone. He had to fight the oil companies, the automobile industry, the power companies—even consumers—when he decontrolled oil and natural gas. It was very difficult. . . .

By the end of Jimmy's term, the energy program he put into effect had already begun to reduce our overdependence on foreign oil supplies and to stop the upward spiral of oil and gas prices. Pat Buchanan, a conservative columnist and commentator, said, ". . . history will say that Jimmy Carter of Plains, Georgia, was the fellow who busted OPEC."

Selection from Rosalynn Carter, *First Lady from Plains.* Published by Houghton Mifflin Company, Boston, copyright © 1984.

CRITICAL THINKING

1. How did Jimmy Carter use the unique qualities of television to suggest ways that Americans could reduce energy consumption?
2. What did the events in the White House indicate about the Carters' personalities and their style of leadership?

2. PRESIDENTIAL ADVISER HAMILTON JORDAN RECALLS THE MORNING HE LEARNED AMERICAN DIPLOMATS WERE BEING HELD HOSTAGE IN IRAN

One of President Jimmy Carter's closest advisers was Hamilton Jordan. In the following selection from his memoirs of his last year at the White House, Jordan recalled his initial reaction to the news that Americans had been taken hostage at the United States embassy in Tehran—news which came while he was one of the leaders of President Carter's reelection campaign against Senator Edward Kennedy of Massachusetts. Early on a Sunday morning—November 4, 1979—he was away from Washington, spending the weekend on the eastern shore of Maryland.

About 4:30 A.M. the phone in my room rang. It took me a minute to recall where I was. I grappled in the dark, and on what must have been the tenth ring, managed to answer it.

"Mr. Jordan, this is the duty officer in the Situation Room," the voice on the other end said. "We wanted to advise you that the American Embassy in Tehran has been overrun by demonstrators and the American personnel are believed to be held in captivity."

"My God," I said. "Are there any injuries? Was anyone killed?"

"Not that we know of, Mr. Jordan—but we really don't have complete information. We'll keep you informed."

I asked if the President had been notified and was told that Secretary of State Vance had called him earlier from the Operations Center at the State Department.

I lay in bed thinking about what I had just heard. This could mean war with Iran. And what would it do to the campaign?

The phone rang again. It was Phil Wise, Carter's appointments secretary, who was always with the President, calling from Camp David. Had I heard the news from Iran? I told him that I had just been called and hadn't had much time to think about it, but obviously the President needed to stay on top of things.

"Don't forget," I said, "the press will be looking at this in the context of the campaign. It'll be over in a few hours, but it could provide a nice contrast between Carter and our friend from Massachusetts in how to handle a crisis."

Wise asked if I thought the President should rush back to Washington. I suggested that he wait a few hours. I reminded him that when the same embassy was overrun the previous February, hostages had been taken but then released several hours later when the Iranian government intervened. This, I told Phil, would end the same way.

I was awakened again at 6:15 by another call from the Situation Room. Nothing had changed in Tehran. The State Department was in direct contact with personnel at the embassy and also with Chief of Mission Bruce Laingen, who was at the Iranian Foreign Ministry when the embassy was seized. The fact that we were talking directly to the people being held seemed to me to be a positive sign. *It takes time to work these things out,* I thought to myself, and went back to sleep.

Later in the morning I got up and jogged on a narrow dirt road that meandered beside the quiet waters of the eastern shore. We all had breakfast together and I told about the calls during the night. Everyone agreed that what was going on in Tehran sounded bad. . . . They hoped that public attention wouldn't be deflected from the weaknesses of the Kennedy program [an interview with the Senator to be held that Sunday evening]. "They'll be released before tonight," I predicted confidently.

Selection from Hamilton Jordan, *Crisis: The Last Year of the Carter Presidency*. Published by G.P. Putnam's Sons, New York, copyright © 1982.

CRITICAL THINKING

1. Summarize Hamilton Jordan's view of the crisis?
2. What reasons did he have for taking this view?
3. Discuss the influence of the campaign on the judgment and concerns of Hamilton Jordan and others in the Administration.

3. PRESIDENT RONALD REAGAN DELIVERS HIS FIRST INAUGURAL ADDRESS

In November 1980, Ronald Reagan won the presidential election. In his inaugural address, on January 20, 1981, President Reagan spoke about the direction in which he wanted to lead the country.

These United States are confronted with an economic affliction of great proportions. We suffer from the longest and one of the worst sustained inflations in our national history. It distorts our economic decisions, penalizes thrift, and crushes the struggling young and the fixed-income elderly alike. It threatens to shatter the lives of millions of our people. . . .

In this present crisis, government is not the solution to our problem; government is the problem. From time to time we've been tempted to believe that society has become too complex to be managed by self-rule, that government by an elite group is superior to government for, by, and of the people. Well, if no one among us is capable of governing himself, then who among us has the capacity to govern someone else? . . .

We hear much of special interest groups. Well, our concern must be for a special interest group that has been too long neglected. It knows no sectional boundaries or ethnic and racial divisions, and it crosses political party lines. It is made up of men and women who raise our food, patrol our streets, man our mines and factories, teach our children, keep our homes, and heal us when we're sick—professionals, industrialists, shopkeepers, clerks, cabbies, and truck-drivers. They are, in short, "We the people," this breed called Americans.

Well, this Administration's objective will be a healthy, vigorous, growing economy that provides equal opportunities for all Americans. . . . Putting America back to work means putting all Americans back to work. Ending inflation means freeing all Americans from the terror of runaway living costs. All must share in the productive work of this "new beginning," and all must share in the bounty of a revived economy. With the idealism and fair play which are the core of our system and our strength, we can have a strong and prosperous America, at peace with itself and the world. . . .

It is my intention to curb the size and influence of the Federal establishment and to demand recognition of the distinction between the powers granted to the Federal Government and those reserved to the States or to the people. . . .

It is no coincidence that our present troubles parallel and are proportionate to the intervention and intrusion in our lives that result from unnecessary and excessive growth of government. It is time for us to realize that we're too great a nation to limit ourselves to small dreams. We're not, as some would have us believe, doomed to an inevitable decline. I do not believe in a fate that will fall on us no matter what we do. I do believe in a fate that will fall on us if we do nothing. So, with all the creative energy at our command, let us begin an era of national renewal. Let us renew our determination, our courage, and our strength. And let us renew our faith and our hope.

Selection from Ronald Reagan, "Inaugural Address," January 20, 1981, in *Public Papers of the Presidents of the United States, Ronald Reagan, 1981*. Published by United States Government Printing Office, Washington, D.C., copyright © 1982.

CRITICAL THINKING

1. What change in direction did President Reagan propose for the government?
2. List three areas in which change was needed and summarize the changes he believed were necessary.
3. What did he believe the effects would be of reducing government involvement in American life?

4. WRITER ELLEN GOODMAN CONTEMPLATES THE DRAFTING OF WOMEN

A subject repeatedly brought up by people opposed to the Equal Rights Amendment was the possibility of women being drafted into the Armed Forces. Writer Ellen Goodman tackles the question head-on. In this unusual essay, "Men, Women and War," she insists that there are no good reasons for not drafting both men and women.

My daughter is 11 years old, and as we watch the evening news she turns to me seriously and says, "I don't like the way the world is doing things." Neither do I.

My daughter is 11 years and 9 months old, to be precise, and I do not want her to grow up and be drafted. Neither does she.

My daughter is almost 12 and worries about unkindness and evil, about slaughtered seals and whales. I don't want her to be brutalized by war—as soldier or civilian.

As I read those lines over they seem too mild. What I want to say is that I'm horrified by the very idea that she could be sent to fight for fossil fuels or fossilized ideas, that I can imagine no justification for war other than self-defense, and that I am scared stiff about who has the power to decide what calls for self-defense.

In recent months there has been talk of registering young people for a possible draft. There has been fervent debate about young women as well as young men. And so I have found myself wondering: Would I feel differently if my daughter were my son? Would I be less anguished at the notion of a son drafted, a son at war?

Would I beat the drums and pin the bars and stars on his uniform with pride? Would I look forward to his being toughened up, be proud of his heroism, accept the risks that he's subjected to as a simple fact of life?

I cannot believe it.

So when I've been asked about registering women for the draft along with men, I've had to nod reluctantly. I don't want anyone registered, anyone drafted, unless we are in a genuine crisis. I am far from convinced we are in a genuine crisis.

But if there is a draft again, it can't touch just our sons, like some civilized plague that leaves daughters alone to produce another generation of warriors.

The courts might not allow a male-only draft anyway. Even with the ERA, the highest courts . . . have passed judgment against most . . . laws that affect only one sex. Alimony is no longer awarded just to women; the Supreme Court ruled that men may receive it also. Social-security rights have been extended to widowers as well as to widows.

If a male-only draft were passed, some man no doubt could challenge it successfully. And would. There are simply no reasonable grounds for a male-only draft today. There are 150,000 women in the military services already. They have proved to be tough and essential members. More than half of the first 62 female West Point graduates requested assignment to combat branches of the Army.

Even if women were not used in combat, there were, I am told, seven soldiers for every combat soldier in Vietnam. Many of the jobs noncombatant soldiers did were precisely the kind we traditionally define as "women's work"—jobs demanding precision, eye-hand motor coordination and mental skills related to technological warfare.

Still, it was ironic to hear Phyllis Schlafly suddenly sounding horrified at the draft and blaming the ERA proponents.

"Carter's proposal proves what we have been saying for the past seven years," she remarks, "that the ERA proponents want to draft women and treat them just like men in the military."

Suddenly this pro-military hawk takes flight as a dove, spreading her verbal wings over women only. Her comments remind me of that harsh anti-male streak that lurks under the thin veneer of femininity in the anti-ERA movement. Many anti-feminists feel a deep reluctance to share the lives and problems of and with men; they express a bitter refusal to "let men off the hook."

I am sure the anti-ERA people know that drafting women would eliminate the very last argument against passing the ERA. The pro-ERA people know this too. But they note again, with irony, that women have "won" virtually all equal responsibilities with men. If women were drafted, we lack only one thing: equal rights.

But I think that if we ever do begin registering again for a draft, in this crisis or any other, women must be included along with men, not only because the courts might demand it, but also because our society demands it. For too long, warfare was seen as men's business only, and was one cause of the rage that so many men have harbored against women.

War is in the mind of the man who yells at an equal rights rally: "Where were you at Iwo Jima?" War is in the mind of the man who is absolutely enraged at a woman who challenges the laws that give job preferences to veterans. War is in the mind of the man who chides his wife for having led a "soft" life.

War has often split couples and sexes apart. . . .

But even more awesome, as a male activity, a rite of passage, a test of manhood, war has been gruesomely acceptable. Old men who were warriors have sent younger men to war as if it were their birthright. Women were supposed to wave banners and sing slogans and be in need of protection from the enemy.

We all pretended that war was civilized, that war had rules and isolated battlegrounds. War did not touch the finer and nobler things of life—such as women.

This, of course, was never true. The civilians among the losers, the enemies, were casualties as surely as were the soldiers. The women in Vietnam were not "safe," nor were the women in Hiroshima. When under duress, or defending their homes, women have always fought. And in a push-button war, women could not be protected.

But perhaps, stripped of its maleness and mystery, its audience and cheerleaders, war can finally be deglorified. Without the last trappings of chivalry it can be seen for what it is—the last, deadly resort.

So if we must ever have a draft registration, I would include young women along with young men. I would include them because they can do the job. I would include them because all women must be in a position to stop as well as to start wars. I would include them because it has been far too easy to send men alone.

I would include them because I simply cannot believe that I would feel differently if my daughter were my son.

Selection from Ellen Goodman, "Men, Women and War," *Redbook*, May 1980.

CRITICAL THINKING

1. List the arguments Ellen Goodman makes for drafting women.
2. According to Goodman, what results come from excluding women from military combat service?
3. According to Goodman, how would drafting women result in the deglorification of war?

5. AND MAY THE BEST WOMAN WIN!

As the 1984 national elections approached, talk about a woman as a vice presidential candidate continued to mount. Six months before the Democrats selected Geraldine Ferraro for second place on its ticket, the New Republic *magazine published an editorial that regarded the idea with disdain. Instead, in an essay called "The Gender Trap," the magazine proposed what it believed would be a more logical alternative for women politicians.*

In this golden age of the gender gap, women are being shamelessly wooed. The Vice Presidency—which has been variously likened to a pitcher of warm spit, a spare tire on the automobile of government, a cataleptic state, and a kind of disgrace—is one prize the Democrats have been dangling with much fanfare. And with much encouragement from women themselves. "Don't call me baby, call me Vice President!" chanted hundreds of conventioneers at the annual convention of the National Organization for Women in October. Their leader, Judy Goldsmith, was just as insistent: "1984 may not be the year for America's first woman President," she proclaimed. "But there is no reason why we should not reasonably look for a woman Vice Presidential candidate in 1984." . . .

Despite the dubious reputation the Vice Presidency has earned, the qualifications for occupying the office are still high and well established: they are, or at least ought to be, the same as the qualifications for the Presidency. Women have made striking gains in politics recently; the number of women in elective office nearly tripled between 1975 and 1981. Yet the Democrats have no woman Senators, and the sole Democratic woman governor, Martha Layne Collins of Kentucky, was elected only last November. The party does have a number of accomplished and respected women in its delegation to the House of Representatives—people like Geraldine Ferraro and Patricia Schroeder. And there is surely nothing wrong with adding sex to the list of irrelevant considerations (region, religion, etc.) which always weigh in the choice. A ticket-balancing formula like "We need a moderate urban Catholic governor from the West" is hardly made worse by the addition of "female." . . .

. . . If there's anything the gender gap should have made clear, but in fact seems to have obscured, it's that women don't need more token gestures. . . .

If women's claims to a place on the ticket are to be credible and constructive, they should start by running for President, not by angling for an unlikely offer of the Vice Presidency. However grueling and often fatuous the long campaign can be, it may be the best way for a woman candidate to establish her qualifications for national leadership. . . . Consider the difference that a serious woman candidate for President would make in 1988 or 1992. Then, instead of making disingenuous offers, men candidates would face actual challenges. Instead of waiting and chanting, women would be gaining exposure and building support. Above all, a bid for the Presidency would prove that women's participation in politics cannot be summed up by the confining rhetoric of a special gender cause.

Selection from "The Gender Trap," *The New Republic*, February 27, 1984.

CRITICAL THINKING

1. What arguments did the editorial give to support its suggestion that women would do better to concentrate on winning the presidential nomination?
2. Cite reasons to support or refute the implication that offering women second place is an example of sexism.

6. THE 1984 SUMMER OLYMPICS— ON YOUR MARK, GET SET, GO!

For many Americans, the Olympic Games held in Los Angeles during August, 1984, symbolized the spirit that President Reagan had called the country's "New Beginning." Even before the games began, Time *magazine described the coming events in superlatives. The subsequent victories of American athletes at those games generated a happy outpouring of goodwill.*

American diver Greg Louganis won two gold medals at the 1984 Summer Olympics.

Eight thousand banners, did you say? Covering 120 miles of Los Angeles? Hanging from 300 different types of lampposts? O.K. Some of the brackets for the banners had to be different too; a real headache. Certainly not, you wouldn't want to use just any colors. Had to be magenta, vermilion, chrome yellow, violet, aqua. "Festive Federalism," the designers call it. . . . Oh, sorry. Please go on. You were talking about construction: 3,500 construction workers at 67 different sites, including Olympic Villages, places for the Games, training facilities, parking lots. That is, if the cars can get there. . . . Fifty-two miles of chain-link fence? Well, you can't be too careful. By all means, read the grocery list for the athletes: Pork, 63,700 lbs.; beef, 206,555 lbs.; 70,000 dozen eggs. (You *do* deliver?). . . .

But where is the center of this thing? No, not the $525 million budget or the anticipated infusion of $3.3 billion into the local economy or the 269,000 dozen cookies. One million new trees planted by a conservation group? Good for them. Nothing like a tree. The question is why. Why, as the magenta was going up at the Los Angeles Coliseum, were 7,800 atheletes from 140 nations loading their gear and kissing Mother goodbye? Numbers? Here's a number. On July 28, 2 billion people of the great trembling bipolar world will lay down their washing and watch these Games.

Selection from "Why We Play These Games," *Time*, July 30, 1984.

CRITICAL THINKING

1. What was the writer's attitude toward the Games?
2. What did the preparations show about the public's attitude toward the Games?

---

7. THE ROBOTS ARE COMING! THE ROBOTS ARE COMING!

In the 1980s, as the field of robotics began to come of age, ideas once associated with science fiction no longer seemed impossible. By 1984, the population of robots in the United States was growing by 30 percent a year, while the human population was growing at about only 2 percent annually. It was estimated that there would be 35,000 robots in America by 1990.

Times change fast, especially in the technological landscape. Twenty years ago, [scientists] would have been laughed out of their laboratories for consorting with robots. Science fiction, not serious science, vouched for the humanlike machines. But within the space of a generation, robots crossed over. The development of microcomputers bolstered the belief that intelligent machines, able to work and act as well as ponder, could be built.

Today they are with us, and in the future, whether they bring prosperity or unemployment, they promise to be omnipresent. In Japan, where more than a half of the world's robot population resides, the government plans to employ them in nearly every field from fire fighting to guiding the blind. The Japanese are calling it a "robolution," a revolution that extends from factory spot welders to devices that slice sushi for overworked chefs to piano-playing home robots (available, with many other talents and a price tag of $42,000, from a leading Tokyo department store).

Americans expect nothing less. . . .

. . . About 6,000 robots work in the United States, most of them lugging parts in factories. They are metal arms that lunge and grab, pivot and relinquish, repeating the motion as perfectly as a replayed film. Some jerk like oil derricks and others bend over backwards like gymnasts. But whether they pick up transistors or engine housings, they are precise and obedient, going only where told to go. Their trump is a glimmer of flexibility; they can do more than one task. . . .

. . . the only walking machine now adaptable to commercial uses [is] the Functionoid. With a cylindrical body and a fishbowl head that rest on six spindly legs, it is a lithe, compact powerhouse. . . . It weighs 375 pounds and presses 1,800 pounds. Considering that strong-armed robots typically lift a fraction of their weight, the feat is impressive. Its delicate and elegant movements make it even more so. It tucks its legs up like an owl, and then stretches them like a cat. On radio command, it plants three legs on the ground and lifts the back end of a pickup truck. . . .

Robotics is breeding a new generation of machines that we may soon meet as pets. . . . BOB, short for Brains On Board . . . scuttles across the room, relying on ultrasonic detectors to avoid walls. When it senses a warm body with infrared detectors, it stops, swaying ever so slightly. BOB does get disoriented, a feature that makes it slightly human. A bop on the head and it speaks—20 words with a mild robot accent.

BOB is cute, a delightful gimmick, but even among those robotics engineers working on more serious problems, there is a singular awe and admiration for the human organism. . . . "The only ones who really appreciate how smart people are," [said an engineer,] "are those who try to do some of these things with a robot."

Selection from Jeanne McDermott, "Robots are playing new roles as they take a hand in our affairs," *Smithsonian*, November, 1983.

CRITICAL THINKING

1. What drawbacks might there be living in a society where machines perform many routine tasks? What advantages?
2. Give pros and cons on how robotics might someday affect people's employment.

GEORGE SEGAL

The sculptures of George Segal [born 1924] depict the modern world by showing anonymous humans living among the objects that fill their homes, their work places, and the public spaces they pass through.

Segal casts his figures directly from living models. First he wraps the fully clothed model in plaster soaked surgical bandages. When the plaster dries, he cuts the mold open and lets his model out. He then reassembles the mold and applies more plaster over the cast to achieve the desired final form and expression. The pure white figures are placed in groups along with objects typical of contemporary American scenes. The final effect is often like a frozen moment, but one which is ordinary, even mundane.

In these works viewers are drawn to the humanity of Segal's plaster humans. Although the frozen poses are authentic, the plaster people portray dramatic isolation in their mummy-like bandages and blank expressions.

While many public sculptures immortalize war heroes and historical figures, "The commuter" shows ordinary Americans awaiting their bus.

CRITICAL THINKING

1. George Segal portrays the anonymity of modern American life. List elements from the photos of his work, shown on these two pages, that support his vision.
2. In what ways are Segal's works both realistic and unrealistic? Contrast his work with Norman Rockwell's.

"The Diner" makes a poignant statement about the loneliness of a community grown so large that even neighbors have become strangers.

Segal captures big city postures in the straight ahead stance of his plaster pedestrians whose eyes seem to avoid contact with others as they obey the commands of a mechanical sign in Segal's sculpture, "Walk- Don't Walk."

The Declaration of Independence

IN CONGRESS, JULY 4, 1776

The Unanimous Declaration of the Thirteen United States of America

When in the Course of human events, it becomes necessary for one people to dissolve the political bands which have connected them with another, and to assume among the Powers of the earth, the separate and equal station to which the Laws of Nature and of Nature's God entitle them, a decent respect to the opinions of mankind, requires that they should declare the causes which impel them to the separation.

We hold these truths to be self-evident, that all men are created equal, that they are endowed by their Creator with certain unalienable Rights, that among these are Life, Liberty and the pursuit of Happiness. That to secure these rights, Governments are instituted among Men, deriving their just powers from the consent of the governed, That whenever any Form of Government becomes destructive of these ends, it is the Right of the People to alter or to abolish it, and to institute new Government, laying its foundation on such principles and organizing its powers in such form, as to them shall seem most likely to effect their safety and Happiness. Prudence, indeed, will dictate that Governments long established should not be changed for light and transient causes; and accordingly all experience hath shown, that mankind are more disposed to suffer, while evils are sufferable, than to right themselves by abolishing the forms to which they are accustomed. But when a long train of abuses and usurpations, pursuing invariably the same Object evinces a design to reduce them under absolute Despotism, it is their right, it is their duty, to throw off such government, and to provide new Guards for their future security. Such has been the patient sufferance of these Colonies; and such is now the necessity which constrains them to alter their former Systems of Government. The history of the present King of Great Britain is a history of repeated injuries and usurpations, all having in direct object the establishment of an absolute Tyranny over these States. To prove this, let Facts be submitted to a candid world.

He has refused his Assent to Laws, the most wholesome and necessary for the public good.

He has forbidden his Governors to pass Laws of immediate and pressing importance, unless suspended in their operation till his Assent should be obtained; and when so suspended, he has utterly neglected to attend to them.

He has refused to pass other laws for the accommodation of large districts of people, unless those people would relinquish the right of Representation in the Legislature, a right inestimable to them and formidable to tyrants only.

He has called together legislative bodies at places unusual, uncomfortable, and distant from the depository of their Public Records, for the sole purpose of fatiguing them into compliance with his measures.

He has dissolved Representative Houses repeatedly, for opposing with manly firmness his invasions on the rights of the people.

He has refused for a long time, after such dissolutions, to cause others to be elected; whereby the Legislative Powers, incapable of Annihilation, have returned to the People at large for their exercise; the State remaining in the mean time exposed to all the dangers of invasion from without, and convulsions within.

He has endeavoured to prevent the population of these States; for that purpose obstructing the Laws for Naturalization of Foreigners; refusing to pass others to encourage their migration hither, and raising the conditions of new Appropriations of Lands.

He has obstructed the Administration of Justice, by refusing his Assent to Laws for establishing Judiciary Powers.

He has made Judges dependent on his Will alone, for the tenure of their offices, and the amount and payment of their salaries.

He has erected a multitude of New Offices, and sent hither swarms of Officers to harass our people, and eat out their substance.

He has kept among us, in times of peace, Standing Armies without the Consent of our Legislature.

He has affected to render the Military independent of and superior to the Civil Power.

He has combined with others to subject us to a jurisdiction foreign to our constitution, and unacknowledged by our laws; giving his Assent to their acts of pretended Legislation:

For quartering large bodies of armed troops among us:

For protecting them, by a mock Trial, from Punishment for any Murders which they should commit on the Inhabitants of these States:

For cutting off our Trade with all parts of the world:

For imposing taxes on us without our Consent:

For depriving us in many cases, of the benefits of Trial by Jury:

For transporting us beyond Seas to be tried for pretended offences:

For abolishing the free System of English Laws in a neighboring Province, establishing therein an Arbitrary government, and enlarging its Boundaries so as to render it at once an example and fit instrument for introducing the same absolute rule into these Colonies:

For taking away our Charters, abolishing our most valuable Laws, and altering fundamentally the Forms of our Governments:

For suspending our own Legislature, and declaring themselves invested with Power to legislate for us in all cases whatsoever.

He has abdicated Government here, by declaring us out of his Protection and waging War against us.

He has plundered our seas, ravaged our Coasts, burnt our towns, and destroyed the lives of our people.

He is at this time transporting large armies of foreign mercenaries to compleat the works of death, desolation and tyranny already begun with circumstances of Cruelty & perfidy scarcely paralleled in the most barbarous ages, and totally unworthy the Head of a civilized nation.

He has constrained our fellow Citizens taken Captive on the high Seas to bear Arms against their Country, to become the executioners of their friends and Brethren, or to fall themselves by their Hands.

He has excited domestic insurrections amongst us, and has endeavoured to bring on the inhabitants of our frontiers, the merciless Indian Savages, whose known rule of warfare, is an undistinguished destruction of all ages, sexes and conditions.

In every stage of these Oppressions We Have Petitioned for Redress in the most humble terms: Our repeated Petitions have been answered only by repeated injury. A Prince, whose character is thus marked by every act which may define a Tyrant, is unfit to be the ruler of a free people.

Nor have We been wanting in attention to our British brethren. We have warned them from time to time of attempts by their legislature to extend an unwarrantable jurisdiction over us. We have reminded them of the circumstances of our emigration and settlement here. We have appealed to their native justice and magnanimity, and we have conjured them by the ties of our common kindred to disavow these usurpations, which, would inevitably interrupt our connections and correspondence. They too have been deaf to the voice of justice and of consanguinity. We must, therefore, acquiesce in the necessity, which denounces our Separation, and hold them, as we hold the rest of mankind, Enemies in War, in Peace Friends.

We, therefore, the Representatives of the United States of America, in General Congress, Assembled, appealing to the Supreme Judge of the world for the rectitude of our intentions, do, in the Name, and by Authority of the good People of these Colonies, solemnly publish and declare, That these United Colonies are, and of Right ought to be Free and Independent States; that they are Absolved from all Allegiance to the British Crown, and that all political connection between them and the State of Great Britain, is and ought to be totally dissolved; and that as Free and Independent States, they have full Power to levy War, conclude Peace, contract Alliances, establish Commerce, and to do all other Acts and Things which Independent States may of right do. And for the support of this Declaration, with a firm reliance on the protection of Divine Providence, we mutually pledge to each other our Lives, our Fortunes and our Sacred Honor.

We the People

of the United States, in order to form a more perfect Union, establish Justice, insure domestic Tranquility, provide for the common defence, promote the general Welfare, and secure the Blessings of Liberty to ourselves and our Posterity, do ordain and establish this Constitution for the United States of America.

Article. I.

Section. 1. All legislative Powers herein granted shall be vested in a Congress of the United States, which shall consist of a Senate and House of Representatives.

Section. 2. The House of Representatives shall be composed of Members chosen every second Year by the People of the several States, and the Electors in each State shall have the Qualifications requisite for Electors of the most numerous Branch of the State Legislature.

No Person shall be a Representative who shall not have attained to the Age of twenty five Years, and been seven Years a Citizen of the United States, and who shall not, when elected, be an Inhabitant of that State in which he shall be chosen.

Representatives and direct Taxes shall be apportioned among the several States which may be included within this Union, according to their respective Numbers, which shall be determined by adding to the whole Number of free Persons, including those bound to Service for a Term of Years, and excluding Indians not taxed, three fifths of all other Persons. The actual Enumeration shall be made within three Years after the first Meeting of the Congress of the United States, and within every subsequent Term of ten Years, in such Manner as they shall by Law direct. The Number of Representatives shall not exceed one for every thirty Thousand, but each State shall have at Least one Representative; and until such enumeration shall be made, the State of New Hampshire shall be entitled to chuse three, Massachusetts eight, Rhode Island and Providence Plantations one, Connecticut five, New York six, New Jersey four, Pennsylvania eight, Delaware one, Maryland six, Virginia ten, North Carolina five, South Carolina five, and Georgia three.

When vacancies happen in the Representation from any State, the Executive Authority thereof shall issue Writs of Election to fill such Vacancies.

The House of Representatives shall chuse their Speaker and other Officers; and shall have the sole Power of Impeachment.

Section. 3. The Senate of the United States shall be composed of two Senators from each State, chosen by the Legislature thereof, for six Years; and each Senator shall have one Vote.

Immediately after they shall be assembled in Consequence of the first Election, they shall be divided as equally as may be into three Classes. The Seats of the Senators of the first Class shall be vacated at the Expiration of the second Year, of the second Class at the Expiration of the fourth Year, and of the third Class at the Expiration of the sixth Year, so that one third may be chosen every second Year; and if Vacancies happen by Resignation, or otherwise, during the Recess of the Legislature of any State, the Executive thereof may make temporary Appointments until the next Meeting of the Legislature, which shall then fill such Vacancies.

No Person shall be a Senator who shall not have attained to the Age of thirty Years, and been nine Years a Citizen of the United States, and who shall not, when elected, be an Inhabitant of that State for which he shall be chosen.

The Vice President of the United States shall be President of the Senate, but shall have no Vote, unless they be equally divided.

The Senate shall chuse their other Officers, and also a President pro tempore, in the Absence of the Vice President, or when he shall exercise the Office of President of the United States.

The Senate shall have the sole Power to try all Impeachments. When sitting for that Purpose, they shall be on Oath or Affirmation. When the President of the United States is tried, the Chief Justice shall preside: And no Person shall be convicted without the Concurrence of two thirds of the Members present.

Judgment in Cases of Impeachment shall not extend further than to removal from Office, and disqualification to hold and enjoy any Office of honor, Trust or Profit under the United States: but the Party convicted shall nevertheless be liable and subject to Indictment, Trial, Judgment and Punishment, according to Law.

Section. 4. The Times, Places and Manner of holding Elections for Senators and Representatives, shall be prescribed in each State by the Legislature thereof; but the Congress may at any time by Law make or alter such Regulations, except as to the Places of chusing Senators.

The Congress shall assemble at least once in every Year, and such Meeting shall be on the first Monday in December, unless they shall by Law appoint a different Day.

Section. 5. Each House shall be the Judge of the Elections, Returns and Qualifications of its own Members, and a Majority of each shall constitute a Quorum to do Business; but a smaller Number may adjourn from day to day, and may be authorized to compel the Attendance of absent Members, in such Manner, and under such Penalties as each House may provide.

Each House may determine the Rules of its Proceedings, punish its Members for disorderly Behaviour, and, with the Concurrence of two thirds, expel a Member.

Each House shall keep a Journal of its Proceedings, and from time to time publish the same, excepting such Parts as may in their Judgment require Secrecy; and the Yeas and Nays of the Members of either House on any question shall, at the Desire of one fifth of those Present, be entered on the Journal.

Neither House, during the Session of Congress, shall, without the Consent of the other, adjourn for more than three days, nor to any other Place than that in which the two Houses shall be sitting.

Section. 6. The Senators and Representatives shall receive a Compensation for their Services, to be ascertained by Law, and paid out of the Treasury of the United States. They shall in all Cases, except Treason, Felony and Breach of the Peace, be privileged from Arrest during their Attendance at the Session of their respective Houses, and in going to and returning from the same; and for any Speech or Debate in either House, they shall not be questioned in any other Place.

No Senator or Representative shall, during the Time for which he was elected, be appointed to any civil Office under the Authority of the United States, which shall have been created, or the Emoluments whereof shall have been encreased during such time; and no Person holding any Office under the United States, shall be a Member of either House during his Continuance in Office.

All Bills for raising Revenue shall originate in the House of Representatives; but the Senate may propose or concur with

THE CONSTITUTION AND AMENDMENTS

INTRODUCTION

The United States is often thought of as a young nation. And, compared to China or Spain or England, it is. But no other country in the world has been governed under the same basic law for so long as the United States has. The American Constitution is two hundred years old. It has been an amazing success. The Constitution has been flexible enough to function well during the past two centuries of change and growth, as the United States developed into a great world power.

Soon after the Revolutionary War began, the Continental Congress adopted a plan of government called the Articles of Confederation. There was no President or Supreme Court under this system. The Continental Congress was responsible for all actions taken in the name of the United States of America.

Under the Articles of Confederation, the individual state governments remained very powerful. In fact, in order to take any important action, the Confederation government had to have the support of delegates from each of the thirteen states. Most American leaders insisted on this. They were rebelling against the actions of a single governing body, the British Parliament. They did not want to create a single powerful government at home that might also mean tyranny.

But the weak Confederation government did not work very well. Congress found it difficult to raise money because at least one state always objected to tax laws. Because they were almost independent of one another, the states quarreled bitterly. European nations did not respect such a *disunited* United States.

Many respected Americans, including George Washington and Benjamin Franklin, wanted to change the system. They wanted a stronger central government that would be able to raise taxes and represent a united nation to the rest of the world.

Nevertheless, when the Constitutional Convention met in Philadelphia in 1787, it was clear that the danger of too powerful a central government was on the minds of many delegates. Most of the debates were concerned with protecting the rights of the states from the powers of the federal government (and vice versa), the small states from large states, the powers of Congress from a strong president, and the rights of minorities from the wishes of the majority.

The men who wrote the Constitution believed in balancing each branch of government against the others. They believed that if one branch of government could *check* (put limits on) the other branches but not completely dominate them, then the central or federal government would be efficient, but it would not be able to take away the liberties of the people. Although the writers of the Constitution had no way of knowing what changes would take place in the United States, they realized that there would be changes. They believed that later generations should be able to change (or amend) the Constitution. Therefore, they designed the Amendment process as part of the Constitution itself.

It was important that the amendment process not be made too easy. If it were, the Constitution would not be a basic law at all. If it could be changed just by a majority vote of Congress, the Constitution would have no more force and dignity than any minor law Congress could pass. Therefore, the amendment process was made difficult but not impossible. As a result, the Constitution as originally written has been amended only 26 times in two hundred years.

 375

Constitution of the United States of America

PREAMBLE

We the people of the United States, in order to form a more perfect Union, establish justice, insure domestic tranquility, provide for the common defense, promote the general welfare, and secure the blessings of liberty to ourselves and our posterity, do ordain and establish this Constitution for the United States of America.

The Constitution derives its authority from the people of the entire nation, not merely from the state governments as under the Articles of Confederation. As stated in the preamble, the major purposes of the Constitution are (1) to create a better balance between state power and national power ("a more perfect Union"), (2) to improve the court system, (3) to prevent outbreaks of civil disturbances or riots such as Shays's Rebellion, (4) to protect the nation from foreign dangers, (5) to encourage national growth and social progress, and (6) to safeguard the freedom of citizens.

ARTICLE 1. LEGISLATIVE BRANCH

The first part of the Constitution, Article 1, concerns the organization and powers of the law-making or legislative branch of government: the Congress.

SECTION 1. CONGRESS

All legislative powers herein granted shall be vested in a Congress of the United States, which shall consist of a Senate and House of Representatives.

The writers of the Constitution decided to divide the law-making power between two houses that were to conduct business separately. Such an arrangement is known as a *bicameral*, or two-house, system for making laws. Though this clause gives "all legislative powers" to Congress, the president shares in law-making when signing a law enacted by both houses of Congress.

SECTION 2. HOUSE OF REPRESENTATIVES

1. *Election and Term of Members.* The House of Representatives shall be composed of members chosen every second year by the people of the several States, and the electors in each State shall have the qualifica-tions requisite for electors of the most numerous branch of the State Legislature.

Every two years, members of the House of Representatives are chosen by the people of the different states. Anyone qualified by state law to vote for a state legislator is automatically eligible to vote for a Representative to Congress. When this clause was written in 1787, all 13 states placed restrictions on who could vote. These requirements have since been removed.

2. *Qualifications.* No person shall be a representative who shall not have attained to the age of twenty-five years, and been seven years a citizen of the United States, and who shall not, when elected, be an inhabitant of that State in which he shall be chosen.

A member of the House must be (1) at least 25 years old, (2) a United States citizen for at least seven years, and (3) a resident of the state in which he or she is elected.

3. *Apportionment of Representatives and Direct Taxes.* Representatives and direct taxes shall be apportioned among the several States which may be included within this Union, according to their respective numbers,* which shall be determined by adding to the whole number of free persons, including those bound to service for a term of years, and excluding Indians not taxed, three-fifths of all other persons. The actual enumeration shall be made within three years after the first meeting of the Congress of the United States, and within every subsequent term of ten years, in such manner as they shall by law direct. The number of representatives shall not exceed one for every thirty thousand, but each State shall have at least one representative; and until such enumeration shall be made, the State of New Hampshire shall be entitled to choose three, Massachusetts eight, Rhode Island and Providence Plantations one, Connecticut five, New York six, New Jersey four, Pennsylvania eight, Delaware one, Maryland six, Virginia ten, North Carolina five, South Carolina five, and Georgia three.

A state's representation in the House is based on the size of its population. The more populous the state, the greater is its number of elected Representatives. Every ten years, a *census*, or official count, is made of the nation's population, and a state's representation in the

*Note: Parts of the constitution no longer in use are crossed out.

House is adjusted accordingly. The current size of the House, 435 members, was fixed by law in 1929. Indians were not counted in the census for purposes of representation until 1940. The practice of counting every five slaves ("all other persons") as equal to only three free citizens was nullified by the adoption of the Thirteenth and Fourteenth Amendments after the Civil War.

4. Vacancies. When vacancies happen in the representation from any State, the Executive authority thereof shall issue writs of election to fill such vacancies.

The governor of a state is the "executive authority" referred to in this clause. When a Representative dies or retires before his or her term expires, the state governor may call for a special election to fill the vacancy.

5. Officers and Impeachment. The House of Representatives shall choose their Speaker and other officers; and shall have the sole power of impeachment.

Members of the majority party of the House select their presiding officer, the Speaker, in addition to other officers. The selection is made every two years after the newly elected House convenes to begin its term.

The Speaker is always a member of the political party to which the largest group of House members belong, and has great influence both in selecting members for important committees and in conducting the business of the House.

To *impeach* an officer of government, such as a president or judge, is to accuse the officer of wrongdoing. Only the House has the power to pass a bill of impeachment.

SECTION 3. SENATE
1. Term and Number of Members. The Senate of the United States shall be composed of two senators from each State, chosen by the legislature thereof, for six years; and each senator shall have one vote.

Since the Seventeenth Amendment was adopted in 1913, senators are elected by the voters of the states at a regular election. Before 1913, senators were elected by state legislatures, and the people had no direct part in their selection. This was because in the early days of the Constitution the senators were supposed to represent the state governments to see that the small states got equal treatment with the large states. Every state is represented by two senators, each of whom serves a six-year term.

2. Three Classes of Senators. Immediately after they shall be assembled in consequence of the first election, they shall be divided as equally as may be into three classes. The seats of the senators of the first class shall be vacated at the expiration of the second year, of the second class at the expiration of the fourth year, and of the third class at the expiration of the sixth year, so that one-third may be chosen every second year; and if vacancies happen by resignation, or otherwise, during the recess of the legislature of any State, the executive thereof may make temporary appointments until the next meeting of the legislature, which shall then fill such vacancies.

Unlike the House, all of whose members are elected at the same time, the Senate has a staggered membership. Only one-third of the senators are elected in any one election year.

If a senator dies or retires in midterm, the current procedure is for the state's governor to call a special election to fill the vacancy. Earlier, before the Seventeenth Amendment was adopted, the state legislature was empowered to make the selection.

3. Qualifications. No person shall be a senator who shall not have attained to the age of thirty years, and been nine years a citizen of the United States, and who shall not, when elected, be an inhabitant of that State for which he shall be chosen.

A Senator must be (1) at least 30 years old, (2) a citizen for at least nine years, and (3) a resident of the state where elected.

4. Vice President's Role. The Vice President of the United States shall be President of the Senate, but shall have no vote, unless they be equally divided.

The only duty that the Constitution assigns to the vice president is to preside over meetings of the Senate. The only time that the vice president may vote on a Senate bill is when there is a tie. Modern presidents have given their vice presidents important political and diplomatic duties to perform, but none of these are required by the Constitution.

5. Other Officers. The Senate shall choose their other officers, and also a President pro tempore, in the absence of the Vice President, or when he shall exercise the office of President of the United States.

The Senate votes for one of its members to preside over debates whenever the Vice President is absent. The position is called *pro tempore* because it is a temporary position. The members of each political party represented in the Senate meet at the beginning of each new Congress and select a "floor leader" and appoint various senators of their own party to help the leader.

6. Trial of Impeachments. The Senate shall have the sole power to try all impeachments. When sitting

377

for that purpose, they shall be on oath or affirmation. When the President of the United States is tried, the Chief Justice shall preside; and no person shall be convicted without the concurrence of two-thirds of the members present.

If a bill of impeachment is passed by the House, then the Senate must act in the manner of a court to try the case of alleged wrongdoing. The Senate sets the date for trial and provides the accused with a written statement of the charges. The accused has the same legal rights of any person on trial.

7. *Penalty for Conviction.* Judgment in cases of impeachment shall not extend further than to removal from office, and disqualification to hold and enjoy any office or honor, trust or profit under the United States; but the party convicted shall nevertheless be liable and subject to indictment, trial, judgment and punishment, according to law.

If the Senate convicts an accused officer of the impeachment charges, that person may be forced to leave office. This is the only penalty that the Senate may impose. However, the person can still be tried in a regular court for any crimes committed.

SECTION 4. MEETINGS AND ELECTIONS

1. *Holding Elections.* The times, places and manner of holding elections for senators and representatives, shall be prescribed in each State by the legislature thereof; but the Congress may at any time by law make or alter such regulations, except as to the places of choosing senators.

Congress set no election requirements until 1842, when it required members of the House to be elected from specific districts in a state. In 1872, it set the same day in even-numbered years as the date for Congressional elections.

2. *Meetings.* The Congress shall assemble at least once in every year, and such meeting shall be on the first Monday in December, unless they shall by law appoint a different day.

Since members of the House of Representatives are chosen every two years, the life of a Congress is considered to be two years. The Twentieth Amendment of the Constitution provides that the Congress shall convene in regular session at noon on January 3 of each year unless it shall pass a law to fix a different date. It meets in the Capitol at Washington, D.C. It remains in session until its members vote to adjourn. The president may call a special session whenever it is necessary.

SECTION 5. RULES OF PROCEDURE

1. *Quorum and Membership.* Each house shall be the judge of the elections, returns and qualifications of its own members, and a majority of each shall constitute a quorum to do business; but a smaller number may adjourn from day to day, and may be authorized to compel the attendance of absent members, in such manner, and under such penalties as each house may provide.

A quorum is the number of members who must be present for either house to conduct business. Currently, in the Senate, a quorum is 51; in the House, it is 218.

2. *Discipline.* Each house may determine the rules of its proceedings, punish its members for disorderly behavior, and, with the concurrence of two-thirds, expel a member.

The rules adopted by each house include procedures for censuring and expelling members. A two-thirds vote is required for expulsion.

3. *Journal.* Each house shall keep a journal of its proceedings, and from time to time publish the same, excepting such parts as may in their judgment require secrecy; and the yeas and the nays of the members of either house on any question shall, at the desire of one-fifth of those present, be entered on the journal.

Two journals, one for the House and the other for the Senate, are published at the end of each session of Congress. A third journal, the *Congressional Record*, is published every day that Congress is in session and provides a complete account of debates, resolutions, and other business conducted in both houses. The purpose of these journals is to make it possible for the general public to watch the conduct of their elected representatives.

4. *Adjournment.* Neither house, during the session of Congress, shall, without the consent of the other, adjourn for more than three days, nor to any other place than that in which the two houses shall be sitting.

This clause gives Congress the power to determine when and where to meet. Both houses, however, must meet in the same city. Adjournment by one house for more than three days is not allowed unless the other house agrees to it.

SECTION 6. PRIVILEGES AND RESTRICTIONS

1. *Compensation and Privileges.* The senators and representatives shall receive a compensation for their services, to be ascertained by law, and paid out of the Treasury of the United States. They shall in all cases, except treason, felony and breach of the peace, be privileged from arrest during their attendance at the session of their respective houses, and in going to and returning from the same; and for any speech or debate in either house, they shall not be questioned in any other place.

The first Congress voted to award members $6 a day in compensation for their services. More recently (1981), the Congress adopted a yearly salary of $60,663 for all regular members and $79,125 for the Speaker of the House.

Members cannot be arrested for what they say in speeches and debates in Congress. They are immune, however, only in the Capitol building itself, and not in their private lives.

2. Restrictions. No senator or representative shall, during the time for which he was elected, be appointed to any civil office under the authority of the United States, which shall have been created, or the emoluments whereof shall have been increased during such time; and no person holding any office under the United States, shall be a member of either house during his continuance in office.

While they are members of Congress, legislators cannot hold positions in either the executive or judicial departments of the government. This clause was intended by the Founding Fathers to uphold the principle of separation of powers.

SECTION 7. HOW BILLS BECOME LAWS
1. Money Bills. All bills for raising revenue shall originate in the House of Representatives; but the Senate may propose or concur with amendments as on other bills.

This clause provides that all tax and appropriation bills for raising money must originate in the House of Representatives. However, the Senate usually amends the money bills voted by the House and may even substitute an entirely different bill.

2. President's Veto Power. Every bill which shall have passed the House of Representatives and the Senate, shall, before it become a law, be presented to the President of the United States; if he approves he shall sign it, but if not he shall return it, with his objections to that house in which it shall have originated, who shall enter the objections at large on their journal, and proceed to reconsider it. If after such reconsideration two thirds of that House shall agree to pass the bill, it shall be sent, together with the objections, to the other House, by which it shall likewise be reconsidered, and if approved by two thirds of the House, it shall become a law. But in all such cases the votes of both Houses shall be determined by yeas and

nays, and the names of the persons voting for and against the bill shall be entered on the journal of each House respectively. If any bill shall not be returned by the President within ten days (Sundays excepted) after it shall have been presented to him, the same shall be a law, in like manner as if he had signed it, unless the Congress by their adjournment prevent its return, in which case it shall not be a law.

After a bill has been passed by both houses, it is sent to the president. The president may approve the entire bill or disapprove it. If the president has not signed the bill within ten days after it reaches him (not counting Sundays), it becomes a law without his signature. However, if Congress adjourns in the meantime, the bill does not become a law unless the president signs it within the ten-day limit. This way of preventing a bill from becoming a law is known as a *pocket veto.*

If the president vetoes a bill while Congress is in session, it does not become a law unless each house passes it over the president's veto by a two-thirds majority vote.

3. Actions Other Than Bills. Every order, resolution, or vote to which the concurrence of the Senate and House of Representatives may be necessary (except on a question of adjournment) shall be presented to the President of the United States; and before the same shall take effect, shall be approved by him, or being disapproved by him, shall be repassed by two thirds of the Senate and House of Representatives, according to the rules and limitations prescribed in the case of a bill.

Besides acting on regular bills, Congress may also adopt resolutions of two different kinds. A *joint resolution* results from a declaration passed by both houses on the same subject. When signed by the President, it becomes a law. A *concurrent resolution* is merely an expression of opinion on the part of either house of Congress. Since it can never become law, this kind of resolution does not require the President's approval.

SECTION 8. POWERS DELEGATED TO CONGRESS
1. Taxes. The Congress shall have power to lay and collect taxes, duties, imposts and excises, to pay the debts and provide for the common defense and general welfare of the United States; but all duties, imposts and excises shall be uniform throughout the United States.

Congress's power to tax may be used only to pay the federal government's debts and to provide for the common defense and general welfare. The taxes it collects must be the same everywhere. An excise or sales tax on gasoline, for example, cannot be higher in Texas than in Hawaii.

 379

2. Borrowing. To borrow money on the credit of the United States;

Selling government bonds is the most common of the government's methods for borrowing money. This clause, extended by Clause 18 below, has enabled Congress to create a national banking system.

3. Commerce. To regulate commerce with foreign nations, and among the several States, and with the Indian tribes;

Congress derives considerable authority from this clause, which gives it exclusive power to regulate trade between the states and trade with foreign countries. Interstate commerce, as defined by the Supreme Court, involves more than transportation and the sale of goods. It also can mean communication by telephone or television across state lines.

4. Naturalization and Bankruptcy. To establish a uniform rule of naturalization, and uniform laws on the subject of bankruptcies throughout the United States;

Naturalization is the process by which foreign-born individuals may become citizens. Bankruptcy is the condition of being unable to pay one's debts to creditors. Congress has power to pass laws on both these matters.

5. Coins and Standards. To coin money, regulate the value thereof, and of foreign coin, and fix the standard of weights and measures;

Under this provision, Congress not only mints coins but also prints and circulates paper money in various denominations. In 1838, Congress adopted the English system of pounds, ounces, feet, and yards as a national standard for weighing and measuring objects.

6. Punishment of Counterfeiting. To provide for the punishment of counterfeiting the securities and current coin of the United States;

The current penalty for counterfeiting American money is a fine of up to $5,000 and/or imprisonment for up to 15 years.

7. Post Offices and Roads. To establish post offices and post roads;

Any turnpike, canal, river, street, and airway may be considered a "post road" if mail travels over it.

8. Patents and Copyrights. To promote the progress of science and useful arts, by securing for limited times to authors and inventors the exclusive right to their respective writings and discoveries;

Congress may protect authors by enacting copyright laws and may encourage scientists and inventors by enacting patent laws. Patents may be obtained on processes as well as products. Copyrights protect an author from acts of plagiarism for the period of his or her life plus 50 years.

9. Lower Courts. To constitute tribunals inferior to the Supreme Court;

From this clause, Congress derives the authority to establish all federal courts except the Supreme Court. Courts created by act of Congress are known as "inferior" or "lower" courts because they are under the final jurisdiction of the Supreme Court.

10. Punishment of Piracy. To define and punish piracies and felonies committed on the high seas, and offenses against the law of nations;

Piracy was common at the time this clause was written. Today, the only significant function that Congress derives from this clause is the power to protect Americans at sea.

11. War. To declare war, grant letters of marque and reprisal, and make rules concerning captures on land and water;

The Founding Fathers probably intended that the power to declare war should lie exclusively with Congress. Many presidents, however, have used their power as commander in chief to carry on acts of war without a formal declaration by Congress.

A letter of marque and reprisal is a commission authorizing private citizens to outfit vessels (privateers) for capturing and destroying enemy ships in time of war. Such letters have been forbidden under international law since 1856.

12. Army. To raise and support armies, but no appropriation of money to that use shall be for a longer term than two years;

13. Navy. To provide and maintain a Navy;

14. Regulation of Armed Forces. To make rules for the government and regulation of the land and naval forces;

Americans in the 1780s were fearful of standing armies like the British army, which had been their enemy. This explains the provision that appropriations for an army be limited to two years. Congress has the power to vote supplies for a navy for an unlimited period.

15. Militia. To provide for calling forth the militia to execute the laws of the Union, suppress insurrections and repel invasions;

A state's militia is its troop of citizen soldiers who may be called into service in time of emergency. Better known as the National Guard, the militia may be called into the federal service by either a vote of Congress or a declaration of the president.

16. *Organizing the Militia.* To provide for organizing, arming, and disciplining the militia, and for governing such part of them as may be employed in the service of the United States, reserving to the States respectively, the appointment of the officers, and the authority of training the militia according to the discipline prescribed by Congress;

The National Guard, when called into federal service, must follow the same rules that Congress has set for the regular armed services of the United States.

17. *District of Columbia.* To exercise exclusive legislation in all cases whatsoever, over such district (not exceeding ten miles square) as may, by cession of particular States, and the acceptance of Congress, become the seat of the Government of the United States, and to exercise like authority over all places purchased by the consent of the legislature of the State in which the same shall be, for the erection of forts, magazines, arsenals, dock-yards, and other needful buildings;

At the time this clause was written, a permanent capital for the United States had not been selected. During Washington's presidency, a piece of land on the Potomac River was named Federal City, and later the District of Columbia. Committees of Congress governed the city until 1874, when presidentially appointed commissioners took over its government. Under the *Home Rule Act* of 1974, the city has governed itself through a mayor and a city council.

18. *Elastic Clause.* And to make all laws which shall be necessary and proper for carrying into execution the foregoing powers, and all other powers vested by this Constitution in the Government of the United States, or in any department or officer thereof.

This is often called the "elastic clause" because its meaning can be stretched to fit many circumstances. The constitutional basis for the concept of *implied powers* is found in this clause. Unlike the other 17 powers directly delegated to Congress, this clause gives no specific grant of power. But its liberal interpretation by both Congress and the Supreme Court has contributed greatly to the federal government's ability to adjust to changing circumstances.

SECTION 9. POWERS DENIED TO THE FEDERAL GOVERNMENT

1. *Slave Trade.* The migration or importation of such persons as any of the States now existing shall think proper to admit, shall not be prohibited by the Congress prior to the year one thousand eight hundred and eight, but a tax or duty may be imposed on such importation, not exceeding ten dollars for each person.

According to this defunct clause, Congress could make no law before 1808 to forbid the sale of slaves. Congress was allowed, however, to place a tax as high as $10 on each slave brought into the country.

2. *Habeas Corpus.* The privilege of the writ of habeas corpus shall not be suspended, unless when in cases of rebellion or invasion the public safety may require it.

A *writ of habeas corpus* ("produce the body") is a court order directing a sheriff or warden who is holding a person in prison to show before a court that the prisoner is being held legally.

3. *Special Bills.* No bill of attainder or ex post facto law shall be passed.

A *bill of attainder* is a legislative act that inflicts punishment without a legal trial. An *ex post facto* law is a law that punishes a person for doing something that was legal before the law was passed.

4. *Direct Tax.* No capitation, or other direct, tax shall be laid, unless in proportion to the census or enumeration herein before directed to be taken.

A direct tax is a tax imposed on each person, such as the poll tax on persons voting. This provision was inserted to prevent Congress from taxing slaves per person for the purpose of abolishing slavery. This clause was overruled by the Sixteenth Amendment, which allows for an income tax.

5. *Export Duties.* No tax or duty shall be laid on articles exported from any State.

This clause also resulted from a commerce compromise. The southern states wanted to make sure that Congress could not use its taxing power to impose taxes on Southern exports, such as cotton and tobacco.

6. *Interstate Commerce.* No preference shall be given by any regulation of commerce or revenue to the ports of one State over those of another; nor shall vessels bound to, or from, one State, be obliged to enter, clear, or pay duties in another.

7. *Treasury Withdrawals.* No money shall be drawn from the Treasury, but in consequence of appropriations made by law; and a regular statement and account of the receipts and expenditures of all public money shall be published from time to time.

Since Congress controls expenditures, it can place limits on a president's powers by deciding how much the chief executive may spend for different purposes. This could well be the single most important check on the president's power in the Constitution.

8. *Titles of Nobility.*
No title of nobility shall be granted by the United States, and no person holding any office of profit or trust under them, shall, without the consent of the Congress, accept of any present, emolument, office, or title, of any kind whatever, from any King, Prince, or foreign State.

This clause prohibits the establishment of a nobility, and also discourages bribery of American officials by foreign governments.

SECTION 10. POWERS DENIED TO THE STATES

1. *Treaties, Coinage.*
No State shall enter into any treaty, alliance, or confederation; grant letters of marque and reprisal; coin money; emit bills of credit; make any thing but gold and silver coin a tender in payment of debts; pass any bill of attainder, ex post facto law, or law impairing the obligation of contracts, or grant any title of nobility.

When this clause was written, Shays's Rebellion was still fresh in the minds of the delegates to the Constitutional Convention. The delegates decided to protect creditors once and for all by denying states the right to pass laws that would impair obligations of contract. During the 1930s, the Supreme Court upheld state laws relieving debtors or mortgagees from paying their debts on the due dates.

2. *Duties and Imposts.*
No State shall, without the consent of the Congress, lay any imposts or duties on imports or exports, except what may be absolutely necessary for executing its inspection laws; and the net produce of all duties and imposts, laid by any State on imports or exports, shall be for the use of the Treasury of the United States; and all such laws shall be subject to the revision and control of the Congress.

A state may not put taxes on goods sent in or out of a state, unless Congress agrees.

3. *War.*
No State shall, without the consent of Congress, lay any duty of tonnage, keep troops, or ships of war in time of peace, enter into any agreement or compact with another State, or with a foreign power, or engage in war, unless actually invaded, or in such imminent danger as will not admit of delay.

States are forbidden to keep troops or warships in peacetime or to make a compact with another state or a foreign nation unless Congress agrees. States can maintain a militia, but a militia's use is limited to internal disorders that arise within a state unless the militia is called into federal service. States can enter into interstate compacts regarding problems that require joint or regional action. These compacts, however, require the approval of Congress.

ARTICLE 2. EXECUTIVE BRANCH

The second part of the Constitution concerns the powers and duties of the president as the head of the executive branch.

SECTION 1. PRESIDENT AND VICE PRESIDENT.

1. *Four-Year Term.*
The executive power shall be vested in a President of the United States of America. He shall hold his office during the term of four years, and, together with the Vice President, chosen for the same term, be elected, as follows:

The Constitution says that the executive power in the federal goverment shall be legally delegated to a president of the United States of America (often called the chief exective). All other executive officers are responsible to the president, and receive from the president the right to perform executive duties as the chief executive's delegates. The president and vice president are the only officers elected by the vote of the whole people.

2. *Electors From Each State.*
Each State, shall appoint, in such manner as the legislature thereof may direct, a number of electors, equal to the whole number of senators and representatives to which the State may be entitled in the Congress; but no senator or representative, or person holding an office of trust or profit under the United States, shall be appointed an elector.

The number of presidential electors is determined by a state's representation (senators and representatives) in Congress. No member of Congress or federal officer may be an elector.

3. *Former System of Election.*
The electors shall meet in their respective States, and vote by ballot for two persons, of whom one at least shall not be an inhabitant of the same State with themselves. And they shall make a list of all the persons voted for, and of the number of votes for each; which list they shall sign and certify, and transmit sealed to the seat of the Govern-

ment of the United States, directed to the President of the Senate. The President of the Senate shall, in the presence of the Senate and House of Representatives, open all the certificates, and the votes shall then be counted. The person having the greatest number of votes shall be the President, if such number be a majority of the whole number of electors appointed; and if there be more than one who have such majority, and have an equal number of votes, then the House of Representatives shall immediately choose by ballot one of them for President; and if no person have a majority, then from the five highest on the list the said House shall in like manner choose the President. But in choosing the President, the votes shall be taken by States, the representation from each State having one vote; a quorum for this purpose shall consist of a member or members from two thirds of the States, and a majority of all the States shall be necessary to a choice. In every case, after the choice of the President, the person having the greatest number of votes of the electors shall be the Vice President. But if there should remain two or more who have equal votes, the Senate shall choose from them by ballot the Vice President.

This clause outlines the original method of selecting the president and vice president. It has been replaced by the method outlined in the Twelfth Amendment. The framers of the Constitution did not foresee the rise of political parties, the development of primaries and conventions, or the broadening of democracy whereby the presidential electors would be elected by the people rather than chosen by state legislatures.

4. *Time of Elections.*
The Congress may determine the time of choosing the electors, and the day on which they shall give their votes; which day shall be the same throughout the United States.

In 1845, Congress set the first Tuesday after the first Monday in November of every fourth year as the general election date for selecting presidential electors.

5. *Qualifications for President.*
No person except a natural born citizen, or a citizen of the United States at the time of the adoption of this Constitution, shall be eligible to the office of President; neither shall any person be eligible to that office who shall not have attained to the age of thirty-five years, and been fourteen years a resident within the United States.

This clause provides that the President (1) must be a natural-born citizen of the United States, (2) must be at least 35 years old on taking office, and (3) must at that time have been a resident within the United States for at least 14 years.

The president's term of office, as provided in the Constitution, is four years. The Twenty-second Amend-

ment to the Constitution limits the number of times a person may be elected president.

6. *Succession of the Vice President.*
In case of the removal of the President from office, or of his death, resignation, or inability to discharge the powers and duties of the said office, the same shall devolve on the Vice President, and the Congress may by law provide for the case of removal, death, resignation, or inability, both of the President and Vice President, declaring what officer shall then act as President, and such officer shall act accordingly, until the disability be removed, or a President shall be elected.

Until the adoption of the Twenty-fifth Amendment, which expressly provides for the vice president to succeed to the presidency, succession was based on a precedent set by John Tyler in 1841. Tyler followed William Henry Harrison as president after the latter's death. He interpreted the ambiguous wording in this clause to mean that the vice president actually became the president, not just a temporary acting head of government.

7. *President's Salary.*
The President shall, at stated times, receive for his services, a compensation, which shall neither be increased nor diminished during the period for which he shall have been elected, and he shall not receive within that period any other emolument from the United States, or any of them.

Originally, the president's salary was $25,000 per year. The president's current salary of $200,000 plus a $50,000 taxable expense account per year was enacted in 1969. The president also receives numerous fringe benefits.

8. *President's Oath of Office.*
Before he enter on the execution of his office, he shall take the following oath or affirmation: "I do solemnly swear (or affirm) that I will faithfully execute the office of President of the United States, and will to the best of my ability, preserve, protect and defend the Constitution of the United States."

On January 20 following election in November, the president begins official duties with a ceremony called the Inauguration. It is customary for the president to go to the Capitol to take the oath of office, which is administered to him by the Chief Justice of the United States.

SECTION 2. POWERS OF THE PRESIDENT

1. *Commander in Chief.*
The President shall be Commander in Chief of the Army and Navy of the

United States, and of the militia of the several States, when called into the actual service of the United States; he may require the opinion, in writing, of the principal officer in each of the Executive Departments, upon any subject relating to the duties of their respective offices, and he shall have power to grant reprieves and pardons for offenses against the United States, except in cases of impeachment.

This provision places the armed forces under civilian control. The president is a civilian but is superior in military power to any military officer. The phrase "principal officer in each of the executive departments" is the basis for the creation of the president's cabinet. Each cabinet member is the head of one of the executive departments. The president chooses the cabinet members, with the consent of the Senate, and can remove any cabinet official without asking Senate approval.

The president may grant a full or a conditional pardon to any person who has been convicted of breaking a federal law, except in a case of impeachment. He may shorten the prison term or reduce the fine that has been imposed as punishment for a crime.

2. Treaties and Appointments. He shall have power, by and with the advice and consent of the Senate, to make treaties, provided two thirds of the Senators present concur; and he shall nominate, and by and with the advice and consent of the Senate, shall appoint ambassadors, other public ministers and consuls, Judges of the Supreme Court, and all other officers of the United States, whose appointments are not herein otherwise provided for, and which shall be established by law; but the Congress may by law vest the appointment of such inferior officers, as they think proper, in the President alone, in the courts of law, or in the heads of departments.

This clause identifies some of the president's major powers, which include the power to make treaties with foreign countries, provided that the Senate gives its concurrence in a vote of two-thirds of its participating members; and the power to appoint ambassadors, Supreme Court judges, and other government officials. Most of the president's appointments to office must be submitted to the Senate for its approval.

3. Vacancies. The President shall have power to fill up all vacancies that may happen during the recess of the Senate, by granting commissions which shall expire at the end of their next session.

When Congress is not in session, the president may appoint people to federal offices for a temporary period. These appointments terminate at the end of the next meeting of the Senate.

SECTION 3. DUTIES OF THE PRESIDENT

He shall from time to time give to the Congress information of the state of the Union, and recommend to their consideration such measures as he shall judge necessary and expedient; he may, on extraordinary occasions, convene both houses, or either of them, and in case of disagreement between them, with respect to the time of adjournment, he may adjourn them to such time as he shall think proper; he shall receive ambassadors and other public ministers; he shall take care that the laws be faithfully executed, and shall commission all the officers of the United States.

In compliance with this clause, it is the president's custom to present to Congress an annual report known as the State of the Union message. In this message, the president sets forth a legislative program for the year, thus giving Congress leadership in solving the nation's problems. In an emergency, the president may call a special meeting of either or both houses of Congress.

This clause also gives the president the duty of meeting with ambassadors and heads of state from other countries. Another presidential duty is to see that federal laws are observed. The president must sign the papers that give federal officials the right to hold their positions.

SECTION 4. IMPEACHMENT AND REMOVAL

The President, Vice President and all civil officers of the United States, shall be removed from office on impeachment for, and conviction of, treason, bribery, or other high crimes and misdemeanors.

Treason means giving help to the nation's enemies. "High crimes and misdemeanors" are serious abuses of political power. For either or both of these offenses, a president and vice president may be impeached (or accused) by the House and removed from office if convicted by the Senate.

ARTICLE 3. JUDICIAL BRANCH

The third branch of the federal government, the judicial branch, is made up of federal courts. It has the duty of explaining and interpreting laws, settling lawsuits between citizens of different states, and punishing those who break the federal laws.

SECTION 1. FEDERAL COURTS

The judicial power of the United States shall be vested in one Supreme Court, and in such inferior courts as the Congress may from time to time ordain and establish. The judges, both of the supreme and inferior courts, shall hold their offices during good behaviour, and shall, at stated times, receive for their services, a compensation, which shall not be diminished during their continuance in office.

The creators of the Constitution did not write the details of the court system into the Constitution. They left to Congress much authority over the federal courts. Congress can decide when to establish more federal courts and judgeships, and what cases each kind of federal court shall hear. It can even change or abolish any federal court except the Supreme Court.

Congress has established two kinds of federal courts (besides special courts). These are (1) the district courts and (2) the courts of appeals for the various circuits. These lower federal courts keep the work of the Supreme Court from becoming too heavy. Congress has passed laws which require that most litigation (trial of cases) in the federal courts shall start in the district courts. If persons in certain kinds of cases are not satisfied with the district court's decision, they can appeal to a higher federal court. Sometimes such cases can be taken directly to the Supreme Court; sometimes they must be appealed to a court of appeals. In some cases, the decision of a court of appeals is final.

SECTION 2. JURISDICTION OF FEDERAL COURTS

1. *Cases Under Federal Jurisdiction.* The judicial

power shall extend to all cases, in law and equity, arising under this Constitution, the laws of the United States, and treaties made, or which shall be made, under their authority; to all cases affecting ambassadors, other public ministers and consuls; to all cases of admiralty and maritime jurisdiction; to controversies to which the United States shall be a party; to controversies between two or more States; between a State and citizens of another State, between citizens of different States, between citizens of the same State claiming lands under grants of different States, and between a State, or the citizens thereof, and foreign States, citizens or subjects.

Cases presented to federal courts for settlement include the following: (1) cases having to do with the Constitution, the laws and treaties of the United States, ships and shipping; (2) cases in which the federal government is one of the two opposing sides; (3) disputes between two or more states; (4) disputes between citizens of different states; (5) disputes about certain claims to grants of land; (6) disputes between a

state and a foreign country; and (7) disputes between an American citizen and a foreign country.

2. *Cases for the Supreme Court.* In all cases affect-

ing ambassadors, other public ministers and consuls, and those in which a State shall be a party, the Supreme Court shall have original jurisdiction. In all the other cases before mentioned, the Supreme Court shall have appellate jurisdiction, both as to law and fact, with such exceptions, and under such regulations as the Congress shall make.

The Supreme Court has *original jurisdiction* in all cases involving a representative from a foreign country or involving a state. It hears the facts of the case and decides which side wins the case. All other cases must be tried in the lower courts first. The decision of the lower courts can then be appealed to the Supreme Court.

3. *Conduct of Trials.* The trial of all crimes, except

in cases of impeachment, shall be by jury; and such trial shall be held in the State where the said crimes shall have been committed; but when not committed within any State, the trial shall be at such place or places as the Congress may by law have directed.

If a person is accused of committing a crime against the United States, he or she has the right to a trial by jury. The accused is tried in a federal court in the state where the crime was committed. If the crime was committed in a territory, not a state, Congress decides where the trial shall be held.

SECTION 3. CASES OF TREASON

1. *Treason Defined.* Treason against the United

States shall consist only in levying war against them, or in adhering to their enemies, giving them aid and comfort. No person shall be convicted of treason unless on the testimony of two witnesses to the same overt act, or on confession in open court.

Treason means carrying on war against the United States or helping enemies of the United States. At least two witnesses must testify in court that the accused person committed the same act of treason. Any confession by the accused must be made in court.

2. *Punishment.* The Congress shall have power to

declare the punishment of treason, but no attainder of treason shall work corruption of blood, or forfeiture except during the life of the person attainted.

Congress has the power to decide the punishment for treason. It can only punish the guilty person. *Corruption of blood* is punishment of the family of a wrongdoer. It is prohibited by this clause.

ARTICLE 4. RELATIONS AMONG THE STATES

SECTION 1. TREATMENT OF OFFICIAL ACTS

Full faith and credit shall be given in each State to the public acts, records, and judicial proceedings of every other State. And the Congress may by general laws prescribe the manner in which such acts, records and proceedings shall be proved, and the effect thereof.

States must honor the laws, records, and court decisions of other states. Regarding judicial proceedings, there are two exceptions. A state does not have to enforce another state's criminal code. A state does not have to recognize another state's grant of a divorce if legitimate residence was not established by the person obtaining the divorce.

SECTION 2. TREATMENT OF CITIZENS

1. *Privileges.* The citizens of each State shall be entitled to all privileges and immunities of citizens in the several States.

This clause means that a resident of one state may not be discriminated against unreasonably by another state. However, a state may require a person to live there for a certain length of time before he or she may vote or hold office.

2. *Extradition.* A person charged in any State with treason, felony, or other crime, who shall flee from justice, and be found in another State, shall on demand of the executive authority of the State from which he fled, be delivered up, to be removed to the State having jurisdiction of the crime.

If a criminal travels from one state to another, the second state, on request of the governor of the first state, will usually send the criminal back to the state in which the crime was committed. In this way, states cooperate in enforcing state laws.

3. *Fugitive Slaves.* No person held to service or labour in one State, under the laws thereof, escaping into another, shall, in consequence of any law or regulation therein, be discharged from such service or labour, but shall be delivered up on claim of the party to whom such service or labour may be due.

This provision applied to fugitive slaves. It was made obsolete by the Thirteenth Amendment.

SECTION 3. ADMISSION OF NEW STATES

1. *Process for Admitting States.* New States may be admitted by the Congress into this Union; but no new State shall be formed or erected within the jurisdic-

tion of any other State; nor any State be formed by the junction of two or more States, or parts of States, without the consent of the legislatures of the States concerned as well as of the Congress.

When a group of people living in a particular area that is not part of an existing state wishes to set up a new state, it petitions Congress for permission to do so. Congress may then tell the people of that area to prepare a state constitution. The people organize to do this and offer to Congress a state constitution, which sets up a representative form of government for the group, and is in no way contrary to the federal Constitution. If a majority of Congress approves of the proposed constitution, it votes favorably on a statehood bill. The new state is then admitted as a member of the national group of states.

2. *Public Lands.* The Congress shall have power to dispose of and make all needful rules and regulations respecting the Territory or other property belonging to the United States; and nothing in this Constitution shall be so construed as to prejudice any claims of the United States, or of any particular State.

For many years, the federal government owned large areas of western lands (territories) that were not part of any state. This clause gave the federal government exclusive right to administer those lands.

SECTION 4. GUARANTEES TO THE STATES

The United States shall guarantee to every State in this Union a republican form of Government, and shall protect each of them against invasion; and on application of the legislature, or of the executive (when the legislature cannot be convened) against domestic violence.

A "republican form of government" is one in which the people choose their own representatives to govern and make the laws in accordance with delegated power.

The federal government can use whatever means are necessary to prevent foreign invasion and to put down domestic violence.

ARTICLE 5. METHODS OF AMENDMENT

The Congress, whenever two thirds of both Houses shall deem it necessary, shall propose amendments to this Constitution, or on the application of the legislatures of two thirds of the several States, shall call a convention for proposing amendments, which, in either case, shall be valid to all intents and purposes, as part of this Constitution, when ratified by the legislatures of three fourths of the several States, or by conventions in three fourths thereof, as the one or the other mode of ratification may be proposed by the Congress; provided that no amendment which may be made prior to the year one thousand eight hundred and eight shall in any manner affect the first and fourth clauses in the Ninth Section of the First Article; and that no State, without its consent, shall be deprived of its equal suffrage in the Senate.

The fifth article of the Constitution provides two different ways in which changes can be proposed to the states and two different ways in which states can approve such changes and make them a part of the Constitution. The Senate and House of Representatives may each approve an amendment by a favorable vote of two thirds of those present. The proposed amendment is then sent to the states for adoption. If, on the other hand, the legislatures of two thirds of the states apply to Congress for an amendment, Congress must call together a national convention to discuss and prepare such an amendment. In either case the consent of three fourths of all the states must be gotten for the proposed change to become effective. In sending the proposed amendment to the states for their consent, Congress may direct that the legislatures of the states shall decide the question or it may call upon the states to hold special conventions.

There have been 26 amendments in all. For all except the Twenty-first Amendment, Congress proposed the amendment and the state legislatures adopted it. In proposing the Twenty-first Amendment, Congress directed that each state call together its own convention.

ARTICLE 6. NATIONAL SUPREMACY

1. Existing Obligations. All debts contracted and engagements entered into, before the adoption of this Constitution, shall be as valid against the United States under this Constitution, as under the Confederation.

This provision assured the nation's creditors that the new federal government would assume the existing financial obligations of the country.

2. Supreme Law. This Constitution, and the laws of the United States which shall be made in pursuance thereof; and all treaties made, or which shall be made, under the authority of the United States, shall be the supreme law of the land; and the judges in every State shall be bound thereby, anything in the Constitution or laws of any State to the contrary notwithstanding.

This "supremacy clause" guarantees that federal law will take priority over state law in cases of conflict. To be valid, however, any law must be constitutional.

3. Oath of Office. The senators and representatives before mentioned, and the members of the several State legislatures, and all executive and judicial officers, both of the United States and of the several States, shall be bound by oath or affirmation, to support this Constitution; but no religious test shall ever be required as a qualification to any office or public trust under the United States.

Almost all government officials must affirm or take an oath to uphold the Constitution. No religious qualification can be set as a requirement for holding public office.

ARTICLE 7. RATIFICATION

The ratification of the conventions of nine States shall be sufficient for the establishment of this Constitution between the States so ratifying the same.

Done in convention by the unanimous consent of the States present the seventeenth day of September in the year of our Lord one thousand seven hundred and eighty seven and of the Independence of the United States of America the twelfth. In witness whereof we have hereunto subscribed our-names.

For the Constitution to become operable, nine states were required to ratify. Delaware was first and New Hampshire ninth, but not until Virginia (tenth) and New York (eleventh) ratified was the Constitution assured of going into effect.

George Washington—President and deputy from Virginia
Attest: William Jackson, Secretary

New Hampshire
John Langdon
Nicholas Gilman

Massachusetts
Nathaniel Gorham
Rufus King

Connecticut
William Samuel Johnson
Roger Sherman

New York
Alexander Hamilton

New Jersey
William Livingston
David Brearley
William Paterson
Jonathan Dayton

Pennsylvania
Benjamin Franklin
Thomas Mifflin
Robert Morris
George Clymer
Thomas FitzSimons
Jared Ingersoll
James Wilson
Gouverneur Morris

Delaware
George Read
Gunning Bedford, Junior
John Dickinson
Richard Bassett
Jacob Broom

Maryland
James McHenry
Daniel of St. Thomas Jenifer
Daniel Carroll

Virginia
John Blair
James Madison, Jr.

North Carolina
William Blount
Richard Dobbs Spaight
Hugh Williamson

South Carolina
John Rutledge
Charles Cotesworth Pinckney
Charles Pinckney
Pierce Butler

Georgia
William Few
Abraham Baldwin

AMENDMENTS

Since the ratification of the Constitution in 1788, it has been modified by amendment a total of 26 times. The first ten amendments, adopted by the first Congress in 1791, are popularly known as the Bill of Rights.

AMENDMENT 1. RELIGIOUS AND POLITICAL FREEDOM (1791)

Congress shall make no law respecting an establishment of religion, or prohibiting the free exercise thereof; or abridging the freedom of speech, or of the press; or the right of the people peaceably to assemble, and to petition the Government for a redress of grievances.

Government is to be kept separate from religion. Citizens are free to join any religious body (or none at all), and each religious body is free to practice its own beliefs and form of worship. The government may not interfere.

This amendment also prohibits any government action that will interfere with a citizen's right to say, write, print, or publish the truth about anything. There are important limitations to the practice of free speech. If false or harmful statements, spoken or printed, unjustly damage someone's reputation, the speaker or publisher may be sued in a court of law. But within these limits, citizens can discuss any question freely and criticize the government.

Furthermore, the First Amendment provides that Congress cannot make laws that stop people from holding peaceful meetings. This is "the right of the people peaceably to assemble." Finally, the amendment guarantees that people may send petitions to the government without fear of penalty.

Originally, all of these guaranteed freedoms applied to Congress and the federal government, not the state governments. Adoption of the Fourteenth Amendment in 1868, as later interpreted by the Supreme Court, guaranteed basic freedoms in the First Amendment against infringement by the states.

AMENDMENT 2. RIGHT TO BEAR ARMS (1791)

A well regulated militia, being necessary to the security of a free State, the right of the people to keep and bear arms, shall not be infringed.

This guarantee, like others in the Bill of Rights, is a limited right. It means more than the citizens' right to possess firearms. It protects their right and duty to serve in the armed forces.

This amendment also prevents the national government from absolutely prohibiting the ownership of firearms by citizens. The federal government has, however, passed laws to exercise some control over the interstate commerce in guns.

AMENDMENT 3. QUARTERING OF SOLDIERS (1791)

No soldier shall, in time of peace be quartered in any house, without the consent of the owner, nor in time of war, but in a manner to be prescribed by law.

The Third Amendment provides that in peacetime no soldiers can be lodged in any private house without the consent of the owners, and in wartime soldiers can be quartered in private houses only according to laws passed by Congress.

AMENDMENT 4. SEARCH AND SEIZURE (1791)

The right of the people to be secure in their persons, houses, papers, and effects, against unreasonable searches and seizures, shall not be violated, and no warrants shall issue, but upon probable cause, supported by oath or affirmation, and particularly describing the place to be searched, and the persons or things to be seized.

Under totalitarian governments, no guarantees of individual privacy are observed. In the United States, the Fourth Amendment and the strictness of courts in upholding it keep citizens free. The word warrant means "justification," and in the legal sense it refers to a document issued by a magistrate indicating the name, address, and possible offense committed. The person asking for the warrant (a police officer, for example) must convince the magistrate that an offense probably has been committed.

AMENDMENT 5. CRIMINAL PROCEEDINGS; DUE PROCESS (1791)

No person shall be held to answer for a capital, or otherwise infamous crime, unless on a presentment or indictment of a Grand Jury, except in cases arising in the land or naval forces, or in the militia, when in actual service in time of war or public danger; nor shall any person be subject for the same offense to be twice put in jeopardy of life or limb; nor shall be compelled in any criminal case to be a witness against himself, nor be deprived of life, liberty, or property, without due process of law; nor shall private property be taken for public use, without just compensation.

Juries are of two types. There are small or *petit* juries consisting of 12 jurors who hear a case tried and decide it. There are also larger, or *grand* juries, made up of as many as 23 persons, who listen to the testimony of witnesses and decide whether enough evidence exists to bring the matter to trial. Indictment by a grand jury means that the jurors think there is sufficient reason to hold a trial. The Fifth Amendment gives all citizens accused of major crimes the right to have their cases considered by a grand jury before being brought to trial.

Furthermore, this amendment states that a citizen who has been tried and acquitted in a criminal case may not be tried for the same offense again. This is his or her protection against "double jeopardy," that is, endangering his or her life or freedom twice. Double jeopardy does not work against a person, however, once he or she has been convicted. The amendment also guarantees protection against "self-incrimination." This clause means that people are not expected to be witnesses against themselves.

The last two sections of the Fifth Amendment provide protection against the violation of "due process" and the arbitrary confiscation of property. The "due process" clause means that all the protections listed in the Bill of Rights and in the body of the Constitution must be extended to the accused person in a criminal action.

AMENDMENT 6. RIGHT TO JURY TRIAL (1791)

In all criminal prosecutions, the accused shall enjoy the right to a speedy and public trial, by an impartial jury of the State and district wherein the crime shall have been committed, which district shall have been previously ascertained by law, and to be informed of the nature and cause of the accusation; to be confronted with the witnesses against him; to have compulsory process for obtaining witnesses in his favor, and to have the assistance of counsel for his defense.

Trial by jury is one of the cornerstones of the American legal system. Accused persons may usually waive this protection if they so choose. If, on the other hand, they demand a jury trial, 12 jurors must reach a unanimous verdict in order to convict. The right to a speedy trial protects citizens from being indefinitely under a criminal charge, something that could cause much hardship.

AMENDMENT 7. CIVIL TRIALS (1791)

In suits at common law, where the value in controversy shall exceed twenty dollars, the right of trial by jury shall be preserved, and no fact tried by a jury, shall be otherwise reexamined in any court of the United States, than according to the rules of the common law.

Either side in a dispute can insist on having a jury trial in cases involving more than $20. On the other hand, both can agree not to have a jury. Judges may not interfere with a jury's decision.

AMENDMENT 8. PUNISHMENT FOR CRIMES (1791)

Excessive bail shall not be required, nor excessive fines imposed, nor cruel and unusual punishments inflicted.

Bail is the money (or property) given to a court by an accused person in order to guarantee that he or she will appear for the trial. This amendment states that bails, fines, and punishments must not be excessive, cruel, or unusual.

AMENDMENT 9. OTHER RIGHTS (1791)

The enumeration in the Constitution, of certain rights, shall not be construed to deny or disparage others retained by the people.

This amendment says that the rights already described in the Constitution and the first eight amendments are not the only rights of the people, and that other rights are not taken away from the people because the Constitution and amendments do not mention them.

AMENDMENT 10. POWERS RESERVED TO THE STATES (1791)

The powers not delegated to the United States by the Constitution, nor prohibited by it to the States, are reserved to the States respectively, or to the people.

Any powers not delegated by the Constitution to the federal government, or definitely taken away from the states, are *reserved* (belong) to the states, and to "the people."

The states pass many laws for the welfare of their citizens under the authority usually known as their "police powers." This means the power delegated to a state by its people to protect their lives, health, and morals and to provide for their safety, comfort, and convenience.

AMENDMENT 11. SUITS AGAINST STATES (1798)

The judicial power of the United States shall not be construed to extend to any suit in law or equity, commenced or prosecuted against one of the United States by citizens of another State, or by citizens or subjects of any foreign State.

Unless it gives its prior consent, a state cannot be sued in the federal courts either by citizens of other states or by foreign countries.

AMENDMENT 12. ELECTION OF PRESIDENT AND VICE PRESIDENT (1804)

The electors shall meet in their respective States, and vote by ballot for President and Vice President, one of whom, at least, shall not be an inhabitant of the same State with themselves; they shall name in their ballots the person voted for as President, and in distinct ballots the person voted for as Vice President, and they shall make distinct lists of all persons voted for as President, and of all persons voted for as Vice President, and of the number of votes for each, which lists they shall sign and certify, and transmit sealed to the seat of the government of the United States, directed to the President of the Senate; The President of the Senate shall, in the presence of the Senate and House of Representatives, open all the certificates and the votes shall then be counted; The person having the greatest number of votes for President, shall be the President, if such number be a majority of the whole number of electors appointed; and if no person have such majority, then from the persons having the highest numbers not exceeding three on the list of those voted for as President, the House of Representatives shall choose immediately, by ballot, the President. But in choosing the President, the votes shall be taken by States, the representation from each State having one vote; a quorum for this purpose shall consist of a member or members from two-thirds of the States, and a majority of all the States shall be necessary to a choice. And if the House of Representatives shall not choose a President whenever the right of choice shall devolve upon them, before the fourth day of March next following, then the Vice President shall act as President, as in the case of the death or other constitutional disability of the President. The person having the greatest number of votes as Vice President, shall be the Vice President, if such number be a majority of the whole number of electors appointed, and if no person have a majority, then from the two highest numbers on the list, the Senate shall choose the Vice President; a quorum for the purpose shall consist of two-thirds of the whole number of Senators, and a majority of the whole number shall be necessary to a choice. But no person constitutionally ineligible to the office of President shall be eligible to that of Vice President of the United States.

In the original Constitution (Article 2, Section 1.3), electors cast a single ballot for president and vice president. This caused confusion in the election of 1800 when Jefferson and Burr as candidates of the same party received an identical number of electoral ballots. The Twelfth Amendment was adopted to prevent this from happening again. It specifies separate ballots for president and vice president.

The amendment provides that at least one of the candidates voted for by the electors must live in a different state. The electors are instructed to make two lists, one that gives the total votes cast for president and another that gives the total votes cast for vice president. The lists are then sealed and sent to the president of the Senate in the nation's capitol.

When the votes are counted, the candidate who receives a majority of presidential ballots is declared the president elect. The same rule applies to the list of vice presidential candidates. On the other hand, if the vote was divided among many candidates and none received more than half the votes, then the House of Representatives must select the president from the three candidates who have the largest number of electoral votes. Each state's delegation in the House casts just one vote. The candidate who receives a majority of the votes of the states is declared the president-elect. A similar procedure is followed in the Senate if no candidate for vice president receives a majority of electoral ballots. In that case, the Senate chooses a candidate from the two candidates with the most votes. A majority of Senators (currently 51 or more) must agree upon one candidate for a vice presidential candidate to be elected. No person can be vice president who lacks any of the qualifications for being president.

AMENDMENT 13. ABOLITION OF SLAVERY (1865)

Section 1. Neither slavery nor involuntary servitude, except as a punishment for crime whereof the party shall have been duly convicted, shall exist within the United States, or any place subject to their jurisdiction.

This amendment was adopted in 1865, after the Civil War, and was aimed at eliminating the ownership of one person by another. Because of the amendment, four million black Americans gained their freedom from bondage.

Section 2. Congress shall have power to enforce this article by appropriate legislation.

Congress has the power to carry out this amendment by enacting appropriate laws.

AMENDMENT 14. RIGHTS OF CITIZENS (1868)

Section 1. All persons born or naturalized in the United States, and subject to the jurisdiction thereof, are citizens of the United States and of the State wherein they reside. No State shall make or enforce any law which shall abridge the privileges or immunities of citizens of the United States; nor shall any State deprive any person of life, liberty, or property, without due process of law; nor deny to any person within its jurisdiction the equal protection of the laws.

The first part of the amendment overruled the Dred Scott decision of 1857 by declaring that a person was a citizen if he was born or naturalized in this country. Americans were to have dual citizenship, on the state and federal levels. The other parts of this section were designed to insure that states would not discriminate against freed slaves. The due process clause, which in the Fifth Amendment limited the federal government, now was used to limit states as well.

The citizenship guarantee means that even children of aliens are citizens of the United States.

The due process clause of the Fourteenth Amendment is intended to protect the citizen from state oppression, through the federal Bill of Rights.

The extremely significant "equal protection" clause makes it unlawful for states to discriminate on unreasonable grounds against any category of citizen. It was this clause which caused the Supreme Court in 1954 to decide that racially segregated schools violated constitutional guarantees.

Section 2. Representatives shall be apportioned among the several States according to their respective numbers, counting the whole number of persons in each State, excluding Indians not taxed. But when the right to vote at any election for the choice of electors for President and Vice President of the United States, Representatives in Congress, the executive and judicial officers of a State, or the members of the legislature thereof, is denied to any of the male inhabitants of such State, being twenty-one years of age, and citizens of the United States, or in any way abridged, except for participation in rebellion, or other crime, the basis of representation therein shall be reduced in the proportion which the number of such male citizens shall bear to the whole number of male citizens twenty-one years of age in such State.

This section voided the provision in Article 1, section 2 about slaves being counted as three-fifths of a free person. Indians were still not counted in the process described here for determining the apportionment of seats in Congress.

Section 3. No person shall be a Senator or Representative in Congress, or elector of President and Vice President, or hold any office, civil or military, under the United States, or under any State, who, having previously taken an oath, as a member of Congress, or as an officer of the United States, or as a member of any State legislature, or as an executive or judicial officer of any State, to support the Constitution of the United States, shall have engaged in insurrection or rebellion against the same, or given aid or comfort to the enemies thereof. But Congress may by a vote of two-thirds of each house, remove such disability.

This clause was designed to penalize southern states by keeping former Confederate leaders out of political office. Such leaders were barred from holding office either in their state governments or the national government. Congress, however, had the power to rescind this prohibition by a two-thirds vote of each house.

Section 4. The validity of the public debt of the United States, authorized by law, including debts incurred for payment of pensions and bounties for services in suppressing insurrection or rebellion, shall not be questioned. But neither the United States nor any State shall assume or pay any debt or obligation incurred in aid of insurrection or rebellion against the United States, or any claim for the loss or emancipation of any slave; but all such debts, obligations and claims shall be held illegal and void.

Neither the states nor the federal government could pay any portion of the Confederate debt. Southern states could not demand compensation for slaves who had been emancipated. Payment of the Union debt, on the other hand, could not be questioned.

Section 5. The Congress shall have power to enforce, by appropriate legislation, the provisions of this article.

Congress had the power after the Civil War to make laws that put this amendment into effect, and it did so during Reconstruction.

AMENDMENT 15. RIGHT OF SUFFRAGE (1870)

Section 1. The right of citizens of the United States to vote shall not be denied or abridged by the United States or by any State on account of race, color, or previous condition of servitude.

After the Civil War, Congress required the former states of the Confederacy to adopt constitutions which provided for universal suffrage of male citizens before they could come back into full partnership with the other states of the Union. Many states did this, but still there was fear that once they had returned to the Union they might then repeal the right to vote from their constitutions. Moreover, even after the Civil War, many northern states denied Negroes the right to vote. To solve these twin problems, Congress adopted the Fifteenth Amendment.

Section 2. The Congress shall have power to enforce this article by appropriate legislation.

Congress may make laws that put this amendment into effect.

AMENDMENT 16. INCOME TAX (1913)

The Congress shall have power to lay and collect taxes on incomes, from whatever source derived, without apportionment among the several States, and without regard to any census or enumeration.

This amendment gives Congress the power to put a tax on income *without* dividing the amount due among the states according to population. Income taxes were collected by the federal government after this amendment was adopted.

AMENDMENT 17. DIRECT ELECTION OF SENATORS (1913)

Section 1. The Senate of the United States shall be composed of two senators from each State, elected by the people thereof, for six years; and each senator shall have one vote. The electors in each State shall have the qualifications requisite for electors of the most numerous branch of the State legislatures.

Section 2. When vacancies happen in the representation of any State in the Senate, the executive authority of such State shall issue writs of election to fill such vacancies: *Provided*, that the legislature of any State may empower the executive thereof to make temporary appointments until the people fill the vacancies by election as the legislature may direct.

Section 3. This amendment shall not be so construed as to affect the election or term of any senator chosen before it becomes valid as part of the Constitution.

This amendment changed the method of selecting senators described in Article 1, Section 3, clause 2 to say that senators would be elected by the people of each state, not by the state legislatures.

AMENDMENT 18. NATIONAL PROHIBITION (1919)

Section 1. After one year from the ratification of this article the manufacture, sale, or transportation of intoxicating liquors within, the importation thereof into, or the exportation thereof from the United States and all territory subject to the jurisdiction thereof for beverage purposes is hereby prohibited.

One year after this amendment was ratified it became illegal in the United States and its territories to make, sell, or carry intoxicating liquors for drinking purposes. It became illegal to send such liquors out of the country and its territories or to bring such liquors into them.

Section 2. The Congress and the several States shall have concurrent power to enforce this article by appropriate legislation.

Enforcement duties were shared by the states and the federal government.

Section 3. This article shall be inoperative unless it shall have been ratified as an amendment to the Constitution by the legislatures of the several States, as provided in the Constitution, within seven years from the date of the submission hereof to the States by the Congress.

This amendment had to be ratified by the state legislatures within a period of seven years. The need for ratification within seven years was written into several amendments.

AMENDMENT 19. WOMEN'S SUFFRAGE (1920)

Section 1. The right of citizens of the United States to vote shall not be denied or abridged by the United States or by any State on account of sex.

Section 2. Congress shall have power to enforce this article by appropriate legislation.

Neither the United States nor any state can keep a citizen from voting because she is a woman. Congress has the power to make laws that put this amendment into effect.

AMENDMENT 20. "LAME DUCK" AMENDMENT (1933)

Section 1. The terms of the President and Vice President shall end at noon on the 20th day of January, and the terms of Senators and Representatives at noon on the third day of January, of the years in which such terms would have ended if this article had not been ratified; and the terms of their successors shall then begin.

Section 2. The Congress shall assemble at least once in every year, and such meeting shall begin at noon on the third day of January, unless they shall by law appoint a different day.

Section 3. If, at the time fixed for the beginning of the term of the President, the President elect shall have died, the Vice President elect shall become President. If a President shall not have been chosen before the time fixed for the beginning of his term, or if the President elect shall have failed to qualify, then the Vice President elect shall act as President until a President shall have qualified; and the Congress may by law provide for the case wherein neither a President elect nor a Vice President elect shall have qualified, declaring who shall then act as President, or the manner in which one who is to act shall be selected, and such person shall act accordingly until a President or Vice President shall have qualified.

Section 4. The Congress may by law provide for the case of the death of any of the persons from whom the House of Representatives may choose a President whenever the right of choice shall have devolved upon them, and for the case of the death of any of the persons from whom the Senate may choose a Vice President whenever the right of choice shall have devolved upon them.

Section 5. Sections 1 and 2 shall take effect on the 15th day of October following the ratification of this article.

Section 6. This article shall be inoperative unless it shall have been ratified as an amendment to the Constitution by the legislatures of three-fourths of the several States within seven years from the date of its submission.

The political term "lame duck" refers to any office holder who expects to be replaced by someone else. Such officials generally lose a great deal of influence. Before 1933, this was true of "lame duck" presidents, who attempted to govern for five months between election day in November and the swearing in of a new president on March 4. Now, because of this so-called Lame Duck Amendment, new presidents are inaugurated in January, thus reducing the lame duck period.

AMENDMENT 21. REPEAL OF PROHIBITION (1933)

Section 1. The eighteenth article of amendment to the Constitution of the United States is hereby repealed.

This amendment repeals Amendment 18. Prohibition is no longer a national law.

Section 2. The transportation or importation into any State, Territory, or possession of the United States for delivery or use therein of intoxicating liquors, in violation of the laws thereof, is hereby prohibited.

Carrying liquor across state boundaries for use in a "dry" state is a crime against the United States as well as against the state.

Section 3. This article shall be inoperative unless it shall have been ratified as an amendment to the Constitution by conventions in the several States, as provided in the Constitution, within seven years from the date of the submission hereof to the States by the Congress.

This amendment had to be ratified by state conventions chosen specifically for their views on the issue. The conventions had to approve the amendment within seven years.

AMENDMENT 22. TWO-TERM LIMIT FOR PRESIDENTS (1951)

Section 1. No person shall be elected to the office of the President more than twice, and no person who has held the office of President, or acted as President, for more than two years of a term to which some other person was elected President shall be elected to the office of the President more than once. But this Article shall not apply to any person holding the office of President when this Article was proposed by the Congress, and shall not prevent any person who may be holding the office of President, or acting as President, during the term within which this Article becomes operative from holding the office of President or acting as President during the remainder of such term.

This amendment wrote into the Constitution a custom begun by George Washington whereby presidents limited themselves to two terms in office. The precedent was not broken until Franklin D. Roosevelt was elected to a third term in 1940 and a fourth term in 1944. The amendment prevents any president from serving more than two terms.

Section 2. This Article shall be inoperative unless it shall have been ratified as an amendment to the Constitution by the legislatures of three-fourths of the several States within 7 years from the date of its submission to the States by the Congress.

For this amendment to take effect, the states were required to ratify it within a period of seven years.

AMENDMENT 23. VOTING IN THE DISTRICT OF COLUMBIA (1961)

Section 1. The District constituting the seat of Government of the United States shall appoint in such manner as the Congress may direct: A number of electors of President and Vice President equal to the whole number of Senators and Representatives in Congress to which the District would be entitled if it were a State, but in no event more than the least populous State; they shall be in addition to those appointed by the States, but they shall be considered, for the purposes of the election of President and Vice President, to be electors appointed by a State; and they shall meet in the District and perform such duties as provided by the twelfth article of amendment.

Section 2. The Congress shall have power to enforce this article by appropriate legislation.

This amendment gives to citizens living in the District of Columbia the right to vote in elections for president and vice president. The District of Columbia is now given three presidential electors. Before this amendment was adopted, it had none.

AMENDMENT 24. ABOLITION OF POLL TAXES (1964)

Section 1. The right of citizens of the United States to vote in any primary or other election for President or Vice President, for electors for President or Vice President, or for Senator or Representative in Congress, shall not be denied or abridged by the United States or any State by reason of failure to pay any poll tax or other tax.

Section 2. The Congress shall have power to enforce this article by appropriate legislation.

Neither the states nor the national government may require a person to pay a poll tax in order to vote in a federal election. For many years before this amendment was adopted, poor citizens were effectively denied the right to vote because they could not pay poll taxes collected by state governments.

AMENDMENT 25. PRESIDENTIAL DISABILITY AND SUCCESSION (1967)

Section 1. In case of the removal of the President from office or of his death or resignation, the Vice President shall become President.

When the President dies, resigns, or is removed from office, the vice president becomes president.

Section 2. Whenever there is a vacancy in the office of the Vice President, the President shall nominate a Vice President who shall take office upon confirmation by a majority vote of both Houses of Congress.

When the office of vice president is vacant, the president appoints a vice president. This appointment must be approved by a majority vote of both houses of Congress.

Section 3. Whenever the President transmits to the President pro tempore of the Senate and the Speaker of the House of Representatives his written declaration that he is unable to discharge the powers and duties of his office, and until he transmits to them a written declaration to the contrary, such powers and duties shall be discharged by the Vice President as Acting President.

When the President writes to the president pro tempore of the Senate and the Speaker of the House declaring that he is unable to perform the duties of office, the vice president serves in the role of acting president.

Section 4. Whenever the Vice President and a majority of either the principal officers of the executive departments or of such other body as Congress may by law provide, transmit to the President pro tempore of the Senate and the Speaker of the House of Representatives their written declaration that the President is unable to discharge the powers and duties of his office, the Vice President shall immediately assume the powers and duties of the office as Acting President.

Thereafter, when the President transmits to the President pro tempore of the Senate and the Speaker of the House of Representatives his written declaration that no inability exists, he shall resume the powers and duties of his office unless the Vice President and a majority of either the principal officers of the executive department or of such other body as Congress may by law provide, transmit within four days to the President pro tempore of the Senate and the Speaker of the House of Representatives their written declaration that the President is unable to discharge the powers and duties of his office. Thereupon Congress shall decide the issue, assembling within forty-eight hours for that purpose if not in session.

If the Congress, within twenty-one days after receipt of the latter written declaration, or, if Congress is not in session, within twenty-one days after Congress is required to assemble, determines by two-thirds vote of both Houses that the President is unable to discharge the powers and duties of his office, the Vice President shall continue to discharge the same as Acting President; otherwise, the President shall resume the powers and duties of his office.

When the vice president and a majority of the cabinet (or some other body designated by Congress) write the president pro tempore of the Senate and the Speaker of the House informing them that the president is unable to perform the duties of office, the vice president immediately becomes the acting president.

The president may resume his duties by writing to the president pro tempore of the Senate and the Speaker of the House informing them that he is able to take up the duties of office. If within four days, however, both the vice president and a majority of the cabinet (or some other body designated by Congress) write the president pro tempore and the Speaker of the House informing them that, in their judgment, the president is still unable to perform presidential duties, Congress must decide the issue. Congress has 21 days to decide, by a two-thirds majority of both houses, that the president is still unable to serve. The vice president then continues as acting president. If Congress determines that the president is able to discharge his duties, the president resumes office.

AMENDMENT 26. VOTING AGE LOWERED TO 18 (1971)

Section 1. The right of citizens of the United States, who are 18 years of age or older, to vote shall not be denied or abridged by the United States or by any State on account of age.

Section 2. The Congress shall have power to enforce this article by appropriate legislation.

No person 18 years of age or older may be denied the right to vote in either a federal or a state election. Congress has the power to make laws for putting this amendment into effect.

395

GLOSSARY OF CONSTITUTION TERMS

abolition The act of doing away with totally; putting an end to.

abridge To cut short.

amendment A legal change made in a law.

appellate A court that has the power to hear appeals from lower courts and to reverse lower court decisions.

bill of attainder A legislative act that judges a person guilty of a serious crime without trial and that carries the death penalty.

commerce Trade; business.

concurrence Agreement.

constitution The basic law of a nation or state.

due process of law Procedure that protects an individual's legal rights.

elastic clause A clause in the Constitution that allows Congress to adjust to changing political and social conditions.

elector One of the individuals who actually elects the President and Vice President.

emancipation Freedom; the act of freeing from bondage.

emolument Money received for performing the duties of an elected or appointed office.

executive The part of government that puts the country's laws into effect.

ex post facto law A retroactive law that punishes a person for having done something that was legal before the law was passed.

felony A serious crime, such as murder.

grand jury A group of 12 to 23 people who decide whether someone should be formally accused of a crime.

habeas corpus, writ of A legal order that can be issued to bring a person to court to determine whether he or she has been lawfully imprisoned.

How A Bill Becomes A Law

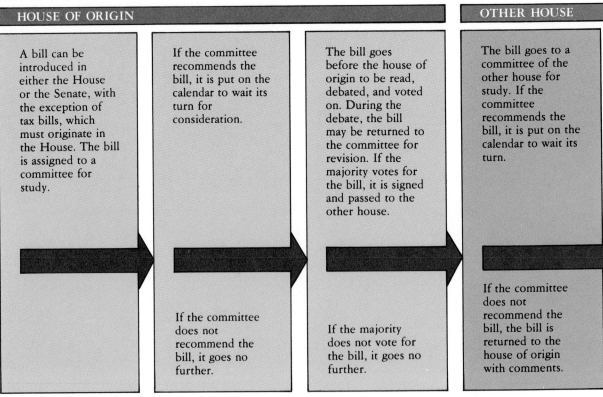

HOUSE OF ORIGIN

A bill can be introduced in either the House or the Senate, with the exception of tax bills, which must originate in the House. The bill is assigned to a committee for study.

If the committee recommends the bill, it is put on the calendar to wait its turn for consideration.

The bill goes before the house of origin to be read, debated, and voted on. During the debate, the bill may be returned to the committee for revision. If the majority votes for the bill, it is signed and passed to the other house.

OTHER HOUSE

The bill goes to a committee of the other house for study. If the committee recommends the bill, it is put on the calendar to wait its turn.

If the committee does not recommend the bill, it goes no further.

If the majority does not vote for the bill, it goes no further.

If the committee does not recommend the bill, the bill is returned to the house of origin with comments.

GLOSSARY OF CONSTITUTION TERMS

impeachment The procedure of charging a public servant with misconduct in office.

imposts and excises Types of taxes.

insurrection An act of open rebellion against an established government.

judicial The part of government that administers justice.

jurisdiction The authority to interpret and apply the law.

jury A group of 12 people who collectively determine guilt at criminal and civil trials.

lame duck An elected official continuing in office for what is usually a brief interim between the election and inauguration of a successor.

legislative The part of government that has the power to make laws.

misdemeanor A less serious crime than a felony, such as theft of a small amount of money.

naturalization The act of granting citizenship to someone from a foreign country.

preamble An introduction to a formal document.

prohibition An order to stop; a law that makes something illegal.

pro tempore Temporarily; for the time being.

quorum The minimum number of members of Congress who must be present in order to transact business.

ratification Official approval.

repeal To withdraw or cancel officially.

requisite Essential; necessary.

resolution Formal statement of a decision adopted by Congress.

suffrage The right to vote.

treason Betrayal of one's country, usually by aiding an enemy in wartime or by plotting to overthrow the government.

OF CONGRESS

The bill goes before the other house to be read, debated, and voted on. If the majority votes for the bill, the bill is signed and sent to the President.

If the other house amends the bill, it is returned to the house of origin for approval.

If the amendments are not approved by the house of origin, a joint conference committee is set up to work out the differences. When this has been done, the revised bill goes to both houses for final approval. If it is passed, the bill is signed and sent to the President.

THE PRESIDENT

The President can sign the bill, and it becomes a law.

The President can hold the bill for 10 days (not counting Sundays) without signing it or vetoing it, and it becomes a law.

The President can veto the bill.

The President can veto the bill and return it to Congress with his objections. Now the bill must pass both houses with a 2/3 majority in order to become a law.

The President can use the "pocket veto." When a bill reaches the President less than 10 days before Congress adjourns, it must have the President's signature to become a law. If the President doesn't sign within that time, the bill does not become a law.

REVIEW OF THE AMENDMENTS

INDIVIDUAL RIGHTS AMENDMENTS

The Constitution said nothing about the rights of individual citizens. The men who wrote the constitution believed it was not necessary to do so because each of the states already included a bill of rights in its state constitution. However, many Americans felt that this was not enough. They had fought a war against Great Britain to preserve their individual liberties as well as to win independence. Because the federal government that the Constitution created was more powerful than the state governments in many ways, they feared that in the future the federal government might attempt to take some civil liberties away. In return for their support for the new government, they insisted that the Constitution be amended immediately in order to guarantee basic freedoms.

The *Bill of Rights*, as the first ten amendments are called, was ratified and became part of the Constitution in December 1791. The *First Amendment* guarantees freedom of religion, freedom of speech, freedom of the press, freedom of people to meet peaceably, and the right to demand change from the government without fear of arrest or other punishment. The *Second* and *Third Amendments* deal with the relationship between the people and the armed forces. The *Fourth Amendment* prevents the government from searching people or their homes without a search warrant. The *Fifth Amendment* guarantees that an accused person cannot be forced to testify against himself or herself in a trial and that if a person is acquitted of a crime, he or she cannot be prosecuted for the same crime again. The *Sixth, Seventh, and Eighth Amendments* guarantee speedy trial, trial by jury, and protection from excessive bail and from torture. The *Ninth Amendment* states that citizens have civil liberties that are not mentioned in the Constitution. The *Tenth Amendment* was designed to protect the powers of the individual states. Any power not given to the United States in the Constitution is reserved to the states.

The Bill of Rights is one of the American people's most cherished possessions for civil liberties have been threatened from time to time. When that has happened, victims have been able to claim their rights as stated in the Bill of Rights.

The *Eleventh Amendment* (1798) deals with the right of people to sue the state governments.

CIVIL WAR AMENDMENTS

In the wake of the Civil War, three amendments were passed to ensure the civil rights of blacks. The *Thirteenth Amendment* (1865) made slavery illegal. The *Fourteenth Amendment* (1868) forbade states to deny equal rights to any citizen. The *Fifteenth Amendment* (1870) prevented states from denying any man the right to vote on the basis of race, color, or previous condition of servitude.

Amending The Constitution

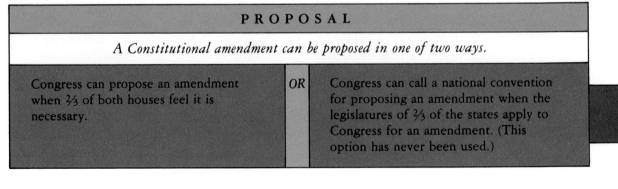

PROPOSAL		
A Constitutional amendment can be proposed in one of two ways.		
Congress can propose an amendment when ⅔ of both houses feel it is necessary.	OR	Congress can call a national convention for proposing an amendment when the legislatures of ⅔ of the states apply to Congress for an amendment. (This option has never been used.)

REVIEW OF THE AMENDMENTS

PROGRESSIVE AMENDMENTS

The next flurry of amendment-making took place during the progressive era, the years of intensive reform in the early twentieth century. The *Sixteenth Amendment* (1913) made possible a graduated income tax, that is, a tax that is heavier on people in upper income brackets than on those in the lower ones. The *Seventeenth Amendment* (1913) required states to elect their senators by popular vote. Previously, state legislatures had elected senators. The *Nineteenth Amendment* (1920) guaranteed women the right to vote.

Only once have Americans amended the Constitution to do what passage of an act of Congress would have done better. This was when widespread enthusiasm for stopping the manufacture and sale of alcoholic beverages led to the ratification of the *Eighteenth Amendment*, called Prohibition (1919). It was soon discovered that the Prohibition Amendment had serious side effects that made it undesirable. However, because it was written into the Constitution, it was necessary to amend the Constitution again, this time with the *Twenty-First Amendment* (1933), in order to repeal Prohibition. The embarrassment of having these two amendments in the Constitution alongside such important matters as the abolition of slavery and votes for women is a good reminder that the amendment process is for fundamental changes in basic law, not for less important matters.

PRESIDENTIAL AMENDMENTS

Another group of amendments deals primarily with the presidency. The *Twelfth Amendment* (1804) specified separate ballots for president and vice president in the electoral college. The *Twentieth Amendment* (1933) moved inauguration day from March 4 to January 20. This was in the midst of the Great Depression when it was believed that, in a time of national crisis, four months was too long a time after election for a new president to take office. The *Twenty-Second Amendment* (1951), limiting a president to two terms, was influenced by President Franklin D. Roosevelt. He had won four elections, and his opponents wanted to ensure that never again would one person dominate the presidency for so long. The *Twenty-Fifth Amendment* (1967) provided means by which a vacancy in the vice presidency can be filled between elections and also by which the vice president can take over for a president who is unable to perform the duties of the presidency.

VOTING AMENDMENTS

The *Twenty-Third Amendment* (1961) made it possible for residents of Washington, D.C. to vote in presidential elections. The *Twenty-Fourth Amendment* (1964) abolished the poll tax, a device that was used in some southern states to prevent poor people from voting. The *Twenty-Sixth Amendment* (1971) changed the minimum voting age to 18.

RATIFICATION

Congress decides who must ratify an amendment.

¾ of special conventions in each state can ratify the amendment. (This option has been used only once—in the repeal of prohibition, the 21st Amendment.)

SUPREME COURT DECISIONS

INTRODUCTION

At the time of the American Revolution, the English Constitution was largely *unwritten*. That is, most of the basic laws by which Great Britain and the colonies were governed had never been formally written down. The British people regarded them as constitutional, or fundamental, simply because they had been practiced for a long time. They were traditional, and to the British, tradition was every bit as binding as written law.

Tradition was not good enough for the citizens of the young United States. During colonial times, their *written* charters were the basis of the rights they claimed. In their quarrel with the British, they believed that Parliament had been able to violate these rights because traditional limitations on Parliament's power *had not been written down*.

Therefore, as soon as they won independence, Americans in each of the thirteen states wrote out their basic laws in clear, simple language. In the Articles of Confederation and the federal Constitution, they did the same. Written constitutions have been an American political tradition since the founding of the republic.

Nevertheless, a few features of our national government are unwritten. For example, the president's cabinet is an important part of our government today. It is hard to imagine the federal government without this assembly of the president's chief advisors. However, while Article 2, Section 2 of the Constitution empowers the president to appoint government officials, there is no mention whatsoever of a "cabinet." The cabinet exists simply because most presidents since George Washington have brought the heads of executive departments together for advice.

A much more important unwritten institution is the Supreme Court's power of *judicial review*. This is the Court's power to declare local, state, and federal laws unconstitutional, and therefore, to cancel them.

Nowhere in the Constitution is such a power even mentioned. It was the Supreme Court that won the important power of judicial review for itself. In the case of *Marbury v. Madison* in 1803, Chief Justice John Marshall ruled that a congressional act, signed by the president, was in conflict with the Constitution. Therefore, it had no force.

President Thomas Jefferson protested Marshall's decision. Marshall himself was cautious about using the power he claimed. While he continued to rule many state laws unconstitutional, he never again overturned a federal law during his thirty-four years as Chief Justice. In fact, it was more than half a century after *Marbury v. Madison* before the Supreme Court ruled another federal law to be in conflict with the Constitution. That was in 1857 in the case of *Dred Scott v. Sandford*.

But the tradition had been established. Although nothing is said about judicial review in the Constitution, no one today denies the right of the Supreme Court to determine the Constitutionality of laws passed by Congress.

Throughout American history, the Supreme Court has had its critics. When the Court has been "conservative," as it was during the late nineteenth century, "liberals" have criticized it. When the Court has been "liberal," as it was during the 1960's, "conservatives" have condemned it. But all admit that if the Supreme Court's power to declare laws null and void is to be limited, it is necessary to amend the Constitution. In this case, tradition has been as strong as written law.

The following table presents eight of the hundreds of landmark Supreme Court decisions. Each case reflects how the Court responded to changing social and political conditions.

LANDMARK SUPREME COURT CASES

CASE
Marbury v. Madison

DATE
1803

SUBJECT
Powers of the Court and of the Federal Government

VOTE
6-0 in favor of Madison

BACKGROUND
William Marbury had been appointed a justice of the peace, but his commission had not been sent to him by the secretary of state, James Madison. Believing that the Supreme Court had jurisdiction in such matters, Marbury went directly to the Court to ask it to order Madison to give him his commission.

The chief justice, John Marshall, had been seeking a way to assert the power of the Supreme Court. The *Marbury v. Madison* case provided him with the opportunity he sought.

DECISION AND CONSEQUENCES
The Supreme Court decided that while Marbury's request was authorized by federal law, it was not authorized by the Constitution. The Court decided unanimously that the federal law was unconstitutional and, thus, refused to grant Marbury's request.

The decision in *Marbury v. Madison* established that the Constitution takes precedence over laws passed by Congress. It also established the right of the Supreme Court to review the constitutionality of laws passed by Congress. This power of the Supreme Court is called the power of *judicial review*.

CASE
Dred Scott v. Sandford

DATE
1857

SUBJECT
Rights of Minorities

VOTE
7-2 in favor of Sandford

BACKGROUND
Dred Scott was the slave of John Emerson of Missouri. Scott went with Emerson to live first in the free state of Illinois and later in the Wisconsin Territory, a territory in which slavery was forbidden by the Missouri Compromise. Emerson died after they returned to Missouri. In 1846 Scott sued Emerson's widow for his freedom in the belief that his residence in a free state and a free territory automatically made him free. While the suit was going on, Scott became the property of John Sandford of New York.

The Missouri Supreme Court ruled against Scott, saying that the laws of other states were not binding on Missouri. Scott's lawyers then took his case to the United States Supreme Court.

DECISION AND CONSEQUENCES
The Supreme Court ruled that Scott was not entitled to bring a suit in federal court because blacks could not become United States citizens, and only citizens could bring suits to the Supreme Court. Therefore, the lower court decision held.

The Supreme Court also ruled that since Congress could not interfere with property, it could not prohibit slavery in any of the territories. Therefore, the Missouri Compromise and, by extension, any future division of land into free or slave territory was unconstitutional.

These rulings were overturned by the Thirteenth and Fourteenth Amendments.
Historical Footnote Scott was sold to a new owner who gave Scott his freedom two months after this Supreme Court decision.

CASE
Plessy v. Ferguson

DATE
1896

SUBJECT
Rights of Minorities

VOTE
7-1 in favor of Ferguson

BACKGROUND
In 1890 Louisiana passed a law requiring railroads to provide and enforce "separate but equal" accommodations for whites and blacks.

Homer Plessy sat in a train car reserved for whites. Plessy, who appeared white but was one-eighth black, was ordered to move. When he refused to do so, he was taken to court. John Ferguson was one of the judges who convicted Plessy of breaking the Louisiana law. Plessy then appealed to the United States Supreme Court for a ruling on the constitutionality of the Louisiana law.

DECISION AND CONSEQUENCES
The Supreme Court ruled that the Louisiana "separate but equal" law was constitutional. The decision in this case was to serve as the basis for 50 years of legal segregation in the United States. This and other Supreme Court decisions that permitted racial segregation began to be reversed in the 1900's— see *Brown v. Board of Education of Topeka*.
Historical Footnote The one Supreme Court judge who disagreed with the majority opinion and thought the Louisiana law was unconstitutional was a former slaveowner.

LANDMARK SUPREME COURT CASES

CASE	BACKGROUND	DECISION AND CONSEQUENCES
CASE Hammer v. Dagenhart **DATE** 1918 **SUBJECT** Regulation of Business and Industry **VOTE** 5-4 in favor of Dagenhart	In the 1800s and early 1900s, children worked in factories. In 1916 Congress tried to stop child labor by passing a law forbidding interstate sale of goods produced by children. Roland Dagenhart had two young sons who worked in a cotton mill. W.C. Hammer, a United States district attorney, acting in accordance with the Child Labor Act of 1916, tried to stop the boys from working. The boys' father obtained a court order, which stopped Hammer from enforcing the Child Labor Act and allowed his sons to continue working. Hammer then appealed to the Supreme Court.	In a close vote, the Supreme Court ruled against Hammer, saying that the Child Labor Act of 1916 was unconstitutional because it interfered with the right of states to regulate manufacturing. **Historical Footnote** Several years after his father won the case, one of the boys said, "I guess I'd have been a lot better off if they hadn't won it. . . . I think the years I've put in in the cotton mills have stunted my growth. They kept me from getting any schooling. . . . From 12 years old on, I was working 12 hours a day—from six in the morning till seven at night." This decision was reversed in 1941.
CASE Schenck v. United States **DATE** 1919 **SUBJECT** Freedom of Speech and of the Press **VOTE** 9-0 in favor of the United States	During World War I, Congress passed several laws against internal opposition that might interfere with the war. The Espionage Act of 1917 made it illegal for a person to interfere with the war effort, including the drafting of soldiers. Charles R. Schenck opposed participation of the United States in the war. In 1917 Schenck mailed thousands of pamphlets to young men, urging them to oppose the draft. A United States District Court convicted Schenck of violating the Espionage Act. His lawyers appealed to the Supreme Court on the grounds that the Espionage Act violated the First Amendment's guarantee of freedom of speech and of the press and was, therefore, unconstitutional.	The Supreme Court unanimously ruled that, because the nation was at war, Schenck's constitutional rights under the First Amendment had not been violated. The Supreme Court's ruling stated, "The character of every act depends upon the circumstances in which it is done." Thus, what Schenck had a right to say when the country was at war was different from what he had a right to say when it was not at war. To judge this and later cases, the Supreme Court used this criterion: Do the words used create a "clear and present danger" of some evil the government has a right to prevent? The Court decided that the use of words harmful to the war effort is not protected by any constitutional right.
CASE Brown v. Board of Education of Topeka **DATE** 1954 **SUBJECT** Rights of Minorities **VOTE** 9-0 in favor of Brown	At the time of this case, the state of Kansas had a law allowing large cities to set up racially segregated schools. Linda Brown was an eight-year-old black girl who attended public school in Topeka, Kansas. Linda's family lived five blocks from an all-white elementary school, but Linda had to ride a bus 21 blocks to an all-black school. Linda's father and the parents of 12 other black children thought that the Kansas law was unconstitutional according to the Fourteenth Amendment. They took Linda's case to the United States Supreme Court.	At this time, the Supreme Court was in the process of transition. The Court, divided on the question of desegregation, was led by Chief Justice Vinson, who was opposed to desegregation. During a postponement, Fred Vinson was replaced as chief justice by Earl Warren, who supported desegregation and was a strong leader. Warren's court delivered the unanimous decision that segregation in public schools was unconstitutional, thus reversing the trend of legal segregation begun with *Plessy v. Ferguson* in 1896.

LANDMARK SUPREME COURT CASES

CASE
Miranda v. Arizona

DATE
1966

SUBJECT
Rights of Persons Accused of Crimes

VOTE
5-4 in favor of Miranda

BACKGROUND

An 18-year-old woman from Phoenix, Arizona was kidnapped and attacked. A few days later the Phoenix police arrested Ernesto Miranda, but they did not inform him of his right to be represented by a lawyer. Miranda was placed in a lineup where he was identified by the woman as her attacker. Miranda wrote a confession to the crime when the police told him that he had been identified by the woman.

Miranda's lawyer argued that the use of Miranda's confession as evidence was unconstitutional because Miranda did not know that he had a right to counsel. The trial judge disagreed, and Miranda was convicted.

New lawyers for Miranda then appealed the case to the United States Supreme Court.

DECISION AND CONSEQUENCES

A sharply divided Court determined that an accused person's right to protection from self-incrimination includes protection from certain forms of questioning by the police. The Court ruled that *before questioning, a defendant must be told that he has a right to a lawyer; if he cannot afford a lawyer, one will be provided for him; he has the right to remain silent; and if he speaks, anything he says can and will be used in court against him. If the defendant chooses to make a statement without the advice of a lawyer, the government must be able to demonstrate that the defendant was competent to make such a decision for himself.* Miranda was granted a new trial.

Historical Footnote Miranda was convicted by the jury in his second trial.

CASE
Immigration and Naturalization Service v. Jogdish Rai Chadha

DATE
1983

SUBJECT
Separation of Powers

VOTE
7-2 in favor of Chadha

BACKGROUND

Since 1932, many laws passed by Congress contain a provision called *legislative veto*. Legislative veto permitted Congress to cancel a decision made by the executive or judicial branches of the government.

Jogdish Rai Chadha was born in Kenya. His parents were British subjects, so he had a British passport. Chadha came to the United States from Kenya in 1966 to attend college. In 1973 immigration officials ordered Chadha to return home (be deported) because his student visa had expired. At the time Kenyan officials refused to allow Chadha to return because they said he was a British subject. But British officials said Chadha would have to wait a year before he could go there. Claiming extreme hardship, Chadha appealed to officials of the United States Immigration and Naturalization Service (a part of the executive branch), and they canceled the deportation order. In June 1974, however, the House of Representatives decided that not enough hardship had been shown and used the legislative veto to reinstate the deportation order. Chadha's lawyers took his case to a federal appeals court, and in 1980 that court canceled the deportation order, saying that the legislative veto violated the separation of powers established by the Constitution of the United States.

DECISION AND CONSEQUENCES

Because of fundamental disagreement between Congress and the courts and between Congress and several presidents about the constitutionality of the legislative veto, lawyers needed a test case to take to the Supreme Court for a final decision. In accepting the Chadha case, the Supreme Court finally agreed to hear and decide the fifty-year-old question of the constitutionality of the legislative veto.

The Supreme Court ruled that legislative veto is unconstitutional, saying that Congress had been usurping powers that rightly belong to other branches of government.

Historical Footnote Jogdish Rai Chadha married an American during the course of this litigation. Thus, he was automatically granted the right to stay in this country. He became a United States citizen in 1983.

INDEX

Italicized page numbers preceded by a *p* refer to a *picture* or *photograph*.

A

Abolition, 11–12, 13, 14, 152–3, 391
"Acres of Diamonds" (Conwell), 186–7
Adams, Abigail, *p104,* 104–5
Adams, John (President), 9, 10, *p93,* 100, *p102*
Adams, John Quincy (President), 7, *p93*
Adams, Samuel, 7, 71
Addams, Jane, 23
Africa, 2, 33. *See also* Slave trade
Agee, James, 296-7
Agnew, Spiro T., 29, 359
Agriculture, 2; American Indian, 1, 2, *p47;* colonial, 4, 5, 44; growth (1870–1900), 17–18; in the 1920s, 291; in the 1930s, 295–6. *See also* Farmers; Plantations
Airplanes, 272, 273
Alamo, Battle of the, 10
Aldrin, Edwin (astronaut), *p30, p352,* 354
Alien and Sedition Acts, 10, 100–3
Allen, Frederick Lewis, 282–4
Allende, Salvador, 30, 359
American Federation of Labor, 18
American Indians, 1–2, 215, 216; colonial period, 36–9, 42–4, *p46–7,* 67–8; Constitution on, 377, 391; removals (1828–42), 11, 133–4; and the War of 1812, 112–13; in the West, 17, 111–12, 215–17, *p222–3. See also* the following tribes and regions: California; Cherokee; Creek; Great Plains; Illinois; Iroquois; Shawnee; Sioux; Wampanoag
André, John (Major), 82–3
Andrews, Sidney, 174–5
Andros, Sir Edmund, 60–1, *p61*
Anthony, Susan B., 209–10
Antin, Mary, 206
Appomattox Courthouse, 15, 172–3
Apportionment, 376–7
Arab-Israeli wars, 30, 355
Armed forces, 380–1, 384
Arms, right to bear, 388
Armstrong, Neil (astronaut), *p30, p352–3,* 354
Arnold, Benedict, 82–4, *p84*
Articles of Confederation, 8–9, 85–7, 375
Asia, 2, 34, 35
Assembly, freedom of, 388
Atlanta (Ga.), *p167*
Atomic bomb, 25, 322–5, 328–9
Attlee, Clement, 328

Audubon, John James, *p142–3*
Automation, 343
Aztecs, 1, 3, 37–9, *p40–1*

B

Bail, 389–90
Balance of power, 343, 355
Baltimore colony, 49–50
Bank of the United States, 10, *p114,* 128, 132
Banks, banking: and the Depression, 300, 304; Jackson's policies, 128–9, 132–3; and World War I, 268
Beauregard, P. G. T. (General), 164
Berlin crisis, 27
Beveridge, Albert J. (Senator), 233–4
Bicameral system, 376
Bicentennial celebration, 31, *p360–1*
Bill of Rights, 9, 91; text, 388–90
Bills, and the legislative process, 379, 396–7
"Billy Yank," 170–2
Black nationalism, 28, 286
Blacks, 11, *p251;* and abolition, 149; in the Civil War, 169–70; in labor unions, 286; lynchings, 285–6; in the 1920s, 284–7; North, emigration to, 285; and Reconstruction, 178–9; school integration, 27, 336; in the West, 17; in World War I, 285. *See also* Civil Rights Movement; Slavery
Blizzard of 1886, 219
Boarding houses, 116
Bonds, 380
Border ruffians, 159
Boston, 60, 157
Boston Tea Party, 7, 71
Boudinot, Elias, 82–4, *p83,* 94–5
Bourget, Charles, 247–8
Bourke-White, Margaret, *p302–3*
Bowen, Ephraim, 70–1
Bowerman, Guy Emerson, 272–3
Bradford, William, 4, 44
Brady, Mathew, *p166–7*
Brain Trust, 304
Broadsides, 100
Brook Farm, 135–6
Brown, John, 162–3, 169, 170
Brown, Joseph (Senator), 210–11
Brown, William Wells, 169–70
Bryan, William Jennings, 19, 240–1

Buchanan, James (President), 159
Buffalo, 11, 17, *p161,* 219
Buffalo Soldiers, 17
Bull Moose party, 21, *p260*
Bull Run, Battle of, 167
Bunker Hill, Battle of, 75, 79
Burnet, William (Governor), 63
Burns, Anthony, 156–8
Bush, George, 31
Business: in the 1890s–1910s, 18, 20, 249–50, 263–4; in the 1920s, 22–3, 290

C

Cabinet members, 384
Calhoun, John C., 12
California, 234; gold rush, 12, 19; Indians, 1; statehood, 156
Calumets (peacepipes), 56–7
Cambodia, 29, 358–9
Canada, 4, 6, 10, 63, 156
Capitalism, 16, 18, 186–7, 196–8, 286. *See also* Monopolies; Trusts
Caricatures, *p72–3*
Carmichael, Stokely, 348
Carnegie, Andrew, 21, 196–7
Carnright, Eldon J., 272
Carson City (Nev.), 220–1, 224–5
Carter, Jimmy (President), 30–1, 313
Carter, Rosalynn, 313
Cartier, Jacques, 4
Castro, Fidel, 28
Catlin, George, *p160–1*
Catt, Carrie Chapman, 274–5, *p275*
Cattle industry, 217–19. *See also* Cowboys
Census, 376–7
Centennial Exposition, *p188–9*
Central America, 1, 3, 6, 7, 20, 294
Central Intelligence Agency, 359
Champlain, Samuel de, 3
Charities, 226
Charles I (King of England), 49
Charles II (King of England), 5
Charles V (King of Spain), 37
Charleston (S.C.), 174–5
Chase, Salmon P., 13, 177
Checks and balances, 375
Cherokee Indians, 133–4
Chesapeake Bay, 49, 60
Chesnut, Mary Boykin, 164–5, *p165*
Chiang Kai-shek, 351
Chicago, 198–9, 229, 253–5
Child labor, 200, 201, *p205*
Chile, 30, 359
China, 24, 26, 29, 30, 34, 35, 351, 356

Chinese immigrants, 16, 19
Chou En-lai, 356
Church and State, separation of, 388
Churchill, Sir Winston, 26, 324
Cities, 20, 288–9; political machines, *p194*, 196, 249–51, 253; slums, 202–3, *p204–5*
Citizenship, 386, 391
"Civil Disobedience" (Thoreau), 136–7
Civil Rights Movement, 27, 28, 332, 337–8, *p340–1*
Civil service system, 192–3
Civil War, xiv, 9, 13–15, *p166–7*, 170–2, 193, 196
Civil War Amendments, 168, 398
Clark, William, 9, 111–12, 160
Clay, Henry, 11, 118, 121, 124
Clay, John, 219
Cleveland, Grover (President), 19, 207–8, *p229*
Clinton, George, 94–5
Clinton, Henry (General), 82
Clothing industry, 199–200
Coaling stations, 233
Cody, William F. ("Buffalo Bill"), 17
Coffin Handbill, 125–6
Coinage, 64, 380. *See also* Currency
Cold War, 26–7, 330–1
Collins, Michael (astronaut), 352, 354
Colonialism, 232–6
Colonial period, 3–6. *See also* Thirteen colonies
Columbia (S.C.), 174, 179–80
Columbus, Christopher, 2–3, 36–7
Common Sense (Paine), 76, 77
Communism, 28, 333
Compromise of 1850, 12, 13, 156
Comstock Lode, 226
Concurrent resolution, 379
Confederacy, xiv, 13, 14–15. *See also* Civil War
Confederation Congress, 85–7
Congress, 376–84; and amendments, 386–7; and federal courts, 385; immunity, 378–9; war declarations, 380, 382. *See also* Confederation Congress; Continental Congress; House of Representatives; Senate
Congressional Record, 378
Congress of Racial Equality (CORE), 340
Conservation movement, 20, 262, 265–6
Constitution, 9, 14, 275, 376–95; amendment process, 386–7; Executive Branch, 382–4; Franklin on, 87–8; glossary of terms, 396–7; Judicial Branch, 384–5; Legislative Branch, 376–82; National Supremacy, 387; Preamble, 376; ratification, 387–8; relations among states, 386; separation of powers, 103, 379. *See also* Bill of Rights; Constitutional Amendments; Constitutional Convention
Constitutional Amendments, 388–95; Equal Rights, 365–7;

Lincoln's proposals, 168–9; Third, 388–9; Thirteenth, 377, 391, 398, 401; Fourteenth, 20, 209–10, 377, 388, 391–2, 398, 402; Fifteenth, 209–10, 392, 398; Nineteenth, 25
Constitutional Convention, 9, 87–91, 375
Consumer goods, 25
Containment policy, 26, 330–1
Continental Congress, 7, 8, 80, 375
Conwell, Russell Herman, 186–7, *p187*
Cook, James H., 217–18
Coolidge, Calvin (President), 22–3, 291, 294–5
Coopy, Robert, 43
Copley, John Singleton, *p58–9*
Copyrights, 380
Corporations, 263–4
Cortez, Hernando, 3, 37–8, *p38*
Cotton Club (New York City), 284
Cotton gin, 117–18
Counterfeiting, 380
Court of appeals, 385
Courts, 380, 384–5. *See also* Supreme Court
Cowboys, 217–19, *p244–5*
Crafts, *p64–5*
Creek Indians, 110
Crime, criminal proceedings, 284, 389–90
Crockett, Davy, 10
Crook, William H., 177–8
Crossword puzzles, 280–1
Cuba, 19–20, 28, 232, 233
Currency, 10, 63. *See also* Coinage
Custer, George A. (Colonel), *p222–3*
Cutler, Manasseh, 105

D

Danforth, Thomas, 60–1
Dare, Virginia, 3
Darly, Matthew, *p73*
Davis, Jefferson, 14, 17, 164
D-Day invasion, 24, 317–18
Declaration of Independence, 8, 11, 14, 80–1, 360; text, 372–3
Delaware, 5, 14, 49, 387
Dellinger, David, 350–1, *p351*
Democracy, 9, 52–3; black faith in, 285–7; Jacksonian, 11, 126–7, *p150–1*; and militarism, 234–5; post-Revolutionary, *p130–1*; Progressive reforms, 251–2; Thoreau on, 137
Democratic party, 13, 193, *p195*, 241
Democratic Republicans. *See* Jeffersonian Republicans
Depression of 1893–97, 208. *See also* Great Depression
Détente, 29, 30, 355
Dias, Bartholomew, 2
Dickinson, John, 80
Dinwiddie, Robert (Lt.-Gov.), 67
Diseases, 203, 253–5
Dix, Dorothea, *p138*, 138–9

Doolittle, Amos, *p78–9*
Double jeopardy, 389
Douglas, Stephen A. (Senator), 13, 17
Douglass, Frederick, 13, 170
Dred Scott case, 391, 400, 401
Drew, Elizabeth, 357–8
Dudley, Thomas, 48
Due process clause, 389, 391
Dulles, Allen, 338
Dulles, John Foster, 26, 338
Dutch colonies, 3, 4, 5

E

Eakins, Thomas, *p190–1*
Eisenhower, Dwight D. (President), 24, 25–7, 338–9, *p339*, 351
Elastic clause, 381
Elections, *p130–1*, 367–8, 378, 382–3. *See also* Presidential elections; Voting rights
Electoral college, 382, 390–1
Ellis Island (New York City), *p212–13*
Emancipation Proclamation, 14, 168, 169–70
Emerson, Ralph Waldo, 12
Energy crisis, 363
Engravings, *p73–4*, *p78–9*
Entrepreneurs, 186–7
Equal protection clause, 391
Equal Rights Amendment, 365–7
Erie Canal, 121
Eskimos, *p46*
Executive Branch, 382–4
Exploration, 2–4, 33–9, 56–7. *See also* Lewis and Clark expedition
Ex post facto laws, 381, 396
Extradition, 386

F

Farmers, 10, 18, *p150;* and the Great Depression, 291, 295–8, 307–9; in the West, 227–8. *See also* Agriculture; Plantations
Farm Security Admin. photographers, *p308–9*
Federal Emergency Relief Act, 305
Federalism, 9
Federalist party, 9–10, 100, 102
Feminine Mystique, The (Friedan), 362
Ferraro, Geraldine, *p31,* 367–8
Fire-eaters, 13
Fishing, 45, 49
Fitch, John, 119–20
Fitzgerald, F. Scott, *p280,* 283
Fitzhugh, William, 60
Fitzpatrick, Thomas, 216
Florida, 107
Football, 247–8

Ford, Gerald (President), 29, 30, 358–9
Fort Laramie (Wyo.), 216
Fort Sumter (S.C.), 13, 14, 18, 164–6
Founding Fathers, 9
Fourteen Points (Wilson), 22, 276, 277
France, 8, 10, 21, 22, 242; colonialism, 233; exploration, 3, 4, 56–7; and Louisiana, 4, 6, 10, 107–8; and World War I, 272–3, 277
Franklin, Benjamin, 7, 72, 73, 87–8, 375, 388
Freedom Riders, p340–1
Free silver issue, 228, 241
French and Indian War, 6, 67–8
French colonies, 3, 4, 6, 56–7, 63, 67
Friedan, Betty, 362
Frontier, 160, p161, 215, p230–1, p244–5
Frost, Robert, 344
Fugitive Slave Act, 12, 156–7, 386
Fulbright, William (Senator), 349
Full faith and credit clause, 386
Fulton, Robert, 120
Fur trade, 6, 49, 62

G

Gandhi, Mohandas K., p303, 346
Gangsters, 279, 284
Garland, Hamlin, p277, 277–8
Garrison, William Lloyd, 152–3
Gaspee incident, 70–1
Gas warfare, 272
Gay Nineties, 248–9
Gender gap, 367–8
George III (King of England), 6, 7, 8, p69, 71, p72, 80, 81
Georgia, 4, 7, 15, 134
Germany, 21–2, 23, 24, 233, 234, 273, 274, 315, 324
Gettysburg Address, xiv, 15
Giacosa, Giuseppe, 198–9, p199
Gibson Girls, p256–7
Gilder, Richard Watson, 196
Gist, Christopher, 67–8
Gladstone, Thomas H., 158–9
Glass, Remley, 295–6
Glenn, John (Senator), 352
Glorious Revolution (1688), 60–1
Gold, 3, 35, 42, 50; California rush, 12, 19; New World, 37–9, p41
Gold standard, 241
Goldwater, Barry (Senator), 28
Gompers, Samuel, 18
Goodman, Ellen, 365–7
Governors, 63, 377
Grand juries, 389
Grant, Ulysses S. (President), 14–15, 172–3, p189
Gravestones, Puritan, p54–5
Great Britain, 219, 236; colonial policies, 6, 10, 11, 62–3, 68–70, 76, 234; constitution, 97, 100; and World War I, 21, 22
Great Depression, 23, 295–309;

bank failures, 300, 304; and farmers, 291, 295–8, 307, 308–9; Hoover's policies, 298–9, 300, 304; photography, p308–9; Roosevelt's policies, 304
Great Plains Indians, 1–2, 17, p160–1
Great Society programs, 28, 344–5
Greece, 330
Grimké, Angelina and Sarah, 140–1
Guam, 312, 313
Guerrilla wars, 315
Gunboat diplomacy, 20

H

Habeas corpus, writ of, 381
Hahn, Dr. Otto, 329
Hamilton, Alexander, 9–10, 84–6, 387
Hamilton, Charles, 348
Hancock, John, 7
Harding, Warren (President), 22
Harlem Renaissance, 284
Harper's Ferry (W. Va.), 162–3
Harrison, W. H. (President), 111, p113, 383
Haskin, Frederic, 242–3
Hawaii, 18, 19, 20, 233–6
Hayes, Rutherford B. (President), 192–3
Hearst, William Randolf, 237–8
Helper, Hinton, 163
Henry, Patrick, 89, 90, 91
Henry the Navigator, Prince, 2, 33
Henson, Josiah, 147–8
Herman, Russell, 186–7
Hersh, Seymour, 358–9
Hiroshima, 25, 323–5, 328, 367
Hitler, Adolf, 23, 24, 316
Hoffman, Charles Fenno, 124–5
Home Rule Act, 381
Homesteaders, 19. See also West
Hoover, Herbert (President), 23, 298–9, 300, 304
Hoovervilles, 300
Horses, 124, 254
House of Representatives, 376–7, 390–1, 393, 394–5; Judiciary Committee, 357; Speaker, 377, 395
Houston, Sam, 11, 154–5, p155
Howe, Frederic, 251–2, p252
Howells, William Dean, p238, 238–9
Hudson River, 4, 120
Hughes, Langston, 284
Hull, Cordell, 304
Hulton, Ann, 75
Hunter, Alexander, 170–2

I

Iles, Elijah, 118–19
Illinois, 118–19; Indians, 56–7

Immigration, 16, p212–13; growth (1860–1910), 19, 200, 206–8; literacy tests, 207–8; 1920s quotas, 287–8
Impeachment, 177, 357–8, 376–7, 384
Imperialism, 19, 232–6
Impressment, 10
Inauguration ceremony, 126–7, 383
Incas, 1, 3
Income tax, 21, 23, 381, 392
Indentured servants, 43
Independence Day, 94–5, p360–1
Indigo, 4
Industrial aristocracy, 248–9
Industrialization, 16, 18, 116–17, 122, 343
Inflation, 365
Ingersoll, Robert, 193
Insane asylums, 138–9
Interstate commerce, 18, 381
Intolerable Acts, 7
Iranian hostage crisis, 30, 364
Irish immigrants, 140, 220
Iron Curtain, 26
Iron industry, p122–3
Iroquois Indians, 2, 57
Isabella (Queen of Spain), 2–3, 36
Isolationism, 21, 24, 268–9, 355
Italy, 2, 13, 22, 23, 24, 315

J

Jackson, Andrew (President), 11; bank policy, 128–9, 132–3; and the 1828 election, 125–6; inauguration, 126–7; Indian removals, 133–4
Jackson, Thomas (General), 14, 155
Jacksonian Democracy, 11, 126–7, p150–1
James I (King of England), 44
Jamestown (Va.), 4
Japan, 23–5, 35, 234, 312, 313–15, 369
Japanese relocation camps, 319
Jefferson, Thomas (President), 9, p93, 100, 130; and the 1800 election, 390; and the Kentucky Resolutions, 102–3; and Louisiana, 10, 107–8; as Secretary of State, 118; on Washington, George, 96–7
Jeffersonian Republicans, 10, 100, 102
Jews, 34, 206–7, 329
Jingoism, 234–5
"John Brown Song, The," 162
"Johnny Reb," 170–2
Johnson, Andrew (President), 175–8, p176
Johnson, Lyndon B. (President), 28–9, 344–5, p345, 350
Johnson, Mordecai, 285–7
Joint Conference committees, 397
Joint resolution, 379
Joliet, Louis, 56–7
Jordan, Hamilton, 364
Judicial Branch, 384–5

Jungle, The (Sinclair), 253–5
Juries, 389. *See also* Trial by jury

K

Kalm, Peter, 62–3
Kansas-Nebraska Act, 13, 158–9, 177
Kennedy, Edward (Senator), 31, 364
Kennedy, John F. (President), 27–8, 343, 344
Kentucky Resolutions, 102–3
Khomeini, Ayatollah Ruhollah, 30
Khrushchev, Nikita, 27
King, Dr. Martin Luther, Jr., 27, 29; "I Have a Dream" speech, 347; on the Montgomery bus boycott, 241–2
Kirkland, Joseph, 199–200
Kissinger, Henry, 29, 30, 355, 358–9
Knights of Labor, 18, 200–1
Know-Nothings, 140
Knox, Henry (General), 95
Korean War, 27
Kublai Khan, 35
Ku Klux Klan, 178–9, 286, 306, 332

L

Labor unions, 18–19, 200–1, 229, 286. *See also* Work force
LaFollette, Robert M., 20, 250–1, 258, 290–1
Land grants, to railroads, 17, 229–30
La Salle, Robert, 6
Las Casas, Bartolomé de, *p42*, 42–3
Latin America, 294, 315. *See also* Central America; South America
Lawrence (Kans.), 158–9
Laws: colonial, 63; and the legislative process, 379; and the Supremacy Clause, 387
League of Nations, 22
League of Women Voters, 274–5
Lee, Clark, 328
Lee, Robert E. (General), xiv, 14–15, 172–3
Legislative Branch, 376–82
Lend-Lease Bill, 314
Lewis and Clark expedition, 9, 111–12
Lexington, Battle of, 8, 74–5, *p78–9*
Liberator, The, 140–1, 152–3
Life magazine, 302, *p320–1*
Life style: 1890s, 248–9; 1920s, *p280–1*, 282–4, 288–9
Liliuokalani (Queen of Hawaii), 235–6, *p236*
Lincoln, Abraham (President), xiv, 13–15, 17, 18, 356; amendment proposals, 168–9; and emancipation, 14, 168; on

Harper's Ferry, 162–3; on the Know-Nothings, 140
Lindbergh, Charles, 26
Literacy tests, for immigrants, 207–8
Literature, 296–7
Little Big Horn, Battle of, *p222–3*
Lloyd, Henry Demarest, 184–5
Locke, John, 96
Lodge, Henry Cabot, 207, 274
Long Drive, 217–19
Louganis, Greg, *p368*
Louisiana Territory, 4, 6, 10, 107–11
Lowell system, *p21*, 116–17
Loyalists, 81–2
Luckner, Felix von, 279
Luther Standing Bear (Sioux chief), 215
Lynd, Robert and Helen, 288–9

M

MacArthur, Douglas (General), 25
MacDonald, Dwight, 328–9
Madison, James (President), 9, 10, 11, *p92*, 103, 388
Mahan, Alfred Thayer, 232
Mah-jongg, 280, *p281*
Maine (battleship), 19–20
Manifest Destiny, 155–6
Mao Tse-tung, 356
Marietta (Ohio), 94
Marquette and Joliet expedition, 56–7
Marquette, Fr. Jacques, *p57*
Marshall Plan, 26, 331–2
Maryland, 4, 14, 49–50
Maryland Toleration Act, 51–2
Massachusetts, 4, 5, 7–8, 48, 51, 64
Massosoit (Indian chief), 44
Mather, Rev. Increase, *p61*
Mauldin, Bill, *p326–7*
May, Col. John, 94
Mayaguez incident, 358, 359
Mayflower Compact, 44
McCarthyism, 333
McClellan, George B. (General), 170
McKinley, William (President), 19–20, 232–3
McNary-Haugen bills, 291
Meatpacking industry, 198–9, 253–5
Mercantilism, 63
Mexican War, 12, 210, 234
Mexico, 1, 3, 154, 155–6
Middle colonies, 5, 52–3, 62–3
Middletown (Lynd), 288–9
Midway I., Battle of, 24
Militias, 380–1, 382, 388, 389
Miller, Merle, 332
Mining, 224–6, 306
Minuit, Peter, 3
Minutemen, 8
Mississippi River, 5, 6, 15, 56–7, 119, 120
Missouri River, 119, 120
Mitchell, Robert Hayes, 178–9
Moley, Raymond, 304

Monarchy, 52–3
Mondale, Walter, 31
Monopolies, 16, 20, 183–5, 250, 290–1
Monroe, James (President), 11, *p93*
Monroe Doctrine, 20, 232
Montezuma (Aztec emperor), 37–8, *p38*, 39
Moon landing, 30, *p352–3*, 354
Morris, Gouverneur, 388
Morris, Robert, 388
Mount, William Sidney, *p150–1*
Muckrakers, 202, 203, 249–55
Muncie (Ind.), 288–9
Munitions industry, 268
Mussolini, Benito, 23, 316

N

Nailmaking, 122, *p123*
Napoleon Bonaparte, 108–9, *p109*, 110
Nast, Thomas, *p194–5*
National Association for the Advancement of Colored People, 337–8
National Organization for Women, 367
National Road, 124–5
National Supremacy, 387
Naturalization, 380
Naturalization Act, 100–1
Navasky, Victor, 333
Naval power, 232
Nazism, 23–4
Nevada, 220–1, 224–5
New Deal Programs, 23, 25, 304–5, 307–9
New England colonies, 4–5, 44–5, 48–52
New England states, 116–17, 135–7, 138–9
New Frontier programs, 27, 343
New Hampshire, 4, 238–9, 387
New Immigration, 19, 200, 206–8
New Jersey, 5
New Mexico, 12
New Netherland colony, 3, 4, 5
New Orleans, 107; Battle (1815), 11
Newport (R.I.), 70
Newspapers: abolitionist, 152–3, 159; and the Civil War, 174–5; and the Spanish-American War, 237, 239; and World War II, 316–18
New World, 2–3, 36–7
New York City, 4, 5, 94, 250, 284, *p361*; colonial period, *p62*, 62–3; political machine, 194, *p194*; slums, 202–3, *p204–5*
Nicaragua, 294–5
Nimitz, Chester A. (Admiral), 25
Nixon, Richard (President), 29–30, 355–9
Normandy invasion, 24, 317–18
Norris, George (Senator), 268–9
North, Lord, 7
North Carolina, 4, 46

Northrup, Solomon, 145–7
Northwest Ordinances, 94
Nuclear weapons, 26, 28. *See also* Atomic bomb

O

Oaths, 175–6, 383, 387
Occupational diseases, 253–5
Ohio Territory, 67
Oil industry, 18, 185–6, 313
O'Keeffe, Georgia, *p292–3*
Old Northwest, 94
"Olive Branch Petition" (Dickinson), 80
Olympic Games (1984), 368–9
Organization of Petroleum Exporting Countries (OPEC), 313
O'Sullivan, John, 155–6
Oswald, Lee Harvey, 27–8

P

Paine, Thomas, 8, 76, 77
Panama Canal, 20, 232, 242–3, *p243*, 295
Panic of 1929, 23
Pardon, presidential, 384
Paris, treaties of: 1763, 6; 1783, 8
Parks, Rosa, *p337*, 337–8
Parliament, 7, 69, 375
Patents, 118, 380
Paterson, William, 387
Patriotism, 196
Patronage jobs, 192
Peace Corps, 27
Peacepipes (calumets), 56–7
Pearl Harbor, 24, 27, 312, 313
Pendleton, Edmund, 90
Pendleton Act, 192
Penn, William, 5, 6, *p53;* "Frame for Government," 52–3
Pennsylvania, 5, 15, 52–3
Philadelphia, 5, 7, 8, *p114, p115;* Centennial (1876), *p188–9*
Philippine Islands, 20, 232–4, 312–13
Photography: and the Civil War, xiv, *p166–7;* and the Great Depression, *p308–9;* and World War II, 302, *p303, p320–1. See also* Bourke-White, M.; Brady, M.; *Life* magazine; Riis, J.
Pilgrims, 4, 5, 44–6
Pinchot, Amos, 258
Pinchot, Gifford, 17, 258, 262, *p262*
Pinckney, Charles, 388
Pirates, 380
Pizzaro, Francisco, 3
Plantations, 4, 60
Plymouth Colony, 4, 5, 44–5
Pocahontas, *p3,* 4
Police powers, of states, 390

Political cartoons. *See* Engravings; Mauldin, B.; Nast, T.
Political machines, *p194,* 106, 249–51, 253
Political parties, 192, *p195,* 196
Poll tax, 136–7, 394
Polo, Marco, 34–5
Populist party, 228–9
Portuguese explorations, 2, 14, 33
Postal saving system, 228
Postal Service, 380
Poster campaigns, *p270–1*
Post roads, 380
Potomac River, 49
Powderly, Terence V., 200–4, *p201*
Presidency, 379; constitutional powers, 379, 382–4; "lame duck," 393; succession to, 394–5; two-term rule, 394
Presidential elections: of 1796, 100; of 1800, 390; of 1828, 125–6; of 1896, 240; of 1912, 264, 267; of 1928, 305–6; of 1932, 298, 300; of 1984, 367–8
Press, freedom of the, 388
Primary elections, 250–1
Prisoner-of-war camp (N.H.), 238–9
Privateers, 380
Progressive Era, 20–1; conservation, 262, 265–6; election reforms, 250–1; government reforms, 251–2, 259, 290–1
Prohibition, 21, 279, 282, 283; Amendments, 387, 392–3
Propaganda, *p270–1*
Prophet, The, 126
Providence (R.I.), 50–1
Public domain, 386
Public schools, *p205;* immigrants in, 206; in the 1930s, 306–7; racial integration, 27, 336; and *Sputnik,* 338
Public Works Admin. (PWA), 23, 307
Puerto Rico, 232, 233
Pullman Company, 197; strike, 229
Purinton, Edward Earle, 290
Puritan gravestones, *p54–5*
Pyle, Ernie, 317–18

Q

Quakers, 5, 52–3
Quartering Amendment, 388–9
Quebec, 4, 6
Quetzalcoatl (Aztec god), 39

R

Racial segregation, 27, 336
Radical Republicans, 177
Railroads, 18, 19; and air brakes, 188; bridges, 197; land grants to, 17, 229–30; monopolies, 183–4, 250; strikes (1880s), 229;

transcontinental, 13, 16–17, 20, 156, 183; Underground, 148, 149
Raleigh, Sir Walter, 3
"Rally Mohawks!" (song, 1773), 71
Randolph, Edmund, 120
Reagan, Ronald (President), 30–1, 359; inaugural address (1980), 365
Reconstruction period, 174–9
Red Cloud (Indian chief), 216–17
Red Scare (1919–20), 282
Reed, Amy, 135–6
Reforms movements: post-Civil War, 192–3; Progressive Era, 250–2, 259, 290–1; Transcendentalist, 135–7; and women, 135, 138, 140–1
Religious freedom, 51–2, 388
Remington, Frederic, *p244–5*
Republican party, 163, 193, *p195. See also* Bull Moose party; Radical Republicans
Resorts, 248–9
Revolutionary War, 6–8, 14, 63, 71, 76–7, 356; battles, 8, 34–5, *p78–9;* caricatures, *p72–3;* and democracy, *p130–1;* loyalists, 81–2; women's support, 74–5
Rhode Island, 4, 5, 50–1
Riis, Jacob, 202, 203, *p204–5*
Roads, 124–5, 380
Roanoke Colony (N.C.), 46–7
Roaring Twenties, 22–3, 279; blacks in, 284–7; fads, *p280–1;* immigration, 287–8; morals, *282–4;* small towns, 288–9
Robots, 369
Rockefeller, John D., 18, 185–6
Rockwell, Norman, *p334–5*
Rogers, William P., 358
Rolfe, John, 4
Roman Catholics, 3, 42, 140, 305–6
Roosevelt, Franklin D. (President), 23–4, 27; Fireside Chats, 304, 313–16; first New Deal, 304–5, 307–8; inaugural address (1933), 301; and World War II, 311–16, 324
Roosevelt, Theodore (President), 20–1, 23, 258, *p260;* and business regulation, 250, 263–5; character, 258; and conservation, 262; memorabilia, *p260–1;* on politics and public service, 259; social reforms, 250; "Square Deal" speech, 264–5; on World War I, 269
"Rosie the Riveter," *p318,* 318–19
Russia, 277. *See also* Soviet Union
Russian immigrants, 206

S

SALT agreements, 30
San Francisco *Examiner,* 237
Saratoga (N.Y.), 248–9
Savannah (Ga.), 80–1
Schlafly, Phyllis, 366
Schurz, Carl, 234–5
Scott, Dred, 16, 391, 400, 401

Scott, Winfield (General), 134
Seal hunting, 265–6
Search and Seizure Amendment, 389
Secotan, p47
Segal, George, p370–1
Self-incrimination, 389
Senate: Constitutional powers, 377–8; direct election to, 21, 392; floor leader, 377; Louisiana treaty debate, 109–11; and presidential elections, 390–1, 393, 394; President pro tempore, 377, 394–5; and treaties, 384
Seneca Falls Convention, 11, 140
Separatists, 5
Seward, William (Senator), 13
Shah of Iran, 30, 359
Shakers, 113
Sharecroppers, 296–8
Shawnee Indians, 112
Shays' Rebellion, 376
Sherman, Roger, 387
Sherman, William T. (General), 15, 167, 174–5
Sherman Antitrust Act, 18
Shipping, 10, 21, 62
Silver: colonial period, 64; free silver issue, 228, 241; mines, 224–6
Sinclair, Upton, 253–5, p255
Sioux Indians, 215–17, p222–3
Slaughter houses, 198–9, 254
Slavery: and the Civil War, 11–15, 168–70; colonial period, 4, 60; life-style, work, 145–7; punishments, 146, 147–8; runaways, 149, 156–8; in the West, 12, 156, 158
Slave trade, 2, 3, 147–8, 381
Smith, Alfred E., 305–6
Smith, John, 3
Smith, Margaret Bayard, 126–7
Social Security system, 23
Sons of Liberty, 7
South America, 1, 3, 4, 6
South Carolina, 4, 128, 174–5, 178–9
Southern colonies, 4
Southern Democrats, 13
Southern states, 13–14, 175–9, 285. See also Civil Rights Movement
Southwest, 3, 12; Indians, 1. See also Mexican War; California
Soviet Union, 24, 26–7, 29, 30, 31, p303, 322, 329, 355
Space program, 30, p352–3, 354
Spain, Spanish Empire, 2–3, 12, 19–20, 36–9, 42–3, 107
Spanish-American War, 19–20, 232, 234, 237, p245; prisoner-of-war camp, 238–9
Speech, freedom of, 388
Spice trade, 2, 34, 35
Sports, 247–8
Springfield (Ill.), 118–19
Sputnik, 338–9, p339
Stagflation, 30
Stalin, Josef, 26
Stamp Act, 7; Congress, 68–70
Standard Oil Co., 185–6
Standish, Miles, 4

Stanford, Leland, 183
Statehood, qualifications for, 386
States, state governments: Confederation period, 8–9; Constitution on, 382, 386–7, 390; free vs. slave, 12–13, 158
Steamboats, p114–15, 119–20
Steffens, Lincoln, 249–50
Steinbeck, John, 316–17
Sterne, Simon, 183–4
Still, William, 149
Stimson, Henry L., 323
Stowe, Harriet Beecher, 13, 147
Stuart, Gilbert, p92–3
Stuyvesant, Peter, 5
Submarine warfare, 21
Suez Canal crisis, 27
Sumner, William Graham, 192
Supremacy Clause, 387
Supreme Court, 384, 385; cases, 400–3; Brown v. Bd. of Education, 336, 402; Dred Scott, 391, 400, 401; Hammer v. Dagenhart, 402; Immigration v. Chadha, 403; Marbury v. Madison, 400, 401; Miranda v. Arizona, 401, 402, 403; Plessy v. Ferguson, 27, 401; Schenck v. U.S., 402
Svinin, Paul Petrovich, p114–15
Sweatshops, 199–200
Swedish colonies, 3, 4

T

Taft, William Howard (President), 20–1, 265–6
Taxation: colonial, 6–7, 68–9, 71; Confederation period, 86–7; Congress's powers, 379–80. See also Income tax
Taylor, Zachary (President), 234
Technology, 188–9. See also Iron industry; Panama Canal; Robots; Space program
Tecumseh, 112–13, p113
Teddy bears, p279
Telegraph system, 228
Telephone system, 228
Teller Amendment, 232
Tenements, 200, 203
Terkel, Studs, 306–7, p307
Texas, 11, 12, 15, 154–6, 164
Textile industry, 116–17
Thanksgiving, 44–5
Thirteen colonies, 4–6, 48–53, 56–63; crafts, p64–5; economy, 48, 49, 62–3; English policies, 62–3, 68–70; ethnic groups, 63; government, 52–3, 60–1, 63; taxation, 6–7, 68–9; wars, 63. See also French and Indian War
Thoreau, Henry David, p12, 136–7, 346
Three-Fifths Compromise, 376–7, 391
Tidewater region, 4
Tippecanoe, Battle of, 112–13
Titles of nobility, 382

Tobacco, 2, 4, 60
Toponce, Alexander, 93
Tories, 81–2
Towns, 288–9
Trade, 10, 11, 62. See also Fur trade; Shipping; Slave trade
Trail of Tears, 133–4
Transcendentalists, 12, 135–7
Transcontinental railroad, 13, 16–17, 20, 156, 183
Transient Relief Program, 304–5
Transportation, 124–5. See also Horses; Railroads; Roads
Treason, 384, 385
Treasury Department, 378, 381–2
Treaties: American Indian, 216; Constitution on, 382, 384; ratification, 110
Trial by jury, 385
Truman, Harry S. (President), 27, 28, p324; atom bomb decision, 322–5, 328; and civil rights, 332; foreign policy, 330–2
Truman Doctrine, 26, 330–1
Trusts, 18, 20, 263–5
Truth, Sojourner, 16
Tubman, Harriet, 149
Turkey, 330
Twain, Mark, 220–1
Tweed, William ("Boss"), p195, 251
Tyler, John (President), p11, 383

U

Uncle Tom's Cabin (Stowe), 13, 147
Underground Railroad, 148, 149
United Nations, 26, 29, 330
Utopian communities, 135–6
U-2 incident, 27, 338

V

Valentino, Rudolf, p281
Versailles, Treaty of, 22
Veto power, 379
Vice-presidency, 10, 367–8, 377, 382, 383, 390–1
Vicksburg, Battle of, 14–15
Vietnam War, 28–9, 349–51, 358–9, 367
Virginia, 3, 4, 43, 86–7, 89–91, 387
Virginia City (Nev.), p224, 224–6
Virginia Resolutions, 103
Voting Age Amendment, 395
Voting rights, 11, 20, 25; ballots, 20, 21, 251; in the Constitution, 376–7, 391, 395

W

Wakarusa War (1855), 158–9
Walsh, David I., p287, 287–8

Wampanoag Indians, 44
War, Constitution on, 380, 382
Ward, Artemus, 224–5
War of 1812, 11, 112–13
War on Poverty, 28
Washington, Booker T., *p22,* 285, 286
Washington, George (President), 8–9, *p92,* 94, 100, 120, 375, 387, 394; artifacts, *p98–9;* character, 96–7; in the French and Indian War, 67–8; inauguration, 94–6; in the Revolutionary War, 83–4
Washington, D.C., 11, 104–5, *p180–1, p360–1,* 381, 394
Watergate scandals, 29–30, 357–8, 359
"Waving the Bloody Shirt," 193
Wealth, 186–7, 197–8. *See also* Monopolies
Webb, John, 304–5
Webster, Daniel, 11, 132–3
Weights and measure, 380
West, 17–18, 215–16, *p244–5;* cattle industry, 217–19; farming, 227–8; Indians, 17, 111–12, 215–17, *p222–3;* housing, *p230–1;* and Manifest Destiny, 155–6; and the Mexican War, 12; mining, 224–6; pioneer settlement, 17–18, 156, *p230–1;* and slavery, 12, 156, 158; transportation, 124–5; women in, 226. *See also* Frontier
West Indies, 36–7, 62

West Point (N.Y.), 82–3
West Virginia, 14
Whig party, 11
White, John, *p46–7*
White, Pelegrine, 64
White House, 104–5, 117–18
Whitney, Eli, 117–18
William III (King of England), 60, 61
Williams, Jim, 178–9
Williams, Roger, *p50,* 50–1
Wilson, Woodrow (President), 21–2; Fourteen Points, 22, 276, 277; "New Freedom" speech, 267; and World War I, 269
Winslow, Edward, 44–5, *p45*
Winthrop, John (Governor), 50
Wisconsin, state government in, 251–2
Wolfe, James (General), 6
Women: in the armed forces, 365–7; in the early 1800s, 124, 140–1; in the 1890s, 248–9; in government, 367–8; in the Industrial Revolution, 116–17; in the labor force, 199–200, 201, *p204,* 318–19; in the 1920s, *p280–1,* 282–3; and reform movements, 135, 138, 140–1; in the Revolutionary War, 74–5; in the West, 226; and World War II, 27, 318–19
Women's liberation, 362
Women's suffrage movement, 11,

21, 25, 209–10, 274–5
Woodcock, Thomas, 121
Woodin, William H., 304
Work force: and the Great Depression, 304–7; in the textile industry, 116–17; wages, 200; women in, 199–200, 201, *p204,* 318–19; working conditions, 198–201, *p204, p205,* 254–5. *See also* Child labor; Labor unions
Works Progress Admin. (WPA), 23, 298, 307
World War I, 21–2, 268–74; and banking interests, 268–9; battles, 272–3; blacks in, 285; dissidents, 268–9; peace terms, 274, 277; propaganda, *p270–1*
World War II, 23–5, *p303,* 311–19, 351; home efforts, 318–19; newspaper correspondents, 316–18, *p320–1;* in North Africa, 315; in the Pacific, 24–5, 312, 313; political cartoons, *p326–7;* and U.S. neutrality, 311
Wright brothers, 24

Y

Yalta Conference, 330
Yankee ingenuity, 121
Yellow journalism, 237
Yorktown, Battle of, 8

ACKNOWLEDGMENTS

ILLUSTRATIONS 1–15, Clyde Risley; 16–31, Lyle Miller

PHOTO CREDITS
The following abbreviations indicate the position of the photographs on the page: *t*, top; *b*, bottom; *l*, left; *r*, right; *c*, center.

FRONT MATTER vi, Lee Boltin; **vii,** The Metropolitan Museum of Art; **viii,** National Museum of American History, Smithsonian Institution; **ix,** The Bettmann Archive; **x,** Culver Pictures; **xi,** The Granger Collection; **xii** (t,b), The Bettmann Archive; **xii** (c), Culver Pictures; **xiii,** The Bettmann Archive; **xiv,** Frank Scherschel, LIFE Magazine, © 1950 Time Inc.; **xv** (t), Jim Goodwin, Photo Researchers, Inc. **xv** (b), Focus on Sports; **xvi,** "George Washington," National Portrait Gallery, Smithsonian Institution, and Museum of Fine Arts, Boston; **xvii** (t) Smithsonian Institution; **xvii** (b), Independence Historical Park Collection.

UNIT 1 32, "The Grand Canyon," Thomas Moran, Thomas Gilcrease Institute of American History and Art, Tulsa, Oklahoma; **38** (r), Culver Pictures; **38** (l), The Bettmann Archive Inc.; **40, 41** Lee Boltin; **42, 45,** The Bettmann Archive Inc,; **46, 47,** Lee Boltin; **48,** Culver Pictures; **50, 53,** The Granger Collection; **54** (l), Farrell Grehan, Photo Researchers; **54** (r), **55,** Michael Cornish; **57,** Culver Pictures; **58** (l), "Self-Portrait," John Singleton Copley, The Henry Francis duPont Winterthur Museum, Winterthur, Delaware; **58** (r), "Governor and Mrs. Thomas Mifflin," John Singleton Copley, Historical Society of Pennsylvania, Philadelphia; **59** (t), "Boy with a Squirrel," John Singleton Copley, Museum of Fine Arts, Boston, Anonymous Gift; **59,** "The Copley Family," John Singleton Copley, National Gallery of Art, Washington, D.C., Andrew W. Mellon Fund; **61** (l, r), The Bettmann Archive Inc.; **62,** Culver Pictures; **64** (l), The Pilgrim Society, Plymouth, Mass.; **64** (r), Corning Museum of Glass, Corning, N.Y.; **65**(tl), Colonial Williamsburg, Williamsburg, VA.; **65** (bl), The Henry Francis duPont Winterthur Museum, Winterthur, Delaware; **65** (tr), The Metropolitan Museum of Art.

UNIT 2 66, "The Hudson Valley, Sunset," Thomas Chambers, National Gallery of Art, Washington, D.C., Gift of Edgar W. and Bernice C. Garbisch; **69,** Culver Pictures; **72,** The Bettmann Archive Inc.; **73** (t), The Granger Collection; **73** (b), The Bettmann Archive Inc.; **78–79,** New York Public Library, The Stokes Collection; **83, 84,** Culver Pictures; **92** (tl), "Gilbert Stuart," Unidentified Artist, after Anson Dickinson, National Portrait Gallery, Smithsonian Institution; **92** (tr) "George Washington," Gilbert Stuart, National Portrait Gallery, Smithsonian Institution, and Museum of Fine Arts, Boston; **92** (br) "James Madison," Gilbert Stuart, National Gallery of Art; **93** (tl), "John Adams," Gilbert Stuart, National Gallery of Art; **93** (tr), "Thomas Jefferson," Gilbert Stuart, National Gallery of Art; **93** (bl), "James Monroe," Gilbert Stuart, National Gallery of Art; **93** (br), "John Quincy Adams," Gilbert Stuart, White House Collection, Washington, D.C.; **98** (l), White House Association, Washington, D.C.; **98** (r), The Bettmann Archive Inc.; **99** (t, br), Smithsonian Institution; **99** (bl), New-York Historical Society; **102,** Library of Congress; **104,** "Abigail Adams," Mather Brown, New York State Historical Association, Cooperstown, N.Y.

UNIT 3 106, "Niagara Falls," Frederick Church, The Corcoran Gallery of Art, Washington, D.C.; **109, 113,** The Bettmann Archive Inc.; **114** (tl), The Granger Collection; **114** (tr), "Winter Scene in Philadelphia," Pavel Petrovitch Svinin, Metropolitan Museum of Art, Rogers Fund; **114–115,** "Deck Life on the Paragon," Pavel Petrovitch Svinin, Metropolitan Museum of Art, Rogers Fund; **115** (r), "Night Life in Philadelphia," Pavel Petrovitch Svinin, Metropolitan Museum of Art, Rogers Fund; **122,** The Granger Collection; **123** (tl), "Interior of a Smithy," Bass Otis, Pennsylvania Academy of the Fine Arts, Philadelphia; **123** (bl), The Bettmann Archive Inc.; **123** (r), National Museum of American History, Smithsonian Institution; **130,** "Election Day at the State House," John Lewis Krimmel, Historical Society of Pennsylvania, Philadelphia; **131** (tl), "Stump Speaking," George Caleb Bingham, The Boatmen's National Bank of St. Louis; **131** (bl), "Election Scene, Catonsville, Baltimore Country," Alfred Jacob Miller, Corcoran Gallery of American Art; **131** (r), "Politics in an Oyster House," Richard Caton Woodville, The Walters Art Gallery, Baltimore; **138,** National Portrait Gallery, Smithsonian Institution; **142** (tl), "John James Audubon," John and Victor Audubon American Museum of Natural History, N.Y.; **142–143,** New York Public Library, Courtesy Scala/Art Resource.

UNIT 4 144, "The Cornell Farm," Edward Hicks, National Gallery of Art, Washington, D.C., Gift of Edgar W. and Bernice C. Garbisch; **150** (l), "Self-Portrait with Flute," William Sidney Mount, The Museums at Stony Brook, New York, Gift of Mr. and Mrs. Ward Melville; **150** (tr), "Long Island Farmer Husking Corn," William Sidney Mount, The Museums at Stony Brook, New York, Gift of Mr. and Mrs. Ward Melville, 150 (br), "Dance of the Haymakers," William Sidney Mount, The Museums at Stony Brook, New York, Gift of Mr. and Mrs. Ward Melville; **151,** "Eel Spearing at Setauket," William Sidney Mount, New York Historical Association, Cooperstown; **155,** The Granger Collection; **160** (l), The Granger Collection; **160** (r), "Assiniboin Girl," George Catlin, Smithsonian Institution, Courtesy Scala/Art Resource; **161** (t), "Catlin Painting the Portrait of Mah-to-Toh-Pa," George Catlin, National Gallery of Art, Gift of Paul Mellon; **161** (b), "Winter Hunting," George Catlin, Smithsonian Institution, Courtesy Scala/Art Resource; **165,** Charles Gay, South Caroliniana Library, University of South Carolina, Columbia; **166,** Culver Pictures; **167,** Library of Congress; **176,** Culver Pictures; **180,** Library of Congress; **181** (t), White House Association; **181** (b), "The Corner of F. Street, Washington, D.C.," Baroness Hyde de Neuville, New York Public Library, Stokes Collection.

UNIT 5 182, "View of Sacramento, California, from across the Sacramento River," George Tirrell, Museum of Fine Arts, Boston, M. and M. Karolik Collection; **187,** The Bettmann Archive Inc.; **188** (l), Culver Pictures; **188** (r), **189** (tl), The Bettmann Archives Inc.; **189** (bl,r) The Granger Collection; **190** (l), The Bettmann Archive; **190** (r), "Gross Clinic," Thomas Eakins, Jefferson Medical College, Thomas Jefferson University, Philadelphia; **191** (tl), "Home Scene," Thomas Eakins, The Brooklyn Museum, Gift of George A. Hearn, Frederick Loeser Art Fund, Dick S. Ramsay Fund, and Charles A. Schieren; **191** (b), "Max Schmitt in a Single Scull," Thomas Eakins, Metropolitan Museum of Art; **194** (tl), The Bettmann Archive Inc.; **194** (tr), Library of Congress; **194** (br), The Granger Collection; **195** (t), Culver Pictures; **195** (b), The Bettmann Archive Inc.; **196, 199** (l), Culver Pictures; **199** (r), **201,** The Bettmann Archive Inc.; **204** (tl), National Portrait Gallery, Smithsonian Institution, Washington, D.C.; **204** (tr), Library of Congress; **204** (br), Museum of the City of New York; **205,** Library of Congress; **212, 213,** Culver Pictures.

UNIT 6 214, "The Lackawanna Valley," George Inness, National Gallery of Art, Gift of Mrs. Huttleston Rogers; **219,** Culver Pictures; **222,** "Custer's Last Stand," Kicking Bear, Southwest Museum, Los Angeles; **223,** Library of Congress; **224,** The Granger Collection; **227, 229,** The Bettmann Archive Inc.; **230, 231** (bl), Culver Pictures; **231** (tl, tr), Nebraska State Historical Society; **231** (br), Arizona State Historical Society, Tuscon; **236, 238, 243,** The Bettmann Archive Inc.; **244** (tl), Benoi Irwin, National Academy of Design, New York City; **244–245,** "Dash for the Timber," Frederic Remington, Amon Carter Museum, Fort Worth, Texas; **245** (tr), "Last Finished Painting," Frederic Remington, Remington Art Museum, Ogdensburg, New York; **245** (b), "Under Which King," Frederic Remington, Remington Art Museum, Ogdensburg, New York.

UNIT 7 246, "Threshing Wheat," Thomas Hart Benton, The Sheldon Swope Art Gallery, Terre Haute, Indiana; **252,** State Historical Society of Wisconsin; **255,** The Bettmann Archive Inc.; **256** (tl), Kenyon Cox, National Academy of Design, New York City; **256** (r), **257** (bl), Culver Pictures; **257** (t), The Granger Collection; **260** (l), The Bettmann Archive Inc.; **260** (r), **261** (br), DeWitt Collection, University of Hartford; **261** (l), Smithsonian Institution; **261** (tr), The Granger Collection; **262, 269,** The Bettmann Archive Inc.; **270–271,** Library of Congress; **275,** The Bettmann Archive Inc.

UNIT 8 278, "Macomb's Dam Bridge," Edward Hopper, The Brooklyn Museum, Bequest of Mary T. Cockeroft; 280 (l), The Granger Collection; 280 (r), Culver Pictures; 281, The Bettmann Archive Inc.; 287, Wide World Photos; 292 (tl), Dan Budnick, Woodfin Camp and Associates; 292 (tr), "East River From the Shelton," Georgia O'Keefe, New Jersey State Museum, Trenton, Gift of Mary Lee Johnson; 292 (br), "Ranchos Church No. 1," Georgia O'Keefe, Norton Gallery and School of Art, West Palm Beach, Florida; 293 (t), "Lake George Barns," Georgia O'Keefe, Walker Art Center, Minneapolis, Gift of the T.B. Walker Foundation; 293 (b), "Black Hollyhock, Blue Larkspur," Georgia O'Keefe, Metropolitan Museum of Art, George A. Hearn Fund; 302 (tl), Margaret Bourke-White, Courtesy Margaret Bourke-White Estate, LIFE Magazine, Time Inc.; 302 (tr, br), Margaret Bourke-White, © 1936 Time Inc.; 303 (t), Margaret Bourke-White, © 1941 Time Inc.; 303 (b), Margaret Bourke-White, © 1946 Time Inc.; 307, Patrick E. Girouard, Courtesy Pantheon Books; 308 (l), Marion P. Walcott, 308 (r), Arthur Rothstein, Library of Congress; 309, Dorothea Lange, Library of Congress.

UNIT 9 310, "American Landscape," Charles Sheeler, Museum of Modern Art; 318, The Bettmann Archive Inc.; 320 (l), Signal Corps Photo, LIFE Picture Service; 320 (r), William Vandivert, LIFE Magazine © 1940 Time Inc.; 321 (l), George Silk, LIFE Magazine © 1943 Time Inc.; 321 (tr), Carl Mydans, LIFE Magazine © 1940 Time Inc.; 321 (br), Eliot Elisofon, LIFE Magazine © 1943 Time Inc.; 324, The Bettmann Archive Inc.; 326 (tl) John Phillips, LIFE Magazine © Time Inc.; 326 (tr), 327, Bill Mauldin and Wil-Jo Associates, Inc.; 334 (tl), Culver Pictures Inc.; 334 (tr), "Town Meeting," Norman Rockwell, Metropolitan Museum of Art, George A. Hearn Fund; 335, "Installing T.V. Set," Norman Rockwell, Los Angeles County Museum of Art, Gift of Mrs. Ned Crowell; 337, Wide World Photos; 339 (l), The Bettman Archive Inc.; 339 (r), 340–350, Wide World Photos.

UNIT 10 342, "Dalles Dam on the Columbia River," Robert Birmelin, Courtesy Sherry French Gallery; 344, Paul Schutzer, LIFE Magazine © Time Inc.; 345, 348, 349, 351, Wide World Photos; 352, 353, NASA; 360, 361 (tl), Jim Goodwin, Photo Researchers; 361 (bl), Tony Korody, Sygma; 361 (r), Ray Ellis, Photo Researchers; 368, Wide World Photos; 370 (tl), Hans Namuth, Photo Researchers; 370 (r), "Next Departure," George Segal, Sidney Janis Gallery, New York; 371 (l), "Diner," George Segal, Walker Art Center, Minneapolis, Gift of the T.B. Walker Foundation; 371 (r), "Walk, Don't Walk," George Segal, Whitney Museum of American Art, Gift of Louis and Bessie Ader Foundation, Inc., The Gilman Foundation, Howard and Jean Lipman Foundation, Inc., and The National Endowment for the Arts; 374, Library of Congress.

A
B 5
C 6
D 7
E 8
F 9
G 0
H 1
I 2
J 3